S. GEORGE WALTERS, Ph.D.
Development Projects Manager, Socony Mobil Oil Company, Inc.,
Formerly Head of the Marketing Section, College of Business Administration,
Lehigh University

MAX D. SNIDER, M.B.A.
Assistant Professor of Marketing, Assistant to the Dean, College of Business
Administration, Lehigh University

MORRIS L. SWEET, M.B.A.
Research Assistant Professor of Business, College of Business Administration,
Lehigh University

SOUTH-WESTERN PUBLISHING CO.

Cincinnati 27 Chicago 44 Dallas 2 Burlingame, Calif. New Rochelle, N. Y.

S30

CONSUMERS
POLICIES
FUNCTIONS
COMMODITIES
CHANNELS
GOVERNMENT

READINGS IN MARKETING

Library of Congress Catalog Card Number: 60-8322

H162

Printed in the United States of America

PREFACE

Readings in Marketing has a threefold purpose: (1) It is designed to be used for supplementary reading in undergraduate marketing courses. (2) It may be used effectively as a basic text or as a readings book in graduate marketing courses. (3) Because it presents a balanced treatment of marketing theory and practice, it is also appropriate for business executives who seek comprehensive insights into the complexities of marketing.

The articles, addresses, research monographs, government reports and hearings, and previously unpublished studies and analyses that comprise *Readings in Marketing* have been carefully selected from a wide range of scholarly and historical sources, as well as from recently presented empirical knowledge and reports of contemporary experience. The readings are organized into seven major topical sections: (1) The Nature of Marketing, (2) The Consumer, (3) Marketing Functions and Policies, (4) Commodity Marketing, (5) Channels of Distribution, (6) Government and Marketing, and (7) International Marketing.

Although topically organized, many of the readings cut across and integrate a number of subject categories. The readings differ considerably in their levels of abstraction, and they sometimes represent conflicting if not contradictory points of view. These readings, therefore, are not unlike the variety of evidence the decision-maker in an imperfect business environment must weigh and upon which he must select a course of action.

Marketing decisions in today's business climate can no longer be made within the framework of knowledge centered around a single business discipline. The very process of analyzing and integrating diverse knowledge is a prime source of business innovation and progress. Thus, a major purpose of this book of readings is to develop in the reader a realization of the need to explore and utilize a number of disciplines in an ever-changing environment. Readings were therefore selected that could demonstrate how the work of a broad spectrum of social scientists and authorities from other areas was transferable and adaptable to the field of marketing.

Contributions from business and other disciplines are presented to provoke further research and thinking. It is hoped that the student, the teacher, and the business manager will be stimulated to examine critically these many promising areas of related activity and then select the most desirable approaches for the analysis of specific marketing problems. If this objective is realized, present and future managers will be better able to cope with the increasingly dynamic and intellectually demanding task of decision-making necessary for the optimum allocation of human, financial, and physical resources.

Integration of diverse areas of knowledge must extent beyond domestic boundaries because business systems abroad do have something to contribute to the development of marketing innovations. In addition, a prerequisite of any trade expansion program in the United States is a full understanding of the total environment in which various marketing systems function. Thus, a section on International Marketing is included.

Many colleagues in academia, business, and government were unusually enthusiastic in providing suggestions that were helpful in formulating the objectives and content of the book. All these individuals have our appreciation and thanks. Special acknowledgment must be made of the support given by Dr. Harvey A. Neville, President, Lehigh University, and by George R. Jenkins, Director of the Institute of Research, Lehigh University. In addition, we must express our grateful appreciation to Dr. Herbert M. Diamond, formerly Head of the Department of Economics and Sociology, now Acting Dean of the Graduate and Undergraduate College of Business Administration, Lehigh University, for his continuing interest and encouragement in our personal and professional development.

SGW / MDS / MLS

CONTENTS

SECTION 3. MARKETING FUNCTIONS AND POLICIES

SECTION 3-A MARKETING RESEARCH

SECTION 3-B MERCHANDISING AND PRODUCT DEVELOPMENT

SECTION 3-C BUYING

SECTION 3-D PRICING

SECTION 3-E SELLING AND ADVERTISING

SECTION 5-B WHOLESALERS

SECTION 5-C RETAIL ORGANIZATIONS

SECTION 5-D RETAIL POLICY CONSIDERATIONS

SECTION 6. GOVERNMENT AND MARKETING

SECTION 7. INTERNATIONAL MARKETING

SECTION 1. THE NATURE OF MARKETING

An understanding of the nature of marketing can be obtained by viewing it from such diverse viewpoints as: (1) its contribution toward the functioning of the economy; (2) its ability to create value; and (3) its relationship to other fields of knowledge.

What is the role of marketing in an economy geared to continuous production? What are the methods necessary to ensure that the constant stream of goods and services is absorbed? Oswald Knauth poses the proposition that a reliable system of distribution is the keystone of the United States economy and that continuous large-scale production is dependent on effective marketing. Marketing may not be a science, but it applies the findings of many varied sciences such as psychology, sociology, and statistics toward solving the problems of the marketing manager.

What is the importance of marketing and how can it be determined? Is marketing—that is, distribution—making any contribution toward increasing the productivity of our economy? Or is manufacturing the only creator of real value? These questions are marketing problems that have been the subject of much study. The study on the "Value Added" concept sponsored by the Chamber of Commerce of the United States provides a better understanding of marketing's importance.

Organization patterns today are in a transition stage, particularly with reference to decentralization of the marketing function. Edward G. Koch analyzes the several basic types that are now well established, traces their common elements, and provides some indication of their probable course of development.

George H. Brown explores the relationships between the economic theorist and the marketing manager. After analyzing similarities and differences in viewpoints, he finds that the managerial approach to marketing provides an effective method of developing a working relationship between the two disciplines.

1. THE ROLE OF MARKETING *

Oswald Knauth

Marketing is a system devised to ensure a constant flow of distribution equal to the flow of production. When it fails to keep pace with production, if efforts to speed up fail, production slows down, orders are canceled, employees are laid off. Disruption and loss are widespread. Marketing is thus a concept more inclusive than the concept of salesmanship. Until the advent of a flow of production, smart salesmanship was sufficient to distribute the goods produced. The great problem was to increase production. The production manager was more important than the sales manager. But with the new technique of the assembly line, production could be increased almost at will. A reliable system of distribution took the center of the stage.

This system is planned in advance and constantly revised in detail as circumstances warrant. Outside consultants are called in. The advertising agency spreads out and establishes a new department of research. A new profession of marketing arises, and at an increasing pace it develops throughout industry. Market research becomes commonplace. The American Marketing Association was formed in 1936; by 1955 it had a total membership of over 40,000, with active groups in many cities. Members exchange experiences and search for underlying principles. Business schools establish divisions of marketing.

Marketing postulates a heterogeneous production and demand. It is concerned with the differentiation of the product and the segmentation of demand. Thus marketing has little or no place in the distribution of standardized products such as wheat, coal, and cement. It comes to its full flower in dealing with those articles tailored to suit individual or group tastes, habits, and uses. It studies the images which consumers have of themselves. It seeks new uses and adaptation for existing articles. It searches for uncultivated fields, for neglected potentialities. It thrives in those areas sometimes (and erroneously) referred to as "imperfectly" competitive but more accurately described as dependent on a strong advantageous trade position.

* Reprinted by permission of Oswald Knauth, *Business Practices, Trade Position, and Competition* (New York: Columbia University Press, 1956), pp. 127-137.

Oswald Knauth, Professor of Marketing, Columbia University; former President and Treasurer, R. H. Macy and Co.

In supplying a segmented demand, the marketer faces a decision of policy. He can offer a variety of choices, each adapted to fit exactly the peculiar needs of each individual; or, he can concentrate on a generalized article, provided he can make it at such a low cost that the price overrides any minor disadvantages. The former is illustrated by the variety of makes, bodies, designs, and colors of automobiles at present; the latter by the Model T Ford. There are relative advantages either way, and they are differently estimated. Such estimates may be right or wrong, proved only by results.

During the 1860s most commodities were of a staple character, with only a sprinkling of imports such as Irish linen, English china, European furniture. These were of limited importance. Markets were local. Classical theory assumed that consumers were rational, so that Jeremy Bentham's theory of the balance of pleasure and pain seemed to fit the situation. Even necessities were in short supply. Bargaining and evaluating were the normal processes of the day. Prior to the 1870s, when the new standards of integrity set by Marshall Field, A. T. Stewart, and John Wanamaker became general, laxness of conscience in exact representation was widespread.

In the 1870s and 1880s the market widened. Railroad systems cheapened transportation. Communication improved. Factories replaced household production. The system of factory-wholesaler-retailer developed. Factories produced individual articles and could increase or decrease the rate of production in accord with orders which they were able to solicit. Local markets became national markets, but they remained simple. Only a few articles in the 1880s were advertised nationally—notably Sapolio, Pears Soap, Ivory Soap, and Royal Baking Powder. Frank Presbrey lists seventy-three items with "more or less" systematic publicity.

In the 1890s national markets began to solidify. Mail-order houses and department stores took on a new importance and began to put forth the claim that they were, in fact, the agent of the consumer. Manufacturers reached out over the heads of distributors to create a demand for their own products, which the distributors were thus compelled to supply. Trademarks multiplied. Independence of choice declined. After 1900, with the increasing range of articles supplied by manufacturers and the increased complexity of materials used, consumer knowledge of value and quality became insufficient. Rational choice was no longer a guide to purchase. Consumers became too unreliable to support a system of production that was increasing in efficiency.

This situation developed in the 1920s into a struggle between manufacturers and distributors for acceptance by the consumer—whether he preferred a specific manufacturer's brand or bought on the reputation of the retail distributor. When the consumer purchases a manufacturer's brand, the store in effect becomes the manufacturer's agent. When the consumer purchases the distributor's brand, the manufacturer becomes subservient to the retail distributor. Local retailers dealing in articles of common use become of necessity subservient to manufacturers to a point analogous with agency. Specialty stores retain independence, but on a petty scale. Small manufacturers lacking a system of distribution thus become dependent on the distributors. The struggle for dominance is between the national manufacturers and the large retailers.

Certain aspects of this evolution, sketched only very broadly, require further examination.

1. With the increased variety and complexity of the articles offered, the consumer is less able to evaluate them intelligently, and he falls back on reputation as a guide. Reputation depends largely on advertising, but it also depends, as in the case of articles of frequent purchase, on the test of use. The manufacturer dares not deviate from his standards, lest dissatisfaction deprive him of the benefit of the habits he has inculcated in the consumer. "Seconds" and "off products" are commonly disposed of under another label, to avoid identification. High standards of integrity are thus essential not only to the formation, but also to the maintenance of habits.

But the consumer is not entirely helpless in so far as selection of quality is concerned. Consumer's Union claims a membership of 750,000 and estimates that it influences 4 per cent of all purchases. Books are reviewed by newspapers and magazines. Clothes, drugs, and food are bought at sufficiently frequent intervals to be subject to the test of use. Pure food laws are stringently enforced. The Federal Trade Commission and Better Business Bureaus are alert to correct inaccuracies in advertising claims.

2. The rise of the new profession of market analysis thus has led to the distinction between salesmanship and marketing. The art of selling has receded in importance before the rise of so-called scientific marketing. The art of selling is old. Daniel Defoe wrote a book in 1725 entitled *The Complete English Tradesman* which is applicable to all times, even to the present. The devices of the itinerant Yankee peddler are well known.

Marketing grew out of and beyond the business of salesmanship. An advertisement of 1890 merely stated in an inch of space that "We have received a shipment of linen from Ireland which we call to the attention of our patrons." A stop-and-start economy. The unsold linen lay on the shelves of the retailer until its turn came, in due course, to be purchased. Meantime, it retained its value in the eyes of the merchant. It was not being crowded out by the arrival of more linen. When one shipment was sold out, more linen was imported. The looms in Ireland may have stood idle until new orders arrived, or they may have had so many orders on hand that they were unable to supply the last order for a year or more. The thought of enlarging their rate of production never occurred to them. But in order to induce continuous sales to meet the necessities of mass production, far greater ingenuity and organization had to be called into being. The professional marketers could not use the whip to drive the mule—they had to lure him with a carrot.

Marketing may not be a science, but it turns to practical account the findings of many sciences such as psychology, sociology, and statistics. The marketers set out to "educate" the consumer with all the skill at their command and through every available channel.

Marketers fitted products to the desires of different classes of consumers. They studied the quantities that were bought. They designed attractive packages, made displays, advertised, wrote jingles. They lubricated the wheels of the ordering mechanism. They wrote stories which seemed to have no relation to the product, but which led up to the point they sought to emphasize. They created circumstances conducive to increased use.

In an economy where industry has solved the problem of production, so that with increased demand production costs can be lowered, distribution may become the conspicuous failure, the gap, in the economy. Marketing attempts to fill this gap. The crude methods of the salesmen of lightning rods have given way to subtle and refined methods of indirection, association, abstraction, appeals of many kinds including vanity and utility.

3. Marketers draw a distinction between core and fringe demand. For every established article there is a solid core of addicted followers. In addition there is a floating population which changes easily under pressure or some supposed advantage. These changes are more fully reflected in trade statistics than ever before. The thorny task of management is to determine whether changes are temporary and random, or whether they reflect a decisive trend. Major interest of

course centers on the building up of a solid core. But the fringe is not ignored; it may be converted into the core.

The extent of impulse buying induced by a display or advertisement, as compared with necessity buying, varies for different kinds of articles and sizes of income. Attempts at measurement have placed it at from $1/10$ to $1/6$ of total normal sales. In either case, it is important.

Even in the purchase of durable goods, Eva Mueller (Consumer Behavior) found a surprising proportion of impulse buying. Over one third of all purchasers had a planning period of less than a month, and one sixth had a period of only a few days. There was no discussion by nearly one half the purchasers, and four fifths of the purchasers had only a little or no discussion at all. In the case of sport shirts, over a third of the purchases were reported as having been made on the "spur of the moment."

Alderson and Sessions note that "In the peculiar terminology of the appliance business, articles of substantial cost such as toasters and waffle irons are now referred to as 'impulse items.' "

A drive by one of the popular brands of cigarettes temporarily increases sales by 20 per cent. The midsummer furniture sales have not only converted a dull season of the year into an average one; they have actually made it the busiest season. Mother's Day was so successful in selling flowers that it was followed by Father's Day for new neckties.

These drives do more than advance the dates of purchase or the advantage of one manufacturer or distributor at the expense of another. They leave an aftermath of increased totals. They spur productive efforts to pay for the increased demand. They create new demands for consumption and form habits which become part of the standard of living.

4. An important part of marketing is the creation of new wants. The range of created demands covers every possible dimension, including adaptation of new methods, labor saving, greater ease of living, pure ostentation. Fear is a major instrument of persuasion. Fear of bad health, bad breath, rough skin, being outdone by neighbors, accident, penury in old age, sickness—all are played on endlessly and with great variety. Different persons would classify them differently, but taken together they form that "education" of the consumer which induces him to purchase the products of mass manufacturing. The consumer is the beneficiary as well as the victim of the speeding-up process.

5. It seems probable that the increase in the skill of marketing has outstripped the skill of the consumer in evaluating purchases. The purchaser is not always the consumer. The purchaser represents the unity—generally the family. When buying for himself, the purchaser thinks not only of immediate but of future consumption, especially when buying durable articles. Articles must be on hand in order to be used sporadically. Purchase and consumption therefore are not synonymous, a point which is greatly stressed in marketing appeal.

Marketing thus goes further than merely supplying the demands of the consumer. It attempts to create new wants and thus to expand all possibilities of distribution. Direct advertising is one of the mainsprings of stimulation for distribution. Therefore the newspapers loom large in such campaigns, and in newspapers the bulk of advertising appears in the Sunday editions. The Des Moines *Register* covers the state of Iowa to a degree that is exceptional. It has a daily circulation of about 200,000, compared with a Sunday circulation of over 500,000. The New York *Times* has a national circulation, especially the Sunday edition, which is replete with advertising. Its weekday circulation outside of New York is about 250,000 compared with a Sunday circulation of 750,000.

Many intelligent researches are undertaken to fill in the uncertain measurements of consumer motivations in different communities and different income groups. The proportion of purchases motivated by necessity, habit, taste, standard of living, impulse, ostentation, both in general and specifically, are anxiously sought after. The knowledge gained pays off. As the result of such a study, a local beer manufactured and used in Philadelphia more than doubled its sales in a few years in competition with the nationally known brands. Compare the lumbering complication of the mail-order blank of 1900 with the streamlined ease of 1950. Orders can be telephoned to a local agent and delivered in a few days from Atlanta or Chicago warehouses. Credit is easier. It has been found that the risk loss of consumer credit is a fraction of one per cent. It is cheaper to accept this loss than to continue the expense and irritation of investigation. Systems of distribution are designed to facilitate purchasing. Credit is dispensed painlessly. Often the price of an article is not quoted, only the monthly rate of payment. Consumer response to all of these methods is so automatic that it can often be forecast with a high degree of accuracy.

6. Most important is the device of installment selling, which has reached large proportions. By this device the time of purchase is

reduced to a minor role, for the payments are spread over a long period. Payments for durable goods thus assume a regularity for the consumer on a par with his purchase of consumable items. The stimulus for having the latest model is turned into an obsession, and the old article exchanged not only becomes the first payment for the new, but also results in introducing the low-priced second-hand article to a new level of purchasers. In these ways the apparent freedom of the consumer to buy or refrain from buying comes into a considerable degree of conformity.

7. The consumption effects of the five-day week have been subjected to scrutiny and are doubtless far-reaching. In the late 1930s a department store offered each of its employees a choice of five or six workdays per week at proportionate pay. The only condition was that once the choice was made it must be adhered to for six months. The result was an almost exact 50:50 choice. In the late 1940s there could scarcely have been such a choice. By that time the five-day week was practically universal, and industry was organized on that basis. How, then, is the extra day utilized? Partly by increased time for consumption. Partly by extra occasional earnings, such as taxi-driving, repair work, odds and ends. It has become customary for certain special needs of individuals to be serviced on Saturday only, when a man is released from his regular work and free to do extra work on his own time. Further study of these proportions would be illuminating.

The increased time for consumption gives opportunity for spending that was previously unavailable. Overnight expeditions for hunting, fishing, swimming at the beaches are possible. Distances no longer present a problem. The Saturday afternoon rush becomes the Friday evening rush. Sport clothes, slacks, and lounging attire replace more formal dress and carry over into everyday life. New necessities and desires are created.

8. Estimates of the rise in productivity cluster around 2 to 3 per cent per year. This is added purchasing power. Alderson and Sessions, using 2.2 per cent as the annual increased hourly percentage of productivity per worker, estimate that some 20 per cent is assignable to increased population, about 60 per cent goes to higher living standards, and 20 per cent to supplying more leisure to the workers.

Marketing has thus become the keystone of the economy. The tremendous prospects of continuous production are dependent on its success. The system of distribution created by the marketers is expensive, but it is more than compensated for by the reduced costs of mass production.

2. VALUE ADDED BY DISTRIBUTION *

The Chamber of Commerce of the United States

The Value Added Concept

The concept of "Value Added by Distribution" is derived from the more general economic concept of *value.* While theories of value differ in detail, there is general agreement on the basic idea. Modern thinking on this subject may be summarized as follows:

1. Value is fundamentally a subjective quality, since it depends on the capacity or *ability of a good or service to satisfy human wants and desires.* For this reason a good or service has value only with reference to human beings and only from their point of view. This is another way of saying that value is not objective and that unless a product or service is wanted by someone it has no value whatever. Such psychological valuations cannot, however, be measured directly, at least with any existing techniques.
2. Since we cannot measure psychological value, a practical measure of the value of a product is its *value relative to other goods and services,* as expressed by the quantity of a given product which exchanges in the market place for different quantities of other products.
3. In practice, value may be measured by the *money price of a product* in the market, using money as a common denominator of value.[1]

The total value of a product, as measured by its price, may be regarded as the end result of the process of "production," which is defined as the *creation of economic value by the addition of utilities to goods.*[2] Now, in a modern and highly developed economic system such as that of the United States, it must be recognized that almost all products pass through several stages of production before they are finally consumed. Iron ore is extracted by the mining industry;

* This report was completed under the sponsorship of the Domestic Distribution and Business Statistics Committees of the Chamber of Commerce of the United States. It was prepared under the supervision of Dr. Theodore N. Beckman, Professor of Business Organization at Ohio State University, who had previously employed the concept in his business consulting work and in testimony before Congressional committees. Research for the report was conducted by Robert D. Buzzell of the Ohio State University staff and by David D. Monieson, formerly of the Ohio State staff and now a member of the Faculty of the Graduate College of the University of Toronto, Canada. Reprinted by permission of The Chamber of Commerce of the United States.

[1] A. L. Meyers, "the price of anything is its value measured in terms of a standard monetary unit," *Modern Economics* (New York: Prentice-Hall, Inc., 1947), p. 69.

[2] *Ibid.*, p. 46.

it then passes through several stages of manufacture, processing, and assembly before it reaches a form in which it is useful to consumers, say, as an automobile. Finally, it passes through several stages of distribution before it is available at the proper times and places and is finally transferred to a consumer. The entire process of mining, manufacturing, and distribution must be included in the term "production," since at each stage a certain amount of *value is added* to the product.

The value added by distribution is simply that part of the final retail price of a product which can be attributed to the marketing stages of the production process. Similarly, the value added by a given marketing institution, such as the retail automobile dealer, is that part of the price which is paid for the contribution made by him. These values added result from the performance of *marketing functions,* which are just as truly productive types of work as are agricultural, manufacturing, processing or factory assembling activities.

Value Added by Distribution may be defined, then, as the dollar value of the functions performed in the marketing process. The value of marketing functions comprises a part, usually estimated at about one half, of the total value of goods and services produced in the United States (Gross National Product).

The most difficult part of the value added concept is its relationship with the concept of *cost.* In one sense, price and cost must always be identical. What an article costs the consumer is its price. Similarly, what distribution costs the consumer is also the value added by marketing. Thus, in a functional sense, value added by distribution is the same thing as the "social cost" of distribution. At this point, however, the difference in attitudes toward distribution and manufacturing or agriculture begins to appear. One seldom hears of the "social cost of manufacturing" or the "social cost of agriculture." The values contributed by these forms of production are clearly recognized, and increases in them are widely hailed as social benefits. If the share of Gross National Product going to distribution increases, however, it is considered undesirable and wasteful. Why? The answer is to be found in the role of distribution in the over-all process of production.

Distribution—the final essential phase of production

Early French economists of the Physiocratic school regarded only agriculture as truly productive and condemned both distribution and manufacturing as "sterile" activities. Later economists included manufacturing as a part of production, but under the Physiocratic influence excluded distribution and all other activities which do not *create tangible products.* Fortunately, most reputable economists have now come to realize that distribution is just as truly a part of production as other economic activities. Production is correctly defined as the *creation of economic utilities,* including those of form, time, place, and possession. Of these four kinds of utilities, distribution creates the last three. Distribution is, therefore, an integral part of production, not a necessary and costly evil which *follows* production. The artificial division between "production" and distribution made in the common usage of the terms has done much to perpetuate the mistaken views of the early and long outmoded economists.

Much of the well-known public antagonism toward distribution stems from failure to recognize the role of distribution in the production process. There seems to be a cultural lag between economic development and public attitudes; and since distribution has only come to be of great importance in the last fifty years, it is not surprising that it has not yet been accorded its proper place. Denunciations of "too high" distribution costs have been common in the press, and not unknown in the writings of otherwise competent economists.

The basic assumption underlying the many attacks on marketing costs is what might be called the "constant margin assumption." The reasoning runs something like this: total production should be measured by the physical volume of goods produced, fabricated, and marketed to consumers. A certain percentage margin is necessary for distribution costs. If this increases, the consumer receives no more value, because he receives the same physical goods; but he is forced to pay more. The cause for the increased margin must be inefficiency in the marketing system, and distribution therefore, costs "too much."

Now, one need not be an economic theorist to see the fallacy of the foregoing argument. In the first place, much of the increase in marketing margins is due to increased specialization in the economic system. Our economy has undergone a dramatic and far-reaching change in organization during the past 100 years, a change which continues and apparently will continue for the foreseeable future. The full development of the factory system, the application of mass production techniques, and the present-day movement toward automation, all operate to shift much of the burden of production from manufacturing to distribution.

One factor is increased distances between factory and consumer, requiring greater transportation of products. Another is the need for marketing research, both because of the separation of factory and consumer and because of the fact that new demands must be discovered and met if our factories are to be kept in operation.

Most significant of all, however, is the need for *demand creation,* a need which did not exist a hundred years ago. As our standard of living advances, more and more production is based on *new products,* on *variations of old products* (many of them minor in character), and on expansion of our *willingness to consume.*[3] All of these dynamic functions are marketing functions, and represent increases in the value added by distribution. It is only natural, therefore, that the share of the consumer's dollar going for marketing should have increased as a long-run trend.

A second factor not taken into account by many of the critics is that more and better marketing services are provided to consumers. Credit, for example, is far more widely used today than at any time in the past. Wider selections of goods require that larger inventories be maintained and financed; and marketing research provides more adequate information concerning the needs and desires of consumers. The point is that distribution costs should be evaluated in relation to the amount and quality of marketing functions performed and services provided, and it cannot be assumed that a constant amount of such work or services is provided per unit of physical output. Yet this is just what the "constant margin assumption" amounts to.

The growth of interest in value added by distribution

Students of distribution have long recognized the problem of measuring output and productivity in this type of production. The fallacies of the one-sided cost approach described above have been pointed out more than once.[4] Only recently, however, has the concept of value added been recognized as a possible measure of output. Value Added by Distribution was the subject of a session at the December, 1954, convention of the American Marketing Association. At that time two papers were presented which have served as the basis for much of this report. The principal contribution to the

[3] For a full exposition of this thesis, see Paul Mazur, *The Standards We Raise.*

[4] See, for example, H. H. Maynard and T. N. Beckman, *Principles of Marketing* (New York: Ronald Press, 1952), pp. 711-12; C. F. Phillips, "A Critical Analysis of Recent Literature Dealing with Marketing Efficiency," *Journal of Marketing,* Vol. V (1941), pp. 360-64.

theory of value added was made by Dr. Theodore N. Beckman of The Ohio State University. Dr. Beckman has made considerable use of the value concept in consulting work with various business firms. In the area of measurement of value added, Mr. David D. Monieson, a contributor to this report, has done considerable research and is presently preparing a doctoral dissertation on the subject.[5]

Several earlier contributions on the subject of value added by distribution deserve recognition. Estimates of value added have been made for the years 1929, 1939, and 1948 by Professor Paul D. Converse and his associates at the University of Illinois.[6] Another contribution was a report prepared by a group under the direction of Mr. Robert J. Eggert of the Ford Motor Company and presented to the Boston Conference on Distribution in 1953.[7]

Value added as a measure of output

It should be apparent from the above discussion that marketing output cannot be measured by the physical quantity of goods marketed. For several reasons, however, it is desirable that this output should be measured. How can this difficult task be accomplished? The value added concept offers at least a partial solution to the problem.

Value added data have been collected for manufacturing establishments and published in the United States Census of Manufactures since 1910. The Bureau of the Census defines value added by manufacture as the value of shipments (sales) minus the cost of materials, supplies, containers, fuel, purchased electric energy, and contract work.[8] The resulting dollar figure is generally accepted as a more useful measure of output than sales because different plants vary in the degree to which the various stages of production are integrated. Some manufacturers have integrated all the steps from raw material processing to final assembly within a single "manufacturing establishment"; while others may perform the function of final assembly only.

In the Federal Reserve index of production, value added is used to measure output but is deflated by the index of prices in order to

[5] These papers are published as part of a volume entitled *Frontiers in Marketing Thought,* Proceedings of the 1954 American Marketing Association Convention (Bloomington, Indiana: Bureau of Business Research, Indiana University, 1955).

[6] See P. D. Converse, H. W. Huegy, and R. V. Mitchell, *Elements of Marketing* (New York: Prentice-Hall, Inc., 1952), pp. 789-92.

[7] Published in the report of the *Twenty-fifth Annual Boston Conference on Distribution* (Boston: Retail Trade Board and others, 1953), pp. 65-71.

[8] *Census of Manufactures*; 1947, Vol. II, *Statistics by Industry* (Washington-D. C.: U. S. Government Printing Office, 1949), p. 18.

eliminate the effects of monetary inflation or deflation.[9] It should be noted, however, that the method of constructing this index for a given industry is based on an assumption similar to the "constant margin" concept described above. Thus, it is assumed that the ratio of value added to sales within an industry remains constant over a period of time unless major changes in industry structure take place.

Value added is a valid measure of production only if a condition of effective competition exists among sellers. This is true because in the absence of competition, buyers might have no choice on which to base their evaluations of different offerings. It seems reasonable, though, to assume a condition of effective competition (not theoretical "perfect" competition) among marketing establishments. This statement is based on (1) the large number of competing establishments in any trading area, (2) the relatively small amount of capital usually required to establish a marketing enterprise, and (3) the fact that buyers are presented with effective choices by marketing institutions with respect to goods offered and to functions performed in the marketing of any one type of goods. It competition does exist, then value added by distribution represents the value placed on marketing services by buyers. As such, it is the best available measure of marketing output.

A final problem has to do with deflating the value added figures, which will be collected in current dollar terms. For this purpose it would be incorrect to use an index of the prices of finished products, since (as noted above in connection with manufacturing) this would amount to assuming a constant margin as the standard of performance. What is needed is an index of the prices of marketing functions themselves. Deflated by this kind of index, value added would measure the *amount of marketing functions performed and services rendered* and comparisons over time could be made. The question of how to account for changes in the *quality* of the service is necessarily left unanswered, just as it has been in indexes of industrial production. One 1955 automobile is still counted the equivalent of one 1924 automobile, and apparently there is no easy escape from this problem. In any event, the system of measuring production in the field of distribution outlined above would be comparable to the present system of measuring manufacturing output and output of the mines, and be a great step forward in the scientific study of distribution.

[9] Bureau of the Census and Board of Governors, Federal Reserve System (joint publication), *Census of Manufacturers*, 1947, *Indexes of Production* (Washington, D. C.: U. S. Government Printing Office, 1953), p. 3.

The Significance of Value Added Data

There would be little point in undertaking the measurement of value added by distribution unless the results were useful in the analysis of economic and business problems. Some of the more important applications of value added data are summarized in this section.[10]

Value added as a measure of economic importance

The original, and still most important purpose of the value added by manufacture column in the Census of Manufacturers, is to obtain an accurate measure of importance of any particular segment of the manufacturing sector. It was felt long ago that the dollar gross sales figure as a criterion of industry importance was quite unsatisfactory because it merely represented the total volume of commercial transactions of the industry, and that it did not represent the final value of the manufactured products of the country.[11] The derivation of the value added by manufactures column was essentially an attempt to eliminate duplications brought about through the compilation of the gross total value of shipments or sales.

A simple example will serve to illustrate this point. Suppose a chemicals manufacturer sells $15,000 worth of chemicals to a plastics manufacturer for $20,000; the plastics manufacturer, in turn, sells for $40,000 these same chemicals in a changed form to a package manufacturer; the package manufacturer sells for $50,000 the packages made from the plastic material. If sales volume were employed as the criterion of economic importance, the packaging manufacturer would be judged most important because he had the largest sales volume. The trouble is that sales volume is a duplicating item that gets larger and larger as the raw material becomes more the finished product. Value added eliminates the duplicating element, so that, in the above example, it would be the plastics manufacturer who added the greatest value to the product, and should be regarded as making the greatest economic contribution, for the greater the dollar value added, the greater the economic contribution of a firm, group of firms, or industry.

[10] Much of this section is suggested by Dr. T. N. Beckman, "The Value Added Concept as Applied to Marketing and Its Implications," *Frontiers in Marketing Thought*, pp. 83-99.

[11] The Twelfth Census of the United States, 1902, *Census of Manufactures*, Volume III, Part I, p. cxxxix.

Value added by distribution can be used as a measure of economic importance in a fashion similar to the use of value added by manufacture described above. In this way it is possible to ascertain the contribution to Gross National Product of a single establishment, a firm, or an industry. Comparisons could also be made between different classes of marketing establishments, such as full-function and limited-function wholesalers, or independent and chain retail establishments. Finally, accurate value added data would permit a true comparison of the entire distribution sector of the economy with other sectors such as manufacturing, agriculture, or mining. Such comparisons would make possible a far more intelligent appraisal of the structure and functioning of the economy as a whole than is possible at present.

. . . Series of rankings based on sales volume, number of employees, and payrolls as published by the Census of Business indicate clearly that none of the criteria available from Census data give a clear picture of the economic importance of the different groups. Among retail establishments, for instance, the Food Group is by far the most important segment if sales volume is used as the criterion. When value added is used, however, the General Merchandise Group (which includes department stores, dry goods and general merchandise stores, general stores, and variety stores) makes just as great a contribution to the economy although its total sales volume is much lower. This is explained by the fact that establishments in the General Merchandise Group earn a much higher proportional rate of value added to sales than do food stores.

In the wholesaling structure, too, similar classifications may be made by use of value added data. Here, again, according to sales volume, the Grocery and Allied Products Group is the most important segment. When value added is employed as the criterion, however, the Machinery and Equipment Group is the most important part of the structure and the Grocery Group is a poor second.[12]. . . In general, the ranking by number of employees tends to correspond with the value added ranking. Divergences between these two rankings probably indicate superior productivity and/or greater capital investments in certain segments of wholesaling and retailing than in others.

[12] This must not be construed to mean that the group with a higher value added to sales ratio is either more or less efficient than the group with a lower value added to sales ratio. After all, value added merely measures *output* of goods or services or the value in goods and services that is created by the group in question, by the single enterprise, by an industry, or by the economy as the case may be. It is only when such output is considered in relation to the *input* (in specific costs for labor or in total costs) that efficiency in a competitive market can be determined.

Value added and productivity

The measurement of productivity or "efficiency" has long been a central problem in applied economics. The importance of measuring productivity can hardly be overstated; productivity indicates the degree of effectiveness attained in the utilization of resources and may be considered the ultimate standard of economic performance. Policy decisions at all levels in the economic system depend on estimates of productivity by alternative methods or institutions. In practice, of course, rough estimates of productivity are used rather than objective measures; the ability to make such estimates probably comprises a large part of what is called "business judgment."

Productivity may be defined as the *ratio of output to input* for an economic institution or process over a given period of time. Calculation of this ratio obviously requires measurement of both output and input; and, as had been indicated in Section I, value added is a measure of marketing output. Input can be measured in physical terms much more easily than output, since only a few factors of production are used to produce a great number and variety of outputs. Labor input, for example, can be measured in man-hours of work, as is done in the many studies of the United States Bureau of Labor Statistics.

All that is required to measure productivity, then, is to express both output (value added) and input as indexes on some common base, and to find the ratio between the two. The problem is not this simple, of course, for a single marketing institution or a small group of institutions. Output in a single institution can be measured by value added, but since the assumption of effective competition cannot be applied to one unit, it must be evaluated in light of a firm's market share. A more useful approach can probably be developed for internal productivity measurement through *work measurement* techniques, which would involve direct measurement of the quantities of various marketing services rendered.

Value added can be used, then, to measure productivity for large groups of marketing establishments and to make comparisons of productivity between different times, places, and kinds of business. Only in this way (if at all) can a meaningful answer ever be given to the question, "Does distribution cost too much?"

Value added and profits

It has already been indicated that the amount of value added by a marketing institution is a measure of the amount of service rendered in the performance of marketing functions. Accordingly, it is reasonable to expect a connection between value added and the amount of profit earned by an institution. Profit, in a competitive free enterprise system, is primarily a return for service rendered. Needless to say, many other factors affect the level of profits in a dynamic economy; but in general, profit returns should be directly proportional to the amount of economic value added by an institution.

It is, unfortunately, impossible to say just what the normal ratio of profit to value added is among marketing institutions. The types and amount of data currently available do not permit any accurate correlation analysis of the two variables. Some preliminary studies do indicate a significant degree of correlation, but the results are by no means clear or unequivocal. An important reason for the collection of more data is to facilitate further study of value added-profits relationships for various kinds of business.

If further study does substantiate the thesis that profits vary with value added, the relationship will have a great deal of significance for the businessman. It will show clearly the fallacy of a one-sided "cost reduction" approach to profit maximization. Profits may be increased at times with costs, at other times by decreasing them. The important thing is the quantity of services rendered for customers and the existence of a demand for these services. A businessman's real objective should be, then, to maximize value added either by earning a wide margin on a low turnover or by earning a narrow margin on a high turnover. This assumes, of course, that every cost dollar spent results in a corresponding quantity of service performed. It should be reiterated that this is valid only for large groups of institutions and not for a single firm. Other methods must be used to control this relationship within a single firm.

To illustrate the application of these concepts to business policy decisions, suppose that a businessman is faced with a choice between a high-margin, full-service policy and a low-margin, limited-service policy. Presumably the limited-service policy would result in a higher volume of sales, but a lower profit margin per dollar of sales. The basis for choice should be the best possible estimate of the value added, in dollars, under the two systems. It might be that the dollar value added would be about the same in either case, in which event dollar profits would probably also be about the same.[13]

[13] It must be pointed out, however, that high sales volume does not necessarily accompany a low margin policy. Department stores are large institutions, but typically operate on very high margins. This indicates a demand for the type of service which they render.

A further application of the relationship between value added and profits has to do with the familiar but vague concept of "fair" or "normal" profits. It is well known that the ratio of profit to sales varies widely among different kinds of business. While the ratio of profit to invested capital is less variable, no specific rate of return has ever been widely accepted as normal. Further investigation may show, however, that a normal rate of profit on value added does exist which could be applied to different types of business activity. Variations in the rate of return on investment would then be accounted for by different degrees of productivity in the use of capital achieved by different firms. Some firms might succeed in achieving a higher ratio of value added to investment than others, which would result in the higher rate of return on investment.

Value added as a basis for normal profit also suggests that the provisions of future excess profits taxes, if they should ever become necessary again, might well be based on value added. The advantage of this approach over either a percentage-of-sales or a percentage-of-investment definition of "excess" profits is that it recognizes differences among firms according to the degree of service performed or contribution made to the economy. Moreover, it would not penalize a company for superior capital productivity, since no arbitrary limitation would be placed on the rate of return on investment.

Value added and taxation

The value added by a business institution, in either distribution or manufacturing, represents its contribution to the gross national product of the economy. For this reason, taxation authorities have suggested that business taxes might be based on value added rather than on sales, profits, or any of the other bases currently employed. The State of Michigan recently adopted a "business receipts tax" based on this same idea and experience with it has apparently been good.[14] Also, a modified value added tax is in use in France, and one was recommended for Japan during the postwar reconstruction but not yet put into effect. The advantage of value added as a basis for taxation is that it provides a non-duplicative allocation of gross national product to individual business enterprises. It would be easier, on such a basis, to evaluate the impact of taxation on different segments of the economy and to adjust taxes in order to equalize their burdens. . . .

[14] See Peter A. Firmin, *The Michigan Business Receipts Tax: An Appraisal:* (Ann Arbor, Michigan: Bureau of Business Research, University of Michigan, 1955).

Measuring Value Added by Distribution

As pointed out in the introduction to this report, it is proposed that the value added concept be implemented through the assembly of adequate quantitative information. Such information is available at present only on a fragmentary basis, through the efforts of various retail and wholesale trade associations. It is highly desirable that fuller coverage be obtained by collecting value added data for the entire marketing system, not just for members of a limited number of trade associations. This section presents a suggested method of gathering such data through the United States Census of Business, together with suggestions for further application by trade associations.

There are two problems involved in the measurement of value added by distribution. The first is the question of the basic approach to be used; the second has to do with the procedure for gathering information. These two questions will be considered in order.

Approaches to the measurement of value added

There are three possible approaches to measuring value added by distribution. These may be called the *commodity, functional,* and *institutional* approaches.

The Commodity Approach. The commodity approach would involve allocating the values added by marketing activities to the various classes of commodities, such as agricultural commodities, manufactured consumer goods, capital goods, and so on. The classification of commodities could of course be carried much further, all the way down to some specific item such as razor blades or toothpaste.

It is not difficult to see the problems which would be encountered in applying the commodity approach. Most products are manufactured and marketed together with other products or with by-products. In consequence, it would be necessary to allocate all costs and profits (to use accounting terminology) to individual products. The experience of the Department of Agriculture in its attempts to do this indicates that it would be an impractical approach to measuring value added. Moreover, it would be much *more* difficult to collect the necessary data for manufactured goods than it has been for agricultural products. Thus, practical considerations prevent the use of a commodity approach on any wide scale, except for special studies.

The Functional Approach. The aim of the functional approach to the measurement of value added by marketing would be to determine the dollar value of income added to the economy by the performance of marketing functions regardless of the commodities involved or the institutions in which the activity takes place. The first task would be to identify all those marketing activities performed, not only by all classes of wholesalers and retailers, but also by manufacturers, farmers, miners, fishermen, and forestrymen. This would be the truest and most comprehensive method of measuring value added by distribution, since "distribution" is defined as a series of functions, rather than as a group of institutions.

However, as the Committee on Business Statistics of the United States Chamber of Commerce pointed out in its preliminary value added by distribution report, the task of measurement by such an approach would be extremely difficult, because not only would all those business institutions performing marketing functions have to be located, but it would also be necessary to segregate marketing functions from manufacturing and processing activities much more accurately than present accounting procedures permit. Just as important would be the need to identify and then place a dollar value on the marketing functions performed by the ultimate consumer.

No estimates of value added by distribution have ever been made on the basis of a strictly functional approach (that is, the addition of the values added by, say, the buying, selling, transportation, storage, grading and labeling, market finance, market risk, and market information functions of marketing). All estimates of value added by marketing activities to date have employed a hybrid functional approach, i.e., the estimators have calculated not only the value added by wholesalers and retailers, but also the value of marketing functions performed in other segments of the economy, such as the manufacturing, agricultural, mining, and transportation industries. One of the most noteworthy attempts along these lines has been Professor Paul D. Converse's series of estimates of value added by marketing activities.[15]

The Institutional Approach. Under the institutional approach, value added by distribution is really that value which is added to goods handled by marketing institutions, namely, the various census classes of wholesale and retail establishments. Obviously, a measure of value added by marketing establishments is less comprehensive than a measure of value added by marketing activities or functions. However, such a measurement would be practical and useful.

[15] Converse, Huegy, and Mitchell, *op. cit.*, pp. 789-92.

The advantages of the institutional approach over either a commodity or a functional approach may be summarized briefly as follows: (1) the necessary data are most readily available on this basis, since accounting records are kept on an institutional basis; (2) it would fit in with the present Census of Business, in which data are gathered on the basis of marketing *establishments*; (3) it would permit comparisons with data from the Census of Manufacturers, which is institutional in scope; (4) it would be most useful for management purposes, since management is largely an institutional function; and (5) it would permit trade associations and similar bodies to participate in applying value added to marketing activities.

. . . In effect, then, value added by wholesale and retail establishments would be the dollar value of their net sales or operating income, f.o.b. plant, less cost of goods sold, supplies, containers, fuel, and purchased energy.

From the above definition, it can be noted that the value added by a given marketing institution is measured roughly by its gross margin. The gross margin, of course, will usually be greater than the firm's value added, the difference arising from the purchase of supplies, containers, fuel, and electricity. The costs of such overhead items, however, do not comprise such a large part of the gross margins as to prevent their use in estimating value added by marketing establishments. Although there are no authoritative statistics in the United States to verify this last statement, it is possible to do so from Canadian data. The Canadian Government issues biennially through the Dominion Bureau of Statistics operating results studies for various segments of the trade industry.[16] From these data one can ascertain the relative importance of the overhead items in question by comparing the gross margin of each trade group with the census concept of value added for the trade group involved. In Canada, value added, by Census definition, comprises about 97 to 98 per cent of the wholesaler's gross margin; about 95 to 96 per cent of the retail chain's gross margin; and about 92 to 95 per cent of the independent retailer's gross margin. While these data are not sufficient to permit any conclusions, they are probably indicative of

[16] For example, the Dominion Bureau of Statistics, Ottawa, Canada, issued the following operating results booklets for 1953: Wholesale Trade—Food, Dry Goods, Piece Goods, Footwear, Automotive Parts and Accessories, Drugs, Hardware, Plumbing and Heating Equipment. Retail Chain Stores—Food, Clothing, Variety, Drug, Hardware. In 1952 the Bureau issued the following independent retail store results: Food, Clothing, Hardware, Furniture, Appliance and Radio Stores, General Stores, Restaurants, Fuel Dealers, Drugs, Jewelry, Tobacco Stores.

the picture in the United States. As a rough figure, then, the firm's gross margin is comparable to its value added, by census definition. Therefore, in the absence of more accurate data, an approximate estimate of the value added by marketing institutions could be made by determining the gross margins of all wholesale and retail establishments in dollar terms.

The procedure described above is not as simple as it may sound. Unlike the Census of Manufactures, the Census of Business does not include value added data for the establishments covered by it; nor does the Census of Business ask for or publish gross margin data. The only government source which publishes any trade gross margin data on a continuous basis is the Internal Revenue Service of the U. S. Treasury Department, through its *Statistics of Income.* There are at least two major limitations to the use of these data. First, the statistics are normally published about four years behind the current year. Second, the information is based on corporation data only, while the census breakdown is by establishments, regardless of ownership. This is of particular importance for distribution, since many retail and wholesale institutions are of the single proprietorship or partnership type.

The most likely sources of existing gross margin data would seem to be individual trade associations, university business research bureaus, and other private institutions. There may be some lack of accounting uniformity among the gathered data, but for the most part these divergences are not serious. Again, the data may not be comparable with the census breakdown by establishments because trade associations gather the data on an ownership or company basis, not on an establishment basis. Also, there is a tendency for only the larger firms to submit such information, thereby introducing a bias into the results. This method, along with the interpolation and addition of net operating profits data to wholesale operating expenses as provided by the Census of Business, are the only two ways which can be at present utilized if any comprehensive or significant study of value added by marketing institutions is to be attempted. . . .

Net Value Added by Marketing Institutions. The Bureau of the Census' definition of value added is not an accurate measure of the actual value which the manufacturing or marketing firm adds to the goods it handles. In theory, value added is the dollar value of income created by the productive activity of an economic institution; it is the income earned by the various factors of production, and distributed to them in the form of rent, wages and salaries, interest, profit, and taxes.[17] The summation of the values added of all the productive factors in the economy would be equal to the economy's gross national product. Therefore, a true measurement of value added by marketing institutions would be equal to the trade sector's contribution to gross national product. . . . If it is desired to measure, as accurately as possible, the value added by the trade industry, or its contribution to gross national product, all income distributed to others than the factors of production must first be subtracted from the firm's gross margin—not merely supplies, fuel, purchased electrical energy. This means that not only purchased goods but also the cost of all purchased services. The following is a list of items to be subtracted from the gross value of output of an industry or net sales of a firm to obtain its contribution to gross national product:

1. Cost of materials and fuels used, and of work given out.
2. Purchased advertising and other selling services.
3. Printing, stationery, and other office supplies.
4. Purchased business insurance premiums.
5. Postage, telegraph, and telephone payments.
6. Expenses for banking, legal, accounting, auditing and similar business services.
7. Cost of materials and parts required for small repairs and maintenance work carried out by the establishment's employees.
8. Cost of small repairs, maintenance, and servicing carried out by outside contractors.

What remains is allocated as income to the various factors of production. The point to remember is that all business taxes are allocated to the government factors, and that depreciation is allocated to the capital factor.[18] If these two allocations are not made, then the true measure of value added is understated, and the resulting dollar value total will be equal to the industry's or firm's contribution to *national income,* rather than its contribution to gross national product.

Suggested course of action

The most desirable course of action for the measurement of value added by marketing would be to incorporate value added data into the United States Census of Business, which covers all retail and wholesale establishments as well as service establishments. It ap-

[17] Government is considered as a factor of Production. See T. N. Beckman, "The Value Added Concept as Applied to Marketing and Its Implications," *Frontiers in Marketing Thought,* Rewoldt, Editor (Bloomington, Indiana: Indiana University, 1955), pp. 97-99.

[18] For a detailed discussion of the problems and methods of measuring net value added by marketing institutions, see David D. Monieson, "On Measuring Value Added by Marketing," *Frontiers in Marketing Thought,* pp. 120-130.

pears that this can be done quite easily and without too much additional expense, since the Bureau of the Census already collects data on sales for both retail and wholesale establishments, and on operating expenses for wholesale places of business.

Every effort should be made, therefore, to add a new section to Census report forms showing value added for each establishment, and to publish this information for the various Census classifications of businesses. It has been noted that this should be done on the basis of a definition of value added consistent with that used in the Census of Manufacturers. . . .

EXHIBIT 1

SUGGESTED METHOD OF COMPUTING VALUE ADDED BY DISTRIBUTION

Census of Business

1. Net Sales and Other Operating Receipts $________

   (This figure is presently collected by the Census of Business for all retail and wholesale establishments.)

2. Deductions from Net Sales and Other Operating Receipts

   (a) Cost of Goods Sold: Cost figures should be computed net of all discounts and allowances; include freight-in. Include the cost of goods sold in 19xx but purchased prior to 19xx; do not include the cost of goods purchased and/or received in 19xx but held over in closing inventories.
   (b) Costs of supplies, materials, parts, and packaging consumed in 19xx.
   (c) Cost of fuel consumed in 19xx.
   (d) Cost of electric energy consumed in 19xx.

   TOTAL, items (a) through (d) $________

   (The items listed in part 2 are recorded by most, if not all, retail and wholesale establishments. It would be necessary only to total them and to report the TOTAL ONLY. Thus only one line need be added to the Census of Business report forms.)

3. Value Added by Distribution: $________

   Net Sales and Other Operating Receipts LESS Total Deductions under part 2.

Trade association action

In addition to the collection of value added data by the Census of Business, it would be helpful if individual retail and wholesale trade associations could participate in the application of the value added concept to business activities. It may be observed that one of the principal activities of such associations has long been the collection of cost data and their use to compare individual firms with typical experience. It would not be a great deal more work to collect data on value added by distribution for member organizations; comparisons of value added ratios would be an eminently useful addition to the types of analysis presently conducted by trade associations.

In addition, associations can go one step further. They can apply techniques of work *measurement* to the operations in their lines, as is already done on a limited scale by the National Association of Wholesale Druggists and by the National Retail Dry Goods Association. While these techniques are not the subject of this report, they are closely related to the value added concept and could be used to show the ultimate relationships between value added, money cost, and efficiency.

Conclusion

Whatever efforts are made to gather and analyze value added information, they should be based on sound concepts of the nature and scope of distribution as a whole and of the various segments of the distribution structure. The Bureau of the Census can, of course, be depended upon for proper classifications and definitions. Unfortunately, this is not true of all government agencies.

Much of the criticism of marketing mentioned in the first section of this report stems from inaccurate uses of concepts and terminology. A prime example is the series of "marketing margin" studies for agricultural products published by the United States Department of Agriculture. In these studies, all costs and profits incurred between the sale of farm products in the raw state and the purchase of finished goods by consumers are attributed to marketing.

Much of this so-called "marketing margin" is, in reality, a manufacturing or processing margin. Thus the USDA grossly exaggerates the share of the consumer's dollar going for distribution.[19] Since scientific study and evaluation of distribution are hampered by misconceptions such as this, it is essential that studies of value added be carefully planned according to appropriate definitions and classification systems.

In summary, then, it is recommended that data be collected and published on value added by marketing institutions, both wholesale

[19] See T. N. Beckman and R. D. Buzzell, "What is the Marketing Margin for Agricultural Products," *Journal of Marketing* (October, 1955), pp. 166-68.

and retail. Later, it may be possible to develop estimates of value added on a functional and/or commodity basis.

Value added data should, if possible, be incorporated into future censuses of wholesale and retail trade and classified according to the present Bureau of the Census system.

In the meantime, various trade associations can and should undertake to collect value added information from their members.

An even greater contribution could be made through sample studies of value added by the Bureau of the Census. . . . The business community can contribute to the progress of research in this area by encouraging the efforts of trade associations and by working for understanding and acceptance of the concept by American businessmen.

3. NEW ORGANIZATION PATTERNS FOR MARKETING *

Edward G. Koch

What's so new about the "marketing concept"? The term has been discussed and written about so much that the uninitiated might be forgiven for assuming that the marketing concept is a dramatic and revolutionary theory that has recently burst upon the management scene; actually, of course, most of the ideas it embodies have been around for some time. What is new—at least for many companies—is the emphasis on making marketing a central part of the business philosophy of the company and elevating the marketing function to a pre-eminent position in the organization.

There was a time when most companies were production-oriented: First they produced the product, then they made a market for it. Selling was thus the important concept—and the difference between selling and marketing is more than a semantic exercise. Selling focuses on the needs of the seller, marketing on the needs of the purchaser. Selling means moving products; marketing means obtaining customers. In production-oriented companies, management tells the sales department, in effect, "You get rid of the products; we'll worry about the profits." In contrast, the marketing-minded company makes every effort to create goods that customers will want to buy at a reasonable profit to the company.

We have had marketing-minded companies with us for some time; such pioneer companies as Sears, Roebuck, John Wanamaker, J. C. Penney, and General Foods have understood and practiced the so-called marketing concept for many years. Today, however, more and more companies are adopting this point of view; management thinking is becoming more customer-oriented, and profitable selling is replacing sales volume as the primary objective of the marketing program.

* Reprinted by permission of the American Management Association, *Management Review*, Vol. 51, No. 2 (February, 1962), p. 4.

Edward G. Koch, Professor of Business Administration, University of California, Los Angeles.

A mature market

The reasons for this changing emphasis are not difficult to determine. During the past decade and a half, the United States market, although by no means saturated, has become mature. A great many U. S. consumers have satisfied their basic needs for products and goods. They have become more discerning buyers, and they can afford to pass up products that do not completely meet their desires and standards. Moreover, they are spending a larger proportion of their income on services than ever before. Thus, producers of consumer goods must compete not only with each other, but with the growing appeal of vacation trips, higher education, better medical care, and the wide array of services that are becoming part of the "good life" to the American consumer.

Focus on the consumer

Faced with this situation, many companies are finding that they cannot afford a hit-or-miss approach to marketing problems. The consumer has become the pivot point about which the entire business must move. This shift in emphasis requires more research expenditures, greater product-development activities, and increased attention to the short- and long-term planning of marketing activities. Marketing plans have become the basis for the design and erection of total corporate planning. Future market plans and sales potentials, for example, serve as premises for the planning of advertising expenditures, sales and promotion efforts, plant expansion and location, financial requirements, and other short- and long-term business commitments.

At the same time, sheer sales volume is no longer considered the key to corporate profitability. As competition increases and profit margins shrink, many companies have found that their marketing plans, policies, and strategies must be designed chiefly for their contribution to profits, rather than predicated on sales-volume objectives alone. And marketing goals must be consistent with over-all company objectives in order to contribute most to the long-range benefit of the firm. This means that the marketing function must be more closely coordinated and integrated with the other activities of the company, and the marketing responsibility has been expanded and reorganized to interlock all functions of the company into greater effectiveness.

Organizational changes

In short, the modern marketing concept demands that the activities of the entire business be directed toward the satisfaction of consumer needs at a profit, and to accomplish this goal it has often become necessary for a company to rearrange its organizational structure. Although the changes that have been made have varied widely from company to company, depending on the peculiar circumstances in which they may operate, enough experience has been logged to identify several basic types of organizational setup that have been established by companies who have adopted this management philosophy.

Simple product line

In companies with a narrow product line, relatively simple problems of distribution, and a single channel of distribution, marketing and selling activities are often diffused among the various functions making up the business. Usually, the product-planning function reports to the production or engineering departments, the pricing function reports to the finance or accounting department, and sales and advertising are separate departments. Sales forecasting and budgeting are often under a separate department or report to the finance or accounting departments.

When such a company adopts the marketing-management concept, all these activities, which obviously bear on the consumer, are properly moved to the direction and control of a marketing director or manager. This executive is under the general supervision of top management and at the same level of delegated authority as production, engineering, and finance.

The specific arrangement of the marketing-management function will be determined by the particular needs and scope of the company's operations. In some companies, for example, some of the technical activities related to the product or product group, such as product development or product research—are not under the direct control of the marketing director but are a responsibility of the production or engineering organization. Other companies place technical product activities in his care, even, in some cases, locating the repair service work with him rather than with production or manufacturing. In all instances, however, the tendency has been toward a task-force approach to departmentalization, giving the marketing director full charge of such activities as market research, advertising, sales promotion, product planning and budgeting, and sales management.

The marketing director

This increased centralization of marketing functions requires a marketing executive who is more than the traditional sales manager. The marketing director must think in corporate terms, rather than confining himself to building up sales volume; he must define problems for research, analyze results, and develop the indicated policies, plans, and strategies. In doing this, he must integrate the activities of other functions into the over-all plans, working harmoniously with all members of top management and with the board of directors.

Such men are not always easy to find; in fact, the chief difficulty many companies experience in adopting the marketing-director form of management is obtaining the right executive for the job. Executive recruiters indicate that the specifications most frequently sought in a marketing manager are these:

1. Ability to plan and coordinate the entire marketing activity on a profit-minded, businesslike basis.
2. Working familiarity with both manufacturing and research.
3. Sufficient knowledge of finance and accounting to be able to judge merger and acquisition possibilities intelligently.
4. Ability to set up and carry out long-range plans for new markets.

Committee systems

It is quite possible that a company lacking such executive talent but desiring to go ahead with a reorganization under the marketing concept might start with a committee system. Indeed, even companies with highly capable managers often prefer the committee approach, believing that it facilitates communication and coordination among the various functions of the business. In the Dennison Manufacturing Company, for example, the president serves as chairman of a marketing committee composed of the marketing manager, the general merchandise manager and his assistant, the research and development director, and the controller. Meetings are held at least every other week to discuss profits, make concrete plans, and decide on course of action. In other companies, marketing committees are composed of the top executives from sales, advertising, market research, finance, and production.

The advantage of the committee system is that it eliminates many obstacles to interdepartmental coordination. The problems of communication between activities are greatly lessened because each, through active participation, is constantly abreast of the problems, needs, and findings of the other activities represented on the committee. But many companies find committees unwieldy, and they prefer to pinpoint the marketing management responsibility under the line authority of a single corporate marketing director.

Diversified companies

Although the reorganizations that implement the marketing concept are significant in functional-type companies, they are even more dramatic in corporations with decentralized operations, many of which have shown a decided movement away from the General Motors type of decentralization. This is not to say that all companies with this marketing approach have changed their organizational patterns; some, like General Electric, adhere to the decentralized structure of self-contained divisions. But more often than not there is a strong trend toward a "recentralized decentralization" under the modern marketing concept.

To see how this trend changes organizational patterns, we can examine the effect of adoption of the marketing-management concept in four types of decentralized companies: (1) those with a package of complementary products or services using the same channel of distribution; (2) those with similar products using separate channels of distribution; (3) those with dissimilar products using the same channels of distribution; and (4) those with dissimilar products using different channels of distribution.

Complementary products—same channels

Companies with a package of complementary products using the same channels of distribution often centralize the marketing-management activity and geographically decentralize selling operations.

In these cases, the pure selling functions are decentralized under regional or territorial line managers for reasons of economy, selective selling, and expanded penetration. Top marketing management reports to the chief executive officer and operates on a staff basis, with "functional authority" over all marketing and selling activities. This pattern of organization is well suited to a company selling complementary products through common distribution channels because the company is often more concerned with marketing a "whole idea" rather than individual products.

It is not difficult to find examples of large corporations that have reorganized in this fashion. Among the companies that are now emphasizing centralized marketing are the following:

• Burroughs Corporation, after a three-year tryout of product-line decentralization in which each division was responsible for its own marketing, manufacturing, engineering, and the like, abandoned this structure and set up a single marketing activity at headquarters to oversee the marketing of almost everything the company produces.

• Illinois Tool Works also centralized its marketing management and decentralized its product groups, which are responsible for their own selling.

• Monsanto Chemical revamped its organization to centralize marketing at the top corporate level. This reorganization was designed to bring marketing and production closer together and to get better-coordinated product planning.

• Humble Oil consolidated six operating affiliates into one, with centralized marketing management at the headquarters office and decentralized field selling operations in four regions across the country. Company management anticipates that over-all sales volume can be increased appreciably in the years ahead through the use of a single marketing organization and a company-wide trademark or symbol. The new organization will be able to make use of national advertising and promotion, to enter new marketing areas where none of the separate affiliates operated before, and to expand the network of marketing facilities in some areas where present representation is comparatively light.

Similar products—separate channels

A second type of marketing organization in decentralized companies can be found in companies with similar products and separate channels of distribution. Under this kind of organization, production and marketing are centralized activities and selling is a responsibility of the divisions. Examples of this pattern are evident in the automobile industry, where Ford Motor Company and Chrysler Corporation—and, to some extent, General Motors Corporation—are moving toward this kind of "recentralized decentralization."

In 1955, Ford Motor Company planned to set up separate, self-contained car divisions to compete line by line with General Motors. Within four years, the company created four new divisions—Continental, Lincoln, Mercury, and Edsel—and dismantled them because sales volume was not robust enough to absorb the divisional overhead. In 1957 and 1958, Mercury, Edsel, and Lincoln were combined into one division. In 1959, Ford dropped the Edsel line and transferred the Lincoln-Mercury division's assembly, purchasing, and production to the Ford division, leaving Lincoln-Mercury merely a sales organization. In 1960, the company took all assembly, purchasing, and production-engineering operations out of the Ford division and placed them in a new centralized automotive activity. This was the final step in centralizing all production, keeping market planning and strategy centralized at headquarters, disbanding self-contained profit centers, and assigning only selling responsibilities to the divisions.

Chrysler Corporation experienced a similar evolution in its organization structure. In 1950, Chrysler was structured on the simple lines of any manufacturing plant of an earlier generation, with a chief executive officer and vice-presidents for finance, engineering, and sales —all operating executives. Reorganizing was a gradual process that started with a program of divisionalization to get control of costs. In 1956, sales responsibilities were taken from the divisions and given to the central staff, evidently to obtain marketing information for headquarters. The system got another upheaval in 1958, when manufacturing operations were taken from the car divisions and put into centralized functional groupings, and the divisions were once more given responsibility for sales. As a result, Chrysler now has a strong policy, market-analysis, and planning staff at the top corporate level, and a centralized manufacturing activity to handle all production. The divisions have no other task than to sell automobiles.

General Motors is the least consolidated of the "Big Three." Each GM car division has its own engine, suspension, and assembly facilities, and Chevrolet and Buick have their own transmission operations. However, a dispersal of activities has started: Now Buick and Oldsmobile share an engine. Chevrolet makes transaxle and rear suspension parts for Pontiac, and Pontiac produces differential parts for Oldsmobile. It is conceivable that the future will see a changing pattern of "recentralized decentralization" in General Motors as it seeks to gain more of the advantages of the modern marketing concept and, along with them, the paring of burdensome divisional overhead costs.

At all three major automotive companies, responsibility for breaching new markets, capitalizing on new-product diversification, and utilizing the modern marketing concept is lodged in a separate office— next door to the chief executive.

Different products—same channels

A third type of recentralization occurs in companies with dissimilar products but common channels of distribution. In this structure, selling operations are centralized under a sales division, because selling methods are the same for all products, but marketing and production functions are delegated to various separate product divisions. Although these divisions are responsible for enterprising efforts and expanded profits on their respective lines, their activities are subject to stringent central-office control by the vice-president of marketing, who oversees marketing management throughout the organization. He approves all short- and long-term planning of the product divisions, including advertising appropriations, sales-promotional deals, pricing policy and strategy, and expense budgets. In addition, he is usually responsible for marketing research, advertising research, and broad consumer-research functions.

Companies with this type of organization—among them, General Foods Corporation, Pillsbury Company, H. J. Heinz Company, and Procter & Gamble Company—depend heavily on consumer and product research to guide them in producing products that meet consumer needs and desires, thus attuning the entire corporate effort to the consumer. Such companies are truly "marketing managed." They utilize research to define needs or desires that a product might be designed to fulfill. New-product ideas come from interpretation of consumer surveys or from astute anticipation of consumer needs. Product divisions, working with the central office of research and development, are responsible for initiating product ideas and improvements; pure research is left to the central R&D activity.

During a product's lifetime, the product division uses research to analyze the quality and value it represents to the consumer, so the company can predict or ward off competitive inroads. Should a product develop trouble, it is the job of the product division and central R&D to determine how much of the problem lies in the product and how much is created by outside pressures. Even when products are successful and trouble-free, product divisions continue to study them for opportunities to redesign or repackage them, or otherwise to improve their salability and expand their market penetration. The "marketing managed" companies are most sophisticated in the use of research and the marketing concept to satisfy today's mature consumer needs at an adequate return to the company.

Different products—different channels

A fourth type of recentralization is found in companies with dissimilar products using different channels of distribution. Even though product responsibilities may be delegated separately—e.g., for consumer and industrial products—they are often controlled by a top management executive operating under the modern marketing concept, as is the case with DuPont, Borden, and General Mills.

Companies with a wide variety of products, both consumer and industrial, must always be alert to the possibility that their profit position may be impaired even while their total sales are growing. Top-heavy selling and marketing activities can be a serious drain on company resources, sometimes to the point where it is actually more profitable to eliminate some lines than to have too many irons in the fire. It is interesting to note that Monsanto Chemical Co. developed an excellent consumer product in "All," a home-laundry detergent, but sold it outright because the product did not fit their line, used a different channel of distribution, and required a separate selling effort.

Recentralized decentralization

All these organizational realignments, different as they are, have a common element: a marked tendency for strong central-office control over marketing and product planning, analysis, and strategy. This strict marketing direction from the top, which is akin to the rigid central-staff financial control found in the General Motors type of organization, is a feature of the organization of an increasing number of companies.

The revolution in marketing management, along with the revolution in information technology, may very well portend a reversal of the trend to decentralization and a strong recentralization of major business functions in the corporations serving the markets of the sixties.

4. WHAT ECONOMISTS SHOULD KNOW ABOUT MARKETING *

George H. Brown

Most economic theorists apparently conceive of the marketplace as a small open square in which producers display their wares, rent free, and to which consumers travel to inspect the offerings and to make their purchases on a cash and carry basis. In this particular world there are no brokers, no wholesalers, no retailers, no railroads, no delivery trucks, no advertising, no salesmen—in short, no marketing. Actually, of course, the marketing functions of transport, storage, communications, etc., would be performed by producers and consumers but the imagined scale of operations is so small that no one agency is specialized in any one marketing function. If the economist were not wrapped so securely in the cloud of comparative statics, he would not only recognize this but would also realize that the problem of introducing the results of technological progress into a big, busy market requires a great deal of advertising and selling.

Unfortunately, the formal study of marketing is a comparatively recent phenomenon. There are several instances of courses in marketing being taught prior to 1915, but the real development did not occur until the rapid evolution of schools of business in the years during and immediately following World War I. In 1923 there were several marketing texts available, and there was enough self-consciousness to warrant the organization of an association of teachers of marketing and advertising.[1] From then on the field has grown steadily.

The institutional approach

In order to understand marketing, it is important to recognize that it emerged as a field of study during that particular period of time when American economists were developing the institutional

* From *The Journal of Marketing*, Vol. XVI, No. 1 (July, 1951), pp. 60-66. Reprinted with permission from *The Journal of Marketing*, published quarterly by the American Marketing Association.

George H. Brown, Marketing Research Manager, Ford Motor Company.

[1] Hugh E. Agnew, "The History of the American Marketing Association," *Journal of Marketing*, Vol. V, No. 4 (April, 1941), p. 377.

approach to their field. Anyone acquainted with the history of economic thought is aware of the reaction against "classical" economics in the period immediately preceding and following World War I and the determined efforts to develop a "real understanding" of economic forces by studying economic activity at first hand. The prominence of such men as Thorsten Veblen, Wesley Clair Mitchell, and John R. Commons, to mention only a few, is sufficient to document the point that this era was strongly institutionalist in its character.

Whether influenced by the developments in economics or whether a product of the same forces that led economic theory into institutionalist channels, the early study of marketing was marked by an effort to describe and measure the exact nature of the activities involved in the marketing of goods. Studies in this direction were stimulated by the discovery that certain basic functions were common to all marketing operations and that the principal difference between the marketing of different goods lay in the allocation of these functions between the various functionaries in the field. This so-called "functional" approach to the study of marketing is today an integral part of all introductory marketing courses.

The development of marketing as a separate study also occurred at a time when changes of considerable magnitude were occurring in the relative importance of various marketing agencies. In the years 1920 to 1930 even the casual observer could recognize the increasing importance of the chain store, the rising importance of direct sales by manufacturers to industrial consumers and large retailers, and the declining importance of the mail-order house and the full-line wholesalers. The problem of documenting these changes, explaining their causes, and estimating their ultimate impact occupied a considerable part of the energies of marketing men during the formative years. The inauguration of the first national census of distribution in 1930 is evidence both of the changes occurring in marketing and of the energy of students of this field who recognized the need for factual information.

The influence of these factors is most clearly seen in the introductory or general textbook in marketing. Almost without exception, these books contain a general statement concerning the scope and magnitude of marketing activities, a statement and discussion of the marketing functions, a description of the major marketing institutions and a statement of their changing relative importance, a description of the agency structure in the marketing of various types of commodities, a discussion of marketing legislation, and an evaluation of cost and efficiency in marketing. The order in which the subjects are presented, the attention devoted to each, and the information on additional subjects varies widely, of course, from book to book.

The managerial approach

In rather sharp contrast to the early study of marketing, which was strongly grounded in institutional economics, the development in recent years has been in the "managerial" aspects of the field. Marketing has always occupied both the general area of the arts and sciences and the less well-known grounds of the professional schools. The aim and purpose of the teaching of marketing has been both the preparation of the individual for an intelligent understanding of and participation in the world in which he lives and the education of a person capable of making good decisions in his capacity as a marketing executive. The advanced courses in marketing have always been strongly managerial in character, but in recent years there has been a tendency for the managerial point of view to reach down into the introductory courses, once the exclusive domain of the institutional economist. An explicit recognition of this situation is indicated by the following paragraph from the preface to Duddy and Revzan's . . . textbook in the field.

> The approach to the study of marketing made in this text is frankly institutional. The authors make no claim to originality since other texts in this field also make use of this approach. Too often, however, the use of this method is obscured by the introduction of "managerial" or "problem" material, or is overshadowed by a commodity analysis or by a theoretical discussion of price determination.[2]

Strangely enough, the increasing importance of the managerial approach actually tends to bring economists and marketing men closer together. In place of the renunciation of formal economic analysis so characteristic of the institutionalists, there is at least a willingness to examine the contributions of economic theory to the managerial problem of price determination and price policy. Quite naturally interest centers in those aspects of economic analysis dealing with the behavior of the individual firm. Discussions of the nature of the demand and cost curves for the firm under monopoly, oligopoly, imperfect, and pure competition have value to marketing men. Even more interesting are the efforts by statisticians and econometricians to measure the shape of these curves from data available to the individual firm. The introduction of the concept of the "kinked"

[2] E. A. Duddy and D. A. Revzan, *Marketing* (New York: McGraw-Hill Book Company, Inc., 1947), p. v.

demand curve, with its implication of price rigidity, has been of particular interest in spite of the recent attacks on this notion. Admittedly, the marketing men who follow these developments are primarily the academic group but the important point is the willingness of these men to apply theories to particular situations.

Shortcomings of economics

While it is difficult to express the opinion of a number of persons, it is probably fair to say that the attitude of those marketing men sympathetic to economic analysis is, in the main, highly critical. Much of the criticism is based on grounds quite familiar to the economist but there seems to be a greater impatience on the part of marketing men with the acknowledged limitations. Whether this impatience is due to a feeling that an ox is unnecessarily being gored as a result of the oversimplifications and wrong assumptions in economic analysis will not be debated here. If this should be the case, however, economists can be sure of a continuing interest on the part of marketing men. If, as is more likely the case, this is not true, the nature of the future relationships is more open to doubt.

For what it may be worth, a brief listing is presented of some of the shortcomings in the usual statement of the demand and cost situation for the individual firm. These are highlighted by the study of marketing. For one thing, the illustrations given in economic theory apply primarily to the simplified case of a single plant producing a single product. Marketing students are keenly aware that the actual situation usually presents a multi-product firm with involved joint cost relationships. Although some very interesting solutions have been worked out for relative prices in the multi-product case in monopoly, the general solution for the multi-product firm in pure competition is not so well known. If it were clearly understood that pricing under pure competition leads to the allocation of a joint cost in proportion to what the market will bear whenever there are fixed proportions in the amount of output (i.e. in a discriminatory manner if any other basis of allocating joint costs is used), it would be considerable help to the marketing executive who is faced with the problem of pricing a new joint product.

Another criticism of the usual analysis is the complete disregard of calendar time. Perhaps this is particularly irritating to the marketing man because he deals with a world in which changes through calendar time are of great importance. A wider use of the concepts of instantaneous demand, intermediate demand, and long-run demand, each with a calendar time connotation, would help the marketing man understand economic analysis, and would give him an insight into the short-run and long-run aspects of his pricing problems.

Declining long-run costs

A more fundamental criticism of economic analysis concerns the assumption, held generally by economists, that the long-run cost curve for the firm is U-shaped. In marketing management, the explicit goal is to secure a larger and larger volume of business with no economic limitations except that the business-getting costs do not exceed the marginal income. This goal carries the implicit assumption that the costs of production for the firm remain the same or tend to fall as the output of the firm increases. Since this assumption is in direct contradiction to the notion held by economists, some effort should be made to reconcile the difference.

Economists have recognized that a monopolist may operate on the declining side of the long-run cost curve and have therefore tended to associate falling costs with the existence of monopoly. Students of marketing can testify, however, that efforts to expand the quantity of goods exist when there are no barriers to entrance into an industry. The theory of monopolistic competition, which recognizes freedom of entrance into the industry, also suggests that equilibrium will be reached with the firm operating on the downward side of the U-shaped cost curve. Even though this theory assumes the existence of a large number of weak monopolists and implies a degree of price flexibility and ease of entrance and exit to industry which does not fit in well with observed facts, the important point is that the theory is consistent with but does not *require* a U-shaped cost curve.

In contrast to these theories, it is clear that no individual firm will devote resources to increasing the quantity of goods sold unless it is faced with both a downward sloping or discontinuous ("kinked") demand curve and a constant or decreasing cost of production. The fact that efforts to increase the quantity sold is characteristic of a very large segment of the economy indicates that declining long-run cost curves are more the rule than they are the exception.

Once the notion is accepted that the long-run cost curve is downward sloping over an indefinite range of output, a whole new area of economic analysis is suggested. Given a declining long-run cost of production and recognizing that transport costs rise as the increasing output of the firm is distributed to the market, emphasis is shifted to the problems of plant location, price discrimination, and nonprice competition. Incidentally, this approach is consistent with the fact that government regulation is necessary when the rate of decline in the cost curve for the plant is so rapid with respect to the size of the market that it produces a "natural" monopoly. Where the rate of decline of the cost curve is not large and when there are a number of substitute products, it appears that freedom of entrance into the industry will serve adequately as the basic technique of social control.

Infinite quality variation

The existence of nonprice competition is another indirect criticism of the assumptions underlying economic analysis. Nonprice competition means the effort to secure a larger share of the market through the improvement of quality, the provision of extra services, large scale advertising, etc. The fact that these activities do occur not only gives further evidence of a declining long-run cost curve, but it brings out clearly that there is a limited number of variations in the quality of goods available on the market. The basic assumption behind "pure" competition is not only that all possible variations in quality and price are available in the market, but that each of the various qualities is produced by a large number of independent firms. In monopolistic competition, it is usually assumed that all quality variations are available, but each variation is produced by a single firm. If either of these assumptions were the case, it would be impossible to engage in nonprice competition because the variations in quality would already be existent in the market.

One of the most difficult problems in marketing management is the determination of product quality; consequently, any attention to this area on the part of economists would be most welcome. Given the nature of the relative preferences for each of the product variations and given the rate of decline of the relevant cost curves, it should be possible to solve for the number of different product qualities that would be produced and the division of the market between them. Moreover, the analysis would reveal the factors tending to increase or decrease the number and nature of the product qualities available in the market and would thus make the existence of nonprice competition a special case of a more general theory.

The maximum growth concept

Perhaps the most serious criticism of economic analysis concerns the basic assumptions by economists that the primary goal of the firm is profit maximization. Marketing men and others who have had an opportunity to deal with the motivation of business managers are inclined to the view that the situation is considerably more complex. Wroe Alderson in his article in "The Theory of Marketing" has suggested that the primary aim of any organized behavior system, including the business firm, is first survival and secondly growth.[3] This indicates that the high interest of businessmen in profits arises from the fact that they are the conditions of survival and growth. If these were true, a monopolist would reduce prices whenever possible to secure growth, but would not reduce prices below cost because this would threaten survival. The actions of the Aluminum Corporation of America of reducing prices during the period it was the sole producer of aluminum is consistent with this hypothesis. Illustrations of situations where business organizations placed survival and growth above maximum profits are found in many areas of marketing. For example, it is well known that firms are unwilling to drop the production and sale of certain products or cease doing business in given areas or with specified customer groups even though it can be shown that profits would thereby be increased. Similarly, there is little interest in the argument that selling or advertising efforts should be reduced whenever there is no clear-cut evidence that the costs produced an equivalent revenue. A firm interested in maximizing its profits would not be likely to balance a doubtful income against a known cost of getting that income.

This is not the place to argue the merits or demerits of the proposition that entrepreneurs are more interested in growth than they are in maximizing profits. The ultimate test is whether or not a theory built around this assumption provides a better explanation of observed events than a theory constructed around some other assumption. If, however, the adoption of this assumption should add to our stock of knowledge, it would demonstrate that the interplay between the economist toolmaker and the marketing man as tool user is a two-way proposition.

Importance of marketing research

Quite apart from their mutual dissatisfaction with the current state of economic theory, marketing men and economists have a common interest in recording and analyzing the economic behavior of the individual consumer. The pioneering work in this direction was

[3] Cox and Alderson, *Theory in Marketing* (Chicago: Richard D. Irwin, 1950), Ch. 4.

undertaken by marketing men in business organizations who introduced the consumer survey. By trial and error, and with help from statisticians and psychologists, these men have worked out the basic procedures for securing a relatively complete and accurate record of individual economic behavior. It is now possible by the use of such techniques as intensive interviewing, store audits, and consumer panels, to measure the rate of purchase and prices paid for a wide variety of goods. In fact there are several organizations that have been recording consumer purchases on a continuing basis for a period of ten years or more.

Marketing research was designed for and will probably continue to serve marketing management. An economist would have little interest in the major findings of marketing research because they deal with problems hidden away in that general category known as *ceteris paribus*. The marketing man knows that the rate of sale of a given product depends not only on its price but upon its availability in the market, the convenience of the package size, the information buyers have about the product, and whether or not that information is based on first-hand experience, hearsay, advertising, etc. In addition, variations in the rate of factory shipments through time may be caused by changes in the amount of inventories carried by dealers or consumers. It is important for marketing policies that the exact cause of a given rate of sale or a given change in the rate of sale be known, hence the need for marketing research.

Although the economist may be unaffected by the difference in factory shipments and actual consumption, he ought to have some interest in discovering the degree to which it is possible to secure information about the economic behavior and intention of consumers. That there is some interest in this direction is indicated by the use of marketing research data in verifying the effects of various economic controls during the last war. A more striking illustration of the possibilities in the use of the method is the wealth of information uncovered in the Survey of Consumer Finances sponsored by the Federal Reserve Board and conducted by the Survey Research Center of the University of Michigan. Other studies using the survey technique are currently being conducted in connection with various economic problems, particularly the business cycle, but the scope and power of the technique is not nearly so well known among economists as it should be. For example, had there been a well-designed consumer panel producing information on a continuing basis, similar to that secured on a periodic basis by the Survey of Consumer Finances, the impact of Regulations W and X would be much more clearly understood than is currently the case.

Whether or not the economist adopts the tool of marketing research, and whether or not he heeds the criticisms of economic theory by those who know the market place, he should be aware of the importance of the managerial approach to marketing. Under the institutional approach marketing and economics are concerned in part with the same ends, but make use of widely different means in reaching those ends. Under the managerial approach, marketing and economics are concerned with different ends but make use, in part, of the same means. If there is to be any fruitful working relationships between the two disciplines, it seems more probable that it will occur under the managerial approach.

SECTION 2. THE CONSUMER

A searching study of the consumer is the basis for any understanding of demand. This study cannot be done by the use of any one discipline. The complex consumer can best be approached by examining initially such basic areas as economics, psychology, and sociology.

Section 2-A
Economic Analysis of Demand

Galbraith's thesis of the affluent society is challenged by Harry S. Johnson. In his critique of the Galbraith thesis, Professor Johnson takes into consideration the diverse viewpoints of Adam Smith, Alfred Marshall, W. W. Rostow, Keynsian economists, and practitioners and theorists of Madison Avenue.

An excellent example of the relationship between marketing innovation and consumption is discussed in Gilbert Burck's article, "Why Do People Buy?" Using recent history, the author considers the Problem of American Capitalism: ". . . will people spend enough to buy back what they produce at a high and rising level of production?"

Major shifts have been taking place in the spending of the consumer dollar. Consumer spending can no longer be considered a passive agent in business fluctuations; instead, it plays a vital role in the maintenance of a healthy economy. Robert Ferber analyzes the impact of this changing pattern of consumer expenditures in "Our Changing Consumer Market."

Section 2-B
Psychological Analysis of Demand

In "The Great Enigma . . . 'Madame X'—," *Grey Matter* points out mistakes made by those marketing people who generalize in oversimplified terms about the so-called "average" consumer. This concept causes a sameness of products and a sameness in advertising that result in great loss to sellers.

Motivation research has gained acceptance as an established method of determining the causes of consumer behavior. Dr. Clawson, in "The Coming Break-Throughs in Motivation Research," is of the opinion that there is considerable room for improvement. He maintains that if the qualitative, quantitative, and ethical break-throughs discussed are achieved, we may secure increased competition as well as greater efficiency in the use of the marketing mix.

A distinguished psychologist applies a wide range of contemporary psychological theory to the problems of consumer behavior. In "Motivation, Cognition, Learning—Basic Factors in Consumer Behavior," James A. Bayton points out that the modern psychologist can help solve a broader type of consumer behavior problem than the one for which he is best known, motivation research.

Section 2-C
Sociological Analysis of Demand

In the "Two-Step Flow of Communication" Dr. Katz discusses the hypothesis, which has been tested in several successive studies, that "ideas often flow from radio and print to opinion leaders, and from these to the less active sections of the population." Each study has attempted a different solution to the problem of how to take account of interpersonal relations in the traditional design of survey research. As a result, the original hypothesis is largely corroborated and considerably refined.

The hypotheses that are presented in the article, "Dress-Buying Behavior of Consumers," attempt to integrate concepts from sociology, psychology, economics, and marketing as they relate to the buying by consumers of differentiated products. How and why does a buyer select one product over another of a similar nature? An effort is also made to distinguish and type consumer behavior patterns and to discover if there are fundamental determinants that underly the more obvious reasons for buying. John E. Jacobi and S. George Walters contend that the degree of awareness and concern with dresses as a status symbol varies significantly within each socio-economic grouping. This conclusion would seem to call for a re-examination of the social class concept as it applies to differentiated goods.

5. THE CONSUMER AND MADISON AVENUE *

Harry G. Johnson

I.

A topic of current and growing interest among economists is the economics of what J. K. Galbraith calls the Affluent Society, and what W. W. Rostow terms the final stage of economic development, the era of high mass-consumption: more simply and recognizably, the economics of the United States today. The distinguishing features of the affluent, high-consumption American economy as an object of analysis meriting special treatment are: on the production side, the corporate form of business enterprise as an instrument for institutionalizing the accumulation of capital and the development and practical application of technical progress; and on the consumption side, the affluent consumer, whose standard of living is already high above anything that can be related to basic needs for food, clothing, and shelter, and is being continuously raised still higher through the creation and satisfaction of new and more demanding wants. The link between the two sides, and the institutional embodiment of the process of want-creation which drives the system on to ever greater heights of production and consumption, is the range of activities broadly describable as "advertising," and symbolized in the concept of "Madison Avenue."

Both distinguishing features of the age of opulence—as I prefer to call it, in deference to Adam Smith—are widely at variance with the concepts used in economic analysis for explaining the functioning of the economic system. The problems of the modern corporation resemble only remotely the problems of the Marshallian entrepreneur, or firm, combining factors of production in a given process to turn out a given product in competition with similar firms, and doomed by Victorian family dynamics to return to shirt-sleeves in three generations. The affluent consumer, whose tastes evolve and whose purchases swell under the mentorship of Madison Avenue, bears still less relationship to the solitary immortal the consistency of whose preferences

* Reprinted by permission of *Current Economic Comment*, Vol. 22, No. 3 (August, 1960), p. 3.

Harry G. Johnson, Professor of Economics, University of Chicago.

is the foundation of both positive and normative economics. Both features, if considered at all seriously, raise grave doubts as to the validity and usefulness of the economist's picture of the economic world; but the second, the affluent consumer, poses by far the more fundamental problem for the economist, by calling into question the very foundations of what economics has to say about economic policy. And it is the license to argue authoritatively about important issues of public policy, rather than the power to discover interesting facts, which has historically provided the study of economics with most of its sex appeal.

The question of the relevance, or rather the assertion of the irrelevance, of economics in the age of opulence has been put most strongly by Galbraith in his recent book, *The Affluent Society*.[1] Galbraith argues, with some injustice to the inventor of the Engel curve and also to those pre-national-income-approach textbook writers who habitually threw in a discussion of the hierarchy of wants, that economists have managed to bind their eyes to the obvious fact that as income rises less urgent wants are satisfied, so that marginal production becomes decreasingly important. Going further, he argues that the wants which are satisfied by increasing production are themselves increasingly created by the increase in production itself, through the passive social process of emulation and envy of one's neighbors, and the active commercial process of creation and stimulation of wants through advertising and salesmanship—processes which he lumps together in the concept of "the dependence effect." Finally, by regarding the production which satisfies such contrived wants as marginal, he reaches the conclusion that "the marginal utility of present aggregate output, ex advertising and salesmanship, is zero" (p. 160). Thus he apparently cuts the ground from under the "conventional wisdom" of economics, according to which extra production is useful because it satisfies wants.

The last part of Galbraith's argument is, of course, sheer semantic chicanery: one might with equal logic argue that the marginal utility of income is negative to a man who supports an administration which spends some of his tax payments on purposes of which he disapproves or to one who reduces his life expectation by heavy smoking. But the thesis which the literary legerdemain is intended to dramatize undoubtedly has substance, and deserves serious attention. This thesis

[1] Boston: Houghton Mifflin Co., 1958.

is most conveniently considered in terms of its two separate parts, since these raise questions of a rather different order. The insistence that, as income rises, the wants which are satisfied are less and less urgent, so that the production which satisfies them is of decreasing significance, raises the question of the importance of economics as the science which studies the want-satisfying system, and of the economists who are its practitioners, in the age of opulence. The contention that increasingly the wants which are satisfied are themselves created in the process of generating the production which satisfies them, with its implication that little or no "genuine" increase in satisfaction results, raises the more fundamental question of the validity of economic science itself, in both its positive and its normative aspects.

Before discussing these questions, I should like to make a general point which is obvious enough but easily overlooked. This is that the logical force and shocking power of Galbraith's argument derives from the challenge it offers to the classical liberal framework of economic analysis, a framework built on the foundations of the principle of consumers' sovereignty; and that the liberal framework is not one which all economists accept, nor one within which avowedly liberal economists habitually do their thinking. Instead, some economists for most of their time, and most economists for some of their time, think about economic problems and policy in pre-liberal mercantilist terms. That is, their thinking about economic aggregates runs in terms of national economic power and prestige, and about domestic economic policy in terms of conflicting group interests. This habit of thinking has been greatly fostered by the economic and political developments of the past thirty years, most notably by the protracted period of the cold war. So far as it is characteristic, the Galbraith thesis becomes irrelevant, since the satisfaction of individual wants is not the standard by which the mercantilist formulates economic policy recommendations and judges economic developments. Indeed, Galbraith's argument provides very handy reinforcement for mercantilist thinking precisely because it appears to undermine the liberal economist's contrary insistence on the primacy of individual satisfactions; it is no accident that some of Galbraith's most enthusiastic reviewers have been socialists, who differ from him only in having a positive policy for disposing of incremental output whose use by consumers they agree in valuing low. Having made this observation, I shall assume in the remainder of this paper that we are concerned with economics as liberally, and not mercantilistically, defined.

II.

The first part of Galbraith's thesis is the proposition that as income rises, less urgent wants are satisfied by marginal production, whose value accordingly is falling. This proposition is from a strictly economic point of view a tautology: less urgent wants are those you do not satisfy until you are rich enough to afford to satisfy them. As Galbraith uses it, however, it is not a tautology but a value judgment, to the effect that as society grows richer, it becomes less and less worth while to try to arrange economic institutions so as to promote maximum efficiency of production. This is a value judgment, of the same sort as the value judgment in favor of more equal distribution of income, and it may be disputed on the same ground, that the activities of the rich are of superior social value to those of the poor. Specifically, it may be argued that a society of typically rich people is so superior to a society of typically poor people, in terms of realizing the values of a good society as liberally conceived, that it is always desirable to take any action which will raise the efficiency with which national resources are used in generating national income, regardless of how well off society is already. This is a tenable position, though the postulated close dependence of goodness on affluence is something of a strain on credulity; but it can hardly be described as a popular one. On the contrary, common sense would seem to be on Galbraith's side on this issue; and the preferences of the community, as revealed both in behavior and in popular attitudes, seem to lie in the direction of tolerating more rather than less wasteful use of resources as income rises.

Whether one accepts this value judgment or not, however, the central fact remains that the kind of policy issues with which economists are typically concerned—issues involving the efficiency or otherwise of resource use—are no longer issues which can plausibly be depicted as basic to the economic welfare of the community; rather, they are peripheral issues determining the location of the margin of a high and rising standard of living. The corollary is that economics, and economists, are not concerned with matters of vital importance to the affluent society. That economists generally pretend otherwise is to be attributed to the conservatism of intellectual tradition and to the more or less fortuitous events of the past 25 years: the great depression and the Keynesian revolution, which gave economists something important to say; the war, which gave them something important to do; and the cold war, which has given them something important to preach about—the economic virtues and vices of free enterprise. In consequence, economics has had a new lease of exciting life, which has been gradually petering out as the fact of affluence has become increasingly well established. The realization that the party is coming to an end is evident both in the diversion of the interests of older economists to the economics of underdevelopment, where exciting usefulness on a grand scale still seems possible; and in the trend toward mathematical and econometric work among the younger economists, and the growth of business schools. The former represents an attempt to transplant the missionary spirit of the 1930's to a more favorable environment, the latter the inevitable transition from intellectual interest into professional competence.

III.

Let us now turn to the second part of Galbraith's thesis, the contention that increasingly the wants satisfied by additional production are themselves created, passively or actively, socially or commercially, by the production process itself, so that the satisfaction of these wants cannot be regarded as a "genuine" increase in satisfaction. If correct, as has already been mentioned, this contention strikes to the heart of liberal economics, which is posited on the independence of consumer wants. How much is there in it?

Note first that the contention is separable into two parts: the observation that the growth of opulence is characterized by the creation and satisfaction of new wants, through social and commercial pressures on consumers, and the judgment that the wants so created are valueless and even contemptible. Of these, it is the observation which presents the serious problem to economics: for if wants are changing in consequence of changes in production, what basis is there for saying that increased production increases welfare? And if wants are changing over time in response to social pressures and the machinations of Madison Avenue, how safely can positive economics build on the assumption that choices are determined by relative prices and incomes? The adverse judgment on the value of created wants is essentially a trivial matter of opinion—a manifestation of Johnson's Law of Social Intransitivity [2]—although, as I shall argue, the assumption that it can be made is a clue to the proper treatment of created wants.

[2] "Everyone has good reasons for considering himself superior to other people."

The notion that economic progress essentially involves the creation of new wants is by no means new in the literature of economics, though it has been steadily pushed into the background by the growing emphasis on mathematical elegance in demand theory, which has finally come up with the result that if people are simply consistent, their demand curves will slope downward, except when they do not. Alfred Marshall was drawing on a long tradition of economic thought when, in introducing his analysis of demand, he wrote:

> Speaking broadly therefore, although it is man's wants in the earliest stages of his development that give rise to his activities, yet afterwards each new step upwards is to be regarded as the development of new activities giving rise to new wants, rather than of new wants giving rise to new activities.[3]

Marshall, be it noted, fully recognized the desire for distinction as an influence on wants—thanks to the backward state of technology, Madison Avenue in his time was just a street and not a business center—but he stressed the desire for excellence as a stronger motive, and he left no doubt of his belief that the trend was upward and not simply sideways. The notion of a desire for excellence was developed much more fully, in his own way, by Knight, who consistently stresses the desire, not merely for the satisfaction of wants, but for the cultivation of better and better wants.

Both Marshall and Knight seem to point, in their respective ways, to the answer to the Galbraith challenge to liberal economics. This answer is, essentially, to admit that the aim of economic activity is not the fuller satisfaction of given wants—wants conceived of as wants for specific commodities do not stay given but instead evolve as the commodities themselves change in the course of economic growth—but to assert that the evolution of wants itself is motivated, fundamentally, by the desire to increase satisfaction. In technical, jargon, progress does not consist solely in improving the production function so as to provide more and better quality goods for consumption; it also consists in improving the consumption function so as to derive more and better satisfaction from production.

To argue this way is to assert that changes in taste are governed ultimately by accepted standards of good and better taste, standards which are capable of being learned and applied by the consumer, and which he does learn and apply in response both to his own maximizing ambition and to pressures from fellow-consumers and from advertising; standards to which, moreover, both the social pressures

[3] *Principles of Economics* (8th ed.; New York: Macmillan Co., 1948), p. 89.

of emulation and invidious distinction and the commercial pressures of Madison Avenue's overt and covert persuasion must ultimately appeal. The notion of standards for recognizing improvements in the consumption function is admittedly much more hazy and imprecise than the notion of standards for recognizing improvements in the production function; nevertheless their existence is, I think, undeniable. It is implied by the very notion, implicit in the second facet of Galbraith's contention about wants, that it is possible to judge the quality of other people's wants and satisfactions in a communicable and authoritative way. But it is not possible, contrary to what Galbraith assumes, to dismiss wants as valueless simply because they have been acquired under the pressures of social emulation and advertising. All economically relevant wants are learned. Moreover, all standards of taste are learned. It is therefore both arrogant and inconsistent to assume that those who have acquired their standards from general culture and advanced education can choose and pass judgments according to standards possessing independent validity, while those who have acquired their standards from social pressures and advertising can neither understand nor learn to understand the difference between good and bad taste.

The general argument is considerably strengthened by the empirical observation that much of both emulation in consumption and the appeals of advertising campaigns is based fairly directly on performance characteristics of commodities, which provide objective standards of quality which the consumer is capable of testing for himself—and does seem to test fairly generally—by experience. Other influential factors are the desire for variety, and for a certain quality of romance in life, neither of which can be dismissed as entirely ignoble. But there remains a certain distasteful residue which cannot be rationalized as part of any beneficial process. So far as emulation in consumption is concerned, this seems to be an unfortunate fact of social life about which there is nothing obvious to be done. With respect to advertising, the problem seems to be not so much demonstrably false or fraudulent claims—which ought to be subject to public control of some kind—as misleading or ambiguous claims. Here there is the possibility of a very difficult choice between the establishment and enforcement of standards of honesty by governmental action, and reliance on competition between advertisers to alert the consumer to dishonest claims. A recent example illustrates the problem: the consumer is probably better served when each cigarette manufacturer is shrieking that his product contains less cancer than any other brand, than when statistical discrepancies in these claims have led to a government-initiated agreement to drop any reference to health effects. One thing is obvious, however: voluntary codes of ethics for the advertising business ought to be viewed with extreme skepticism.

IV.

The argument I have been presenting is concerned with the welfare problem raised by created wants, and leads to the comforting conclusion that the fact of want-creation does not invalidate the assumption that an increase in national income carries with it an increase in welfare. It also has implications for positive economics: so far as the evolution of wants is guided by generally accepted standards of what constitutes an improvement in the quality of wants, changes in wants as affluence progresses will have an underlying rationality or regularity which should make it possible to discover empirical regularities of economic behavior. This proposition can also be supported by an application of economic principles to the process of emulation and the activities of Madison Avenue themselves. So far as emulators are rational in their pursuit of invidious distinction, one would expect them to make a show of the possession of goods whose prices have only recently fallen to within their economic means; and so far as advertising agencies are rational in their pursuit of profits, one would expect them to seek their clients among producers who are able to satisfy potential wants cheaply and profitably. Hence one would expect that the forces of emulation and advertising would be concentrated on creating those wants whose cost of satisfaction is being most steadily and rapidly reduced by the process of opulence itself—the process of want-creation may be rational even though the wants created may not themselves be rational. Furthermore, the progress of production in an opulent society has a definite pattern which suggests a similar pattern for the evolution of wants: both the accumulation of capital and technical progress imply a general trend toward the reduction of the prices of commodities in terms of labor, and this in turn implies a tendency toward the substitution of capital-intensive for labor-intensive methods of satisfying consumer desires.

In closing, I should I suppose say something more concrete about the prospects for the consumer and Madison Avenue in the affluent sixties. From what I have already said, it should be clear that I expect Madison Avenue to prosper in the future as it has in the recent past: nationwide mass advertising is an essential instrumentality of the era of high mass-consumption. Aside from the necessity for the consumer's wants to progress with the economy's productive capacity, there are two other cogent reasons for predicting new highs for huckstering. First, as Martin Mayer points out in his *Madison Avenue, U.S.A.*,[4] advertising is a form of insurance for the corporation against the risks of managerial mortality; as corporations prosper, their advertising appropriations are likely to grow, for reasons unconnected with demonstrable profitability of advertising. Second, the rise of Madison Avenue to date has been associated on the one hand with technical progress both in communication and in the techniques employed by communications media, which has made possible the elaborate centrally planned and executed advertising campaign, and on the other hand with the rising relative cost of labor, which has given a progressive cost advantage to "absentee salesmanship" by means of advertising aimed at the buyer. Both factors will continue to favor Madison Avenue. With respect to the kind of appeal characteristically made by advertising campaigns, my argument would suggest a trend toward more emphasis on discriminating taste, on what used to be called "the art of gracious living." But the more disturbing type of appeal epitomized in the phrase "hidden persuasion" is also likely to spread: psychiatric treatment has long been a superior type of luxury consumption good among the affluent elite, and it seems probable (and not too deplorable) that the less affluent will choose to buy it with their groceries. Finally, it seems likely that the major consumption goods on whose advertisement the largest sums of money are spent will continue to be food and soft drinks, soaps, drugs and toiletries, alcoholic drinks, and tobacco (where advertising promises the producer substantial and sustained profits if successful, while offering the consumer the gratification of ennobling the humdrum routine of consumer existence) together with automobiles (where potential producer profits are equally tangible and the consumer is offered his last chance to buy a piece of the frontier spirit). But it is also likely that increasing affluence will manifest itself in increasing expenditures on advertisements for household durables on the one hand, and recreational equipment and facilities on the other—the former as a reflection of the falling relative price of durables in terms of labor already referred to, and the latter as an expression of the fact that leisure is a prime luxury good, so that as opulence progresses efforts to sell the complements of leisure will multiply.

[4] New York: Harper & Brothers, 1958.

6. WHY DO PEOPLE BUY? *

Gilbert Burck

The most illustrious economist of our times, the late Lord Keynes, made his reputation largely on the proposition that people do not automatically buy enough to maintain prosperity. He wrenched the thinking of the capitalist world away from production and toward consumption; his theories were built around the behavior of the consumer. Yet Lord Keynes never seriously considered the possibility that "selling"—the persuasive element in distribution—might have a measurable effect on how much people buy.

And Keynes is not the only one who neglected salesmanship. Few economists before or since have paid much attention to it, to say nothing of taking it seriously. Selling and advertising, writes Harvard's J. K. Galbraith in his . . . book *American Capitalism*, "may be waste but they are waste that exists because the community is too well off to care." Most economists, indeed, tend to regard selling as an excess of capitalism, a kind of bug in the distribution process. They make no functional distinction between distribution and selling. If the distribution process were ordered rationally, they imply, it would consist almost entirely of packaging, shipping, warehousing, and sending goods to market. They do not grant that selling or the art of persuading people to buy can affect appreciably the over-all volume of consumption. To them the consumer buys for a variety of causes, but rarely if ever because he is sold.

In eighteenth- and nineteenth-century Europe, where most economic ideas originated, distribution without persuasion was natural. The problem there was (and often still is) to produce enough to maintain a subsistence living. The U. S. today is uniquely different. The standard of living is so far above subsistence that it is fair to say that production is no longer a problem—in the sense that it is *the* problem in all the rest of the world. Distribution, in the mechani-

* Reprinted from the April 1952 issue of *Fortune* magazine by special permission; Copyright 1952 by Time, Inc.

Gilbert Burck, Editor, *Fortune* magazine.

cal sense of moving the right goods to the right market, is not a problem. In the years ahead, barring the deluge of war, the problem of American capitalism is clear: will people spend enough to buy back what they produce at a high and rising level of production?

The economists' answer: not necessarily. And the economists should not be airily dismissed; they may be right. But have the economists overlooked something, the new something called selling? Is the consumer really predictable? Does he act with the rational self-interest of "economic man"? And finally are economists correct in assuming that the whole apparatus of American selling is powerless to move the index of consumption by the relatively few points that spell the difference between prosperity and depression?

These are some of the questions that need to be asked about American selling. There are no pat answers; perhaps the questions can't be answered satisfactorily until much more is known about the consumer. But there is in very recent history a storehouse of experience: the "saving spree" of 1951. It is a good place to start asking the questions. This phenomenon, the most stunning economic surprise since 1929, provides a vivid demonstration of the unpredictability of the unsold consumer, the narrow margin between boom and recession, and the role that salesmanship *can* play.

The "saving spree," significantly, was preceded by the spending spree that began immediately after the Korean war broke out in June, 1950. Never, probably, has the outbreak of war been so violently inflationary. Everybody remembered all too clearly what happened "last time"—the shortages, the rationing, the black markets. Everybody acted as if he had to stock up for a war of indefinite duration. One hotel proudly announced that it had laid in a 10-year supply of liquor. One government agency bought a 247-year supply of loose-leaf binders.

The stampede

All this was not helped by the warnings and homilies of the experts. Thought control in a democracy must be very subtly executed if it is not to end up by defeating its own aim. The Department of Agriculture kept assuring people that there was plenty of everything, which of course made them doubt there was. The C. I. O. set up picket lines to stop scare buying, which probably started a lot of scare buying. Economists, bankers, and columnists "clarified" inflation, and of course the more they "clarified" the subject the greater the inflationary pressure became. And Mr. Truman and his CEA, though never averse to a little inflation, came in like a Greek chorus, predicting catastrophe unless a whole roster of direct controls were invoked. No wonder prices rose violently, some of them faster than ever before—and even before very much was spent on munitions. And no wonder selling languished.

But an urge to save lurked underneath all the furor, and amazingly strong it seems to have been. The very excesses of the boom naturally strengthened that urge. In any event, inventories began to increase faster than sales even in the latter part of 1950. With General MacArthur's advance to the Yalu River in October, savings increased and buying dropped sharply. Although China's entry into the war sparked a new buying wave, this wave began to peter out by early 1951. It was in March, 1951, that the consumer clutched his pocketbook to his breast, spat in the face of world economic forces, and began to save a higher proportion of his disposable income than he ever had in peacetime. By April his reaction was in full swing, and in the second quarter he was piling up net savings at the phenomenal rate of nearly $20 billion a year, almost a tenth of disposable income. He did even better in the third and fourth quarters. To put it another way, the increase in his savings alone nearly canceled out the increase in defense spending during 1951. Prices remained steady.

The flabbergasted Di Salles and Keyserlings rubbed their noses and tried to connect the miracle with price and wage controls. Counting on a decline in the rate of savings, they kept insisting that the situation was still inflationary. They also reminded everybody that the consumer's urge to save was a lucky thing for the country, which indeed it was. It is frightening to think of what would have happened if the predictions of inflation had materialized. But like missing the plane that later crashes, what happened in 1951 hardly provides a method for avoiding future disaster.

And a survey made in November, 1951, by the Survey Research Center of the University of Michigan indicated that people were still cautious. Unlike the experts, they did not see their dollars going to hell in inflation, and were in no rush to buy. Just which classes are doing the saving is not precisely known; as *Fortune* suggested in its March, 1952, Roundup, the continued growth in time payments, presumably by low-income groups, indicated that upper-income groups, which normally account for most savings, were again doing so. At all events, the high rate of saving continued for more than a year.

The bad good times

Rarely has an economic phenomenon been so pulled apart, dissected, analyzed, and mulled over. There is even a school of thought that pooh-poohs it. The year 1951, this school says, was after all the second best (after 1950) in peacetime history; the noise was made by retailers, who always judge this year's sales not by, a ten-year average, but by last year's. One expert has essayed to show that in reality 1951's department-store sales were normal, and that stores should not be surprised if the current ratio of sales to disposable income continues indefinitely.

Other analysts, particularly those in department-store organizations, sharply question the accepted figures on savings, openly arguing that the only remedy for the sales lag is less government spending and reduced taxes. That the savings figures are not wholly satisfactory there is no doubt. "Savings" figures generally include insurance, payments on homes, and social-security contributions, most of which could not have been arbitrarily spent on goods. But the facts belie most such arguments. Had people bought in 1951 as they did in 1950, there would be nothing to argue about. And the fact also remains that in 1951 the consumer's savings in cash, securities, and net debt liquidation (but not life-insurance premiums) came to $6.5 billion more than the same categories of savings amounted to in 1950. The consumer, in other words, would have spent $6.5 billion more in 1951 had he saved as he did in 1950.

This may no longer seem like big money to a people accustomed to talk in an offhand way about hundreds of billions. But it has a tremendous leverage. Between October, 1950, and May, 1951, retail inventories rose by $3.2 billion. If the consumer had spent $6.5 billion more in 1951, business probably would have "boomed." Prices would have stayed firm or advanced—in short, much of the inflation that everyone predicted with such cocksure sagacity probably would have materialized.

One of the things that most people have yet to appreciate adequately is the incredibly small difference between "over-supply" and "scarcity." In 1951 the auto industry made 5,300,000 cars, or just enough to keep a "scarcity" from developing. Another 500,000 automobiles, everything else being equal, would have meant "oversupply." In 1950 refrigerators were "scarce"—yet manufacturers sold 6,200,000 of them. "Scarcity" quickly becomes "oversupply" when the consumer is possessed by the urge to save and is permitted to indulge it, and "oversupply" quickly becomes "scarcity" when he is possessed by the urge to buy and is permitted to indulge it.

But why didn't the consumer buy as much as he could have in 1951? Practically every expert, recognized and self-appointed, has a reason. One such reason is the "fact" that many consumers balked at buying because they felt insecure about the future. Another is that they balked because of high prices—just as high prices of soft goods in England have caused even the austerity-ridden Britons to go on a kind of buyers' strike. A related reason is that people, though their wages had more than doubled, still thought in terms of 1940 prices: the traveler outraged at the 25-cent redcap fee, the housewife by Boy Scout shoes at $9 a pair and beef at $1.25 a pound.

Still another related reason given for the reluctance to buy is the perverse but psychologically sound one that people buy when goods seem to be growing scarce. Finally, there is the notion that the average consumer today can buy so many things with his money that he has become, in the words of Arno Johnson of J. Walter Thompson, a man with great discretionary spending power. Beardsley Ruml likes to talk about consumer *un*necessities. "Today as never before," he says, "the ordinary individual can get along without purchasing for his day-to-day requirements. . . . The consumer is free—free to postpone, free to reduce, free to anticipate, free to switch from one *un*necessity to another."

But these reasons by themselves afford only partial clues to the consumer's behavior. Who is this consumer, and why *does* he behave as he does? On this question, alas, it is possible to throw only a meager and fitful light. We know there are roughly 53 million "spending units" in the country—a "spending unit" being defined as all related persons living at the same place who pool their incomes for major expenses. We know how these "spending units" break down by income, how much each income group saved or spent in any year, and, as the result of special surveys, what each of these groups did or intended to do under certain circumstances. But we still lack many elementary statistics such as who owns what brand of autos, stoves, etc., and when they were purchased. And as yet we have few valid generalizations on consumer behavior under common circumstances—for instance, which individuals increase their savings and for what reason.

That man Keynes again

The most important or at any rate the most consistent work in "psychological-economic" fact gathering is being done by the Survey Research Center of the University of Michigan, under Professor

George Katona, author of *Psychological Analysis of Economic Behavior*. The center not only does considerable investigation in its own right; it makes the field surveys for the Federal Reserve Board's highly regarded annual "Survey of Consumer Finances." Well aware that consumer behavior has been generally regarded as a bunch of immeasurables, Professor Katona nevertheless thinks consumer behavior can be investigated empirically, and that someday the Research Center may be able to suggest under what circumstances a certain pattern of consumer behavior is likely to appear. But not enough of this investigation has been done to formulate sound generalities. Anyone wanting to account for the consumer and his proclivities in a large way must perforce turn (as indeed Katona himself has turned) to the late Lord Keynes, who built his doctrines around a theory of how the consumer behaves. Not many sales executives are students of Keynes; the time has come for them to get out the books again.

It was the core of Keynes's Theory of Employment that unemployment and depression come because people save more than business at the time is willing to invest in capital goods. When a man saves $10,000, Keynes's argument went, he reduces by $10,000 the demand for certain consumer goods and thus, of cource, reduces employment in the industries that make them. The trouble is that the $10,000 is not necessarily or immediately put to work creating new jobs in heavy goods. Then there are fewer jobs and fewer purchases, and the downward drift toward depression commences. Savings without works, Keynes kept emphasizing, are distinctly bad; and the ultimate remedy for too much saving is government spending.

To account for the propensity to save, Keynes decided that a "fundamental psychological law" governs human spending and saving. He stated the law thus: "Men are disposed, as a rule and on the average, to increase their consumption as their income increases, but not by as much as the increase in their income. . . . For a man's habitual standard of life usually has the first claim on his income, and he is apt to save the difference which discovers itself between his actual income and the expense of his habitual standard; or, if he does adjust his expenditures to changes in his income, he will over short periods do so imperfectly. Thus a rising income will often be accompanied by increased saving, and a falling income by decreased saving, on a greater scale at first than subsequently."

And how has this "law," which has been accepted by most economists if only because nothing else is more acceptable, worked out in actual practice? Is there any correlation between it and sales effort? The figures before the 1930's do not lend themselves to a reliable interpretation one way or the other. But during the 1930's the trend seemed generally to uphold Keynes. From 1932 to 1935, consumer expenditures followed Keynes and exceeded disposable income, as well they might have, since people were using up savings to live. Between 1935 and 1940 consumer savings increased faster than income. And during the war Keynes's law fulfilled itself with a vengeance. Incomes rose swiftly, but savings rose still more swiftly. The consumer saved what till then had been unheard-of sums, at unheard-of rates. In 1942 he saved $25 billion, or 22 per cent of the national disposable income; in 1943 and 1944 he saved more than $30 billion, or nearly 24 per cent. But the wartime increase, of course, proves little one way or the other, for the consumer was under unusual and heavy pressures to save. (Surveys indicated that the "shortages," contrary to general opinion, did not play a large role in his decision to save.)

It is hardly to be expected that a close analysis of consumer spending *after* the war would verify Keynes's thesis. No matter how much the consumer's income was increasing, he would not be likely to continue to save after having saved so much and bought so little during the war. And so it was. An analysis of "dissaving" (spending in excess of income) in 1946 and 1947 by Professor Katona shows that although disposable income increased by 6.6 per cent, over-all savings did not increase, as Keynes's law says they should, but actually declined (from 18.5 per cent of disposable income in 1945 to 2.3 per cent in 1947). What is more, there was a vast increase in "dissaving." And it all happened without much sales effort on the part of American business, which as a whole almost forgot how to sell between 1941 and 1949. But the survey noted that this abnormal spending would probably be followed by saving. In another analysis Professor Katona examined the effect of income changes on the rate of postwar savings. This was inconclusive, contradicting Keynes at points and verifying him at others. The most significant conclusion emerging from such studies was that people's buying seems governed by expectations: when they expect good times, they buy more than when they are dubious or pessimistic.

Taking everything together, Keynes's law seems hard to verify by experience. But in so far as it suggests an underlying desire to save on the part of consumers, it can claim a certain validity. Surveys made by the Michigan center as early as 1946 indicated that people might start to save again once they had filled their wants. From 1947 there seems to have been a definite swing toward savings. In 1948, net consumer savings, thanks to a second- and third-quarter spurt, advanced to $10.5 billion, or 5.6 per cent of disposable income. In 1949, owing to the resumption of buying after the "inventory recession," net savings declined to $6.3 billion, or 3.4 per cent of disposable income. But despite the wild spending and dissaving after the Korean war started, savings were $10.7 billion in 1950. And the "Survey of Consumer Finances" made by the center in January and February, 1951, printed in the *Federal Reserve Bulletin* of April, 1951, gave clear indications that people were planning to buy less, not more, durable goods. In retrospect it seems that anyone who had noted these signs with Keynes's law in mind might have guessed what was coming. And it is perhaps arguable that what happened in 1951 might be interpreted as a kind of delayed fulfillment of that law.

The real reason

Actually no economic theory anticipates what was possibly the most important and relevant explanation for 1951. And in the sense that all the other reasons commonly given for 1951's savings are only excuses, they do not anticipate the important explanation either. The explanation: people buy for a number of reasons, a major one being that they are sold; and business wasn't selling as it should have been. It hadn't been, indeed, since prewar days. Just as salesmanship was caught napping in the short "inventory" slump of 1949, it was caught wanting in 1950 and 1951. True, many companies had organized for the selling that they knew lay ahead. But even the most determined of them found their resolution softening in the heat of the sellers' picnic "after Korea."

Some of them were caught by circumstances. Most department stores built up inventories so much that they suddenly found themselves forced to liquidate inventory rather than do a well-rounded job of selling, in which price is only one of several ways of attracting a customer. "When your people are trying to unload," says one department-store executive, "they just don't bother to balance up customer preferences."

Earl Puckett of Allied Stores laments the tendency of inventory to grow old too soon. "To create want in people," he says, "you need something new and not merchandise that's six months old. High inventories always make for decelerated selling." In a way, of course, these reasons beg the question. Would stores' inventories have been as cumbersome if stores had sold harder?

Or take the auto business. Anticipating a shortage of cars because of material shortages, dealers neither built up their sales forces nor offered their customary trade-in allowances. They speculated in inventory. Some of them were therefore caught with more cars than they could sell easily. "If the industry had sold aggressively," an auto sales manager explains the industry's dilemma, "it could have disposed of half a million or three-quarters of a million more cars than it did. But it couldn't equip itself to sell like that because it didn't have, or wasn't sure of having, the cars to sell."

Unlike the auto manufacturers, who managed to use up all the materials allocated them, makers of many consumer durables like refrigerators seem to have been caught by their own neglect. They found themselves unable to sell all they could make because they coasted along trying to sell the same old staples. In 1950, for instance, they sold 6,200,000 refrigerators; in 1951, 4,075,000. In 1950 they sold 7,463,800 television sets; in 1951, 5,100,000. Yet other more expensive durables sold *better* in 1951 than in 1950.

The lesson is clear. It seems fair to say that if manufacturers had concentrated (so far as materials supply allowed) on turning out better new products and selling them harder, the total sales of consumer durables other than autos might have been much higher than they were. Besides being caught long on inventories, the hard-goods business was caught short on timing, design, and value. It turned out the same old models at ever higher prices in the expectation that buyers would not be choosers. And it is still suffering from the effects of its errors.

The difference between boom and stability in 1951, as we have noted, was a matter of some $6.5 billion. If salesmanship were as highly organized and proficient as it has been and should be, might it not have persuaded people to spend $6.5 billion more than they did? Unless the American selling apparatus is nothing but a luxury that only an inordinately wealthy and somewhat insane nation would tolerate, the answer is obvious. Selling could have. The government's fiscal policies being what they were, the U. S. can thank its luck that under the circumstances it did not.

. . . Many experts, particularly department-store owners and durable-goods makers, take a dogmatically optimistic view of the long-term prospects. The events of the past years, they say, are abnormal; the long-range trend is not toward saving but just the opposite. With all people sharing more equally in the national income, the argument goes, there will be less to save on the part of the upper-income groups because there will be fewer large incomes. Pension programs, old-age insurance, unemployment insurance, and so on have fostered and will continue to foster a feeling of security that will result in a continuous and high level of spending.

It is nevertheless possible to make an excellent case for just the opposite, that people will feel the urge to save more and more. True, incomes have tended to become equalized. But it is also true that no less than 44 per cent of the personal income is still earned by those making more than $5,000 a year, and that as a group they have more to save than ever. And many people who never could save can now do so, for the equalization of U. S. incomes is being achieved while the real per capita income is steadily advancing.

Consumers' discretion

Thus it may be that the absolute savings potential is greater now than it ever has been. As Mr. Ruml and others keep insisting, the area of optional or discretionary buying is growing immensely rather than contracting. Just what percentage of the nation's income is spent optionally is almost anybody's guess. Arno Johnson of J. Walter Thompson defines it as what is left after the bare necessities of food, clothing, and shelter are paid for. He estimates it at around $105 billion, or more than 45 per cent of 1951's disposable income, or two and a half times as great as in 1940. Other estimates are considerably smaller, for they place a more liberal interpretation on the cost of food and clothing and include some transportation.

But in the sense that discretionary purchasing power represents goods whose purchase can be *postponed* it does not have to be large to be important. When people delay purchasing goods, they do not necessarily accelerate their buying later on to compensate for what they didn't buy earlier. As Keynes observed, "An act of individual savings means—so to speak—a decision not to have dinner today. But it does not necessitate a decision to have dinner or buy a pair of boots a week hence or a year hence or to consume any specified thing at any specified date." Such is the kind of saving that can throw a monkey wrench in the economic machine. It is the margin between "oversupply" and "scarcity," and it is no more certain than the unsold consumer's whim.

Thus on the one hand we have the Keynesian uncompensated saving, whose ultimate solution may be capital formation by government works. On the other, we have the forces of salesmanship striving to prevent accelerated saving, indeed to keep savings down to the minimum needed for capital formation.

Does selling raise demand?

The alternative, of course, may not be quite that sharp. It is just possible that the system can jog along without real selling and without running into a depression. All Keynes tried to prove with his Theory of Employment was that the system might stabilize itself at less than full employment. And it is not straining probability to imagine a prosperous, stabilized economy in which people regularly save 10 per cent or more of their disposable income—i.e., an economy with a high rate of capital formation or "donation diplomacy."

On the other hand, nobody has proved that Keynes's basic analysis is wrong. It is a commonplace that businessmen do not like to expand when consumption is declining. Even the progressive motor industry does not plan vast expansion of production facilities when the outlook for sales is bad, and even the boldest and most resourceful dress manufacturer prefers to spend a year at Miami Beach when business in general is bad. There is no reason to suppose industry will change its habits in the near future. It was this entrepreneurial reluctance to buy capital goods, indeed, that drove Keynes into his partiality for more or less permanently low interest rates. High interest rates may encourage savings, he argued, but they do not encourage capital formation when capital formation should be encouraged most.

Why didn't Keynes pay more attention to the role of selling? Because selling had not rescued the U. S. from the depression, he may have concluded (as some of his followers have concluded) that selling is so much wind and noise generated by what Americans stubbornly insist on calling competition. Most economic thought, as a matter of fact, has tended to regard selling primarily as a device for increasing one company's sales over another and has tended to doubt that it has any important effect on the *aggregate* consumption.

Not even the most enthusiastic exponent of the art would claim that selling can turn depression to boom. But doesn't it really play a preventive role? Isn't it or couldn't it be a means of sustaining aggregate national demand?

To answer these questions in the affirmative, the businessman obviously must behave as if a major aim in life were to demonstrate that Keynes and the other economists were wrong. Defining salesmanship, as *Fortune* has defined it, as everything that contributes to the salability of a product from the time it is conceived until it is finally used up or worn out, the businessman must practice salesmanship as he never has practiced it before.

Who does buy?

That means, among other things, not merely going back and resurrecting all the prewar devices and the conventionally *ad hoc* approach of sales departments and advertising agencies. It means augmenting them with something more in the way of a clear picture of just who the consumer is and precisely what he has bought or intends to buy under given conditions. . . . Despite the libraries of statistics that Americans have collected, despite the millions of dollars they have spent on "market research," they know little or nothing about many vital facts like these.

They also need less theorizing on the behavior of consumers and more verifiable knowledge about it. They need more knowledge, to the extent that such knowledge can be ascertained, about consumer reaction patterns. What the Survey Research Center at Michigan has done so far is only a little more than an introduction to this important and potentially valuable subject.

If selling is to keep consumption in line with production, it needs all possible breaks. Then it may well give the lie to the economists and establish itself as a prime economic force upon which the health of the economy depends.

7. OUR CHANGING CONSUMER MARKET *

Robert Ferber

Had anyone predicted ten years ago that the mainstay of postwar prosperity was to be consumer spending, he would have been ridiculed. Traditionally, business investment in plant and equipment and in inventories had been the spark plug, as well as the foretoken, of business conditions; it helped determine consumer income, which then led to a more or less predetermined level of consumer expenditures.

The experience of the last decade has shown, to almost everybody's surprise, that the process can also work the other way around. In 1948-49, and then again in 1953-54, it was consumer spending that remained high and paved the way for further prosperity, while activity faltered in other sectors of the economy.

These developments have been among the most spectacular and widely publicized characteristics of consumer spending in the postwar years. Yet, they reflect in large measure more basic changes that have been taking place over many years, and particularly during the past two decades. These include changes in the characteristics as well as the number of consumers, changes in consumer income and assets, and changes in consumer wants and preferences—all of which add up to a strikingly different present-day market structure for consumer goods, and which presage additional changes yet to come.

The slowing down of the postwar boom and the concomitant availability of a major new set of data on consumer expenditures make this a convenient time to take stock of these changes and to evaluate their effects in relation to possible future trends in business conditions. These new data were obtained in the course of a nationwide survey of consumer income and expenditures completed in 1957 under the sponsorship of *Life* magazine. They represent the most

* Reprinted by permission of *Business Horizons,* Vol. 1, No. 2 (Spring, 1958), pp. 49-66.

Robert Ferber, Director of the Consumer Savings Project, Inter-University Committee for Research on Consumer Behavior; Research Professor of Economics and Acting Director of the Bureau of Economic and Business Research at the University of Illinois.

extensive private study of this market ever undertaken to date, and rival in scope the mammoth 1950 consumer expenditures study of the

Much of the Rise in Incomes After Taxes . . .

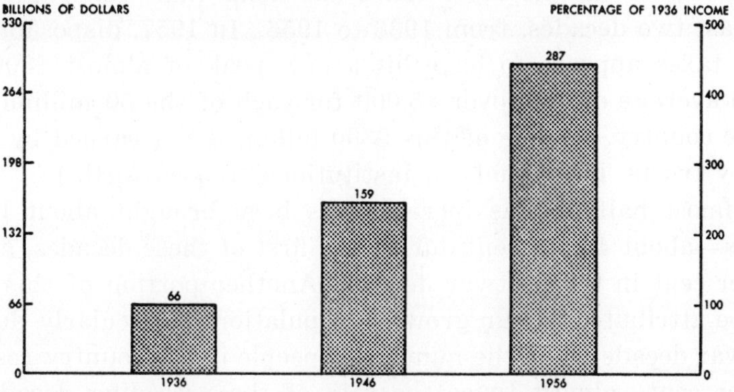

. . . Is Attributable to Higher Prices and a Larger Population.
Nevertheless, Purchasing Power Has Risen Substantially Too.

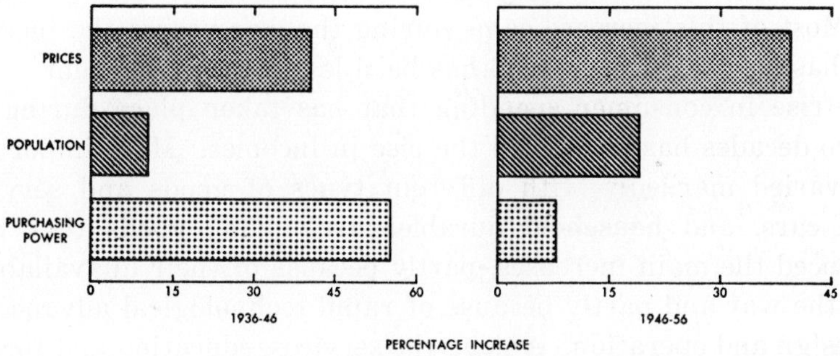

SOURCE: *Computed from U.S. Department of Commerce:* SURVEY OF CURRENT BUSINESS *and various supplements; U.S. Bureau of the Census,* CENSUS OF THE UNITED STATES *and various supplements.*

Figure 1

U. B. Bureau of Labor Statistics.[1] Comparable in many respects with these earlier government studies, the *Life* data enable us to bring up

[1] Some pertinent statistics are: The *Life* sample contained 17,173 households selected by an area probability design from the population at large. Of this number 15,003 supplied some of the information requested, and 10,243 supplied all information. Data were collected from each household in four "waves" of interviews conducted between October, 1955, and the end of 1956. All together 110,314 interviews were carried out during the course of the study, each interview averaging about two hours.

to date the broad developments that have been taking place in the consumer market and to examine the current state of affairs.

Money, Money, Money

Consumer income after taxes has more than quadrupled during the past two decades, from 1936 to 1956. In 1957, disposable income after taxes appears to have hit a new peak of almost $300 billion, or an average of well over $5,000 for each of the 50 million families in the country. (Some of this $300 billion is not earned by families, but by trusts, individuals in institutions, and so forth.)

Almost half of this increase has been brought about by rising prices—about 40 per cent during the first of these decades, and about 60 per cent in the postwar decade. Another portion of this increase can be attributed to our growing population, particularly during the postwar decade when the number of people in the country rose almost 20 per cent—almost twice the rate of the preceding decade. However, even after allowance is made for these increases in prices and population, the fact remains that consumers' purchasing power has undergone a rather hefty increase; in 1956, the real income of the average consumer was 71 per cent more after taxes than it was in 1936. Most of this increase came during the war years; the increase in purchasing power since 1946 has been less than 10 per cent.

The rise in consumer spending that has taken place during the past two decades has paralleled the rise in incomes. More important, it has varied markedly with different types of goods and services. Homes, cars, and household durables are among goods that have experienced the main increases, partly because of their unavailability during the war and partly because of rapid technological advances in their design and operation. Among the services, education and foreign travel have registered the largest gains, reflecting the newly found discretionary spending of millions of families and the growing popularity of overseas vacations. Consumer spending has risen much less than average for rental housing and for purchased local and intercity transportation, which have suffered because of the shift to home and car ownership; for clothing, which has lost for the time being much of its former glamor; and for domestic service, which has declined as a result of the widespread labor shortage, enabling workers in this field to make more money elsewhere.

Of course, much of this rise in expenditures—approximately 60 per cent of it—is due to increases in price and population. However, much the same pattern of consumer spending emerges when allowance

The Effect of Prosperity on the Consumer Budget

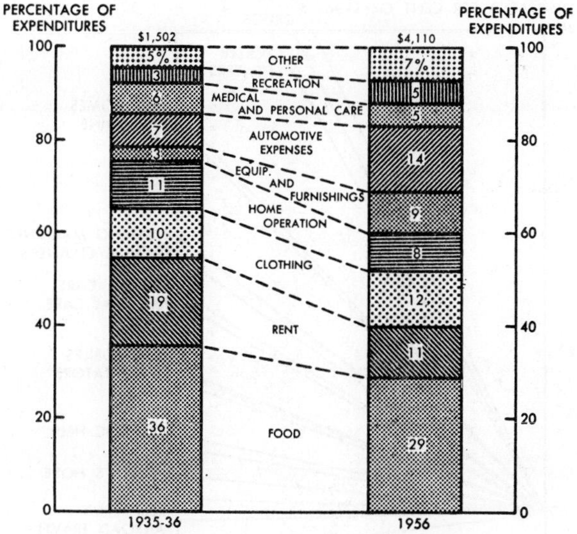

SOURCE: *Percentages for 1935-36 are derived from National Resources Committee,* CONSUMER EXPENDITURES IN THE UNITED STATES, ESTIMATED FOR 1935-1936; *and supplementary reports by the Department of Labor, Bureau of Labor Statistics. Percentages for 1956 are derived from* LIFE STUDY OF CONSUMER EXPENDITURES, *copyright 1957 by* TIME, INC.

Figure 2

is made for the effects of price and population changes. This is supported by a comparison of household expenditures in 1936 with the corresponding *Life* magazine data for 1956.

Such a comparison shows that gadgetry, particular in the form of durable goods, and pleasure have been occupying an increasingly important position in the American family budget. The average urban household in 1956 went in relatively more for home furnishings and equipment (including appliances), recreation, and automobiles, and related expenses (much of which in turn can be charged to recreation), and less for clothing, rent, and household operation.

In fact, symptomatic of the great postwar prosperity has been the decline in the proportion of the family budget devoted to the traditional necessities of life—food, clothing, and shelter. American families roughly doubled their outlays on food, clothing, and shelter between 1936 and 1956, but during the same period their over-all expenditures on other items of family living nearly quadrupled. As

Trends in Purchases of Selected Goods and Services

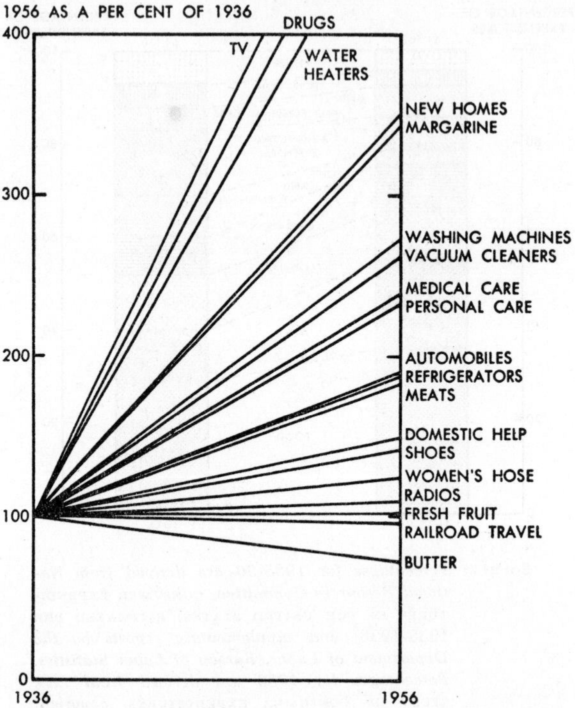

SOURCE: *Percentages for 1936 are computed from U.S. Department of Commerce,* NATIONAL INCOME, 1954 EDITION: A SUPPLEMENT TO THE SURVEY OF CURRENT BUSINESS. *Percentages for 1956 are computed from U.S. Department of Commerce,* SURVEY OF CURRENT BUSINESS, *July, 1957.*

Figure 3

a result, the importance of food, clothing, and shelter in the family budget fell from nearly two-thirds of the total in 1935-36 to just a little over half in 1956—and this is without allowance for the sharp increase in purchases of such luxury items as fancy foods and air conditioning.

When we get down to individual products, differences between family outlays then and now become much more pronounced. For some products, such as fresh fruit, potatoes, railroad travel, and domestic service, expenditures have risen hardly at all in dollar terms, and have actually declined, once price increases are taken into account. However, purchases of such items as new homes, washing machines, and margarine have risen in some cases almost fourfold. Perhaps the most striking indication of the changes that have taken place in consumer markets is the growing proportion of the family budget going to new products that had no counterparts in 1936—air conditioning, television, clothes dryers, and frozen foods.

The Story Behind the Story

Essential to an understanding of the nature of these changes and what they portend for the future is a consideration of the factors responsible for the changes. In general, among such factors there seem to be four principal ones:

- income
- population
- assets
- credit

Income

The tremendous rise in the level of consumer incomes alone would have been sufficient to bring about pronounced changes in consumer spending. This rise has been reinforced by the decline in the concentration of incomes. There has been in particular an increase in the proportion of middle-income families brought about by the needs of a full-employment economy. Higher wages, especially for unskilled labor, serve to increase the earnings of those already employed and, at the same time, induce more family members to enter the labor force.

These developments have produced a more equal distribution of incomes. Thus, in 1935-36 the 10 per cent of families with the highest incomes accounted for 36 per cent of total family income in that year, whereas in 1956, according to the *Life* data, the same highest 10 per cent of families accounted for only 24 per cent of total incomes. More families were above what would be defined as a subsistence income in 1956 too—about 44 per cent in 1956 as against 24 per cent in 1935-36 (taking $4,500 and $1,750 as the corresponding respective subsistence levels). The result has been not only higher levels of spending but the creation of mass markets for goods previously in the luxury category.

Population

That more people need more goods is axiomatic. However, when characteristics of the population that are closely related to spending patterns change markedly, shifts in consumer markets are an almost inevitable consequence. The changes in the present instance are indeed pronounced. During the past two decades, our population has become more educated; more white collar and professional in class; more suburban; older, yet, paradoxically, with more children and larger families.

These changes, interacting with the growth and redistribution of incomes, have led to a growing sophistication in tastes and preferences (or at least so people like to believe), as well as to substantial expansion in markets for various products. The current boom in hi-fi sets, in foreign goods, in sports cars, in white shirts (as against colored shirts), and in wines and brandies is largely a manifestation of these changes. When a family moves into a different income or population group, its spending patterns invariably tend to conform to those of the new group, albeit with some lag.

The growth of suburban living has led especially to pronounced shifts in consumer purchases; producing, among other things, a booming market for home improvement and do-it-yourself materials, a not unrelated surging market for bandages and medical supplies, and a fertile new field for novelists in search of material.

Assets

When a person has money in the bank, he is more likely to spend liberally out of current income than when his pocket is holding his last dollar. If, in addition, his holdings have risen well above customary levels because of a scarcity of goods and pressure to accumulate government bonds, he is likely to spend very well indeed once the emergency lets up; and this is what appears to have happened in the postwar years.

The high proportion of aggregate consumption expenditures to personal disposable income during this period—nearly 94 per cent—would hardly have been reached had most consumers not had a cushion to fall back on in case of sudden reversals. This cushion not only has been a comfortable one but, what may not be widely realized, has been increasing throughout the postwar period. Thus, savings (time) deposits of individuals rose from $232 per capita at the end of 1936 to $771 per capita in 1946 and then further still to $1,077 per capita at the end of 1956. At the same time, there is some evidence that liquid asset holdings (savings and checking accounts and U. S. government bonds) have become more concentrated during the past decade. Ten per cent of American households were reported to have

$5,000 or more of liquid assets in early 1956 as against 6 per cent in 1946. At the same time, the proportion of households without any assets rose slightly, to one-fourth of the total.

Credit

To a large extent, the expansion of consumer credit can be alleged to be an outgrowth of these other changes. After all, really poor people are not able to borrow! The most frequent users of credit in recent years have been households in the middle-income brackets, earning between $4,000 and $7,000 per year. Many of these households have liquid assets as well but prefer to borrow anyway, treating repayment of the loan as a form of disciplined saving. The cost of this borrowing seems to be of little consequence to the consumer as long as his income is sufficient to cover the payments.

On the whole, there is little doubt that credit expansion has served as a major stimulus to consumer spending, bringing about many purchases which would not otherwise have been made—especially of cars, homes, and other durable goods. In effect, this credit expansion can be interpreted as a reflection of the growing importance of capital goods in family living, spurred in part by the sharp decline in the availability of competent household help at reasonable prices. As in business operations, outright purchase of consumer capital goods is often too costly. The consumer therefore follows the alternative of purchasing these goods on credit, thereby obtaining for himself the services and pleasures provided by these capital goods well before the time he can actually afford to own them. Whether one likes it or not, paying in the future for present enjoyment is becoming an increasingly popular way of life.

Other factors

Diverse price movements could to some extent be labeled a fifth factor accounting for the present structure of our consumer market. It is not so considered here because during a period of rapidly rising incomes such as have characterized the last two decades, price considerations become of secondary importance in most purchase decisions. There have been notable exceptions, however, when the price of a product went completely out of line with that of competing products. This invariably has had disastrous results—as in the case of butter.

Many other factors have also contributed in one way or another to the present state of our consumer market. Most notable of these is perhaps technology, which has spurred demand for new or improved products, often at the expense of other, more prosaic products. Advertising, changing styles, and mass communications (especially the homogenizing influence of mass media) have also contributed in one way or another. Competitive pressures for mass production and standardization are also not to be ignored. Indeed, some maintain that these are the principal factors impelling consumers to "be alike and live alike."

A Telescopic View

The present consumer market can be eulogized in terms of a tremendous variety of adjectives. It is bigger, better, broader than at any time in our history. There are more different goods and services for sale, more of most items available, more people and more money bidding for the goods—and, of course, more advertising exhorting us to buy still more goods.

Huge as this present market may be, all indications are that it will be dwarfed by consumer markets of the future. Estimates of the size of these markets can be obtained by extrapolating past aggregate growth trends, a favorite parlor exercise of business analysts. Such an approach may yield a rough idea of the general size of these markets, but it tells us little about their characteristics—how expenditures will be distributed among different types of consumers, how expenditure patterns will be adjusted to different economic circumstances, how competition will affect expenditure patterns, and many other questions. These questions can only be answered by studying current expenditure patterns of a cross section of the population and using this as a springboard for insights into the future. Such data, if current enough, can also throw considerable light on the structure of the present consumer market and thereby serve as a basis for gauging shortrun market potentials, guiding the use of promotional efforts, constructing more effective sales territories, and determining investment plans.

In a rapidly moving economy such as ours, expenditure patterns can change substantially within a few years, and it is therefore of particular importance to have data recent enough to yield an up-to-date cross section of the consumer market. It is in this sense that consumer expenditure studies, such as the recent *Life* survey, come in so handy. Changes in early postwar consumer expenditure patterns have already been pinpointed by the 1950 Consumer Expenditures Study of the U. S. Bureau of Labor Statistics and the University of Pennsylvania, and this new study indicates the extent to which further changes have taken place.

Diminishing influence of income

One of the striking characteristics of the present consumer market brought out by this study is its apparent homogeneity. This is true, on the whole, even with regard to income; for within a few percentage points, high-income households distribute their expenditures in much the same way as do low-income households. The only exception of any consequence is the tendency for the higher-income households to spend less on food and more on automobiles, home, furnishings, and appliances.

The principal effect of income on the household budget seems to lie in determining how large a proportion goes for food; the allocation of the budget among other types of expenditures is determined by the homogenizing influence of mass tastes and preferences, modified by specific social and demographic factors affecting particular households.

Of course, this is a very general tendency, and numerous exceptions will be found when data for individual households are examined. In addition, we have to consider that although households in different economic and social circumstances may allocate their expenditures among different categories in the same manner, this does not mean that the same products are bought. Not only may altogether different products be bought, for example, steak and lobster as against hamburger and smelt, but the quality of product may differ substantially: The high-income family may purchase a Cadillac or an Imperial while the low-income family goes in for a Ford or a Studebaker. It may well be these quality differentials that constitute the main difference between household expenditures at different levels of income; for preliminary examination of the distribution of household budgets among individual products shows, on the whole, surprisingly small differences.

Further evidence of the declining role of income is provided by the large number of expenditures that seem to be relatively insensitive, or *inelastic,* to income changes. As incomes move up, manufacturers and distributors of goods possessing high income elasticities are in a favored position, since a given rise in income produces proportionately more outlays on these goods than on others. This approach has also provided a basis for sales forecasting and gauging market potentials, by estimating the income elasticity of demand for a good from consumer expenditure surveys and then applying it to alternative projections of future income levels and distributions.

In 1956, however, only a few of the 65 groups of goods and services used in the *Life* study exhibited elastic demand:

CATEGORIES WITH ELASTIC DEMAND

Between low (0-$2,000) and middle ($4-5,000) income levels	*Between middle and high ($7,000 up) income levels*
Miscellaneous home improvements	Wines, brandies, liquors
Small appliances	Miscellaneous home improvements
Furniture	Floor coverings
Automobiles	Photographic equipment
Photographic equipment	Sport goods
Games and toys	
Sport goods	

If finer classifications were used and individual products treated separately, this list would become many times longer. It is nevertheless apparent from the above and from what has been said before (Figure 3) that the importance of income, although still great, is diminishing and will continue to do so as incomes rise further.

This is not to say that income effects can be ignored. Clearly, without income there could be no purchases, and even at present levels of income, substantial variations in purchases exist among different income levels. This is particularly true when quality considerations are taken into account. Then, too, income effects interact at times with other characteristics, so that the direction of change in consumer expenditures shifts as the level of income is varied. Thus, expenditures for infants' clothing are higher among low- and middle-income families whose heads have more education, but the reverse is true among high-income families.

Concentration of markets

The present-day consumer market is highly concentrated. This has been brought about on the one hand by the steady migration of the population to urban centers, particularly to metropolitan areas and their environs, and, on the other hand, to the not unrelated fact that incomes are highest in these areas. Nearly six out of every ten American households resided in metropolitan areas in 1956. These families earned on the average over $5,000 apiece in that year (in the suburbs of the large cities nearly $6,000), while household incomes in other parts of the country were averaging not much over $4,000.

This huge metropolitan market of nearly 30 million households accounted for two-thirds of the total purchases of goods and services by American households in 1956. More than three-fourths of household expenditures for beer, liquor, housing, and floor coverings took place in this area. As one would expect, there are substantial variations in the market shares of various goods and services between the central cities and the suburbs of metropolitan areas. Central city households accounted for disproportionately large shares (in relation to their number) of expenditures on liquor, women's and girls' clothing and footwear, accessories and clothing care, housing, spectator fees, and writing equipment; while expenditures in the suburbs were disproportionately high for nearly all housing items, appliances, and house furnishings; as well as for liquor (those exurbanites again!), automotive items, sporting goods, and pet foods—all reflecting the emphasis in the suburbs on comfortable living.

The consumer market is also highly concentrated in various other ways. Thus, households with children spent considerably more than other households, particularly on most food items (not to mention baby food!), clothes, decorating material, and writing equipment.

Concentration by income is also pronounced: The one-third of households with the highest incomes accounted for nearly half of the total household expenditures for goods and services. However, this percentage was actually greater when incomes were lower and more unequally distributed. Geographic concentration is a much more recent development.

Despite this concentration, the fact remains that the consumer market has become so large that even the smaller segments comprise substantial markets in themselves. A commodity that appealed to only 1 per cent of this market would still have a sales potential of half a million units, representing a population exceeding that of all but four of our cities. It is largely for this reason that markets for such specialty goods as custom-made furniture, motor scooters, and such canned "delicacies" as maggots and rattlesnakes have been able to do so well alongside the development of the homogenizing mass market.

Emergence of other forces

Occupation, education, family size, and other social forces have always influenced consumer expenditures to some extent. Now, however, with income gradually losing its traditional role as the principal, almost sole, determinant of the types of goods and services a household will buy, these social and demographic factors are assuming positions of new importance. Differences in expenditure patterns already appear to lie about as much between households of different social characteristics, different age levels, different educational attainments and sources of livelihood, and different geographical locations, as between households of different income levels.

Many of these differences become especially pronounced when comparisons are made of expenditure patterns of households possessing different social and demographic characteristics but at the same levels of income. Thus, whether a household is earning less than $3,000 a year or over $10,000 a year, we find that the one headed by a college graduate spends relatively less on food, clothing, and medical and personal care, but spends more on the home and on automotive expenses. Again irrespective of income, families headed by younger people spend proportionately less than older families on food and medical and personal care but spend more on clothing and automotive supplies.

Region and marketing location seem to exert special influences of their own on the allocation of household expenditures. Households in the Northeast devote more of their expenditures to food than households in the South or West. At the same time, as the size of the community increases, more of the household budget goes to food, shelter, education, and recreation expenses and less to automobile expenses.

Indicative of the growing importance of other factors is the diversity of changes in household expenditures between households at the same levels of income but with differing social and demographic characteristics. Substantial variation at the same level of income is evident more often than not for each of the five characteristics [more education, older household heads, presence of children, south to north (metropolitan areas only), and metropolitan (versus nonmetropolitan areas)]. In fact, for some expenditure categories, the relative variation in purchases is larger for one or more of these characteristics than it is for income; this is true of several food products, beer and ale, tobacco, some clothing items, laundry soaps, radio and TV, medical supplies, writing equipment, and building materials. Yet these are not the only relevant characteristics that influence consumer expenditures, and indeed for some of the products listed in the table, none of these may be the most *relevant* characteristic. Again, much more frequent and substantial variations can be expected when individual product purchases are considered.

The Consumer in the Bright New World

There is little doubt that the consumer market of the future will, with occasional setbacks, be still bigger and more grandiose than anything yet seen. Rising incomes and standards of living will take care of that. The implications of these trends are many, but perhaps the principal ones are the following:

1. *Consumers are becomingly increasingly able to act differently from each other, yet in practice they seem to act more like one another.* This paradoxical behavior of the consumer may well be such as to give market analysts and psychologists alike a completely new set of frustrations. For as incomes rise and consumers obtain more leeway in allocating expenditures, the former emphasis on subsistence gradually fades into the background. Already, probably not much more than half of the average household income goes for subsistence expenditures, and this proportion will undoubtedly decline further. Thus, consumers will have at their command an ever increasing latitude in allocating expenditures, so that consumer budgets might be expected to differ increasingly from each other.

But what has been happening? Despite the growing potential for increasing heterogeneity between consumer budgets, the trend seems to be in the other direction. Consumer budgets on the whole are very similar to one another, even when comparisons are made by income levels; the main differences appear to lie in the qualities of the goods and services that are bought rather than in what is bought. Whether it is due to mass communications, to a pervading desire for conspicuous consumption, to pressures from manufacturers, or to some other forces, consumers appear to be becoming more homogeneous in an era when they are being endowed increasingly with the capacity to behave differently.

To be sure, individual exceptions are numerous, as is only to be expected in an economy containing 50 million households. Hardly ever are we likely to reach a stage when the behavior of all individual consumers conforms to the average. In the present situation, dispersion about the average is yet to be determined, but indications are that the same tendency toward uniformity will be found to exist.

2. *New concepts of market analysis are needed.* The growing impact on consumer expenditures of a host of factors other than income means that the past practice of predicting sales by deriving a simple relationship between income and expenditures will yield increasingly inferior results as time goes on. Accurate forecasts will entail the use of methods that take into account the effects on expenditures of

a number of different factors simultaneously. This is not the place to go into such methodological issues, but it might be mentioned that some "multivariate" techniques already exist for handling such problems and other techniques are in developmental stages.

3. *The role of the consumer as a purely passive agent in business fluctuations is a relic of the past.* With incomes well above subsistence levels and with enormous reserves of unneeded spending power in the form of durable assets and unused credit, consumers are much more free to spend as they please. Concomitantly, consumer expenditures are less likely than before to vary with moderate fluctuations in income. A substantial portion of the national income is brought about by sales at the consumer level. If incomes in other sectors of the economy dip but consumers keep on spending, the net effect can be a considerable boost to these other sectors and renewed prosperity. Postwar experience, particularly in 1949 and 1954, has demonstrated conclusively how effectively consumer spending can support the economy and mitigate the effects of recessions.

To be sure, consumer spending can work the other way, and precipitate a recession when one might not otherwise have occurred. Then, again, consumer spending may at times assume a passive role while more traditional forces, such as business investment or government spending, call the turn. The point is that the consumer has become, with these other forces, a potential catalyst in business fluctuations. His influence cannot be ignored. Whether he will choose to take the initiative at a particular time may well be the $64 billion question of the future!

8. THE GREAT ENIGMA . . . "MADAME X" *

Everybody claims to know her, but nobody *understands* her. The chronicles of her daily doings read like mystery tales. Yet she's considered the most *important* person in America. She's the "average consumer."

Anthropologists, sociologists, psychologists, as well as nose-counters and head-shrinkers, vie with one another in telling us just *who* the "average" consumer is and *how* she acts.

Something like 10 million dollars a year are spent on prying into her psyche, measuring her buying pressure, testing her impulses. (We say "her" not because we underrate the male of the species, but because there is supposed to be less mystery about the "mister" of the family than about the "missus.")

Composite of the "average" consumer

If you like to form a picture of who the "average" consumer is and what she looks like, try to do so from these descriptions:

> Some experts tell us that "the average consumer has an underlying fear that we do not *deserve* the good life we have had . . . we feel *guilty*, and to be sold we must be given a *rational* justification for buying and using a product."
>
> Others say that "the consumer doesn't buy by *reason*. Emotional stimulation is the *only* trigger for the buying impulse."
>
> Some "experts" proclaim that "the middle class aspires to ape the *upper class* in social behavior and in the possession of conveniences."
>
> And others says: "Once people reach the upper middle class, they lose the *zest for buying* consumer goods."
>
> We could fill pages with what "experts" tell us about the psychology, motivation, and behavior of the "average" consumer.

A very pretty package

Too often the "experts" on mass behavior hand out neatly-wrapped packages tied with pretty ribbons and labeled "Average Consumer, U. S. A."

And too often marketers accept those packages as gospel. The resulting loss to business is *incalculable millions.*

In actuality, the "typical consumer" is a *figment of fancy.* She (or he, if you wish) does not exist.

Let's take as an example the young suburban housewife who is so frequently cited as the "typical consumer." She is described as

* Reprinted from July, 1958 issue of the National Advertisers' Edition of *Grey Matter*, published by the Grey Advertising Agency, Inc., New York.

"*young*, lives in a ranch style home in the *suburbs*, has one or two cars, is busy raising a family, wants all the conveniences and comforts of modern home appliances, and is ready to mortgage her future to get them."

It's true that between 1950 and 1957 the suburbs have grown in population seven times as fast as the rest of the United States. Hence, marketers fall over each other to woo her.

Yet while this suburban phenomenon has been developing, the percentage of married *working couples* increased in 1957 to 10.8 million, that is, 28 per cent of the estimated 38.9 million married couples in the United States. How "typical" a consumer, then, is the suburban housewife?

The point of this one example is that the concept of the "typical American consumer" or of the "average American consumer" can lead to many pitfalls.

Perhaps some day we may reach a *valid* knowledge of mass buying behavior. Perhaps some day the social sciences will provide us with a *common denominator* for mass motivation. Possible. (For those of us who have lived through the past half-century, nothing is impossible of achievement by the human mind.) But we sure don't have it now. The probability of evolving a *practical* theory of mass human behavior is remote because such a theory pre-supposes either a *stable* or *controlled* society.

Built-in mobility

There is nothing stable about American society. The desire for *change* has become ingrained in the American character.

Even in suburbia there is a restless urge to be *different* while conforming to the pattern. There are social, intellectual and economic islands in apparently homogeneous suburban communities. The urge to *surpass* is often much more powerful than the desire to conform.

The noted sociologist, David Reisman, of the University of Chicago, put his finger on the problem recently when he said: "Differentiation is as strong as homogenization in the market, and the very effort to get *everybody* will alienate *many* bodies."

The automobile industry may be cited as an example of marketers being swept off their feet by visualizing the consumer as a *composite* personality and then keying their styling, designing, marketing and advertising to this image. A look at the 1958 cars is ample evidence of this automotive marketing thinking. An analysis of the price brackets of 11 makes of cars in the "big 3" families also reveals that they've taken a bead on this so-called "average consumer."

The concept of concentration

For companies with limited budgets it is often a matter of survival to discover and concentrate on a segment of the market which presents the richest potentials. For large volume advertisers, too, it is often sound strategy to aim at *groups* instead of shooting the works at the nonexisting "average" consumer.

In aiming at a specific group you're shooting at an audience which can return the "mostest" in sales with the "leastest" in expenditures. Instead of spreading advertising dollars in a thin layer to create an awareness of your product, you *break through* this layer of awareness to the layer of *acceptance* and then into the magic circle of *buying.*

In the vast expansion predicted for our economy, the concept of the "average" consumer will become more *complex* and more *puzzling.* The tremendous increase in population will result in larger heterogeneous groups of consumers who will have to be taken into account in marketing strategy. Marketers and advertisers who accept the *packaged* "average consumer" will then go even further astray.

However, as markets grow larger and more complex, there will be *less need* for trying to find the "average" consumer. For specific segments of the total market will be large enough in themselves to be cultivated profitably by mass marketers. Fact is that even today astute advertisers are finding it profitable to pick *segments* of the market and to develop them deeply and intensively.

A few examples: (It just happens that they're Grey clients.)

The Mennen Company is concentrating for its baby products advertising appeal on "The Lady-in-Waiting," instead of trying to influence *all* women who have babies. With great success.

Everybody is a prospect for bus travel. But the automobile owner is a *prime* prospect. Hence The Greyhound Corporation is aiming successfully at people who use their cars for trips, with a campaign built around the appeal: "It's such a comfort to take the bus . . . and leave the driving to us."

Coffee is a universal drink. But Chock Full O' Nuts chose for its special market the segment of our population which prides itself on being *coffee lovers.* The appeal: "Don't spend the extra money for Chock Full O' Nuts Coffee unless you're just plain crazy about good coffee." Result: an *impressive share of the markets* where this brand is distributed.

Discovery and identification

How will these specific market segments be found and identified?

1. Improvement and development of research to determine *personality differences* in specific segments of the consumer market.
2. More investigation of *family spending habits.* (Such a study is projected by the Inter-University Committee for Research on Consumer Behavior with a grant from the Ford Foundation.)
3. Research on a *continuous basis* instead of being confined only to specific product problems.
4. Research to discover what George Romney, President of American Motors Corporation, calls "neglected areas of consumer demand," as a means of side-stepping the *deadly conformity* which characterizes so many products.
5. Refinements of techniques in *quantitative research* and development, of greater ability to draw sound conclusions from the findings.
6. Skillful evaluation of pseudo-scientific research which peddles notions borrowed from psychoanalysis as honest-to-goodness clues to *mass* consumer motivation.
7. Recognition of the value of true qualitative research as a *supplement* and not as a competitor of quantitative research.

Summing it all up

There are too many people in the world of advertising and marketing who have named themselves spokesmen for an ephemeral "average consumer" and who pontificate on how this "average" consumer *thinks* and *acts.*

These pronunciamenti are too often taken as gospel, and marketing planning is based on them at *terrific costs.*

The "average consumer" *doesn't exist.* She's only a statistic. Building marketing plans around her, addressing advertising only to her, is like shooting rockets into the void.

The concept of the "average consumer" causes a *sameness* of products and a *sameness* in advertising which result in terrific *loss* to advertisers.

Finding large segments of the consumer market with similar characteristics is the answer for *many* (not *all*) *advertisers.*

As our population grows and our economy expands, many more such segments will in themselves constitute *huge profitable markets.*

More and more *effective* research will *find* and *identify* segments of the mass market with large enough common denominators to make them *unified* marketing and advertising targets.

Perhaps some day research will enable us to *predict* mass behavior accurately. As of now, the "average" consumer is a mirage.

9. THE COMING BREAK-THROUGHS IN MOTIVATION RESEARCH *

C. Joseph Clawson

Vance Packard's much-discussed best seller, *The Hidden Persuaders,* has turned the American public's attention to a snowballing revolution which has been under way for over ten years. This is a revolution in the methods of finding out what makes consumers buy or not buy. It involves a group of projective techniques borrowed from clinical psychology, collectively called "motivation research."

As scores of cocktail party guests can now tell you, "M.R." induces consumers indirectly to reveal their concealed motives, and even their subconscious ones, toward a product by getting them to discuss other people's motives and personalities. The Thematic Apperception Test, incomplete sentences, word association—all have helped unearth a rich new vein of facts about consumers which could not be reached economically, if at all, through more conventional survey techniques.

The Complex Consumer

Despite the confusing mixtures of triumphs and blunders, praise and scorn, which have accompanied the new developments, they have made a lasting impression on the business community. They have shown that this wondrously confusing, God-created, man-embroidered being—the consumer—is complex beyond the wildest imaginings of the old-time advertising copywriter and the free-wheeling sales manager of yesteryear.

Advertising, selling, and other marketing people are beginning to realize the tremendous complexity and intelligence of the consumer, and they are discovering that soaking up information—in addition to Scotch on the rocks—is a tremendous aid to creative inspiration.

Some business firms, indeed, are buying motivation research today with an enthusiasm which almost sweeps the researchers off their feet. Thoughtful motivation researchers, while pleased with the size

* Reprinted by permission from Alderson Associates, Inc., *Cost and Profit Outlook,* Vol. XI, Nos. 5 and 6 (May-June, 1958), pp. 1-6.

C. Joseph Clawson, Principal, Alderson Associates, Inc.

of this burgeoning demand, are beginning to feel and quietly express concern over the nature of the demand and the problems of delivering the results which are being expected of them.

Room for Improvement

In short, motivation research is off to a blinding start with flaming exhausts. But there is reason to be concerned whether this man-made satellite will go into orbit and stay there, or burn up as it re-enters the atmosphere and plunges to earth, its charred remains to be studied in the future as relics of a fantastic fad. The outcome will depend on whether or not certain improvements are made in this powerful new research weapon.

The purpose of this article is to reaffirm that motivation research represents a genuine scientific break-through in the field of marketing research, and to point out at the same time that there are greater break-throughs which must be and, I believe, can be achieved in this field.

There are seven such needed break-throughs. The first three involve improvements in the *quality* of motivation research. The next two refer to the *quantification and cost* of motivation research. The last two involve *concepts and standards.*

1. *Motivation research must be designed to uncover ALL the types of motives which affect purchase of a given product, not just the psychological or social motives.*

The recent long-overdue success of projective research methods (often wrongly called "motivation research" as if there were no other way to discover motives) has so far led to a dangerous over-emphasis on the social and biological motivations, with frequent disregard of economic motives.

Economic Man Not Extinct

A tremendous amount of money has been spent on research into the motivations of potential customers emphasizing social status, ego identification, and sex-imagery connected with the products involved. In many of these studies few questions if any are asked by the researchers about the motivational influence of cost of upkeep, cost of operation, rising insurance rates, growing irritation with products too large for the storage space available, and so on. Some serious marketing blunders have resulted.

Please understand, I am not rejecting psychoanalytic concepts nor am I calling Freud a fraud. Normal people also have deep subconscious and concealed motivations. But why must the pendulum swing so far in this direction? And why did we have to swing so far in the opposite direction, as we used to, and say that all consumer behavior was explainable in terms of income, prices, and home inventories, with perhaps a condescending nod to something called "preferences"?

Clearly necessary, therefore, is some sort of a check list of the broad categories as well as the specific motives which may influence behavior for or against a particular product. The research plan can then be designed to give an opportunity for all such motives to be expressed (or not expressed) through the proper selection of methods and specific questions.

Six Hundred Motives

It has been my pleasure for the past three years, both at the Graduate School of Business Administration at the University of California at Los Angeles and more recently at Alderson Associates, Inc. to have engaged in making up a compilation of American consumer motives. These are motives which have been revealed in actual marketing and motivation research studies conducted by scores of organizations throughout the country. We have reduced to punch-card form the motivational findings of all these available studies.

One of the most important preliminary observations is that consumers are influenced at some time, to some degree, and for some products by at least 600 different motives. These include not only a host of *biological* and *social* motives, but a great variety of motives in other categories such as the *artistic, political, religious, intellectual,* and *economic* types of motives. To these should be added the *general* motives which cut across all of the other categories.

When designing a consumer research study for a particular product I have found it helpful as a matter of routine to run a card-sort of motives from our nationwide compilation to pick out those motives which have been found by any firm to affect the demand for this type of product or similar products. The motives which are sorted out help in developing a well-rounded set of hypotheses to be tested, which in turn help in tailor-making the set of research tools which will be the most productive. At the same time, freedom to follow new leads is unhindered.

2. *Motivation research will check all the behavioral links in the "chain of motivation" leading up to and extending beyond purchase of a product.*

Another vitally needed type of check list which a well-rounded research design should utilize is that of the *chain of motivation.* This comprises the 24 "problem-solving functions" which the consumer household must perform or have performed for it in the sequence of decisions and actions associated with every purchase. The chain stretches out from initial recognition of need for a satisfaction all the way through to final disposition of used resources. Every buying motive is attached to at least one of these problem-solving functions, such as price motivation being associated with the function of procurement and concern over available refrigerator space being associated with the storage function.

The problem-solving functions of purchasers are described in greater detail in the September and October, 1957, issues of the COST AND PROFIT OUTLOOK, together with examples of additional motives attached to various functions.

CHAIN OF BUYING BEHAVIOR

The important point to be emphasized here is that in many motivation research studies there has been far too much emphasis on the benefits or disadvantages which a consumer expects to receive while he is *using* the product, and too little recognition that the consumer realizes from the outset that *he has to perform a large number of prior functions before he can use the product, and some subsequent functions also have to be performed after he has used it.*

The consumer must see a "clear track" or unbroken chain ahead of him reaching all the way from the present stage in which he finds himself on through all of the functions which he expects to have to perform at some time or other in connection with the product. Just as a chain is only as strong as its weakest link, the demand for a high-quality, low-priced product may be weakened, for instance, by the consumer's fear that he may lack a place to store it properly.

A well-designed research plan should provide for investigating all the links in the chain of buying behavior, above all in studies intended to explain a declining market share, assist in new product development, or provide a comprehensive "new look" at a firm's entire marketing program.

3. *Motivation research will employ a full kit-bag of tools, not just projective tests by themselves.*

There are many techniques for investigating motives, but some advocates of projective tests and depth interviews have tried and almost succeeded in expanding from a corner *of* motivation research to a corner *on* the whole idea. It is almost as if the airlines had managed to patent the word "transportation" for their sole use, barring automobiles, railroads and others from using the term. Heated opposition comes from distinguished pollsters who see no room at all for projective and depth methods, since conventional survey methods, they say, can do the job adequately alone.

Both extreme views illustrate the third great qualitative defect of consumer research today. Much of it is done by specialized research houses which have built fine reputations on one particular method or group of methods. Hence, they are often prone to engage in mortal and, if at all possible, public combat with the enemy to defend their research tool as the One True Method.

Full Kit-Bag of Tools

It is my view that motivation research is in many cases exactly what the marketing executive needs, and at Alderson Associates, Inc. we do not hesitate to prescribe it. But in other instances an entirely different research tool—or additional tools—would be more advisable. *The firm which gathers information for a business client should not be committed to a single method or group of methods.* It should be in possession of a "full kit-bag of tools," and it should know when and how to use each one of these market research techniques, both separately and in combination. A given client may need motivation research using projective techniques, or it may need a time-line study of usage, advertising cost analysis, operations research, straight attitude survey, customer clinic, statistical forecasting, shopping games, controlled experimental tests, or some other technique which has the greatest bearing on its particular problem. Out of the repertoire of techniques the research director should select one or more methods and combine them in the most skillful and economical fashion.

Often these different methods are used on different kinds of respondents and in separate studies, although all may have a bearing on a particular problem of a given firm.

It is also desirable, in many cases, to employ a blend of methods in a single interview. In analyzing consumer motivation and behavior, for instance, interviews will undoubtedly be designed more frequently to use a gradual "surfacing approach," with the *deep projective* techniques (such as the Thematic Apperception Test) coming near the beginning of the interview, followed by *semi-projectives* (such as sentence completion), and concluding with *fully subjective* devices (such as Time-Line Interview, Consumer Jury, Motivation Ratings, and classifying questions about family size, income and so on).

The Surfacing Approach

This approach dredges up the deepest subconscious and concealed motives before the real purpose of the interview can be guessed, and warms up the respondents so they can discuss these motives in personal terms later. Then it sweeps rapidly across a broad range of activities, preferences, and motives which are less profound. It concludes by skimming off the conscious, public data which lie on the psychological surface, such as what, when, where, and how the respondents have purchased and what their future plans are. In the last stage, in fact, motives of all types—subconscious or conscious—concealed or public—biological, political, social, religious, intellectual, artistic, economic, or general—can be measured in comparable terms.

The surfacing approach to interview design helps, in short, to integrate research methods which are in reality complementary rather than alternatives to one another. And instead of merely providing clever ideas for copy themes, it furnishes the comprehensive factual basis needed to help the marketing manager and his department heads develop a coordinated, effective marketing program, meshed with but not limited to the new copy theme.

4. *Motivation research will become highly quantitative, in addition to providing qualitative insights.*

The pioneers of motivation research have made a contribution of tremendous value to the field of marketing research, but they have not gone nearly far enough. The most important of all breakthroughs now needed is the quantification of findings. It is my belief that this development is not only necessary, but highly feasible—and almost upon us. Yet it could just fail to happen.

The failure would be highly regrettable, perhaps even fatal. *Marketing executives have always needed and will continue to need to know how many people of what types in which regions feel what way, why, how intensely, and how much difference this makes in their behavior.* The results which executives must explain, predict and control are *quantitative* ones, so the motives and other influences which cause these results must be expressed in quantitative terms too. Bright qualitative insights are welcome but far from sufficient for forecasting behavior and planning action to influence it.

A Ladder of Usefulness

To understand where motivation research is today and where it probably will go, we may visualize a ladder of quantitative usefulness.

Today, we are not yet firmly on even the lowest rung. But we have laid a solid *foundation* on which the ladder can rest. Motivation research is now able to determine fairly well what *kinds* of motives affect the demand for a product or service, as already described in earlier paragraphs.

The *first rung* of the quantitative ladder can be reached when most M.R. studies utilize the *fully structured interview* in the main test. Since all the interviews will then be comparable, cover the same broad topical areas, and show responses to the same set of pictures, incomplete sentences, or direct questions, they can be tabulated to show the per cent of respondents who give each response. Even in small samples, as Mason Haire showed eight years ago, statistically significant differences can be obtained in this way.

The fully structured interview will also permit larger samples to be drawn, providing greater representativeness as well as permitting cross-tabulations of subgroups of respondents. This would tell the executive whether he is hearing about an overwhelmingly powerful motivation or a transitory, trivial—albeit fascinating—motivation.

While showing the per cent expressing a motive is the first rung, showing *intensity of motivation* is the second rung on the ladder. The first rung described above secures motives in qualitative form at the level of the individual interview, then quantifies the motives by tabulating how many respondents reveal each one. The second rung, in contrast, secures motives in *quantitative* form at the level of the individual interview. Then the distribution of these intensities is calculated for the whole sample.

The Greatest Break-Through

We often need to know a variety of *quantities* from each respondent, in addition to what *kinds* of motives influence him. We may inquire how far he would like to go toward any particular goal or satisfaction, where he thinks he now stands in relation to that satisfaction, and how far forward or backward he expects a certain brand will put him.

We also need to know in many cases how strongly a given motive actually influences him as compared with other motives, how desirable one brand is as compared with other brands, and so on. Even more vitally, we frequently wish to determine the extent to which a current advertising campaign has affected these quantities, or the degree to which a proposed campaign will affect them.

Measuring these vital quantities will be, in my opinion, the next great break-through—judged both in terms of the public attention it will attract and its contribution to scientific marketing. How will these quantities be measured? What new tools are needed?

Actually the tools are already in existence and waiting to be applied to a greater degree than they have been so far. Many of the tools may be lumped together under the phrase "psychometric methods." These include any orderly technique of converting individual motives and attitudes into numbers. They range all the way from the now-familiar rank-order method to the increasingly exotic paired-comparisons, Thurstone equal-appearing intervals, semantic differentials, and on up to the highest type of scale—the ratio scale—such as the Guttman scale, the Likert scale, the "Q-sort," and Motivation Ratings. The latter term refers to a particular version of motive measurements used at Alderson Associates, Inc.

Computers Are Ready

Once the motivation measurements of different types are actually secured from respondents, there is a great body of mathematical and statistical techniques for processing them, and these techniques are also highly developed and immediately available. Particularly valuable will be the techniques of *Operations Research*, the *analysis of variance*, and *multiple and partial regression*. The moment these computational procedures are put to work *electronic computers* can be utilized to speed them up.

The application of all these mathematical and statistical devices for processing motivational data is awaiting only two major developments. As soon as quantitative measurements are secured on the full range of appropriate motives at the level of the *individual interview*, through psychometric methods, the other applications will follow like a chain reaction. The application of psychometric methods, in turn, is delayed only by the lack of certain improvements in the theory or analytical model of the decision-and-action process, to be discussed under point six later. Some developments of this sort are currently being tested at Alderson Associates, Inc. and in a few other organizations as well.

Forecasting by Simulation

Because of these imminent advances, I predict that the decision process of individual respondents in a sample of consumers will be "simulated" in some detail within the next five to ten years. As in the simulation of the flight of an ICBM, it will be possible to forecast with greater accuracy than at any time in history what the behavior of individual consumers, samples of consumers, and consumer universes will be.

Since a "closed system" is not yet and may never be possible, current data on influences outside the semi-closed model will of course always need to be fed in periodically.

Also, since behavior responding to various possible changes in advertising appeals, media, product improvements, price changes, retail outlets, income changes, family sizes and structures and many other influences will soon have a good chance of being predicted, it follows that "optimum marketing mixes" will be more accurately computed and recommended for the guidance of marketing executives. Promotional programs can be given "trial flights" on electronic computers.

Verification by Experiment

Finally, it is safe to forecast that the "psychometric-and-operations-research revolution" will induce more and more firms to conduct *controlled experiments* using the most intricate experimental designs. Only in this way can the formulas be made more accurate and the motivational influences actually proved in the market place. Gone will be "validation" by faith, and "proof" by the semi-sophisticated judgments and present-day "success stories" like those reported in Vance Packard's book.

5. *The cost per interview of motivation research studies will be reduced sharply.*

The high cost per interview of present-day motivation research studies has prohibited the gathering of such information from "large" samples (running from 500 into the thousands of consumers). This, in turn, has reduced the statistical projectability of the findings to the total population of consumers being studied, as well as limiting the breakdown of the findings to compare users versus non-users, geographical regions, income groups, and so on.

Some of the advances described above, particularly the "fully structured interview" and the use of psychometric methods, are already making possible sharp reductions in the cost per interview and an increase in the economic size of samples, based on our experience.

Usually the two greatest components of total cost are field interviewing expenses and tabulating costs. Let us look at the first of these. The *fully structured interview* is proving to be productive of high-quality information, at the same time as permitting shorter interviews by less expensive interviewers, in place of lengthy interviews of an unstructured nature requiring graduate training in psychological interviewing. This does not, of course, eliminate the need for such interviewers in the exploratory and pre-test phases.

Another great saving based on the coming methods is in permitting coding and punch-card tabulation by less expensive clerical workers, rather than hand tabulation by analysts at the professional level. This, too, does not eliminate the necessity of code development and analysis of findings by the more highly trained workers.

Better Data at Less Cost

High costs were perhaps inevitable in the pioneering phase from which we are just emerging, but they are not inherent in this new science. I predict that within five years most motivation research firms will be able to offer their services at only slightly higher cost per interview than is involved in a straight opinion survey, as the term is now understood in market research. Planning and analytical costs would undoubtedly remain somewhat higher than in straight surveys, but field interviewing and internal tabulating expenses may very well be equal to or even below those for comparable, direct surveys which contain a fair number of open-end questions.

In brief, the coming technical break-throughs in motivation research point hopefully to improved quality, larger samples, greater variety of cross-tabulations, greater representativeness and more statistical tabulations of the data as compared with present-day M.R. studies. They also augur well for reducing motivation research costs to a point only slightly above the cost of straight surveys. Most important of all, the greater utility of the findings for purposes of forecasting behavior and developing more effective marketing programs will be incalculable.

6. *Motivation research will develop an improved framework of theoretical concepts.*

Far from being visionary or impractical, one of the most down-to-earth tools required but still missing in motivation research is an adequate theoretical model. In a discipline which aspires to become an orderly science, able to *explain* and *forecast* demand and *recommend* programs for influencing it, an absolute "must" is a theoretical framework which specifies the interacting variables involved. These range all the way from price, income, and present supply to subconscious and concealed motivations. With this information, the research planner will be able to build into his study design the topical coverage which the problem requires, with some assurance that significant factors which could influence the outcome unpredictably will not be overlooked. Once the topical areas are clearly specified for a particular client's problem, the selection of research tools becomes much easier.

This would seem obvious both to the researchers and their more sophisticated clients. How, therefore, can this deficiency be remedied?

Social Sciences Must Be Integrated

Probably an integrated conceptual framework for describing consumer motivation and behavior will arise in a situation in which specialists in different fields, such as economics, psychology, sociology, anthropology, statistics, mathematics, and engineering can sit together for the *precise and unique purpose* of developing a unified doctrine, as well as a research plan which will help them test and improve such a body of common doctrine. It is not likely to arise as a *by-product* of an applied research project.

Where is such a group most likely to come together for such a purpose? It can happen, and is on its way to happening, in a few of the largest business firms in the country. More probably, however, it will occur in leading universities, operating under financial grants from foundations.

Why have the universities not accomplished more in this direction already? *I believe the main source of the present gaps in our conceptual framework lies in the present archaic, all-too-slowly fading university system, which compartmentalizes the various disciplines in the behavioral sciences.* Therefore, we do not yet even pretend to produce a "whole man" in the behavioral sciences. A few nonconformists attempt to make themselves into an imitation of such a person, but in general find themselves regarded as part of the "lunatic fringe" by the more respectable, orthodox professors working within the established confines of the several disciplines.

Although the various social disciplines have not yet come together in a "United Nations of the Behavioral Sciences," they are beginning to form regional pacts. We see psychology, sociology, and anthropology coming together in Departments of Social Relations. We see courses in economics required by Sociology Departments (but rarely vice versa). We see some universities allowing and even suggesting that economics and marketing students take courses in social psychology and in motivation, but we do not see many instances in which they are requiring them to do so.

So the old compartments are fusing, but at a maddeningly slow pace. The present pace of integration among the social sciences needs to be vastly accelerated within the universities and large corporations. This will occur only under the impetus of heavy financial grants to both groups, with enthusiastic support from business executives and motivation researchers.

7. *Motivation research will be guided by professional standards of skill and ethical standards of usage.*

Professional standards of *skill* will become increasingly important in the field of motivation research. However, this is still young enough a field that it would be infanticide for any body of "industry experts" to pass upon the training and experience of practitioners of motivation research in order to determine whether they should be stamped with some sort of seal of approval or granted a license. Some practitioners with no advanced degrees at all are doing a fine job of motivation research, and possession of a Master's degree or a Ph.D. degree is not a guarantee that the client will get the sort of job done for him which he deserves.

Some of the recent "neighborhood brawls" in the motivation and marketing research fields have been somewhat undignified, although they might be good exercise. They have also been highly confusing to business executives, who must make decisions as to which school of thought they will accept and which firms they will hire. This internecine warfare tends to cast doubt upon the qualifications of all market researchers, in the same way that a heavy propaganda campaign by one branch of medicine warning people against "quacks" sometimes results in patients staying away from the "approved" as well as the "disapproved" groups.

Evolving Standards and Ethics

Attempts to establish internal standards of professional skill in motivation research will undoubtedly be made in the next few years. It is more likely, however, that a workable set of interim standards will be set up by associations of clients who have accumulated some experience in the purchase of motivation research. A few attempts of this sort are already being made and published, but they are highly tentative.

The *ethical* issue in motivation research is one which will become more and more important in the future. Certainly projective research methods and other ways of studying motivations constitute weapons of enormous power, and only a fraction of their potential has been demonstrated so far. When some of the break-throughs I have discussed take place—and I believe they will and must take place in the very near future—the public concern which will then be awakened will make Vance Packard feel he was worrying about civilization being destroyed by the psychological equivalent of a crossbow.

No Thought-Control

It is normal and it is essential for all of us to worry about the possible misuse of powerful new tools on the part of rascals. Motivation research is not in *itself* moral or immoral. It is amoral. But narcotics do sometimes fall into the hands of dope peddlers, automobiles *can* be driven by gangsters, and armies can be misused by dictators.

The answer, however, is not to abolish motivation research and all other dangerous things. There are compelling reasons why we should not do this. A research tool which can determine what people are really thinking, make forecasts about what they are likely to do under varying circumstances, and provide guidance as to the most acceptable products and most effective forms of mass persuasion, if employed for decent purposes by democratically controlled government and business leaders, could lead to a wonderful increase in the prosperity and peacefulness of our world. We must, therefore, be very careful to control the uses to which motivation research is applied.

For the moment, however, I trust that thinking members of the public will refuse to tremble in terror or hide beneath their beds after reading the ominous passages in Vance Packard's book. He seems to suggest that the day of complete thought-control by Big Business, politicians, or even more "sinister" groups is already here. This definitely is not the case.

Safeguards Exist

There are many safeguards which our society has carefully "baked in," which of course need to be safeguarded and, where necessary, strengthened. For one thing, the competitive economic system acts as a major control device. Most firms have competitors, and the competitors are able to purchase motivation research too. Most politicians have opposing candidates, who are just as able to read *The Hidden Persuaders.* All groups have access to information-gathering and information-disseminating media in our society, with its reasonably free communications.

What is more significant, consumers perform the buying function with increasing skill, as research studies have shown, and are careful to judge a piece of information by its sponsorship.

Further safeguards come from vigilant consumer-protection organizations. We also have strong government bodies such as the Federal Trade Commission and others to help protect the public from flagrant distortions of the truth. Self-policing to reduce unethical practices will also undoubtedly develop among motivation researchers themselves, in the form of penalties and expulsions from respected associations, criticism in technical journals, and the use of many other control devices.

Benefits Ahead

In conclusion, if the qualitative, quantitative, and ethical break-throughs I have listed are achieved in consumer motivation research, they point to several great marketing benefits. First, they point to the potentiality of greatly improved products for the American market. Merchandise can be better suited to the real needs and desires of consumers. This would also benefit business through increased efficiency by eliminating expensive frills and furbelows. Competition will continue to prevent the business firms from permanently taking these gains in the form of unduly high profits.

Second, the break-throughs will help to bring forward a tremendous burst in the effectiveness and usefulness of advertising, both to the business firms and to consumers.

Finally, motivation research can help to an increasing extent in the transformation of outmoded channels of distribution and methods of marketing in numerous industries.

I cannot guarantee that these happy results *will* be achieved. But the fact is that business firms and other organizations are ordering more and more marketing and motivation research studies, and they seem to be making more and better use of the information than they used to.

However, I firmly believe, unless motivation research makes the advances I have listed—which are so necessary and so close—it may go down in commercial history as the Frivolous Fad of the Fifties.

10. MOTIVATION, COGNITION, LEARNING—BASIC FACTORS IN CONSUMER BEHAVIOR *

James A. Bayton

Motivation, Cognition, Learning

The analysis of consumer behavior presented here is derived from diverse concepts of several schools of psychology—from psychoanalysis to reinforcement theory.

Human behavior can be grouped into three categories—motivation, cognition, and learning. Motivation refers to the drives, urges, wishes, or desires which initiate the sequence of events known as "behavior." Cognition is the area in which all of the mental phenomena (perception, memory, judging, thinking, etc.) are grouped. Learning refers to those changes in behavior which occur through time relative to external stimulus conditions.

Each broad area is pertinent to particular problems of consumer behavior. All three together are pertinent to a comprehensive understanding of consumer behavior.

Motivation

Human needs

Behavior is initiated through needs. Some psychologists claim that words such as "motives," "needs," "urges," "wishes," and "drives" should not be used as synonyms; others are content to use them interchangeably. There is one virtue in the term "drive" in that it carries the connotation of a force pushing the individual into action.

Motivation arises out of tension-systems which create a state of disequilibrium for the individual. This triggers a sequence of psychological events directed toward the selection of a goal which the individual *anticipates* will bring about release from the tensions and the selection of patterns of action which he *anticipates* will bring him to the goal.

* From *The Journal of Marketing*, Vol. XXII, No. 3 (January, 1958), pp. 282-289. Reprinted with permission of *The Journal of Marketing*, published quarterly by the American Marketing Association.

James A. Bayton, Projects Manager, National Analysts, Inc., Philadelphia; Professor of Psychology, Howard University.

One problem in motivation theory is deriving a basic list of the human needs. Psychologists agree that needs fall into two general categories—those arising from tension-systems physiological in nature (biogenic needs such as hunger, thirst, and sex), and those based upon tension-systems existing in the individual's subjective psychological state and in his relations with others (psychogenic needs).

Although there is not much disagreement as to the list of specific biogenic needs, there is considerable difference of opinion as to the list of specific psychogenic needs. However, the various lists of psychogenic needs can be grouped into three broad categories:

1. *Affectional needs*—the needs to form and maintain warm, harmonious, and emotionally satisfying relations with others.
2. *Ego-bolstering needs*—the needs to enhance or promote the personality; to achieve; to gain prestige and recognition; to satisfy the ego through domination of others.
3. *Ego-defensive needs*—the needs to protect the personality; to avoid physical and psychological harm; to avoid ridicule and "loss of face"; to prevent loss of prestige; to avoid or to obtain relief from anxiety.

One pitfall in the analysis of motivation is the assumption that a particular situation involves just one specific need. In most instances the individual is driven by a combination of needs. It seems likely that "love" brings into play a combination of affectional, ego-bolstering, and ego-defensive needs as well as biogenic needs. Within the combination some needs will be relatively strong, others relatively weak. The strongest need within the combination can be called the "prepotent" need. A given consumer product can be defined in terms of the specific need-combination involved and the relative strengths of these needs.

Another pitfall is the assumption that identical behaviors have identical motivational backgrounds. This pitfall is present whether we are thinking of two different individuals or the same individual at two different points in time. John and Harry can be different in the motivational patterns leading to the purchase of their suits. Each could have one motivational pattern influencing such a purchase at age twenty and another at age forty.

Ego-involvement

One important dimension of motivation is the degree of ego-involvement. The various specific need-patterns are not equal in significance to the individual. Some are superficial in meaning; others represent (for the individual) tremendous challenges to the very essence of existence. There is some evidence that one of the positive correlates of degree of ego-involvement is the amount of cognitive activity (judging, thinking, etc.) involved. This means that consumer goods which tap low degrees of ego-involvement will be purchased with a relatively lower degree of conscious decision-making activity than goods which tap higher degrees of ego-involvement. Such a factor must be considered when decisions are made on advertising and marketing tactics.

At times the ego-involvement factor is a source of conflict between client and researcher. This can occur when research reveals that the product taps a low degree of ego-involvement within consumers. The result is difficult for a client to accept; because *he* is ego-involved and, therefore, cognitively active about his product, consumers must certainly be also. It is hard for such a client to believe that consumers simply do not engage in a great deal of cognitive activity when they make purchases within his product class. One way to ease this particular client-researcher conflict would be for the researcher to point out this implication of the ego-involvement dimension.

"True" and rationalized motives

A particular difficulty in the study of motivation is the possibility that there can be a difference between "true" motives and rationalized motives. Individuals sometimes are unaware of the exact nature of drives initiating their behavior patterns. When this occurs, they attempt to account for their behavior through "rationalization" by assigning motivations to their behavior which are acceptable to their personality structures. They may do this with no awareness that they are rationalizing. There can be other instances, however, in which individuals are keenly aware of their motivations, but feel it would be harmful or socially unacceptable to reveal them. When this is the case, they deliberately conceal their motivations.

These possibilities create a problem for the researcher. Must he assume that every behavior pattern is based upon unconscious motivation? If not, what criteria are to be used in deciding whether to be alert to unconscious motivation for this behavior pattern and not that one? What is the relative importance of unconscious motives, if present, and rationalized motives? Should rationalized motives be ignored? After all, rationalized motives have a certain validity for the individual—they are the "real" motives insofar as he is aware of the situation.

The situation is even more complicated than this—what about the dissembler? When the individual actually is dissembling, the researcher must attempt to determine the true motives. But, how shall we determine whether we are faced with a situation where the respondent is rationalizing or dissembling? In a given case, did a projective technique reveal an unconscious motive or the true motive of a dissembler? Conceptually, rationalized motives and dissembled motives are not equal in psychological implication; but it is rare, if ever, that one finds attempts to segregate the two in consumer research directed toward the analysis of motivation. This failure is understandable, to some extent, because of the lack of valid criteria upon which to base the distinction.

Cognition

Need-arousal

Motivation, thus, refers to a state of need-arousal—a condition exerting "push" on the individual to engage in those activities which he anticipates will have the highest probability of bringing him gratification of a particular need-pattern. Whether gratification actually will be attained or not is a matter of future events. Central to the psychological activities which now must be considered in the sequence are the complex of "mental" operations and forces known as the cognitive processes. We can view these cognitive processes as being *purposive* in that they serve the individual in his attempts to achieve satisfaction of his needs. These cognitive processes are *regulatory* in that they determine in large measure the direction and particular steps taken in his attempt to attain satisfaction of the initiating needs.

The ego-superego concept

The ego-supergeo concept is pertinent to a discussion of cognitive activities which have been triggered by needs. Discussions of the ego-superego concept usually come under the heading of motivation as an aspect of personality. It is our feeling that motivation and the consequences of motivation should be kept systematically "clean." In the broadest sense, ego and superego are mental entities in that they involve memory, perceiving, judging, and thinking.

THE EGO. The ego is the "executive," determining how the individual shall seek satisfaction of his needs. Through perception, memory, judging, and thinking the ego attempts to integrate the needs, on the one hand, and the conditions of the external world, on the other, in such manner that needs can be satisfied without danger or harm to the individual. Often this means that gratification must be postponed until a situation has developed, or has been encountered, which does not contain harm or danger. The turnpike driver who does not exceed the speed limit because he sees signs saying there are radar checks is under the influence of the ego. So is the driver who sees no cars on a straight stretch and takes the opportunity to drive at excessive speed.

THE SUPEREGO. The superego involves the ego-ideal and conscience. The ego-ideal represents the positive standards of ethical and moral conduct the individual has developed for himself. Conscience is, in a sense, the "judge," evaluating the ethics and morality of behavior and, through guilt-feelings, administering punishment when these are violated. If a driver obeys the speed limit because he would feel guilty in doing otherwise, he is under the influence of the superego. (The first driver above is under the influence of the ego because he is avoiding a fine, not guilt feelings.)

Specific examples

Credit is a form of economic behavior based to some extent upon ego-superego considerations. It is generally felt that one cause of consumer-credit expansion has been a shift away from the superego's role in attitudes toward credit. The past ego-ideal was to build savings; debt was immoral—something to feel guilty about, to avoid, to hide. These two superego influences restrained the use of credit. For some cultural reason, credit and debt have shifted away from superego dominance and are now more under the control of the ego—the primary concern now seems to be how much of it can be used without risking financial danger.

The purchasing of specific consumer goods can be considered from the point of view of these two influences. Certain goods (necessities, perhaps) carry little superego influence, and the individual is psychologically free to try to maximize the probability of obtaining satisfaction of his needs while minimizing the probability of encountering harm in so doing. Other goods, however, tap the superego. When a product represents an aspect of the ego-ideal there is a strong positive force to possess it. Conversely, when a product involves violation of the conscience, a strong negative force is generated against its purchase.

Let us assume that, when the need-push asserts itself, a variety of goal-objects come into awareness as potential sources of gratification. In consumer behavior these goal-objects may be different brand names. The fact that a particular set of goal-objects come into awareness indicates the generic character of this stage in the cognitive process—a class of goal-objects is seen as containing the possible satisfier. What the class of goal-objects and the specific goal-objects within the class "promise" in terms of gratification are known as "expectations."

There are, then, two orders of expectation: generic expectancies, and object-expectancies. Suppose the needs were such that the individual "thought" of brands of frozen orange juice. Some of the generic expectations for frozen orange juice are a certain taste, quality, source of vitamin C, protection against colds, and ease of preparation. The particular brands carry expectations specifically associated with one brand as against another. The expectation might be that Brand A has a more refreshing taste than Brand B.

In many instances, cognitive competition occurs between two or more generic categories before it does between goal-objects within a generic category. Much consumer-behavior research is directed toward the investigation of generic categories—tires, automobiles, appliances, etc. But perhaps not enough attention has been given to the psychological analysis of cognitive competition between generic categories. An example of a problem being studied is the competition between television viewing, movie going, and magazine reading. For a particular producer, cognitive competition within the pertinent generic category is usually of more concern than cognitive competition between his generic category and others. The producer usually wants only an intensive analysis of consumer psychology with respect to the particular generic category of which his product is a member.

Let us now assume that under need-push four alternative goal-objects (Brands A, B, C, and D) came into awareness. Why these particular brands and not others? Why are Brands E and F absent? An obvious reason for Brand E's absence might be that the individual had never been exposed to the fact that Brand E exists. He had been exposed to Brand F, however. Why is it absent? The problem here is one of memory—a key cognitive process. The producers of Brands E and F obviously are faced with different problems.

Two sets of circumstances contain the independent variables that determine whether a given item will be remembered. One is the nature of the experience resulting from actual consumption or utilization of the goal-object. This will be discussed later when we come to the reinforcement theory of learning. The other is the circumstances present on what might be called vicarious exposures to the goal-object—vicarious in that at the time of exposure actual consumption or utilization of the goal-object does not occur. The most obvious example would be an advertisement of the goal-object. Of course, the essential purpose of an advertisement is to expose the individual to the goal-object in such a manner that at some subsequent time it will be remembered readily. The search for the most effective methods of doing this by manipulation of the physical aspects of the advertisement and the appeals used in it is a continuing effort in consumer-behavior research. Finally, for many consumers these two sets of circumstances will be jointly operative. Experiences with the goal-object and subsequent vicarious exposures can coalesce to heighten the memory potential for an item.

Making a choice

With, say, four brands in awareness, the individual must now make a choice. What phsychological factors underlie this choice? The four brands could be in awareness due to the memory factor because they are immediately present in the environment; or some because they are in the environment, and the others because of memory.

The first problem is the extent to which the items are differentiated. The various goal-objects have attributes which permit the individual to differentiate between them. The brand name is one attribute; package another; design still another. These differentiating attributes (from the point of view of the consumer's perceptions) can be called signs or cues. All such signs are not equally important in consumer decisions. Certain of them are depended upon much more than others. For example, in a study of how housewives select fresh oranges, the critical or key signs were thickness of skin, color of skin, firmness of the orange, and presence or absence of "spots" on the skin.

The signs have expectancies associated with them. Package (a sign) can carry the expectancy of quality. Thin-skin oranges carry the expectancy of juice; spots carry the expectancy of poor taste quality and insufficient amount of juice. Often sign-expectancies determined through consumer research are irrelevant or invalid. Signs are irrelevant when they do not represent a critical differentiating attribute of a goal-object. Certain discolorations on oranges have nothing to do with their intrinsic quality. Expectancies are invalid when they refer to qualities that do not in fact exist in association with a particular sign.

The different goal-objects in awareness can be assessed in terms of the extent to which they arouse similar expectancies. This phenomenon of similarity of expectations within a set of different goal-objects is known as generalization. One goal-object (Brand A, perhaps), because of its associated expectancies, can be assumed to have maximum appeal within the set of alternative goal-objects. The alternates then can be ordered in terms of how their associated expectancies approximate those of Brand A. Is this ordering and the psychological distances between the items of the nature of:

Brand A		Brand A
Brand B		
	or	
		Brand B
Brand C		Brand C

These differences in ordering and psychological distance are referred to as generalization gradients. In the first case, the expectancies associated with Brand B are quite similar to those for Brand A, but are not quite as powerful in appeal. Brand C has relatively little of this. In the second case, the generalization gradient is of a different form, showing that Brand B offers relatively little psychological competition to Brand A. (There will also be generalization gradients with respect to cognitive competition between generic categories.) In addition to the individual producer being concerned about the memory potential of his particular brand, he needs to determine the nature of the generalization gradient for his product and the products of his competitors. Mere ordering is not enough—the "psychological distances" between positions must be determined also, and the factor determining these distances is similarity of expectancy.

The discussion above was concerned with cognitive processes as they relate to mental representation of goal-objects under the instigation of need-arousal. The items brought into awareness, the differentiating sign-expectancies, and the generalization gradient are the central factors in the particular cognitive field aroused under a given "need-push." One important dimension has not yet been mentioned—instrumental acts. These are acts necessary in obtaining the goal-object and the acts involved in consuming or utilizing it. Examples are: "going downtown" to get to a department store, squeezing the orange to get its juice, ease of entry into service stations, and the operations involved in do-it-yourself house painting.

Instrumental acts can have positive or negative value for the individual. One who makes fewer shopping trips to downtown stores because of traffic and parking conditions displays an instrumental act with negative value. Frozen foods are products for which much of the appeal lies in the area of instrumental acts. The development of automatic transmissions and of power-steering in automobiles are examples of product changes concerned with instrumental acts. The point is that concentration upon cognitive reactions to the goal-object, *per se,* could be masking critical aspects of the situation based upon cognitive reactions to the instrumental acts involved in obtaining or utilizing the goal-object.

LEARNING

Goal-object

Starting with need-arousal, continuing under the influence of cognitive processes, and engaging in the necessary action, the individual arrives at consumption or utilization of a goal-object. Using our consumer-behavior illustration, let us say that the consumer bought Brand A and is now in the process of consuming or utilizing it. We have now arrived at one of the most critical aspects of the entire psychological sequence. It is with use of the goal-object that degree of gratification of the initial needs will occur.

Reinforcement

When consumption or utilization of the goal-object leads to gratification of the initiating needs there is "reinforcement." If at some later date the same needs are aroused, the individual will tend to repeat the process of selecting and getting to the same goal-object. If Brand A yields a high degree of gratification, then at some subsequent time, when the same needs arise, the consumer will have an increased tendency to select Brand A once again. Each succeeding time that Brand A brings gratification, further reinforcement occurs, thus further increasing the likelihood that in the future, with the given needs, Brand A will be selected.

This type of behavioral change—increasing likelihood that an act will be repeated—is learning; and reinforcement is necessary for learning to take place. Continued reinforcement will influence the cognitive processes. Memory of the goal-object will be increasingly enhanced; particular sign-expectancies will be more and more firmly established; and the generalization gradient will be changed in that the psychological distance on this gradient between Brand A and the competing brands will be increased.

Habit

One of the most important consequences of continued reinforcement is the influence this has on the extent to which cognitive processes enter the picture at the times of subsequent need-arousal. With continued reinforcement, the amount of cognitive activity decreases; the individual engages less and less in decision-making mental activities. This can continue until, upon need-arousal, the goal-obtaining activities are practically automatic. At this stage there is a habit.

Note this use of the term "habit." One frequently hears that a person does certain things by "*force* of habit," that habit is an initiator of behavioral sequences. Actually, habits are not initiating forces in themselves; habits are repeated response patterns accompanied by a minimum of cognitive activity. There must be some condition of need-arousal before the habit-type response occurs. This has serious implications in the field of consumer behavior. The promotional and marketing problems faced by a competitor of Brand A will be of one type if purchase behavior for Brand A is habitual, of another if this is not true. If the purchase is largely a habit, there is little cognitive activity available for the competitor to "work on."

Frequency of repeating a response is not a valid criterion for determining whether or not a habit exists. An act repeated once a week can be just as much a habit as one repeated several times a day. The frequency of a response is but an index of the frequency with which the particular need-patterns are aroused. Frequency of response also is often used as a measure of the *strength* of a habit. The test of the strength of a habit is the extent to which an individual will persist in an act after it has ceased providing need gratification. The greater this persistence, the stronger was the habit in the first place.

Problem—Concept—Research

The above views integrate concepts in contemporary psychology which seem necessary for a comprehensive explanation of human behavior, and apply these concepts to the analysis of consumer behavior. Each psychological process touched upon contains areas for further analysis and specification.

Some type of comprehensive theory of human behavior is necessary as a *working tool* to avoid a lack of discipline in attacking problems in consumer behavior. Too frequently a client with a practical problem approaches a researcher with an indication that all that is needed is a certain methodology—depth interviewing, scaling, or projective devices, for example.

The first step should be to take the practical problem and translate it into its pertinent conceptual entities. This phase of the problem raises the question of motivations. Here is a question involving relevance and validity of sign-expectancies. There is a question dealing with a generalization gradient, etc. Once the pertinent conceptual entities have been identified, and only then, we arrive at the stage of hypothesis formulation. Within each conceptual entity, a relationship between independent and dependent variables is established as a hypothesis to be tested.

Often the relation between conceptual entities must be investigated. For example, what is the effect of continuing reinforcement on a specific generalization gradient? Within the same research project, one psychological entity can be a dependent variable at one phase of the research and an independent variable at another. At one time we might be concerned with establishing the factors associated with differential memory of sign-expectancies. At another time we could be concerned with the influence of remembered sign-expectancies upon subsequent purchase-behavior.

Discipline requires that one turn to methodology only when the pertinent conceptual entities have been identified and the relationships between independent and dependent variables have been expressed in the form of hypotheses. Fundamentally this sequence in the analysis of a problem serves to delimit the methodological possibilities. In any event, the methodologies demanded are those which will produce unambigious tests of each particular hypothesis put forth. Finally, the results must be translated into the terms of the original practical problem.

We have used the term "discipline' 'in this phase of our discussion. The researcher must discipline himself to follow the above steps. Some find this a difficult thing to do and inevitably their data becomes ambigious. They must resort to improvisation in order to make sense of the results *after* the project is completed. A research project is truly a work of art when the conceptual analysis, the determination of the hypotheses, and the methodologies have been developed in such an "air-tight" sequence that practically all that is necessary is to let the facts speak for themselves.

11. THE TWO-STEP FLOW OF COMMUNICATION: AN UP-TO-DATE REPORT ON AN HYPOTHESIS *

Elihu Katz

Analysis of the process of decision-making during the course of an election campaign led the authors of *The People's Choice* to suggest that the flow of mass communications may be less direct than was commonly supposed. It may be, they proposed, that influences stemming from the mass media first reach "opinion leaders" who, in turn, pass on what they read and hear to those of their every-day associates for whom they are influential. This hypothesis was called "the two-step flow of communication." [1]

The hypothesis aroused considerable interest. The authors themselves were intrigued by its implications for democratic society. It was a healthy sign, they felt, that people were still most successfully persuaded by give-and-take with other people and that the influence of the mass media was less automatic and less potent than had been assumed. For social theory, and for the design of communications research, the hypothesis suggested that the image of modern urban society needed revision. The image of the audience as a mass of disconnected individuals hooked up to the media but not to each other could not be reconciled with the idea of a two-step flow of communication implying, as it did, networks of interconnected individuals through which mass communications are channeled.

Of all the ideas in *The People's Choice,* however, the two-step flow hypothesis is probably the one that was least well documented by empirical data. And the reason for this is clear: the design of the study did not anticipate the importance which interpersonal relations would assume in the analysis of the data. Given the image of the atomized audience which characterized so much of mass media research, the surprising thing is that interpersonal influence attracted the attention of the researchers at all.[2]

* Reprinted by permission of *The Public Opinion Quarterly* (Princeton, New Jersey: Princeton University), Vol. XXI, No. 1 (Spring, 1957), pp. 61-78.

Elihu Katz, Sociologist Professor, University of Chicago.

[1] Paul F. Lazarsfeld, Bernard Berelson and Hazel Gaudet, *The People's Choice,* New York: Columbia University Press, 1948 (2nd edition), p. 151.

[2] For the discussion of the image of the atomized audience and the contravening empirical evidence, see Elihu Katz and Paul F. Lazarsfeld, *Personal*

In the almost seventeen years since the voting study was undertaken, several studies at the Bureau of Applied Social Research of Columbia University have attempted to examine the hypothesis and to build upon it. Four such studies will be singled out for review. These are Merton's study of interpersonal influence and communications behavior in Rovere;[3] the Decatur study of decision-making in marketing, fashions, movie-going and public affairs, reported by Katz and Lazarsfeld;[4] the Elmira study of the 1948 election campaign reported by Berelson, Lazarsfeld and McPhee;[5] and, finally, a very recent study by Coleman, Katz and Menzel on the diffusion of a new drug among doctors.[6]

These studies will serve as a framework within which an attempt will be made to report on the present state of the two-step flow hypothesis, to examine the extent to which it has found confirmation and the ways in which it has been extended, contracted and reformulated. More than that, the studies will be drawn upon to highlight the successive strategies which have been developed in attempting to take systematic account of interpersonal relations in the design of communications research, aiming ultimately at a sort of "survey sociometry." Finally, these studies, plus others which will be referred to in passing, will provide an unusual opportunity to reflect upon problems in the continuity of social research.[7]

Findings of *The People's Choice*

The starting point for this review must be an examination of the evidence in the 1940 voting study which led to the original formula-

---

Influence: The Part Played by People in the Flow of Mass Communications (Glencoe, Illinois: The Free Press, 1955), pp. 15-42; Eliot Friedson, "Communications Research and the Concept of the Mass," *American Sociological Review*, Vol. 18, (1953), pp. 313-317; and Morris Janowitz, *The Urban Press in a Community Setting*, (Glencoe, Illinois: The Free Press, 1952).

[3] Robert K. Merton, "Patterns of Influence: A Study of Interpersonal Influence and Communications Behavior in a Local Community," in Paul F. Lazarsfeld and Frank N. Stanton, eds., *Communications Research, 1948-9* (New York: Harper & Brothers, 1949), pp. 180-219.

[4] Elihu Katz and Paul F. Lazarsfeld, *op. cit.*, Part Two.

[5] Bernard R. Berelson, Paul F. Lazarsfeld and William N. McPhee, *Voting: A Study of Opinion Formation in a Presidential Campaign* (Chicago: University of Chicago Press, 1954).

[6] A report on the pilot phase of this study is to be found in Herbert Menzel and Elihu Katz, "Social Relations and Innovation in the Medical Profession," *Public Opinion Quarterly*, Vol. 19, (1955), pp. 337-52; a volume and various articles on the full study are now in preparation.

[7] Other authors who have drawn upon the concepts of opinion leadership and the two-step flow of communication, and developed them further, are Matilda and John Riley, "A Sociological Approach to Communications Research," *Public Opinion Quarterly*, Vol. 15 (1951), pp. 445-460; S. N. Eisenstadt, "Communications Processes Among Immigrants in Israel," *Public Opinion Quarterly*, Vol. 16 (1952), pp. 42-58 and "Communication Systems and Social Structure: An Exploratory Study," *Public Opinion Quarterly*, Vol. 19 (1955), pp. 153-167; David

tion of the hypothesis. Essentially, three distinct sets of findings seem to have been involved. The first had to do with *the impact of personal influence.* It is reported that people who made up their minds late in the campaign, and those who changed their minds during the course of the campaign, were more likely than other people to mention personal influence as having figured in their decisions. The political pressure brought to bear by everyday groups such as family and friends is illustrated by reference to the political homogeneity which characterizes such groups. What's more, on an average day, a greater number of people reported participating in discussion of the election than hearing a campaign speech or reading a newspaper editorial. From all of this, the authors conclude that personal contacts appear to have been both more frequent and more effective than the mass media in influencing voting decisions.[8]

The second ingredient that went into the formulation of the hypothesis concerned *the flow of personal influence.* Given the apparent importance of interpersonal influence, the obvious next step was to ask whether some people were more important than others in the transmission of influence. The study sought to single out the "opinion leaders" by two questions: "Have you recently tried to convince anyone of your political ideas?", and "Has anyone recently asked you for your advice on a political question?" Comparing the opinion leaders with others, they found the opinion leaders more interested in the election. And from the almost even distribution of opinion leaders throughout every class and occupation, as well as the frequent mention by decision-makers of the influence of friends, coworkers and relatives, it was concluded that opinion leaders are to be found on every level of society and presumably, therefore, are very much like the people whom they influence.[9]

A further comparison of leaders and others with respect to mass media habits provides the third ingredient: *the opinion leaders and*

Riesman, *The Lonely Crowd* (New Haven: Yale University Press, 1950); Leo A. Handel, *Hollywood Looks at its Audience* (Urbana: University of Illinois Press, 1950). The program of research in international communications at the Bureau of Applied Social Research has given considerable attention to opinion leadership; see Charles Y. Glock, "The Comparative Study of Communications and Opinion Formation," *Public Opinion Quarterly*, Vol. 16 (1952-53), pp. 512-523; J. M. Stycos, "Patterns of Communication in a Rural Greek Village," *Public Opinion Quarterly*, Vol. 16 (1952), pp. 59-70; and the forthcoming book by Daniel Lerner, Paul Berkman and Lucille Pevsner, *Modernizing the Middle East.* Forthcoming studies by Peter H. Rossi and by Robert D. Leigh and Martin A. Trow are also concerned with the interplay of personal and mass media influences in local communities.

[8] Lazarsfeld, Berelson and Gaudet, *op. cit.*, pp. 135-152.

[9] *Ibid.*, pp. 50-51.

the mass media. Compared with the rest of the population, opinion leaders were found to be considerably more exposed to the radio, to the newspapers and to magazines, that is, to the formal media of communication.[10]

Now the argument is clear: If word-of-mouth is so important, and if word-of-mouth specialists are widely dispersed, and if these specialists are more exposed to the media than the people whom they influence, then perhaps "ideas often flow from radio and print to opinion leaders and from these to the less active sections of the population." [11]

Design of the Voting Study

For studying the flow of influence as it impinges on the making of decisions, the study design of *The People's Choice* had several advantages. Most important was the panel method which made it possible to locate changes almost as soon as they occurred and then to correlate change with the influences reaching the decision-maker. Secondly, the unit of effect, the decision, was a tangible indicator of change which could readily be recorded. But for studying that part of the flow of influence which had to do with contacts among people, the study design fell short, since it called for a random sample of individuals abstracted from their social environments. It is this traditional element in the design of survey research which explains the leap that had to be made from the available data to the hypothesis of the two-step flow of communication.

Because every man in a random sample can speak only for himself, opinion leaders in the 1940 voting study had to be located by self-designation, that is, on the basis of their own answers to the two advice-giving questions cited above.[12] In effect, respondents were simply asked to report whether or not they were opinion leaders. Much more important than the obvious problem of validity posed by this technique is the fact that it does not permit a comparison of leaders with their respective followers, but only of leaders and non-leaders in general. The data, in other words, consist only of two

10 *Ibid.*, p. 51.
11 *Ibid.*, p. 151.
12 Strictly speaking, of course, if a respondent reports whether or not he is a leader he is not speaking for himself but for his followers, real or imagined. Furthermore, it ought to be pointed out for the record that it is sometimes possible for a respondent to speak for others besides himself. The voting studies, for example, ask respondents to report the vote-intentions of other family members, of friends, of co-workers, though this procedure is of undetermined validity.

statistical groupings: people who said they were advice-givers and those who did not. Therefore, the fact that leaders were more interested in the election than non-leaders cannot be taken to mean that influence flows from more interested persons to less interested ones. To state the problem drastically, it may even be that the leaders influence only each other, while the uninterested non-leaders stand outside the influence market altogether. Nevertheless, the temptation to assume that the non-leaders are the followers of the leaders is very great, and while *The People's Choice* is quite careful about this, it cannot help but succumb.[13] Thus, from the fact that the opinion leaders were more exposed to the mass media than the non-leaders came the suggestion of the two-step flow of communication; yet, manifestly, it can be true only if the non-leaders are, in fact, followers of the leaders.

The authors themselves point out that a far better method would have been based on "asking people to whom they turn for advice on the issue at hand and then investigating the interaction between advisers and advisees. But that procedure would be extremely difficult, if not impossible, since few of the related 'leaders' and 'followers' would happen to be included in the sample." [14] As will be shown immediately, this is perhaps the most important problem which succeeding studies have attempted to solve.

Designs of Three Subsequent Studies

To this point, two aspects of the original statement of the two-step flow hypothesis have been reviewed. First of all, the hypothesis has been shown to have three distinct components, concerning respectively the impact of personal influence; the flow of personal influence; and the relationship of opinion leaders to the mass media. The evidence underlying each has been examined. Secondly, the design of the study has been recalled in order to point up the difficulty that arises from attempting to cope with the fundamentally new problem of incorporating *both* partners to an influence transaction into a cross-sectional study.

From this point forward, the major focus will turn to those studies that have succeeded *The People's Choice*. We will first report

[13] There is an alternative procedure which is something of an improvement. Respondents can be asked not only whether they have given advice but whether they have taken advice. This was done in the Decatur and Elmira studies which are cited below. Thus the nonleaders can be classified in terms of whether or not they are in the influence market at all, that is, whether or not they are "followers."

[14] Lazarsfeld, Berelson and Gaudet, *op. cit.*, pp. 49-50.

the different ways in which three of the four studies selected for review approached the problem of designing research on interpersonal influence.[15] Thereafter, the substantive findings of the several studies will be reviewed and evaluated so as to constitute an up-to-date report on the accumulating evidence for and against the hypothesis of the two-step flow of communication.

1. THE ROVERE STUDY. Undertaken just as the 1940 voting study was being completed, the earliest of the three studies was conducted in a small town in New Jersey. It began by asking a sample of 86 respondents to name the people to whom they turned for information and advice regarding a variety of matters. Hundreds of names were mentioned in response, and those who were designated four times or more were considered opinion leaders. These influentials were then sought out and interviewed.[16]

Here, then, is the initial attempt, on a pilot scale, to solve the problem of research design posed by *The People's Choice.* To locate influentials, this study suggests, begin by asking somebody, "Who influences you?" and proceed from the persons influenced to those who are designated as influential.

Two important differences between this study and the 1940 voting study must be pointed out. First, there is a difference in the conception of opinion leadership. Whereas the voting study regards any advice-giver as an opinion leader if he influences even one other person (such as a husband telling his wife for whom to vote), the leaders singled out by the criterion employed in Rovere were almost certainly wielders of wider influence.

Secondly, the voting study, at least by implication, was interested in such questions as the extent of the role of interpersonal influence in decision-making and its relative effectiveness compared to the mass media. The Rovere study took for granted the importance of this kind of influence, and proceeded to try to find the people who play key roles in its transmission.

A final point to make in connection with the design of this study is that it makes use of the initial interviews almost exclusively to *locate* opinion leaders and hardly at all to explore the *relationships* between leaders and followers. Once the leaders were designated,

15 The Elmira study will be omitted at this point because its design is essentially the same as that of the 1940 voting study except for the important fact that it obtained from each respondent considerably more information about the vote-intentions of others in his environment, the kinds of people he talks with, etc., than was done in *The People's Choice.*

16 Merton, *op. cit.*, pp. 184-185.

almost exclusive attention was given to classifying them into different types, studying the communications behavior of the different types and the interaction among the leaders themselves, but very little attention was given to the interaction between the leaders and the original informants who designated them.

2. THE DECATUR STUDY, carried out in 1945-46, tried to go a step further.[17] Like the voting study, but unlike Rovere, it tried to account for decisions—specific instances in which the effect of various influences could be discerned and assessed. Like Rovere, but unlike the voting study, it provided for interviews with the persons whom individuals in the initial sample had credited as influential in the making of recent decisions (in the realms of marketing, movie-going, and public affairs). The focus of the study this time was not on the opinion leaders alone, but (1) on the relative importance of personal influence and (2) on the person who named the leader as well as the leader—the advisor-advisee dyad.

Ideally, then, this study could ask whether opinion leaders tended to be from the same social class as their followers or whether the tendency was for influence to flow from the upper classes downwards. Were members of the dyads likely to be of the same age, the same sex, etc.? Was the leader more interested in the particular sphere of influence than his advisee? Was he more likely to be exposed to the mass media?

Just as the dyad could be constructed by proceeding from an advisee to his adviser, it was also possible to begin the other way around by talking first to a person who claimed to have acted as an adviser, and then locating the person he said he had influenced. The Decatur study tried this too. Using the same kind of self-designating questions employed in the voting study, persons who designated themselves as influential were asked to indicate the names of those whom they had influenced. By "snowballing" to the people thus designated, there arose the opportunity not only to study the interaction between adviser and advisee but also to explore the extent to which people who designated themselves as influential were confirmed in their self-evaluations by those whom they allegedly had influenced. Proceeding in this way, the researchers hoped to be able to say something about the validity of the self-designating technique.[18]

[17] Katz and Lazarsfeld, *op. cit.*, Part Two.

[18] About two-thirds of the alleged influences confirmed the fact that a conversation had taken place between themselves and the self-designated influential on the subject-matter in question. Of these, about 80 per cent further confirmed

The authors of *The People's Choice* had said that "asking people to whom they turn and then investigating the interaction between advisers and advisees . . . would be extremely difficult if not impossible." And, in fact, it proved to be extremely difficult. Many problems were encountered in the field work, the result of which was that not all the "snowball" interviews could be completed.[19] In many parts of the analysis of the data, therefore, it was necessary to revert to comparisons of leaders and non-leaders, imputing greater influence to groups with higher concentrations of self-designated leadership. Yet, in principle, it was demonstrated that a study design taking account of interpersonal relations was both possible and profitable to execute.

But about the time it became evident that this goal was within reach, the goal itself began to change. It began to seem desirable to take account of chains of influence longer than those involved in the dyad; and hence to view the adviser-advisee dyad as one component of a more elaborately structured social group.

These changes came about gradually and for a variety of reasons. First of all, findings from the Decatur study and from the later Elmira study revealed that the opinion leaders themselves often reported that their own decisions were influenced by still other people.[20] It began to seem desirable, therefore, to think in terms of the opinion leaders of opinion leaders.[21] Secondly, it became clear that opinion leadership could not be viewed as a "trait" which some people possess and others do not, although the voting study sometimes implied this view. Instead, it seemed quite apparent that the opinion leader is influential at certain times and with respect to certain substantive areas by virtue of the fact that he is "empowered" to be so by other members of his group. Why certain people are chosen must be accounted for not only in demographic terms (social status, sex, age, etc.) but also in terms of the structure and values of the groups of which both adviser and advisee are members. Thus, the unexpected rise of young men to opinion leadership in traditional groups, when these groups faced the new situations of urbanization and indus-

---

that they had received advice. The extent of confirmation is considerably less in the realm of public affairs than it is in marketing or fashion. *Ibid.*, pp. 149-161 and 353-362.

19 Partly this was due to inability to locate the designated people, but partly, too, to the fact that original respondents did not always know the person who had influenced them as is obvious, for example, in the case of a woman copying another woman's hat style, etc. See *Ibid.*, pp. 362-363.

20 *Ibid.*, p. 318; Berelson, Lazarsfeld and McPhee, *op. cit.*, p. 110.

21 This was actually tried at one point in the Decatur study. See Katz and Lazarsfeld, *op. cit.*, pp. 283-287.

trialization, can be understood only against the background of old and new patterns of social relations within the group and of old and new patterns of orientation to the world outside the group.[22] Reviewing the literature of small group research hastened the formulation of this conception.[23]

One other factor shaped the direction of the new program as well. Reflecting upon the Decatur study, it became clear that while one could talk about the role of various influences in the making of fashion *decisions by individuals*, the study design was not adequate for the study of fashion in the aggregate—*fashion as a process of diffusion*—as long as it did not take account of either the content of the decision or the time factor involved. The decisions of the "fashion changers" studied in Decatur might have cancelled each other out: while Mrs. X reported a change from Fashion A to Fashion B, Mrs. Y might have been reporting a change from B to A. What is true for fashion is true for any other diffusion phenomenon: to study it, one must trace the flow of some specific item over time. Combining this interest in diffusion with that of studying the role of more elaborate social networks of communication gave birth to a new study which focused on (1) a specific item, (2) diffusion over time, (3) through the social structure of an entire community.

3. THE DRUG STUDY. This study was conducted to determine the way in which doctors make decisions to adopt new drugs. This time, when it came to designing a study which would take account of the possible role of interpersonal influence among physicians, it became clear that there were so few physicians (less than one and one-half per 1,000 population) that it was feasible to interview all members of the medical profession in several cities. If all doctors (or all doctors in specialties concerned with the issue at hand) could be interviewed, then there would be no doubt that all adviser-advisee pairs would fall within the sample. All such pairs could then be located within the context of larger social groupings of doctors, which could be measured by sociometric methods.

Doctors in the relevant specialties in four midwestern cities were interviewed. In addition to questions on background, attitudes, drug-use, exposure to various sources of information and influence, and the like, each doctor was also asked to name the three colleagues he

[22] See, for example, the articles by Eisenstadt, *op. cit.*, and Glock, *op. cit.*; the Rovere study, too, takes careful account of the structure of social relations and values in which influentials are embedded, and discusses the various avenues to influentiality open to different kinds of people.

[23] Reported in Part I of Katz and Lazarsfeld, *op. cit.*

saw most often socially, the three colleagues with whom he talked most frequently about cases, and the three colleagues to whom he looked for information and advice.[24]

In addition to the opportunity of mapping the networks of interpersonal relations, the drug study also provided for the two other factors necessary for a true diffusion study: attention to a specific item in the course of gaining acceptance, and a record of this diffusion over time. This was accomplished by means of an audit of prescriptions on file in the local pharmacies of the cities studied, which made it possible to date each doctor's earliest use of a particular new drug—a drug which had gained widespread acceptance a few months before the study had begun. Each doctor could thus be classified in terms of the promptness of his decision to respond to the innovation, and in terms of other information provided by the prescription audit.

Altogether, compared with the earlier studies, the drug study imposes a more objective framework—both psychological and sociological—on the decision. First of all, the decision-maker himself is not the only source of information concerning his decision. Objective data from the prescription record are used as well. Secondly, the role of different influences is assessed not only on the basis of the decision-maker's own reconstruction of the event, but also on the basis of objective correlations from which inferences concerning the flow of influence can be drawn. For example, doctors who adopted the new drug early were more likely to be participants in out-of-town medical specialty meetings than those who adopted it later.

Similarly, it is possible to infer the role of social relations in doctor's decision-making not only from the doctor's own testimony concerning the role of social influences but also from the doctor's "location" in the interpersonal networks mapped by the sociometric questions. Thus, on the basis of sociometric data, it is possible to classify doctors according to their integration into the medical community, or the degree of their influence, as measured by *the number of times* they are named by the colleagues as friends, discussion-partners, and consultants. They can also be classified according to their membership in one or another network or clique, as indicated by *who* names them. Using the first measure makes it possible to investigate whether or not the more influential doctors adopt a drug earlier than those who are less influential. From the second kind of analysis one can learn, for example, whether or not those doctors who

[24] See footnote 6.

belong to the same sub-groups have similar drug-use patterns. In this way, it becomes possible to weave back and forth between the doctor's own testimony about his decisions and the influences involved, on the one hand, and the more objective record of his decisions and of the influences to which he has been exposed, on the other hand.

Note that the networks of social relations in this study are mapped "prior" to the introduction of the new drug being studied, in the sense that friendship, consultation, and so on, are recorded independently of any particular decision the doctor has made. The study is concerned with the potential relevance of various parts of these sociometric structures to the transmission of influence. For example, it is possible to point to the parts of the structure which are "activated" upon the introduction of a new drug, and to describe the sequence of diffusion of the drug as it gains acceptance by individuals and groups in the community. While the Decatur study could hope to examine only the particular face-to-face relationship which had been influential in a given decision, the drug study can locate this relationship against the background of the entire web of *potentially* relevant relationships within which the doctor is embedded.

The Findings of Studies Subsequent to *The People's Choice*

Having examined the *designs* of these studies, the next step is to explore their *findings* insofar as these are relevant to the hypothesis about the two-step flow of communication. It will be useful to return to the three categories already singled out in discussing *The People's Choice*: (1) the impact of personal influence; (2) the flow of personal influence; and (3) opinion leaders and the mass media. Evidence from the three studies just reported, as well as from the 1948 Elmira study [25] and from others, will be brought together here; but in every case the characteristics of each study's design must be borne in mind in evaluating the evidence presented.

A. The impact of personal influence

1. Personal and the Mass Media Influence. The 1940 study indicated that personal influence affected voting decisions more than the mass media did, particularly in the case of those who changed their minds during the course of the campaign. The Decatur study went on to explore the relative impact of personal influences and the mass media in three other realms: marketing, fashions and movie-

[25] Berelson, Lazarsfeld, and McPhee, *op. cit.*

going. Basing its conclusions on the testimony of the decision-makers themselves, and using an instrument for evaluating the relative effectiveness of the various media which entered into the decisions, the Decatur study again found that personal influence figured both more frequently and more effectively than any of the mass media.[26]

In the analysis to date, the drug study has not approached the problem of the relative effectiveness of the various media from the point of view of the doctor's own reconstruction of what went into the making of his decision. Comparing mere frequency of mention of different media, it is clear that colleagues are by no means the most frequently mentioned source. Nevertheless, exploration of the factors related to whether the doctor's decision to adopt the drug came early or late indicates that the factor most strongly associated with the time of adoption of the new drug is the extent of the doctor's integration in the medical community. That is, the more frequently a doctor is named by his colleagues as a friend or a discussion partner, the more likely he is to be an innovator with respect to the new drug. Extent of integration proves to be a more important factor than any background factor (such as age, medical school, or income of patients), or any other source of influence (such as readership of medical journals) that was examined.

Investigation of why integration is related to innovation suggests two central factors: (1) interpersonal communication—doctors who are integrated are more in touch and more up-to-date; and (2) social support—doctors who are integrated feel more secure when facing the risks of innovation in medicine.[27] Thus the drug study, too, provides evidence of the strong impact of personal relations—even in the making of scientific decisions.

2. Homogeneity of Opinion in Primary Groups. The effectiveness of interpersonal influence, as it is revealed in the studies under review, is reflected in the homogeneity of opinions and actions in primary groups. The medium of primary group communication is, by definition, person-to-person. Both of the voting studies indicate the high degree of homogeneity of political opinion among members of the same families, and among co-workers and friends. The effectiveness of such primary groups in pulling potential deviates back into line is demonstrated by the fact that those who changed their vote intentions were largely people who, early in the campaign, had

[26] Katz and Lazarsfeld, *op. cit.*, pp. 169-186.

[27] On the relationship between social integration and self-confidence in a work situation, see Peter M. Blau, *The Dynamics of Bureaucracy* (Chicago: University of Chicago Press, 1955), pp. 126-129.

reported that they intended to vote differently from their family or friends.[28]

The drug study, too, was able to examine the extent of homogeneity in the behavior of sociometrically related doctors, and was able to demonstrate that there were situations where similar behavior could be observed. For example, it was found that, when called upon to treat the more puzzling diseases, doctors were likely to prescribe the same drug as their sociometric colleagues. The study also showed that, very early in this history of a new drug, innovating doctors who were sociometrically connected tended to adopt the new drug at virtually the same time. This phenomenon of homogeneity of opinion or behavior among interacting individuals confronting an unclear or uncertain situation which calls for action has often been studied by sociologists and social psychologists.[29]

3. THE VARIOUS ROLES OF THE MEDIA. The 1940 voting study explored some of the reasons why personal influence might be expected to be more influential in changing opinions than the mass media: It is often non-purposive; it is flexible; it is trustworthy. It was suggested that the mass media more often play a reinforcing role in the strengthening of predispositions and of decisions already taken. Nevertheless, it was assumed that the various media and personal influence are essentially competitive, in the sense that a given decision is influenced by one *or* the other. The Decatur study tended toward this assumption too, but at one point the study does attempt to show that different media play different parts in the decision-making process and take patterned positions in a sequence of several influences. The drug study elaborates on the roles of the media even further, distinguishing between media that "inform" and media that "legitimate" decisions. Thus in doctors' decisions, professional media (including colleagues) seem to play a legitimating role, while commercial media play an informing role.

B. The flow of personal influence

The 1940 voting study found that opinion leaders were not concentrated in the upper brackets of the population but were located

[28] Lazarsfeld, Berelson and Gaudet, *op. cit.*, pp. 137-145; Berelson, Lazarsfeld and McPhee, *op. cit.*, pp. 94-101, 120-122.

[29] That men, faced with an unstructured situation, look to each other to establish a "social reality" in terms of which they act, is a central theme in the work of Durkheim, Kurt Lewin and his disciples, H. S. Sullivan ("consensual validation"), and in the studies of Sherif, Asch and others.

in almost equal proportions in every social group and stratum. This finding led to efforts in subsequent studies to establish the extent to which this was true in areas other than election campaigns and also to ascertain what it is that *does* distinguish opinion leaders from those whom they influence.

The first thing that is clear from the series of studies under review is that the subject matter concerning which influence is transmitted has a lot to do with determining who will lead and who follow. Thus, the Rovere study suggests that within the broad sphere of public affairs one set of influentials is occupied with "local" affairs and another with "cosmopolitan" affairs.[30] The Decatur study suggests that in marketing, for example, there is a concentration of opinion leadership among older women with larger families, while in fashions and movie-going it is the young, unmarried girl who has a disproportionate chance of being turned to for advice. There is very little overlap of leadership: a leader in one sphere is not likely to be influential in another unrelated sphere as well.[31]

Yet, even when leadership in one or another sphere is heavily concentrated among the members of a particular group—as was the case with marketing leadership in Decatur—the evidence suggests that people still talk, most of all, to others like themselves. Thus, while the marketing leaders among the older "large-family wives" also influenced other kinds of women, most of their influence was directed to women of their own age with equally large families. In marketing, fashions, and movie-going, furthermore, there was no appreciable concentration of influentials in any of the three socio-economic levels. Only in public affairs was there a concentration of leadership in the highest status, and there was some slight evidence that influence flows from this group to individuals of lower status. The Elmira study also found opinion-leaders in similar proportions on every socio-economic and occupational level and found that conversations concerning the campaign went on, typically, between people of similar age, occupation, and political opinion.

What makes for the concentration of certain kinds of opinion leadership within certain groups? And when influential and influencee are outwardly alike—as they so often seem to be—what, if anything, distinguishes one from the other? Broadly, it appears that influence is related (1) to the *personification of certain values* (who

30 Merton, *op. cit.*, pp. 187-188.

31 For a summary of the Decatur findings on the flow of interpersonal influence, see Katz and Lazarsfeld, *op. cit.*, pp. 327-334.

one is); (2) to *competence* (what one knows); and (3) to *strategic social location* (whom one knows). Social location, in turn, divides into whom one knows within a group; and "outside."

Influence is often successfully transmitted because the influencee wants to be as much like the influential as possible.[32] That the young, unmarried girls are fashion leaders can be understood easily in a culture where youth and youthfulness are supreme values. This is an example where "who one is" counts very heavily.

But "what one knows" is no less important.[33] The fact is that older women, by virtue of their greater experience, are looked to as marketing advisers and that specialists in internal medicine—the most "scientific" of the practicing physicians—are the most frequently mentioned opinion leaders among the doctors. The influence of young people in the realm of movie-going can also be understood best in terms of their familiarity with the motion picture world. The Elmira study found slightly greater concentrations of opinion leadership among the more educated people on each socio-economic level, again implying the importance of competence. Finally, the influence of the "cosmopolitans" in Rovere rested on the presumption that they had large amounts of information.

It is, however, not enough to be a person whom others want to emulate, or to be competent. One must also be accessible. Thus, the Decatur study finds gregariousness—"whom one knows"—related to every kind of leadership. The Rovere study reports that the leadership of the "local" influentials is based on their central location in the web of interpersonal contacts. Similarly, studies of rumor transmission have singled out those who are "socially active" as agents of rumor.[34]

Of course, the importance of whom one knows is not simply a matter of the number of people with whom an opinion leader is in contact. It is also a question of whether the people with whom he is in touch happen to be interested in the area in which his leadership is likely to be sought. For this reason, it is quite clear that the

[32] That leaders are, in a certain sense, the most conformist members of their groups—upholding whatever norms and values are central to the group—is a proposition which further illustrates this point. For an empirical illustration from a highly relevant study, see C. Paul Marsh and A. Lee Coleman, "Farmers' Practice Adoption Rates in Relation to Adoption Rates of Leaders," *Rural Sociology*, Vol. 19 (1954), pp. 180-183.

[33] The distinction between "what" and "whom" one knows is used by Merton, *op. cit.*, p. 197.

[34] Gordon W. Allport and Leo J. Postman, *The Psychology of Rumor* (New York: Henry Holt & Co. Inc., 1943), p. 183.

greater interest of opinion leaders in the subjects over which they exert influence is not a sufficient explanation of their influence. While the voting studies as well as the Decatur study show leaders to be more interested, the Decatur study goes on to show that interest alone is not the determining factor.[35] In fashion, for example, a young unmarried girl is considerably more likely to be influential than a matron with an equally great interest in clothes. The reason, it is suggested, is that a girl who is interested in fashion is much more likely than a matron with an equally high interest to know other people who share her preoccupation, and thus is more likely than the matron to have followers who are interested enough to ask for her advice. In other words, it takes two to be a leader—a leader and a follower.

Finally, there is the second aspect of "whom one knows." An individual may be influential not only because people within his group look to him for advice but also because of whom he knows outside his group.[36] Both the Elmira and Decatur studies found that men are more likely than women to be opinion leaders in the realm of public affairs and this, it is suggested, is because they have more of a chance to get outside the home to meet people and talk politics. Similarly, the Elmira study indicated that opinion leaders belonged to more organizations, more often knew workers for the political parties, and so on, than did others. The drug study found that influential doctors could be characterized in terms of such things as their more frequent attendance at out-of-town meetings and the diversity of places with which they maintained contact, particularly far-away places. It is interesting that a study of the farmer-innovators responsible for the diffusion of hybrid seed-corn in Iowa concluded that these leaders also could be characterized in terms of the relative frequency of their trips out of town.[37]

C. The opinion leaders and the mass media

The third aspect of the hypothesis of the two-step flow of communication states that opinion leaders are more exposed to the mass media than are those whom they influence. In *The People's Choice*

[35] Katz and Lazarsfeld, *op. cit.*, pp. 249-252.

[36] It is interesting that a number of studies have found that the most integrated persons within a group are also likely to have more contacts outside the group than others. One might have expected the more marginal members to have more contacts outside. For example, see Blau, *op. cit.*, p. 128.

[37] Bryce Ryan and Neal Gross, *Acceptance and Diffusion of Hybrid Seed Corn in Two Iowa Communities* (Ames, Iowa: Iowa State College of Agriculture and Mechanic Arts, Research Bulletin 372), pp. 706-707. For a general summary,

this is supported by reference to the media behavior of leaders and non-leaders.

The Decatur study corroborated this finding, and went on to explore two additional aspects of the same idea.[38] First of all, it was shown that leaders in a given sphere (fashions, public affairs, etc.) were particularly likely to be exposed to the media appropriate to that sphere. This is essentially a corroboration of the Rovere finding that those who proved influential with regard to "cosmopolitan" matters were more likely to be readers of national news magazines, but that this was not at all the case for those influential with regard to "local" matters. Secondly, the Decatur study shows that at least in the realm of fashions, the leaders are not only more exposed to the mass media, but are also more affected by them in their own decisions. This did not appear to be the case in other realms, where opinion leaders, though more exposed to the media than non-leaders, nevertheless reported personal influence as the major factor in their decisions. This suggests that in some spheres considerably longer chains of person-to-person influence than the dyad may have to be traced back before one encounters any decisive influence by the mass media, even though their contributory influence may be perceived at many points. This was suggested by the Elmira study too. It found that the leaders, though more exposed to the media, also more often reported that they sought information and advice from other persons.[39]

Similarly, the drug study showed that the influential doctors were more likely to be readers of a large number of professional journals and valued them more highly than did doctors of lesser influence. But at the same time, they were as likely as other doctors to say that local colleagues were an important source of information and advice in their reaching particular decisions.

Finally, the drug study demonstrated that the more influential doctors could be characterized by their greater attention not only to medical journals, but to out-of-town meetings and contacts as well. This finding has already been discussed in the previous section treating the *strategic location* of the opinion leader with respect to "the world outside" his group. Considering it again under the present

---

see Ryan and Gross, "The Diffusion of Hybrid Seed Corn in Two Iowa Communities," *Rural Sociology*, Vol. 8 (1942), pp. 15-24. An article, now in preparation, will point out some of the parallels in research design and in findings between this study and the drug study.

[38] Katz and Lazarsfeld, *op. cit.*, pp. 309-320.

[39] Berelson, Lazarsfeld and McPhee, *op. cit.*, p. 110.

heading suggests that the greater exposure of the opinion leader to the mass media may only be a special case of the more general proposition that opinion leaders serve to relate their groups to relevant parts of the environment through whatever media happen to be appropriate. This more general statement makes clear the similar functions of big city newspapers for the Decatur fashion leader; of national news magazines for the "cosmopolitan" influentials of Rovere; of out-of-town medical meetings for the influential doctor; and of contact with the city for the farmer-innovator in Iowa [40] as well as for the newly-risen, young opinion leaders in underdeveloped areas throughout the world.[41]

Conclusions

Despite the diversity of subject matter with which they are concerned, the studies reviewed here constitute an example of continuity and cumulation both in research design and theoretical commitment. Piecing together the findings of the latter-day studies in the light of the original statement of the two-step flow hypothesis suggests the following picture.

Opinion leaders and the people whom they influence are very much alike and typically belong to the same primary groups of family, friends and co-workers. While the opinion leader may be more interested in the particular sphere in which he is influential, it is highly unlikely that the persons influenced will be very far behind the leader in their level of interest. Influentials and influencees may exchange roles in different spheres of influence. Most spheres focus the group's attention on some related part of the world outside the group, and it is the opinion leader's function to bring the group into touch with this relevant part of its environment through whatever media are appropriate. In every case, influentials have been found to be more exposed to these points of contact with the outside world. Nevertheless, it is also true that, despite their greater exposure to the media, most opinion leaders are primarily affected not by the communication media but by still other people.

The main emphasis of the two-step flow hypothesis appears to be on only one aspect of interpersonal relations—interpersonal relations

[40] Ryan and Gross, *op. cit.*, choose to explain "trips to the city" as another index of the non-traditional orientation of which innovation itself is also an index. In the case of the drug of-town meetings, trips to out-of-town centers of learning, etc., but the latter were also mentioned as key sources of advice by doctors who were innovators and influentials.

[41] See the forthcoming book by Lerner, *et al.* cited above.

as channels of communication. But from the several studies reviewed, it is clear that these very same interpersonal relations influence the making of decisions in at least two additional ways. In addition to serving as networks of communication, interpersonal relations are also sources of pressure to conform to the group's way of thinking and acting, as well as sources of social support. The workings of group pressure are clearly evident in the homogeneity of opinion and action observed among voters and among doctors in situations of unclarity or uncertainty. The social support that comes from being integrated in the medical community may give a doctor the confidence required to carry out a resolution to adopt a new drug. Thus, interpersonal relations are (1) channels of information, (2) sources of social pressure, and (3) sources of social support, and each relates interpersonal relations to decision-making in a somewhat different way.[42]

The central methodological problem in each of the studies reviewed has been how to take account of interpersonal relations and still preserve the economy and representativeness which the random, cross-sectional sample affords. Answers to this problem range from asking individuals in the sample to describe the others with whom they interacted (Elmira), to conducting "snowball" interviews with influential-influencee dyads (Decatur), to interviewing an entire community (drug study). Future studies will probably find themselves somewhere in between. For most studies, however, the guiding principle would seem to be to build larger or smaller social molecules around each individual atom in the sample.[43]

[42] These different dimensions of interpersonal relations can be further illustrated by reference to studies which represent the "pure type" of each dimension. Studies of rumor flow illustrate the "channels" dimension; see, for example, Jacob L. Moreno, *Who Shall Survive* (Beacon, N. Y.: Beacon House, 1953), pp. 440-450. The study by Leon Festinger, Stanley Schachter and Kurt Back, *Social Pressures in Informal Groups* (New York: Harper & Brothers, 1950), illustrates the second dimension. Blau, *op. cit.*, pp. 126-129, illustrates the "social support" dimension.

[43] Various ways of accomplishing this have been discussed for the past two years in a staff seminar on "relational analysis" at the Bureau of Applied Social Research. The recent study by Seymour M. Lipset, Martin A. Trow and James S. Coleman, *Union Democracy* (Glencoe, Ill.: The Free Press, 1956), illustrates one approach in its study of printers within the varying social contexts of the shops in which they are employed. The study by Riley and Riley, *op. cit.*, is another good example.

12. DRESS-BUYING BEHAVIOR OF CONSUMERS *

John E. Jacobi and S. George Walters

THEORIES OF CONSUMER-BUYING BEHAVIOR

The major limitation of all theoretical approaches is the tendency to treat each one as a separate independent explanation. However, the hypotheses of other writers on consumer-expenditure behavior can be classified under the following headings: biologically and psychologically based values, needs, drives and instincts; social-cultural situations; institutional availability, that is, the consumer could buy only merchandise made available by the manufacturer; immediate influences, that is, special opportunity to buy, price cuts, salesmanship, etc.

A THEORY OF DRESS-BUYING BEHAVIOR OF CONSUMERS

The theory proposed here concerns a short-run explanation of how and why consumers buy a dress at a given time. It briefly considers the long run process by which consumers accept or reject certain social-economic status symbols which affect dress purchases.

The narrowing concept

At the time of any particular dress purchase, the consumer has oriented herself to the stores appropriate for her in terms of price, style, and store personality. During this first stage in the process of selection, a certain amount of "narrowing" is almost automatic. The consumer is not aware of the full range of dresses available in various stores, or made available by various manufacturers. Ignorance of styles and availability of styles automatically reduces the number of dresses from which a choice can be made.

* From *The Journal of Marketing*, Vol. 23, No. 2 (October, 1958), pp. 168-172. Reprinted with permission from *The Journal of Marketing*, published quarterly by the American Marketing Association.

John E. Jacobi, Associate Professor of Sociology, Lehigh University, and S. George Walters, Development Projects Manager, Mobil Oil Company.

Critical-attribute phase

After the "narrowing process" has reduced dress choice, the purchaser has four or five dresses from which to choose. Which does she select and why? This is the critical-attribute phase.

All product attributes are of equal importance in this phase. If one is missing, a purchase probably will not occur. Therefore, the attribute least available becomes critical. If the selection has been narrowed to two dresses similar in style, color, and price, but differing in fabric, then fabric becomes the critical attribute because it is least available in the range of combinations.

The symbol-acceptance concept

The symbol-acceptance concept visualizes the dress buyer as moving through several levels throughout her dress-buying history. The individual buyer makes value judgments on appropriate outer-apparel symbols, that is, a dress with particular features for her.

The essence of this concept is the buyer's degree of style awareness. Buyers may be typed on the basis of: (1) awareness and ownership of current style; (2) partial awareness and ownership of current style; (3) lack of awareness or ownership of current style.

People at every income range are permanently located at, moving into, or moving through various levels. These levels may be differentiated by the degree of acceptance of status symbols shown by dress purchases. The present analysis limits these levels to three. Narrower definitions of these levels could result in more. These levels may be defined by social-cultural symbols to which dress buyers subscribe, for example, specific styles, fashions, fads, labels, store personality.

Whether three social-cultural dress levels are used for the entire range of consumer income, or dress levels for any particular income bracket, three types of buyers or social-cultural dress levels may be distinguished. The type-1 buyer group comprises those who have spent some time buying within this particular level. They have assimilated appropriate social-cultural group-status symbols; and some are in the process of or about to shift into the next higher social-cultural dress level group. Women in type 1 are familiar with but probably less dependent upon store names, label, and brand than the other types. They are more concerned with the subtle aspects of all product attributes, such as fabric quality, pattern, etc.

Type 2 includes those who have not completely assimilated appropriate status symbols. Since they have not fully assimilated the group-status symbol, greater reliance is placed on store name, brand, and label, as well as on the price of a particular dress. Price for type 2 may be a limiting factor (since the marginal utility of their income may be high), or price may serve as a symbol of style as well—for instance, a dress costs $20.00 and, therefore, it is a style dress.

Type 3 is a group little concerned with style. A large segment is made up of elderly persons. Expectations and actual purchase patterns indicate no movement in either direction, either into a higher or lower social-cultural economic group.

The structure is further complicated by the continual movement of people from type to type. Shifts are probably caused by changes in status objectives, or limitations imposed by income, or both.

Examination of the Theory

Each part of the theory leads to a number of implications. The following analysis is based on a survey of the literature, a study of research projects completed to date, and an exploratory survey designed specifically to throw some light on these tentative proposals and some of the theory implications.

Implications relating to the concept of the "narrowing process"

(1) The number of stores, brands, labels, and dress prices is narrowed and the range of appropriate dresses reduced to a small number, possibly four or five or less. One narrows the choice of available dresses by relating dress price to income, as well as by chance. Chance is involved because it is impossible for the average consumer to shop all stores and thus to be aware of all styles made available by stores and manufacturers. Nor is it possible for any one store to stock full lines of all manufacturers. Those who have narrowed their store choices to one or two or three stores will generally be ignorant of offerings in the other outlets.

(2) A second aspect of the narrowing process occurs when the consumer relies in part on magazines, newspapers, television and other media for information on what constitutes appropriate outer apparel. One individual relies almost entirely on television programs for ideas of appropriate styles; others depend upon the traditional fashion magazines. Thus, those who are particularly style conscious, or who rely on certain media because of uncertainty about what constitutes appropriate outer apparel, will in part have the narrowing process performed by media.

(3) Institutional availability is a third aspect of the narrowing process; this relates to the dresses released to retail store outlets by manufacturers. The institutional coverage in any retail trading area itself limits range of available choices. In one exploratory study in the East, a respondent eliminated all available styles within her trading area. She made it a point to buy dresses not normally available to her neighbors by shopping in a nearby trading area where a California dress line was available.

(4) The specific situational need is the fourth characteristic of this narrowing process. A large segment of women select dresses for a particular use situation. The narrowing process is made largely on the basis of exactly what the dress is going to be used for. This seems to be a particularly important concept and a major part of the narrowing process. A greater portion of the women in one exploratory survey were primarily concerned with securing a "transitional dress," to be used in the closing weeks of the summer and on into fall. As a result, the particular feature sought was three-quarter length sleeves. In another area, younger women were interested in this physical aspect as well. Three-quarter length sleeves had three uses: to cover arms and elbows, to provide warmth, and to convey modesty. Certain types of retail dress outlets specialized in certain use dresses. Some stores are regarded as carrying good sportswear, others good formal wear. The consumer wants a dress type appropriate for a particular use situation, and goes to those stores which she believes excel in that type of dress.

(5) The store buyer's influence is the final aspect of this narrowing process. This came to light in studies dealing with a small limited-line store. A significant percentage of the respondents let the store buyer perform the selecting process for them. Rejections by consumers were amazingly small. In two cases the women had no idea of buying a new dress, but did so when the store buyer told them that a particular dress was ideally suited for them. The concept of the narrowing process has been verified in the exploratory study. The most frequent combination of variables at work in the first phase of the narrowing process appears to be price, media, chance, institutional availability, and use situation. The situation in which the store buyer is called upon to perform the narrowing process for the respondents has occurred frequently enough to warrant inclusion.

(6) Phase 1 of the narrowing process results in a reduction of the number of dresses available to the individual consumer. After the dress choice has been narrowed to a relatively small number, the critical-attribute phase, or stage 2 of the narrowing process of

selection becomes operative. How does the buyer select one particular dress from among the three or four left? As indicated earlier, this phase of the narrowing process involves a decision on the part of the consumer in which she must give a priority to some special feature of a dress. In effect, the final decision rests on the fact that there is one dominant attribute that shifts the scale in favor of a particular dress.

Visualize two dresses comparable in style, color, price, and fabric. One dress has a full skirt and the other a sheath skirt. If the consumer prefers the full skirt, and the two dresses are similar in all other respects, then the dress with the full skirt will be purchased. That attribute least available in the range of combinations becomes the critical attribute; purchase is made on the basis of the critical attribute. It is important to make a distinction between the kinds of things that the consumer weighs in phase 1 of the narrowing process, and the kinds of things the consumer gives weight to in phase 2 of the narrowing process.

In most consumer studies, where the consumer ranks or assigns weights to reasons for buying a particular dress, it has not been possible to assign proper weights to these variables. If a consumer reports that she bought a dress because of style, the fact is that there are many other dresses of the same style available to the purchaser.

These studies also fail to recognize the difference in the use of the word "style" in connection with phase 1 and phase 2. Recognition that this is a two-stage process permits a more realistic examination and understanding of consumer dress-buyer behavior.

The respondent who mentions "style" in phase 1 of the narrowing process is talking about something quite different than when she mentions "style" in phase 2. In an exploratory study, when the respondent oriented to phase 1 was asked to discuss the factors she looked for in the purchase of any dress, style was frequently cited. Certain types of respondents are articulate about what particular style they are looking for. But when the respondent is asked to think about the dress just purchased, she is unable to identify it as belonging to any particular style. At this phase (the critical-attribute stage), the term style generally referred to some special characteristic of the dress, for example, a bow with streamers at the rear of the dress, or a bow at the bustline. "Stylish" was the word that was frequently heard.

Two exploratory studies indicate the variations which may take place in phase 2 of the narrowing process, termed the critical-attribute phase. In one area, women had purchased a $12.98 nylon jersey dress with an autumn-leaf pattern, available in various sizes, and in three colors, plum gray, blue, and cinnamon. Some of the women interviewed purchased the $12.98 nylon jersey because it had three-quarter length sleeves. This raised the question as to why they bought the dress they did, since, after all, there were three colors available in the three-quarter length. Thus, the critical attribute became one of color.

Summary of critical-attribute phase

In this second phase of purchase, all product attributes are of equal importance. If one is missing, the purchase probably will not be made. The critical attribute is that attribute least available in the range of combinations, and determines the ultimate purchase. When the individual has selected one dress, it is the result of a cumulative assessment of a number of factors relating to the product attribute and also to use situations and institutional availability. Media, other social groups, and other standards of living may be emulated. All these factors operate in phase 1 of the narrowing process. In short, psychological-biological drives, institutional availability, and the immediate influences help to narrow down the range of dresses until the consumer reaches phase 2 of the narrowing process, the critical-attribute phase.

While there is a relationship between the critical attribute selected and the reason why it was selected, this relationship is most tenuous. It is extremely difficult to get the respondent to connect the critical attribute with a fundamental reason why.

The term "dress-purpose" can be used both in the sense of use situation (sportswear, eveningwear, cocktail wear) and in the sense of use situation *plus* subtle aspects of personality. A dress may be wanted for a cocktail party, as well as to call attention to one's self.

Implications relating to the symbol-acceptance concept

In exploratory surveys, respondents were grouped in line with the procedure described earlier.

Respondents in type 1, having largely assimilated the style-status symbol, were relying chiefly upon subtle aspects of product attributes. They were not overly concerned with label or store name, although for the most part they knew both.

Comments made by type-2 respondents included: "I buy all of my clothes at this store," or "the store buyer selects the dress with my personality in mind" and "she knows what looks good on me," or "I have confidence in the store." Thus, the hypothesis about type-2 people found some support.

Product attributes were examined by type-3 respondents in a way that showed no style consciousness. This group was characterized by a stable purchase and use-situation pattern of apparent long standing.

Relationship between the narrowing process and the symbol-acceptance concept

The product attribute finally selected as the critical attribute is partly determined by the symbol concept. It is not the only determinant but is a principal one. For example, those in the type-1 category give critical attention to the subtle aspects of the product attributes. To illustrate the second part of the statement that the symbol concept is one of the principal determinants, but not the only determinant, women may select a particular dress in line with the symbol-acceptance and critical-attribute concepts, and the critical attribute will be related to some aspect of the individual's personality. Consequently, the narrowing process and the critical-attribute concept are interdependent, rather than separate and distinct from the symbol concept.

SECTION 3. MARKETING FUNCTIONS AND POLICIES

The purpose of Section III is twofold: first, to provide background and analytical material about the marketing functions and policies involved in the process of distributing goods and services; second, with the exception of channel policies, as discussed in Section V, this material has been combined to convey a general picture of the process and magnitude of marketing planning.

Many lists of marketing functions and policy areas have been developed. It is well to remember that such a list will vary according to the purposes and methods of analysis. The design and execution of marketing strategy may involve only several of the areas discussed in this section, or they may involve the entire marketing complex.

Section 3-A
Marketing Research

From the standpoint of the firm marketing research may be defined as action research. In fact, Wroe Alderson in his "A Systematics for Problems of Action" suggests that it should be distinguished from both pure science and applied science. Marketing research in this sense does not contribute directly to the advancement of knowledge as pure science does. The purpose of marketing research is to minimize uncertainty, to point to the most efficient way of utilizing the firm's resources, and to preserve the power to act. The general problem of marketing strategy, kinds of action problems, investigative procedures and boundary limitations are also discussed by Mr. Alderson.

Professor S. F. Otteson in his article, "Research and the Science of Marketing," uses marketing research in a somewhat broader sense than does Mr. Alderson. He develops the idea that marketing research, whether it utilizes the "Method Concept" or the "Fund of Knowledge" approach, centers on problem solving. One concentrates on method, the other on result. While Professor Otteson emphasizes controlled experimentation as illustrative of the method concept, the term might well include other techniques of operations research. In his definition the author indicates that "marketing research embraces all methods and techniques of inquiry that can be applied in the solution of marketing problems." In order for marketing research to aid in the development of a science of marketing, attention must be given to three areas: the scope of inquiry, the technique of inquiry, and the depth of inquiry.

"Operations Research as Applied to Marketing Problems," by John F. Magee, presents a definition of operations research and examples of how operations research teams have been contributing to the solution of marketing problems. A number of the techniques of experimental science are discussed and illustrated.

Martin Goland and Boyd Ladd discuss the present role and limitations of operations research and electronic data processing. Their article, "Operational Thinking in Management," also identifies OR techniques, presents additional examples of OR applications, and discusses some of the difficulties of securing widespread acceptance of OR within the business firm.

Section 3-B
Merchandising and Product Development

Merchandising and product development, as well as advertising and selling and in fact the whole marketing complex, are kept dynamic as a result of creativity. There is general agreement that the most important aspect of marketing is the mind of the marketing man. Since the publication of Graham Wallas's volume, *The Art of Thought*, a great deal of attention has been devoted to considering the questions posed by James Webb Young's book, *A Technique for Producing Ideas.* Of course, one must not overlook Poincaré's *Science and Hypothesis or Science and Method.* There are many others. Most of us, not being geniuses, can probably benefit by knowing how to go about developing merchandising, product, or advertising ideas. Perhaps by considering the ways in which others have developed these ideas, one can receive some guidance on how to proceed and thus become productive earlier than if forced to learn by the wasteful method of personal experience.

According to Joseph G. Mason in "How to Develop Ideas" creative men have four main traits. He points out how anyone can acquire or develop them to some extent. The four characteristics are Problem Sensitivity, Idea Fluency, Originality, and Flexibility. In relation to these characteristics consideration should also be given to those factors that keep the average person from being creative.

Richard W. Dalzell discusses whether there is a need for product diversification, the desirability of so doing, and the best approach in "Diversification: Watch the Pitfalls." The firm that does not make a searching study before diversifying may be assuming new problems which can lead to disastrous consequences.

Martin Mayer, the author of *Madison Avenue, U. S. A.*, and *Wall Street Men and Money*, analyzes, "Planned Obsolesence: RX for Tired Markets." Mr. Mayer suggests that there is something that the manufacturer can do to increase the apparent rate of consumption of a durable good and hence increase his replacement market. The task is to make his product seem older, and three courses of action are open: (1) functional obsolesence, (2) style obsolesence, and (3) materials failure. As for planning obsolesence, the author finds that "The more one studies the question of Planned Obsolesence, the more certain it seems that the phenomonon occurs because businessmen react to changing conditions, rather than because they plan." The mandate seems clear—the market demands newness, and producers must react swiftly to market changes.

Liquidation, shifts to new lines of business, major product modifications, and bankruptcy are alternative courses of action confronting the firm that is outdistanced in the competitive race. Professor O. K. Burrell considers the situation of "Industrial Adaptation." The author draws on the automobile industry for case material to illustrate the various efforts made by firms gradually being overtaken by competitors. The most dramatic of these cases is that of the Peerless Corporation. The efforts to secure new financing, the shift from fine cars to fine beer, and the conversion process—both financial and marketing—are analyzed.

Section 3-C
Buying

The function of buying comprises the processes of estimating demand, locating sources of supply, negotiation of terms, and finally transfer of title and delivery. Buying and selling are the very essence of marketing.

Innovation extends to all phases of business activity. One innovation recently adopted by an industrial distributor is the blanket purchase order. Alfred P. Koch and S. George Walters in their article, "The Blanket Purchase Order," utilize the experience of a wholesaler with the blanket purchase order to point up the necessity of anticipating the significant areas of risk and uncertainty associated with the adoption of innovation.

Professor Kalman Joseph Cohen in "Determining the 'Best Possible' Inventory Levels" presents a system of establishing inventory levels and several examples of how the system was applied practically. In addition to outlining the conceptual framework of his "simulated optimal branch inventory levels" system, he indicates graphical and computational techniques which could be used in implementing the procedure.

Industrialist H. Thomas Hallowell, Jr. in his article, "Reducing Costs Through Purchasing," discusses the role of the purchasing executive. This executive is in a position to exercise constructive guiding influence on the research programs of his suppliers. Sometimes out of this consumer-supplier relationship there develops a standard product that has industry-wide application.

William B. Fynes in "An Analysis of Purchasing Methods Used in Army Ordinance Procurement" reports the results of his study of the effectiveness of government procurement arrangements under negotiated and sealed bid contract procedures. He concludes that the government's procurement program cannot be evaluated by the usual yardsticks of efficiency or economy used by industrial purchasing authorities.

Section 3-D
Pricing

This material on pricing develops some of the principal pricing methods and goals viewed primarily from the standpoint of the individual marketing manager. Concepts taken from economic analysis as well as from several noneconomic areas are examined.

Professor Alfred R. Oxenfeldt in his paper, "Cyclical Implications of Private Pricing Policies," examines some of the major aspects of industrial pricing. The author considers pricing objectives, policies, methods, and strategy; he also covers businessmen's perception of the business scene, their knowledge of developments in the marketplace, their expectations, as well as their actual market behavior; the interrelationships among prices at different levels in the industrial structure and the relationship of retail, wholesale, and service prices are also cited. Professor Oxenfeldt concludes that "social objectives

—whether they be economic stability or economic growth—cannot be pursued effectively through private pricing policies." After examining the conditions under which prices may be adjusted during a recession, the timing and form of such price reductions, and the effect of these price changes on the firm's sales, the author suggests that the objectives and policies of the firm are neither regularly consistent or inconsistent with broad social objectives. Further that if these broad social objectives are to be realized, national policy will have to be developed in spheres outside of the pricing area.

The use of odd prices or "charm" prices is illustrative of a non-economic concept of pricing. Lawrence E. Fouraker in his article, "Oligopolistic Equilibrium in the Retailing of Produce," poses this question: "Is the average buyer of foodstuffs significantly influenced by the final digit of the price tag above the commodity being bought?" The question of the customer's psychological interpretation of a 39-cent price tag as compared with a price of 40 cents is examined in the light of several studies. It is suggested that the use of odd-cent price endings in the produce industry is the result of entrepreneurs following the rule of thumb of moving to the nearest price ending in nine after their initial approximation. Though it may be difficult to defend with logic, odd pricing may nevertheless perform the necessary function of introducing some order into an industry characterized by perishable products, low margins, and considerable rivalry.

Another aspect of setting price differentials is that which occurs when the location of the buyers varies. J. A. Guthrie in his article, "Impact of Geographical Price Discrimination on the Buyer," examines the problem of shifting from multiple basing-point pricing to f.o.b. mill pricing. Four separate cases are considered, and some of the theoretical aspects and affects of the change from unequal mill net to f.o.b. mill basis are established. The effect of these changes on price is of primary importance to the buyer.

Professor A. J. Alton's paper, "The Influence of Manufacturers' Price Policies upon Price Determination by Wholesalers," considers the type and degree of influence exerted by manufacturers upon wholesalers' attempts to establish prices. It is concluded that the wholesaler's pricing freedom is impinged upon by manufacturers when they utilize resale price maintenance or suggested resale prices.

The author contends that it is possible for wholesalers "to improve their profit picture by a careful examination of their present pricing practices as they are affected by manufacturers' policies regarding suggested resale pricing and freight charges."

The spectacular growth of discount houses in the United States in the past two decades has frequently been linked to the existence of resale price maintenance or what is popularly termed "fair trading." It is generally agreed that the discount house has been able to flourish because of the wide margins granted to retailers by resale price maintenance. Professor Fritz Machlup in discussing discount house operations before the Subcommittee of the Select Committee on Small Business of the United States Senate examines the discount house situation in the light of fair trade legislation. Professor Machlup contends that fair trade laws indirectly support the monopoly position of manufacturers. A very small, special interest group (only 10 per cent of all retailers have more than one half of their business in fair traded goods) is getting a favor at the expense of 175 million consumers. Not only does fair trade result in giving a bonus to a small group of favored retailers by taking money out of the pockets of a great number of workers, government employees etc., but it also results in a reduction of the total efficiency of the economy, holds down real national income, and retards the economic growth of the nation. Professor Machlup contends in his committee statement that when there is a bad law which prevents what is good for people, the time comes when some people find a way out. And the discount house was a way out. "I think the American people owe a great deal to those who pioneered it. Indeed there are things of which discount houses sell as much as 80 or 90 per cent of the total volume in certain branded goods." Professor Machlup also suggests that any survey of economists on retailers' protection by way of resale price maintenance would show an overwhelming majority in opposition to any such type of legislation.

One of the duties of the Federal Trade Commission is to protect the public from the abuses of misrepresentation in advertising. In recent years certain pricing practices have so flagrantly tended to mislead the consumer that it has been necessary to define and control certain types of pricing practices. The "Guides Against Deceptive Pricing" is an example of how the Federal Trade Commission attempts to elicit voluntary collaboration from business, so as to minimize the need for legal proceedings.

Section 3-E
Selling and Advertising

The first step in planning the activities of a firm is the development of a sales forecast. The short-term forecast may be used not only as a basis for planning, but also as a basis for coordination and control of production, inventories, and purchasing, as well as to set standards of performance for selling and advertising. The long-term sales forecast is frequently used as a basis for planning long-term financing and plant development. Almost all types of company budgets flow from the initial sales forecast. A third kind of forecasting is commonly called general business forecasting. Frequently companies will evaluate the over-all business outlook as a first step in preparing the sales forecast.

One may place, as Professor James H. Lorie has, all sales forecasting methods into two classes. One class may be labeled the guesses of experienced observers, that is, company economists and business executives; and the other may be referred to as statistical and mathematical manipulations. Professor Lorie's paper, "Two Important Problems in Sales Forecasting," considers the problem of combining these two approaches and the problem of an economic evaluation of forecasts. While the problem of economic evaluation of alternative forecasting methods is difficult, a continual economic evaluation is necessary and worthwhile.

Personal selling and advertising can be considered alternative ways of communicating information to the consumer. Determining the size of the advertising and selling budget may thus be viewed as a common problem. Frank D. Robinson, Vice President and Treasurer of Diebold Company, considers this problem in his paper, "The Advertising Budget." This paper utilizes "Game Theory" to decide which of several advertising budgets maximizes profits and minimizes losses in the light of a competitor's advertising. After establishing pertinent advertising principles and the steps that should be taken in setting up the advertising budget of a product whose sales tend to fluctuate in line with the business cycle, a mathematical model is built. The author indicates that this model takes into account two factors frequently overlooked—the impact of competitor's advertising and the variation in the degree of advertising effectiveness as related to changes in the business cycle.

In his article, "General Semantics: Tuning Ad Men," Harry E. Maynard states his belief that more advertising practitioners should familiarize themselves with the concepts of general semantics. The need for greater familiarily stems from the fact that general semantics is the best science for communicating information and ideas to move people to act.

Accounts of brainwashing and subliminal advertising have raised the spector of manipulation or hidden persuasion. Raymond A. Bauer, a social scientist who has been active in the field of psychology, considers the "Limits of Persuasion." He concludes, "I am skeptical about the extreme pictures of hidden persuasion that have been drawn for either the present or future of business or politics."

Professor of Marketing Edward C. Bursk, Editor of the *Harvard Business Review* looks at persuasion in another way. He agrees that it is helpful to know the boundaries of persuasion and to appreciate that it is difficult if not impossible to control society through subconscious manipulation. However, Mr. Bursk suggests that in devoting all this attention to motivation research there may be a danger that marketers will come to rely on scientific techniques and forget to go out and sell. Therefore, his title, "Opportunities for Persuasion." The situations which Professor Bursk examines would suggest that rational motives after all turn out to be the best device for securing the buyer's patronage. If a firm is selling the mass market, is it not true that rational buying motives will best cover that market as compared with an irrational want or feeling which is not necessarily common to a large part of the market? Professor Bursk concludes that any irrational resistance, even if it is in the subconscious, will be handled by the healthy prospect himself—"and will be, if he is provided with a sufficient rational motive as incentive."

Dr. Steuart Henderson Britt, Psychologist, Advertising Agency Executive, Professor of Marketing, and Editor of the *Journal of Marketing* in his article, "Subliminal Advertising," considers subliminal advertising in the light of the results of several experiments, the nature of the design of these experiments, and the ethical and practical considerations. Professor Britt as well as Professor Bauer point out that experiments conducted in the laboratory or in any situation in which it is possible to control the individuals environment have demonstrated, "that perception can be produced." Whether these experiments result in overt action, and whether it is possible for subliminal stimuli to cause a person to do something which he does not desire to do are questionable. But the laboratory is quite different from a large society. Dr. Britt suggests that there is a need for well designed experiments to be conducted outside of the laboratory. Until extensive basic work is done and until the complete design of any experiments are made public, "subliminal advertising is not likely to engulf us."

Section 3-F
Transportation and Storage

Transportation and storage, generally considered as functions of physical supply, involve those operations which move goods through space and hold goods through time.

In his article, "Selecting Transportation Services," Richard M. Boyd, General Traffic Manager of the Pittsburgh Plate Glass Company, concludes that the selection of transportation services has become quite complex. He believes that the systematic, if not scientific, selection of the means of transportation and of the best carrier within that means is basic to any successful manufacturing or distributing operation.

Stanley Ferguson in "Pattern of U.S. Freight Traffic Changing Fast" sheds new light on the emerging pattern of United States freight traffic through his analysis of "revenue carloadings."

A group of technical specialists in private business have prepared an article, "How Field Warehousing Concerns Help Small Business," for the United States Small Business Administration. Field warehousing makes it possible for a manufacturer or processor with national or regional distribution to place a full stock of products with distributors at little or no credit risk. The role of field warehousing in securing loans on inventory from banks and other lending agencies is well known.

Section 3-G
Risk and Finance

A major factor in obtaining distribution and sales is the availability of financing at all levels of the marketing process. Sydney D. Maddock in "Industrial Financing—Its Role in Distribution" graphically illustrates the importance of industrial financing by using as examples the movement of various commodities, such as shrimp from the ocean to the consumer's table.

"Floor Planning" is an analysis of a form of wholesale credit whose historical roots developed with the financing of automobile dealers and now extends to the wholesale financing of appliances, boats, mobile homes, and other big ticket items. Though these articles are concerned primarily with the major distributive channels, financing is also of importance in the performance of the facilitating functions.

Financing is closely interwoven with the movement of cash in a going concern; and if the enterprise is successful, the flow of cash will be greater than the drain of cash for manufacturing, and for such marketing activities as selling, advertising and research. Risk and uncertainty is endemic in varying degrees to all of the marketing activities examined in this volume, and therefore consideration of risk and uncertainty is not confined to the articles in this section.

13. A SYSTEMATICS FOR PROBLEMS OF ACTION *

Wroe Alderson

Bertrand Russell, in one of his gentler jibes at the pragmatists, says that this school would obviously prefer Othello, the man of action, to Hamlet, the man of thought.[1] This figure is singularly inept since Hamlet brought about the death of six people through violent action. That more than equalled the score rolled up by the presumably more active Othello. What Hamlet lacked was not the power to act but an adequate theory of action. Having first attempted to avoid the issue presented by the murder of his father, he is swept up in a gale of violence because of that very attempt at avoidance.

Russell has suggested elsewhere that philosophers can be classified according to a tripartite division based on whether their chief interest is a theory of knowledge, a theory of action, or a theory of value.[2] He places himself in the first category and points to Dewey and his fellow pragmatists as prime examples of the second. Actually in some of its versions pragmatism is a theory of knowledge promulgated by thinkers who are impressed with the importance of action. When philosophers really make action primary they are inclined to emphasize its irrational character, whether they end by deploring it like Schopenhauer or glorifying it like Nietzsche and Bergson. A theory of rational action which would provide an adequate perspective for the executive and policy-maker has yet to be formulated.

Experimental psychology has made some progress toward providing a scientific foundation for a theory of action. For a long time the most attractive clue for a science of behavior appeared to be the conditioned reflex. The loftiest reaches of human activity were felt to be reducible to habit and impulse, to fumbling trial and error and simple conditioning. More recently the purposive element in behavior

* Reprinted by permission from *Philosophy of Science*, Vol. 18, No. 1 (January, 1951), pp. 16-25.

Wroe Alderson, Professor of Marketing, University of Pennsylvania.

[1] Bertrand Russell, *Twentieth Century Philosophy* (New York: Philosophical Library, 1943), p. 236.

[2] Bertrand Russell, *History of Western Philosophy* (New York: Simon & Schuster, 1945), p. 792.

has been given greater emphasis and much of the activity of animals as well as men has been dignified with the label of problem-solving. Tolman has pointed out that experimenters tend to conclude that behavior is more largely rational or irrational according to whether their laboratory animals are apes or rats.[3] Tolman himself takes the side of the apes and hence of reason.

Relation of Inquiry to Action

John Dewey, as the philosopher of problem-solving, has both helped and hindered the development of a theory of rational action. He has properly stressed the importance of beginning with the problem in any inquiry. The present discussion accepts his dictum that problem-solving is the essence of rational action. He has created confusion by his tendency to merge the roles of the man of action and the scientist. Dewey defines science to include every orderly approach to judgments, whatever the nature of the problem. He goes on from that position to assert that inquiry effects the objective transformation of the situation.[4]

This formulation could scarcely be accepted by either the responsible man of action such as the business executive or by the market analyst and consulting economist who conducts investigations on his behalf. The scientific investigator undertakes to predict what may be expected under stated conditions. The man of action makes a commitment of resources in order to realize stated expectations. The investigator cannot accept or discharge responsibility for these commitments. The man of action, whether he be a business executive, a government administrator, or a military commander, may sometimes choose with complete rationality to get along without the services of the investigator.

A helpful distinction has been drawn by Northrup in criticizing Dewey's conception of the problem-solving process.[5] He says that Dewey attempts to move directly from the statement of the problem to the formulation of hypotheses to be tested by research. Northrup asserts that there is a missing step, namely, the analysis of the problem. The outcome of this analysis is the identification of the factual situation corresponding to the problematic situation. It is the factual situation which is to be explored through investigation in order to

[3] E. C. Tolman, *Purposive Behavior in Animals and Men* (New York: Appleton Century, 1932), p. 3.

[4] John Dewey, *Logic, The Theory of Inquiry* (New York: Henry Holt & Co., Inc., 1938), p. 104 and following.

[5] F. C. S. Northrup, *The Logic of Science and the Humanities* (New York: The McMillan Co., 1947), p. 30.

provide guideposts for action. In drawing this distinction Northrup is in effect distinguishing between a problem of action and a problem of knowledge.

Another useful approach is the recognition of the three stages of the act as proposed by Mead.[6] These stages are perception, manipulation, and consummation. In relation to this framework there would appear to be three types of investigative procedure which might or might not be included in a given inquiry. One procedure consists of an extension of perception in the direction of more precise and quantitative observation and utilizing means other than the unaided senses for recording and measurement purposes. A second procedure is the test manipulation of a small sample of the objects which may eventually be manipulated in full scale action. Such test manipulation is called experiment. A third procedure is the manipulation of symbols rather than of the ultimate objects of action in a manner that is thought to parallel the manipulation of the objects themselves. A large part of mathematical physics and also of mathematical economics illustrates this procedure of the manipulation of symbols.

Another major consideration as to the relation of inquiry to action is the status of the so-called pragmatic test of truth. The man of action, who will hereafter be called the executive, would have little patience with the notion that a statement is true because it works. The writer has had long experience in research of the kind that is designed to serve the ends of action in the economic sphere. His clients would not be happy with the assertion that only by applying survey findings could their truth be determined. They would say that the investigator had been retained in the hope of avoiding the costly procedure of trying out plans of action to see if they would work.

What the executive wants from the investigator is general statements of fact which he can rely upon in framing a program of action. Executives who are accustomed to use the results of inquiry are increasingly concerned with the question of reliability. They would understand and approve Churchman's fundamental principle for all science, namely, that the general goal of science is the progressive reduction of errors of measurement toward the limit of zero.[7]

The executive would applaud such efforts to provide data which he could accept with confidence. He would not understand or accept the pragmatic test of truth since it is not the data which must work

[6] George H. Mead, *The Philosophy of the Act* (Chicago: University of Chicago Press, 1938), pp. 1-25.

[7] C. West Churchman, *The Theory of Experimental Inference* (New York: The MacMillan Co., 1948), p. 173.

but a program of action framed with the data in mind. It is the full scale manipulation of the objects of action which affects the "objective transformation of the situation." Facts alone, or facts and generalization together cannot dictate the shape of action or relieve the executive of his ultimate responsibility for the commitment of resources to action.

The Nature of a Problem of Action

Before discussing the special problems of "action" research, it is necessary to comment briefly on the nature of a problem of action. Mead's analysis of the act pertains most directly to a single project or major decision. The executive normally operates within a system of action which has the character of a going concern. In such an action system the manipulation of the objects of action is proceeding from day to day according to prescribed methods which may have been largely reduced to repetitive routines. The executive undertakes to keep the system functioning by maintaining balance among its various parts, by improvising means for meeting emergency developments not covered by established procedures, and by adapting the system to changes in underlying conditions. He tends to identify his own interests with the survival and successful adaptation of the system. To act is to direct and perpetuate the functioning of a system of action. The executive's power to act rests upon the operating capacity of the system.

The executive entertains certain expectations concerning the outcome of the system of action. A problem arises when he experiences uncertainty as to the realization of these expectations. At any given moment the executive relies on the normal functioning of most of the established procedures which are integrated into a system of action. He concentrates his attention on parts of the system which have become infected with uncertainty. Sometimes his sense of uncertainty may spread until he has doubts about the system as a whole. In any case it is this uncertainty which is the essential ingredient of a problem of action.

Efficiency and Power

The general problem of the executive can be defined as the problem of efficiency so long as he takes the goals of action as settled. For any specified goal there is presumably a most efficient way of accomplishing it, or a most effective way of employing his available resources toward that end. Uncertainty about the methods now in use will ordinarily stimulate a search by the executive for more efficient methods.

As for the operations of a business firm in a market economy, it is helpful to conceive of executive action in terms of opportunity and effort. From his judgment of the market, often supplemented by detailed market analysis, the executive determines which segment of the market his firm can serve most effectively with its skills and resources. A move toward capitalizing on market opportunity parallels at the level of deliberate and rational choice the occupation of an ecological niche by an animal species. Having selected certain opportunities in the market, the firm's efforts to exploit them must take specific form in order to equal or exceed the efficiency of competitors. This stage in the process of adaptation to the market parallels the specialization of an animal species in the process of making the occupation of its niche effective.[8]

The rational executive must avoid over-specialization for his firm. This is an important qualification of the principle that he seeks maximum efficiency. While his general goals such as profit-making may remain unchanged, opportunity is subject to continuous change and sudden shifts. Thus over-specialization is an even greater hazard for the business firm than for an animal species since market opportunity can disappear or change its character much more quickly than an ecological niche. Furthermore, production and marketing techniques are undergoing rapid development. The executive will not invest a large amount in equipment designed to make his plant the most efficient in his industry today if he knows that much more effective techniques will be available tomorrow.

These considerations lead directly to the fundamental principle of rational action. The executive will act in such a way as not to dissipate the power to act. Whatever may be the more immediate and limited objective which he is pursuing, the overriding objective is the perpetuation of power. The gravest uncertainty as to the outcome of action is not whether it can achieve its immediate goal but whether it can do so without impairing the power to act. The more serious form of waste as compared with the waste of effort is the waste of capacity.

This principle provides a rational criterion which is inherent in the nature of action. Many issues can be decided by direct reference to this criterion. A proposed course of action might so clearly impair the power to act that it can be quickly discarded. Routine decisions

[8] Julian Huxley, *Evolution, The Modern Synthesis* (New York: Harper & Brothers, 1943), p. 263 and following.

can be made promptly because they do not have any significant bearing on the power to act. A third class of decisions may be designated as strategic decisions because of the possibility that the power to act is seriously involved. Rationality, which is a scarce resource at best, economizes itself by giving prior consideration to strategic decisions.

Formal inquiry is often undertaken when a strategic decision is to be made. New conditions or new objectives may call for an adaptation of the system. Established routines may be discarded and new routines devised to replace them. In carrying out such changes the ruling consideration is that the system as a whole shall continue to survive as a balanced set of potencies. Investigation is directed toward minimizing uncertainty as to the preservation of the power to act during the course of the adjustments and modifications in the system.

The Diversity of Action Situations

The problems of the executive have so far been discussed only with relation to uncertainties which affect the use of resources under his direct command. It has been stated that the rational executive will use these resources in such a way as not to dissipate the power to act. Efficiency alone is not an adequate criterion for rational action. There are risks involved in striving for the utmost efficiency in a single direction. The executive may prefer to retain a certain amount of versatility in order to have the power to effectuate other objectives as they arise and to meet changes in operating conditions.

The power precept is also fundamental in considering the use of resources which are not under the direct command of the executive. Uncertainties as to realization of expectations may arise because of the absence of essential cooperation or the presence of effective opposition. Rational action must consider means of obtaining cooperation and eliminating or neutralizing opposition. Action then takes the form of persuasion or coercion in order to maintain or extend the operating system.

Fact-finding is often employed as a means of dealing with this type of uncertainty. Surveys are undertaken for the frank purpose of proving a point. This type of study tends more and more to obey strict canons of scientific research technique. Those who are to be influenced by survey results are increasingly knowing judges of what constitutes valid research findings.

Perhaps the oldest use of fact-finding has been in situations involving potential coercion such as criminal trials. Some methods of determining guilt were very crude, such as obliging the accused to walk across a bed of hot coals and then examining his feet to see whether they had blistered. There is a long subsequent history as to rules of evidence and the admissibility of certain classes of facts. In recent years the courts have been struggling with the problem of admitting statistical data as evidence in cases involving economic issues.

The point with respect to such fact-finding in the present instance is that evidence is used to arrive at judgments which are then to be enforced by a higher authority. Aside from court action there are many special types of arbitration bodies which may utilize fact-finding. Within a restricted system of action, such as a business firm, the chief executive may have to arbitrate disputes between subordinates in order to keep the system operating. The facts may have nothing to do with personal culpability since the disputes may be concerned with different positions as to policy. Very extensive surveys are sometimes made which from the executive viewpoint primarily serve the purpose of restoring or improving cooperative relations within the system of action.

The role of fact-finding in connection with this phase of action, namely, in the use of force or persuasion, is clearly quite distinct from science in the ordinary sense. While scientific techniques may be used in the collection of data, the determination of what facts are to be collected rests squarely on what is needed for purposes of persuasion or arbitration. However objective the research may be that is used for these purposes, there is no question that the arts of persuasion enter in a critical way into this kind of problem of action. In such cases the issue facing the executive cannot possibly be reduced to a question of inquiry alone. To remove uncertainty from his outlook he is obliged to influence or to predict the actions of key individuals which is in sharp contrast with the problem of predicting mass behavior.

The three kinds of action problems which have been discussed are those of operating decisions within the domain of direct executive control, the necessity of obtaining cooperation through persuasion, and the similar need for eliminating opposition or conflict by means of arbitration or legal decision. This division resembles the list of occasions on which the policy-maker may resort to inquiry as developed by Robert Merton.[9] Actually the categories are not usually so

[9] Robert K. Merton, "The Role of Applied Social Science in Formation of Policy," *Philosophy of Science*, (July, 1949), p. 161.

distinct in practice. Persuasion and coercion merge into each other in various ways. Their complex relationships in economic activity have been described by John R. Commons.[10] Similarly it is difficult to set a definite boundary between the domain of control and the parts of an action system which the executive does not command directly.

There are also qualifications to be made in the application of this general point of view to various kinds of action systems. Individuals are associated in some behavior systems primarily because of the congenial nature of their contact with each other. In systems which have specific operating goals, association is largely instrumental or there may be various combinations of congenial and instrumental membership character. There is also a difference as to whether an action system has a specified date or result as its anticipated point of termination. Thus a group of individuals consisting of two parties to a negotiation will generally cease to exist as a system of action when the negotiation is concluded. The concepts of effort and opportunity, of specialization and versatility, of efficiency and the power precept would require appropriate interpretation for application in different types of action systems.

Action Research and Science

The use of scientific research techniques is more and more prevalent in what is here designated as action research. In that sense research designed to serve the ends of action may be designated as a phase of science. For purposes of clarity and to promote the development of this field on its own merits it should be distinguished from both pure science and applied science as those terms are usually employed.

Action research does not contribute directly to the broad objective of pure science, namely, the advancement of knowledge. The immediate urgency which prompts the executive to authorize an investigation is uncertainty concerning his operating situation. He administers his action system on the basis of a set of operating assumptions. These assumptions have to do with the facts about his situation and about the adaptation of his program of action to the facts. His confidence may be shaken by failure of the program to fulfill his expectations. He may propose to venture into new fields and therefore contemplate modifications in the program.

[10] John R. Commons, *Institutional Economics* (New York: The MacMillan Co., 1934), pp. 336-339.

In many cases of this kind the executive specifies the information that should be gathered by investigation. He is, in effect, selecting certain of his operating assumptions to be tested. These are the beliefs which must be reaffirmed, revised, or definitely refuted, before the executive will be ready to frame a new program of action.

In other cases the executive expects diagnosis as well as fact-finding from the investigator. The logical first step is for the investigator to make a comprehensive list of the operating assumptions which the executive appears to be making. He undertakes to make his own selection of assumptions which may be erroneous or seem doubtful enough to suggest that they should be tested. This is the stage which corresponds to the framing of a hypothesis. In fact the investigator may set alternatives for one or more of the executive's operating assumptions and design his study so as to provide a basis for choosing between the alternatives in each case.

This method of choosing hypotheses for testing differs from methods that would ordinarily be followed in pure science. Instead of canvassing every aspect of a single situation the scientist would be more likely to consider a single aspect or factor as it might apply to many situations. His study might produce a generalization which would be useful to many executives. Thus applied science might furnish some of the tested operating assumptions in any action situation. In most cases the executive has to make additional assumptions of a very specific character which could only be tested by direct inquiry. The social sciences are still very young and their applications are correspondingly uncertain. The place for direct inquiry may be narrowed as social science advances or with the multiplication of broad fact-finding programs such as those of the Bureau of Census. In the meantime the competent investigator makes use of such general data but often finds that they have to be supplemented with information from inside or outside the client firm.

The assignment to the investigator or consultant often goes beyond either fact-finding or diagnosis. He may be asked to make recommendations as to new operating programs to meet the problem situation. He must recognize in undertaking to make recommendations that he is working in an area that lies outside the field of research proper. Factual information provides the framework within which a program of action must be devised but there may be several programs which are equally feasible with these limits. Further research cannot go very far toward facilitating the final selection among plans. It would not be economically feasible to pre-test every detail of an operating plan in advance. More than that it is not the details that will have to be subjected to an ultimate test but the integrated operation of the plan as a whole. There is no difference between testing the plan and installing it.

Instead of testing a plan in operation there is the device of manipulating symbols which are believed to work together in a manner paralleling the interaction of forces and objects under the plan. Several kinds of models are available for this kind of analysis as will be discussed presently. There is also the possibility of a pilot plant operation to locate and eliminate operating difficulties which do not show up in the laboratory. Some sales testing is done in marketing but there is drastic limitation on the disclosure of an operating plan through such tests because of considerations of sales strategy and the danger of arousing opposition prematurely.

Measurement, Experiment, and Model Building

The previous section mentioned three broad types of investigative procedure which may now be reviewed briefly from the standpoint of general methodology. These procedures are measurements, experiment, and model building. In the field of marketing, the area in which the writer has had his own research experience, rapid progress is being made in techniques of measurement and in understanding what constitutes valid measurement techniques. Probability sampling has become the established norm even though it offers special difficulties because of the wide areas from which samples must be drawn, in many cases embracing the continental United States. Various kinds of bias are being recognized and methods are being sought to eliminate them.

One of the great weaknesses of marketing research at present is that only limited progress has been made in the direction of developing experimental methods. Most surveys of consumer demand rely on respondents as informants concerning quantities consumed, attitudes toward products, buying plans and many other matters. Progress is being made on the first point by establishing panels to keep purchase records. Attempts are being made to devise experiments in which an attitude is indicated by a behavior response rather than by a mere statement of attitude. Interest in the experimental method is strong and great advances may be seen in the near future.

Another aspect of methodology is the use of models in attempting to determine how a plan will operate. Mathematical models have long been employed in theoretical economics but mostly at a level of generality which threw little light on operating plans in specific situations.

The econometric approach has been somewhat more flexible and has had an increasing number of applications to business problems. The use of the calculus has been supplemented by other types of mathematics such as a set theory in some recent theoretical model building.

Of more immediate importance in helping the executive to reach a decision is the use of small-scale three dimensional models. The demonstration table is a standard tool of the engineer in planning factory layout and similar devices have been used in some phases of marketing. Lacking a type of model which can throw light on the processes comprising a plan of operation, reliance must still be placed on a detailed verbal description of a plan which can be subjected to the informed judgment of the executive and his associates. Such descriptions are often supported by charts, diagrams, and maps to assist in visualizing the plan in operation.

There is believed to be a place in constructing models of action systems for the use of modern symbolic logic. Some applications have been made to engineering and organizational problems. Preliminary explorations in marketing give promise of a new field of usefulness for logic. At the very least it should be helpful in identifying the principal possibilities for action within a system obeying certain stated restrictions. This development in marketing, as well as measurement and experimental techniques, falls within the field of interest of the philosophy of science.

The Power Precept and Ethical Principles

Some version of the power precept, namely, "Act so as not to dissipate the power to act" has been advocated by thinkers of such different bent as Macchiavelli and Edgar Singer.[11] The real distinction is whether or not the precept is held to be an ethical principle. The present view is that the power precept is not an ethical principle any more than the scientific precept of seeking progressively to reduce errors of observation to zero is an ethical principle. It has only been asserted with respect to the power precept that it is the fundamental principle of rational action. Power is not set up as the basic goal of action in the preceding discussion. The point is that preservation of the power to act is a necessary condition of success whatever objectives are chosen.

The subject matter of ethics is responsibility rather than knowledge or action in themselves. The search for a satisfactory ethics

[11] Edgar A. Singer, Jr., *On the Contented Life* (New York: Henry Holt & Co., Inc., 1936), p. 147.

grows out of the human sense of responsibility and the effort to cope with diversified responsibilities which are not always consistent with each other. The individual's ethical need cannot usually be resolved in terms of loyalty to a single organization. Each individual belongs to a number of action systems, each making claims upon him. The problem of conflicting claims as it impinges on the business executive has been cogently analyzed by Chester Barnard.[12]

The individual may try to live with this pattern of conflicting responsibilities in a variety of ways. He may give a relatively high rating to one claim and a low one to another. He may make an effort to meet all claims or to meet only those which are backed up by inescapable compulsions. One possibility is to adhere to a fundamental principle which may serve as the criterion against which all claims may be evaluated. Different individuals may choose this principle in different ways. In a given culture there may be some convergence toward a single principle based on what appear to be successful lives within that culture.

A basic characteristic of our own culture is that many individuals pursue their purposes within the same system of action. In order for each to maximize the realization of his own expectations he makes commitments to others about what they may expect from the system. Among these commitments are those which concern the status expectations of the individual since the substance of his status is power to act in various directions. This use of the term commitment is not inconsistent with the earlier discussion of commitment of resources. The executive commits resources under his direct command and prevails on others to commit their resources in return for reciprocal commitments concerning their expectations as to goods or status.

Individuals communicate with each other within a system of action and the certainty or uncertainty of their expectations depends upon the reliability of these messages. Much of what we accept as knowledge is communicated rather than observed. The messages may vary in content from simple operating signals to detailed commitments concerning future status. Because of the impact of communication on expectations an important phase of responsibility is responsible communication.

Frustration results from the failure of expectations to be realized in accordance with commitments. There is a strongly subjective aspect in frustration so that the executive could hardly be held respon-

[12] Chester I. Barnard, *The Functions of the Executive* (Cambridge: Harvard University Press, Cambridge, 1938), pp. 258-284.

sible for all feelings of frustration within the action system. The emphasis here is on what might be called objective frustration. This term is meant to designate failure to realize expectations despite the fact that the individual has put forth effort and has lived up to his own commitments. From this viewpoint the fundamental ethical principle might be stated as follows: The responsible individual will choose his commitments and his communications in a way that is calculated to minimize objective frustration. As an ethical principle this precept lies somewhere in the broad expanse between Kant and the Utilitarians, between duty for its own sake and the greatest good for the greatest number. Unless the sense of responsibility is in some degree innate in human life and culture, there is no ethical problem but only a problem of expediency. The power precept then becomes an adequate rule of life.

The proposed ethical principle is socially oriented but unlike the utilitarian principle it presents a program rather than a common goal. It recognizes plurality of purposes in its criterion of minimizing frustration. It states a basic condition for meeting this criterion, which may be approached through a more favorable distribution of knowledge, power, and responsibility.

The principle of rationality inherent in action itself is preservation of the power to act. The shape of action is further determined by science and ethics. The theory of action must not usurp the role of either. Its central concern is the strategy of decision in a world of scarce resources and multiple objectives.

14. RESEARCH AND THE SCIENCE OF MARKETING *

S. F. Otteson

Among the words that rate high on the list of popularity in the marketing profession are these: "science," "theory," "principles," and "research." There is a rather general feeling that it would be nice to have marketing classified as a science. This is evidenced in many ways, including the statement which sets forth the purpose of the American Marketing Association, "An association for the advancement of science in marketing." [1] A review of new courses in marketing theory and a flood of articles bearing that label provide ample testimony to the fact that several members of the marketing profession consider theory important and highly desirable. Likewise, titles of introductory marketing books, together with statements in their prefaces, indicate the desire for more marketing principles. Finally, the interest in research manifests itself in many ways, and some members of the American Marketing Association criticize the society for being what they call a marketing research assoication. What does all of this mean? The writer wishes to develop the idea that these various interests are closely inter-related, and though sometimes misguided, they point toward a general improvement in the stature of marketing as a profession.

To begin with, why is there the desire to call marketing a science? Perhaps the term connotes sophistication; perhaps some marketers and kindred souls believe that such a label puts them on a professional and academic plane along with the natural and physical sciences, assuming they have not already reached or surpassed such levels. On the other hand, perhaps there are more significant reasons for the interest in developing marketing into more of a science. An exploration into the nature of a science may cast further light upon this possibility.

* Reprinted by permission from S. F. Otteson, *Marketing: Current Problems and Theories*, Indiana Business Report No. 16 (Bloomington: University of Indiana School of Business, December, 1952), pp. 11-18.

S. F. Otteson, Professor of Marketing and Chairman, Department of Marketing, University of Indiana.

[1] *National Roster 1950-51*, The American Marketing Association, p. 17.

The problem of semantics must always be reckoned with. One group of scholars looks upon a science as a method of dealing with basic problems and of seeking general truths through an orderly process of inquiry. For purposes of brevity this is referred to as the "method concept" of science. A second group of scholars considers a discipline to be a science to the extent that a body of theories, principles, and laws have been formulated. They consider a discipline as a science to the extent that a fund of organized and systematized knowledge has been developed. Again for purposes of brevity, this is referred to as the "fund of knowledge" concept of science. Both of these general approaches center around problem solving. One emphasizes method and the other lays stress upon the results. Each of these is now examined in somewhat greater detail.

The "method concept" places great emphasis upon the evolutionary nature of things. We are constantly examining and re-examining the known body of knowledge, discarding old concepts and adding new ones, and striving to reach universal truths. The process is dynamic rather than static. What is considered a final answer or explanation today may be discarded tomorrow as a result of new evidence or further examination. Those who stress this point of view quite logically place their emphasis upon the method of inquiry rather than the results of inquiry.

Some students who adhere to this approach or point of view believe that the method itself must be experimental, which requires that all variables in a given study be isolated and controlled, except for the one variable being observed. It should be possible to measure the latter with a high degree of accuracy. Such a restriction would exclude any of the so-called social sciences from the realm of science. If these lines are to be drawn, perhaps the scholars in such fields as biology and zoology should be reminded that there are only a few objects to which complete experimental control can be applied. Certainly each of the various elements in the guinea pig cannot be measured nor can they be compared in an absolute manner for homogeneity, or diagnosed with finality to determine their interrelationships, particularly if the pig is to live for further experimentation on a following day. Control is relative, and while the field of marketing and similar fields recognize the difficulty of much control, there are, and always must be, efforts made in that direction.

Now let us examine the "fund of knowledge" concept of science and the way that it relates to marketing. In the field of marketing, as in most other fields, we are continually solving or attempting to solve problems. Some of these problems may be entirely unique, distinctive, and dissimilar to all others. These must be analyzed and studied on an individual basis, and each solution is completely limited to the problem at hand. This may be slow, expensive, and often times subject to much guesswork. The desire, then, is to classify problems into groups so that those in each group have common solutions. Once a workable solution is reached, it can be applied to every problem that comes up, providing that the problem fits the group. These solutions or generalizations are known as hypotheses, theories, principles, or laws.

Many definitions of these terms can be found. There seems to be some agreement that they are all considered to be generalizations or general solutions to a class of problems. Some students prefer to speak of them as statements of cause and effect relationship, but in the social sciences we sometimes have difficulty in determining what is the cause and what is the effect. The concept that is set forth in this chapter is certainly not the only one, but it is believed to be highly useful and is rather generally accepted. As indicated in Exhibit I, this concept draws a distinction between these four types of knowledge on the basis of the degree to which they have been verified and accepted.

A hypothesis is merely a tentative solution which has not been verified and is not accepted. A theory is a generalization that has been verified at least in part and is accepted by some but not all students in the field. A principle has greater verification than a

EXHIBIT I

DISTINCTION BETWEEN HYPOTHESIS, THEORY, PRINCIPLE, AND LAW

Hypothesis	Generalization	Not verified	Not accepted
Theory	Generalization	Partially verified	Partially accepted
Principle	Generalization	Verified	Generally accepted but understood to have some exceptions
Law	Generalization	Completely verified	Universally accepted and has no exceptions

theory and is generally accepted but with the understanding that there may be some exceptions. A law has been appropriately referred to by Dr. T. N. Beckman of Ohio State University as "a principle with whiskers." In other words, in terms of our present understanding, it has been fully verified, is universally accepted, and has no exceptions.

In line with this concept, one might wonder why there is so much interest in marketing theory. Some people may be intrigued with the word itself, as they are intrigued with the word "science" because they believe that it sounds sophisticated. Others may think that it represents advanced learning. This may very well be true. New hypotheses, and upon some verification new theories, often result from a new or further synthesis of existing knowledge. Perhaps, then, there should be as great an interest in formulating new hypotheses in the field of marketing as there is in developing new theory.

There are those, of course, who look upon theory or "the theoretical" as being the impractical. This is a rather interesting bit of confusion. Where do theories come from? Are they not an explanation of practice? To the extent that they are verified, are they not based, at least indirectly, upon an observation of practice? Can you label a generalization about practice as being a theory unless it explains or describes that practice? If theory does not explain practice, then it is not good theory!

In terms of this "fund of knowledge" concept, do we actually have a science of marketing? Very few would agree that we have marketing laws. Most students seem to think, however, that a body of marketing principles exists, and most introductory texts are concerned with principles of marketing. How many principles are actually contained in some of these books? Are not many of these so-called principles only theory, at best? Upon close examination, should not a great number of them be classified merely as hypotheses? How much genuine effort has been expended in verifying many of these so-called principles? So far as acceptance is concerned, could it be that they are generally accepted because the reader has little basis for making his own appraisal, has little information about how the author attempted verification, or has little interest anyway in the principle per se?

If a body of theories, principles, and perhaps laws is to evolve, the means is through research. Inasmuch as confusion also seems to surround this activity, its nature and scope are often misunderstood. Some conceive of marketing research as a survey; others believe it to connote a questionnaire; and there are those who even confuse it with public opinion polls. Such confusion is detrimental because it tends to limit the scope of problems that may be investigated and also the scope of method that may be employed. Examining the definition itself, we find marketing research defined as any purposive investigation which has as its objective the obtaining of knowledge of any business activity necessary to affect the transfers in the ownership of goods or to provide for their physical distribution. Thus, marketing research embraces all methods and techniques of inquiry that can be applied in the solution of marketing problems. Likewise, its scope encompasses all problems or facets of problems in this field.

Quite apparent then, the extent to which marketing is a science is determined in great measure by the nature and exhaustiveness of research in the field. From the methodological approach, the method and techniques of marketing research form the basis for the method of science in this field. From a "fund of knowledge" point of view, the extent to which a body of theory, principle, and law is developed is limited by research.

If this is the case, then how can the method of inquiry in marketing be improved upon so that the science of marketing can be augmented? The answer seems to lie in three parts. The first is concerned with the scope of inquiry, the second with the technique of inquiry, and the third with the depth and thoroughness of inquiry.

Much progress has been made in recent years to treat marketing research in its proper perspective. But there is still too much emphasis upon consumer surveys, sales analysis, and a few other important but narrow and somewhat isolated aspects of the field. The argument is not that these aspects should be given less attention, but that much additional attention should also be given to many other things. We must apply much more research and seek tested solutions to the broad social and economic problems in marketing. The problems considered in the various chapters of this book are indicative of those that come within the province of research. We must pay more attention to buying, financing, and other marketing functions. They are just as worthy of research as is the function of selling. Likewise, considerably more effort can be expended upon research directed at improving our marketing institutions. These are but a few illustrations of the many areas in marketing that could greatly benefit by further scientific inquiry.

Considerable criticism has been heaped upon the social sciences, and marketing in particular, for their lack of proper research techniques. Some is warranted while some is perhaps exaggerated. To begin with, the marketing profession is criticized for its slowness in accepting new statistical tools and for its failure to use the tools of statistics correctly. Many of the latest techniques of small sampling have been accepted by the quality control people in the manufacturing field, and certain government agencies have done much to incorporate advanced statistical method in their research. But the marketing profession, except for isolated instances, has been slow to adopt the more recent developments in statistics, particularly in sampling and "analysis of variance" in analyzing its problems.

So far as the correct usage of statistics is concerned, the mail questionnaire probably comes in for the greatest criticism. This criticism is often justified, particularly so when only a small portion of the questionnaires are returned, yet those that are received are used as a basis to describe the entire group, including nonrespondents. A further criticism of usage is aimed at the sampling techniques often used in marketing studies. The "purposive" or sometimes called "in-ratio" sample, such as used in most public opinion polls, is often used in marketing studies. Serious valid objections are raised to this method of sample design. Also, once a sample is extracted, even a good one, many marketing studies are criticized for failing to recognize sampling error. This is particularly important when conclusions are reached for a portion of the sample, e.g., one state or one type of respondent, since the sampling error could be particularly great in such circumstances. A further criticism of statistical usage is directed at those who accept statistical measures categorically as the final answer or explanation. While good statistical procedure can give a clear quantitative picture or measure of relationship, within defined limits, it cannot prove cause and effect relationship. Even more important, social statistics represent what has happened under a given set of circumstances, with almost an infinite number of variables entering into play. Since these variables are so numerous, and many of them cannot be controlled, we must assume a great amount of stability and order if this picture of the past is to be useful in solving problems for the future. Fortunately, there is a great deal of order and consistency that surrounds a considerable share of issues in marketing. But every statistical measure must be seasoned with judgment if it is to be used properly in a given situation. Perhaps this phase of the discussion can be summarized by stating that statistical method provides an invaluable tool for reasoning, but it is absolutely no substitute for reasoning.

While several other objections have been raised concerning marketing research and the science of marketing, the final criticism discussed in this chapter is leveled at the lack of precision and finality in our findings. The so-called principles are said to be clothed in so many "tends to" and "other things being equal" that they lack usefulness. This can be explained rather easily. Any relatively new profession which encompasses such a broad field of practice is faced first with the task of gaining perspective and of dealing in some manner with the general problems that exist. Solutions to such problems in this state of development must at best be tentative. Within each broad problem lies many unsolved problems; each of the latter has many complicated facets. After all, the human being is just one unit in much of our work, and we have psychologists and psychiatrists who spend their entire professional lifetime trying to understand this one unit, freely admitting that they are just scratching the surface. But as the science of marketing develops, we can concentrate more and more upon exploring the detailed facets of the problems which have been treated rather superficially for the lack of time, resources, or sufficient knowledge. While the zoologist patiently spends years to study the genes of the fruit fly, the economist or marketing man is studying such problems as the general causes and cures of the public cycle. To the zoologist, the latter is analogous to studying the causes of death. While these very broad basic problems must be spelled out, and the social scientist should not be criticized for doing so, there comes a time in the development of a science when great efforts are needed to explore the many detailed facets. This is our next step in the march of marketing toward becoming a science.

One of the approaches that should prove extremely useful to such an accomplishment is the case study method of inquiry. The medical profession, and to some extent the field of sociology, has already benefited from this approach and has achieved some excellent results. Surely there are many other existing techniques and there will be many new ones which will improve our method of inquiry in marketing. Only through the persistent and diligent application of proper method will we augment and refine our body of theory, principles, and perhaps laws in this field.

15. OPERATIONS RESEARCH AS APPLIED TO MARKETING PROBLEMS *

John F. Magee

A well-known student of marketing problems, in a recent article, says: "If all operations analysts were shot at sunrise tomorrow, company market researchers would live longer and die happier."

Needless to say, I am not at all in sympathy with the suggestion implied, and I hope those of you who are on the fence will in time take a firm stand in opposition to capital punishment for the members of the Operations Research Society. I sincerely believe, based on our experience, that market research and operations research people can live and work together profitably, and that jointly they can make substantial additional contributions to the efficiency of marketing and distribution problems.

Most of the examples which have appeared in the literature about operations research have been concerned with work in production planning and inventory control, traffic and communications problems, military tactics, or data-handling methods. Not much has been said about work in problems with a strong marketing flavor. In some ways this is a compliment, indicating as it does the importance placed on it by the companies who have had operations research teams working in the marketing area, and their desire to keep details of what they are doing under cover. The only two companies that I know have mentioned their work in this area are the Lamp Division of the General Electric Company, and Imperial Oil. Actually, in our group we find ourselves putting more effort into problems centered about marketing than into any other single area. If the interest in and growth of work on marketing problems in our own group is any measure, I would predict that in the future, marketing will be one of the most fertile areas for use of the experimental and analytical skills of operations research to complement the knowledge and techniques of present-day marketing research.

* Reprinted by permission of John F. Magee, from a talk delivered before the Chemical Market Research Association in Boston, November, 1956.
John F. Magee, Arthur D. Little, Inc.

Examples of marketing problems

Here, in brief, are some examples of what operations research teams have been doing in marketing problems.

The executive committee of a company making a line of light machines questioned the amount of money spent for missionary salesmen calling on customers. Studies and experiments were made which resulted in numerical statements of (1) the relation between the number and types of accounts called on and the effect on sales volume, and (2) the relation between sales and manufacturing and distribution costs. These were brought together, and by using the methods of differential calculus, tables were set up which could be used for picking the level of promotion in each area, depending on economic and marketing conditions, which would maximize company net profits. The results showed that nearly a 50 per cent increase in promotional activity was economically feasible and would allow substantial profits.

An operations research team has been engaged in a continuing program of study for a manufacturer of chemical products. This has resulted in measurement of the sales impact of various types of trade advertising and promotion of a number of the company's products. The most important result has been the development of a pretest method. This allows the company to determine, using some short experiments, the responsiveness of new products to advertising, and their expected market life. These pretest results give the company a rational basis for setting up promotional campaigns on new products to get the degree of market penetration which will maximize long-run profits.

A research program was undertaken for a shoe manufacturer operating a captive chain of retail outlets. The job was to find out how the chain could best be operated to maximize the return on investment of the parent company. The studies resulted, among other things, in a cost control method based on statistical concepts similar to quality control. It also brought to light an important but previously unrecognized inconsistency between the basis for store manager compensation and the goals of the company. It turned out that store managers had a much greater incentive to sell clothing and accessories purchased on the outside than to sell the company's own manufactured products. This turned out to be just the wrong thing to do, from the point of view of company-wide return on investment.

One of the most difficult problems in many types of retail chain operations is getting an accurate estimate of what the potential volume of business at a particular site may be in the light of expected traffic and existing competition. An operations research team has been working on this problem for one chain operator and has developed a preliminary mathematical model or theory which appears to tie together a lot of hitherto unexplained marketing data, and on a trial basis appears to improve ability to predict volume very substantially. Work is continuing to test out the method, and if the initial promise holds up, it will represent a substantial breakthrough for this company in planning their marketing investments.

Another operations research team attacked price problems for a manufacturer of basic chemicals. This company is not the dominant figure in its field; and though demand is currently keeping capacity fully employed, the company was concerned about what would happen when new units of capacity were installed, in view of the existing price structure. The research team worked out a pricing basis which would permit the company to capitalize on certain location advantages it had, and to defend its market position against larger suppliers in the event of excess capacity. The company has implemented these results and has seized the pricing initiative in its field. For what it's worth, one of its major competitors had dismissed operations research until the results of this study went into effect. Since the word leaked out that the new pricing system was based on an operations research study, the competitor has moved rather quickly to plan its own operations research activity.

It is perhaps misleading to characterize these problems as marketing problems, if one implies that these are the sole or primary concern of a marketing function in a business. Attack on these problems characteristically requires not only a study of marketing operations and customers' reactions to marketing effort, but also an investigation of cost and operating characteristics in the production and distribution system. In short, while these problems have a strong marketing flavor, in the sense that detailed investigation of marketing operations is required and that the work frequently results in modification in marketing methods or plans, they are really company problems, and company-wide interests must be taken into account. This suggests an important objective of operations research—to reduce the pressures bearing on particular plans or decisions as far as possible to numerical quantities, so that company management will be in a position to reconcile these pressures to the best advantage of the company as a whole.

Several other companies, including a large financial house, a petroleum company, and one of the large food processors, have undertaken studies by operations research teams in the marketing area. These include studies of advertising effectiveness, competitive problems, location of facilities to improve market service and penetration, and product line.

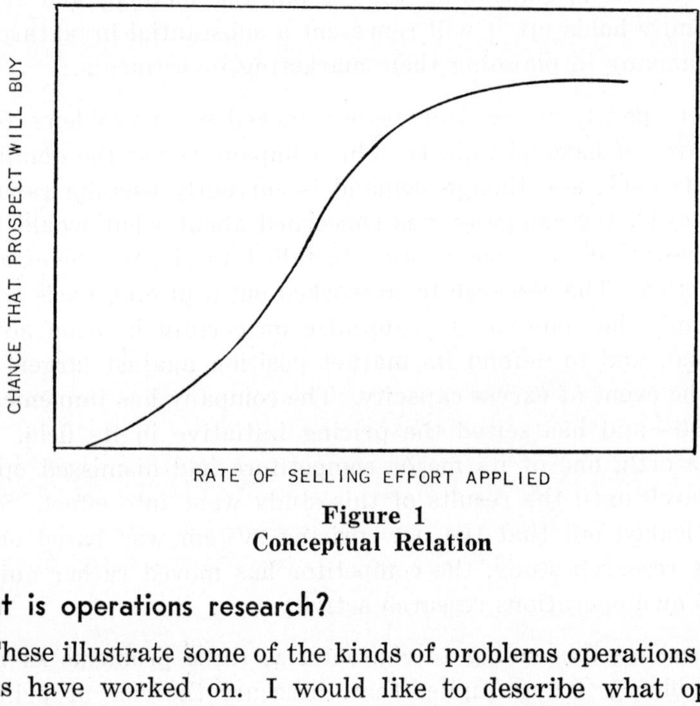

Figure 1
Conceptual Relation

What is operations research?

These illustrate some of the kinds of problems operations research teams have worked on. I would like to describe what operations research is and what it does, in terms of a typical marketing problem—budgeting sales effort. I realize that this covers only a small part of the complex of problems facing management in marketing. In many industrial concerns, this problem may not be important—for example, where products are sold on very long-term contracts, or where geography has an overwhelming effect on sales. I think it will illustrate the kinds of things operations research teams do. In the course of this discussion, I would like to use some illustrative charts and graphs. I have necessarily been forced to disguise the products and the scales used in these graphs; otherwise, the relationships and the data shown are real and are the result of work on real business problems.

Operations research teams use the techniques of experimental science and men trained in these techniques to do these things:

1. By experiment and observation, to define and measure important relationships needed for management planning and control—for example, the relation between the amount of selling effort and the payoff in sales;
2. Using numerical or mathematical techniques, to analyze these relationships to predict the effect of alternative operating methods and strategies—for example, changes in assignment of selling time, or changes in the promotional budget;
3. To check by experiment the accuracy of these predictions; and
4. To recommend to management improved operating methods, based on these tests and analyses.

I would like to look first at the problem of experimentally measuring basic relationships. For example, it is generally conceded that a salesman must put in effort to sell a prospect, and in many cases, the more effort put in, the more likely is the salesman or promotion to complete the sale.

One idea as to what the relation between selling effort and outcome or payoff might look like is illustrated in Figure 1. The horizontal scale represents the rate or amount of selling effort applied to an account or prospect, and the vertical scale represents the chance that a sale will be made as a result of that effort. Figure 1 is pure imagination; the first job of an operations research study of many selling operations is to find out by experiment what this relation really looks like and how to measure the horizontal and vertical scales. What are the numbers that characterize this relationship? What is meant by "effort," or payoff? How fast does it rise? Does it level off? When? What does the relationship depend on? Is it different, for example, for different types of products or for customers of different size, or under different conditions of competition, or in different economic circumstances, or for different salesmen?

There are indeed many difficulties in trying to locate and measure any relationship of this sort—difficulties due to differences in salesmen, in customers, in economic and competitive conditions. Happily, however, the measurement difficulties that arise in this problem are not at all unique to sales problems; they arise in other fields that are equally vague and equally difficult to explore. Techniques for designing experiments and making measurements are being built up and are available for use. Analysis of variance and covariance is one such type of technique that can be used to sort out the various effects of different circumstances and conditions on this fundamental relation between effort and results.

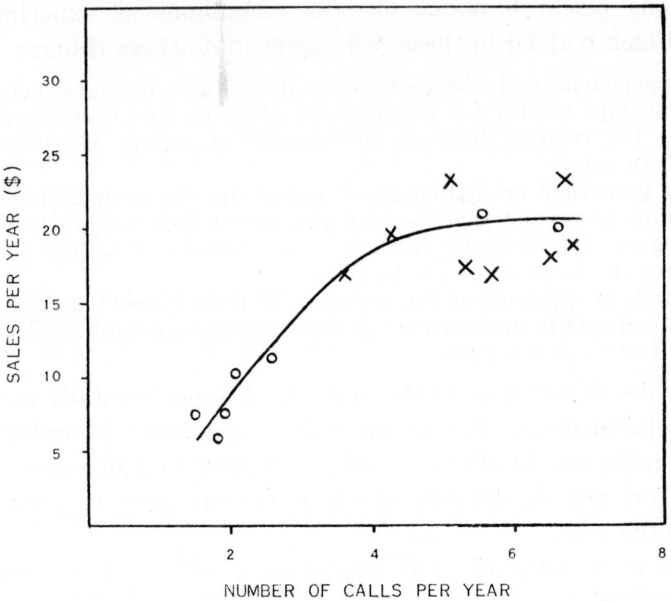

Figure 2
Annual Sales Per Customer vs. Frequency of Calls

To illustrate, Figure 2 shows what was found in the case of a consumer product. This product is sold door-to-door, and the estimate of this payoff function was constructed by analysis of salesmen's call records. The horizontal scale in this case is the frequency of calling on a particular customer, i.e., the number of calls per year; the vertical scale is the average amount purchased per call. The apparent relationship indicated by Figure 2 shows a characteristic form, similar to Figure 1—low return for very small effort, a sharply rising area when effort really begins to pay off, and the flattening out of results at high rates of effort.

In many cases, life is not as simple as indicated by the last example. A number of different selling approaches may be used, with the selling approach a combined effort on the part of salesmen and advertising campaigns. There is usually a line of products, and advertising and selling effort have different effects depending on the product characteristics. Display and availability are important, particularly in consumer retail items. Another important point is the question of who is to be sold—whether the dealer or consumer, in retail items, or the buyer or user, in industrial items. These may make measurement and experimentation more difficult, but the same experimental methods will still work. I don't want to leave with you

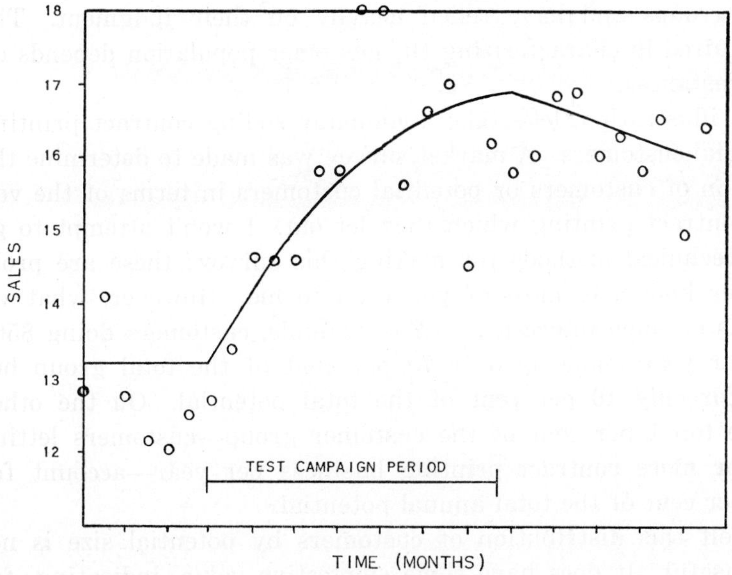

Figure 3
Growth in Sales vs. Time under Promotion

the impression that I think running experiments of this type is easy; I don't. These experiments are time-consuming and delicate. On the other hand, they can be made, and meaningful results can be obtained. It is important that they be made, because getting a measure of the relation between effort put in and the results obtained from a particular customer or prospect is fundamental in getting a real grasp on selling problems.

Here is another dramatic illustration in Figure 3. The product is a technical service type product, such as a grease, which is sold through promotion to equipment dealers who recommend the product for the equipment servicing which they do. There are a number of competitive products, and it is fairly easy for a dealer to shift from one to another. The result of the promotion is a rapid rise when dealers are converted to the use of the product promoted, and then a slow decay in sales as the dealers are gradually won away to competitive products.

Another type of experiment and measurement has to do with building a numerical picture of sales operations describing the customer population—in terms of number of customers, potential business, and other characteristics which may be identified as important. This, of course, is an area where market research methods are particularly valuable, where we have worked closely with market research groups and have relied heavily on their judgment. The detail required in characterizing the customer population depends on the circumstances.

As an illustration, let's take a company selling contract printing to industrial customers. A market survey was made to determine the distribution of customers or potential customers in terms of the volume of contract printing which they let out. I won't attempt to go into the technical methods for making this survey; these are probably better known to most of you than to me. However, what we found was of some interest. . . . For example, customers doing $500 or less per year make up over 70 per cent of the total group but account for only 10 per cent of the total potential. On the other hand, the top 1 per cent of the customer group—customers letting $10,000 or more contract printing business per year—account for over 30 per cent of the total annual potential.

In itself this distribution of customers by potential size is not directly useful. It does have some suggestive value, indicating, for example, the tremendous importance of the few large printing buyers. However, combined with the results of the experiments and the experimental measurements of the relation between sales effort and payoff, this distribution puts us in a position to make some significant progress. On one hand, we have an estimate of the chance of gaining a customer or holding a customer, related to the amount of sales effort put in; on the other hand, we have a distribution of customers according to volume, which gives us a basis for knowing how many customers of any given size we have to work with. We can now begin to play these relationships one against another, to decide just how much of the market we should attempt to tap, how much of our effort should go into trying to gain large new customers vs. trying to hold moderate-sized existing customers. This brings us to the second job of an operations research team: to use numerical and mathematical methods to manipulate the relationships that have been found and measured, and in this way to uncover improved operating methods or strategies for management to consider.

For example, with the measurements and relationships described before, we are now in a position to begin to answer questions like these: How and where should sales effort be used? How much sales effort should be devoted to various types and sizes of customers? How many accounts and prospects should be assigned to a particular salesman? How many salesmen in total can be effectively employed in view of the estimated revenue they will produce and their cost?

There are a number of techniques for attacking these questions once the relation between effort and payoff is known, and we have some description of the customer population. These techniques range from arithmetic to more complex methods. The classical methods of the calculus may be used, and in some cases even more esoteric approaches such as game theory may have a place. In some cases it may be satisfactory to attack these problems with pencil and paper, while in others it may be productive to use computing equipment. An analyst who is well versed in a range of these techniques and has a good sense for the physical realities of the problem can use the ideas and basic principles which are common to these techniques fairly readily in getting at answers to operating questions of the type I have posed.

There is one principle which is fundamental to all of these; that is to adjust the use of effort in order to get an equal added profit or return on the advertising investment from the last dollar spent on each medium or customer. This is by no means a new principle; it is very similar to the principle underlying the economist's marginal analysis. What is new or added is this: first, we have isolated and measured the relationships needed to apply this principle, and have changed these from abstract concepts to numerical quantities; second, we have techniques to manipulate the numerical relationships in order to apply marginal principles in practice.

For example, using mathematical or arithmetic techniques of the type mentioned, it is possible to construct a chart like Figure 4 [page 180], relating sales obtained to promotional effort in total. This chart was derived for the problem I mentioned earlier of door-to-door selling of customer products. The solid line shows the derived relationship based on the detailed measurements of results obtained vs. effort put in and on the statistical analysis of the customer population. The points show various experimental checks that were made in field trials.

One might ask: Why go to the bother of working out the derived relationship? Why not obtain the relationship directly from experimentation? There are at least three reasons why building up this relationship from detailed analysis was fruitful:

1. Any relation between effort expended on promotion and results obtained implies a determination of how different increments of promotional effort would be used. The preliminary analysis was necessary to arrive at an efficient answer to this question.
2. Preliminary analysis gave us a close enough understanding of individual customers' behavior to permit accurate adjustments for dif-

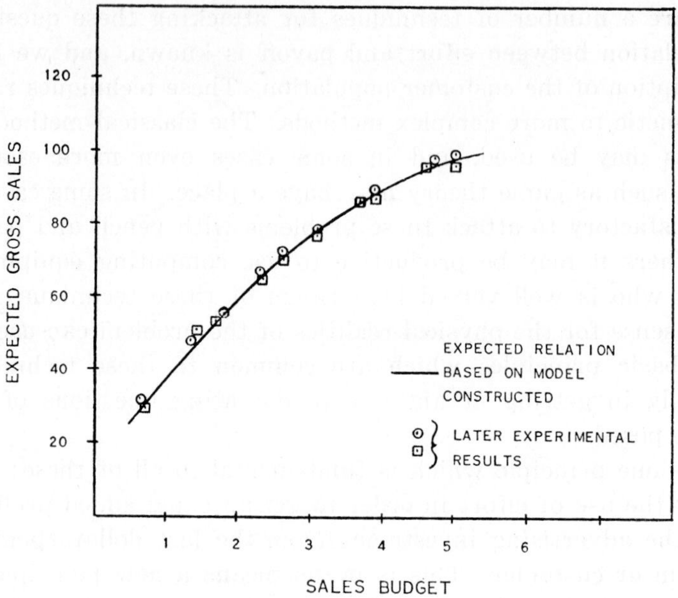

Figure 4
Expected Gross Sales vs. Sales Budget

ferences in sales results due to economic or geographical differences. Without the preliminary work, it would have been extremely difficult to interpret the experimental results to account for extraneous influences.

3. A check between the derived relationship based on detailed analysis and the experimentally observed relationship gave us confidence both in the analysis which had gone before and in the validity of the experimental results.

In Figure 5 [page 181] I have tried to illustrate how these pieces tie together into a coherent picture of a marketing operation as a whole.

Digging out, measuring, and building up relationships of the types described is one of the prime jobs of an operations research team in helping business management program sales activities. With relationships of this type stated and measured, together with analyses of production, distribution, and promotion costs, the team is in a position to look into such questions for management as: How big should the promotion budget be? At what products or customers should it be directed? What media or promotion methods should be used? What sales and profits can be expected? How can tests be set up to measure and control results on existing products and sales areas, or to spot the characteristics of new products or customer markets which are developed?

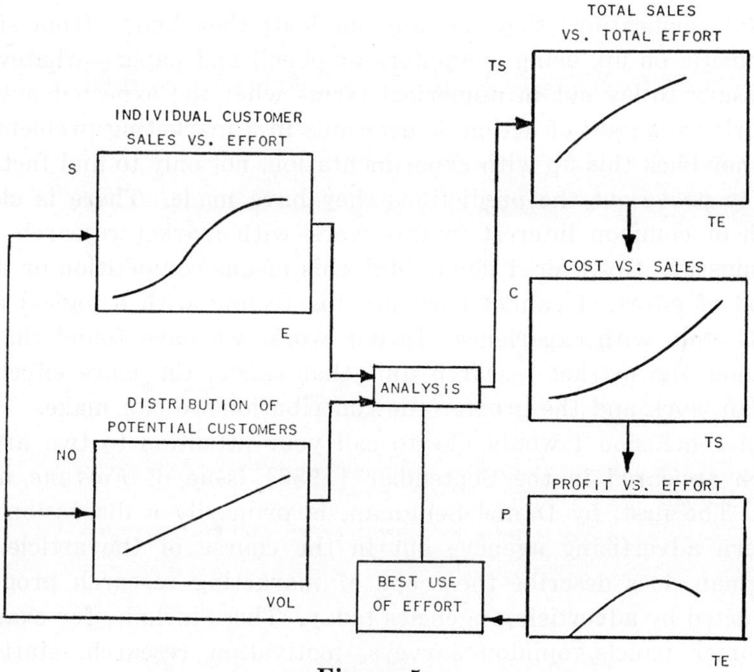

Figure 5
Illustrative Model of Sales Budgeting

1. First, as shown by the graphs to the left, we must start with a measure of the relationship between effort spent on an individual customer or prospect and the payoff expected, and with measurement of the distribution of customers as a whole.
2. Then, by numerical or mathematical analysis of these, we can measure the relation between total effort expended and total sales expected, on the upper right. This may be checked experimentally.
3. Analysis of operating and distribution costs related to volume, and knowledge of the effort required to get a given sales volume, gives the raw material for measuring total operating cost vs. sales volume or, alternatively, the total operating profit.
4. The relations between volume and profit, and between effort and volume, give the relation between effort and profit. From this we can choose the optimum range of total effort.
5. The analysis which yielded a measure of total sales resulting from a given amount of effort can indicate how best to use the level of effort agreed on; i.e., which customers to concentrate on, and how much effort to spend on each type.

Conclusion

The examples I have given do illustrate the sorts of things operations research teams try to do in the marketing area: they experiment; they dig out relationships tying together action and outcome; they state these in numerical terms suitable for analysis and experimental verification; they use any methods they know, from simple arithmetic on up, using computers or pencil and paper—whatever is necessary to lay out in numerical terms what the expected outcome of various courses of action or decisions in a marketing problem will be; they back this up with experimentation, not only to find facts but also to prove out the predictions they have made. There is clearly much of common interest in this work with market research units in industry. However, I don't think this means competition or duplication of effort. I cannot back up this feeling with a logical argument—only with experience. In our work, we have found that the stronger the market research unit that exists, the more effectively we can work and the greater the contribution we can make.

In conclusion I would like to call your attention to two articles which appeared in the September [1956] issue of *Fortune* magazine. The first, by Daniel Seligman, is primarily a discussion of a modern advertising agency; but in the course of the article, Mr. Seligman does describe the scope of marketing research programs conducted by advertising agencies today. These include, for example, consumer panels, opinion surveys, motivation research, statistical studies of market potential and characteristics, advertising readership measurements, and the use of the results of this work in guiding media selection, advertising campaigns, product policy, packaging, promotional appeal, and other aspects of merchandising programs. These research programs cover much of what I as a layman understand to be meant by the term marketing research.

By way of contrast, there is the second article in *Fortune,* entitled, "How I sold Listerine," by Gerard B. Lambert. Mr. Lambert describes the experiments and test methods he used to get a measure of the sales response to promotions and how these results in turn were used to devise advertising strategies. Mr. Lambert gives a large share of the credit for his success to the meticulous experimental and analytical work done. You, as marketing people, might feel that Mr. Lambert's point of view was rather narrow, and I wouldn't quarrel about that. Nevertheless, it is safe to say that his approach was different from that normally taken in marketing research, and it was clearly successful in supporting or buttressing his marketing genius. Mr. Lambert's point of view toward experimentation and analysis, backed up with modern experimental and analytical techniques, epitomizes to me the role of operations research in marketing problems.

16. OPERATIONAL THINKING IN MANAGEMENT *

Martin Goland
Boyd Ladd

To those of us in executive and administrative pursuits, our ability to remain in intelligent control of our work reduces to three basic requirements: we must have pertinent background information readily available when a problem arises; we must have at our disposal useful techniques for interpreting the data; and we must use data appraisal and experience-based judgment in proper proportions when evaluating the factual background and when arriving at the final decision.

One approach to the problem of having information available and interpreted is to appoint a staff assistant, or other form of adviser, with the assigned responsibility of keeping abreast of the company-wide activities and of being immediately available for the conduct of special studies. An alternative approach to the information problem, and one which is daily gaining acceptance in business and industry, constitutes a refinement in the manner in which the company history is recorded and scrutinized. This approach can be best summed up as a company-wide, coordinated effort to collect, preserve, and analyze those data which define and govern the company dynamics—the underlying mechanisms which determine its daily conduct of business.

The tools which are adding this new management dimension are the much-discussed methods of electronic data processing (*EDP*) and operations research (*OR*).

EDP AND OR

OR. The literature on operations research thus far has been concerned principally with demonstrating the types of services this new discipline offers. A variety of tools has been developed which permits the exercise of the scientific method when dealing with certain of the semitechnical and nontechnical management problems encountered

* Reprinted by permission from *Western Business Review*, Vol. 2, No. 2 (May, 1958), pp. 90-95.

Martin Goland, Vice President, Southwest Research Institute.
Boyd Ladd, Research Faculty, Operations Research Office, Management System Division, The Johns Hopkins University.

in business and industry. The basis for the scientific method is the process of careful observation of the facts relating to a problem, the formulation of a hypothesis which apparently ties the available facts together by a rational cause-and-effect argument, and finally the experimental check of the hypothesis to assure its validity and determine its range of usefulnes. With a dynamic hypothesis deduced, the operations researcher is then able to assess with confidence the effects of changing conditions. He is then able to seek the optimum solution to the problem under study.

An *OR* model is dynamic in the sense that it represents causal relationships. Once the factors entering into a situation are known, the sequence of consequences may be inferred with definiteness and with known precision. This cause-and-effect basis for *OR* is simultaneously its greatest strength and its greatest practical weakness. The strength is derived from the conviction with which a prognosis can be made. The weakness is that few management problems are completely determined by the identified causes, nor are they completely rational and reducible to mathematical terms. Hence, at best, *OR* will offer a valuable, yet circumscribed, view of the "best" solution. The executive, the decision-maker, must fill in the gaps and supply the final judgment which enables study to become action.

Within the bounds of its capabilities, *OR* performs several valuable functions. To begin with, expensive trial-and-error empiricism is replaced by the collection of minimum experimental data required to substantiate the underlying hypothesis. Second, knowledge is formalized, so that similar or analogous problems encountered in the future can be solved directly and with relative ease. Finally, it enables management to view its problems from a position closer to the strictly logical viewpoint of the mathematician. This accomplishment adds new horizons to the ability to deal with complex problems governed by many interrelated influences.

EDP. In electronic data processing, it appears that the time has come to transfer some of the planning responsibility from the shoulders of the computer specialist to the management group. *EDP*, it must be recognized, is a business force which is here to stay. Because of the far-reaching importance of *EDP* in determining the character of information-handling throughout the organization (a significant factor in the expense of doing business and in the effectiveness of business performance), it becomes a management responsibility to understand and interpret the role of *EDP* in his company.

In technical research, the laboratory director is often called upon to direct programs which are outside his immediate scientific experience; a chemist, for example, may find himself responsible for the success of certain mechanical engineering research. Despite his lack of specific engineering training, it would be folly for him to rely wholly on his staff for decision-making. His general knowledge of the conduct of research, coupled with his unique understanding of how the program mates with the overall company objectives, makes his participation vital to the success of the undertaking. If the laboratory director is so completely lacking in appreciation of mechanical engineering as to be incompetent to guide the overall research, then perhaps we must conclude that he is incapable of filling his job.

Analogously, the modern executive must be able to fathom the forces which are gathering to alter the practice of management.

Comments on the Current Operations Research Scene

A great deal of writing on *OR* and *EDP* has been widely distributed in recent years. For this reason, no attempt is made here to repeat what has been said many times over. However, it may be useful to offer some comments on the current scene, pointing out what progress is being made in the practical utilization of both techniques.

The practicality of undertaking *OR* analyses is being aided significantly, in many cases, by the growing availability of *EDP* services. In a recent management conference on "Electronics in Action," for example, papers are listed on the use of linear programming for gasoline blending activities, on the use of linear programming for the planning and expansion of plant facilities, and on the use of Monte Carlo methods for the study of inventory controls. It should not be inferred, of course, that automatic computers are essential for the conduct of *OR* studies, although the problems investigated are often of sufficient complexity to require some aid from automatic data processing equipment.

The chief obstacle to an even more widespread acceptance of *OR* appears to be a continuing lack of empathy between some practitioners and some company executives. In talks with a number of executives who have investigated the possibility of using *OR* services within their organizations, we find that all too many have been repelled by an excessively autocratic attitude on the part of those who propose to do the work. As one company president expressed himself after a meeting with a potential consulting group: "If I pay them a large sum of money each month, they'll agree to look into my affairs, with the hope they'll be able to help with some of my problems. Of course, they insist on a completely free hand to meddle where they please. No objectives stated—no cost estimate given. No thanks, not for me!"

While there is some legitimacy to the idea that an operations research team cannot guarantee results, just as no research team can assure important new findings, there is little justification for the idea that *OR* cannot be approached in the same manner as any other form of applied research. Goals can be established at the outset and cost estimates made in the manner that investigators in chemistry, engineering, and physics use experience and judgment to appraise the requirements of an applied research goal. Modifications of the end objective and the costs may become necessary as events unfold, but these will emerge as logical topics of discussion when the *OR* team presents its progress reports to the company executives.

The *OR* team may sometimes be forced to report unusual difficulty in arriving at a solution, either because a suitable *OR* model has not been deduced, or because data cannot be collected as easily as originally thought. Once again, it is a matter of executive decision as to how far the research gamble should be continued.

At any instant, however, an applied research team should have a definite program in mind—one that can be made to appear reasonable to those bearing the costs. The classification of *OR* as a "pure" science, in which the investigator is permitted the luxury of drifting wherever his research may lead, does not appear to us to be valid. Operations research in practice is an applied science, and it must conform with the same rules and philosophy which have been found to be successful in the purely technical branches.

OR problems. Some of the difficulties in putting *OR* to work can be ascribed to the unfortunate tendency of practitioners to insist that *OR* is "new." Many operating executives fall in with this fallacy and expect the results from *OR* to be spectacularly novel. The realistic point of view is that careful thinkers always have been present in business and industry. It is hair-splitting to classify their performance in the past as not having been within the spirit of operations research.

Techniques available. The *OR* worker of today can, however, improve on the past. He can take advantage of recent developments in mathematical techniques. Linear programming, for example, makes it possible to calculate the most commercially advantageous flour mix, or the cheapest way of routing a fleet of trucks over a prescribed delivery route, or the optimum production schedule for a factory. Queuing theory ("waiting-line" theory) enables the precise analysis of traffic problems, whether the traffic consists of automobiles on roads, paper-work traveling through a secretarial department, or material being handled in an inventory system. Monte Carlo methods permit the field reliability experience with a new product to be tested in advance of actual sales. These are only illustrations of the special tools available today which give powerful insight into long-established problems. *OR* is "new" only in the sense that past thinking has been formalized within a mathematical framework; the same elements are present, but the formalism of mathematics enables small elements of the problem to be captured and held intact until the overall fabric can be woven and the final pattern determined.

Since common sense is the fundamental approach of *OR*, none should be mystified by the techniques used as tools. Whether or not the executive follows the details—and doing so is the business of the specialist—an *OR* analysis need not be obscure or frustrating. If the thinking person cannot, with guidance, appreciate the methodology and understand the findings, it is the analysis which is at fault, not the viewer.

Examples of OR application. To conclude this brief overall view of the current *OR* scene, it may be worthwhile to mention some of the areas where the technique has convincingly demonstrated its utility in practice.

In inventory problems, *OR* is now an accepted study technique. Even a cursory glance at the inventory problem shows its obvious relationship to the production and sales functions of the company. It is hardly surprising, therefore, to find that many *OR* studies which commence in the inventory area end in penetrating analyses of production capabilities and sales policy. Minimum inventory cost at the expense of more frequent, expensive production runs is hardly an overall economy. Similarly, the inventory level should not be reduced so sharply as to involve undue risk of unavailability, either of subcomponents on the production line or of finished products for delivery to customers. In regard to customer deliveries, it is evident that forecasts of the coming market and company policy in regard to delivery speed are both factors which directly affect the required inventory level. The balancing of these varied items, and many more, for optimum effect is by now a classic problem in the *OR* library.

The influence of sales policy on company profits is another type of problem in which *OR* teams have met with considerable success.

An increase in the sales budget reflects itself throughout the organization, for greater sales mean more production, a greater volume of accounting and other services, and increased capital commitments. What, then, is the best policy for a particular company to follow? *OR* may not provide the final answer, but it will disclose how sensitive company operations are to the overall volume of business, and it will illuminate points where sales effort is not in balance with the other branches of the organization.

TRANSPORTATION. Transportation problems have often been solved with signal success by the *OR* techniques of linear programming. The routing of truck fleets has already been mentioned as a problem in this category. Where warehousing is employed in the delivery system, the planning of warehouse locations has been integrated into the study. Even the size and location of new production facilities has been determined by the *OR* approach, which affords a picture of the interrelationships between raw materials, market areas, labor costs, transportation costs, and other influences. Additional transportation solutions on record include the optimum routing of bus systems and the best methods for designing port facilities for marine freight handling.

Product optimization for greatest profits, as exemplified by the flour-mix and the gasoline blending operations, is also a standard application of *OR* techniques. In cases where the properties of the components to be blended continuously vary, or where price fluctuations in the blending components or final mix are rapid, the optimum-mix problem has been coded for speedy solution on automatic computers. Frequent rescheduling of the production process to meet the product requirements with best cost advantages is then possible.

STATISTICAL ACCOUNTING. Statistical accounting, now in use by the airlines and railroads, may also be classed as an *OR* innovation. Where large numbers of counter-billings between two parties must be handled, a carefully planned statistical sampling in place of complete unit accounting has been found to yield excellent (and predictable) accuracy in determining the final credit balance, with considerably reduced accounting costs. Probability sampling in controlling the accuracy of unit charging (as in the case of airline ticket pricing) is also a logical area for the use of statistics in accounting.

It is interesting to note that the *OR* movement within airline management has grown to impressive proportions. The manner in which high-cost aircraft and engines can be employed with minimum traffic loss should be a most suitable area for operations research. The distribution of maintenance facilities and spare parts over the route, in order to ensure minimum schedule disruption due to mechanical difficulties, is typical of the problems receiving attention. New-route studies are also appropriate areas for the *OR* approach. Within the airline industry a consistent effort is being made to integrate *OR* and *EDP*, so that information availability and information analysis can be combined the better to serve the needs of a highly technological enterprise in which speed is essential.

The scheduling of production lines is another classic *OR* problem. In plants producing a variety of items, the older and simpler methods for determining the most economical lot sizes for individual products are giving way to a more comprehensive visualization of the entire production entity. Plant scheduling can be determined for the best overall effect, taking into account the relative desirability of replacing old equipment with new, the influences of overtime policies and changing labor rates, and so forth.

GAME THEORY. Finally, brief mention should be made of the growing powers of game theory in appraising competitive situations. Not yet a truly practical tool, save in special circumstances, considerable research attention is being given to adapting the powers of game theory to throw light on such problems as the best use of advertising and the establishment of optimum pricing policies to permit one company to "defeat" another in the competitive and changing game of free enterprise.

EDP today

The current scene in electronic data processing hardly requires review here, since the breathtaking speed with which *EDP* is altering information handling is well known even to those who follow its development only casually. It is sufficient to say that new equipment is appearing daily, specifically designed to meet the needs of both small and large companies. Older equipment—and here age is counted on a scale of very few years—is already at work in scores of organizations to good effect. It is significant to note that a recent government decision permits the submission of quarterly reports of wages taxable under the Federal Insurance Contributions Act in the form of reels of magnetic tape.

Indicative of the range of new equipment being offered is the recent appearance of a small computer priced at around $40,000 and incorporating most of the essential automatic features of even the largest machines, including the capability of punched paper-tape input and output.

The computer manufacturers, for their part, have squarely faced the need of tailoring their equipment to the requirements of commerce as well as science. Those who use computers, on the other hand, have overcome their first impulse to seek quick answers to whether, and how, they should make use of this new tool. The idea is now commonly accepted that the relative advantages of introducing *EDP* into a company should be evaluated by detailed study, aimed at determining whether the unique requirements of the organization can be efficiently mated with the performance capabilities of the available equipment.

One area which will probably grow in importance in the coming years is the development and use of special-purpose management computers, whose function will be described through an illustration. In a public utility, management was interested in studying the complex problem of overall system operation on a continuing basis. In the particular case in mind, inputs into the system could be drawn from a number of alternate points, with the most economical operation resulting when these points were balanced with the changing market requirements. In addition to this dispatching function, it was desired that the computer enable the study of the relationships between company profits and such factors as changing local and federal tax structures, capital requirements, and fluctuations in total sales.

The one stipulation placed on the design of the machine was that it should be operable by the company executives themselves, with no requirements for specialized computer training of any kind. The inputs were to be presented in a form which would permit immediate visualization of their significance, and the answers were to be displayed with immediate clarity.

The solution of this problem introduces the interesting possibility of using a general-purpose data processing unit to perform rapidly the computing functions of each trial, and of arranging the inputs and outputs on a special-purpose computer panel which would meet the requirements of operation by the executive unconcerned with technical details. While the use of such a computer does not entirely conform with *OR* principles, in that it involves a trial-and-error approach as the basis for seeking the optimum answer, it does have the distinct advantage of enabling the executive to participate directly in formal studies of company dynamics.

The management computer may well provide one practical means for integrating the experience of management people with the more mathematical analysis of the Operations Research staff. Without an effective way of doing this, the firm's program of analyzing company dynamics may fail. But management people trying various combinations of operating inputs and side-conditions in the effort to find a "maximum return" position are likely to detect rapidly those respects in which the model built into the computer seems to be not entirely in agreement with experience. Thus the *OR* model, which always suffers from oversimplification, will be improved by building in new factors suggested by the operators' experience. Conversely, trial-and-error experimentation by managers on the computer is likely to engender respect for the power of analytic methods and the desire to extend their effective application.

Summary

Management's job is decision-making. Key elements required in systematic decision-making are: *facts, finding relationships among facts,* and the *feel for the situation* (i.e., executive discretion). Integrated Data Processing can provide the facts in quantity, rapidly, currently, and economically. Operations Research is sophisticated common sense, the tool for interpreting the facts and relating them to one another and to hypotheses about company dynamics. Executive judgment must guide the applications of *EDP* and of *OR* in the firm, must formulate the hypotheses, must establish the goals and the yardsticks.

The needs include: respect by *OR* practitioners for the management function; managerial self-respect and exercise of command in the face of technical details of electronic machines or of mathematical solutions; more effective exchange of information about applications; and tailored use-studies for data-processing planning. Management computers seem to offer a feasible technique for combining management experience and intuition with formal *OR* analysis and high-speed information-handling. Further research is justified, in our view, on developing objective guide lines for judgment, especially in formulating hypotheses as to company dynamics and in the empirical search for a best solution on the management computer.

New technologies assist management in the relatively routine fact-finding analysis and hence make more critical and more productive the creative work of devising alternatives and weighing the choices.

17. HOW TO DEVELOP IDEAS *

Joseph G. Mason

Ideas are vital factors in business survival today. Business, science, and government need all the ideas they can get. But in any type of organization, creativity must come from the top. Top and middle management executives must set the example.

If an executive himself is not a spectacular idea man, he must at least have enough knowledge and understanding of the creative processes that he does not inadvertently block or discourage fresh or different kinds of thinking within his organization.

This article covers two areas of creative thinking: the factors affecting creativity in you, as an individual; and some practical operational techniques of deliberate creativity—devices and procedures you can use to prime your imagination when you need ideas.

All studies to determine what makes a person creative point to four principal characteristics:

Problem sensitivity.
Idea fluency.
Originality.
Flexibility.

Experiments have demonstrated that all four of these can be acquired or developed to some degree in any individual. This does not mean, of course, that a person who rates low in using his imaginative faculties can suddenly be turned into a creative ball-of-fire. But he can, through application, learn to do more with what he has. At the same time, the naturally creative person can, through experience, learn to raise his already high creative output even higher.

* Reprinted by permission from *Nation's Business*, Copyright 1958, reprinted from the January, 1958 issue of *Nation's Business*.

Joseph G. Mason, Batten, Barton, Durstine & Osborn, Inc., Minneapolis, Minnesota.

Problem sensitivity

This is basically the ability to recognize that a problem exists; or to be able to cut through misunderstanding, misconception, lack of facts, or other obscuring handicaps, and recognize the real problem.

An example of an initial lack of problem sensitivity occurred during a course in creative thinking being conducted for a major research organization. As a homework exercise, the scientist-students were given six cartoons from magazines and instructed to write new captions for them. One young chemist turned in a particularly good set. After class, the instructor complimented him.

"Thank you," replied the student, "but those were just switches on someone else's ideas. I want to learn to think up new things."

To the instructor, this was the tip-off that the student, who had demonstrated an ability to be imaginative, had not learned to use his imagination to find opportunities for applying ideas. At the next class session, the instructor pointed out opportunities for chemists. Right in the room were the paint on the walls, finishes on furniture, composition ceiling tiles, flooring material, window glass, even the clothing the students were wearing and the textbook materials they were using. All of these represented opportunities for chemical improvements in either basic materials or methods of manufacture. He then gave the students the assignment of bringing in a list of 10 such opportunities the next week.

When, the next week, he asked the young chemist how he had made out on this assignment, he received a self-satisfied smile and the reply: "I've got a couple of ideas that I'm not even going to tell you about—I'm taking them home to work on myself!"

Find a better way to do it

Write it down

Actually, the easiest way to improve your problem sensitivity is simply to keep in mind that nothing is ever as well done as it could be. Every man-made article, every business operation, every human relations technique can be improved and someday will be. In every situation you encounter as an executive, no matter how many times you have met and handled it before, an opportunity exists to find a better way. If you can once learn to recognize these problems as challenges to your own creative effort, you will be half-way to finding creative solutions to such opportunities.

Idea fluency

This term simply means that a person can pile up a large number of alternative solutions to a given problem in a given time. The value of this lies in the fact that the more ideas you have, the greater your chances of finding a usable one; the more plentiful your opportunities to get out of the same old ways of doing things.

Idea fluency depends largely upon personal mental habits. It is an attribute that can be developed or improved by nearly every person who will consciously apply himself to it. The theories covering fluency development are simple:

First, remember that it is quantity you are after. Second, don't mix evaluating with your idea gathering. Get your ideas first—worry about whether they are good or not later on.

Devices to aid fluency development are just as simple, but more plentiful. Here are a few of the more common ones. Don't be surprised if you find that you already use one or more of these. Most executives use such techniques from time to time. The value of having them formalized lies in the confidence it gives you to know that these tools exist, that they have a purpose, that you can use them whenever you feel the need of them.

MAKING NOTES. The use of notebooks, or "think books" or "idea traps," as they are sometimes called, is almost universal. Nearly every businessman carries at least one pocket notebook or some substitute such as 3x5 index cards or scratch pads. Unfortunately, carrying it is often as far as he gets. Or, if used, it is merely a recording device for statistics such as names, addresses, or what to tell the serviceman about the car next time it goes in.

Note-making can be a big help in idea producing if the right kinds of notes are made and the right uses made of them. The first useful kind of note to make is one that captures any stray idea. Write it down. You have probably had the experience of "going to sleep on a problem," and waking in the middle of the night with a good idea. It was so obviously good that you knew you would remember it in the morning. But came the dawn and disappointment. The problem was still there, but the idea was gone. Idea men who really mean it keep pencils and pads all over the house and office to capture those stray ideas immediately, before they have a chance to get away.

Record your observations of circumstances: plant operations . . . personnel conflicts . . . office procedures . . . production problems. Later, when you find yourself with even a few free minutes, you can use such at-the-moment notes as a base for giving the circumstance some thinking time.

Record your conclusions or opinions on problems you have been thinking about. Frequently, a person spends hours, even days, working on a problem. After reaching some good conclusion (an idea or decision), and acting on it, he puts the problem out of his mind to work on the next one. Later, the first problem may recur in the same or a different form. The man may recall that he had thought that problem through once, but without a record of why he did what he did, chances are he will have to do it all again . . . or else take the risk that all conditions are still the same and the same action is still appropriate.

The statistical note does, of course, have a place. You should certainly form the habit of noting anything that may have possibilities for future use to you, however remote those possibilities may seem at the moment. In this class of notes may be included clippings from newspapers, magazines, books, etc. Psychological tests have established that on information of average interest (i.e., neither slight nor vital), the rate of forgetting is 25 per cent within the first 24 hours; 85 per cent within a week. In the face of this, pure memory-substitute notes do make sense.

But along with your note-making system, you will have to develop a note-using system to which you transfer your spur-of-the-moment notations at the earliest opportunity. This can be as simple or as elaborate as the problems you are making notes on. Actual systems used by successful and creative executives range from a simple cigar box (which never fills up because the owner constantly pulls out and uses his ideas) to an elaborately indexed and cross-indexed library of loose-leaf notebooks used by a leading physicist. (He does the filing and indexing himself—claims he gets the same pleasure and relaxation out of it that other men get out of arranging stamp catalogs.)

Whatever system you devise, remember that the objective is to enable you quickly to gather everything you have seen, read, heard, or experienced on a problem or problem area when you need it. Then, when you have the problem, be sure to use the notes. Frequently, the hardest part of solving a problem is just getting started on it. Your notes can provide a take-off or starting point to get you going. They will help stimulate your imagination as you begin the search for ideas.

PICK YOUR TIME TO BE CREATIVE. Every individual runs on a daily cycle. Each of us has a time during the day or night when he is most capable of creative or imaginative thinking. Conversely, you probably also have a time when you are most capable of cold-blooded analytical thinking. Your personal cycle is something you will have to analyze for yourself. Once you find it, however, set it aside and guard it zealously for ideating—use it for thinking about problems with a view to getting ideas.

Pick a time to be creative

Set a deadline

In the same vein, you may find that you create best in some special location. If so, try to use that location for creating. It is probably too much to hope that your day-to-day working schedule can be arranged to let you use both your favorite time and your favorite place for idea collecting, but if you should be fortunate enough to be able to have it this way, by all means do so. You want to give yourself every break in going after ideas.

SET A DEADLINE. It is human nature to procrastinate on problems. Yet prolific idea men find they are at their most creative in spurts—they get their best ideas when they really go all out to get them.

Sometimes, of course, there is a real and practical deadline to supply the urge to push yourself mentally. But you can also simulate such pressure by setting a deadline for yourself. If you really want to get yourself emotionally involved in meeting that deadline, just tell someone else that you are going to come up with 10 or 20 new ideas at such and such a time. This brings up another good individual spur:

GIVE YOURSELF A QUOTA. Remember that the aim of developing fluency is to build up your capacity to generate quantities of ideas. So start shooting for quantity right away. Don't set an impossible task for yourself, but if you can usually think up two or three ways something might be done, try setting a quota of at least five ways. When you can make five, up your quota to 10. When you get to 10, try 15 or 20. You shouldn't have to keep this up long before you will notice that, when a problem presents itself, your mind will automatically begin to run through many different ways of handling it.

You will probably find that the quality of your ideas is improving right along with the quantity. This gets back to the basic advantage of idea fluency: If you have a problem, and you have only one idea as to how to solve it, then good, bad, or indifferent, one idea is all you have. If it happens to fail, then you are right back with no ideas. If you have two ideas, chances are one will be better than the other. If you have 20 or 50 or 100 ideas, your biggest problem may then be to decide which is the best.

Originality

In the problem-solver this assumes many degrees. Ideas can range in value from the completely new abstract mathematical theory, down to a way to save 10 cents a day in the mail room. In practical, everyday business problem-solving, complete newness, or pure originality, is usually not what is needed. In fact, it may not even be wanted. The originality required of the business executive is more likely to be that of finding new ways to vary existing conditions, or new ways to adapt existing ideas to new conditions, or a new modification of something that will fit in an existing condition. The difference between a great business executive and an ordinary one is often his ability to produce these original variations to meet existing conditions.

The creative attribute of originality can also be developed, or at least simulated, to the point where it meets the requirements of successful business operation. The secret is in the systematic use of questions.

Challenge the obvious

One of the most noticeable characteristics of highly creative people is their overwhelming curiosity. These people are always asking themselves, and others: "Why is this made this way?" "Why do we follow this procedure?" "Is this object really necessary?" "How can we improve the way we do this?" Charles Kettering calls it "systematically challenging the obvious."

The person who does not have this questioning ability will probably never be creative. But such a questioning approach to life, or to business operations, is largely a matter of habit. Therefore, it is something that can be learned. Almost every business organization or business executive makes use of checklists in one form or another. Usually, these are just to remind us not to make any mistakes in an accepted procedure. But another form of checklist can also be used to remind us not to forget to be original. This is made up of operational questions that challenge the obvious aspects of a problem. Using such checklists to spur ideas can be the basis for forming the questioning habit in an executive.

Before going any further on this subject, it should be said that the executive should never forget that his questioning must be done in a positive frame of mind. Too many people use such questions as a way of establishing their presence in an organization. They never go after the answers—they just raise the questions. The object of creative questioning is to uncover new possibilities for better ways of doing things. The person who asks a creative question does so with the intention of trying to find the answer himself.

The best type of checklist is one you make up yourself to fit your own types of problems of a recurring nature. Using such a checklist takes a certain amount of initiative, however. Just a mechanical use of a checklist does not produce originality. The purpose of such questions is to provide challenges to obvious ways of doing things. Therefore, the answers to these questions must be well thought out—even if the final answer is: "No; this is the best we can do right now."

Idea checklists can often be improvised, too. For instance, a sales manager looking for new customers might get real benefit out of just leafing through the yellow pages of a telephone directory with an open mind. An office manager, trying to develop a more efficient utilization of office space, might get some ideas by paging through a trade publication devoted to hotel or kitchen planning. Since you are simply trying to find new or different ways of solving a particular problem, you can never tell when or where you will find an idea you can borrow. The originality may consist of the fact that this has never been used in your particular field before—and if it will solve your problem, settle for that.

Creative flexibility

The quality of creative flexibility is largely that of being willing to consider a wide variety of approaches to a problem. This, in turn, is largely a matter of attitude. Rather than obstinately freezing onto one particular idea, or a single approach to a problem, the flexible person starts out by remembering that if one solution won't work, he can always approach the problem from another angle. This is also called "creative expectancy"—meaning, the creative person just plain expects to solve the problem, no matter how many failures temporarily delay the solution.

You can't go far on the subject of creative attitudes before running into the mental blocks that restrict or hamper creativity. Dr. James E. Gates, dean of the School of Business Administration, University of Georgia, has summed up these psychological quirks rather succinctly as "the way we feel about things . . . the way we see things . . . the way we think we ought to go about things."

One quick pencil-and-paper demonstration will probably suffice to show common mental blocks can hamper you in a search for ideas. Let's consider the way we see things:

Here are two drawings of an object—the front view and a side view:

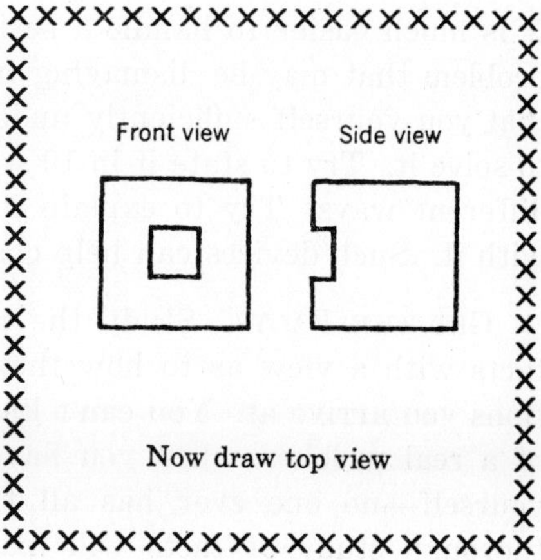

Now, before you read any further, take your pencil and, in one minute, draw the top view of this object.

You will find the top view, and also a cross section view, at the conclusion of this article. Chances are, you have drawn the top as a square or rectangular shape. Or, if you suspected a trap, you may have taken a wild stab at some variation of a straight-sided figure. However, this particular object is a cylinder. The square on the front representation and the notch on the side view show a small area milled off the side of the cylinder. Therefore, the top drawing should be a circle.

Why did you try to make a square or straight-sided figure? Because you were probably hampered by a perceptual block. Because two dimensions of the object appeared to be square, your mind immediately short-circuited to make the third dimension square also. Now translate this simple demonstration into a business problem, where two or three known factors are given to you, and you can easily see why it is sometimes difficult to prevent yourself from being forced into an obvious assumption about a third factor that may completely mislead you as to the course of creative action you should take.

Overcoming such mental blocks to creativity is, again, largely a matter of developing a healthy skepticism about the obvious. And the necessity to avoid being blocked makes a good case for having a systematic approach to solving problems.

As in checklists, the chances are no one method for processing problems is going to serve every businessman's needs.

Again, the best method you can use will probably be one that you make up yourself to suit your own types of problems. Therefore, the following method should be considered only as an example of what you might consider developing.

DEFINE THE PROBLEM. If it is large and complex, break it down. It is much easier to handle a series of small problems than one big problem that may be dismaying in its apparent complexity. Be sure that you yourself sufficiently understand the problem before you try to solve it. Try to state it in 10 words or less. Try to state it several different ways. Try to explain it to someone completely unfamiliar with it. Such devices can help clarify your own thinking.

GET THE FACTS. Study the conditions and relationships of the facts with a view as to how they will affect the value of any solutions you arrive at. You can't know too much about the background of a real problem when you have the job of solving it, but resign yourself—no one ever has all the facts. Sometimes just a good, thorough study of facts will make the problem solution apparent.

Go after ideas

Sit on it

If so, you can then forget the rest of these steps. But if, after studying the background and conditions of your problem you still don't see a solution, then . . .

GO AFTER IDEAS—but lots of ideas—all you and anyone you can get to help can think up. It is characteristic of any kind of problem susceptible to creative solution that there are many feasible solutions. The only guarantee you have that you will eventually pick the best solution to a problem is by making sure that you have thought of every possible solution. This is where idea fluency pays off. It is in this stage of the problem-solving that you use the various spurs and idea-starting mechanisms already outlined. And remember, don't at this stage let evaluation interfere with your idea collecting.

USE INCUBATION. If you have labored over a problem, and haven't as yet found a satisfactory solution, you run the risk of frustration. The best thing to do then is to get away from the problem—let up on your mind. Your conscious mind is only a small part of the mental powers at your disposal. Back in the memory cells of your mind may be dozens of facts and associations that you have completely forgotten about, and so haven't brought them into use on your particular problem. But they are still there in the subconscious. If you can just give them a chance, they may help you find the solution to your present problem.

Incubation is commonly referred to as "sleeping on the problem." In actual practice, however, it may be just a matter of breaking away from your desk to take a walk to the water cooler, or timing yourself so that you can knock off your concentration to go to lunch.

Evaluate Your Ideas. No collection of ideas, by itself, is worth anything until something is done with them. This means that plenty of cold-blooded judicial thinking has to be exercised and some decisions made. If you follow the procedure of starting with a quantity of ideas, it is probably best to do the evaluating in two stages: first, screen the ideas roughly for "possibles," "probables," and outright "impossibles." Then, tighten up your evaluation on the probables and possibles. There is also plenty of room for imagination in this decision-making phase. Often a seemingly impossible idea may be susceptible to a switch to make it usable. Asking creative questions about bad ideas can often develop new ideas or approaches that will be usable.

A final word on evaluating: You must learn to be objective. Too often, a person with a problem will go through all the motions of being organized and methodical in orienting the problem, gathering his facts, collecting literally dozens of ideas, and then will throw all the previous work out the window by adopting the idea he favored in the first place simply because he couldn't maintain his objectivity to the end.

Everything mentioned so far has concerned itself with what the executive can do to promote his own creativity. But no executive operates in a vacuum. A good executive realizes that he must operate through other people. In trying to inspire other people to be more imaginative or more creative, there are a few factors you will have to cope with. Recognizing that these exist is really the key to overcoming them, because an understanding of the situation will help you in planning your approach.

Here are a few of the things that keep the average person from being creative:

People prefer status quo

Laziness. Getting out of a rut requires effort. Creative thinking entails the hardest kind of mental effort. Unless there is some great incentive, and money is often not enough, people prefer the status quo. Life is so much simpler that way.

Natural Resistance to Change. People get in a rut. They like the ruts they are in because they know them so well.

LACK OF CONFIDENCE. This comes from lack of experience. The organized effort to promote more creativity is a relatively new force in our culture. You may as well assume that, up to now, no one has ever tried to encourage your workers to use their imaginations; no one has ever made them conscious of ideas, or what ideas are, or how to go about having them. You have the job of developing the confidence if you want the creativity.

FEAR OF RIDICULE. This is ingrained in most people through having, at some time in the past, had their ideas laughed at or ignored. It is still common practice today to criticize or laugh at unusual or different ideas before we have taken the time really to think about them and determine whether they are good or not. The executive who wants more ideas from his organization first has to create the atmosphere of encouragement and appreciation of creativity—the climate of safety—the freedom to fail.

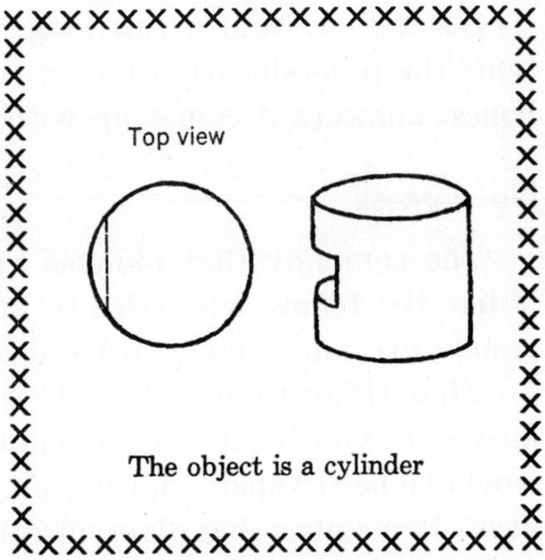

The object is a cylinder

No executive can inspire creativity if his own attitude toward it is skeptical.

The creative atmosphere cannot be accomplished through a complete organization overnight—no matter how sold or willing the management. This is even more so in the case of a company that may not have been paying too much attention to workers and their ideas in the past. But one thing we do know: Creativity must come from the top.

It could easily be that the road to success, fame, and fortune for an aspiring executive will be that he has used his own imagination to analyze, develop, and solve the problem of infusing his company with the necessity and the means of getting all-out, imaginative, creating thinking from everyone.

18. DIVERSIFICATION: WATCH THE PITFALLS *

Richard W. Dalzell

The road to product diversification can be rocky or smooth. But it's seldom easy. And the pot at the end of the rainbow can hold ashes as well as gold. On the record, there have been more failures than successes in this business of introducing new products.

Success or failure can hinge on how many soul-searching questions the diversification bound company asks itself—and how many honest answers it comes up with.

No cure-all

The company that plunges in without a close look at all angles is like the fellow who tries to break the bank at Monte Carlo. The results are more likely to be disastrous than rewarding.

First thing to ask yourself is whether diversification is the only answer to your problem. It could be that the time, effort, and money would be better spent shoring up weaknesses in your present business area. Remember that diversification is no cure for management shortcomings. It's more likely to aggravate the disease by generating new management challenges.

And don't be ashamed to back away if the proposition is not so rosy after close inspection as it looked at first glance. Too many times, managements have decided to enter a new business to justify the time and money spent on a program. Usually, these ventures lead to unhappy consequences.

Here are two basic areas you should look into before a new product is taken into the family:

1. What are the general objectives of your business as a whole? Do management and stockholders want to continue it on a long-term basis? Is capital buildup or current return more important to the owners? Are the stockholders in a mood to take on more of a risk than that involved in the existing business? Are there any operating characteristics of the business, such as seasonality, which should be remedied for the long-range good of the business?

* Reprinted by permission from *The Iron Age*, Vol. 178, No. 2 (August 16, 1956), pp. 51-55.

Richard W. Dalzell, Arthur D. Little, Inc.

These fundamental, long-term objectives should be clearly defined by management, of course, for general business planning. But it's particularly important that they be agreed upon before considering a new business venture.

2. Make sure you're doing as well as you should in your present business before shouldering new problems.

How to do it

If answers to the foregoing questions don't rule out diversification, here's how to go about it:

The first step is to take stock of your corporate strengths—and weaknesses. These resources may be human or physical and include such factors as acceptance in specific markets, established distribution channels, design and engineering skills, plant facilities, natural resources, highly skilled management in a given business area, and many others.

In our experience, we have found that management, technical skills, distribution channels, and market acceptance are generally the most important resources.

Production facilities and know-how, particularly in the metalworking industry—are a resource. But diversification based on production resources alone is usually risky because of the highly competitive situation in most areas of metal fabricating.

Strength versus weakness

Production-oriented companies, particularly those whose operations have been concentrated in contract manufacturing, many times prefer to diversify by buying a going business. In this way they obtain ready-made sales organizations, market acceptance, product design skills, and the like.

It is just as important to assess weaknesses as it is to recognize strengths. Frank recognition of deficient areas, such as lack of merchandising or product engineering skills, need not lead to a negative decision regarding diversification. However, it can lead to a program geared to overcome them.

In adding up strengths and weaknesses the management group might well consider one more factor: It should determine whether there is any type of business even remotely related to the current one which it finds interesting and stimulating. This human interest factor has been a prime contributor to success in several company diversification programs. Of course, no matter how much enthusiasm is generated by this approach, the new venture should still make business sense.

Product guideposts

After you've found out where your strengths and weaknesses lie, your second step is to formulate a set of rules for a new product or line. Such yardsticks are invaluable both in directing product search and in evaluating opportunities. From a practical standpoint, you can't expect to find a product that will satisfy all your requirements. So it helps to separate the requirements in at least two groups, say, major and desirable. Products under consideration can then be judged on the basis of these yardsticks.

Once you've set up the yardsticks, the third step is to find a line or product to fit them. The new line or product can originate from one of three general sources: (1) internal development, (2) product acquisition, or (3) taking over a going business.

1. INTERNAL DEVELOPMENT. Internal development of a product and of the business organization needed to promote it is generally a high risk situation—unless it is related closely to existing management, design, engineering, and marketing skills and facilities. Employment of one or several key persons with extensive experience in the proposed new field makes the job easier.

2. PRODUCT ACQUISITION. Acquiring a license or other rights on a product available for manufacture and sale. This can sometimes provide a short-cut, particularly from a product design standpoint. However, in most instances it still requires substantial engineering, tooling, and market development investment.

3. TAKING OVER A GOING BUSINESS. If the company is adequately evaluated and is operating at a reasonable profit in relation to contemplated investment, this course probably involves the least risk of any diversification method.

But regardless of where they originate, new product areas should be screened and the possible range narrowed by exploratory research and evaluation with respect to product requirements. This process then should be carried on to a finer degree; identifying, exploring, and evaluating specific product lines within a chosen area.

It's possible that after a close look, changes in certain standards, or the addition of others, will be justified. It is not too important that the original product rules first be strictly followed. But it is important to have and to use a set of standards which will provide objective guides for each major decision to be made. It's easy to become too enthusiastic over a product or company on its own merits and to overlook the fundamentals of diversification.

Narrowing field

There are a number of tools available for use in product search. Probably the broadest is the Standard Industrial Classification Manual, published by the Executive Office of the President, Bureau of the Budget, and obtainable from the Superintendent of Documents, U. S. Government Printing Office, Washington 25, D. C., at a cost of $1.25. This is a complete list of major classifications and types of manufactured products that are produced and marketed in the United States. It may well suggest fields which ordinarily would not come to attention.

For more directed search, directories and encyclopedias for many specific industries are available which furnish specific details on products and companies in, or serving, these fields. Trade magazines also provide information on new products and businesses, some of which are frequently available to a company with financial and other resources.

Once product search has been narrowed to a fairly specific product or market situation, discussions with distributors or even major users regarding their experience and needs are generally profitable.

Of particular interest to metal-working firms, a number of the basic metals producers, both ferrous and nonferrous, make available to potential customers the services of their market development departments.

Diversification pitfalls

There have been more failures than successes in introducing new products. The major reasons for failures are:

1. Inadequate knowledge of markets and buying habits.

2. Inability to finance an adequate development program, particularly for market development. Market development costs often exceed those of development engineering, and facility additions or modifications.

3. Lack of appreciation of the market acceptance and general resources of competition—particularly where one or two companies control a given market. It is generally more difficult to enter a market dominated by relatively few companies.

4. Nonprofessional approach in management, design, and marketing. Many times, a highly qualified management and organization in its own field has failed in a new business area, simply because of

lack of experience and/or adaptability in another type of business. For example, it is difficult for a firm in a field of highly engineered industrial products to utilize the same management philosophy, engineering skills, marketing approach, or manufacturing facility to serve even its current markets with a low-cost, volume-produced product. . . .

Organizing a development program

If you've decided to develop a new product internally, a development program, timetable, and budget should be set up before any major steps are taken. Here's what it should include:

1. Define the product in terms of function, price, services, and other matters of interest to the distributor and user.

2. Determine by market research: (a) distributive and consumer acceptance; (b) market potential; (c) requirement for, and availability of distribution channels; (d) pricing, discount, and financing practices; (e) competitive activity; (f) long-term market trends; (g) design and engineering features to maximize acceptance.

3. Complete design and produce prototype models.

4. Make final market tests.

5. Complete production engineering and prepare facilities.

6. Set up market development and distribution program: (a) sales organization; (b) advertising and sales promotion; (c) other sales support, e.g. technical service.

7. Project investment, earnings, and cash flow over a three- to five-year period.

Sizing up a going business

If you're thinking of buying a going business, examine it thoroughly before committing yourself. Here are three important steps:

1. An accountant should verify assets, liabilities, and earnings records.

2. Legal examination of indentures, corporate charters, stock restrictions, executive compensation contracts, and other pertinent legal documents related to assets, liabilities, and corporate equity rights and obligations.

3. An operational analysis to study those segments of business that will contribute in a major way to future profits. The following situations should be analyzed: management, market potential and trends, product strength, engineering evaluation, user and distributive acceptance, distribution, research and development, patent position, manufacturing, competition.

19. PLANNED OBSOLESCENCE: RX FOR TIRED MARKETS? *

Martin Mayer

We see before us a most perplexed person, a man who is wondering how he ought to feel at this moment. He is the controller of a large corporation which makes electrical products, mostly big-ticket items, for the consumer market. And he is visiting the home of a friend, who is just now showing him the kitchen. Over against the wall, he sees an electric stove which his company made more than twenty years ago when electric stoves were a relatively new idea. The stove gleams. It is obviously in steady use and carefully kept up. Somebody loves it.

"That was one of ours, wasn't it?" says the controller.

"Yes," says his friend happily. "It's a wonderful stove."

The controller's automatic reaction is a feeling of pride in the quality of the product his company turned out twenty years ago—but then a sudden shaft of gloom descends upon him. All that money spent on planning wall ovens, automatic controls, clocktimers, griddles, deep-fat fryers—all that money spent on advertising the remarkable new product features, styling, choice of colors. Why does his friend still *want* the old stove? Has he no feeling for progress? How could the company survive if everyone were happy with an old stove?

Goods, as J. K. Galbraith has recently pointed out in his book, *The Affluent Society*, are produced to be consumed—and "consumed," in this case, has a specific meaning. Once something has been "consumed," the value is gone out of it. Paintings in a museum can't be consumed by the patrons of the museum, because the paintings are as good as ever after the art lover has looked at them. However, what is left of a steak after you have eaten it isn't much use to anyone but a dog.

* Reprinted by permission from *Dun's Review and Modern Industry*, Vol. 73, No. 2 (February, 1959), pp. 40, 70-74.
Martin Mayer, author of *Madison Avenue, U.S.A.* and others.

Between the imperishable work of art and the evanescent beef steak, there is, in a highly-developed community, a wide range of "durable" goods. The more durable the item, the more slowly it will be consumed and the fewer units any one consumer will require over a period of time. Coffins, to take a special case, are one to a customer. Manufacturers of durable goods must, therefore, sell most of their output to a limited market of first customers.

Theoretically, it would seem, there is nothing the manufacturer can do to remedy this situation. Once an item is produced and sold, its rate of consumption depends upon the use the consumer makes of it. Obviously, a manufacturer can't hope to make a five-year-old refrigerator or automobile as valueless as an eaten ice cream cone or a combusted gallon of gasoline. But a manufacturer *can* hope to increase the *apparent* rate of consumption of a durable item—and thus automatically increase his replacement market—if he makes his older product seem "obsolete." The trick isn't foolproof, but it ought to work a good part of the time—and perhaps it can even be planned, assuring the manufacturer of a large, steadily increasing replacement market. Such planning could proceed in three directions:

1. Functional Obsolescence. Refrigerators are a good example. New refrigerators with effective, self-contained freezer compartments—and trouble-free automatic defrost mechanisms—make older refrigerators far less valuable, despite a great continuing consumption-potential. The addition of a new function and a new convenience are persuasive reasons for the market to discard old units still in perfect working order. The more important the new function—or the more important it can be made to seem by advertising—the closer to "obsolete" the old units become, and the more willing customers will be to replace what they have. When television sets with 21-inch screens first became available, many people discarded relatively new 17-inch sets.

2. Style Obsolescence. The ladies' garment industry was, of course, the pioneer in this area. And the automobile industry has followed in its high-heeled footsteps, developing a kind of style obsolescence by social pressure. Upper-income elements of the market have been encouraged to believe that they are socially declassed if they are seen driving an old automobile. To make sure that the age of a car can be dated at a glance, models have been changed—superficially in most cases—every year. And the technique unquestionably has been effective in certain markets. There are communities

Object lesson in obsolescence: Phonograph's humble beginnings . . .

. . . were soon eclipsed by imposing console models, which very soon . . .

. . . yielded to the electric models. Then, only a short decade ago . . .

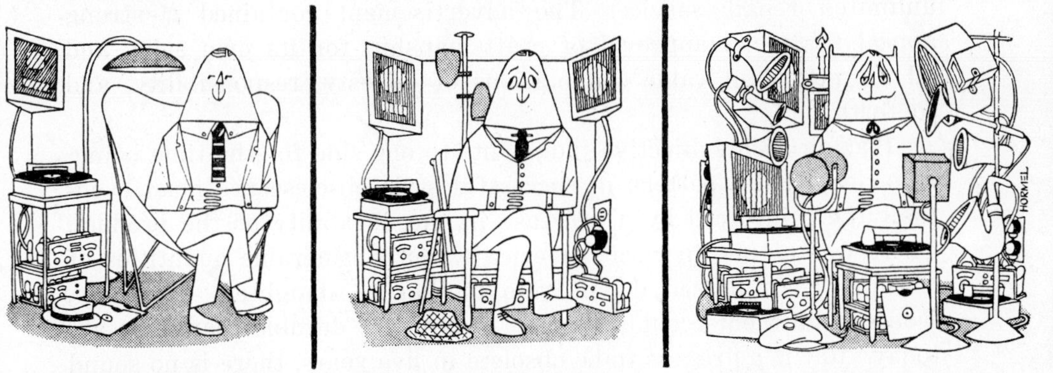

. . . the long-playing record ushered in the dawn of the hi-fi era . . .

Today we have stereophonic sound, and as technology marches on . . .

. . the consumer may soon vanish in the maze of his own home music system.

in this country where a wealthy man can get a reputation for stinginess simply by driving an older car. It must be kept in mind that this situation is exclusively American. Citroen, in France, made an automobile that was exactly the same on the outside from 1938 to 1956. It is not possible to date a Jaguar, a Mercedes, a Rolls-Royce, or even a Volkswagen, simply by the appearance of the vehicle. In France, England, and Germany, productive capacity has remained below effective demand for automobiles. Thus the manufacturer has had no reason to attempt to heighten the consumption rate of his product.

3. MATERIALS FAILURE. Obviously, one way to increase the replacement market for durable goods would be to make products in such a manner that they would function less well as they got older. This

area of possible planned obsolescence is so highly charged emotionally that it is virtually impossible to get accurate evidence of actual procedure—and positively libelous to suggest possible examples. Items which are made to wear out more quickly than they must are, by definition, shoddy goods. A manufacturer who puts his name on shoddy goods risks a destructive reaction from the market which could more than offset his possible gains from increased consumption.

Durability still sells

There are some areas, indeed, where durability is regarded as a major selling point. Fountain pens are still guaranteed "for life" or even "forever." One of the most effective advertisements appearing last year was for Zippo cigarette lighters, which offered free, unlimited repair service. The advertisement contained a strong appeal for social approval of craftsmanship for its own sake, and all the attendant value connotations of honesty, responsibility, and so forth.

Placing such subjective judgments to one side for the time being, it is clear that a pattern of successful style obsolescence must eventually be reinforced by a decrease in the durability of the product. There was a time in rural America when considerable quantities of clothing were passed down from mother to daughter. Certainly, women's garments could be made to be more durable than they are today. But if a dress is to be obsolete in five years, there is no sound economic reason to make it durable for ten. Indeed, under these conditions, the achievement of maximum durability for the product would be wasteful. If the decreased cost of making the less durable product is passed on to the consumer in the form of lower prices—which is likely in most situations—the "shoddy" product will be more attractive, not only in the market, but also by standards of community interest.

Such an analysis assumes that all members of the community feel style obsolescence at the same rate—an assumption which is not valid. There must be women somewhere who would be content to wear older fashions if the clothes held out. To the extent that the majority sense of obsolescence diminishes the durability of the available product, these women are discriminated against. It is this minority, presumably (there is also a political element here), that voices the complaints about defective workmanship which are fairly often lodged against the clothing industry.

Fins, fashion, and craftsmanship

Where such complaints are common, it is at least possible that goods are not being made for maximum durability. Thus the charge against the automobile industry is worthy of a hearing—especially since the evidence indicates that European cars, which are not produced under conditions of repeated style obsolescence, tend to give somewhat longer service. Except for the Rambler, which has done a minimum of restyling in recent years, no American make of automobile stresses durability as a major selling point. Dodge once concentrated its promotional fire in this area, but the 1959-model Dodge is being sold with the bald argument that "the old must make way for the new." The theoretical conditions necessary for the calculated use of materials failure to reinforce campaigns of style obsolescence are present in the industry.

Nevertheless, it seems unlikely that the automobile companies are, in fact, using such an approach. The brand names of automobiles are probably better known than the brand names of any other product, and a proved accusation of shoddiness could be competitively catastrophic. Again, while very few women would wish to be seen in any but the latest fashions, a large section of the community still desires a durable automobile, and is quite willing to drive something old. (The existence of an active used-car market still is vital to the selling of new automobiles.) If social philosophers find the contemporary American automobile less durable than might be ideally desirable, the blame is less likely to lie in the shoddiness concomitant with style obsolescence than in the difficulties of maintaining high standards of quality control when the labor force is strongly unionized.

Functional obsolescence and style obsolescence are also very closely related. Even in the area of quickly-consumed goods—drugs and toiletries, for example—modern marketing procedure calls for a change in style whenever there is a change in function to heighten awareness of the "new" product. Again, a style change will be far more effective in creating obsolescence if an improvement in function can be associated with it. Thus Chrysler advertised the "aerodynamic" values of fins, and electric stove manufacturers found reasons why wall ovens do a better job of roasting turkeys. In the advertising of consumer durables, the most important single task is to convince those who already own such goods that the new styles are functional, not just decorative.

Chance takes a hand

Not everything that happens in the world is necessarily "planned." Artificial obsolescence is clearly in the self-interest of the durable goods manufacturer, and its occurrence in the market place is plainly visible. The fact that things happen as an intelligent manufacturer would wish them to happen argues strongly that there is an *intent* toward obsolescence. But intentions and plans are greatly different breeds of cat.

Continuing reactions to continuing changes in market conditions could create patterns of "planned obsolescence" with no more long-term planning than that performed by, say, a football coach. It is always hard to determine whether or not a given business achievement was really *planned* to happen as it did. A great deal of on-the-spot decision-making is involved even in a thoroughly planned operation, and only someone who has lived with the situation can say for sure how greatly these small decisions made under the impact of market conditions have influenced the course of the larger plan. And when these lucky experts come to speak, one usually finds that the notoriously selective human memory has interpreted past actions by the value of present results. If the operation was a failure, luck was bad; if the operation was a success, the planning was splendid.

A case in point

One of the clearest examples of intended obsolescence in recent years was the introduction of the "stereo" phonograph record and associated playing equipment. The change from conventional records and phonographs was functional. Though a considerable technological change was involved, no alteration in the appearance of either record or playing equipment was required. The new technique involved an undoubted potential for improving accuracy in the recording and the reproduction of sound, and it could honestly be maintained that stereo made existing equipment "obsolete."

Economically, some considerable functional advance was much to be desired by the manufacturers of phonographs. Despite the popularity of "high fidelity," the rate of increase in the market had slowed, and by the Winter of 1957-58, the pipelines from factory to consumer were well clogged with slow-moving items. Stereo offered manufacturers the chance to build a new replacement market and also to force rapid, sale-price disposal of stock-in-being on distributors and retailers.

The first successful demonstrations of stereo records and playing equipment were performed in the Fall of 1957 by Decca Records (Britain) in London and by the Westrex Corporation in New York. Almost immediately, the larger manufacturers proclaimed their intention to proceed as quickly as possible with the manufacture of stereo goods. The fact that the techniques had been developed by relatively small companies (Westrex was a subsidiary of Western Electric, but AT&T had agreed to divest itself of the subsidiary as partial answer to an antitrust problem) meant that secrecy was out of the question. Manufacturers, in this case, didn't want secrecy anyway, because part of their aim was to use the threat of obsolescence to push existing goods through the channels at increased speeds.

An initial delay developed because the two systems, British and American, were different in several details. Two meetings of the engineering staffs of all the potentially important producers of stereo phonograph records were held in January and February of last year. (The meetings were not publicized because of a well-founded fear that the Justice Department might take an interest.) Significantly, the meetings failed to produce general agreement on the best technical approach to stereo. Nevertheless, the largest single company in the market—RCA Victor—decided to go ahead with the Westrex system as refined by its own engineers. All the other companies shortly fell into step behind the leader in the approved fashion, and marketing departments prepared to introduce stereo to the public in the Fall.

Many a slip

No engineering department in the industry was really happy with the decision to market stereo in the Fall of 1958—although, as the head of the largest such group said, "We'll get through it all right. We've learned to invent on schedule." Marketing departments, however, were convinced that delay increased the danger of the competition coming in first and slicing off an unduly large share-of-market. This fear was well-founded. Even before the policy decisions had been made in executive offices, one of the smaller record companies had come out with a line of stereo records (though the equipment on which they could be played did not yet exist, even in prototype). In the early Spring of 1958, one of the larger phonograph manufacturers held a press showing of its new stereo line and even advertised to the public that its stereo equipment was now on sale in the stores. If any appreciable demand had been stirred up by this announcement, the company would have had explanations to make to both its dealers and the public because the production lines were not yet in operation. But the gamble paid off. The company managed to tie its name to the new development without arousing the ire of disgruntled prospective purchasers.

All off schedule

In the end, nobody met delivery dates. RCA Victor engineers refused to release their designs for production on the deadline day. Westinghouse stylists were still unable to decide on cabinetry as late as mid-June, although introduction was scheduled for a trade fair in July. General Electric, which had manufactured the largest-selling quality "pickup" for conventional high fidelity installations, did not even begin production on its stereo pickups until the last week in September. As the result of the rush to meet release deadlines, the first stereo phonographs on the market were not—to put it mildly—of the quality expected from their eminent manufacturers. Moreover, phonograph dealers, noting that the stereo items were not coming through on schedule, refused to be hustled into store-wide inventory sales, so that the anticipated clean-up of older models was not achieved.

Time will not only heal these wounds; it will turn them into battle ribbons. In two or three years, when stereo is solidly established, authorities will look back on the frenzied days in Spring and Summer 1958, and cite the introduction of stereo records and phonographs as an example of "planned obsolescence." And fair enough, too, for the obsolescence of conventional phonographs was certainly the industry's *intention*. But nobody who sat up with the patient through the feverish preintroduction nights—as I did—could ever honestly say that the obsolescence was *planned*.

Planning vs. flexibility

One of the oddest features of the current business thinking is the prestige which the word "plan" has achieved among men who are most vocal in their loyalty to the concept of a free market economy. It was only a few years ago that Peter Drucker assured the nation that deep recessions were no longer possible because the essential cause of serious economic setbacks was a decline in business investment, and that long-range planning had now made such declines inconceivable. Nevertheless, the recession of 1957-58 was characterized by a very severe slash in business investment in reaction to prior overproduction of capital goods. (Partly due, by the way, to an unsuccessful pattern of artificial obsolescence in the capital goods market, especially in equipment for the manufacture of steel, non-ferrous metals, and automobiles.) Planning, which is unresponsive to the market conditions, would be indistinguishable from the socialist administration of business. But Mr. Drucker thought such planning was a good thing, a sign of the maturity of our business leaders and the excellence of our present semicompetitive business structure.

The genius of capitalism is, in point of fact, its ability to react swiftly to market changes, and to the extent that any "planning" tends to lengthen that reaction time, it places the company involved at a severe competitive disadvantage. Notwithstanding the virtues of long-range planning as taught in business schools and reported at management conferences, it is unlikely that corporate policy-makers will carry the concept of long-range planning to the point of renouncing all flexibility of corporate action and reaction. Rigid long-range planning would be an especially severe handicap if it were applied to withhold innovation until some later time. The more one studies the question of "planned obsolescence," the more certain it seems that the phenomenon occurs because businessmen react to changing conditions rather than because they plan.

Competitive free-for-all

The introduction of stereo illustrates some of the problems involved. Even technical discussion on an industry-wide basis was regarded as risky under the antitrust laws, and any large-scale agreement on marketing procedures would surely have called down the wrath of the Federals. Without a better espionage system than most businesses are willing to support, therefore, no company can be entirely sure how its competitors are proceeding with any innovation. The safest course is to rush ahead, full speed, and get your own version on the market as quickly as possible. Even where an entire industry starts with everybody at scratch—with a public announcement of a new process available to all by license, as the Westrex announcement of its stereo devices—each company scrambles forward at full tilt. The scramble gets even more frenzied when an individual company's research department comes up with something new and has no way of knowing for sure whether the competition has hit upon the same idea.

Haste can be risky

"Planning," if the word means anything at all, implies that something is held back for the future. In a competitive consumer market, holding back can be profitable only if the item in question is not yet perfected—or, to put the matter more precisely, if it cannot be made to function properly when produced in large quantities. (RCA Victor gained nothing whatever by being first on the market with a gremlin-ridden color television set.) Otherwise, the overriding marketing necessity is to be *early*. Each year, as technical advances are made, companies vie with each other to be the first to get their new products before the public. Such a process is the essence of competition, but it prohibits meaningful planning.

Style obsolescence is more subject to planning than functional obsolescence—partly because it is less dependent on the accidental timing of technical innovation, partly because the discontinuance of a style tends to frighten the market (as Chrysler found out in the 1930's), and may even lead prospective purchasers to cherish rather than to disdain what they already own. Even here, however, the trick is to arrive at the preferred style ahead of the opposition, and the market researchers must work with the stylists to determine how quickly appearances can be altered.

The disastrous 1958-model automobiles led critics to wonder whether obsolescence, as a marketing device, had not finally lost its place in the American economy. Such a development, while not inconceivable, would be revolutionary and thus surprising. The feeling that last year's furniture is now "obsolete" has deep roots in the American past, in the psychology of mobility, the love for the frontier, the belief in progress. If ten years of depression did not interfere with the American notion that the new is better than the old, it seems unlikely that a one-year recession, however deep, can wield such influence.

The case against obsolescence

Regarded critically, patterns of obsolescence show many unfortunate facets. The discarding of "perfectly good" used wearing apparel and machinery is a well-known sin-and-shame. Nobody likes waste. Constant stress on the importance of newness diminishes respect for craftsmanship. It would be sad to think, as *Time* magazine does, that Americans are now buying cheap rather than good wrist watches because they wish to have something they can discard painlessly when fashions change. (One could also argue that high-priced watches have simply been losing ground to other big-ticket items in a period when consumers have had to think twice about major expenditures.) And within industry itself the need to get there first with anything new may produce diminished quality and some strikingly odd product features—like the first refrigerator cold controls, which were not connected to anything.

Nevertheless, the market wants newness, and producers must react to the market. Perhaps there would be less uproar over "planned obsolescence," from both conservative and radical social critics, if businessmen stopped stressing the very minimal amount of true planning that can, in reality, be applied to the problem of enlarging replacement markets.

20. INDUSTRIAL ADAPTATION *

O. K. Burrell

When a business enterprise, large or small, is outdistanced in the competitive race, there are only four things it can do. It can attempt to catch up by making necessary modifications in the product and in merchandising or other policies; it can be stubborn and go on losing money until its resources are completely exhausted, and it ends up in bankruptcy; it can liquidate the assets, pay off the creditors, and divide the remainder, if any, among the owners; or it can attempt to shift its resources into an entirely new and profitable line of business.

The least desirable of these alternatives is, of course, to be stubborn and end up in bankruptcy as a result of a refusal to recognize the necessity for adaptation to the changed competitive world. But even if the changed situation is recognized before bankruptcy becomes inevitable, the decision as to the proper course of action is a difficult one. Should the enterprise attempt to sharpen up the product, modify merchandising practices, and reduce costs; or should it undertake the difficult and perhaps impossible job of shifting resources to an entirely different, although perhaps related line? The decision to simply liquidate is one that is rarely made since it is contrary to the interests of the management group and since liquidation of an unsuccessful enterprise would not normally be expected to yield very much.

Such a decision as this cannot be wisely and safely made on the basis of precedent alone. The fact that a particular decision worked badly or well for a particular enterprise at a particular time does not mean it will produce the same results for another enterprise at another time. Each enterprise is unique and timing is extremely important; any alternative would have proved to be less than satis-

* Reprinted by permission from *Business Topics* (East Lansing: Michigan State University, Bureau of Business and Economic Research), Vol. 7, No. 2 (Spring, 1959), pp. 40-49.

O. K. Burrell, Professor of Finance, School of Business Administration, University of Oregon.

factory if undertaken in 1930. Nevertheless, examination of the efforts of unsuccessful companies to adapt to changed circumstances may be useful even though it is not possible to construct a formula with which to solve these difficult adaptation problems. After all, business decisions can rarely be solved by formula. Nevertheless, study of decisions made by other enterprises can be useful at least as background material, especially when the varying attendant circumstances are taken into account.

Case Material in the Automobile Industry

Competition has really separated the men from the boys in the business of automobile making. Since the automobile industry was born about the turn of the century, more than two thousand makes of cars, from the ABC and the Abbott to the Zimmerman and the Zentmobile, have sought public favor.[1] Something over a hundred of these were steam cars and a lesser number were powered by electricity; by far the greater number were gasoline powered. Only a few survive.

The automobile manufacturers who have not survived did not run typically million-dollar enterprises. Most of them were simply promotions that didn't make the grade—a few cars were assembled, some may have been sold, but the car cost more than the public could be persuaded to pay. Entry into the automobile industry in its early years was not especially difficult. The market for automobiles was not as large as it is now, but it was an unsaturated market; moreover, capital requirements were low. In the early years of the industry, automobiles were not so much manufactured as they were assembled. The first Ford, for example, was almost entirely an assembly job: the engines, transmissions, and axles were purchased from the Dodge Brothers, the bodies and cushions from the Wilson Carriage Company, and the wheels from the Prudden Company.[2] The financial practices of the new industry kept the capital requirements down. There was a tremendous demand for cars; in return for exclusive territorial dealer rights, the producers were able to obtain substantial cash deposits on orders, and to receive full payment upon delivery. And liberal credit terms could be obtained from the well-established parts makers.

Most of the makers of these early cars went out of business in a very short time. In other cases the product caught on, and the

[1] From the list of automobiles once manufactured in the United States included in *A Chronicle of the Automobile Industry in America, 1892-1936*, published for private circulation by the Eaton Manufacturing Co.

[2] *Combustion on Wheels*, by David L. Cohn (New York, 1944).

company prospered for a decade or two. In many cases only a very few cars were produced by ambitious machine shop proprietors, and operations were suspended when it was found that the car had mechanical defects and could not be sold, or costs were too high to yield a profit. Even as late as 1923 a rather substantial number of automobile manufacturers were producing cars, but after this date the competitive struggle in the industry became more intense, making it difficult for the smaller units to survive as automobile manufacturers. For this reason most of the instances of attempted shifts out of the industry occurred in the period following 1923.

Automobile manufacturing as a sideline

In a surprising number of cases the transition from automobile manufacturing was made relatively easy by the fact that car making was a sideline. It was only necessary to drop the sideline and concentrate on the main product. Today the automobile companies manufacture many other products and no one regards this as in any way peculiar. Probably few people remember that it was once the other way around: manufacturers of bicycles, wringers, wagons and buggies, sewing machines, farm implements, and railroad locomotives set up "automobile departments" and manufactured automobiles as a sideline business.

In some cases this venture soon became the main product rather than an incidental part of the business. The Winton (1898), the Pierce-Arrow (1901), and the Jeffery (which became the Nash; 1903) developed out of bicycle manufacturing enterprises; the bicycle lines were dropped as the automobiles became popular. The Willys Overland Co. began as a buggy manufacturing enterprise, but buggy making was soon forgotten after the company was rescued from financial difficulties by an early supersalesman by the name of John Willys. Measured by present standards, the rescue required no vast amount of money: Mr. Willys supplied $500 to meet a payroll.

Sewing machines and steam automobiles might not appear to be very closely related; nevertheless it was the White Sewing Machine Co. of Cleveland, Ohio, that developed the well-known White Steamer. In 1907 the White family decided that automobiles and sewing machines really didn't fit together very well and so the White Co. was organized to take over the "automobile department" of the sewing machine company.

The leading maker of railroad steam locomotives, the American Locomotive Co., manufactured and sold the Alco car, but it was powered by gasoline rather than steam. The car was massive as well as expensive ($7,250) and boasted a "Pullman" ventilator in the top which gave it some faint resemblance to a railroad passenger coach. The car had "illuminated steps" and the upholstery was said to be ten inches deep.

At least three farm implement manufacturers had a fling at the automobile business. The Moline Plow Co. manufactured the Stephens. The J. I. Case Co. of Racine, Wisconsin, made the Case. The International Harvester Co. manufactured, in its plant in Akron, Ohio, a so-called "auto-buggy" with high wheels and an air-cooled motor. This vehicle was apparently designed for the farm market and was made to appear as nearly like a horse-drawn buggy as possible. In none of these cases did the implement manufacturers succeed in the passenger-car business, although International Harvester has long been an important factor in the truck business.

How did it happen that in so many cases cars were manufactured as a side-line by concerns in other lines of business? In the first place, in the early years of the industry very little specialized capital was required in automobile making. In the pre-assembly line days a car could be built in a good machine shop, especially if enough of the parts could be purchased from others. Many of the early car makers did little more than assemble parts purchased elsewhere; indeed the advertising of many of these early cars boasted of the excellence of these components. Prominently mentioned were such essential parts as Bosch magnetos, Atwater Kent ignition systems, Driggs-Seabury frames, and Warner Gear Co. transmissions.

The farm implement makers as well as the carriage and wagon makers perhaps felt that they might have a potential advantage in the sale of automobiles through their established dealers. Perhaps the automobile might be just a welcome and profitable addition to the regular line of merchandise. While this may have appeared to be good reasoning, it certainly grossly underestimated the dynamic nature of the new industry. The automobile, as it turned out, was not just another line of merchandise for buggy dealers to sell.

Indeed it was not easy to appraise the future of the new automobile industry in the first decades of the century. This was an industrial revolution that is still impossible to measure. Periods of competitive stress forced manufacturers to take decisive steps of various natures in order to stay in business. While many firms, having taken on car manufacturing as a sideline, could withdraw from this field and concentrate on their original undertakings, other concerns in similar circumstances resorted to different means for remaining in the automotive field.

Attempts to recover market position

It is understandable that an automobile manufacturing company which found itself at a competitive disadvantage would make vigorous efforts to recover its former position. Some of these attempts were successful; others seemed to be successful for a few years and in a few cases for a decade or two; in at least two instances, the shift appears to have been made with complete success. Most of the efforts involved a more or less radical shift in car design and construction. This, too, is understandable: a successful enterprise is not likely to make sudden radical changes in design, but an unsuccessful one has everything to gain by such an undertaking.

Those enterprises that persisted to the point of ultimate bankruptcy were usually the smaller units with little operating history that have left scant public record. But one larger company, the H. H. Franklin Manufacturing Company, of Syracuse, New York, makers of the well-remembered car with the air-cooled motor, elected to be stubborn. It produced a rather expensive but exceptionally fine car, and it kept on producing it in the face of persistently recurring operating losses. The company lost all the stockholders' money and most of the creditors' money as well: in the 1934 bankruptcy the general creditors received only slightly more than ten cents on the dollar for their claims.[3]

It will be remembered that Walter P. Chrysler was associated with two successful efforts to rejuvenate unsuccessful automobile manufacturing enterprises. In the earlier instance, Mr. Chrysler was employed, at what appeared at the time a fabulous salary, to undertake the reorganization of the Willys-Overland Company. His second effort was concerned with Maxwell Motors, which was eventually reconstituted and given the Chrysler name. In both cases it was apparently Mr. Chrysler's engineering genius that was responsible for the successful turn of events. In fact, in the case of Maxwell, there was a frank admission that previous models had been less than desirable. The new models introduced after Mr. Chrysler was brought into the company were advertised as "The Good Maxwell."

The great importance of timing is to be seen in the relative experience of American Motors and the old Graham-Paige. In both cases the method adopted was to make striking changes in car design.

[3] *Commercial & Financial Chronicle*, February 16, 1935.

(In the case of Graham-Paige a great deal of fresh capital was also a feature of its change period.) The shift has been, apparently, highly successful in the case of American Motors with its new Rambler car; but the effort was entirely unsuccessful in the case of Graham-Paige. American Motors was lucky enough, or perhaps wise enough, to undertake extensive changes in a period of generally active business; Graham-Paige undertook its comparable changes just at the onset of a great depression.

The tax factor

The economic value of large accumulated losses to profit-making enterprises has permitted some automobile manufacturing concerns to retire from the industry without complete loss to stockholders in recent years of high corporate income taxes. When Kaiser Motors found it could no longer operate profitably in the automobile industry, the dominant interest in the company was able to combine the enterprise with certain profitable ones and recover the monetary value of the accumulated losses. In the case of Studebaker it is also the monetary value of the accumulated losses that has operated as a powerful stimulant to transition. In order for the value of these losses to be recovered it is necessary under present laws for the company with the losses to absorb profit-making enterprises.

Several automobile manufacturing enterprises have succeeded in varying degrees in shifting completely out of the automobile manufacturing field. Reo, for example, continued to make trucks for some years after the manufacture of the Reo Flying Cloud passenger car was discontinued. Eventually truck-making became unprofitable and for a time the company shifted to various metal specialties, including a power lawn mower. Then there was a period of litigation and indecision with the result that the company distributed to stockholders a liquidating dividend of $28 per share and then merged the corporate shell with an enterprise in the electronics business. The White Motor Company shifted out of the manufacture of the well-known White Steamer, but has continued to manufacture trucks successfully. Both Graham-Paige and Hupp are still operating, although not in the automobile business. But in none of these cases was the shift as successful and as astonishing as the shift of the Peerless Motor Car Corporation from automobile manufacturing to the brewing of beer. So unusual a chapter in the industrial history of this country is made up of the story of the Peerless enterprise that the account of the firm's change of direction is given here in considerable detail.

Transition at Peerless

For many years it was said that the three great cars in the United States were the three P's: Peerless, Packard, and Pierce Arrow. This was an oversimplification, but it was certain that the Peerless was a fine and dependable car. The first Peerless was built in Cleveland in 1900;[4] from the beginning the company made no effort to turn out cheap cars for the mass market. The company was not beset by ambition—it was content to build and sell good cars, to maintain a comfortable financial position, and to let others slug it out for the mass market. The Peerless owner could feel confident that his car would not be depreciated by radical year-to-year changes; to own a Peerless was something of a mark of distinction.

But Peerless and the other small units in the industry found it more difficult to operate profitably after 1920. There were a few good years. Nineteen twenty-three was a good automobile year, even for the smaller companies in the industry, and Peerless made quite a satisfactory profit. Perhaps because of lessened competition from the Ford Motor Company, the year 1926 was a year of profitable operation for Peerless, as well as for most other units in the industry. But profitable as the 1920's were for business generally, it was not a boom period at Peerless. The new Ford Model A was introduced in 1927, and seemed to many people to set a new standard of value, and the Peerless Corporation, along with others in the industry, found it difficult to compete. By 1929 it was clear that something had to be done; the problem could not be solved by waiting.

New financing

To provide sufficient working capital to expand operations, the management arranged for new financing in April 1930, obtaining about $1,400,000[5] by offering new stock to stockholders. Each was permitted to buy, at $8, one new share for each share held. There was, however, no rush to take advantage of the offer. Of the some 258,000 new shares offered, less than 170,000 were sold, and most were not taken by stockholders. About half of the issue was placed with nationally known investor-industrialists who had been favorably impressed with the Peerless prospects. These major investors were, of course, quite aware of the risks inherent in the enterprise;

[4] Annual reports of the company; various volumes of *Moody's*.

[5] Facsimile of the statement to the Committee on Stock List of the New York Stock Exchange in connection with the stock offering; also report of the Wall Street Survey, a financial news service.

the management had disclosed all known conditions in the company and in the industry, but had expressed confidence that the affairs of the company could be conducted so as not to lose the additional capital brought in by the sale of stock. It was also indicated that, if the market expansion hoped for did not materialize, it would be the policy of the company to repay investors. It was recognized, however, that repayment to stockholders would have to be on a pro rata basis, and that it would be impossible to repay only new investors.

It is noteworthy that, in spite of worsening economic conditions generally and in the automobile industry in particular, the new economies in production and the general belt-tightening enabled the Peerless company to show a small profit for the year ending September 30, 1930. But the handwriting was on the wall. It became apparent that the economic depression would be of undeterminable duration and severity. Management formed the opinion that shareholder interests would not be served by expansion or even by continuation in the automotive industry. This is the kind of decision not often made by corporate management. The decision was not a forced one; when it was made, the working capital brought in by the April 1930 financing had not been dissipated by operating losses and was largely intact. Moreover, it was a decision against the immediate personal interest of the management team, whose experience had been largely in the automotive industry.

From fine cars to fine beer

Once having determined that it was not feasible to continue in the automotive industry, the management gave some attention to possible alternatives. Should the Peerless Company liquidate the assets, pay off what debts it had, and divide the remainder among the stockholders? Or should it attempt to find some other line of business? Surprisingly, it was the conclusion of the Executive Committee that the best program for the company would be found in the production and distribution of a product which "cost less than ten cents and was either consumed or thrown away." After several months of investigation the directors concluded that the production of beverages would be the most suitable use of the company's resources. Since this decision was made shortly before the repeal of the Prohibition Amendment, it was inevitable that management should consider the production and sale of beer. A firm of architects and engineers specializing in the construction of breweries was employed to make a survey of the feasibility of converting all or part of the Cleveland plant to a brewery. This firm reported that in three or four months, at a cost of a little more than a half million dollars, a portion of the plant could be converted to a brewery with an annual capacity of 150,000 barrels, and that this could be increased to a capacity of 264,000 barrels merely by increasing storage space.[6]

Once it had been decided that the company would go into the production and distribution of beer as soon as this was legally possible, it was agreed that the capital raised in 1930 involved a rather special shareholder obligation. This capital had been raised on the representation that the company would continue in the automobile business and that, if expected opportunities in the industry did not materialize, it would be the policy of the company to return all or part of the additional capital advanced. But it was legally impossible to return capital to some stockholders and not to others. As a partial solution to this problem, the company, early in 1932, offered to purchase stock at $3.50 per share; about 159,000 shares of treasury stock was thus acquired from stockholders. Later in 1932, the company paid a liquidating dividend of $4.50 per share on the stock still outstanding. While the liquidating payment was less than the price at which the additional stock had been sold in 1930, the company actually returned, in stock purchase and liquidating dividend, an amount larger than had been received in the sale of stock in 1930.

Assets and skills

The manufacture of Peerless cars was discontinued in 1931, and the company waited out the repeal of the Prohibition Amendment, which would permit the legal manufacture and distribution of beer. After the payment of the liquidating dividend and the purchase of treasury stock in 1932, the company's working capital was largely depleted; the principal asset was the well-located Cleveland plant site of about twenty-two acres and buildings, mainly of modern steel and concrete construction, with a floor area of 658,000 square feet. Another asset, not recorded on the balance sheet, was a fierce desire to survive. The corporate belt was tightened, and during the transition period costs were drastically reduced. The salary of the president was fixed at "not more than" $10,000 and other salaries scaled down from this figure.

The skills required in making automobiles are, of course, not the same as those required in making beer and ale; a skilled machinist

[6] *Commercial & Financial Chronicle*, July 1, 1933.

cannot easily be converted into a brewmaster. Moreover, the selling of beer and ale presents fundamentally different problems and requires different skills. It was clear that Peerless had to have help—both money and technical know-how.

After extended search an arrangement was worked out with the Brewing Corporation of Canada, now known as Canadian Brewers, Ltd., makers of the well-known Carling's Black Label Beer and Carling's Red Cap Ale. The Peerless Company issued 25,000 shares of its nearly worthless stock to the Canadian company for the exclusive rights to its brands, copyrights, and labels, and also for the exclusive sales agency for Carling products in the United States.[7] In addition, in order to replenish working capital, the Cleveland company sold some 178,000 shares of treasury stock at $3 per share.

The conversion process

With the money from the stock sale, the complicated business of turning an automobile factory into a brewery began. Prices and costs were not high, but nevertheless the conversion cost a bit more than expected, so it was not long before still more working capital was needed. In October 1933, while the conversion was still in progress, the company attempted to sell more stock. This effort must be labeled as a failure. The stock was offered to stockholders at $5 per share, in the ratio of one new share for each five shares held; if all stockholders had purchased stock to which they were entitled a total of 92,348 shares would have been sold. The actual sale amounted to only 20,277 shares. Because of the failure of this financing and because the plant conversion cost more than expected, the suppliers of some of the brewery equipment were unable to collect immediately and had a prolonged and anxious wait,[8] but in spite of these difficulties, the conversion was finally completed. The Canadian company sent a brewmaster and a cadre of skilled workmen to Cleveland to train the employees of the Peerless Company in the new art.

Everyone knows, of course, that no business organization called the Peerless Motor Car Corporation is in the beer business. It would look a bit silly for an automobile company to advertise beer and ale. But the only reason a company called the Peerless Motor Car Corporation is not advertising beer and ale is that the Cleveland company found it desirable to change the corporate name several times. The corporate name was first changed to the Peerless Company about the time that the manufacture of automobiles was discontinued. Even

[7] *Ibid.*, October 14, 1933.
[8] Letter of Mr. A. W. Fritzsche, son of a former director.

the proud old name, Peerless, was eliminated in 1933, and the company became the Brewing Corporation of America; later the present name, the Carling Brewing Company, was adopted.

After the new enterprise became profitable, the Canadian company began to buy up the stock of the Cleveland company; gradually, over a period of years, Canadian Brewers increased its proportion of ownership. By 1946 its ownership was 71 per cent of the total; this had increased only to 78 per cent by 1951, when the Canadian company made a formal offer to the remaining stockholders of the Cleveland company to exchange two shares of Canadian Brewers for each share of the Cleveland company. As a result of this offer and further purchases the proportion of ownership by Canadian Brewers is now more than 98 per cent.[9] This buying resulted in sale prices that were highly satisfactory to Peerless stockholders.

Hey, Mabel!

In these days, industrial diversification is almost a fad. Railroads have gone into the trucking and pipeline businesses; copper mining enterprises have taken up uranium, oil, and metal fabrication; coal mining companies have shifted to machine tools. But such industrial diversification was uncommon until fairly recent years. Perhaps the Peerless experience helped to point the way.

In the process, the fine old name Peerless was lost. The spirit of the company may also have undergone some changes in the shift to the new line. The advertising of the Peerless car was very restrained and sedate. It was sometimes called "the car for aesthetes;" usually the advertising carried a picture of a black Peerless that seemed to exude quiet respectability; under the name Peerless appeared the phrase "all that the name implies." All this is certainly in contrast to the advertising program of the beer-making corporate successor to the Peerless Motor Car Corporation. A typical ad shows a genial shirt-sleeved man, who has evidently just returned from the grocery, holding up a bottle of beer and shouting to his wife, "Hey Mabel! Black Label." All advertising, however, is less sedate than it was in the heyday of the Peerless car. If the Peerless Motor Car Corporation were still selling cars, it is certain that not all of them would be painted black, and that the styling would be more streamlined than the 1928 model. It is equally certain that the advertising would not be dull and restrained and factual, but colorful, entertaining, and perhaps a bit loud. After all, the world has changed.

[9] The several exchange and purchase offers by Canadian Brewers were traced through various issues of the *Commercial & Financial Chronicle* and *Moody's*.

21. THE BLANKET PURCHASE ORDER *

Alfred P. Koch
S. George Walters

Selling in today's highly competitive markets necessitates new ideas and new methods. One innovation of recent origin is the blanket purchase order. In order to maintain present sales volume, to secure new or additional sales volume, to get an edge on or to squeeze out competition, an increasing number of vendors, manufacturers and industrial supply firms utilize the blanket purchase order.

Constant source of supply from a reputable vendor, prompt delivery, lower cost of buying and handling, etc.—these advantages may be found in the blanket purchase order. However, there may be certain concessions which the inexperienced supplier may unwittingly grant that may be questionable and economically unsound.

In this appraisal of the blanket purchase order, the technique and the advantages and disadvantages accruing to buyer and seller are identified and discussed. A case history involving the use of a blanket order by a long-established industrial supply firm serves to underscore the fact that even an experienced innovating entrepreneur may fall victim to the siren song of the blanket purchase order.

Among advantages under a blanket order, the supplier acts as a storekeeper inasmuch as the customer's inventory requirements are stocked. As a result, a customer is required to carry only a skeleton inventory of material for, perhaps in some extreme instances, no more than daily current production needs. In effect, the customer requisitions from the supplier's stockroom, instead of his own stockroom. The sometimes crucial element of prompt delivery is virtually guaranteed in the blanket order, and reputable suppliers conveniently located may fulfill requisitions even on a daily basis.

Advantages to the buyer

A blanket-order policy in purchasing may result in the elimination of certain cost, expense, and capital requirements. An impressive number of advantages may be given including:

* Reprinted by permission of *The Controller*, Vol. 271, No. 11 (November, 1960), p. 534.

Alfred P. Koch, Professor of Accounting, Lehigh University; Consultant; CPA.

S. George Walters, Development Projects Manager, Mobil Oil Company.

1. Prices may be guaranteed for a negotiated period of time.
2. Quantity discounts may be granted on the basis of quantities shown on the blanket order.
3. Cancellation charges may be eliminated since a supplier meets the demands of other customers.
4. Capital requirements for stock inventory, land, building, shelving, and material-handling equipment may be decreased by stocking a skeleton inventory.
5. A skeleton inventory would require less storekeeping, and the resultant effect would be a decrease in the number of employes.
6. Record keeping and accounting for inventory would be decreased since fewer different types and smaller quantities of stock items would be inventoried.
7. Losses and costs resulting from theft, shrinkage, damage, fire, obsolescence, depreciation, and miscellaneous risks would be held to a minimum.
8. Since certain capital requirements may be reduced, the cost of borrowing may be lessened.

In addition to these and other possible cost and expense advantages, a blanket order puts a customer in a better position to meet budgetary allotments and perhaps improve cash flow by requesting deferred billing. An uninterrupted production schedule may be assured since the supplier carries tools and materials to meet future production needs.

These considerations are the dollar-and-cents reasons for the purchasing agent to buy under a blanket order.

Advantages to the supplier

The blanket-order method of doing business also may be profitable to the supplier since long-term orders build up a backlog of guaranteed future sales. The supplier is in a position to earn or bargain for favorable quantity discounts with the manufacturer on the basis of consolidating quantities of like material from the blanket orders of many customers.

The cost of making sales may be reduced since the order may cover a long period of time and could contain in one order what ordinarily would encompass one hundred separate orders. The sales time and effort saved may be used in procuring new business from present and new customers. By rendering good service and assuring delivery on time, future orders may be received from the same customers for items not covered by the blanket order.

The supplier also may have the advantage of negotiating a blanket order with his manufacturer for a negotiated period of time at guaranteed prices.

Possible hazards to the supplier

Under normal conditions, the blanket order is advantageous to both the customer and the supplier. However, many suppliers may not be on the so-called preferred list and are unable to secure a blanket order because of the ever-increasing intensity of competition. In order to squeeze out competition, to get an edge on competition, or to secure new business or increase present volume, a supplier may use this blanket-order technique in a fashion detrimental to financial soundness. A situation covering many pitfalls may arise through the improper use of a blanket order. Such a situation involving an actual case history is illustrated below. The order was accepted by a supplier to secure a competitive advantage at a time when a price increase was anticipated, although no price protection was granted by the manufacturer.

A manufacturers' distributor of industrial tools and supplies negotiated a blanket purchase order with one of its customers for a period of a year and a half from July 31, 1958, to December 31, 1959. The order read as follows except that only a partial list is shown in *Exhibit 1* of some 1,000 items that were ordered in varying quantities. The usual mark-up on these items to the distributor was 20 per cent. Pertinent data from the blanket purchase order follow.

> Delivery—In accordance with our releases. Price list in effect on July 1, 1958, less 10%.
>
> To cover our estimated needs of reamers, twist drills, taps, and dies as shown on the attached list for the period July 1, 1958, to December 31, 1959.
>
> NOTE: The attached list was compiled from the best historical information available to us, our actual usage for 18 months ended June 30, 1958. If our requirements do not materialize to the extent of the attached list, we are relieved of any obligation in this contractual relationship.

EXHIBIT 1

A PARTIAL LIST FROM THE BLANKET ORDER

Quantity	High Speed Drills	Selling Price (Each)	Supplier's Material Cost July 1, 1958	Oct. 1, 1958	July 15, 1959
72	25/64″	1.86	1.66	1.87	2.24
400	13/64	1.86	1.66	1.87	2.24
100	27/64	2.03	1.81	2.05	2.40
72	7/16	2.03	1.81	2.05	2.48
252	29/64	2.22	1.98	2.24	2.60

The buyer in this circumstance was freed entirely from the risk of a price increase. Purchases that are made for other than specific or known requirements are to a degree speculative. The appendent note to the purchase order freed the buyer from ordering the quantities specified if the need did not materialize. In addition, this blanket order not only freed the buyer from the speculative risk of a price rise, but the appendent note permitted that, in the event of a price decrease, the buyer could shift to other sources of supply to secure lower prices. In order to prevent such a shift, most suppliers will automatically pass on price decreases. This condition is conceivable; however, in today's period of inflation and higher labor costs, decreases seem unlikely.

The buyer secured in this instance the advantage of quantity discounts although the size of his releases did not entitle him to a quantity discount. He was also assured of an adequate inventory without the cost of maintaining that inventory.

The industrial distributor was convinced that his own manufacturer would guarantee to hold prices in the event of a price increase. Pressures of competition and time forced the distributor to negotiate the blanket purchase order without obtaining formal assurance from his manufacturer. However, contacts with junior executives led him to believe that the price would be held. This belief bolstered his hopes that the business deal would be a very lucrative one. While the industrial distributor appreciated the possibility of having to absorb a price increase, he felt that there was a psychological advantage to be gained which would result in additional purchase orders. Such possible gains may not offset the possible losses incurred by poor marketing strategy.

On October 1, 1958, a price increase was announced for the trade. A second price increase was made on July 15, 1959. The distributor was forced to absorb these price increases since no price-protection guarantee was made by his manufacturer. Unfortunately, the industrial distributor was able to furnish only 50 per cent of the requirements from inventory before the first price increase went into effect; 25 per cent was secured at the price effective October 1, 1958; and 25 per cent was secured at the price effective July 15, 1959. Thus it was necessary to purchase 50 per cent of the requirements at a cost in excess of the guaranteed selling price.

Circumventing the hazards

Since specific brand names were not given for the items listed in the blanket purchase order, it might have been possible for this supplier to protect himself, or at least modify the impact of the price increases, by procuring items of comparable quality from inventories being liquidated or from foreign sources which might have been available at lower prices. If such alternatives are not available to the supplier to alleviate such a dilemma, it becomes necessary to sit out the storm at a loss, if financially able, or face liquidation or possible bankruptcy because of an inexcusable, self-imposed, precarious position.

It is glaringly apparent that the foregoing blanket order contained seemingly unbelievable flaws, flaws to which one would say experienced business managers would not fall victim. Yet, this story is taken from an actual case history, concerning a long-established industrial supply firm.

The writers' observation is that the supplier might have been influenced by the customer on the basis of an implied promise that "you'll have your foot in the door on a permanent basis." Calculated risks resulting from questionable deviations from a normal blanket order may be too great to assume and may be economically unsound.

There are definite economic benefits to both the supplier and buyer under normal blanket-order conditions. But there are certain points which are well to remember when negotiating such an order. If the price is guaranteed to the buyer, the order should cover a relatively short period of time so that the supplier may plan and estimate with a fair degree of accuracy the least and greatest effect of a possible price increase or some other economic setback. If the price is guaranteed to the buyer for a relatively long period of time, the supplier should obtain protection by receiving a price guarantee from his source of supply, the manufacturer. Such price guarantees are known to be made. This concession, however, may prove disadvantageous to the manufacturer. A blanket order covering a long period of time should include a clause to protect the supplier from an unfavorable price change. The buyer should not impose on the supplier by expecting him to suffer losses or absorb price increases such as evidenced in the case history illustrated. A supplier's long-term success is a buyer's success.

22. DETERMINING THE "BEST POSSIBLE" INVENTORY LEVELS *

Kalman Joseph Cohen

Introduction

We shall be concerned here with the problem of how inventory levels should be established. This is an important problem, for inventories play a role in all phases of business and industry, whether retail, wholesale, or manufacturing. Rather than considering all aspects of inventory problems, however, we shall concentrate on the function of inventories in the distribution of commodities, in particular, in the wholesaling operations, and we shall not be concerned with the part that inventories play in manufacturing.

In a distributional business, the reason for having any inventory is to sell goods. Usually, you cannot sell anything to a customer unless you have it in stock. These considerations would tend to make wholesalers or retailers carry large inventories, for the more items there are in stock, the greater are the chances of having what customers want when they want it.

However, there are limits to the size of the inventories which any business would want to have, these limits arising because it costs money to hold inventory. Inventories can be considered to be too large when the costs of carrying the commodities exceed the benefits obtained from having them in stock. On the other hand, inventories are insufficient when the additional gains from having more inventory are greater than the additional costs which would be generated. Somewhere in between there exists the *best possible* level of inventory, i.e., that level of inventory which results in the largest possible profit for the business. How to find the level of inventory which *is* best is the subject of this article.

* Reprinted by permission from *Industrial Quality Control,* Vol. XV, No. 4 (October, 1958), pp. 4-10.

Kalman Joseph Cohen, Assistant Professor of Economics and Industrial Administration, Carnegie Institute of Technology.

The Warehouse Network

The particular work which we shall discuss was done for the Replacement Division of Thompson Products. This Division does no

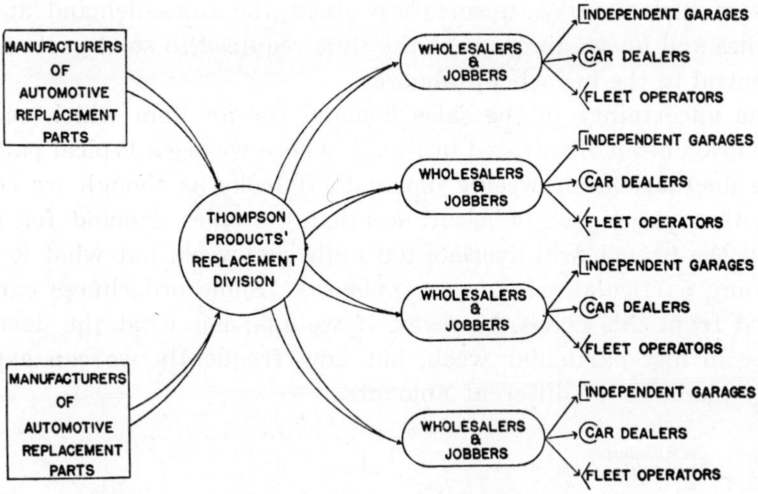

Figure 1—Physical Flow of Replacement Parts

manufacturing, so we need not consider the functions of inventories in manufacturing operations. Replacement Division is a large distributor of automotive engine and chassis parts for replacement use, as is indicated in Fig. 1. This Division buys these parts in bulk from various manufacturers and sells them to wholesalers or jobbers, who in turn sell them to independent garagemen, car dealers, and fleet operators.

Replacement Division has one central warehouse in Cleveland and 36 branch warehouses scattered throughout the United States. Most of the sales are made at the branches. The central warehouse serves mainly as a supply depot, from which all branch stocks are sent.

The inventory problem at the branch warehouses consists in determining the best possible amounts of inventory which should be carried in stock. The magnitude of this problem can be appreciated from the fact that approximately 15,000 items are sold at each of the 36 branches, so there are more than half a million branch warehouse inventory levels to be established.

Sales Demand at the Branches

If it were possible to say exactly how many parts would be sold each week at every branch and how long it would take to get these parts to the branches from the central warehouse, then it would be relatively easy to specify the best possible inventory levels at each branch warehouse. The problem that we have to deal with is considerably more difficult, however, because of two unavoidable elements of uncertainty: uncertainty about the sales demand at the branches and uncertainty about the time required to send parts from the central to the branch warehouses.

The uncertainty in the sales demand for an item which occurs at the branches is illustrated in Fig. 2, where we see a typical pattern in the fluctuations of weekly demand. It looks as though we could say with some degree of assurance that the sales demand for that part at the branch will average ten units per week, but what it will be in any particular week, we cannot say. Some orderliness can be derived from this chaos, however, if we ask, not what the demand will be in any particular week, but how frequently we can expect weekly demands of different amounts.

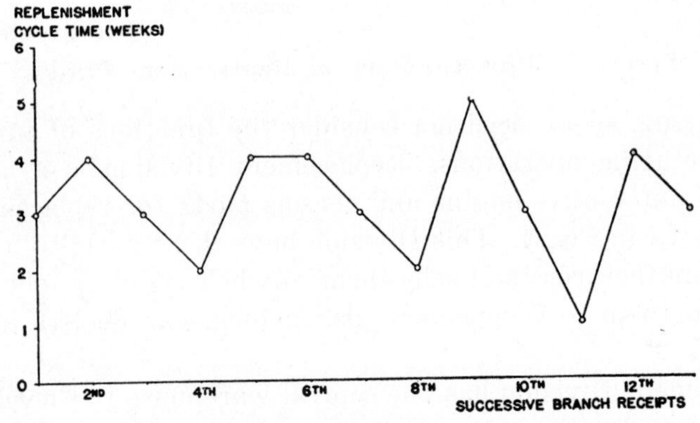

Figure 2—Variations of Demand for an Item at a Branch

If we look at the weekly demands for a part at a branch over a large enough number of weeks, there will become evident a stable pattern of the relative frequencies with which different levels of demand occur. Over a long enough period of time, the pattern of weekly demand that we saw in Fig. 2 will build up into the frequency distribution of weekly demand shown in Fig. 3. Here we see that the most frequently occurring weekly demand is the average demand of ten units per week, the next most frequently occurring demand is nine units per week, and so forth. Furthermore, a weekly demand of ten units occurs three times as frequently as a weekly demand of five units, etc.

Statisticians apply the name "Poisson distribution" to describe the type of frequency distribution shown in Fig. 3. For our purposes, we need know only that the shape of the Poisson distribution is completely determined by its average value, and that we can use this distribution to describe the uncertainties in the weekly demand for a part at a branch warehouse.

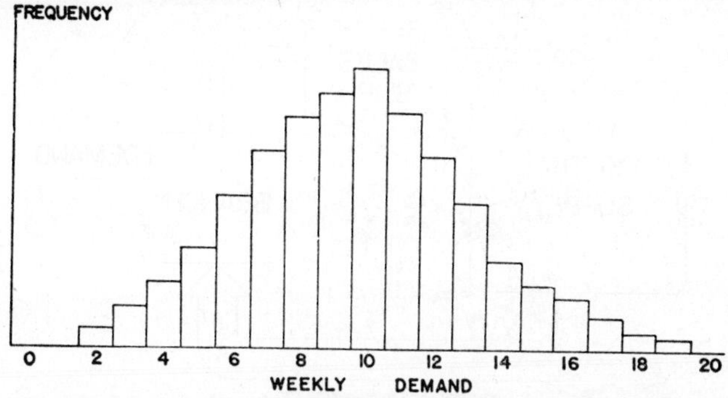

Figure 3—Frequency Distribution of Weekly Demand for an Item at a Branch

Because of the fluctuations in sales demand, it sometimes happens that a branch is out of stock on an item when a customer wants it. This results in a *lost sale,* for when a customer cannot immediately obtain a particular part from the local branch warehouse, he will usually purchase it from a competitor. Thus, lost sales are lost business, and if a branch is out of stock when an item is requested, Replacement Division foregoes the profit that could have been made by selling that item.

The Replacement System

The branch warehouses are not autonomous in their operations. The central warehouse maintains rigid inventory control over the branches, determining what their inventory levels should be and actually shipping all stocks for the branches from Cleveland. The relation between the central and branch warehouses is shown schematically in Fig. 4. Whenever a part is sold at a branch, a copy of the sales slip is immediately sent to Cleveland, so that the central warehouse can prepare an invoice for the customer. Cleveland accumulates the sales slips from a branch for a whole week, and it then prepares a replenishment shipment to restore the branch warehouse's inventory, replacing each part which has been sold during the week on a one-for-one basis. Thus, sales of all parts for a week are automatically replaced on a weekly basis, and a replenishment shipment is sent each week to every branch warehouse.

Replenishment Cycle Time

The period between the first sales slip for a week being sent from a branch to Cleveland and the receipt of the corresponding replenishment shipment at the branch can be called the *replenishment* cycle. Another major element of uncertainty in the system is the length

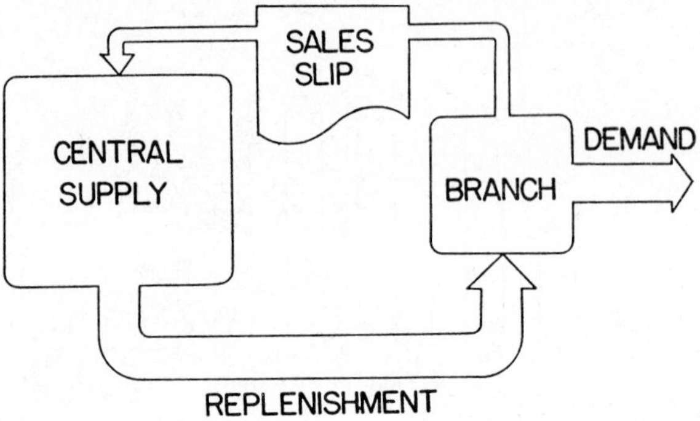

Figure 4—Branch Warehouse Supply System

of the replenishment cycle, for this varies from week to week. Fig. 5 shows a typical pattern in the fluctuations of replenishment cycle times. While the average replenishment cycle time shown here seems to be three weeks, there are substantial variations from one week to another. We can deal with the uncertainty of the replenishment cycle time as we dealt with the uncertainty in weekly sales demand. That is, we shall ask not what the replenishment cycle time will be in any particular week, but how frequently we can expect replenishment cycles of different lengths.

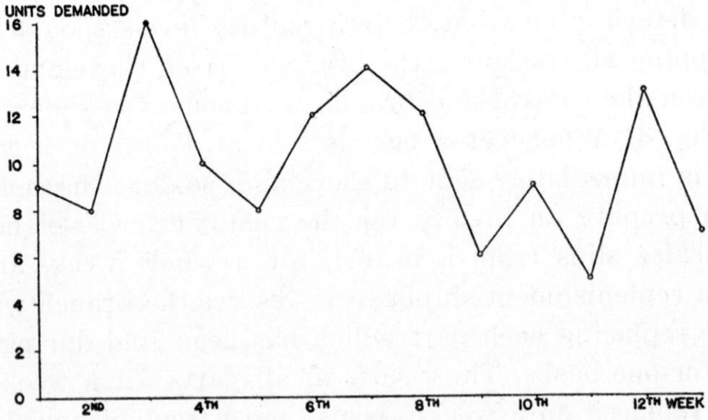

Figure 5—Variation of Replenishment Cycle Time for a Branch

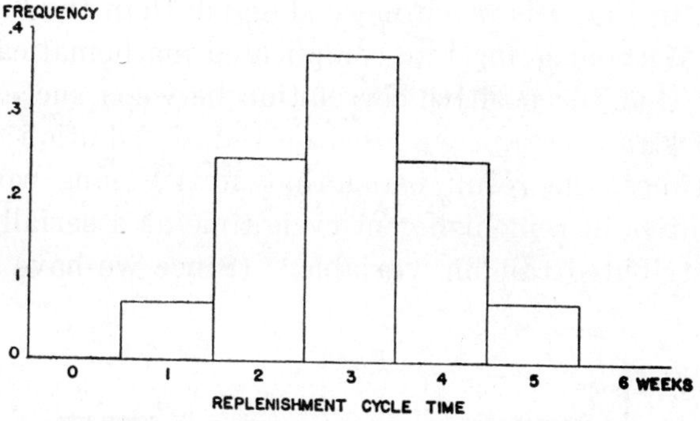

Figure 6—Discrete Frequency Distribution of Replenishment Cycle Times

If we look at the replenishment cycle time over a large enough number of weeks, there will become evident a stable pattern of the relative frequencies with which different lengths of replenishment cycles occur. Over a sufficiently long period of time, the pattern of replenishment cycle times that we saw in Fig. 5 will build up into the frequency distribution of replenishment cycle times shown in Fig. 6. Here, we see that the most frequent replenishment cycle time is three weeks, which occurs about 38 percent of the time. Replenishment cycles of two or four weeks each occur about 24 percent of the time, and replenishment cycles of one or five weeks each occur about 7 percent of the time.

Statisticians apply the name "normal distribution" to the type of frequency distribution shown in Fig. 6. For our purposes, we need know only that the shape of the normal distribution is completely determined by its average value and its standard deviation, and that we can use this distribution to describe the uncertainties in the replenishment cycle time at a branch warehouse.

The uncertainties in replenishment cycles are actually somewhat more complicated than those indicated by the distribution shown in Fig. 6. How long the replenishment cycle will be in one week seems to depend on how long it was in the previous week, since there is a positive correlation in the lengths of successive replenishment cycles. Although over a long period of time, the relative frequencies with which different replenishment cycles occur is adequately described by the normal distribution, the positive correlation between successive replenishment cycle times means that the magnitude of the weekly fluctuations will be lessened. Figure 7 illustrates the difference in replenishment cycle patterns which occurs depending on whether this correlation is present or absent. The "correlated" time series shown in Fig. 7 is much more sluggish than the "independent" time series. Without going into complicated mathematical details, we can say only that the positive correlation between successive replenishment cycles can be superimposed on the distribution of replenishment cycle times, the result being that statisticians would describe the uncertainties in replenishment cycle time as a serially correlated, normally distributed random variable.[1] (Since we have momentarily

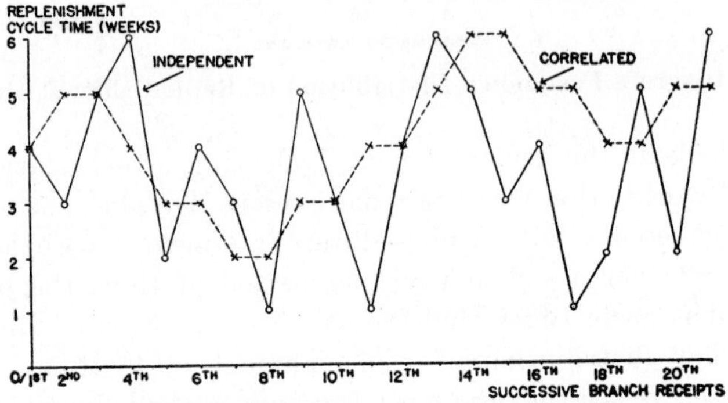

Figure 7—The Effect of Serial Correlation on Replenishment Cycle Times

lapsed into statistical jargon, we can mention in passing that statisticians would similarly describe the uncertainties in weekly sales demand as a Poisson distributed random variable.)

The Relation Between Lost Sales and Inventory Levels

Let us once again look at the schematic relation between the central and branch warehouses. This is illustrated in Fig. 8, where we have introduced roulette wheels to indicate the uncertainties in weekly sales demand and replenishment cycle time. These two elements of uncertainty make it impossible for a branch always to have parts in stock when customers want them. The frequency with which a branch is out of stock on items that customers want depends upon the size of that branch's inventories, for the branch warehouse inventories function as buffers which mediate the uncertainties of sales demand and replenishment cycle time. Therefore, a necessary step in determining the best possible levels for branch inventories is first to

[1] A method for handling the serial correlation in replenishment cycles has been developed in Jack Weinstock and David Young, "The Influence of Correlation of Replenishment Times on Inventory Control Systems," Operations Research Society of America, Tenth National Meeting, November 15-16, 1956, San Francisco, Calif. Figure 7 was taken from the Weinstock and Young paper.

determine the relation between lost sales of an item and the level of inventory for that part at a branch.[2]

If sufficient historical data were available, it would be possible to determine directly how lost sales depend upon inventory levels. The required data were not available, however, so it was necessary to adopt an alternative approach. Essentially, what we did was to reconstruct or simulate the history of branch warehouse operations on a high-speed electric computer.[3] From this reconstructed history, we were able to obtain the required data, and thus, the dependence of lost sales on inventory levels.

Technically, this simulation of history on a computer is called a "Monte Carlo" approach, after the gambling casino of the same name. Anybody who has watched the roulette wheels at Monte Carlo or Las Vegas can understand the reasoning behind this approach.

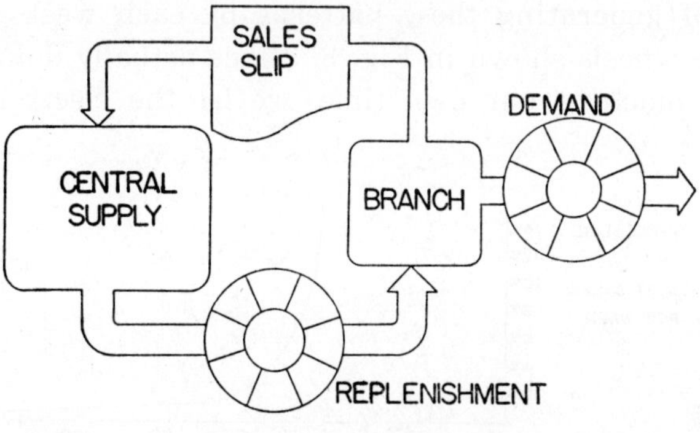

Figure 8—Branch Warehouse Supply System

[2] An analytical method for determining the relation between average lost sales and inventory level for the special case in which successive replenishment cycle times are uncorrelated has been developed in William Karush, "A Queuing Model for an inventory Problem," *Operations Research*, Vol. 5, No. 5 (Oct. 1957), pp. 693-703, and in Philip M. Morse, *Queues, Inventories and Maintenance*, New York: John Wiley and Sons, Inc., 1958, pp. 139-146.

[3] This Monte Carlo approach has been discussed in: (a) Kenneth C. Lucas and Leland A. Moody, "Electronic Computer Simulation of Inventory Control," pp. 107-121 in *Electronics in Action: The Current Practicality of EDP*, Special Report No. 22, American Management Association, New York, 1957. Figures 2, 4, 5, 8, and 9 were taken from the Lucas and Moody paper; (b) Jack K. Weinstock, "An Inventory Control Solution by Simulation," pp. 65-71 in *Report of System Simulation Symposium*, (Sponsored by the American Institute of Industrial Engineers, The Institute of Management Sciences, and the Operations Research Society of America, held in conjunction with the 8th National Convention of the American Institute of Industrial Engineers, New York, May 16, 17, 1957), 1958; (c) Andrew Vazsonyi, "Electronic Simulation of Business Operations (The Monte Carlo Method)," Second Annual West Coast Engineering Management Conference, May 27-28, 1957, Los Angeles, California, sponsored by the Management Division, Southern California Section, The American Society of Mechanical Engineers.

Let us look again at Fig. 8, which shows the relation between the central and branch warehouses. With the one-for-one replenishment system which is being used, the number of sales during any week of a part at a branch (and the number of lost sales) depends only upon the sales demand during that week and the inventory on hand at the start of the week. This starting inventory depends, in turn, upon sales during previous weeks, the lengths of time required for replenishment cycles during preceding weeks, and the level of inventory which was initially established.

Thus, in order to determine the actual sales and lost sales which can be expected to result from a given initial inventory level, it is necessary to know only the patterns of sales demand and replenishment cycle times which occur. Both demand and replenishment times are uncertain, but typical patterns for them can be constructed from the frequency distributions which describe them. Conceptually, we can think of generating these patterns by each week spinning the two roulette wheels shown in Fig. 8. Since actually doing this would require too much of our own time, we let the electronic computer

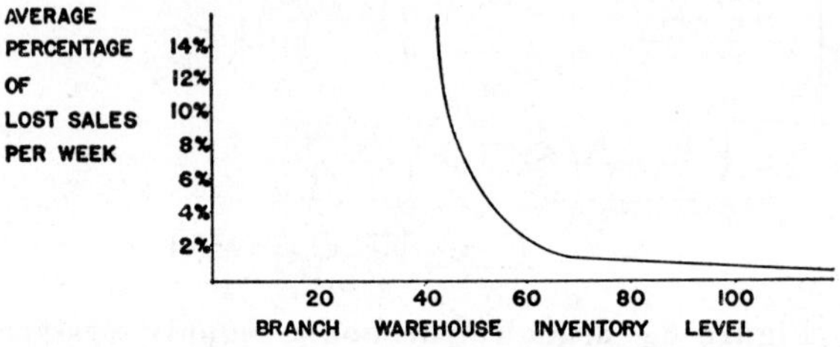

Figure 9—Expected Weekly Lost Sales as a Function of Branch Inventory Level, for Average Demand of Ten per Week

calculate the values which result from spinning the roulette wheels. A high-speed computer can run through calculations of this type very, very quickly, and in a brief time it is possible to determine the average number of lost sales which will occur each week for any particular initial inventory level.

Using the computer to simulate history resulted in a set of curves similar to the one shown in Fig. 9. For a given average weekly sales demand, the percentage of sales which will be lost decreases as the inventory level increases. However, as we see in Fig. 10, the exact relation between the average percentage of lost sales per week and branch inventory level depends upon the average weekly demand.

The SOBIL (Simulated Optimal Branch Inventory Levels) System

Once we know the relation between average lost sales and inventory levels, we are ready to use this knowledge to establish the best possible branch warehouse inventory levels. By "best possible" inventory levels, we mean those levels of inventory which will result in the largest total expected profits from the operations of the branches. By balancing the expected gain resulting from the sales that branch warehouse inventories will support against the expected cost of carrying this inventory, normal inventory levels can be established for every part at each branch in a way which leads to the largest possible total profits. For convenience, we have invented the name "SOBIL System" to refer to the use of the simulation curves of Fig. 10 for establishing branch warehouse inventory levels which are optimal in accordance with the expected profit maximization criterion.

The gross gain each week from holding inventory is the product of the average weekly sales that will result from this inventory and the gross margin per unit sold, where the gross margin on a part is

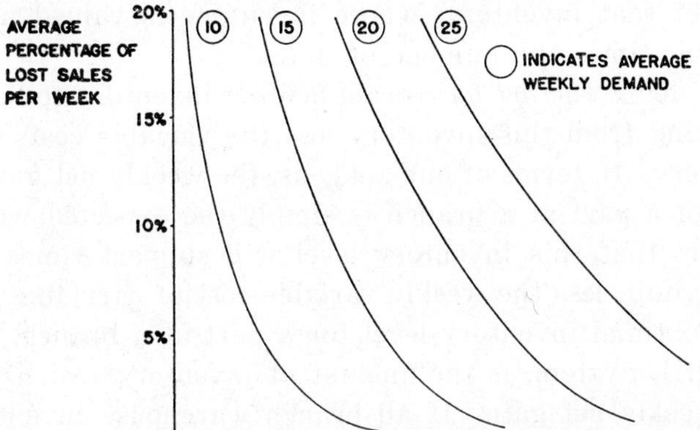

Figure 10—Expected Weekly Lost Sales as a Function of Branch Inventory Level, for Various Average Weekly Demands

the difference between its selling price and material cost. The reasonableness of this can be seen from the following three considerations.

First, lost sales, as measured by the simulation curves of Fig. 10, are lost business. This is substantially true, for customers are usually unwilling to wait for a part when a branch is out-of-stock. Of course, for very minor delays of a day or two pending receipt of a shipment already in transit, some customers may be willing to wait, but this possibility has in fact already been taken into account by the manner in which the simulation curves were derived.

Second, in those rare instances when a customer who requests a part from a branch which is out of stock is willing to experience a substantial delay in obtaining it, i.e., to allow his order to be backlogged, there are considerable extra costs incurred in processing, expediting, handling, and shipping this order. These extra costs probably eliminate profit which would have accompanied a normal sale of the item.

Third, the administrative and processing costs of handling customer orders are the same regardless of whether those customer orders result in direct sales or lost sales.

On the opposite side of the ledger, the penalty attached to holding inventory is the cost of carrying this inventory. Specifically, we must consider those variable elements of inventory carrying costs which depend upon the size of inventories actually held, as e.g., the cost of invested capital, obsolescence, insurance and taxes, handling and labor costs, and space costs. In Replacement Division, the variable costs of holding inventory at a branch warehouse are proportional to the value of that inventory, where inventory is valued at material cost per unit times the number of units.

We can define the *net gain* from holding inventory to be the gross gain resulting from this inventory less the variable costs of holding this inventory. In terms of our analysis, the weekly net gain from an inventory of a part at a branch is simply the expected weekly sales of that part that this inventory level will support times the gross margin per unit, less the weekly variable cost of carrying this inventory. The optimal inventory level for a part at a branch, as defined by the SOBIL System, is the amount of inventory which will maximize the weekly net gain. If all branch warehouse inventory levels were established according to the SOBIL System, then the overall expected profits of the operation will be maximized.

The procedure for establishing the best possible inventory levels is shown symbolically in Fig. 11. The weekly net gain from holding an inventory of a part at a branch is a function of the size of that inventory. In order to find the optimal size of that inventory, we can set the derivative of the weekly net gain from holding inventory equal to zero, and then solve this equation for the optimal inventory level. When we do this, it turns out that the best possible inventory levels do not depend upon the height of the simulation curves of Fig. 10, but, rather, they depend upon the *slopes* of these curves. In particular, in order to establish the optimal inventory levels, we have to know the relation between the rate of increase in average weekly sales and branch warehouse inventory levels. The form of this relation is shown in Fig. 12, where we see that for any given level of average weekly demand, the rate of increase in average weekly sales decreases as the inventory level increases. The electronic computer can be used to produce these new curves shown in Fig. 12, as well as the simulation curves shown in Fig. 10.

To determine the optimal inventory level for a part at a branch, we first select the curve from Fig. 12 which corresponds to the average weekly sales demand for the item. Suppose that this particular curve is the one shown in Fig. 13. Next, we divide the variable cost of carrying one unit of inventory for a week by the gross margin on the part. The resulting value, as we see in Fig. 13, is found on the vertical axis. From there, we move horizontally from the curve, and then we move vertically from the curve to the horizontal axis. The level of inventory which is then indicated on the horizontal axis is the best possible inventory level for the part at the branch.

If desired, rather than using this graphical procedure, the determination of optimal branch inventory levels can readily be programmed for an electronic computer.

It must be emphasized that while the SOBIL System provides an automatic way of determining branch warehouse inventory levels, this neither restricts management's prerogative nor eliminates the need for sound business judgment. Management always has the discretion to establish branch warehouse inventory levels other than those indicated by the SOBIL System, if policy considerations should so dictate. Indeed, management might want to do so because of a desire to give exceptional service to favored customers, to maintain a particular share-of-the-market, or aggressively to develop a new market. In such cases it is easy to determine the net gain from holding inventory *which is foregone* by establishing a branch warehouse inventory at some level other than that indicated by the SOBIL System. This provides additional information which management would not otherwise have, information which can help management decide whether the special policy considerations are worthwhile. Figure 14 shows the form in which this information could easily be provided if the calculations of optimal branch warehouse inventory levels are done on an electronic computer.

Forecasting Requirements for the SOBIL System

In order to make effective use of the SOBIL System, is is necessary to forecast the average weekly demand for every item at each

D = average weekly demand for an item at a branch warehouse
X = branch warehouse inventory level for the item
$l(X)$ = average weekly lost sales for the item at the branch, as a percentage of the demand
P = selling price of the item
C = material cost of the item
v = weekly variable inventory carrying costs, as a percentage of branch warehouse inventory value
$G(X)$ = weekly net gain from a branch warehouse inventory level of X for the item

Criterion: the optimal branch warehouse inventory level for the item is that X that maximizes $G(X)$. This value of X must satisfy the inequality

$$G(X - 1) < G(X) > G(X + 1),$$

where

$$G(X) = (P - C)[1 - l(X)]D - vCX.$$

The inequality is equivalent to

$$(P - C)Dl(X - 1) - vC > (P - C)Dl(X) < (P - C)Dl(X + 1) + vC.$$

The value of X that satisfies this inequality can be closely approximated by solving the equation obtained by setting the derivative of $G(X)$ with respect to X equal to zero. This leads to

$$-\frac{dl(X)}{dX} = \frac{vC}{(P - C)D}.$$

This means that the solution is equal (or very nearly equal) to the value of X where the negative slope of the $l(X)$ curve is equal to $vC \div (P - C)D$.

Figure 11—The SOBIL System

branch. This may not be easy to do, for these average weekly demands slowly change over time.

Over a long period, the local demand for an automotive replacement part will vary because of the changing size and age distribution of the existing stock of automobiles and trucks, the changing number of models in which the part has been used, competition, seasonal factors, and random fluctuations.

Many alternative methods for forecasting demand by item by branch should be investigated. Perhaps the simplest procedure is to use a moving average or linear trend extrapolation based on recently experienced demand. More sophisticated would be the use of a life cycle growth and decay curve based on the number of models in which a part has been used and the elapsed times since the part was first and last incorporated in a new model.

Even more elaborate would be a mortality, age-distribution, share-of-the-market model. The size of the market for a replacement part would be estimated by considering the size and age distribution of the existing stock of automobiles and trucks, the probability of the part becoming defective as a function of the age of the machine

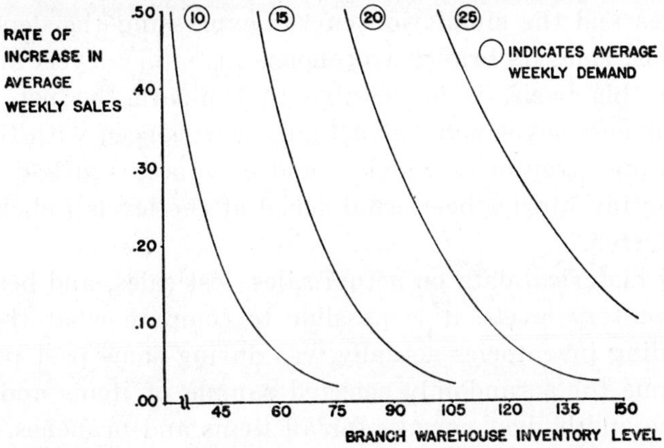

Figure 12—Rate of Increase in Expected Weekly Sales as a Function of Branch Inventory Level, for Various Average Weekly Demands

in which it is housed, and the models in which the part has been incorporated. The size of the market for the part is then multiplied by each branch warehouse's assumed share-of-the-market to yield the forecasts of the average demand for that part at the various branch warehouses.

Any or all of these forecasting procedures might be improved by making adjustments for seasonal variation.

How often the forecasts of average weekly demand should be revised depends upon how frequently the branch warehouse inventory levels should be changed. This, in turn, depends upon the clerical and data-processing costs required to reset the branch inventories, the net gain from holding inventories which is foregone because of using incorrect estimates of average weekly demand, and any changes which might occur in the values of critical parameters, such as the means or variances of the replenishment cycle times, the cost of capital, or other inventory holding costs.

Testing the SOBIL System

Before completely accepting the worthwhileness of the SOBIL System, it is desirable to estimate the magnitude of the increased profits which should result from the use of this procedure. There are two general ways of making such an estimate, either through a careful analysis of historical data or through a program of controlled experimentation.

The cheapest and fastest way of estimating the amount of increased profits which should result from adopting the SOBIL System is to assume that the equation defining the net gain from holding inventories and the simulation curves expressing the dependence of average lost sales on branch warehouse inventory levels are all accurate. On this basis, it is possible to compare the net gain from holding inventories which was actually experienced with the net gain from holding inventories which would have occurred had the branch warehouse inventories been established at the levels indicated by the SOBIL System.

Using historical data on actual sales, lost sales, and branch warehouse inventory levels, it is possible to compute what the net gain from holding inventories actually was during some past period. This can be done for a randomly selected sample of items and branches, or, if time and budget permit, for all items and branches.

From the same historical data on actual demand, it is possible to determine the potential performance of the system, i.e., the net gain from holding inventories which would have resulted from optimal inventory levels. The results of these two calculations should then be compared. The difference between the net gain from holding inventories had optimal branch warehouse inventory levels been established and the actually experienced net gain indicates the increased profits which should result from using the SOBIL System.

The conclusive test of the SOBIL System can come only from a controlled experiment, however. Using proper experimental design principles, a randomized sample of branch warehouses should have their inventory levels established as indicated by the SOBIL System. In the remaining branches, the inventory levels should continue to be determined by the present system. The worthwhileness of the SOBIL System can then be determined by comparing the profitability of those branches where it was employed with the remaining branches. In order to get a meaningful basis of comparison which is independent of size, what should be considered is the percentage change in profits of the branch warehouses, not the absolute profits themselves. Then, the measure of effectiveness of the SOBIL System would be the ratio of the percentage change in profits of those branches using this new system to the percentage change in profits of those branches using the present method.

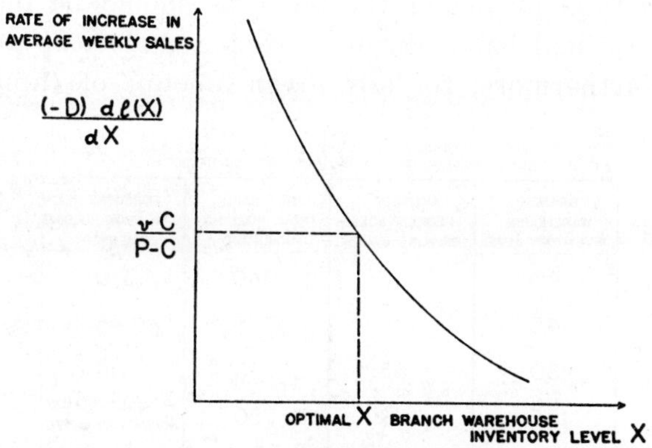

Figure 13—SOBIL System, Graphical Determination of Optimal Branch Inventory Levels

Conclusion

In this article we have described a procedure, which we have called the SOBIL System, for establishing the best possible branch inventory levels in a network composed of one central and several branch warehouses using a one-for-one replenishment system. Since the branch warehouse inventories function as buffers mediating the uncertainties of weekly sales demand and replenishment cycle time, there is a probabilistic dependence of weekly lost sales on branch inventory levels. A Monte Carlo approach, that is, a simulation of the history of the system on an electronic computer, was used to determine the relation between average weekly lost sales and inventory levels. By balancing the expected gain resulting from the average weekly sales that branch warehouse inventories will support against the expected cost of carrying inventories, our knowledge of the relation between average weekly lost sales and inventory levels can be used to determine optimal branch warehouse inventories, i.e., the levels of inventory which yield the longest possible net gains from holding inventory.

In addition to outlining the conceptual framework of the SOBIL System, we have indicated graphical and computational techniques which could be used in implementing the procedure, discussed the nature of the forecasts which must be made, and presented ways of determining the amount of increased profits which should result from adopting this system.

In a warehouse network such as we have described, adoption of the SOBIL System should result in several advantages. First and foremost, the total profits of the business should be increased, because of the optimal balancing of revenues and costs generated by inventory. Furthermore, for any given amount of capital invested

PART P BRANCH WAREHOUSE B AVERAGE WEEKLY DEMAND 10

BRANCH WAREHOUSE INVENTORY LEVEL	AVERAGE PERCENTAGE OF LOST SALES	NET GAIN FROM HOLDING INVENTORY	FOREGONE NET GAIN FROM HOLDING INVENTORY
40	20.0	6.40	1.10
45	11.5	7.05	.45
50	6.5	7.35	.15
55	3.0	7.50	OPTIMAL BRANCH INVENTORY LEVEL
60	1.7	7.43	.07
65	.8	7.32	.18

Figure 14—SOBIL System, Computer Print-Out

in inventory, the best possible distribution of this inventory can be obtained between the branches and for the different items, and the total investment in inventory can be controlled merely by changing the cost of capital. Finally, when policy considerations dictate establishing branch warehouse inventories at levels other than those indicated as optimal by the SOBIL System, the amount of short-run profit which is foregone by this policy is readily calculable.

Acknowledgements

This article discusses some continuing research which is being done for the Replacement Division of Thompson Products by the Management Sciences Department of The Ramo-Wooldridge Corporation. This work represents a team effort, and it is difficult adequately to delineate the parts for which various people are responsible. The members of the Ramo-Wooldridge team who, at various times, were involved in this project include Mr. W. R. Hydeman, Dr. William Karush, Mr. L. A. Moody, Mr. A. F. Moravec, Dr. A. Vazsonyi, Mr. Jack K. Weinstock, and Dr. David M. Young. The author's own contributions, conceived in close collaboration with Mr. Moravec, were mainly connected with developing the decision rules for determining optimal branch warehouse inventory levels (based on the relation between expected lost sales and inventory) and the general economic analysis of the Monte Carlo model's relevance to the Replacement Division's operations.

23. REDUCING COSTS THROUGH PURCHASING *

H. Thomas Hallowell, Jr.

There now exists so many more ways to do any given job that we tend to become confused as to what is old and tried in contrast to the new and unproven. Of course, the only right way to progress is to use the very best course available, which consists of the best of the old ideas and the best of the new ideas.

With things changing so fast, due to the multiplying effect of new and changing ideas and so many new people in our management jobs—brought about by the rapid expansion of our economy—it is quite easy to be diverted by the glamour, "hoopla" and advertisements of "pie in the sky" promised by the would-be creators of tomorrow's necessities.

Let us not discourage this dynamic atmosphere, but let's go to work to bring the pie in the sky down to earth so that we can enjoy it as pie on the table. And, of course, let us do this in such a way that we can afford it and bring it about profitably so all can benefit.

We do know, and we should instinctively know by this time, that we have had continuing long-term world-wide inflation, and it will probably continue on a controlled basis or semi-controlled basis.

And by this time we should know that using capital is a lot cheaper than using people's efforts and by using larger doses of capital in new plants with modern methods and the latest machines, with enlightened management and cooperative workers, we can make possible low costs brought about by large-scale standardized production and in this way we can combat inflation.

The output of our modern industrial progress produces goods faster in terms of human effort than hourly wages rise. From this phenomenon we get our increasingly higher living standards.

* Reprinted by permission from *Advanced Management*, Vol. 22, No. 8 (August, 1957), pp. 5-7.

H. Thomas Hallowell, Jr., President, American Standards Association and Standard Pressed Steel Company, Jenkintown, Pennsylvania.

I said, "large-scale production of a standardized product." And to bring about this large-scale production we need a product that can be used by more than one person or organization and will have as wide-spread a use as possible.

Where there has been large-scale production of standardized products and we've used plenty of capital in latest plant, tools and equipment, we've been pretty well able to keep costs down and prices under control.

To illustrate that an enlightened management can do this job, in our own company on our standard products—Unbrako socket screws, Flexloc locknuts, Hallowell work benches, Cleveland cap screws, Cooper Precision Products items and our other standard lines—the over-all prices have gone up less than 30 per cent since 1940, while wages have gone up over 135 per cent; steel prices up about 85 per cent and freight rates up approximately 45 per cent in the same period!

However, by the same rules with the same economics at work, today on non-standard items or a way of filling requirements by custom-built methods, costs and prices are many times higher than 20 years ago!

Capital assets are not high production items and tend to be made by custom methods, therefore, the cost of capital assets has probably gone up several times whereas production items have gone up only a few per cents. And chances are the capital items—machines, buildings, tools, etc.—will continue to rise greatly in the future.

Small lots of special items are not produced economically by any supplier when honestly compared to the situation costwise and pricewise with the closest standard substitute.

Furthermore, an informed supplier prices his standard items at such a low price as to not bring undue competition into the field, and today in progressive companies, costs and prices and profits on standard items are kept separated from the same elements of our nonstandard items' production—and there is good reason for this.

The throwing of a volume of good, standard peaches into the same basket with a few non-standard lemons can make such a formidable brew that its effects can be extremely corrosive to a company's profits. For example:

$1,000	Sale of standard high production stock items (peaches)
900	Costs
$ 100	Profits

\$ 150	Cost of a non-standard short lot special (lemons)
50	Sales price
\$ 100	Loss

On a combined sale of \$1,050 of standard peaches and non-standard lemons, the profit can be 00000! However, if we eliminate the lemon, the profit goes back to 10 per cent—or by increasing the price of the lemon even 3 times, the profit on the entire transaction would be 9½ per cent! (Just breaking even on the special!)

Even with a constant campaign on converting special users to standards, we do a very large volume of special item business. A whole division of our company is set up to handle these variations from standards in a most prompt and economical manner. We have taken every step to minimize the pain of a necessary special, both in our own organization and our customer's.

Now, Mr. Executive, these simple facts of industrial life today apply not only to your suppliers but you'll find even more graphic illustrations in your own manufacturing and company operations. How long can a situation such as this continue? As long as your profits and your management will allow!

Management is the planning, organizing, directing and controlling force in the use of capital and efforts in our American industrial set-up and management decisions require a dollar tag on them.

There is no one management group more enlightened and expert at getting the best prices on things bought in the market than our purchasing executives and their purchasing personnel. People both inside and outside your organization can be educated rather promptly through their pocketbooks!

To lower purchasing costs you, more than ever before, are the people who can put the price tag on the wastefulness of the non-standard requirements of specials required by your company.

Specials need special treatment all along the line. They must be screened and estimated. They require special engineering, expediting, processing, time-study, supervision, inspection, testing and packaging. They require special tools, gages, materials and set-ups on the machine tools. And they're usually produced by slower methods due to the low volume per order.

Fewer specials mean higher volume, longer runs, continuity of operations justifying more mechanization, special purpose machines and better tools.

I have found that there are four types of variations from standards:

Class 1:

A specially-engineered item that serves a very necessary, useful purpose, needed in large quantities, and by using it, improves the performance of the end assembly in such a way that its increased cost or nuisance value is more than offset by greatly improving the end performance of the products.

Class 2:

A specialty item required which perhaps could be eliminated or converted to a standard if sufficient time and thought were put on the problem, and whose extra cost can be economically justified by a slightly or marginal increased utility of the end product.

Class 3:

A specially-designed item which does not serve any very useful purpose, however, the extra cost is definitely not made up in increased utility of the end product.

Class 4:

The "god-awful" type of special whose costs are completely out of keeping with the economics of the assembled product and the elimination of such item can bring about savings many times greater than the cost of *engineering man years* if required to bring about the elimination.

Purchasing executives are in a position that it is necessary for them to have sufficient standing in an organization so that they have freedom to be uninhibited in helpful suggestions to the engineering department. Probably more than half of the special items (variations from a standard) could be eliminated if someone were to ask, "Is this really necessary?" If it were totally eliminated or converted to a standard article just how would it adversely affect the performance of the assembled product?" Let me encourage you to do this even more often than I think you've done in the past.

Just why does anyone need a special length of thread on a cap screw? We find that this is usually the result of some engineer's designing. He should have looked at a cap screw standards book! Why is a very long hollow set screw necessary? It's a special. It costs a great deal more than a standard. Why not screw two short hollow sets in the hole, one on top of the other? This approach can bring about untold savings.

The problem of organizational status is equally important in the engineering department as it is in the purchasing end of the business. Furthermore, engineering specifications bear a signature of some responsible person and so does the requisition for the material.

Standardization can proceed at a much more rapid rate for the benefits of all concerned if there is a company atmosphere reflecting top management thinking which makes possible an intelligent interchange of ideas in both directions between engineering, stores and purchasing, with the proper dollar tags attached so that the most economic way is achieved before the final decision is made.

Purchasing executives are in a unique position because their job is to select their supplier. They can, therefore, do business with enlightened, progressive suppliers who have large research divisions in their organizations. And purchasing executives are in a position to be a most constructive guiding influence on the research programs of their suppliers, particularly when they represent the purchasing requirements of a large user of the supplier's products.

He can take advantage of these research facilities by first giving such a supplier a part of his business and secondly, by bringing the supplier's research men in contact with his own engineering and development men in such a way that there can be an interchange of ideas so that everyone learns.

In this way new products and components can be devised so that they will have the greatest chances of serving a useful need, and quite often a supplier-consumer relationship can develop a standard product which can have an industry-wide application.

Today a first-class supplier must be able to furnish complete data as to specifications and performance and satisfactory proof of testing on his product. By so doing he eliminates the necessity for the user to do this checking in a field in which the user is not a specialist.

Titanium aircraft bolts which we currently produce in quantity are the outcome of a three year experimental program which cost us more than ½ million dollars. These bolts are 56 per cent as heavy as their steel counterpart yet they have the same tensile and shear values as heat-treated alloy steel, and the fatigue characteristics are equal or better.

The control techniques on this item are so unusual that no customer at this time has adequate facilities to check the finished item. Therefore, our organization has taken on the added responsibility of furnishing all information required by the customer and we certify that the facts are correct on each individual item shipped. This procedure is being used on an increasing number of our new items.

Research and standardization practices in the Standard Pressed Steel Co. and its subsidiaries have allowed us to constantly improve our products and develop new ones so that today with ten plants in three countries and 5000 employees, we can manufacture and have in stock more than 500 million pieces.

Standardization makes it possible for approximately 75 per cent of our total business volume of more than $50 million per year to be stocked by our distributors all over this country and in other parts of the world, so that immediate service can be furnished to any one of our tens of thousands of end consumers who have shown their confidence in our company by working with us so that together we both can prosper and continue to grow. Yes, these ideas work! Our company seems to be growing at the rate of doubling its size each five years.

A standard product means, Mr. Executive, that you need much less investment in inventory and still can have a prompt, adequate shipment.

One further step your leadership might accomplish in your own company is the education of top management as to the importance of standards in today's industrial economy. Too many chairmen, presidents and vice presidents still look upon standardization simply as a technical function of production. And top management usually delegates technical functions to the experts in charge of the various departments of the company. In a complex, inter-related economy like ours, this delegation can be overdone.

Standardization today is a true management function that should not be completely delegated to others because some of our greatest future areas of cost reduction with corresponding increases in profits lay in the area of the more development and use of American Standards.

The concept and use of standards is a key element in management control, coordination, integration, planning and continued profits. Your purchasing executives have a most important responsibility to constantly drive for more standardization among your outside contracts and within your own company, your associates and higher management. Your continued efforts for maintaining standardization will result in reducing costs and increasing profits through purchasing.

24. AN ANALYSIS OF PURCHASING METHODS USED IN ARMY ORDNANCE PROCUREMENT *

William B. Fynes

This study provides an analysis of the basic methods of purchasing used in the United States Department of Defense by the Army. It was performed to determine whether the government's aims in establishing formal advertising as the accepted method of purchasing were being met.

The government regulations by their emphasis on formal advertising as opposed to negotiation in the conduct of procurement are intended to insure that favoritism in awards will be prevented and that competition will be assured. It may well be that the requirements of the procurement regulations, if properly implemented, would accomplish these ends. However, it does not necessarily follow that the actual practice of the government in the accomplishment of its procurement mission attains the objectives established by the regulations. An evaluation of the results obtained on a sample of contracts of one technical service of the Department of the Army, thus, was the purpose of this study. In addition, the study also seeks to determine whether the government's emphasis on formal advertising as a means of attaining these ends is reasonable.

Importance of Procurement Methods

The importance of procurement lies in the fact that the government's buying methods may affect, to a considerable extent, the return on its dollar. This, in turn, has a significant effect on the civilian economy. A. N. Weecksler has clearly and pointedly indicated the importance of military buying and its direct relationship to the national economy.[1] He notes that historically the procurement of

* Reprinted by permission from the *Economics and Business Bulletin* of the School of Business and Public Administration, Temple University (March, 1959), pp. 17-24.

William B. Fynes, Plans and Programs Assistant in the Plans and Programs Office; Major, U. S. Army Reserve.

[1] A. N. Wecksler, "Warring on Waste in War Procurement," *Purchasing*, XXXIII, November, 1952, p. 122.

supplies has been looked upon as a military function and has been regarded, as other functions of war, as being wasteful. Now, under conditions of a continuing cold war with the necessity for maintaining a major military defense establishment, there is no longer any room for waste in military buying. In the future, Wecksler predicts, the percentage of the economy which will go to the military may vary as the threat to peace blows hot or cold, based on Soviet maneuvers; but he indicates that somewhere between 15 to 20 per cent of the gross national product will probably be required to meet military requirements.

Mr. Roger M. Kyes, past Deputy Secretary of Defense, has made it very clear that military and economic strength are inseparable.[2] The sustained striking power of the military is no greater than the economic body from which it draws its vitality. He points out that we must maintain sufficient military posture to deter our potential enemies and to do this our economic capabilities must not be weakened by an inefficient approach to national security. President Eisenhower also has stated that the role of the purchasing executive is crucial in the important task of eliminating waste and extravagance in the operation of the government.[3]

Methods used in this study

The materials used in this study included the procurement regulations, procedures and laws applicable to the Department of the Army and the contracts and details concerning their performance for a sample of 184 Army procurement contracts. The latter were limited to those contracts resulting from formal advertising without dollar limitations and negotiated contracts exceeding $2,500 which were awarded during the period from January 1, 1954 to December 31, 1956.[4] To these data were added the opinions and experiences of purchasing personnel from two commercial concerns. The data from the contracts were secured by a detailed examination of and the completion of an individual data sheet on each of them. Information concerning commercial purchasing positions and policies resulted from interviews in the offices of the firms.

[2] R. M. Kyes, "Impact of Wasteful Military Procurement," *The Commercial and Financial Chronicle*, CLXXVIII, July, 1952, p. 112.

[3] *New York Times*, November 10, 1953, p. 54.

[4] The two Army Ordnance installations involved are the Frankford Arsenal, Philadelphia, Pennsylvania, and Ordnance District Office, Philadelphia, Pennsylvania.

Present Regulations

The Department of Defense Agencies are restricted in their buying practices by three sets of regulations, i.e., The Armed Services Procurement Regulation, the Army, Navy, Air Force Procurement Procedures, and the procurement instructions issued by each of the technical services of the Department of the Army. All of these regulations find their origin in a large number of statutes promulgated over the years by the Congress and particularly in one act known as the Armed Services Procurement Act of 1947 (Public Law 413, 80th Congress). These statutes, in connection with government contracts, foster such policies as buy-American goods, fair labor standards, protection of small business, protection against "kick backs," renegotiation of war contracts, and protection against discrimination in employment because of race, color or creed. The Armed Services Procurement Act of 1947 prescribed that formal advertising be a requirement for letting of government contracts, with certain exceptions, and detailed the requirements and conditions governing those cases where negotiation would be permitted.

Since 1861, the standard government practice has been to handle all procurement by means of formal advertising. The authority was contained in the basic law which was codified in Section 3709 of the Revised Statutes. Generally, the law required that all purchases should be made by formal advertising, except in emergencies.[5] Over the years the basic law has been amended to include a number of exceptions to the rule requiring advertised bids. However, these exceptions were haphazard and uncoordinated. Furthermore, experience during and after the First World War made it apparent that certain procedural requirements of government contracting had not been used during the war because of emergency pressures.

As a result, during World War II steps were taken promptly to provide procurement procedures compatible with the speed required in war contracting. The President was empowered by the First War Powers Act[6] to make contracts, amendments, and modifications of contracts without regard to the present provisions of law relating to the making, performance, amendment or modification of contracts, whenever he deemed such action necessary.

With the cessation of hostilities, it became apparent that contracts would no longer be negotiated on the premise that such action

[5] It may be noted that this law was enacted March 2, 1861, at the outbreak of the Civil War.

[6] 55 Statute 838 (1941), 50 U.S.C.

would facilitate the prosecution of the war. Therefore, the War Department initiated an intensive study of the problems which would be involved in getting procurement back to a normal, peacetime basis. Recommendations were submitted by each of the technical services, on the basis of which a preliminary bill was drafted. About this time, the Civilian Production Administration set up an Interdepartmental Procurement Policy Committee, the primary purpose of which was to determine what methods of procurement developed during the war should be retained during peacetime.

That Committee decided that procurement by advertising and competitive bidding should be the "normal" method of purchasing supplies and services. It was felt that this method would assure the government the advantage of competition, prevent favoritism, and permit all persons an equal opportunity to share in government business. However, it was also recognized that there were certain situations in which advertising would not serve the best interests of the government. Accordingly, while the Committee recommended that procurement by advertising and competitive bidding be continued as a general rule, it provided for certain stated exceptions to meet the situations where procurement by negotiation would be most advantageous to the government.

A bill was drafted and sponsored by the War and Navy Departments. It was endorsed by the Comptroller General and introduced as HR 1366 into the House of Representatives. This bill was subsequently passed and became The Armed Services Procurement Act of 1947. The law followed the Committee recommendation in that it required procurement by advertising and competitive bidding, but it contained seventeen exceptions or circumstances where the specific conditions under which negotiation of a contract was permitted in lieu of the standard practice of formal advertising.

Formal Advertising and Negotiation

The basic mechanics of the two methods of purchasing employed by the government, i.e., formal advertising and negotiation, will be explained briefly at this point. The formal advertising process begins with acceptance by a purchasing agency of a purchase requirement. The requirement includes a description of the item, the quantity required, and an estimate of what the item should cost, with an indication of the possible source(s) of supply which are able to fabricate, construct, or manufacture the item or perform the service. At this point, the requirement is examined from the standpoint of which method of purchasing can be employed. When formal advertising is used, an invitation to bid is prepared and distributed to the known available sources of supply; it is also advertised through conventional news media. Any firm interested can bid on the proposal. A certain time limit within which bids can be prepared is stated.

The bids are sealed by the bidders and, upon receipt by the government are clearly noted as to the time of receipt. They are then placed under lock and key and held until the time previously established for the formal opening. On the day set, the bids are opened in the presence of specified government witnesses and any bidders who may care to attend. The pertinent data from each invitation to bid are noted on a government abstract of bids form. Evaluation of the data then takes place with the contract being awarded to the lowest bidder, all other considerations being equal.

The mechanics of the negotiation process are quite different. After the purchase request is received and a determination that one of the circumstances permitting negotiation prevails, a request for a proposal from industry is prepared. This proposal is forwarded to the selected sources together with the request that each submit an offer in terms of price, delivery and other specified considerations. Upon the receipt of these proposals, the process of negotiation begins.

In these negotiations a contractor must weigh his position relatively with his estimates of the positions of the rest of his competitors on the particular procurement involved. Although the profit motive is assumed to underlie the actions of the contractor, one must note that other considerations are also evident. For example, an initial contract may be taken, not for the profit it may be expected to generate but for the "know how" it would develop in his plant for future contracts. Contractors are usually aware of the fact that other firms are bidding on the procurement, but they are not aware of their bid positions, especially with regard to price, during the course of the negotiations. The official award of the contract to one of the contractors terminates the negotiations. The award in this case, unlike that under the formal, competitive bid method, hinges on a variety of factors and normally becomes a much more complex determination than the award of a contract to the low bidder.

The interests and role of the government

The functions and influence of government, especially those of the national government, have grown in the past few generations. H. J. Abraham states that:

"Gone long ago are the days when the role of government was viewed as solely that of preserving law and order. Gone also are those days when a government's chief concern was simply the maintenance of unbridled free competition. Today governments intervene in the economy in order to attain certain economic objectives. The reign of genuine laissez faire, if, indeed, it ever existed at all, has been on the decline for almost a century." [7]

It might be said that the objective of a good government purchasing policy should be to maximize the utility received for the dollars spent in processing and consuming the goods it needs, and by minimizing any losses from shortages caused by untimely deliveries. The government today has the interest of the national economy uppermost in mind. However, unlike commercial concerns, it purchases with two purposes in mind, i.e., obtaining full value for dollars spent and controlling the effects which the purchases are likely to have on the economy. For example, W. J. Baumol states:

"In choosing a procurement method, a government may have an eye on economy as well as the achievement of its ultimate purpose in making the purchase, and the simultaneous achievement of both these aims might involve more difficulty than the attainment of just one of them." [8]

The government's purchasing policies require that certain contracts be awarded only to small business concerns; it will not permit other contracts to be awarded to any firms except those in labor surplus areas; in other cases, its contracts legally bind the contractor with whom it is doing business to purchase items of supply only from American firms, one impact of the Buy-American Act.

Thus, in thinking of the government's emphasis on any particular method of procurement, its role as a stabilizer, social and economic guardian, and in enforcing democracy must always be kept in mind.

Contract Data Findings

As noted above, the contract data for this study were obtained from a random sample of Army contracts. The sample was made up of two parts. The first included 25 contracts, each selected randomly from a total of 357 negotiated contracts located in the District Office; the second group included 164 contracts which were selected randomly from the file of the Ordnance Mission Arsenal. The sample selected in this case involved 56 negotiated and 108 sealed bid docu-

[7] H. J. Abraham, *Government as Entrepreneur and Social Servant*, Washington, D. C.; Public Affairs Press, 1956, p. 1.

[8] W. J. Baumol, "Notes on the Theory of Government Procurement," *Economica*, XIV, February, 1947, p. 2.

ments. Altogether a total of 184 contracts were reviewed and analyzed to provide the data used in this study.[9]

As each contract was reviewed, a schedule based on its terms and performance was completed. The data collected were designed for presentation in tabular form which would facilitate evaluation and provide answers to the following critical questions:

1. Are small business firms given a proportionate share of government business?
2. What is the degree of restriction expressed in the selection of sources for government contracts?
3. Does a price comparison of certain selected items purchased by both negotiated and sealed bid purchasing methods indicate any reasonable variance?
4. How do sealed bid and negotiated contracts compare in terms of delinquency on delivery schedules?
5. How do sealed bid and negotiated contracts compare in terms of the processing time required to finalize the contract (administrative lead time)?

Effects on small business

An analysis to determine whether small business firms were given a proportionate share of government business yielded significant results. Of the total awards made (184), both sealed bid and negotiated, 65.9 per cent were awarded to small business and 34.1 per cent went to large business. In the case of sealed bid contracts, 76.4 per cent of the awards went to small business, 23.6 per cent to large business.[10] In terms of dollar value, of the total sealed bid awards within the sample that went to large business (25), 56.0 per cent were valued between $1,000 and $2,500; 32.0 per cent, from $2,501-$10,000; and 12.0 per cent, from $10,001-$100,000. None was over $100,000 in value. On the other hand, of the dollar value of the total sealed bid awards that went to small business (81), 42.0 per cent were valued between $1,001 and $2,500; 40.7 per cent, $2,501-$10,000; and 17.3 per cent, $10,000-$100,000. None was $100,000 and over. Because of the small size of the sample no statistical conclusion as to significance could be drawn concerning the dollar value of sealed bid contracts awarded to small or large business at any dollar value level.

[9] The total sampling initially represented 190 contracts, 109 of which were sealed bid contracts and 81 negotiated contracts. Of the 25 contract numbers revealed by the random sampling in the District Office, all contract files were located. Of the 165 contract numbers revealed by the systematic sampling in the mission arsenal, 159 of the contract files were located, 106 of which were sealed bid contracts and 53 of which were negotiated contracts. Therefore, the contractual data for the study were ultimately extracted from a total of 184 contracts, 78 of which were negotiated and 106 of which were sealed bid contracts.

[10] Small business is defined as one employing less than 500 and/or as one so classified by the Small Business Administration.

In negotiated procurements, 51.3 per cent of the awards surveyed (76) were made to small business and 48.7 per cent went to large business. The awards appeared to be evenly divided. Of the dollar value in the negotiated awards to large business, none was under \$2,500; 54.1 per cent were awards of \$2,501-\$10,000; 24.3 per cent were awards of \$10,000-\$100,000; and 21.6 per cent were awards of \$100,000 or more. Of the 39 contracts awarded to small business, 53.9 per cent were for \$2,501-\$10,000; 35.9 per cent were for \$10,001-\$100,000; and 10.3 per cent were for \$100,000 and over. No statistically significant difference could be found to exist, although large business would appear to be favored dollar-wise.

It may be concluded that small business firms received a greater number of awards in both the negotiated and sealed bid procedures. In addition, small business firms received a relatively larger proportion of sealed bid than negotiated contracts. It is also apparent that the proportion of total value awarded to large business was larger than that for small business. No statistical conclusion as to significance could be reached regarding dollar value distribution, however, because of the small sample size.

Restrictions on sources of supply

The data presented were classified by number of contracts in terms of the number of sources solicited and according to whether the responses were received from negotiated proposals or sealed bids.

Of the total negotiated contracts, in 50.0 per cent of the cases only one source was solicited; in 25.6 per cent of the cases there were 2 to 5 sources; in 16.7 per cent, 6 to 10 sources; and in 7.7 per cent, more than 10 sources. In the case of sealed bid contracts, 71.7 per cent of the contracts represented solicitation of not less than 10 sources. It can be concluded that, generally, the sealed bid (advertised) contracts gave evidence of a much wider participation by proposers than did negotiated contracts.

Price comparisons, certain selected items

By comparison of certain selected items purchased by both techniques, an analysis of results was made. Such comparisons were made only when the items were found to be completely identical at the time of purchase by one method as compared with the time of its purchase by the other method. Contract dates were then compared since price changes might be the cause of the difference in cost as between two points in time. Quantities of items purchased in both cases were compared since this difference could also account for price variations. Similarly, contract date sequences were analyzed since a higher price is sometimes paid on the original purchase of an item. After allowance for these variables, the data supported the conclusion that, on the basis of prices paid for the particular items selected, sealed bid contracts were more advantageous.

Comparisons of delinquency status

The data collected showed that 52.8 per cent of the sealed bid contracts surveyed were delinquent, in the sense of not performed on the contract date, as compared with 39.7 per cent of the negotiated contracts. It also indicated that the duration of the period of nonperformance past the due date was greater for sealed bid contracts than negotiated contracts. About 42.0 per cent of the delinquent negotiated contracts remained in that status for less than 30 days, while 28.6 per cent of the delinquent sealed bid contracts were in this time category. Of the balances, 16.1 per cent of the delinquent negotiated contracts and 21.4 per cent of the delinquent sealed bid contracts were delayed from 30 to 59 days; 6.6 per cent of the delinquent negotiated contracts and 12.5 per cent of the delinquent sealed bid contracts, 60-89 days; and 35.5 per cent of the delinquent negotiated contracts and 37.5 per cent of the delinquent sealed bid contracts, 90 days or more.

In order to determine the percentage of delinquent sealed bid and negotiated contracts within the population from which the sample was taken, a statistical analysis was made using the 95 per cent confidence level. It was determined that the percentage of sealed bid contracts that were delinquent within the population from which the sample was drawn fell within 43.3 and 62.4 per cent of all the sealed bid contracts in the population. With regard to negotiated contracts, it was determined that the percentage of negotiated contracts delinquent within the population from which the sample was drawn fell within 28.8 and 50.7 per cent of all the negotiated contracts in the population.

Thus, while it was evident that sealed bid contracts did not necessarily have a higher delinquency rate than the negotiated contracts, the significant conclusion was that both could have come from a population having a delinquency rate as high as 50.0 per cent.

Administrative lead time comparisons

An analysis of administrative lead time tends to place the sealed bid contracts in a more favorable light. In the administrative lead time groups of between 15 and 89 days were 78.3 per cent of the sealed bid contracts and 53.4 per cent of the negotiated contracts. Relatively more of the negotiated contracts had less than 45 days of lead time, but this was probably due, in the main, to the regulation requiring that sealed bids be advertised for a minimum of 30 days, except in an emergency.

Methods Used by Two Large Companies

As was indicated previously, purchasing practices and policies of two commercial concerns were examined for the purpose of comparing information and results with those obtained by government; both were corporations employing over 10,000 employees. Each had sales of over one billion dollars in 1956, and in both firms purchasing is a major function.

In the case of both concerns, negotiation was the accepted method of purchasing, with formal advertising used to an extremely limited degree. In one, formal advertising was limited to the area of construction contracts. In the other, it was rarely, if ever, used. The reasons given for this approach were that industry desires first to go out only to specific and preselected sources of supply and second, that firms desire to have freedom to negotiate the quoted price downward, if possible. They are opposed to granting the contract to the low bidder and accepting the low bid as the "best" bid.

There were similarities between the purchasing methods and programs of the firms and the government. Industry, as represented by the cases of the two companies studied, and the government both were interested in obtaining the best "buy," with price and other factors considered. The "other factors considered" represent the major difference between industry and the government. In industry, the overriding emphasis was on price. Quality and time play important, though lesser roles. Even if the price is "right" and the item either is not delivered on time or does not perform properly when delivered, then a "good" price is really of little benefit.

In the government, on the other hand, price and quality were important factors, but social, economic and political objectives seemed to assume an almost equal level of importance in the placement of contracts. The legal requirements upon government agencies, including aid to small business, distressed labor areas, and domestic producers, were typical of these objectives.

Both industry and the government maintained lists of what some considered to be competent sources of supply. Industry's attitude toward poor or delinquent producers appeared to be more severe than government's. It was found that if a contractor should fail to deliver according to the agreement, the government might place him in default status and terminate the contract. If the government had to buy the same items from another contractor and pay a higher price, the difference in price between the defaulted contract and the new contract was charged against the defaulted contractor. However, the investigation indicated that the contractor, in most instances, had to be quite unable to deliver before his contract was terminated for default. It was also found that such a contractor might receive another government award subsequently. In industry, on the other hand, poor producers were found more often than not to be completely eliminated as sources of supply.

Industry and government both were found to utilize an indefinite quantity (open end) type contract for items of a commercial nature which were not made in accordance with specifications and drawings but were readily available on the open market.

In both industry and government there was evidence of a large amount of centralized buying. However, the trend in industrial concerns seemed to be toward decentralization. In government, on the other hand, the trend was toward greater centralization. The decentralization trend in industry was also a key finding in a recent survey conducted by the National Industrial Conference Board among 212 manufacturing companies.[11] That study found that one firm in three had made some change in the organization of its purchasing operations during the past five years, and in 60.0 per cent of these the shift was in the direction of dispersing purchasing authority.

Concluding Observations

The primary conclusions from this study are summarized below. Because of sampling and case study methods, the conclusions relate only to this specific study and the data covered, although it is believed to have general applicability.[12]

[11] "Current Trends in Purchasing; A Survey," *The Management Review*, Vol. XLV, July, 1956, pp. 556-67.

[12] The complete study is available in the Library of Temple University and may be reviewed there by those interested.

The study indicates that sealed bidding appears to offer the advantages contemplated by Congress. Invitations for bids are distributed on a wider basis and participation by a larger number of sources was obtained. This tended to encourage competition and to minimize favoritism. Although there is no absolute criterion for judging whether small business is favorably treated, it appears that small business firms do obtain a relatively large number of awards under both types of procedures, but their position is better apparently under sealed bid than negotiation procedures.

Both negotiated and sealed bid contracts show a high delinquency rate in government, with negotiated as opposed to sealed bid contracts showing somewhat less frequent delinquencies. Formal advertising appears to result in the best prices to the government on an individual contract price basis, although the data were sufficiently limited to make this generalization tenuous. Lastly, the administrative lead time in finalizing contracts was found to be greater for negotiated than sealed bid contracts.

Comparing government and industry procedures, as represented by the two cases studied, showed many similarities and a few differences of significance. In general, the same procedures were used by both, although as a policy matter industry tends to use the negotiation form almost exclusively. It is also evident that government tended to appear less demanding and to be guided by social and political-legal objectives while industry was more likely to be governed by economic considerations. Divergent trends were also evident in greater centralization of purchasing by government, greater decentralization by industry.

The one overriding conclusion evident from this study is that the government's procurement program cannot be measured by the usual yardsticks of efficiency or economy recognized as determining factors by industrial purchasing authorities.

25. CYCLICAL IMPLICATIONS OF PRIVATE PRICING POLICIES *

Alfred R. Oxenfeldt

I. Scope of method

This paper is focused on a few aspects of industrial pricing policies. It is oriented particularly around industrial price behavior during recession. Accordingly, little will be said about pricing during a business upswing or about economic growth aspects of pricing.

This paper does not deal specifically with the present recession, but is intended rather as a more general analysis of pricing during recession. However, this discussion applies to the present and to future recessions—rather than to those of the past. The phenomenon of "inflationary recession" must deter us from generalizing on the basis of economic fluctuations during the 1920's and 1930's, let alone those of an earlier period. The combination and balance of forces operating in the pricing sphere apparently has changed substantially since, say 1930. Consequently, notions that were appropriate in an earlier decade would probably lead us to misunderstand and mismanage the present recession. Since we have had very little experience with our substantially altered economic system, we are unlikely to understand it thoroughly; we must not therefore rely very confidently upon any general conclusions we are tempted to reach.

This paper is confined primarily to industrial prices and therefore discusses retail, wholesale and service prices only indirectly. However, interrelationships among prices at different levels in the industrial structure must not be overlooked. Pressure on prices at retail often are shifted back to the manufacturer and by him to suppliers of major raw materials. These vital interrelationships should not be passed over lightly as a consequence of having different people discuss retail and industrial prices; they shall be touched on here only in passing.

* Reprinted by permission from Compendium of Papers Submitted by Panelists Appearing before The Joint Economic Committee, *The Relationship of Prices to Economic Stability and Growth* (Washington, D. C.; United States Government Printing Office, 1958), pp. 461-475.

Alfred R. Oxenfeldt, Professor of Marketing, Columbia University.

Further, this paper discusses industrial pricing during recession primarily from the standpoint of the price-setter. It revolves around a consideration of businessmen's pricing objectives, policies, methods and strategy; it deals also with their perception of the business scene, their knowledge of market developments, their anxieties and hopes, as well as their actual market behavior. This view of pricing stands in sharp contrast with studies by others for this Committee which are based upon a broad statistical analysis of price quotations or of announced price changes. A thorough understanding of the total pricing picture requires the use of both methods.

The study of pricing from the standpoint of the individual businessman overcomes the grave weaknesses that arise when one uses price quotations or announcements about price as the basis for study. Especially during periods of recession, these often do not represent the prices actually paid. This approach to an understanding of pricing offers other advantages also. First, it makes much clearer the causes for price behavior, for at bottom they do lodge in the objectives, framework of analysis and perceptions of the individuals responsible for setting price. Second, it frees us from dependence for basic data upon experience during earlier business recessions which may differ substantially from the present one, and from those we can anticipate in the future.

On the other hand, this method of studying prices during recession suffers two major difficulties: In the first place, it limits one to the small number of cases with which any individual can have close personal contact; second, and related to the first, it forecloses generalizations about the effects of such things as differences in industrial structure, the nature of the product, the age of the industry, rate of technological change on price behavior during recession.

II. Businessmen's price objectives—with particular reference to periods of recession

Businessmen have a whole hierarchy of conscious objectives that come into play during recession. Uppermost is the goal of survival for the firm. If this is assured, profitability will be a primary objective. About on a par with profitability in the minds of most businessmen is the maintenance of the firm's market share. A minority of business executives will consciously endeavor, in addition to pursuit of the foregoing objectives, to adopt courses of price action during recession that will ease the firm's marketing problems when business ultimately revives.

Beyond these objectives for the business, business executives' goals include some more personal aims. They want to maintain and advance their own positions within the firm; in addition, they will want to avoid blame for the decline in sales and profits and will try to get credit for pulling the firm out of its decline. Also, they may favor policies which make a minimum drain on their time and energies.

These many objectives are not necessarily consistent with one another; conflicts of objectives are likely to arise during recession. For example, it might prove immediately expedient to liquidate a large inventory by a drastic price reduction, but such action might make the maintenance of price on other sales more difficult and also cause difficulties in raising price once the recession ends. Sometimes, also, considerations of profit would dictate that a firm accept a reduced market share, posing a choice among conflicting goals held by management. Similarly, many business executives fear that top management or the Board of Directors will demand a report on what they have been doing to combat a decline in sales; at such times they are more comfortable if they can point to some concrete action they have taken. A reduction in prices often satisfies persons prodding for some action, even though it may involve a sacrifice of both short and long-run profits.

The existence of potentially inconsistent pricing objectives results in diversity of behavior, for individual firms and executives attach different weights to their various goals. Also, decisions made involving multiple and conflicting goals generally are made by less rigorous and systematic methods than less complex choices, and therefore are extremely difficult to unravel and understand.

III. Businessmen's main pricing policies during recession

Businessmen's pricing objectives, pricing policies, pricing strategies, and pricing methods shade off into one another. Also, they are closely interconnected for particular objectives require special policies; these in turn dictate the use of specific pricing strategies and sometimes even the particular pricing method to be employed. It is possible to distinguish four main combinations of pricing objectives-policies-strategies-methods that are prevalent among business managements in the United States. (For want of a better term, these combinations of related pricing goals and methods will be called "pricing syndromes.")

One widely employed "pricing syndrome" aims primarily to minimize price disturbances in both the selling and buying industries. This syndrome calls for stabilized prices during both recession and revival, for it rests upon the conviction that stable prices are beneficial to buyer and seller alike. The main benefits from stable prices are that the selling industry will not suffer sharp erratic spurts and declines in sales as buyers speculate in inventory; and, buyers will be spared the risks of loss from unavoidable inventory speculation. The pricing method implied by this pricing syndrome is that of adhering to past prices as long as possible. An important rationalization for this syndrome is that management should be obliged to forego price increases during periods of active business and in compensation should be spared price reductions during recession. The strategy required by this pricing syndrome is that customers should be persuaded that they gain from this pricing policy so that they become its advocates.

A second pricing syndrome has as its chief objective the maximization of profit in the fairly short run. With this objective, a seller reduces prices voluntarily only when he expects it to result in a fairly prompt rise in his sales and profits. He does not worry about possible long range effects of his price reductions because he is convinced that there is no stable connection between present and future prices and short-run and long-run profitability in his business. With this pricing objective, sellers will reduce price only when they have strong reason to believe that unit sales would be strongly stimulated thereby. Inasmuch as the sales of many products (though we do not know just how many) are quite insensitive to changes in price, this pricing syndrome rarely calls for prompt reductions during early recession. Indeed, one would expect unit sales to become less sensitive to price reductions during recession for price considerations would then be diluted with such factors as financial liquidity, the exception of further price reductions and the like. Moreover, it is difficult to understand why firms would be able to profit by price reductions during early recession, unless they had been charging too much for their own good before recession struck. Accordingly, one would expect firms to profit from a price reduction during recession only when it had a reasonable hope of winning customers away from rivals and keeping many of them. This hope would be unreasonable in most important industrial situations because it has become established practice for customers to ask their usual suppliers to match price concessions offered by other sources. Thus, efforts to maximize short-term profits during recession generally lead businessmen to avoid price reductions as long as possible. This pricing syndrome often includes outspoken espousal of price maintenance combined with the expressed determination to match price cuts by rivals.

A third pricing syndrome might be termed "an early yielding to the inevitable." This view of pricing involves a conviction that no firm can resist the basic economic forces at work during recession and that these forces are saluatory—even though painful. Thus, the objective underlying this pricing syndrome might be termed the goal of playing the game according to the rules, because one would ultimately "get caught" if he were to violate them. Given this objective, the firm's pricing policy would require a reduction in price when it became clear that the economy was undergoing general recession. Several strategies are compatible with this pricing syndrome: first, the firm may try to gain an advantage over its rivals by being the first to cut price; or, second, it may refrain from price reduction itself, figuring that even though a price decline is inevitable, the later it comes the better. If the second strategy is adopted, the firm will make special efforts to learn what its competitors are charging and stand ready to adjust its prices very speedily; with this view of pricing, a businessman is not likely actively to discourage price reductions by his rivals.

A fourth pricing syndrome calls for adherence to the firm's "basic pricing method." The objective of this pricing syndrome is to maintain what management believes to be sound business practice, and to avoid unplanned expedients. Underlying this pricing syndrome is the conviction that management has selected a pricing method after careful deliberation, presumably management took account of the fact that general business is variable and the "regular" pricing method meets the needs of such conditions. Thus, a recession would not call for any revision of the *method* used to establish price—though it might require a change in *price* itself. The most commonly employed method of arriving at price is some variation of the "cost-plus" method. For some businessmen, this pricing method rests upon the conviction that a manufacturer simply processes materials obtained from others and his rewards are a fee above the costs of the things he requires in his processing activities; beyond repayment of his costs, he is "entitled" to a "fair" profit for taking the risks involved in his business. Given this view, the price-setter should not be expected—and will not feel obliged—to reduce price unless his costs decline; on the contrary, if his costs were to rise at a time when business was declining, he would feel entitled to raise his price.

The foregoing discussion does not describe each pricing syndrome in its full complexity and passes over the many sub-types that exist. However, the main concepts involved in each of the four discussed are quite familiar and require no further elaboration for the purpose at hand, which is to explain the circumstances under which prices are altered during recession and the timing, form, and typical consequences of those changes. These four pricing syndromes may not cover all important pricing policies, though they probably do account for the overwhelming majority of cases.

IV. Conditions under which prices are reduced during recession

A. WHEN THE "WEAK LINK" BREAKS. Implicit in every pricing syndrome is the axiom that one must match price reductions by rivals if they do, or threaten to, make heavy inroads on sales. A businessman may deplore a price reduction by a rival, consider it poor business from his rival's standpoint and a misfortune for the entire industry, but he cannot ignore it if his sales suffer as a result. Consequently, one must expect price reductions to become general in an industry once they have been made by any firm that accounts for a significant proportion of the business. (The dependence of any firm's sales upon the prices charged by rivals depends primarily upon the proximity of the products to one another—either geographically, when transportation costs are heavy—or in the qualities and features that buyers believe inhere in them.)

An unsystematic study of announced price reductions during the present and the last recession suggests that the most important cause of price reductions these days is that a competitor has already done so. Thus, to explain a general price reduction for a product requires that one seek out the firms which were the first to reduce price and account for their actions. The result is the "weak link" explanation for price declines.

Price reductions during recession generally are initiated by firms that have been very hard hit by the business decline. They may have suffered a larger reduction in sales than most firms in their industry due to accidents of product mix or because they did not have a popular "line" as their rivals at the time that recession developed. Or, they may be firms with the lowest financial liquidity—or with the largest obligations coming due. Sometimes the "weak links" are firms whose managements are prone to panic under pressure; they may be executives of low intellectual caliber who are unwilling to reason through the consequences of their price actions. We do not consider as "weak links" those firms which hope to divert business from many rivals without stirring them up to retaliate or those that hope to "beat their rivals to the punch" and make a minor "killing" before the others do something to protect themselves. The "weak link" is a firm that is, or imagines itself to be, in danger of being driven out of business or of sustaining extremely heavy financial losses or of suffering a loss of standing (as, for example, a loss of a high credit rating or a reputation for uninterrupted dividends) that is extremely valuable to continued operation.

Under such circumstances, the management of a stricken firm will almost always feel compelled to take *some* action that promises speedy relief. The only policy that is clearly intolerable at such times is that the firm do nothing to save itself. One of the most potent and speedy sales promotion devices is a price cut. Other measures, like an advertising program, redesign of product, the addition of more salesmen, etc., involve added expenditure when the firm is suffering a shortage of funds; also they are slow to produce benefits—even when they are ultimately beneficial. Consequently, the price cut is the favored remedy of a stricken business. Very frequently, one might say almost always, price reductions under such circumstances only aggravate the situation of the firm making the price cut; moreover, the management making the price reduction could reasonably have been expected to recognize that it would not get additional business in response to the price cut. However, it is one of the established facts of industrial history that prices will be cut under such circumstances.

There is a close connection between the "weak link" case of price reduction and industrial structure. Prices are most volatile in industries where there are some firms of small size and limited resources which cannot withstand a sharp decline in revenues or a prolonged modest drop in sales. The financial pressure which builds up on them ultimately is converted into a price reduction which ultimately (sometimes it spreads slowly) exerts pressure on the entire industry to which they belong.

Industries that have no "weak links"—that is, even their weakest links are very strong—are likely to avoid price changes throughout a recession. If prices are reduced in these industries, it is only because they hold reasonable promise of stimulating sales greatly. Also, if recession is short and mild; or, if it follows on a prolonged period of highly profitable prosperity during which firms accumulated large liquid resources, "weak links" may never develop or will develop late in recession.

Other factors than the existence of "weak links" explain price reductions during recession. Among the more important occasions for price reductions are: first, a decline in a major cost element; second, pressure from large buyers; third, recognition that a general recession has begun.

B. When a Major Cost Element Is Reduced. Many price reductions occur during recession when a major cost item declines. However, not all industries would reduce price under such circumstances, as was explained in the foregoing discussion of the main pricing syndromes. There are two main types of situation in which prices will ordinarily be lowered if a major cost element were to become significantly cheaper: first, where prices are traditionally based upon costs and the pricing formula would call for a price reduction; second, where the industry is extremely prominent in the economy and failure to lower price would give rise to a Congressional investigation or an expensive anti-trust indictment.

One must not overlook the diverse behavior of costs during recession. On one hand, average costs ordinarily rise markedly due to the drop in unit sales volume because fixed charges cannot be reduced for a substantial period. Reductions in variable costs, if there be any, often would not offset the higher per unit *fixed* costs. Consequently, it is only an exceptional firm whose average costs will decline during early recession, even if it were one of the few whose variable costs fell substantially at such times.

However, industrial firms employing a "cost-plus" method of pricing do not base their prices upon full average cost, but use a special cost base for price. These special cost computations usually are unaffected by variations in sales volume, for they include costs plus profit at some "standard" volume. In the case of distributors, prices are almost always based upon invoice costs of merchandise and are therefore unaffected by variations in costs of operation due to fluctuations in sales volume.

The fact that average unit costs generally rise during early recession—and often throughout recession—explains the reluctance of businessmen to pass on modest reductions in their variable costs. They recognize that their unit costs have increased and therefore tend to delay a price reduction even when strict adherence to their pricing formula would require one.

C. When a Large Buyer Brings Strong Pressure to Bear. Buyer pressure sometimes results in price reductions. In part, the skilled buyer seeks out the "weak link" among suppliers and hastens the break by bringing his full bargaining power to bear upon him. Pressure by buyers on their suppliers frequently will lower price in the absence of a weak link; the main situations referred to here are: first, the buyer has himself been compelled to reduce price because of the "weak links" in his own industry and feels pressure to get his suppliers to assume part of the burden of the price cut; second, the buyer is convinced that a reduction in the price of the items he sells would stimulate sales greatly and he endeavors to win the cooperation of his many suppliers to a coordinated program to reduce price for mutual benefit.

Generally a buyer cannot persuade his suppliers to reduce price simply by showing that his own prices have been reduced; he must convince his suppliers that they would benefit from a price reduction rather than seek sympathy and a form of charity. (For example, he may promise them a larger share of his business.) Actually, his suppliers are likely to have suffered greater sales reductions than he did and therefore to seek rather than extend sympathy.

Buyers sometimes try to inspire price reductions by producers of the many important elements that enter into their final product. They recognize that the price they charge depends heavily upon the prices they are compelled to pay; also, that the amount they pay any single supplier has relatively little effect on the total cost of the final product. Consequently, their only hope of stimulating sales by a price reduction is to persuade all of their suppliers to participate in a cooperative program in which all lower price. Such a program is extremely difficult to institute and is even of questionable legality. However, some manufacturers apparently do attempt to persuade suppliers to reduce prices by committing themselves to reduce their own "markup" and thereby to gain the benefits of a larger price reduction and possibly a larger sales increase than would be possible by the unilateral action of either.

Often the large skillful buyer wins a secret concession for himself rather than a general price reduction for all buyers; his concession may not take the form of an outright price cut but some other form that is less vulnerable to attack on grounds of legality. Indeed the seller would favor selective price reductions during recession—that is, concessions only when and to those for whom they are unavoidable. However, price concessions tend to spread fairly rapidly when the existence of recession is unmistakable.

D. Some price reductions seem to result simply from the fact that sellers recognize that a recession is in progress. Many of these price cuts can be traced to the opinion that price reductions are inevitable during recession. Just about every businessman one meets is familiar with and frequent exponent of the "law of supply and demand." Even though he must *know* that he decides about price himself, he also feels that price is set for him by the forces of "supply and demand." During a recession businessmen find their sales volume declining and they anticipate further reductions in sales. This condition they describe as a "drop in demand" which, according to the law of supply and demand, dictates that they reduce price. By this line of reasoning, some businessmen conclude that a price reduction either is in their financial interest or is inevitable or is required of them by the logic and ethics of a free enterprise system.

If these businessmen were to view "demand" as a statement of the relationship between their price and the amount they would sell, they might recognize that their profits would be lowered by a reduction in price; and, it might also do other types of damage to the firm's market position as well. Faced with a conflict between their self-interest and their conception of what is inevitable and ethical, they might decide to resist any price reductions. Many apparently do not recognize the possibility of such conflict and lower price simply because there is a recession. The prevalence of this line of reasoning is re-enforced by history. Prices have fallen in most industries during past recessions, suggesting to some that price must fall anyway and therefore they might just as well reduce them.

Thus far, businessmen's pricing objectives during recession and the pricing policies, strategies and methods they employ have been described along with the main circumstances that lead to price reduction during recession. Three further matters require discussion to round out this brief sketch of how prices behave during recession, as viewed from the standpoint of the price-setter. The first is the question of timing; specifically, can we reasonably hope that prices will be adjusted at the very onset of recession? Do price adjustments follow speedily upon a decline in sales or do they follow, if at all, only after a long delay? Second, what different forms do price reductions take and are they similar in their economic effects? Third, under what circumstances do price reductions stimulate sales?

V. Timing of price reductions during recession

One is able to date the beginning of a recession only on hindsight, and even then only with great difficulty. The same reasons that make it difficult to know when general business has started to decline make it difficult for a businessman to answer the question, "how's business?" He too can only know the right answer long after he was asked.

Apart from the very real difficulties of analyzing business developments to discern underlying changes in the course of events, one must reckon with the strong subjective elements in all interpretations of current business conditions. To a large extent, people see what they expected would happen, what they want to see, or what they most fear will take place. As a crude rule, the first executives to recognize recession are those who had been expecting it; conversely, those who thought business would remain strong will recognize it last for they will attribute the first signs of sales weakness to any of the many special circumstances that can reasonably explain a decline in sales.

What a businessman does about price depends mainly upon his view of what is happening to the economy, his industry, and to his firm in particular. For example, if he believes his sales decline is confined to his own firm—that it was not due to general business recession—he usually would consider a price cut more appropriate than if he believed the business decline was general throughout the industry or the economy. Businessmen are unable to learn what is happening to the entire industry's sales in many cases. Consequently, they find it extremely difficult to diagnose their own sales declines. And, once they do learn the level of sales in the entire industry, and become convinced that a general industry decline is under way, they still face great difficulties in determining whether it has resulted from recession or from some other cause. That is, they can learn their own industry's experience much more rapidly that they can learn what is happening to the economy generally.

One important fact must be emphasized: a considerable period must be expected to lapse before a businessman can identify a drop in sales as the result of general economic recession. It is impossible to fix any exact time period that it takes for a recession to be recognized but six months after the start of recession probably is a conservative average.

It emphatically is not suggested that price will be affected in six months after the start of recession, but simply that the existence of recession will be acknowledged by most in that time. Many may, even when they accept the fact that a recession had started, also hold the opinion that business will revive very speedily. In other words, we must recognize that not only will businessmen take a considerable period to recognize a period of recession, but many will expect a revival of business in the near future that would discourage them from price actions that they might take if they expected recession to continue and worsen. Of course, "weak links" that are under severe pressure will be driven to take action almost no matter what they think. We must never underrate the great uncertainty that surrounds any business decision. When high officials of government, whose opinions are based upon the advice of staffs of technicians, disagree about the business outlook, one can be certain that businessmen will hold diverse views about the future of business.

Thus, one must become reconciled to a belated recognition of recession by businessmen. Consequently, even in the unusual case in which their pricing syndrome would call for reduction in prices during recession, their price changes will be very delayed. Certainly, they would not come early enough to nip a recession in the bud—even if price reductions were (and we shall see presently that they probably are not) an effective antidote for recession.

VI. The forms that price reductions take during recession

As was already discussed, most businessmen will recognize the possibility that an on-going recession may be extremely brief. (There will almost always be some authority or high government official to cite as basis for such a view.) Consequently, if they feel compelled to reduce price they will strongly favor price reductions that are of a temporary character and avoid as long as possible a change in price quotations—and most especially a revision of their price lists. As a result, businessmen have developed a wide variety of price concessions that differ in their apparent permanence. Some of the more common forms of price reduction that prevail at present will be listed, with brief indication of the potency and general economic efforts of some of them.

One form of price reduction involves making up "special merchandise" for the buyer which costs the supplier less than his usual line of wares. On such deals, the supplier may take a thinner markup than he usually obtains, though such need not be the case. In effect, this type of price reduction involves a change in the range of offerings available to buyers without any significant reduction in the prices paid to suppliers for their services as processors of raw materials. Also, such arrangements are "one-shot deals" which need not be repeated and need not be offered to other customers. (Such special merchandise may be passed off to the ultimate consumer as "regular goods".)

Price reductions sometimes take the form of giving higher quality merchandise at the same price. Selected customers may be offered their "pick" of items, if the product is not completely standardized. On occasion, suppliers will ship a higher quality of product, formerly selling at a higher price, at the same price the buyer paid for goods of lower quality previously. Where the buyer is given "first pick" his gain comes at the expense of other buyers; however, if they notice the decline in the average quality of goods offered them (ordinarily, they would not notice the change promptly because they generally will buy without inspection and only their subordinates would actually see the merchandise when delivered) the seller might be forced to reduce price to move it. In the second case—where goods of a higher grade are sold at the price of a lower grade—there has been a genuine price reduction, but a very restricted one. In the first place, it has been a secret concession, rather than one offered to all buyers equally; in the second place, it has required the buyer to purchase goods of higher quality when he may not have wanted to do so; in the third place, because it does not reduce the buyer's outlays, it probably does not stimulate purchases as much as a reduced price for goods of the quality he formerly purchased.

Perhaps the most common and speediest form of price reduction is the secret price concession, which offers one or more—but not all—buyers a lower price than they had been paying. For legal protection (and to "prove" to unfavored customers that no concession was given to other buyers) the reduced price might not even be recorded on the customer's invoices. Occasionally, recipients of secret price concessions are forced to give up some desired features in the product or to accept poor service—thus partly offsetting the gains from the price reduction. Sometimes this concession is not explicit, but the supplier feels entitled to send the poorer quality of product to the buyer getting the reduced price on the belief that, "he has no right to complain."

Other common types of special price concessions include:

1. Special credit accommodation, including a longer period in which to make payment, a delayed billing for the merchandise, etc.
2. Special return privileges, allowing the buyer to obtain full credit on unsold merchandise.

3. Increased discounts for prompt payment.
4. Increased quantities at the same price—giving 13 bottles to the dozen, etc.
5. Absorption of freight.
6. Provision of services free.
7. Extension of price guarantees.

VII. The effect of price reductions on a firm's sales

Classical economists simply assumed that firms could increase their sales by reducing price. We know however that the effects of a price reduction are not simple or predictable. What are the likely responses of buyers to a price reduction? Can many firms reasonably expect to gain substantial benefits by reducing price during recession? Second, do price reductions during recession increase *total* purchases? This section is concerned with the first question only; the second is discussed in the following section.

A price reduction by a single firm is likely to have three types of effects—and an even larger number of possible combinations of effects. First, it might cause buyers to patronize different sources. Second, it might cause buyers to alter the quantity they purchase. Third, it may shift the timing of purchases. The firm making price reductions will hope to win new customers, sell more to old customers and speed up the purchasing of old and new customers. What reactions to a price reduction are most usual?

No comprehensive study has been made of this subject. (One survey, conducted by *Purchasing* magazine, is in process.) One can be confident that not all buyers in a trade will react similarly to a price reduction; possibly substantial differences in usual response are found among industries. However, the concensus of informed opinion holds that the most typical effect of a price reduction is to induce buyers to seek (and they almost always obtain) the lower price from their usual supplier. Under such circumstances, the price reduction will not have helped the firm making it.

To understand this prevailing practice, one must recognize that there are many intangible benefits to be gained from continuing to deal with the firm one has patronized over a long period. Also, there often would be some personal embarrassment in shifting suppliers after a long period of pleasant dealings. Thus, it has come to be expected—the "polite" thing to do—that a buyer will offer his regular supplier an opportunity to match a concession tendered by another source. Indeed, it seems that buyers will fail to do so only when they have been quite dissatisfied with their present supplier and really welcome an excuse to shift sources. Where as a buyer might be embarrassed to tell a long-time supplier that he is no longer going to buy from him under ordinary circumstances, he would find it relatively easy to do so if he felt that his regular supplier was charging him "too much"—even though he knew he could have obtained a similar reduction from his regular supplier if he had demanded it.

Another fairly common buyer response to a price reduction seems to be to refrain from purchasing as long as possible in the expectation that further price reductions can be won from the same or other sources later. Generally, buyers are confident they would be notified before prices were returned to their earlier level, though their confidence would vary with the form of the price concession they had been offered. The effect of a price reduction in such a case is to lower current sales—precisely the opposite effect to the one desired by the price-cutter.

Some buyers may respond to a price reduction by increasing their purchases out of fear that the price reduction would be withdrawn speedily since no other firm has yet offered it. Certainly, the seller would try to achieve this effect, but he is unlikely to succeed in many cases. The greater the optimism about the future outlook, the stronger the inclination of the buyer to hasten the purchases. However, optimism is one of the rarest of commodities during recession.

If the foregoing discussion is valid, individual sellers have little reason to expect to gain substantially by cutting price; consequently, there is little basis for expecting that many will do so voluntarily. Moreover, as is explained in the following section, price reductions apparently do not do much to spur purchasing and therefore cannot be expected to be a brake to recession or to speed revival.

VIII. The general economic effects of price changes upon sales during recession

The conventional, and probably the majority, view holds that prompt price reductions would offset wholly or in part the original causes of a sales decline. In its simplest terms this view holds that people can afford to buy more at low than at high prices, and price reductions increase the cost of savings by requiring the saver to forego the consumption of more goods to save a given sum. For these reasons, price reductions are believed to increase unit sales and total expenditure and ultimately stimulate production.

Some eminent economists hold precisely the opposite view. They regard price reductions as unstabilizing and likely to intensify a recession. The main basis for this conclusion is that many buyers may interpret price reductions as heralds of further reductions in price. If these men are right, price reductions are signals to hold current purchases to a minimum. Similarly, price reductions are very disquieting to investors for they lower the anticipated rate of return.

Clearly, it is essential that this conflict be resolved and preferably not by further assertions, however embellished they might be by ingenious reasoning. At issue is a factual question and one that can and should be settled by reference to facts. Namely, how do persons responsible for purchasing—whether on behalf of households, retail establishments, distributors, manufacturers, or producers of raw materials—interpret and respond to price changes during early recession? This Committee could render a valuable service if it were to sponsor, or at least inspire, empirical investigations to illuminate this question. It probably is not too late to make such a study now because the memories are very fresh, the recession is not very old (even though we hope it is near its end) and because in the case of business buyers there may exist some documents which state the firm's buying policies and indicate how they have been affected by the existence or absence of price changes.

This writer emphatically does not know whether price reductions stimulate or inhibit revival or balance; it is doubtful that their effects are the same in all industries and they are unlikely to be the same as they were even 25 years ago. Futhermore, the effect of a price reduction may depend primarily upon whether it comes before the fact of recession is generally acknowledged or comes as belated acknowledgment of a general weakening in demand.

Clearly an investigation of business pricing policies during recession becomes almost pointless if there is no clear gain or loss from either stable or highly volatile prices. For that reason, concentrated study of buyer reactions to price changes would seem to be a necessity. If such a study were made, it should be made of all levels of industry and of consumers and rely heavily upon personal interviews of a moderately "deep" type. Also, such an investigation would particularly seek out memoranda and policy statements that disclose management's thinking about when to buy and how management actually interpreted specific price reductions made by suppliers.

IX. Are businessmen's private pricing policies consistent with public policy during recession?

Since we do not know the effects of price reductions on sales in all market situations, we cannot tell whether businessmen would be benefited or injured by speedy price reductions with the onset of recession. Conceivably, businessmen would gain even as would the economy generally from speedy price adjustments; in that case, there would be a happy harmony of private and public interest. Proper public policy would then simply require that businessmen be given assistance and encouragement to do what was good for them.

If public policy is to be served by speedy price cuts during recession, either of two effects must be achieved. First, sales of that product must increase without lowering the sales of anything else; or second, savings on the purchase of that product must be devoted to the purchase of something else—rather than to the reduction of debt or just saved. High sensitivity of sales to a price reduction in itself would not make a price reduction beneficial either to the economy or to the individual businessman. Very possibly, his gain in sales at the lower price would come at the expense of virtually certain sales at a future date and at a higher price.

Thus, it is not clear that the public interest is served best simply by a speedy increase in sales during recession that was induced by price reductions. One must inquire also into the full and longer run effects. Specifically, a price reduction might speed up sales but not increase them. Thus, to apply a brake to a decline might come at the expense of delaying or taking the steam out of the upswing. Revival might be impaired in two ways: first, by having shifted purchases forward in time and thereby lowering the level of demand at a later date; second, by making prices low and production unprofitable with the effect that investment becomes less attractive. In this round about way we see that a proper public policy regarding price during recession should not be framed solely with respect to stopping recession. The measures used must be such that subsequent revival is not impaired. One would want to avoid a policy that stopped a recession moderately quickly but kept output on a reduced level.

It is beyond the scope of this paper to discuss the economic developments during a recession that foster subsequent revival. Recessions do, in some ways, though not in all, set the scene for revival. They generally are characterized by inventory decumulation, postponement of purchases, deferred maintenance, etc., which ultimately result in increased purchasing. If, by some change in pricing arrangements, these developments do not take place or are cut short, one must expect the subsequent revival to be altered, if it comes at all. The vital distinction suggested here is between price actions which would prevent a business downswing from cumulating—which produces no benefits for the future—from developments which contribute to revival. Recession cumulates as reductions in income suffered by one group spread to other groups as they curtail purchases. Perhaps the most direct and effective remedy does not lie at all in the area of price changes but in changed money dispersements.

Thus, there is no necessary conflict between public and private interest with respect to pricing during a recession. On one hand, the public interest is not always served simply by applying a brake to recession. On the other hand businessmen might gain by price reductions which strongly stimulate sales and which shorten a general recession. We have found no basis for expecting many businessmen to reduce price voluntarily during recession. Price reductions contrary to the businessman's interest will be resisted—often successfully. Since most major industries are characterized by close interdependence of rivals, no one could hope to effect a gain at his competitor's expense by cutting price. Consequently, only dire necessity (a shortage of cash or an actual threat of bankruptcy) and short sightedness will lead businessmen to cut prices in such situations. If we were to try to combat recession by compelling early price reductions, it would be necessary to rely upon extensive government price fixing—a solution that would create far more problems than it would solve.

Another alternative—that of creating markets where there are so many producers that they will not strongly be affected by the actions of any one—would involve even drastic governmental actions. You just cannot chop up existing firms into lots of smaller ones; what is more, Congress wouldn't do it even if it would mitigate recessions.

We must accept a structure of industry much like the one we have at present for quite a few recessions to come; we must also accept the fact that price reductions will be as delayed and as small as businessmen can make them. We must therefore find a solution for recession in another area—namely by changing expenditures and income through tax, monetary and social security policies. We just do not know enough about the effects of price reductions to undertake the drastic programs needed to insure that they come about. There is even a real danger that volatile prices during recession injure rather than benefit the economy. There is no need to completely overhaul the nation's industrial structure to mitigate recession. We have far quicker, easier, and more promising solutions.

X. Private pricing policies and the distribution of the burdens of recession

The discussion up to this point has dealt with the relationship between private pricing policies and the duration and severity of recession. Recessions have another aspect that must be considered: the distribution of the burden of recession among individuals and economic groups. Business pricing policies influence the distribution of personal income, for a reduction in prices shifts income from the seller to the buyer; conversely, when prices are increased, the seller gains to the detriment of the buyer. Accordingly, private pricing policies have a fairly straight-forward effect upon income distribution and an unclear influence upon the course of a recession. Thus, a mitigation of recession could possibly require an aggravation of income inequality. Faced with such a choice, there might be genuine reasons for knowingly accepting a somewhat longer and more severe recession, if it shared its economic and human costs very equitably.

The foregoing discussion has stressed that prices are reduced very late and unwillingly during recession by most businessmen. To the extent that businessmen maintain prices in the face of declining personal income, they aggravate the loss of real income by persons whose income has been reduced by recession beyond what it would be if prices were to decline. A reduction in prices would compel businessmen to share the burden of recession with other groups whose personal incomes were reduced.

It must therefore be recognized that pricing policies during recession must not be evaluated exclusively by the test of how they would influence the duration and severity of recession. However, it probably would turn out that even concern for equitable sharing of the burdens of recession would not call for a change in existing pricing methods; measures that operate through changes in the income stream would seem far more appropriate and efficient. Whatever methods one favors, it does not alter the point that the economic costs of recession must be shared as equitably as possible.

XI. Relationship between pricing policies for recession and for economic growth

Private price policies are, and inevitably must be adopted largely without regard to broad national objectives, as was explained. If private pricing policies either quicken or impair economic growth, it is quite by accident. Indeed, even if prviate businessmen tried conscientiously to adopt pricing policies that would spur economic growth, it is not clear how these policies would be identified. In some cases, growth would be fostered most by prices that made investment in the industry very attractive; such prices presumably would be relatively high compared to costs. In other cases, low prices relative to costs would spur growth most by speeding buyer acceptance of the product. It is very difficult to know in any specific case which policy would be most favorable to economic growth. A businessman who is financially involved in the product is not likely to be a good judge. Moreover, it is not clear that the nation can legitimately expect him to add this concern to his others—even if he were competent to do so and could be objective.

Thus, the conclusion again emerges that social objectives—whether they be economic stability or economic growth—cannot be pursued effectively through private pricing policies. Business objectives and policies are neither regularly consistent or inconsistent with these broad social objectives. If those objectives are to be attained, a national policy will have to be devised in spheres outside the pricing area. Otherwise, it will be necessary to build so many constraints into our present industrial arrangements that we will erect a fundamentally changed economic system. Such an outcome would not be objectionable if the changed economy were superior to the present one. I would expect it to be far worse!

26. OLIGOPOLISTIC EQUILIBRIUM IN THE RETAILING OF PRODUCE *

Lawrence E. Fouraker

Is the average buyer of foodstuffs significantly influenced by the final digit of the price tag above the commodity being bought? Does he (or more likely she) feel that green beans at 29c per pound are a considerably better buy than green beans at 30c per pound? Or does the odd-cent price ending serve another purpose? Recently C. R. Brader, a graduate student at Pennsylvania State University, included the following table in a term report:

Retail Price Endings for Produce in Pittsburgh Chain Grocery Stores (six-month period)

Price endings	1	2	3	4	5	6	7	8	9	0
Per cent of frequency	.5	0	5.4	.5	25.2	0	1.7	.2	65.5	1.2

In conjunction with another investigation, seven chain-store grocery executives and their assistants were interviewed. These men were responsible for ordering and pricing produce in the organizations. During these interviews, the executives were asked to explain their preference for produce prices ending in "9." Six of those interviewed provided the customary "psychological" interpretation, which is that 39c, for example, gives the impression of a bargain; the customer is likely to feel that the price has been shaved from 40c, or even 50c.[1]

While this may in fact be the case, there are some dissenting viewpoints: (1) An executive in a major mail-order house maintained that their profits were neither increased nor lessened by rounding their odd-cent prices to the next highest figure.[2] (2) Another Pennsylvania State graduate student, John Early, constructed

* Reprinted by permission from *The Southwestern Social Science Quarterly*, Vol. 37, No. 3 (December, 1956), pp. 271-272.

Lawrence E. Fouraker, Assistant Dean for Research, Pennsylvania State University.

[1] H. H. Maynard and T. N. Beckman, *Principles of Marketing* (5th ed., New York, The Ronald Press Company, 1952), p. 656; C. F. Phillips, *Marketing by Manufacturers* (rev. ed., Homewood, Ill., Richard D. Irwin, Inc., 1946), p. 457; R. S. Vaile, E. T. Grether, and R. Cox, *Marketing in the American Economy* (New York, The Ronald Press Company, 1952), p. 452; P. D. Converse and H. W. Huegy, *The Elements of Marketing* (5th ed., New York, Prentice-Hall, Inc., 1952), p. 209.

[2] E. Ginzberg, "Customary Prices," *American Economic Review*, Vol. 26, p. 296.

two sheets with thirty prices (associated with abstract items) on each sheet. One set of prices had endings in the same proportions as used in Brader's table. The other set of prices had endings equally proportioned from 0 through 9. The sum of the prices on the first sheet was equal to the sum of the prices on the second sheet. A total of 137 women were asked to indicate which store they thought was cheaper, or if there was no difference. The results are as follows: 46.7 per cent thought the store with the equally proportional price endings was cheaper; 31.4 per cent thought the store with the odd-cent price endings was cheaper; 21.9 per cent thought there was no difference. These differences are not statistically significant. (3) Many economists contend that a consumer's buying skill and acumen are in direct proportion to the frequency with which the object is purchased.[3] If this is correct, the customers of chain grocery stores are not likely to be misled by such a simple ruse as odd-cent pricing, for food items are purchased with great regularity and frequency.

The seventh of the executives interviewed suggested an explanation for the odd-cent price endings that is not to be found in standard texts on marketing. It was his contention that the customary preference for prices ending in 9 enables the industry to achieve price uniformity on many items. Thus, the trade, knowing approximately how much of a markup could be placed on different categories of produce items, would price their products approximately the same even in the absence of the odd-cent convention.

"Close," however, is not good enough in the pricing of produce. A price differential of a few cents may cause a substantial shift in customers, which is disastrous for an industry marketing a perishable product. But independent calculations, even though crude, can produce identical results if all entrepreneurs follow the rule of thumb of moving to the nearest price ending in 9 after their initial approximation (or the ending may be 5 for some items whose prices and margins are relatively low). This practice introduces an element of order into the chaos of an industry characterized by aggressive rivalry, low margins, perishable products, and perceptive customers.

The Trobriand people of Melanesia masked the trade between their islands with ceremonies based upon superstition.[4] There may be a counterpart in modern business practices that, though defended with poor logic, nevertheless perform necessary functions.

[3] G. J. Stigler, *The Theory of Price* (New York, The Macmillan Company, 1947), p. 66.

[4] B. Malinowski, "Traders of the Trobriands," *A Reader in General Anthropology*, ed. C. S. Coon (New York, Henry Holt and Company, 1948), pp. 293-321.

27. IMPACT OF GEOGRAPHICAL PRICE DISCRIMINATION ON THE BUYER *

J. A. Guthrie

As a result of the Supreme Court's decision in the Cement Case [1] and the action of the cement and iron and steel industries in shifting to f.o.b. mill pricing, attention has been directed to the incidence of geographical price discrimination, particularly in relation to existing pricing systems. Most theoretical discussions of price discrimination have been concerned primarily with the conditions necessary to discrimination; its influence on production, profits, and business policy; the special circumstances under which it is practiced, and the peculiar problems it raises.[2] Some writers have assumed that discrimination may be beneficial to all concerned, including consumers; others feel that it is generally harmful to the consumer.[3] In view of the cement case decision, the impact of discrimination on consumer [4] price has taken on added significance. If existing pricing practices, which allow unequal mill nets to the seller, are to be outlawed or drastically restricted, and if sales are to be largely or entirely on an f.o.b. mill basis, the effect of these changes on prices is of considerable concern to the buyer. The purpose of this article is to focus attention on some theoretical aspects of this problem and to draw a few tentative conclusions. No attempt is made to pass judgment on the merits or demerits of discrimination.

In the analysis that follows, the usual conditions associated with discrimination are assumed to be present. These are separable mar-

* From *The Journal of Marketing*, Vol. XIV, No. 4 (January, 1950), pp. 538-543. Reprinted with permission from *The Journal of Marketing*, published quarterly by the American Marketing Association.

J. A. Guthrie, The State College of Washington.

[1] Federal Trade Commission *v.* Cement Institute, 333 U. S. 683 (1948).

[2] A. C. Pigou, *The Economics of Welfare* (London: MacMillan & Co., 1929), Chapter XVII; Joan Robinson, *The Economics of Imperfect Competition* (London: MacMillan & Co., 1938), Chapters 15 and 16; A. R. Burns, *The Decline of Competition* (New York: McGraw-Hill, 1936), Chapters VI and VII; Ralph Cassady, Jr., "Some Economic Aspects of Price Discrimination under Non-Perfect Market Conditions," *Journal of Marketing*, Vol. XI, No. 1, July, 1946; Ralph Cassady, "Techniques and Purposes of Price Discrimination," *Journal of Marketing*, Vol. XI, No. 2, October, 1946.

[3] V. A. Mund, *Open Markets* (New York & London: Harper & Bros., 1948), Chapter XII; T.N.E.C. Monograph No. 1, "Competition and Monopoly in American Industry" (Washington, D. C., 1941), p. 147.

[4] "Buyer" and "consumer" are here considered to be synonymous.

kets with differing elasticities of demand; some degree of monopoly in the production of the commodity or service involved; appreciable economies of scale with consequent declining average total costs, and output at a point where total revenue is maximized. Output will generally be at or to the left of lowest average cost, though this is not a necessary condition for maximizing revenue. The ATC curve is considered to be the long-run average, although the situation would be in general the same in the short run period inasmuch as the short run ATC curve has the same general shape as the long-run curve. For simplicity it is assumed that there is one commodity which is sold in only two markets, the local and the distant market. Because of greater competition from other producers, the demand is more elastic in the distant than in the local market.[5] In practice, under industrial pricing systems there are frequently as many markets as there are buyers, each with a different elasticity of demand. When the combined demand curve is being considered, reference will be made to the less elastic portion and the more elastic portion. Price, which is here considered to be the net amount paid by the buyer after freight, etc. is deducted, is always higher in the local market than in the distant market when there is freight absorption by the seller.

I.

Four separate cases may be considered. In Case I (Fig. I) the assumption is made that neither the less elastic demand curve D_1D_2,

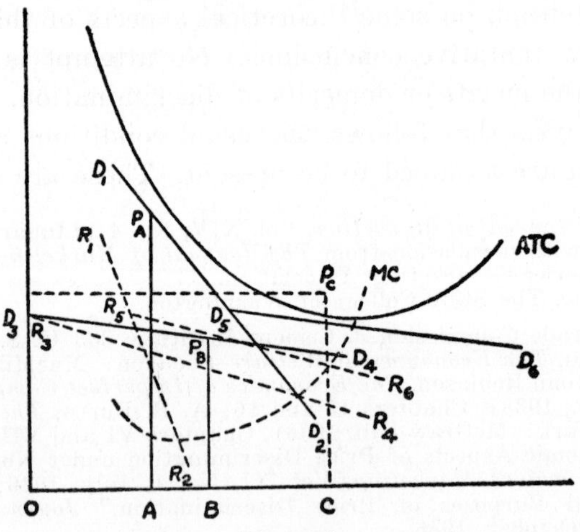

FIGURE I

[5] This condition is assumed here, although invasion of the local market by other producers may result in elastic demand locally.

the more elastic demand curve D_3D_4, nor the aggregate curve $D_1D_5D_6$ will touch or cut the average total cost curve ATC. Hence, no price can be charged which will equal or exceed average total costs.

If, however, quantity *OA* is sold in the less elastic market at a price AP_A and quantity *OB* in the more elastic market at price BJ_B, a total of $OC (= OA + OB)$ will be sold at an average price.

$$CP_C = \frac{(OA \times AP_A + OB \times BP_B)}{OA + OB}$$

which is sufficient to cover *ATC*. Since output *OC* is at the point where marginal cost equals the aggregate marginal revenue in both markets R_5R_6, returns will be maximized.[6]

Thus by charging different prices in the two markets, production and sale can result, and consumers will in general be able to purchase at lower *average* prices than if supplied from some other source, for if buyers are forced to purchase from a more distant source instead of having the option of buying either from a distant or a nearby source, they will normally have to pay a higher price.[7] It may happen, of course, that a distant producer is able, through economies of scale, to produce and supply a market more cheaply than a nearby producer. Under those circumstances the nearby producer will be unable to compete, and discrimination by him will not result.

In Case II it is assumed either (a) that the less elastic demand curve D_1D_2 (which is also the less elastic portion of the aggregate curve) touches but does not cut the *ATC* curve, and the more elastic

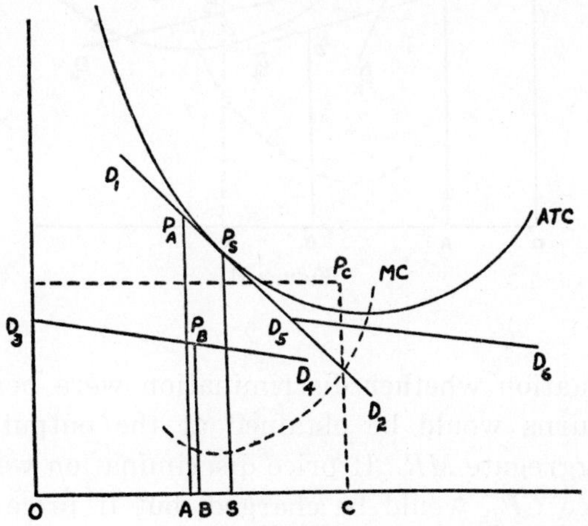

FIGURE II

[6] Joan Robinson, *op. cit.*, p. 183. Aggregate marginal revenue, R_5R_6, is the lateral summation of the two individual marginal revenue curves. It is not necessarily marginal to the aggregate average revenue curve.

[7] *Ibid.*, p. 203.

portion D_5D_6 does not touch (Fig. II), or (b) the less elastic portion cuts the *ATC* curve, and the more elastic portion just touches or does not touch the *ATC* curve.

In this case, whether or not price discrimination were permitted, production would result. In the event there was no discrimination a single price SP_S would be charged which would normally be higher than the average price of CP_C under discrimination. However, with discrimination the price AP_A in the less elastic market would generally be greater than SP_S and the price BP_B in the more elastic market less than SP_S.[8] Thus buyers would be charged a higher average price if the seller were not permitted to discriminate than if discrimination were allowed. But discrimination would generally mean higher prices in the local and lower in the distant market.

In Case III (Fig. III) it is assumed that the less elastic portion of the curve D_1D_5 will either not touch or will just touch the *ATC* curve, and the more elastic portion D_5D_6 will cut or touch the *ATC* curve.

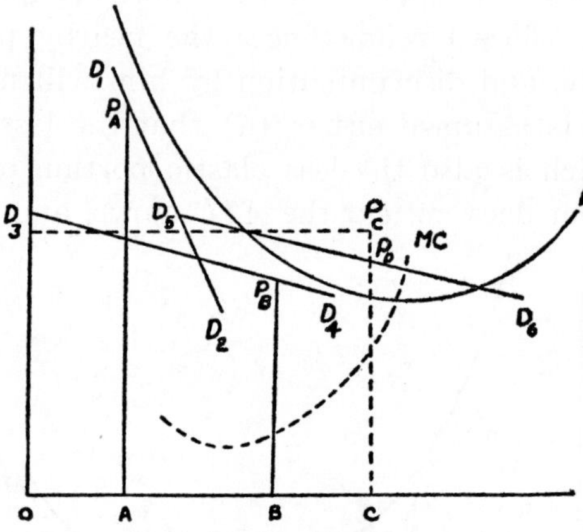

FIGURE III

In this situation whether discrimination were permitted or not, maximum returns would be obtained at the output *OC* at which point $MC =$ aggregate *MR*.[9] If price discrimination were not allowed, the single price CP_D would be charged, but if price discrimination were permitted, the higher average price CP_C would be charged.

[8] There could, of course, be exceptions to this depending on the shape of the *MC* curve.

[9] With straight line demand curves the output would be the same under simple as under discriminating monopoly. See Joan Robinson, *op. cit.*, p. 190.

In Case IV (Fig. IV) it is assumed that both the less elastic and the more elastic portions of the combined curve would cut the *ATC* curve.

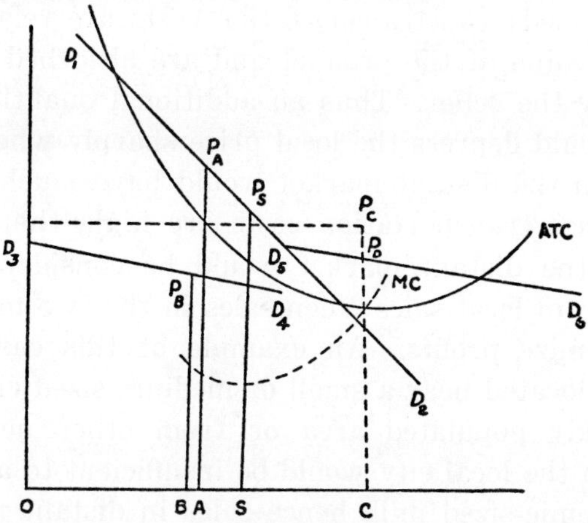

FIGURE IV

In this case, maximum profits are obtained either under simple or discriminating monopoly at an output OC where $MC =$ aggregate MR provided the profits under simple monopoly are greater than can be obtained by selling in the less elastic market alone. But if selling at one price under simple monopoly yields less profits than selling in the less elastic market alone, the most profitable price to the seller in the less elastic market is charged. Thus, under Case IV if price discrimination is allowed, the average price CP_C would be charged. If discrimination is not allowed, and the largest profits can be made by combining the two markets, the price CP_D (less than CP_C) would be charged. But if profits by selling in the combined market are less than in the less elastic market alone, the price SP_S which would maximize profits in that market alone would be charged. This price would probably be greater than CP_C and less than AP_A, the price in the less elastic market under discrimination.

Thus in Cases I and II discrimination would generally result in lower average prices to consumers; in Case III higher average prices; and in Case IV sometimes higher and sometimes lower average prices to consumers. In Cases II, III, and IV discrimination would also generally mean higher prices in the less elastic market.

II.

Let us consider further these four cases in relation to industrial pricing practices and the conditions under which they may be expected to prevail.

Case I would be the situation where (1) the demand in the local (less elastic) market is only slightly elastic or is inelastic; (2) the local market is small relative to the output at which average total costs are minimized; (3) transportation costs are relatively high in relation to the value of the product and are absorbed completely or in large part by the seller. Thus an additional quantity sold on the local market would depress the local price sharply whereas the same quantity sold on the distant market would have much less effect on price. Also, since transportation costs are high, the price received from sales in the distant market would be considerably less than that received from local sales when sales in the two markets are adjusted to maximize profits. An example of this case would be a newsprint mill located near a small or medium sized city and distant from any thickly populated area or from other newsprint mills. Consumption in the local city would be insufficient to absorb the output of an economic-sized mill, hence sales in distant markets would be a necessary condition of operation. Under these circumstances local consumers of newsprint would generally be charged lower prices if the mill were allowed to practice price discrimination.

Case II exists when (1) the local market is larger, relative to the output at which costs are minimized, than in Case I (that is, the less elastic demand curve is further to the right) and (2) transportation costs represent a significant proportion of the total price and are largely or entirely absorbed in sales in the distant market. An example would be a newsprint mill located close to a city or area which consumes enough to support the operation of an economic-sized mill. However, because of the limit in size of the local market or because of competition from other mills, profits could be increased by selling also in a distant market at a lower mill net. In this case also consumers would generally pay a lower average price under discrimination. The benefit of lower prices, however, would be realized by the distant consumer, and the local consumer would frequently pay higher prices under discrimination.

Case III is the situation where (1) the local market is small, relative to the output at which costs are minimized and (2) transportation costs constitute a small proportion of the price, or if large, they are absorbed to a lesser extent, so that there is less difference between the mill nets in local and distant markets than in Cases I or II. Sales in the distant market are also relatively large. An aluminum rolling mill selling predominantly in a distant market would illustrate this case. In this situation, prohibiting discrimination would benefit the consumer, particularly the local consumer, for the single price so charged would be lower than the average under discrimination and still lower than the price in the local market, although it would be somewhat higher than the price in the distant market with discrimination.[10] It is true, of course, that in this case prohibiting discrimination might, in some instances, have the effect of forcing or inducing the producer to move his plant away from the small local market, particularly if his distant market were much more important. The aluminum rolling mill operator, if forced to charge a uniform price to all buyers, might find it to his advantage to move his mill near his principal market. This could occur when the costs of raw materials, power, labor, etc., are not significantly different in the two areas and the cost of transferring the mill is not excessive.

Case IV can be subdivided into two categories, Case IVa and IVb. Case IVa exists when (1) the local market is larger relative to the output required to minimize costs than in Cases I and III and (2) transportation costs either constitute a relatively small proportion of the price, or if a large proportion, freight absorption by the seller is small. An illustration of this situation would be an aluminum mill located near a large consuming area.

As in Case III, prohibiting discrimination would result in a lower price to the consumer, for the single price CP_D would be lower than the average under discrimination. Unlike Case III, however, prohibiting discrimination would probably not result in moving the plant to the more distant market, for the local market alone would be large enough to make sizable profits.

Case IVb exists when (1) the local market is relatively large and (2) transportation costs are also large and are absorbed entirely or in large part by the seller. The difference between the mill net received in the local and distant markets would therefore be considerable. This case is much like Case II, and could also be illustrated by a newsprint mill located in a large consuming area. Under these circumstances prohibiting discrimination would likely result in the seller giving up the distant market entirely and selling only in the local market at the price SP_S, which would probably be higher than the average under discrimination, but lower than the price AP_A charged to the local buyer under discrimination.

[10] It can be proved mathematically that with straight-line demand curves and output such that returns are maximized, the single price CP_D under simple monopoly would be higher than the BP_B in the more elastic market under discriminating monopoly.

In the four cases considered, static demand curves have been portrayed. Actually, however, these curves are constantly shifting. Any one of the four cases may become one of the other three as demand changes.[11] An expanding local market will change Case I into Case II, or Case III into Case IV.

It is apparent that pressure on the part of sellers to practice discrimination is likely to be greater during periods of reduced total demand and less during periods of increased demand. The sizable increase in price discrimination involved under the NRA codes reflected in part the desire of sellers to obtain reduced costs by greater utilization of capacity. On the other hand when total demand and profits are large, the sellers will be less likely to resist being forced to desist from the practice of freight absorption, particularly if the local market represents a large fraction of their total sales. When the local market is large and profits from it are appreciable, the seller may in fact prefer to give up the practice of price discrimination and sell only at one price, that charged in the local market. The action of the iron and steel industry in shifting to f.o.b. mill pricing possibly came as a result of this situation and probably meant higher average prices to the consumer. Sales at lower prices in distant markets were given up, and all buyers, local or distant, were required to pay the local price.

The conclusions reached in this article are briefly as follows: if the difference in mill nets from selling in local and distant markets is small, either because transportation costs are a relatively small proportion of the price of the commodity or, when large, they are absorbed only to a small extent, discrimination will generally result in higher average prices to the consumer, and prohibiting it will mean lower consumer prices. If, on the other hand, the difference between mill nets in local and distant markets is large because transportation costs are a large part of the price and are largely or entirely absorbed, price discrimination will generally mean lower average prices to the consumer. In most instances, also, discrimination probably means that prices to the local buyer are higher than they would otherwise be.

[11] Changes in transportation rates or the amount of freight absorbed will, of course, also cause a shift in the demand curve in the more elastic market.

28. THE INFLUENCE OF MANUFACTURERS' PRICE POLICIES UPON PRICE DETERMINATION BY WHOLESALERS *

A. J. Alton

The importance of wholesalers in the marketing structure is clearly indicated by a comparison of sales of wholesale establishments with retail store sales. The U. S. Census of Business—1954 reports sales of $247 billions for wholesale establishments while retail store sales amounted to $170 billions for the same year. Such a tremendous volume of sales shows the importance of the wholesaler's strategic position with respect to price determination.

Of course the amount of freedom in pricing which these middlemen possess depends largely upon the degree of influence which wholesalers' customers and sources of supply are able to exert upon wholesalers in their attempt to arrive at prices for the thousands of commodities which they resell. The object of the study reported here was to ascertain the type and degree of influence exercised by manufacturers upon wholesalers' attempts to establish prices.

Methodology of the Research

Research was carried on in three of the traditional "jobbing" or wholesaling lines which have been important in the marketing structure for many years. They are the hardware, dry goods, and drug wholesalers. Nine wholesale establishments were selected for study, three from each of the trade categories. The majority of firms included in the study are located in the Miami Valley and all are in the Midwest of the United States. Because of this geographical concentration, all of them are affected by reasonably similar external conditions.

Although the sample is limited, it is believed that the value of a study of this type does not necessarily depend upon an extensive sampling. Intensive probing into the pricing processes of 38 buyers

* Reprinted by permission from *Miami Business Review,* Vol. XXIX, No. 1 (October, 1957), pp. 1-4.

A. J. Alton, Associate Professor of Marketing, Miami University, Oxford, Ohio.

in nine wholesale establishments will cast considerable light upon the topic. The wholesale establishments selected for study are all general-line, full-function wholesalers, each performing all of the functions normally associated with the term wholesaler. These firms are very similar and are believed to be representative of the numerous wholesalers found in each category.

A judgment selection of 60 merchandise items for each of the trade categories was made. These items were selected on the basis of their representing a kind of merchandise subdivision in a commodity group classification. Each group of 60 items was to be a cross section of the kinds of merchandise items which the respective wholesalers carried.

To insure the highest degree of accuracy in obtaining the correct invoice cost, incoming freight charges, and wholesalers' selling price for each item, appropriate records were examined. Markup percentages were then calculated for all items. After cost, selling price, and markup data had been determined, it was feasible to interview each buyer to learn how he had arrived at the selling price for a particular item. The interview was characterized by the "open end" type of question. The merchandise item in question was mentioned and the price the buyer had established was cited. The buyer was then asked to explain how he arrived at each price. There were 515 individual pricing explanations related by 38 buyers.

Use of Fair Trade Legislation By Manufacturers

All wholesalers in the study carried manufacturers' branded or trademarked merchandise which they sold at prices stipulated by manufacturers. One method utilized by manufacturers to establish wholesalers' selling prices was the use of the provisions of state resale price maintenance or fair trade statutes and the federal McGuire Act. Not only do these laws permit manufacturers to set prices on branded or trademarked goods below which no retailer can resell to his customers, they also allow manufacturers to set prices below which no wholesaler can resell to his customers. Some state resale price maintenance laws provide that a minimum price may be established, while others permit the establishment of an absolute price at which a commodity must be sold.

Fair-traded merchandise items, which preclude any pricing freedom on the part of wholesalers, were not included in the three groups of products selected for intensive study since one of the primary purposes of the research not discussed in this paper was to discover how prices were determined when buyers enjoyed freedom in pricing. Nevertheless, it is obvious that the use of resale price maintenance legislation by manufacturers is an important example of manufacturers' price policies affecting wholesalers.

TABLE 1

IMPORTANCE OF NINETEEN FACTORS MENTIONED VOLUNTARILY BY BUYERS IN PRICING 515 REPRESENTATIVE ITEMS CARRIED BY THREE HARDWARE, THREE DRY GOODS, AND THREE DRUG WHOLESALERS, MIDWESTERN UNITED STATES

FACTOR	Times Cited				Per Cent of Total			
	Total	Hardware	Dry Goods	Drugs	Total	Hardware	Dry Goods	Drugs
Suggested resale price	214	54	36	124	30.4	24.7	13.0	59.1
Competition	146	63	54	29	20.7	28.8	19.5	13.9
Intense	62	22	26	14	8.8	10.0	9.4	6.7
Average	80	38	27	15	11.4	17.5	9.8	7.2
Low degree	4	3	1	0	0.5	1.3	0.3	0.0
Average markup	96	53	29	14	13.6	24.3	10.5	6.7
Retail price	65	0	64	1	9.3	0.0	23.2	0.5
Established trade practice	53	24	23	6	7.6	11.0	8.4	2.8
What the traffic will bear	41	2	26	13	5.9	0.9	9.4	6.1
Rate of stock turnover	31	12	13	6	4.4	5.5	4.7	2.8
Slow	15	8	4	3	2.1	3.7	1.5	1.4
Fast	16	4	9	3	2.3	1.8	3.2	1.4
Accommodation merchandise	25	5	11	9	3.6	2.3	4.0	4.2
Seasonal merchandise	6	3	2	1	0.8	1.3	0.7	0.5
Hidden value	6	0	6	0	0.8	0.0	2.2	0.0
Staple merchandise	6	0	5	1	0.8	0.0	1.8	0.5
Fashion merchandise	5	0	3	2	0.7	0.0	1.0	1.0
Purchased at lower price	3	1	1	1	0.4	0.4	0.3	0.5
Perishable	3	0	0	3	0.4	0.0	0.0	1.4
Probable markdown	2	0	2	0	0.2	0.0	0.7	0.0
Lower grade merchandise	1	1	0	0	0.1	0.4	0.0	0.0
Annual model change	1	1	0	0	0.1	0.4	0.0	0.0
Recognized brand	1	0	1	0	0.1	0.0	0.3	0.0
Merchandise odds and ends	1	0	1	0	0.1	0.0	0.3	0.0
TOTALS	706	219	277	210	100.0	100.0	100.0	100.0

Source: Interviews of wholesalers included in the study.

One consequence of this type of resale price maintenance is the shifting of the buyer's price-making function to the manufacturer. As a result, less time is required of buyers in determining hundreds of resale prices and in evaluating competition and other pricing factors. This is especially true in the drug trade, one of the most outstanding areas where fair trade legislation is utilized.

MANUFACTURERS' USE OF SUGGESTED RESALE PRICES

A manufacturer's policy of suggesting the price at which his merchandise is to be resold by a wholesaler was frequently mentioned by buyers in explanation of the price they had established. This method of attempting to influence the price-making process was quite successful and widespread as shown by the data in Table 1. In 214 of 515 examples of pricing, buyers, in the three lines of trade, determined the selling price of merchandise by following manufacturers' suggested resale prices. Buyers in dry goods houses determined price this way in 20 per cent of the examples. The practice was much more prevalent in the hardware and drug trades. Buyers in the hardware trade utilized a suggested resale price in 33 per cent of the pricing examples, while buyers in the drug trade followed such a practice in 59 per cent of the pricing examples.

The suggestions of manufacturers with respect to wholesalers' resale prices were made with varying degrees of strength and insistence. Some manufacturers printed suggested prices in the form of list prices in their catalogue, or price sheet, but did not make any other attempts to insure that wholesalers would follow the list price. Other manufacturers were more aggressive and employed phrases such as "recommended resale price," or "suggested resale price." This variation is significant, for whether or not wholesalers followed the recommended prices depended, in part, upon the degree of insistence by the manufacturer.

At the other extreme, some manufacturers not only indicated the recommended resale price in print but engaged in an active policing program. Thus, some buyers stated that a manufacturer would take away his line if a recommended resale price was not followed. The policy of granting exclusive distributorships to wholesalers provided manufacturers an excellent opportunity to insist that favored wholesalers follow suggested resale prices. Although exclusive distributorships from manufacturers were relatively few in number, their importance is magnified when wholesalers purchase from exclusive dealing manufacturers with long merchandise lines.

Effect of Suggested Resale Prices Upon the Wholesaler

Although manufacturers suggested resale prices, the suggestions were not always followed. It is believed that a sizable number of products not priced by buyers according to a manufacturer's suggested resale price were listed in the manufacturer's catalogue or price sheet according to the list price method. For in 20 instances buyers voluntarily mentioned that they disregarded some form of a manufacturer's suggested price: either a list price or a price merely described as "suggested" or "recommended."

Buyers followed manufacturers' suggested resale prices in 214 of 515 examples of pricing. They may have disregarded a manufacturer's suggested price in as many if not more instances. Data are not available to show the number of times buyers disregarded manufacturers' suggested resale prices. However, Table 2 contains evidence that buyers compare the possible advantages in either following or not following manufacturers' suggested resale prices.

The considerations involved in such decisions were mentioned by buyers in a sufficient number of examples to shed some light upon this topic. Buyers' comments shown in Table 2 pertain only to pricing examples for which the selling price was determined by following a suggested resale price of the manufacturer. In 27 occasions buyers mentioned that manufacturers were very insistent that recommended resale prices be followed. Buyers weighed the following considerations when deciding upon a course of action involving a manufacturer's suggested resale price: the sales volume of the product concerned, the adequacy of the gross margin, the amount of advertising, and the demand for the product by retailers. Buyers sometimes resold the

TABLE 2

COMMENTS OF BUYERS IN PRICING REPRESENTATIVE ITEMS CARRIED BY THREE HARDWARE, THREE DRY GOODS, AND THREE DRUG WHOLESALERS ACCORDING TO MANUFACTURERS' SUGGESTED RESALE PRICES, MIDWESTERN STATES

Comments of Buyers	Number of Times Mentioned	Per Cent of Total
Markup adequate	34	23.4
Manufacturer very insistent that suggested resale price be followed	27	18.6
Manufacturer not insistent that suggested resale price be followed	19	13.1
Would raise price but competition prevents such action	14	9.6
Good sales volume	13	8.9
Product is advertised	11	7.5
Markup inadequate	10	7.0
Sold under distributorship arrangement	6	4.2
Poor sales volume	5	3.5
Merchandise is presold	4	2.8
Manufacturer would take line away if suggested resale price not followed	2	1.4
TOTAL	145	100.0

Source: Interviews of wholesalers included in the study.

item at a price higher or lower than the suggested resale price if the manufacturer did not object.

The data in Table 2 show that buyers would have sold at a price higher than the recommended resale price on 14 occasions if competition had not prevented them from so doing. Competing wholesalers followed the suggested price, and in order to be competitive, a buyer had to follow suit. A situation was created in which wholesalers followed the suggested resale price even though the manufacturer was not insistent.

A desire to sell at a higher or lower price than that suggested was thwarted by the following considerations: the manufacturer's insistence upon a set resale price, the existence of an exclusive territorial distributorship, or the threat to take away the line. Some buyers indicated that a satisfactory situation existed even though the margin was lower than they would normally like if the merchandise was "presold," heavily advertised, or the sales volume great. On several occasions buyers volunteered the statement that "we help pay for the advertising with our smaller margin." In other instances buyers stated that markup was inadequate for products which manufacturers insisted be sold at the suggested resale price.

Management and buyers both stated that in the past heavily advertised lines had been fewer, brand names had not been as important, and consumer recognition of, and insistence upon, branded merchandise had not been as great. It had been easier for a buyer to "average" his markup among many merchandise items and categories to arrive at an over-all satisfactory gross margin. He had greater freedom to price as he thought best. In more recent years the buyer's freedom to price, and to average his markup, was curtailed to a considerable degree with the advent of advertised lines and "preselling" of merchandise. Although data are lacking to confirm the opinion of buyers and management, they felt that a considerable percentage of the branded lines and products had margins below those which commonly had been associated with such merchandise in the past. The dry goods trade seemed to be more concerned, and perhaps more affected, by this turn of events.

Approximately two thirds of the markup percentages of pricing examples involving a suggested resale price are so-called average markup percentages. Since these average markup percentages were a percentage of invoice cost in 70 per cent of the pricing examples when inward freight was paid by wholesalers, it resulted in wholesalers realizing less than the typical or average markup. This is an unfortunate situation in light of wholesalers' increasing operating expenses and decreasing gross margin.

Effect of Inward Transportation Costs and Cash Discounts

Although policies of manufacturers with respect to transportation charges and cash discounts are, in the main, cost modifiers, they were not entirely overlooked in the pricing process. Data indicated that buyers followed no uniform practice in first determining a landed cost for merchandise and then considering pricing factors enumerated in Table 1. Buyers often disregarded incoming freight in pricing, and worked from invoice cost. At times buyers frankly stated that they did not consider freight, and analysis shows that when average markups were used they frequently were a percentage of invoice cost and not of landed cost.

One of the decisions that a manufacturer had to make which could affect the pricing process of a wholesaler, concerns the responsibility for payment of transportation costs from the factory to the wholesaler. If manufacturers universally prepaid freight charges, buyers in wholesale establishments would all price from a landed cost and would automatically include freight costs. The manufacturers in this study, however, prepaid freight in only 45 per cent of the 515 examples of pricing. Freight was prepaid in 62 per cent of the examples in the drug trade, 26 per cent in the dry goods trade and 60 per cent in the hardware trade.

It would seem logical to believe that a majority of manufacturers selling similar merchandise would follow the same policy in regard to prepayment of freight. The data support this contention. In 106 instances involving merchandise items at least one of the three wholesalers in a trade category purchased an item from a different source of supply. In approximately 85 per cent of these cases, manufacturers had similar policies regarding prepayment of freight.

Since wholesalers had to pay freight costs in 55 per cent of the 515 examples of pricing, buyers in those cases had one more variable to contend with in their task of determining a selling price. As previously mentioned, evidence shows that this variable was not handled in a uniform manner by buyers. Whether or not a buyer is keenly aware of the effect of transportation costs upon the margin of each item, such costs are an important additional variable confronting buyers. Data show that, in most instances, manufacturers prepaid freight, partially or entirely, only if a minimum quantity were ordered. The minimum usually was expressed in terms of weight or dollar amount. If a buyer was attempting to achieve a particular gross margin for an item, this variable certainly had an effect, since it modified the cost.

Although cash discounts were not considered as closely related to buyers' pricing processes as incoming transportation charges, buyers did on occasion mention such discounts when explaining how particular prices were established. In a few instances, buyers said that a markup for a particular item was better than it appeared since, for example, a manufacturer offered a cash discount of 3/10 net 30, whereas the house offered its customers 2/10 net 30 on the same item. On the other hand, it was pointed out that a markup was not as good as it appeared because the manufacturer sold the item on a net basis and the wholesaler offered his customers a cash discount of 2/10 net 30. Since a small minority of buyers mentioned the cash discount so infrequently during interviews covering 515 examples of pricing, it appears that the cash discount is of little significance as a factor in pricing merchandise.

Summary

It is apparent that the pricing freedom of wholesalers is curtailed in varying degree by manufacturers, depending upon the line of trade. Manufacturers accomplished this by the utilization of resale price maintenance legislation and the employment of suggested resale prices. To a much lesser degree the wholesaler was affected in his pricing by inward transportation charges and the cash discount.

The extent to which manufacturers' suggested resale prices were followed by wholesalers depended upon the degree of insistence by manufacturers which varied to a considerable degree. Wholesalers considered such variables as markup, competition, advertising, sales volume, and exclusive distributorships in deciding whether to follow suggested resale prices and in evaluating the profitableness of an item or line of merchandise sold according to suggested resale prices. The study indicates that it is possible for wholesalers to improve their profit picture by a careful examination of their present pricing practices as they are affected by manufacturers' policies regarding suggested resale pricing and freight charges.

29. RESALE PRICE MAINTENANCE *

Fritz Machlup

If one wants a strong defense of so-called fair-trade protection—resale-price maintenance—on economic grounds, one must not turn to an honest economist. If such an economist is asked whether price fixing in retail trade is in the national interest, not just in the interest of special groups in the economy, he has only one answer: "No; it is not in the national interest." If he has to explain why so many legislatures in almost all countries have seen fit to pass legislation for retailers' protection from price competition, he will have to point to two political factors—that retailers are an organized pressure group commanding many votes, and that the argument for fair-trade legislation can easily be put so that someone untrained in economics is persuaded, or at least able, to acquiesce.

Special-Interest Groups

In this respect, protection from retailers' competition through restrictions on price reductions is much alike to protection from foreign competition through import restrictions. Save in a few exceptional circumstances, protection of domestic producers against imports cannot be honestly defended as being in the interest of the national economy, but, since such protection is demanded by politically strong and vocal groups pressing their special interests, and since those untrained in economics can easily be persuaded by arguments which are fallacious but sound plausible, the legislatures of almost all countries in the world have passed tariff laws and other trade restrictions to protect domestic producers from competition by foreign producers.

If you poll all economists, or those whose special field is international trade, you will find them overwhelmingly opposed to higher

* Reprinted by permission from hearings before a Subcommittee of the Select Committee on Small Business, United States Senate, 85th Congress, Second Session on Competitive Impact of Discount-House Operations on Small Business, June 23, 24, and 25, 1958, pp. 170-186.

Fritz Machlup, Walker Professor of Economics and International Finance, Director of International Finance Section, Princeton University.

tariff and quota protection. A poll of economists on retailers' protection through fair-trade laws would, likewise, show an overwhelming majority in opposition to any such program.

This committee could easily make such a poll by sending a short questionnaire to all members of the American Economic Association, whose field is industrial organization and market structure. I would expect the result to be at least 9 out of 10 in favor of repealing our fair-trade legislation and restoring price competition to all sectors of the market.

The special interest group for which this kind of legislation is urged is much smaller than it is widely believed to be. For by no means all the retail trade, let alone all trade, is affected by fair-trade protection. According to a report of this committee, made in July 1956, 71 per cent of a significant sample of retailers have 10 per cent or less of their business in fair-traded goods. Almost a third of all retailers carry no such goods at all. Only 10 per cent of all retailers have more than one half of their business in fair-traded goods. In short, what we have here is a small special interest group getting a favor at the expense of 175 million consumers.

Now if this merely meant that you take some money from the consumers and give it to the retailers as an extra profit, if it were only a transfer of income from the American people to the group of retailers which you love better than the rest of the population of this country, I could say nothing as an economist.

As a citizen I could complain about such favoritism; I could squawk about your scheme of taking money out of my pocket and out of the pockets of all the workers, government employees, schoolteachers, and all the rest, in order to give a bonus to a small group of favored retailers. But as an economist I have to be neutral—as long as your scheme does not reduce the total efficiency of the economy, does not hold down real national income, and retard the economic growth of the Nation. Price fixing does exactly that. And it thus costs the American people a lot more than it benefits the few sellers of branded goods protected from competition under the price-fixing umbrella.

Competition Among Retailers and Among Manufacturers

I do not have to point out here what every Member of Congress has been saying hundreds of times, that restriction of competition reduces economic efficiency, and that we are dedicated to the maintenance of a competitive free-enterprise economy.

Some people say that competition among retailers is not so important, provided there is vigorous competition among manufacturers. This is wrong on two counts. First, price competition in retail distribution can be very important as a spur to efficiency and a check to inefficiency within the field of distribution, quite apart from the presence or absence of competition among the producers.

Secondly, the reduction of price competition among retailers results in a reduction of price competition among the producers of the goods concerned. This is probably the chief reason why some manufacturers are so anxious to help the retailers to maintain a fair-trade program.

You will want me to present supporting arguments for these two statements. The first can best be understood by imagining for a moment—what fortunately is contrary to fact—that all consumers goods were "fair traded." How could retailers compete, if their freedom of charging lower prices is taken away? The only ways in which they could try to get bigger shares of the business would be through luxury service, fancy store decoration, air conditioning, more green stamps, better looking sales girls, free delivery, charge accounts with longer credit. In other words, instead of giving the consumer lower prices and thus enabling him to buy more goods, productive resources are being used to give the consumer luxuries which he does not really want and would gladly exchange for what they cost.

Moreover, since the fixed retail prices allow a comfortable margin for the least efficient of the retailers, the most important function of competition—to eliminate inefficiency—is cut out of the system.

The second statement, concerning the effect of resale price maintenance upon competition among producers, shows why fair-trade legislation is the most absurd inconsistency in our whole antitrust program.

If retailers were to fix prices among themselves—that would be unlawful restraint of trade. If manufacturers were to fix prices among themselves, that, too, would be unlawful restraint of trade. But if both manufacturers' and retailers' prices are fixed at the same time through fair-trade price lists—this is perfectly lawful under the fair-trade laws.

Naive laymen sometimes believe that price fixing is done by a group of people actually meeting and debating and agreeing on the prices they will charge.

In actual fact it is much simpler: All that is necessary is that a manufacturer publishes a list and makes people understand that he will not soon reduce his prices below the list. Then all the other manufacturers' lists cannot be maintained very long. Some of the manufacturers will find it expendient to lower their prices. Others will follow suit, and the consumers will get more goods for their money.

However, if the retailers are compelled by law to stick to the list prices, then the manufacturers can maintain their lists. The result is a more effectively cartelized economy, where high prices all around protect the least efficient and least industrious.

The antitrust laws forbidding restraint of trade are made a shambles because the government undertakes to restrain trade by helping the cartelists to police the fixed prices. The irony of it all is that the supporters of this scheme pose as high-minded believers in a competitive free-enterprise economy, although no one dealing with fair-traded goods is to be left free to be enterprising and to compete for business by passing on to consumers the economies of his greater efficiency.

Freedom To Change Prices

Perhaps I may add at this point that my opposition to fair-trade price policing is based not only on economic principles—efficiency and economy—but also on the moral principle of individual freedom.

I consider it an outrage that—in peacetime, in an otherwise competitive field—a seller should be prohibited from deciding and asking the price at which he is willing to sell. In the case of public utilities—natural monopolies—we have accepted systems of price regulation in order to prevent monopolists from charging exorbitant prices. In wartime, we have accepted systems of price control chiefly in order to prevent producers of civilian goods from bidding up the prices of productive resources needed for the production of military goods. But when neither natural monopolies nor wartime emergencies are involved, the abrogation of the freedom of pricing, without collusion, in free competition with others, should be intolerable to all defenders of freedom, and especially to the defenders of a free-enterprise economy.

That this aberration of a depression period—the first fair-trade law with enforcement of list prices was introduced in 1933—should have been allowed to continue for as long as 25 years in this country with its tradition of freedom is hard to understand, even when one realizes that the price-fixing interests have maintained a bureau of education on fair trade to re-educate the public to accept coercive pricing.

THE THREE ARGUMENTS

Three arguments have been used in support of the fair-trade system of fixing and policing the retail prices of branded or trademarked goods.

Argument 1: The practice of using loss-leaders is an unfair method of competition, which should be prohibited.

Argument 2: The practice of selling branded or trademarked goods below the list prices suggested by the manufacturer or wholesaler reduces the property value of his trade name or trademark, which should be prevented.

Argument 3: The practice of selling at prices which do not include a fair profit margin for the retailer is predatory competition, leading to the extermination of small business.

Do these three arguments have a firm basis of both factual evidence and economic reason?

THE LOSS-LEADER PRACTICE

The loss-leader practice must be examined for its effects upon (*a*) the consumer, (*b*) the small retailer, and (*c*) the owner of the trade name or mark.

(*a*) The assertion that consumers are injured by this practice because they are "lured" by it to purchase from the same store overpriced or inferior goods lacks any evidence. Of course, the store which offers a bargain does so in the hope that people will buy other things besides; but no one has proved (i) that the loss leader really costs the store more than what it is sold for, (ii) that most stores offering such bargains really try to palm off overpriced or inferior goods on their customers, and (iii) that many customers are so careless or dumb as to be switched to inferior goods or to be talked into paying excessive prices.

It is not our custom to send a policeman with each customer to make sure that he is not cheated and, moreover, there is no reason for believing that customers will more likely be cheated by a store that offers bargains than by one that spends large sums on advertising or by one that does neither and handles only a small volume of business.

In most instances in which complaints about loss-leader selling have been checked, it was found that the stores in question had not lost at all on the articles offered at low prices, but merely were satisfied with smaller margins. It is deceptive language to speak of loss leaders in such cases. (A British Royal Commission stated a few years ago that the term "loss leader" was applied so vaguely as to make it impossible to find any basis "for reconciling the frequently divergent features attributed to loss-leader selling." An even stronger statement on the loose use of the term by business is found in the Canadian inquiry into loss-leader selling.) But, in any case, the assertion that the consumer is put at a disadvantage through bargain or loss-leader selling rests on the assumption that, as a rule, he is stupid.

This assumption is untenable and has always been rejected by those who were responsible for framing our legal and economic institutions.

Few people are unable to learn a lesson; American consumers are quite cagey and not easily fooled. As Professor Adelman once said:

> The supposed evils of loss-leader selling rest fundamentally on the idea that the consumer is so dumb that, if he is lured into the store with a few low prices, and prices have been raised on other things, he will never know the difference.

(*b*) There is more to the point of view of the small retailers who complain that they lose business to the large store that attracts customers through loss-leader sales, and they may even find it expedient to discontinue carrying the article sold elsewhere at a bargain price.

No doubt it must be aggravating to retailers to lose business to a chiseler. But is this a good reason for the Government to rush to their aid?

The careful inquiry by the Canadian Restrictive Trade Practices Commission, published in 1955, came to the conclusion that "in the course of this lengthy inquiry" no "serious shortcomings from the public viewpoint" had been shown, and that instances of real loss-leader selling had been extremely rare and without "any significant effect."

I am satisfied that this conclusion applies equally to the situation in the United States. But, just for the sake of the argument, let us ask whether legislative remedies would be indicated in the public interest if real loss-leader selling—not merely competitive price cutting—were frequent and effective in diverting business to those who practice it. Granted that small retailers may not be able to afford the cost of selling anything below the price at which they buy it; but similarly they cannot afford the expensive advertising that is done regularly by chain stores and department stores, nor the free customer parking and all the rest. But this does not mean that they cannot continue in business. They enjoy offsetting advantages, both on the cost side and on the side of customer attitudes. No one has ever shown that loss-leader practices of large stores would make the difference between death and survival of small retailers.

(*c*) If, when some stores have sold a branded or trademarked article at a bargain price, many retailers discontinue stocking this article or at least stop pushing its sale, the producer has a real grievance. How serious a grievance is it? The Canadian Commission answered this as follows:

> If a manufacturer loses some dealers who are unable to adapt their handling of his product to a competitive market, it does not follow that his overall sales volume will suffer. The interest of large-volume sellers to maintain and increase sales volume and the widening of the market through lower prices will be potent factors in sustaining trade in the manufacturer's product. There is also the factor that dealers who wish to maintain patronage will find it undesirable to discontinue a line which is in strong demand by consumers, even if the margin which they can obtain is not as large as they previously enjoyed. No proof satisfactory to the Commission was offered that overall sales volume had in fact suffered in any instance in Canadian business.

Some manufacturers may complain about the loss of orders from retailers irked by cut-rate sales of the article, and may fail to note at the same time that orders from other distributors, namely from those who are satisfied to work with smaller margins, have increased enough to overcompensate for the loss.

Other manufacturers, however, have been smart enough to discover the connection, have realized that lower distributor's markups are favorable to larger sales, and, in consequence, they have become cool toward fair-trade price policing.

The Loss of Goodwill

The second argument—the need for protection of the property value of trade names and trademarks against the loss of goodwill as a result of price cutting below official list prices—appears so strong and plausible to many that they consider anchoring the entire fair-trade program onto the trademark law.

On the other hand, one of the foremost trademark lawyers, Mr. Derenberg, has been moving in the opposite direction, stating that "the argument for fair trade as a means of protection of the manufacturer's goodwill has lost some of its force" with him and that he is "beginning to come to the conclusion" that the goodwill argument is not quite so important to the manufacturers as it has been alleged by the defenders of fair trade.

There are two separate steps in the argument: (*a*) That the goodwill of a trade name or mark suffers when the article which they identify is sold below the price announced by the manufacturer, and (*b*) that the public interest requires prevention of such loss of goodwill. The first is a question of fact, the second a question of political philosophy.

It would be difficult to understand why a consumer should lose confidence in the quality of a product when he finds that one or more retailers in their competition with other retailers sell it at a lower price.

But if for me the retailer's profit margin is no reflection on the quality of the product, perhaps it is for other people; and perhaps somebody has not contented himself with introspective reasoning and has made inquiries. The Canadian Commission has done so, and this is what their report says in the summary chapter:

> It was frequently represented to the Commission during the hearings by some representatives of both manufacturers and dealers that price competition in the sale of a particular branded article had the effect of lessening consumer preference for the article and reducing purchases. In other words, it was suggested that the affording to the consumer of an opportunity to purchase a branded article on a competitive price basis as between dealers would lessen the consumer's goodwill toward the manufacturer's brands. The Commission considers that the weight of the evidence in the inquiry does not support these representations. No positive evidence was submitted which would indicate that a consumer's attitude toward a branded article became less favorable if he found that he could purchase it at a lower price, and in fact the evidence which was given as to the quantities of certain branded articles, which were bought in brief periods when a substantial price reduction was advertised, points in the opposite direction.

Since the question of fact is answered in the negative, the question of policy becomes a moot one. But I should like to stick my neck out by making the provocative statement that even a serious loss of value of "trademark property" as a result of price competition should be of no public concern and would not call for preventive or remedial measures in the public interest.

The trademark law has one ultimate objective; to protect the consumer against deception; the protection afforded to the owner of the trademark is only instrumental to the ultimate objective, in that the owner can be expected to look out for his own interest and to sue those who by unauthorized use of identifying devices deceive consumers. But where no consumer interests are jeopardized, the public interest does not call for action in support of the value of the industrial property in question.

Thus, resale price maintenance for the purpose of maintaining the value of trademark property would be objectionable in any case. It is doubly so, since, according to all available evidence, no real danger to the value of industrial property arises from price competition among retailers.

Predatory Competition

Before we can examine the assertion concerning the dangers of predatory competition, we must know what it is; we must know when competition is "predatory" and when it is not. This can be known best after we call to mind what functions the socially useful type of competition is supposed to perform. In order to work well in a way that benefits society, competition should—

(1) keep producers and distributors under constant pressure, giving them no chance to relax in their efforts to serve the public as well as possible;

(2) force them thereby to be ingenious and to think of ever more efficient ways of producing and distributing;

(3) force them to be satisfied with the margin of receipts over cost that is just compatible with the survival of that number of firms which the best service to the public requires;

(4) force those who relax, who are not constantly improving their methods, and who try to charge more than is needed for an economically operated enterprise to survive, to go out of business and do something more useful instead.

Thus, that it eliminates the least efficient or the least satisfied is one of the socially desirable functions of competition. In some industries it is possible, however, for a less efficient but financially powerful firm to drive a more efficient but financially weak firm out of business by selling for a considerable time at substantial out-of-pocket losses.

All the firms will lose money in the process, but the richest ones will survive. After the poor rivals are killed off, the survivors are left in monopolistic control of the market and can recoup their losses by gouging the consumers. This is "predatory competition"; it can exist only in industries where it is very difficult and very expensive to start a business, or to re-enter once you are out.

For, surely, no sane person would ever dream of throwing away money for years in order to kill rivals if they can come back into business, or others in their places, as soon as prices are raised.

Retailing is typically the kind of business where entry and re-entry is easy and cheap and, therefore, predatory competition cannot exist. If some people in the retail trade use that term, they do so either because they do not know what it means or because they hope that it will make a big impression on others who are ignorant of its true meaning.

Even when the term "predatory" is used in a loose sense to refer to all discriminatory practices of a large firm that are seriously injuring their smaller competitors, there is little or no evidence that such competition has actually killed off many small retailers. Thus one economist, apparently annoyed by the horror stories circulated by fair-trade advocates, exclaimed:

> Oceans of ink have been spilled on the supposed evils of loss-leader selling, local discriminatory selling, and so on. But what I am still looking for is one authentic example of somebody's being put out of business by the discriminating sharpshooting of a chain store. I have yet to find the one example—to be able to offer it to my students as a museum piece.

This does not mean that this expert wants to deny the high mortality rate in retail trade. It has been general knowledge that retailing has a very high mortality rate. But it has also a very high birth rate. This is why we do not have to worry about the emergence of one retail-monopolist controlling a market for any length of time.

If the claim that, because of the prevalance of predatory competition, small retailers cannot survive without fair-trade laws is taken seriously, we can easily look whether there is any evidence for it.

Three states, Missouri, Texas, and Vermont, and the District of Columbia, have never had fair-trade laws. Surely there cannot be any small retail businesses left if that claim is right; they must all have died off in the last 25 years. Have they? And since during the last years, the fair-trade laws have been invalidated or have become inoperative in some 15 other states, we should see in these states an enormous jump in the bankruptcy rates for retail businesses. We should see it—if the fair-trade advocates were right.

Equalize Rights In Distribution

One additional argument ought to be examined, partly because it has been advanced by the one reputable economist of my acquaintance who defends fair-trade legislation, partly because it has been incorporated into the title and preamble of H. R. 10527, a bill introduced this year in the House of Representatives. This bill intends "to amend the Federal Trade Commission Act—so as to equalize rights in the distribution of identified merchandise."

The point is that very big manufacturing concerns can become wholly integrated and own their retail outlets; since they sell directly to the consumer they need not dictate their prices to anybody else. Likewise, large and powerful firms can sell through their own agents or through their consignees. Small manufacturers and wholesalers may not be able to afford such schemes; if they want to control the retail prices of their products, they need fair-trade laws which prevent retailers from engaging in price competition.

In other words, since we cannot prevent every manufacturer from controlling the retail prices of their products, we are told that we should prevent none.

The logic of this argument can be easily shown by an analogy, also in the antitrust laws. Congress has not found a good way of preventing very large firms from achieving a measure of control of their market. But our laws have been prohibiting firms from combining to achieve collective control of the market.

This prohibition of contracts in restraint of trade obviously deprives small firms of an opportunity which the very big one may have. Hence, if we set out to equalize the opportunities of the small and the big, we must hurry and repeal the Sherman Act and allow all firms to get together and form cartels and other combinations to restrain trade to their hearts' content. Then the rights will be equalized. I trust that this argument will not convince many Members of the Congress.

30. GUIDES AGAINST DECEPTIVE PRICING

Federal Trade Commission

The following guides have been adopted by the Federal Trade Commission for the use of its staff in the evaluation of pricing representations in advertising.[1] While the guides do not purport to be all inclusive, they are directed toward the elimination of existing major abuses and are being released to the public in the interest of obtaining voluntary, simultaneous and prompt cooperation by those whose practices are subject to the jurisdiction of the Federal Trade Commission.

In determining whether or not pricing practices are violative of the laws administered by the Commission, the facts in each matter are considered in view of the requirements of the Federal Trade Commission Act, as amended, and principles enunciated by the Courts in the adjudication of cases. The foremost of these principals are:

1. Advertisements must be considered in their entirety and as they would be read by those to whom they appeal.
2. Advertisements as a whole may be completely misleading although every sentence separately considered is literally true. This may be because things are omitted that should be said, or because advertisements are composed or purposely printed in such a way as to mislead.
3. Advertisements are not intended to be carefully dissected with a dictionary at hand, but rather to produce an impression upon prospective purchasers.
4. Whether or not the advertiser knows the representations to be false, the deception of purchasers and the diversion of trade from competitors is the same.

* *Guides Against Deceptive Pricing*, Federal Trade Commission, Adopted October 2, 1958.

[1] For the purposes of these Guides "Advertising" includes any form of public notice which uses a claim for a product, however such representation is disseminated or utilized.

5. A deliberate effort to deceive is not necessary to make out a case of using unfair methods of competition or unfair or deceptive acts or practices within the prohibition of the statute.
6. Laws are made to protect the trusting as well as the suspicious.
7. Pricing representations, however made, which are ambiguous will be read favorably to the accomplishment of the purpose of the Federal Trade Commission Act, as amended, which is to prevent the making of claims which have the tendency and capacity to mislead.

THE GUIDES

In considering particular types of pricing practices for the purpose of determining whether terminology and direct or implied representations, however made, i.e., in advertising or in labeling or otherwise, may be in violation of the Federal Trade Commission Act, the following general principles will be used: [2]

I. Saving claims

No statement, however expressed, whether in words, phrases, price figures, symbols, fractions, percentages or otherwise, which represents or implies a reduction or saving from an established retail price, or from the advertiser's former price, should be used in connection with the price at which an article is offered for sale unless,

(a) the saving or reduction statement applies to the specific article offered for sale as distinguished from similar or comparable merchandise,
(Note: Where a comparison is made between the price of the article offered for sale and the price of comparable merchandise Guide III applies.)

AND, (b) OR (c)

(b) the saving or reduction is from the usual and customary retail price of the article in the trade area, or areas, where the statement is made,
Examples of phrases used in connection with prices which have been held to be representations of an article's usual and customary retail price are:

[2] Pricing practices in connection with the sale and offering for sale of fur and fur products are governed primarily by the provisions of the "Rules and Regulations Under the Fur Products Labeling Act."

"Maker's List Price"
"Manufacturer's List Price"
"Manufacturer's Suggested Retail Price"
"Sold Nationally At"
"Nationally Advertised At"
"Value"

(c) the saving or reduction is from the advertiser's usual and customary retail price of the article in the recent, regular course of business,

Examples of words and phrases used in connection with prices which have been held to be representations of the advertiser's usual and customary retail price are:

"regularly"
"usually"
"formerly"
"originally"
"reduced"
"was____now____"
"made to sell for"
"woven to sell for"
"our list price"
"____% off"
"save up to $____"
"special"
"you save $____"
"$50 dress—$35"

AND

(d) the statement clearly shows whether the saving or reduction is from the usual and customary retail price of the article in the trade area or from the advertiser's usual and customary retail price of the article in the recent, regular course of business.

II. Limitations

No statement which represents or implies a reduction or saving from an established retail price or from the advertiser's usual and customary retail price should be used if,

(a) an artificial mark-up has been used to provide the basis for the claim, or

(b) the claim is based on infrequent or isolated sales, or

(c) the claim is based on a past price (i.e., one not immediately preceding the price used in the recent, regular course of business) unless this fact is clearly and adequately disclosed.

III. Comparable and similar merchandise

Nothing in these guides is intended to preclude an advertiser from comparing his selling price for an article to the price at which similar and comparable merchandise is currently offered for sale, or sold, provided that,

(a) it is clearly and conspicuously disclosed in the statement, however made, that the comparison in price is being made between the article offered for sale and similar and comparable merchandise so that it is made clear that the comparative price is not the former or usual and customary price of the advertised article but is the price of such similar and comparable merchandise.

AND

(b) the merchandise, to which the sales price of the advertised article is compared, is at least of like grade and quality in all material respects,

AND

(c) said similar and comparable merchandise is generally available for purchase at the comparative price in the same trade area, or areas, where the claim is made, or, if not so available, that fact is clearly disclosed.

An example of a statement which would be proper within the provisions of Guide III if based on facts is:

"Dacron suit $20.00—
Comparable suits $25.00"

IV. "Special sale, etc."

No statement which represents or implies that because of some unusual event or manner of business, an article is offered for sale to the consuming public at a saving from the usual and customary retail price in the trade area, or areas, where the claim is made, or at a saving from the advertiser's usual and customary price for the article in the recent, regular course of his business should be made unless the claim is true.

Examples of words and phrases illustrative of representations to which Guide IV has reference are:

"Special Purchase"
"Clearance"
"Marked Down From Stock"
"Exceptional Purchase"
"Manufacturer's Close-Out"
"Advance Sale"
"Sale"

V. "Two for one sales"

No statement or representation of an offer to sell two articles for the price of one, or phrase of similar import, should be used unless the sales price for the two articles is the advertiser's usual and customary retail price for the single article in the recent, regular course of his business.

(Note: Where the one responsible for a "two for the price of one" claim has not previously sold the article and/or articles, the propriety of the advertised price for the two articles is determined by the usual and customary retail price of the single article in the trade area, or areas, where the claim is made.)

VI. "½ price"—"1¢ sale" conditioned on purchase of additional merchandise

No statement or representation of an offer to sell an article at a saving through claims such as "½ price" or "50% off" or "1¢ sale," or expressions of similar import,[3] should be used when the offer is conditioned upon the purchase of additional merchandise, unless:

(a) the terms or conditions imposed are conspicuously disclosed in immediate conjunction with the offer,

AND

(b) the represented saving in price is in fact true, and when the claim is "½ price," or an expression of similar nature, the saving is from the advertiser's usual and customary retail price for the article in the recent, regular course of business.

[3] Similar claims, not conditioned upon the purchase of other merchandise, are governed by the provisions of Guide I (b) and (c).

AND

(c) the price charged for the additional merchandise required to be purchased is the usual and customary retail price for the merchandise in the recent, regular course of the advertiser's business.

(Note: Where the one responsible for the saving claim has not previously sold the article and/or the additional merchandise, the propriety of the claim will be governed by the usual and customary retail prices of the article and the additional merchandise at retail in the trade area, or areas, where the claim is made.)

VII. "Factory or wholesale prices"

No statement should be made in connection with the offering for sale of a product to the consuming public of a "factory" or "wholesale" price, or other such expression, which represents or implies that the consuming public can purchase the article at the same price that retailers regularly do, and provides a saving from the usual and customary retail price for the article in the trade area, or areas, where the claim is made unless such statement is true.

VIII. "Pre-ticketing"

No article should be "pre-ticketed" with any price figure, either alone or with descriptive terminology, which exceeds the price at which the article is usually and customarily sold in the trade area, or areas, where the "pre-ticketed" article is offered for sale.

(a) Those who disseminate "pre-ticketed" price figures for use in connection with the offering for sale of articles at retail by others (even though they themselves are not engaged in retail sales) are chargeable if the price figures do not meet the standard set forth in this Guide. As such, they are chargeable with knowledge of the ordinary business "facts of life" concerning what happens to articles for which they furnished "pre-ticketed" prices. One who puts into the hands of others a means or instrumentality by which they may mislead the public, is himself guilty of deception.

(b) For the purposes of this Guide "pre-ticketing" includes the use of price figures,

(1) affixed to the article by tag, label or otherwise, or

(2) in such a form as to be affixed to the product by others, or

(3) in material, such as display placards, which are used, or designed to be used, with the article at point of sale to the consuming public.

IX. "Imperfect, irregular, seconds"

No comparative price should be quoted in connection with an article offered for sale which is imperfect, irregular, or a second, unless it is accompanied by a clear and conspicuous disclosure that such comparative price refers to the price of the article if perfect. Such comparative price should not be used unless (1) it is the price at which the advertiser usually and customarily sells the article without defects, or (2) it is the price at which the article without defects is usually and customarily sold at the comparative price in the trade area, or areas, where the statement is made, or if such an article is not so available, that fact is clearly disclosed.

Nothing contained in these Guides relieves any party subject to a Commission cease and desist order or stipulation from complying with the provisions of such order or stipulation. The Guides do not constitute a finding in and will not affect the disposition of any formal or informal matter before the Commission.

31. TWO IMPORTANT PROBLEMS IN SALES FORECASTING *

James H. Lorie

This paper is about two important problems in sales forecasting: (1) the problem of combining objective statistical analysis with subjective judgment in making forecasts and (2) the problem of evaluating economic forecasts.[1]

Combining Statistical Analysis with Subjective Judgment

At the cost of spectacular oversimplification, methods of sales forecasting can be placed in two classes. Into the first goes all the variety of subjective, intuitive appraisals of the market outlook which comes to economists and business executives after spending many years trying to forecast the sale of some commodity or group of commodities. Into the other class goes all the variety of statistical and mathematical manipulations, usually carried out by young men not long out of graduate school and not long in the business world.

These young men, typically, are intolerant of the unquantified and imprecise speculations of their elders, and this intolerance is usually not significantly mitigated by the fact that their elders often seem to make more accurate forecasts. The elders, on the other hand, often doubt that young men can know enough about the peculiarities of any particular business—peculiarities which even surprise the graybeards from time to time—to make good forecasts. The graybeards often hire statisticians, particularly in periods of high corporate income-tax rates, in order to see what they can produce; but, when there are serious conflicts between the statisticians' equations and the graybeards' insights, the equations are equally disregarded.

* Reprinted by permission from *The Journal of Business*, Vol. XXX, No. 3 (July, 1957), pp. 172-179. Copyright 1957, University of Chicago.

James H. Lorie, Associate Dean, School of Business, University of Chicago.

[1] On this point there have been some interesting papers. See R. Ferber, "Sales Forecasting by Correlation Techniques," *Journal of Marketing*, XVIII (1954), 219-32, and his "Measuring the Accuracy and Structure of Businessmen's Expectations," *Journal of the American Statistical Association*, XLVIII (September, 1953), 385-412; and Harry V. Roberts, "A Technique for Appraising and Improving Forecasts," *Proceedings of the Conference of the American Marketing Association*, June, 1956, pp. 97-102.

It is unfortunate that the intolerance of the two groups is so great and communication between them so difficult. Each can make an important contribution to sales forecasting. Undoubtedly, something can be learned from the competent analysis of historical data, of survey data, and of data resulting from experimentation. It is equally clear that men of long experience in a business can make important contributions to sales forecasting, even though their perceptions cannot be quantified and the interrelationships among them are neither consciously recognized nor clearly stated.

A very important problem in sales forecasting is combining the wisdom of experienced businessmen with statistical analysis, which can be conducted at low cost, in order to achieve better forecasts. The combination of these two sources of enlightenment will probably be even more valuable in the development of accurate forecasts if the combination is achieved through some objective process. This paper describes two methods for combining intuitive appraisals with statistical analysis. Both achieve objectivity in the process of combination. Because the "operations research" label seems capable of attracting widespread attention to useful processes which were largely neglected under their former designations of "applied statistics" or "business economics," it may be worth noting that these methods of forecasting can be legitimately termed "operations research."

Before describing these two methods, however, the more conventional methods of statistical analysis will be discussed very briefly to indicate some of the reasons for their very moderate successes in the past and why it is unreasonable to expect that more complicated massaging of numbers according to conventional statistical techniques is likely to produce very much more successful results in the future.

A. Some conventional methods of statistical analysis

1. Regression Analysis. Regression analysis is certainly one of the most widely used means for forecasting sales. Very few respectable research staffs fail to grind out substantial quantities of regression analyses in which sales of various commodities are the dependent variables. Usually the independent variables include such things as some measure of aggregate economic activity, some measure of industry activity, some measure of prices or relative prices, and often some indication of family formation or particularly relevant changes in demographic data.

Although such analyses provide some information about average relationships in the past or about average relationships between variables at one time but in different places, such analyses are subject to several important limitations, especially when used uncritically. The ordinary linear multiple-regression model involves the following assumptions when used for forecasting: (1) the "dependent variable" is, except for random deviations, a linear function of the "independent variables;" (2) the random deviations are normally and independently distributed with the same standard deviation, regardless of the values of the "independent variables." Simple modifications of this model will accommodate some of the violations of these assumptions that are met in practice, such as departures from linearity and non-constant standard deviation of the dependent variable about the regression line. A more serious problem is that of non-independence of the residuals. There is no general agreement on ways of dealing with this problem, though certain rough-and-ready methods, such as use of first differences of all variables, seem often to be useful.[2]

Perhaps a more fundamental objection to regression analysis as a means for forecasting is that it merely transforms the forecasting problem from the dependent variable to the independent variables. It requires that the analyst forecast the levels of the independent variables such as national income or industry sales rather than the level of the dependent variable, sales of a particular company's product. There is certainly very little reason to believe that forecasters have been markedly more successful in forecasting the kinds of variables which are typically considered to be independent in forecasting equations than they have been in forecasting the variables which are considered dependent.

Further, regression analysis as it is usually and perhaps as it always is practiced provides no objective means for permitting the injection into the forecasting mechanisms of the influence of short-run factors which may be believed by business executives to be of decisive influence for any particular forecast.

In spite of the grave limitations of correlation analysis, it will undoubtedly continue to be widely used. One of the reasons is that

[2] Another point often mentioned is that the "independent" explanatory variables are not "independent" of one another. This statement confuses two completely different meanings of "independent"—functional and statistical independence, respectively. The linear multiple-regression model does *not* assume statistical independence among the "independent variables." However, intercorrelations among the "independent variables" do have the effect of increasing the error of estimates.

it is one of the very few techniques which can be readily learned by people receiving low wages and which has the comforting—albeit superficial—appearance of "scientific" precision.

2. SALESMEN'S FORECASTS. Many companies place substantial reliance on sales forecasts by salesmen, which may or may not be filtered through district and regional sales managers. The variety of ways in which these forecasts are made and subsequently adjusted is great. Some remarkable improvements in salesmen's forecasts have been achieved by educating salesmen both regarding the economic determinants of fluctuations in sales and regarding their own record in forecasting. Further, it is possible to improve the accuracy of salesmen's forecasts by adjusting them to compensate for systematic biases which have been revealed through analysis of previous experience with these forecasts.

This technique of sales forecasting has much to commend it. It is based upon a systematic collection and analysis of the opinions of men who, among all the company's employees, are in closest contact with dealers and ultimate consumers. Nevertheless, there are inherent deficiencies in this method of sales forecasting for which it may be impossible to devise effective remedies. The technique makes no provision for discovering what can be learned from the competent statistical analysis of historical data on sales. Second, it seems unreasonable to expect that salesmen can ever be made to have the breadth and depth of understanding of pervasive economic influences on the economy as a whole, on the industry in which the company operates, or on the company itself that can be possessed by either executives or professional staff analysts. Third, the turnover in sales forces is often substantial, with the possible consequence that forecasts would be built upon the deliberations and analyses of relatively inexperienced men whose biases could not be determined by historical analysis. Fourth, the method as here described and usually used makes no provision for the objective combination of the wisdom of technical analysts and executives with that of the sales force.

3. CONSUMER SURVEYS. Consumer surveys have been used with increasing frequency in recent years in forecasting, especially in forecasting sales of consumer durable goods. Some of this popularity is undoubtedly attributable to a widespread publicity which has been given in various business publications to the successes of the surveys of buying intentions which are one of the products of the *Surveys of Consumer Finances* of the Board of Governors of the Federal Reserve System in forecasting the direction of change from year to

year in the volume of purchases of specified consumer durable goods. Perhaps the most remarkable successes were in 1949, when a sustained volume of purchases was forecast in spite of reduced personal income, and in 1951, when a reduction of volume was forecast in spite of a substantial inflation and increased personal income.[3]

Asking people what they are going to do is an attractively simple approach to the forecasting problem. To the comment that people often do not know what they are going to do, the answer might come that the *Surveys of Consumer Finances* seem to have worked very well in spite of the undoubted validity of that fact. Before embracing the technique wholeheartedly on the basis of this success, the success should be scrutinized a bit. The following comments seem worth making:

(*a*) Such surveys cost a great deal of money.
(*b*) Only the direction of change and not its magnitude has been forecast.
(*c*) The data on buying intentions have been interpreted subjectively by a person of great experience in such interpretations. It is doubtful whether less skilled interpreters could achieve the same success.
(*d*) The predictive value of buying intentions has not been tested during a period of serious recession.
(*e*) No evidence exists regarding the value of the technique in predicting the sales of nondurables.

These shortcomings indicate that it may still be worthwhile looking for other predictive techniques which are more objective, more precise, less costly, and more generally applicable.

B. Two solutions to the problem of combining statistical analysis with unquantified forecast

1. THE FILTER TECHNIQUE. This technique is called the "filter technique," since, by mechanical application of a statistical formula, it is possible to filter out the regular, recurring causes of fluctuations in sales and cast into relief for identification, study, and possible eventual incorporation into the forecasting mechanism those irregular causes of sales fluctuations which may not have been suspected and yet which may have been of decisive importance. The technique works like this:

(*a*) Select a simple statistical model. For example, the model might be that sales next month will be the same as in the corresponding month in the preceding year. Alternatively, and better, the model

[3] See Irving Schweiger, "Forecasting Short-Term Consumer Demand from Consumer Anticipations," *Journal of Business*, XXIX (April, 1956), 90-100.

might be that next month's sales will differ from last month's sales by the same percentage that marked the difference between sales in the corresponding months in the preceding years. Note that this process automatically takes into account of seasonal, cyclical, and secular influences.

(*b*) By use of this model, generate an artificial or historical forecast in order to see for some extended period of time into the past what the sales forecast would have been if this model had been the forecasting mechanism.

(*c*) Compare forecast sales during this historical period with actual sales.

(*d*) Identify those periods in which the discrepancy between forecasts and actual sales exceed tolerable levels.

(*e*) Subject these periods of too-great discrepancy to intensive study in an attempt to find explanatory variables.

(*f*) Incorporate what appear to be the most promising explanatory variables into the simple statistical model. These variables could be unusual price changes in the products of the company of or the company's competitors, strikes, model changes, etc. These new explanatory variables can be introduced into the forecasting mechanism either through some formal device such as regression analysis or by subjective evaluation of their importance. For example, the regression could be between price differences and historical discrepancies between actual sales of the product and the sales that were forecast through the use of the statistical model that served as the filter. Regression analysis could also be used when the explanatory variable was promotional activity. When the explanatory variable is not easily quantified or has occurred so seldom as to make regression analysis impossible, some other device must be used. Such explanatory variables could be the introduction of new models by either the company making the forecast or its rival or strikes at the plant of the company making the product or at the plants of its rivals. When variables such as these seem to explain historical discrepancies, recourse must be had to the use of judgment as to their effect or to the use of simple averages of historical discrepancies between the series being forecast and the forecast itself generated by the filter device.

(*g*) Generate a new series of artificial, historical forecasts and repeat the steps outlined above until a model of sufficient accuracy—as measured by retrospective forecasts—is secured.

(*h*) Test the model by forecasting the future.

This method has a number of desirable characteristics not possessed by the older and more conventional techniques already discussed. It provides an objective means for combining wisdom which cannot be quantified and expressed symbolically with statistical analysis. It does this in such a way that the very valuable time of the men who possess this wisdom is rigidly economized and is drawn upon only to the extent that the efforts of staff personnel—often at relatively low levels—have proved inadequate. In the second place, it starts with an extremely simple and cheap process to which additional time and money are devoted only up to the point at which the process becomes satisfactory. Third, the process provides an objective record of both sales forecasts and the methods by which they are made so that study of this record can be a means for continual improvement in the forecasting process.

2. THE SKEPTIC'S TECHNIQUE.[4]—This technique is based upon a healthy skepticism regarding the ability of experts to foresee the future. Yet the technique implies limited faith—faith in the persistence of historical forces which have been affecting sales and which might be assumed to have a continuing effect. This latter limited faith reflected itself in a simple statistical projection of least-squares trend lines—usually linear—of historical time-series data on sales of individual company products.

The problem is to combine the intuitive wisdom of experts with the mechanical projection of data on sales. It has been done in the following way.

For each of the large number of products for which a company requires sales forecasts, the forecaster projects least-squares trend lines—usually linear—and computes two standard deviations on each side of this trend line, providing a range within which future sales could be expected to fall a vast majority of the time if historical forces continued to work in the same way. This work, incidentally, could be done by statistical clerks whose rate of pay is substantially less than that of barbers or plumbers.

At the same time the forecaster asks his experts to retire to their offices and engage in whatever mystical rites they deem appropriate to enable them to foresee the future volume of sales of the products about which they are allegedly expert. These experts, incidentally, usually receive substantially more than barbers or even plumbers.

If the experts' forecasts fall within the range indicated by the projection of the historical time series, the forecast is accepted. If not, the expert is asked to go back and reconsider, perhaps to ask the gods for another omen. If the expert still cannot provide a forecast within the limits indicated by the work of the statistical clerk, the forecaster has to make a decision—something which, it will be observed, he has avoided up to this point.

It is not necessary to dwell upon the way in which he makes this decision but merely to indicate that experience has indicated that the forecast in a vast majority of the cases would have been more

[4] This technique was developed though not named by Ashley Wright, of the Standard Oil Company of New Jersey.

accurate if the experts' forecast had arbitrarily been moved to the nearest control limit provided by the statistical clerk rather than being accepted as it was.

The filter and skeptic techniques have five important characteristics in common:

(*a*) Both involve the creation of a written record of specific forecasts and the methods by which they were made.
(*b*) Both involve statistical analysis of available data.
(*c*) Both involve very simple assumptions in making use of the statistical analyses. Complications are avoided until they seem to be necessary.
(*d*) Effort is expanded only when results fall short of requirements.
(*e*) Both methods provide a means for bringing together formal statistical analysis with a less formal appraisal by men of experience whose perceptions are often valuable though not susceptible to quantitative expression and analysis.

The Evaluation of Forecasts

Progress comes most rapidly in any pragmatic discipline when adequate testing devices are available for measuring the success of current theories and procedures. Only by such testing is it possible to discard what has not succeeded and to cling to what has succeeded, for the purposes of further elaboration and refinement. These facts are considered self-evident in the field of meteorology, where most of the practitioners make their living by forecasting. As a consequence, a very extensive literature devoted to problems of evaluation has developed during the last seventy-five years.[5] Further, the people who write this literature seem to have learned something from one another and seem to have something to say to one another. The same is not equally true of economists.

There are two main problems in evaluating forecasting devices: (1) determining accuracy and (2) determining economic usefulness. There are three principles which may be helpful in solving these two problems.

A. The superiority of written forecasts

Forecasts should be written to indicate without ambiguity what is being forecast and how the forecast was made. These requirements are met surprisingly infrequently. Too often, forecasts are not written at all, with the usual consequence that the forecasts seem to

[5] An excellent summary of this literature containing a summary of fifty-five articles on verification, chronologically arranged and beginning with 1884, was published by the American Meteorological Association (R. H. Muller, "Verification of Short-Range Weather Forecasts [a Survey of the Literature]," *Bulletin of the American Meteorological Society,* XXV [1944], 18-27, 47-53, 88-95).

become more and more accurate as they recede into the past where memory is inexact and usually comforting. For this reason—and perhaps for others—the accuracy of oral forecasts often appears to be superior, in retrospect, to the accuracy of the written forecasts.

Even when forecasts are written, they are often so vague that it is difficult to decide if experience confirms or fails to confirm what was forecast. This fuzziness occurs primarily because of the emphasis on adjectives and adverbs to designate the nature of movements in the series being forecast. Words such as "much," "little," "great," "small," "sharply," "moderately," etc., often permit a substantial amount of subjective evaluation in judging the accuracy of forecasting.

Even worse than the use of such words as these is the failure to designate without ambiguity what statistics are being forecast. The financial analysts are perhaps particularly guilty of this crime. It is distressingly easy to find examples of forecasts which refer to "markets" or "business activity" or the "state of business" or "sales" or "conditions." Such broad designations often include a variety of statistics with divergent time patterns so that the accuracy of the forecasts cannot be judged. Their usefulness, however, can; their usefulness is negligible.

It is also disheartening to people interested in improving the quality of the economic forecast to find that often written forecasts of objectively determinable accuracy have not been presented together with a detailed explanation of the method by which the forecast was made. The absence of a record of the forecasting method makes it extremely difficult to judge what has been successful and what unsuccessful among the techniques for peering into the future. It is usually worthwhile trying to set down with as much accuracy as possible the process of reasoning by which forecasts are made, even though the process includes a great deal of intuitive or subjective appraisal of economic evidence. Sometimes these appraisals, when scrutinized carefully, will be found to have a common pattern which might suggest a principle of analysis of substantial value. In fact, the descriptive process is even more important for subjective appraisal than for objective analyses whose results sometimes permit a reconstruction of the method by which they were achieved.

B. The statistical evaluation of forecasting techniques

In one sense the statistical accuracy can be determined by measuring the percentage discrepancy between the unambiguous forecasts of specified data and the recorded changes in these data. This operation can be performed and the results of it can be studied. This kind of statistical evaluation is not very useful, however, as can be seen from the following example. There was once a weather forecaster in St. Petersburg, Florida, it is alleged, who forecast every day that the following day would be clear and sunny. Some people believe that this forecaster made up his forecasts for a year in advance, leaving his time free for fishing and other rewarding activities. Forecasts made in this way were right and would continue to be right about 95 per cent of the time. There is also a story that a team of trained meteorologists in Chicago had been peering intently at modern meteorological instruments and considering a variety of relevant meteorological data in making their forecasts. These forecasts have been correct only 80 per cent of the time. There is probably no overwhelming evidence to support the conclusion that meteorologists make better forecasts than fishermen, but it is also probably true that few people would be content to let their evaluation of these different forecasting techniques rest entirely on a comparison of 95 per cent with 80 per cent.

If there is a point to the preceding example, it is that the statistical evaluation of forecasting techniques must take account of the variability of the series being forecast. Undoubtedly, the variability of weather in Chicago is much greater than that in St. Petersburg, with the result that the forecasting task in Chicago is much more difficult.

In taking variability into consideration for the purpose of evaluating the contribution of the forecasting technique, it is important that "variability" be properly understood. What is desired is measurement of the "marginal" contribution of the forecasting technique. What is desired is an indication of the extent to which one can forecast better because of the use of the forecasting technique than would be possible by sole reliance on some simple, cheap, and objective forecasting device. Clearly, when there is no variability in the series being forecast—as was almost true in St. Petersburg—forecasting methods which insisted that the future would always be like the past would work perfectly, with the consequence that the marginal contribution of any other forecasting technique would be zero. The meteorologists have devised several simple, objective forecasting techniques which they use for the purpose of measuring the marginal contribution of more complicated and pretentious techniques. In economics it is not hard to think of some simple statistical models which can be used for this purpose. Two of these models have already been suggested in this paper in the discussion of the filter technique.

When choosing among alternative simple statistical models, the guiding principle should be to choose the one which accounts for the most variability in the series being forecast. It is usually not worthwhile to make a careful determination of which is the "best" forecasting device. A simple and intuitive appraisal is usually not significantly worse than a more painstaking discrimination.

C. The economic evaluation of forecasts

Of even more importance in economic forecasting than a statistical evaluation is an economic evaluation. The difference between them, of course, lies in the fact that the economic evaluation attaches monetary consequences to the discrepancies between the forecast and subsequent behavior of the series being forecast, while statistical evaluation does not. This distinction is obviously of importance only when some kinds of statistical errors or discrepancies are more costly than others. This is frequently true.

A forecasting technique is judged to be superior to alternatives according to an economic evaluation if the consequences of decisions based upon it are more profitable than decisions based upon the alternatives. Gringorten discusses this problem with regard to weather forecasts and gives a fine example with reference to the economic consequences for airlines of mistaken weather forecasts.[6] The problem of economic evaluation is often difficult but usually worthwhile.

[6] Irving I. Gringorten, "The Verification and Scoring of Weather Forecasts," *Journal of the American Statistical Association*, XLVI (September, 1951), 279-96.

32. THE ADVERTISING BUDGET *

Frank D. Robinson

Because of our ability to determine a definite mathematical relationship between costs and activity at various operating levels, our budgeting for the manufacturing or production function of the business is reasonably accurate and is a powerful management tool. With a properly set fixed and variable budget it is possible to provide for profit control by (1) setting forth where and how variable costs should fluctuate with volume and (2) by establishing limits on so-called "fixed" costs.

Basically, we are free to operate the manufacturing function in line with the profit plan (or budget) because we more or less know precisely the effect on profits that any of our possible courses of action will have.

The marketing cost elements of rent, telephone, commissions and sales salaries are likewise relatively easy to budget, for they, too, fall into the familiar fixed and variable elements. With these elements of marketing costs we again feel free to set forth a profit plan, knowing with reasonable accuracy the effect on profits that any of our possible courses of action will have.

The advertising element of marketing costs is completely different, because we cannot accurately measure the effects of our possible courses of action and, equally important, the benefits of any course of action we take with respect to the advertising program may be greatly influenced by the advertising activities of our competitors. In other words, a course of action we elect to take with respect to advertising may be a good one if competition takes one course of action, and a poor course if the competitor takes another.

Therefore, there is a very important distinction between budgeting for manufacturing and marketing costs other than advertising on the one hand, and advertising costs on the other. The first group of costs are under our own power to optimize for profit.

* Reprinted by permission from *The Controller*, Vol. XXVI, No. 8 (August, 1958), pp. 368-389.

Frank D. Robinson, Vice President and Treasurer of Diebold, Inc., Canton, Ohio.

The advertising cost levels established may or may not be at optimum profit levels depending upon forces beyond our control—that is, the advertising efforts of our competitors coupled with changes in the direction of the business cycle that have taken place in the time between the authorization of the expenditure and its actual occurrence.

A properly set advertising budget, therefore, is one in which the "diluting" effects of competitors' advertising are evaluated and a course of action—i.e., strategy—is selected so that at least fair results will be achieved even if competition chooses the worst possible course of action against our cause, and where excellent results will be obtained if competition chooses the course of action least damaging to our cause. In addition, the budget should be "set" for the direction that it is anticipated the business cycle will take.

Mathematical techniques have been developed to solve problems involving the determination of the best of several alternate courses of action, the benefits of which courses will vary depending upon the action taken by competitors. These mathematical techniques are known as "game theory."

Before setting up a mathematical model of the problem, however, we must establish the advertising principles that we have considered valid in setting forth the ranking of the benefits and losses used in the mathematical model.

1. The basic justification for advertising is that with such expenditures, sales can be increased at an advertising cost that yields an additional contribution to operating profit that is beyond the profit that would have been achieved without the advertising. At some point the cost of advertising will increase to the level that the increased sales cease to be worth the additional advertising costs. Increased sales due to advertising can be either increased unit sales at constant prices or increased unit selling prices above those that could be obtained without an "advertised product."

For example, a retailer who buys a unit for $60, resells it for $100, and pays a 10% ($10 unit) commission cannot afford to spend more than $30 for advertising for each *additional* unit sold. A $3,000 advertising campaign, therefore, would require the sale of 100 additional units just to break even.

2. Different products vary greatly in the way that their sales can be increased by the use of advertising. Caskets are an example of a product the over-all sales of which are "inert" to promotion.

3. However, even if additional over-all demand for the products cannot be created, it is possible to increase one's own share of the

fixed market. This means that the advertising of such inert products should be slanted at improving "market share"—we should not attempt to sell the product as a product, but should sell the benefits of our particular version of the product or the value of dealing with our particular firm.

4. Different products vary greatly in the length of time that the purchasers of such products react to past advertising. For example, a seller of college class rings has a different lot of customers each year. A seller of bank vaults has purchasers that tend to remain in their jobs for considerable periods of time. Therefore, the risks involved in curtailing advertising are much less with some products than they are with others. In addition, a decision to reduce advertising efforts is much safer on the part of a firm which has built up a high degree of advertising retention than one which has not.

5. While no conclusive studies have been made, it appears that during past downswings in the business cycle, firms which increased advertising maintained rates of volume higher than those of competitors who did not increase advertising, but that such advertising did not increase the profits of those who increased advertising over those who did not.

On upswings in the business cycle, firms who increased advertising increased both their volumes and profits over those who did not. We believe that it is vital to increase advertising on the upswing of the business cycle, attempt to find an optimum level of advertising during the boom, and drop off sharply on the downward side of the business cycle. We would define "sharply" as at a rate greater than the forecasted rate of drop in sales volume.

TABLE 1

	200 units sold @ $100.00 each		$20,000	100.0%
Less:	purchase costs 200 @ $60.00 each	$12,000		
	Commissions @ $10.00 each	2,000		
	Advertising	2,400	16,400	82.0%
			$ 3,600	18.0%

TABLE 1-a

	100 increased units sold @ $100.00 each		$10,000	100.0%
Less:	100 units cost @ $60.00 each	$ 6,000		
	100 units commission @ $10.00 each	1,000		
	Advertising	1,200	8,200	82.0%
			$ 1,800	18.0%

TABLE 1-b

	100 units sales @ $100.00 each		$10,000	100.0%
Less:	100 units cost @ $60.00 each	$ 6,000		
	100 units commission @ $10.00 each	1,000		
	Advertising	1,000	8,000	80.0%
			$2,000	20.0%

6. The effect of competitors' advertising is to dilute one's own advertising efforts. Therefore, the benefits from any program we undertake will vary in accordance with the intensity of competitors' advertising. One element of justification for the advertising budget should be a factual exhibit of competitive advertising practices and cost levels over past periods.

7. In our opinion, the advertising budget should not be set on an annual basis in companies where volume will probably vary with the business cycle; quarterly budgets would seem most reasonable.

Using the above listed principles, the following steps should be taken to set the advertising budget of a product line whose sales tend to fluctuate in the same general path as the over-all business cycle:

1. Develop, assuming operations at the top of the business cycle, the advertising cost level that will produce additional sales dollars sufficient to yield the firm's required rate of marginal contribution to income on the increased sales dollars forecast. Obviously, this can only be a guess. However, the requirement to determine "plus" volume, "plus" operating profit after the increased advertising expense, and to set an objective is, in our opinion, most beneficial to the company despite the inaccuracies that are present.

For example, we previously discussed the retailer who resold a unit with a $60 cost for $100 and paid a 10% or $10 commission. If he assumed he could move 200 "plus" units as a result of an advertising campaign, and had an objective of an 18% marginal contribution to income, then he could spend only $2,400 for advertising *(Table I)*.

A summation of the budgets for each of the individual product lines would be the over-all company advertising budget in good times expected to continue long enough to recoup the advertising outlay.

A corollary benefit of this approach is that it tends to get dollars spent promoting items with high marginal income contribution rates and/or those items whose sales are expected to be most greatly increased by advertising.

2. Determine the probable immediate direction of the business cycle—horizontal, up or down.

3. Estimate the probable level of competitors' advertising activity:

a. If he will decrease advertising, we are safe to spend at a lesser rate.

b. If he will increase his activity, we may require more funds to attain any given objective.

c. Either earmark some of the budget for a programmed direct counterattack or, in any event, hold some of the budget uncommitted for possible counterattack. Experience is the only guide as to how much of the budget to reserve for this safety factor.

4. Having established the optimum level of the advertising budget assuming favorable business conditions, held back a reasonable portion for counterattack, and adjusted the total for probable increased or decreased competitive activity, the next step is to decide whether to increase, decrease, or hold the budget constant in view of the direction of the business cycle. Our decision to increase, decrease, or hold constant must also recognize that our competitor has the same three alternatives as ourselves. As we said earlier, the aim is to select a course of action so that at least fair results will be obtained if the competition selects the course of action least favorable to us, and which will give us excellent results if the competition selects a course most favorable to us.

5. In calculating our best course of action, we obviously cannot set actual dollar and cents values or other quantitative values in measuring the benefits of one course of action versus those of another. This does not mean that game theory cannot be applied to the solution of the problem if we will accept a ranking of the order of benefits. Using this ranking—the process is called "ordering"—we rank benefits in the order of from "excellent" to "very poor." In other words, while we cannot make quantitative estimates of the net results of each of our alternative courses of action as they will be affected by competitors' activities, we are usually able to set qualitative values in the same way as we know boiling water is warmer than water at room temperature, which is, in turn warmer than ice water.

6. Example of model *assuming decline* in business cycle, assuming:

a. Our objective is to maximize profits rather than sales.

b. Our product volume has fluctuated in the past with the general business cycle.

c. In business cycle downswings, advertising costs do not produce enough additional sales to justify the additional advertising costs. That is, the company which increases advertising does not increase its profits over one which does not increase its advertising costs, even though it may increase sales volume.

d. Our customers are a stable lot in terms of the time period over which they remain in the market—i.e., risks in cutting back advertising are justified.

e. Our products are not unduly sensitive to advertising promotion.

We set forth the general advertising level possibilities open to us and to our competition. In this case, we simplify the problem by considering competition as one player against us, because we assume the competition is not in a coalition against us. A coalition of competitors directed against us would require different calculations. Our rank of the alternatives is shown in *Table II* (remember, this ranking is for downswings in the business cycle, only).

For calculation of our optimum course, or combination of courses, we set forth the preceding in a matrix, as shown in Table II-a. Because the lowest of the column maxima and the highest of the row minima are the same (f) we should never vary our strategy; we should always follow strategy #1, cut expense in a declining business cycle. The worst result we can obtain will be fair, and could be excellent if the competition cuts along with us. A coalition in which *all* industry members took part to reduce advertising would seem to be an excellent economic, although probably illegal, maneuver.

The foregoing example is a simple one because, while we ranked the alternatives in line with our best judgment, the result came out "f" in both the lowest of the column maxima and the highest of the row minima.

If we had ranked any of the nine possible alternatives differently, a matrix may have resulted in which the highest of the row minima was different from the lowest of the column maxima. In such case, a combination of our three basic courses of action should be taken according to proportions that can be developed by relatively simple solutions of matrixes using game theory in which arbitrary values are assigned to the various letters, for example:

Excellent	=	+10
Good	=	+ 5
Fair	=	0
Poor	=	− 5
Very Poor	=	−10

Substituting these arbitrary values for the letters would enable a person familiar with the solution of game theory matrixes to tell you the proportion in which each of the three strategies should be used.[1]

The reason we would have to vary strategies in some optimum proportion is because, where there is no "balancing" of "maxmin" and "minmax" indicating one best strategy that should always be followed, the competition will probably become aware of our unvarying reactions under given circumstances and take the course of action that will help them most at our expense.

7. An example of model assuming upswing in business cycle and its matrix of alternatives are shown in *Tables III* and *III-a.* Once again, under our ranking of alternatives, we have a situation where we have "f" as the maximum of the row minima and "f" as the minimum of the column maxima. Here too, we should follow only one course, alternate #3, as a result of which we will always come out with at least a fair result, and can possibly achieve an excellent one.

Other individuals might very well rank some of the nine alternatives differently, with the result that the maxmin and the minmax may not be the same. In such a case, as we mentioned before, arbitrary values can be assigned to the letters and optimum combinations of the three basic courses open to ourselves can be determined.

In the preceding examples, the ordering of benefits was based upon one company's assumptions; each company must set its own order of benefits according to its own good judgment. The important thing is that an ordering of benefits be arrived at.

Let's look back at the retailer who decided that, in good times, he could increase his sales of the $100 unit by 200 units *(Table I)*. We had calculated an advertising budget of $2,400 so as to enable him to buy the unit at $60.00, pay 10% commission on sales, and yield an 18% contribution to income. This retailer, would, in our opinion, be foolish to go blindly ahead with the $2,400 program if general business were falling or if he knew that a competitor would advertise the same product at the same time. Frequently, such advertising is pro-

[1] A primer on this method, requiring only a knowledge of arithmetic is "The Compleat Strategyst" by J. D. Williams, a Rand Corporation Research Study published in 1954 by McGraw-Hill Book Company, New York.

moted or partly subsidized by the product manufacturer and there is great risk that competitors will avail themselves of the same promotion aid.

Assuming general business going along fine, the retailer who believed his competition would also promote the item to the extent of diluting the increased sales expected by 50% would have to cut the advertising costs 50% if he wanted to retain his required 18% rate of marginal contribution to income *(Table I-a)*.

The retailer faces a more difficult problem in downswings in the business cycle. If past experience has shown that demand is harder to increase under such conditions, he has to decide whether to spend more money than he would in good times to go after the full 200 plus units or cut back his advertising expenditures, using maximum quality media to hold his advertising to a level that will maintain his 18% gross profit objective. If the retailer decided that 100 units was a realistic level of plus volume, then he could, again, spend only $1,200 on advertising to maintain his 18% marginal contribution to income objective. The problem is further complicated because, while he will aim at the 18% rate of marginal contribution to income, he may actually need a rate greater than 18% in business downswings because his marginal contribution to income in absolute dollars (at the 18% rate) will probably be declining faster than his ability to lower his so-called "fixed" expenses. If the retailer decided he would need a 20% rate, then the advertising expenditure in the preceding example would have to be reduced to $1,000 to yield $2,000 marginal contribution to income on $10,000 of sales *(Table I-b)*.

We set forth the preceding examples of the retailer's problem to show in simple terms that advertising programs must take into consideration the two elements that seem to be frequently overlooked —the effect of competitors' advertising and the fact that the degree of advertising effectiveness fluctuates in some relationship to the general business cycle.

In our opinion, while sales promotional efforts must be increased during downswings in the business cycle, as advocated by most of the management counsellors, care must be used to differentiate advertising from sales promotion.

And, above all, in periods of declining sales do not confuse increased sales with increased profit; those last few dollars of increased sales have to be paid for and may very well not be worth their cost.

TABLE II

DOWNSWINGS

1. We cut, competition cuts	Excellent—Because we know we will cut expenses and have reasonable assurance that our market share will remain the same.
2. We cut, competition holds even	Good—We take steps to cut our outlays, and the competition should not pick up too many sales that would otherwise have gone to us.
3. We cut, competition increases	Fair—While we have cut expenses, there is a chance that the competition might put together our decrease and his increase to net enough volume to hurt us slightly.
4. We maintain, competition cuts	Fair—We have at least a chance to maintain our profit level.
5. We maintain, competition maintains	Poor—We both maintain our advertising costs while sales will decline. Profit level will probably decline.
6. We maintain, competition increases	Fair
7. We increase, competition cuts	Fair—We will get a real chance of picking up volume and may pick up a profit.
8. We increase, competition maintains	Poor
9. We increase, competition increases	Very Poor—We both increase our advertising costs with little or no chance to increase volume. Can anyone win?

TABLE II-a

		OUR COMPETITION			
		1 (cut exp.)	2 (maint. exp.)	3 (inc. exp.)	Row Min
	1 (cut exp.)	e	g	f	f*
OUR	2 (main. exp.)	f	p	f	p
COMPANY	3 (inc. exp.)	f	p	vp	vp
	Column max	e	g	f*	

TABLE III

UPSWING

1. We cut, competition cuts	Good—Basically, the product was assumed to be relatively inert to advertising. Other products would rate a different grade. Profits should increase.
2. We cut, competition holds even	Fair—The competition will get the jump on us but we will probably at least maintain our past profitability.
3. We cut, competition increases	Very Poor—We stand to lose a golden opportunity and add value to our competitors' advertising program.
4. We maintain, competition cuts	Fair—We have probably lost a chance to pick up profitable volume, but we should not lose ground, profitwise.
5. We maintain, competition maintains	Fair—We should hold our present position, both industrywise and profitwise.
6. We maintain, competition increases	Poor—We may lose an opportunity due to inertia on our part.
7. We increase, competition cuts	Excellent—We will probably increase profits and volume faster than the competition.
8. We increase, competition maintains	Good—We will gain ground but at a lesser rate than 7 above.
9. We increase, competition increases	Fair—We will hold our own only, but the increased volume should at least break us even profitwise.

TABLE III-a

		OUR COMPETITION			
		1 (cut exp.)	2 (maint. exp.)	3 (inc. exp.)	Row Min
	1 (cut exp.)	g	f	vp	vp
OUR	2 (main. exp.)	f	f	p	p
COMPANY	3 (inc. exp.)	e	g	f	f*
	Column max	e	g	f*	

33. GENERAL SEMANTICS: TUNING AD MEN *

Harry E. Maynard

What can a study of general semantics teach the advertising man? In my opinion, general semantics hold the key to what are undisputably the two most important processes involved in our modern advertising era: creatively and successful communication.

There are many current definitions of creativity. Among them, my favorite is that of Jules Porsche, manager, central research department of the Armour Co. He writes:

"Creativity is the faculty possessed by human beings for integrating facts, impressions, or feelings resulting from experience into a new form. It is the ability to establish new connections between facts and symbols. It is the capacity for gaining new insights into the relations between bits of existing knowledge."

1. New relationships

General semantics specifically proposes to study how human beings establish these "new connections between facts and symbols" and how the creative person symbolically manipulates these new connections. Or, stated another way, general semantics is the study of how we perceive or "size up" the world and then symbolically relate to it; that is, talk about it, write about it, or mathematize about it.

By now the perceptive reader will have realized that general semantics is not classical semantics. Classical semantics is an important branch of philology and deals with the historical evolution of word usage. I call it "verbal etiquette."

General semantics, on the other hand, is concerned with the total reaction of the individual to the world—only part of which touches him through what is commonly called language.

To see the world afresh and to perceive these new relationships we must rid ourselves of what John Kenneth Galbraith calls the "vested

* Reprinted by permission of *Printers' Ink* Vol. 272, No. 10 (September 2, 1960), p. 38.

Harry E. Maynard, Associate Advertising Director of LIFE International.

interests of the mind." This is not essentially a physical problem. It is usually a psychological and intellectual problem.

It is not only a verbal or symbolic problem, it is problem of premises. That is why I call the title of my projected book, "The Tyranny of Assumptions." The problem of the legitimate assumption is of more primary importance than the problem of the words we use to symbolize our world ("The Tyranny of Words"). Our words are merely an outgrowth of our assumptions. Or worse, our assumptions can become the outgrowth of our words, losing all contact with reality. It is in our conscious and unconscious premises that the whole line of our reasoning process begins. Here we succeed or fail. That is why I would like to cite four of the basic assumptions of general semantics.

1—We are living in an ever-changing-process world. Many of our so-called facts may be rapidly aging. To quote philosopher Alfred North Whitehead, "Today's heresy is tomorrow's orthodoxy." Thus the advertising man must be perpetually posing these questions: What situations are changing? What are the important trend lines? The advertising man should be perpetually inventorying rates and degrees of change. The perpetual questions he should be asking in the world he deals with are: How much is it changing? How fast? How important a change is it?

2—Another assumption of general semantics is called the principle of nonidentity. Stated simply, it means that so far as we have been able to discover, there are no two things exactly alike in the world. An expert is one who has investigated a lot of facts and things, has seen the important similarities, but who has also spotted the significant differences.

3—Your symbolic map must fit the territory. The question to ask here is whether your symbolic maps, including verbal ones, adequately represent the territory. If they do, you can rely on them. You can predict from them. Your plans will work. If your symbolic maps do not represent the territory, trouble is apt to lie ahead.

4—Finally, meaning is never in a thing, or in a word or symbol, or in the speaker, listener, writer or reader, *but solely in the relationship between the word or symbol and the human nervous system reacting to it.* I could swear at you in Chinese, for example, and you would not respond because the words have no meaning for you. There's just no relationship between the sounds and your antenna for perception.

Another example: The redness of an apple is not in the apple itself, nor, strictly speaking, in the eyes of the observer. The redness is really the relationship between the color wave-length emanating from the apple and the human nervous system which interprets it. Incidentally, no two people get precisely the same reading of the redness of the same apple—that is, they don't get precisely the same meaning.

For communicators this is a very important point. It should make you ask of everything you write, "How could this conceivably be misunderstood?" When you realize that the answer is "thousands of ways," you've come a long way on the road to becoming a good communicator.

The truth is, as general semantics warns, that no one is ever completely tuned in on anyone else. No one ever gives anyone else 100 per cent attention, and no one ever completely understands precisely what is on your mind. Through all our senses—and there is now evidence we have a total of more than 50—we receive a signal from someone else, whether it be orally, visually, or however. That signal starts traveling along our nerves to our brain—and is immediately distorted by all sorts of blocs, short-circuits, weak currents, stored experience, memory, prejudices, fears, desires and previous conditions of servitude. The signal beamed at us, through whatever sense, may have been a simple one delivered calmly and clearly—or so the other fellow thought. But we only half get it, for before it reaches our brain we have already reacted to it, grabbed some specific from it, made an uncritical inference, and turned it into an inadequate premise from which we proceed to draw conclusions.

II. Structuring ideas

General semantics teaches us that if we want to inform or influence other minds we must first put our own mind in order. If there's a clutter in our minds, that clutter is bound to show up in our communication. Especially in mass communication (which is advertising) we must structure everything clearly in our own minds before we even begin to attempt to transmit it to others. We must make all the elements of our message fit together, work together toward a single impression. We will fail as communicators unless we have put our message in a sharper, clearer focus and are able to show someone else how it's done.

Suppose you are preparing an advertisement whose purpose is to give the impression that your firm has strength, dignity, and reliability. To give that impression, you make all the elements of your ad conform to the governing idea. Copy, illustration, type face, layout, choice of colors—you will engineer everything to contribute its part to the whole. When you've done your ad this way it will say what you mean and only what you mean.

And when you've done the ad this way you'll have the answer to the fellow somewhere along the line who wants to include a bathing beauty, or wants to blow up the headline three times, or mortise in a list of distributors. You can explain to him why you did what you did and why his idea, excellent though it may be, is a *different* idea, not the one you're working on at the moment.

Now extend this idea to all your work. Before you produce a single brochure, newsletter, direct-mail piece, trade ad, speech for the vice-president, news release, new-product campaign or a series of full-color ads in your favorite magazine, you as sculptor should carefully structure the kind of personality and reputation you are trying to project for your company first of all, and then the kind of related personality each of your products should have.

This, of course, is not easy. Think for a moment of the many definitions of a single product that exist in a single corporation. As I read recently in a new book called "The Management of Time," the president sees the product as something respected by reputable banking establishments and by business colleagues. The sales vice-president sees it as something that will fulfill the wants of buyers, look good at conventions, and lend itself to merchandising at the point of sale. The controller sees the product as one of the chief variables in the great game of figures he plays, and is interested in keeping the product stable so his figures will come out right. The manufacturing head sees the product as the embodiment of a long and careful process. To the purchasing agent it is the final form of raw materials. To the man at the machine, the product is something he does something to after the fellow before him has done his bit and before the fellow after him does his. To the maintenance man, the product is something that wears out his bearings and tires his machines.

III. Empathy: the passkey

These many definitions illustrate another cardinal principle of general semantics—namely, that each of us sees the world from his own private, individual vantage point which is never precisely the same as the vantage point of anyone else. They also illustrate what I call "corporate multiphrenia"—the successor to that old-fashioned disease called schizophrenia which resulted from a split personality.

Now each one of these many images of a product is legitimate, but only one of them takes into consideration the customer who buys your product in preference to another. There still must be an image of the product which you project to your prospects and which, if understood and accepted, will motivate them to try it. This is primarily your job of sculpturing—to stand back from all the narrow definitions within your shop and to look at the product from the viewpoint of the customer—speaking in psychiatric terms, to empathize. What is there about your product, you must ask, that could conceivably make a person want to buy it? What basic or transitory human need does it fulfill? Will it make him rich or save him money, increase his stature or his potency, mark him as a man of distinction, improve or preserve his health, make him beloved or admired—what? What *idea* is there in our product that makes it preferable to another product that does the same thing but emanates a different idea? What idea can you build into your presentation of the product that will make it attractive to people?

IV. Know his premises

The great communicator is the man who has thought or researched his way into the mind of his customer—who knows what makes the customer tick. In general semantics terms, the good communicator makes sure, before he transmits, that he has tuned in on the other man's wave length, that he knows what the other fellow's premises are.

What are premises? To repeat what we said before, they're the basic assumptions from which a person starts an argument or a line of reasoning and from which a course of action will result.

Premises are of two kinds—conscious and unconscious, and the unconscious ones are, as you know, the hardest to discover. If a man doesn't even know what his own unconscious premises are, it takes a trained observer to get at them.

But get at them we must—through observations, through depth interviews, through all the techniques of modern market research. We've got to know our prospect so well that we can think as he thinks, go along with him for a while to win his friendship, find some common ground on which his premises meet ours, and then—and this is the supreme art—we must slip him our premises and get him to accept them as his own if we want him to take the action we want, which is to buy our products or think well of our company.

One finding that interests me particularly as a general semanticist is the fact that ordinary people like me tend to think in words whereas geniuses tend to think in pictures. This fact hasn't been scientifically explained yet, but I believe it's because pictures show structure better and define relationships more sharply—and as the philosopher Northrup puts it, "the ultimate reality is relationships." Korzybski, the father of General Semantics, put it this way: "The only possible link between the objective world and the linguistic or symbol world is found in structure and structure alone."

Next time you have a brilliant idea, try to trace back how it came to you. One word that will occur is "flash." All of a sudden a lot of items swimming around in your brain took up a certain relationship and—flash—the idea was there. Actually, the idea is a new relationship—putting the same old parts together in a new way.

V. A science of behavior

As communicators, your part is deliberately to play the part of a potential customer whenever you have something to tell him. There are always plenty of people around the office who can see the company's side, but all too often there's no one around to represent the customer. That person should be you. You are the one to keep your company from missing contact with customers.

If you put this science to work for you, you will be in the best of company. The largest advertising agency in the U. S. today is McCann-Erickson, and McCann got where it is under the leadership of Marion Harper. Now listen to this from *Printers' Ink*: "Marion Harper has probably made better use of the science of general semantics in advertising than any other man in the profession. Harper discovered general semantics in the early '40s, and saw in it what might possibly become the best science for understanding why people behave as they do . . . the best science for communicating facts and ideas to move people to act. Harper wants his executives to study general semantics."

To sum up: I basically regard general semantics as attitudinal therapy. It gives one a method of improving one's thinking and communicating ability. To do this we have constantly to toss aside these attitudes and premises which are strangling our creative and communication processes. General semantics is a perpetual inventorying system to help us achieve this task.

34. LIMITS OF PERSUASION *

Raymond A. Bauer

Man seems to live in perpetual hope and horror that infallible means have been developed whereby one man can control another's behavior. As usual, the hope and the horror are opposite sides of the same coin:

> On the hopeful side, some selfishly see the possibility of advantage for themselves in gaining control over their fellow men. Others, more idealistically, look to a "science of man" as the basis for establishing a Utopia which will be optimally efficient in the production of both material goods and human happiness.
>
> On the side of horror, some fear that they themselves will be "manipulated" to the advantage of someone else. Others fear the motives for their own relations to their fellow men. The image of a potential Utopia gets turned inside out, and we see that the reverse image is that of *1984*—the totalitarian state of George Orwell's novel—in which the best qualities of man are lost.

Recent developments in the science of psychology, and the publicity given to some of its more sensational applications—such as "subliminal advertising" or "brainwashing"—have strengthened our anxiety. The significance of these developments is of particular concern to businessmen, for they, along with politicians, will be responsible for the use of the new techniques. But there is no reason for panic. Anxiety stems, in part, from ignorance of the causal relations between the "persuaders" and the "persuaded." To show this relationship, and the limitations it imposes on the techniques, we must consider three broad areas of application:

- Propaganda and human relations.
- Appeals to "noneconomic" motives.
- Appeals to "unconscious" motives.

With a better understanding of the functioning of these techniques, we will be in a stronger position to evaluate them realistically.

* Reprinted by permission from *Harvard Business Review*, Vol. 36, No. 5 (September-October, 1958), pp. 105-110.

Raymond A. Bauer, Ford Foundation Visiting Professor at the Harvard Business School.

New Fear or Old Scare?

The specter of "manipulation" and "hidden persuasion" has stalked all the lands that man has ever inhabited. The most primitive manifestation of the deep anxiety which we feel on this issue is represented by Nightmare Alice, the witch of Li'l Abner Land. From time to time, Nightmare Alice makes an effigy of one of the "good people" of Dogpatch and places this person under her hidden control. Black magic is found among most nonliterate peoples, and the fear of it persists. In the Middle Ages, people were "possessed by the devil"; in our own colonial times we went back to "witches."

In recent decades, to be sure, we have done away with such superstitions and become more "scientific." Or have we simply dressed up our old fears in modern fashions? Remember how during the 1920's and 1930's we worried about the mysterious powers of the mass media, particularly as manipulated by such practitioners as George Creel and Ivy L. Lee? My point is that although this century has led to tremendous progress in our knowledge of the human mind, our fear that this knowledge will be misused is as old as the history of man.

But what are the facts? Does modern psychology give us the tools to control each other? The full range of considerations is, of course, beyond our purview here. Moreover, any discussion of psychological techniques of persuasion and manipulation must, of course, be done without knowing what new knowledge may be developed. It is my belief, however, that what I have to say must hold in principle for almost any conceivable situation that may develop.

Ratio of Resistance

Let me begin my positive assertions with what may seem like a paradoxical statement. Without doubt we have, largely on the basis of improved social science knowledge in the fields of psychology, sociology, and anthropology, developed increasingly refined and effective means of persuasion. It does not follow, however, that even in the field of advertising we are able to effect more persuasion. How can this be? Simply because the increased knowledge benefits not only the persuader but also the target of persuasion. As the persuaders become more sophisticated, so do the people to be persuaded.

One way of reading the history of the development of techniques of persuasion is that the persuaders have been in a race to keep abreast of the developing resistance of the people to be persuaded. Thus:

In the decades following World War I, we were very excited about the power of propaganda. We came close to saying that if it were possible to get a story in the newspapers or on the radio, people would automatically believe it and act on it. But what happened? Many people became so suspicious of propaganda that they would scarcely believe the news on the sports page.

As a result, World War II propaganda in the Western countries was markedly different from that of World War I. Propagandists—that is, "persuaders"—were scrupulously careful not to test the credulity of their readers and listeners; they also avoided more blatant emotional appeals.

Why? People had become more sophisticated, and more resistant to "persuasion." Social science research on the effects of communications, by the beginning of World War II, had pretty well destroyed the myth of propaganda's omnipotence.

We see today similar developments in advertising. There is still some advertising that is reminiscent of the old-fashioned pitchman selling snake oil. However, the development of the "soft sell" seems to me a tacit acknowledgment of the developing resistance of the potential consumer.

Manipulation more difficult

Within business and industry we have witnessed the evolving concern with human relations and communication. These events also have been viewed with horror as evidence of the growth of manipulation. But the viewers-with-horror naively assume that the knowledge on which this presumed manipulation is based is limited to the manipulators. Without in any way deprecating the desirability of the human relations approach—I not only favor it but even try to practice it—I doubt if it has produced any increase in manipulation.

As a matter of fact, all this new concern must have made the process of interpersonal communications more complicated. It is traditional that, as people become more diplomatic, their communications become more subtle. Perhaps we are all reaching the point of the diplomat who, on being informed of the death of his opposite number, queried: "I wonder what he meant by that." So in the absence of any long-run trend statistics on the number of effective persuasive and manipulative acts in business and industry, I shall remain content with pointing to the obvious mechanisms of resistance to persuasion; noting that manipulation has become more difficult; and suggesting there is no more reason to believe that the actual practice of manipulation has increased than that it has lessened. The data to prove me wrong are unobtainable.

Hidden Persuaders?

Our main fear, however, is not that we will be taken in by the persuasive logic of a Madison Avenue salesman but that, through appeals to deep, unconscious motives, we can be manipulated without even knowing it.

A book such as Vance Packard's *Hidden Persuaders* [1] generates a good deal of soul searching, both among the general public and within professional circles. This book, for the benefit of the fortunate few who are not familiar with it, tells *a* story, though certainly not *the* story, of how psychology has been applied in market research. By determining people's unconscious motives "via the principles of modern dynamic psychology," researchers are able to devise methods whereby mysterious and miraculous marketing results are produced. The consumer is powerless to resist these techniques, and he just buys and buys without knowing why. From this it is, of course, only one step to applying these techniques in politics, and *1984* will arrive at least twenty years ahead of schedule. Packard's picture, needless to say, is a trifle stylized.

Packard wrote his book to warn the public. The net impact of the volume is that there has been a complete revolution in market research in the form of motivation research, the term for the intensive exploration of the psychological factors involved in consumer behavior and product usage. But it is only the *intensity of concern* that is new. So far as I can see, the major practical result has been—as one might expect—an increased and unrealistic demand for motivation research. Packard succeeded in painting the picture of psychological demonology so persuasively that motivation researchers are now concerned with giving their clients a more realistic notion of what they can do.

But Packard also succeeded in creating again the primitive anxiety that we are on the verge of being able to establish complete control over human behavior to the extent that the victims of this control will not have a chance to resist it because they do not realize it is there.

Noneconomic motives

In the first place, people *do* have some chance to resist the motives associated with the new techniques. People buy many things for *noneconomic* reasons, but such motives are not necessarily *unconscious*.

[1] New York, David McKay Company, Inc., 1957.

It is a serious mistake to equate the two; and the use of the term *irrational* makes the confusion even worse. Once you label noneconomic motives irrational, you imply that they are unreasonable, and you are well on the way to assuming they are unconscious.

When I say that people do things for noneconomic reasons (what others might call "irrational"), I am talking about the fact that people may buy a particular automobile because they desire status, the esteem of themselves and others; because they like products which fit their own self-image; or even because a man likes the feeling of potency which comes from driving an overhorsepowered vehicle. But I can see no reason to say a man is more "rational" to want transportation than to want self-respect and the esteem of others—though if it helps you to understand why he is doing what he is doing, you can say he is being less economic.

It is true that most of the motives I have just mentioned are not usually cited in response to the direct question: "Why did you buy that product?" In our culture, the accepted reasons for buying a product bear on its primary economic function: for instance, the cost of transportation provided by the car, the cleaning effectiveness of a soap, and so on. Accordingly, we are not as likely to think of the noneconomic motives as reasons for buying, bearing as they do on the secondary functions (or "added value") of products. Or, if we do, perhaps we feel a little ashamed and so are reticent about them. But in no meaningful sense are these motives unconscious. With a little stimulation almost every one of us recognizes their existence.

Practical consequences

This is no mere quibble. The fact that people can and do acknowledge the existence of these motives has considerable practical consequence. The use of appeals directed to such motives—as well as the widespread discussion, which we have already witnessed, of the concern given such motives in product design and merchandising—is bringing them into the center of consciousness as buying motives even if they were not there before. Some people will come to accept these as proper buying motives, and will probably learn to shop as astutely for the product that gives them the most prestige as for the product that has the lowest price, best mechanical qualities, and so on. Other people will resist these appeals, not accepting the secondary functions as a legitimate reason for buying.

Appeal to such motives may still serve, as in the past, to win the merchandiser a temporary advantage. However, as such appeals become customary and the public becomes generally aware of them, they will leave the merchandiser just about where he was to start with as far as his "persausive advantage" is concerned.

Just because marketing and product design are based increasingly on psychologically oriented market research, it does not follow that products will continue to be sold increasingly on the basis of their secondary functions or "added value." At this time merchandisers are becoming more and more alert to the power of the secondary characteristics of products to satisfy consumer wants. As a psychologist I can have no conceivable objection in principle to people's non-economic wants being satisfied. But we must look seriously at the possibility that this trend may reach the point of saturation.

Even now, the "irrationality"—a word I detest—of the consumer may be grossly overestimated. In few, if any, of the discussions of consumer motivation is there any mention of the growth of such consumer information services as Consumer's Research and Consumer's Union. The notion that people are not concerned with and do not understand the technical aspects of the products they buy may have to be tempered in the future. Today's consumers are almost certainly more interested and better informed on the technical features of products than they have been in the past.

There is something ironical in depicting the housewife shopping in the supermart as being indifferent to economy, being cozened by hidden persuaders into spending 15% more for her market basket than some stringent criterion says is necessary. Remember, the corner grocery store offers the housewife psychological rewards that the supermart does not. Yet in the interests of economy housewives have deserted the corner grocery store for the more impersonal, but more economical, supermart. This very same group of housewives has patronized discount houses, which scarcely give them the same psychological satisfactions as do department and high-class specialty stores.

One of the established arguments for stressing the secondary functions of a product is that all products in a given line are virtually identical with respect to their primary economic function. But suppose all automobiles in a given price range become virtually identical with regard to their symbolic value: this might drive the manufacturers to strive again for differentiation on the basis of the primary function of transportation. This notion is far from facetious. While Chrysler may indeed have gotten into difficulty a few years ago by de-emphasizing styling, today it is the small economical car—

American Rambler or a foreign make—that is making inroads into the market, not the cars with "sex appeal."

This is not to brush aside the importance of the motives that the motivation researchers have stressed. I am merely suggesting that we keep our image of the consumer in somewhat clearer perspective. The merchandiser who concentrates too much on the secondary characteristics of products will find himself in as much difficulty as the one who ignores them completely. Motivation research may indeed become indispensable *because* of the very trends in the population I have been describing. The merchandiser will probably need increasingly detailed psychological knowledge of consumers as the years go on, if only to know what difficulties he is up against and how far he must stay away from noneconomic appeals.

Unconscious Motives

This is not the whole picture. All that I have said to this point is that many of the motives with which motivation research deals are *not* unconscious *in any meaningful sense*; and that, as these particular motives are appealed to, the consumer recognizes them more explicitly as motives linked to consumer behavior, and develops the capacity for a critical appraisal of appeals to such motives.

But there *are* some truly unconscious motives—that is, motives which the individual would not acknowledge consciously *to himself* even if, or especially if, they are called explicitly to his attention. To illustrate:

> One of the most spectacular of the claims for the exploitation of unconscious motives is the development of the hardtop convertible. The hardtop is labeled as a compromise between the male buyer's dual attachment to the stable, reliable wife, symbolized by the sedan, and the flashy unreliable mistress, symbolized by the convertible.
>
> Certainly, in psychoanalytic thinking, it is accepted that the male child has conflict over thinking of his mother as a sexual object, and develops a split image of women. But I cannot conceivably take a stand on whether or not this is the complete story of the hardtop, or what substantial portion of the story it may comprise. I use it only as an example of appealing to a motive that is meaningfully referred to as unconscious.

There is something very plausible in the notion that if we understand another person's unconscious motivation, then we can appeal to his motives and get him to do something without his knowing why he did it. Certainly, he ought to be powerless to resist. To some extent this is true. But the entire picture is more complicated. Remember that there is a reason for certain motives remaining unconscious; in general, conscious acknowledgment of these motives would produce intolerable anxiety. Hence, appeal to such motives may backfire, and backfire violently. Thus, on an *a priori* basis, combining the "mistress and the wife" in the form of the hardtop convertible *could* have aroused anxiety and caused people to stay away from this model in droves.

My concern is not hypothetical. Research projects give us evidence that this happens, as in the following cases:

One of the most deep-seated motives that is postulated in Freudian psychology is fear of castration. Furthermore, our anxiety over dental work is asserted to be due to a displacement of this castration anxiety. Again, I ask you to take this interpretation on its face value. It is only if you take it seriously that there is any issue at all. Presumably any message directed at relieving this anxiety ought to be met with prompt and vigorous positive response. Thus, instructions on oral hygiene ought to be listened to attentively, remembered, and acted on. However, experiments at Yale show that highly emotional messages on oral hygiene are less effective than detached, less emotional ones in conveying information on proper methods of preserving teeth.[2] Furthermore, the persons who heard the more emotionally charged lectures were *less* resistant to counterpropaganda.

While the psychologists who did this work have been conservative in interpreting these results, in the context of this discussion I am willing to put myself out on a speculative limb. I would argue that this finding suggests that what I have already indicated may be true, that strong appeals to unconscious motives *may* evoke a great deal of anxiety, with resultant strong resistance to the message directed at the person. Thus, appeal to unconscious motives is a subtle and complex business which may well backfire.

Much has been made of the possibilities of subliminal advertising—the presentation of messages at an intensity low enough so that the individual at whom they are directed is not aware of their presence. Work on subliminal perception is extremely controversial within the profession of psychology, and the particular data on which subliminal advertising was promoted are more questionable than most. However, what is significant is that Professor George Klein of New York University, on whose basic research subliminal advertising was built, reported in the public press that his own experiments gave evidence that some people responded *negatively* to the purportedly unseen stimuli.

There are innumerable difficult technical problems involved in subliminal advertising, and I do not want to pass judgment one way or another on the effectiveness of this phenomenon—although I have some profound doubts. All I want to point out is that to the extent we have firm knowledge in this area, some of that knowledge at least suggests that the individual may resist even "unperceived" messages. My guess would be that extensive use of subliminal advertising—again begging the technical question of what it is and whether it could be pulled off—would increase the strength and pervasiveness of resistance.

[2] Carl I. Hovland, Irving L. Janis, and Harold H. Kelley, *Communication and Persuasion* (New Haven, Yale University Press, 1953), pp. 56-98.

Power to Resist

I am not arguing for or against the effectiveness of any of these techniques of persuasion. I have merely indicated that individuals have the capacity to resist even on the unconscious level. I *am* arguing that the individual's resistance to persuasion probably increases in proportion to the efforts made to persuade him against his own perceived interest. We may even go further than that. Our primitive anxiety concerning the possibility of being manipulated leads us to resist persuasion by others, even in some instances where it may be *in our own interest.* Thus we have the automatic response, "Nobody's going to tell me what's good for me."

My guess is that over the years the American people have developed resistance to manipulation at about the same rate that our techniques of persuasion have become more sophisticated and effective. I mean, of course, that *if the audience had remained the same,* our new techniques would be more effective than our old ones. But the audience has not remained the same. The pace of the race has grown swifter, but it is difficult to say who has gained on whom.

Another point to remember is that merchandising is a competitive activity, and any technique of research or persuasion is about equally available to anyone who wants to make use of it. Even the vaunted subliminal advertisements would tend to cancel out each other if all refrigerator manufacturers, for example, were to use them on television. Competition among persuaders, indeed, is very much like that between the persuader and the object of his persuasion. Adoption of a new technique may well give a momentary competitive advantage, but this advantage lasts only until competitors have also adopted that technique. As long as there is a multiplicity of advertisers, it is difficult to see how the public at large can become the passive puppets of "hidden persuaders."

Omnipotent control?

But there is still one other dread possibility to dispose of, if we can. Let us consider what might happen if there were *no* competition—if the tools of manipulation were in one group's hands. This would be *1984,* the society in which an elite group will direct the behavior of everyone else, in so subtle a way that no one is aware that it is happening. Perhaps it has already happened? How could we tell when it began?

I would not say for a moment that there are no situations in which one person can exercise absolute control over another. Give one man a gun (known in the vernacular as a "persuader"), and he can do a pretty good job of directing the activities of an unarmed man. True, some people in such a situation have escaped, taken the gun from the man, or got themselves shot. But I would not like to quibble about such a small minority, particularly in view of the fact that the effectiveness of this persuader depends on its presence being known, not hidden.

Accounts of brainwashing and similar phenomena indicate that—with a considerable expenditure of effort, careful control of a man's environment (which includes isolating him and getting him in a state of fatigue), good intuitive psychological insight, and a great deal of patience—it *is* possible to change the beliefs of a large proportion of one's victims. There is even some threat in the offing that the use of drugs and of electrodes implanted in the brain may make such procedures more effective.

Although I have some modicum of competence on such subjects, I frankly do not know exactly how far one can go now or in the immediate future with such procedures of influencing people. But look at how remote this is from the notion of controlling *a large society* via psychological techniques. Not only is it doubtful if strictly psychological practices would effect a considerable amount of brainwashing in the absence of all the other factors of control over the individual's environment, but there is the very practical matter that the amount of time and energy expended on each individual must be at least equal to his own time and energy. In short, the influencing of a single individual in a confined situation and by a large number of people is an entirely different case from that of a small number of people influencing a large number of people on a societal level. The Soviet Union is the closest approximation to this latter circumstance that we have seen, and I can say from my own studies of that society that the persuasion was far from hidden, far from total, and, possibly, far from desirable for the efficient functioning of the society.[3]

To be quite realistic, I do not see how anyone who has observed or operated any large-scale organization can take seriously the notion of complete control of behavior. In particular, social science has taught us at least as much about the *necessity* of permitting initiative—which a *1984* society by definition cannot do—as it has taught us about directing behavior.

[3] See, for example, Raymond A. Bauer, "Brainwashing, Psychology or Demonology," *Journal of Social Issues*, Vol. 13, No. 3, 1957, p. 41.

Conclusion

In sum, I am skeptical about the extreme pictures of "hidden persuasion" that have been drawn for either the present or future of business or politics. This does not mean I am indifferent to the prospects of individual instances of the unscrupulous use of psychological or other social science knowledge. What I have been attacking is the notion of the possibility of omnipotent control over the behavior of large numbers of human beings. That such a notion rears its head repeatedly comes, I believe, from our primitive anxiety over manipulation. This anxiety is caused, on the one hand, by our fear that other people may be doing it to *us*, and therefore that we have lost control over our own destiny. It comes, on the other hand, from the notion that *we* may be doing it to others; and here we have a sense of guilt concerning our own motives and behavior toward those others.

I may be fighting a straw man in the sense that this particular *object* of people's fears is not real. But the *fears* exist; they are real. To date most people have not recognized that the threat of omnipotent control over man's behavior *is* a straw man. It may be that my contribution here is that of pointing out that the "hidden persuaders" in their exaggerated form are, in fact, made of straw.

35. OPPORTUNITIES FOR PERSUASION *

Edward C. Bursk

It is helpful to know the limits of persuasion: to realize that gains in motivation research techniques are accompanied by gains in individuals' discernment and ability to resist; and to learn that it is difficult, if not impossible, to exert mass control of people through subconscious manipulation. Raymond A. Bauer's article makes this clear.[1] But there is another way of looking at persuasion—at its opportunities rather than its limitations, particularly when it is practiced openly and rationally.

In fact, I think it can be argued that psychological limitations come into operation only to the extent that persuasion is misapplied. Resistance may be a reaction to attempts at persuasion; however, persuasion does not always produce resistance. I have seen plenty of instances where persuasion is effective largely because it reduces resistance. Sometimes buyers even take positive delight in being sold. And then other times they react unfavorably to too much persuasion or too little persuasion or the wrong kind of persuasion.

What is the right amount and kind of persuasion? That is a difficult question, since different ideas (or different products and brand features) have different reaction factors in people's minds. The potentialities for securing acceptance, as well as the difficulties of overcoming resistance, vary over a wide range. So it is useful to have the clearest possible understanding of why consumers buy or do not buy.

Consumer Motivations

The mistake is to think that knowing consumer motivations means being able to shape them to specific ends, such as getting people to go out and buy a particular product or reach for this brand in pref-

* Reprinted by permission from *Harvard Business Review*, Vol. 36, No. 5 (September-October, 1958), pp. 111-119.

Edward C. Bursk, Professor of Marketing, Graduate School of Business, Harvard University; Editor, *Harvard Business Review*.

[1] See "Limits of Persuasion," p. 354.

erence to that brand. I claim that persuasion is more a matter of strategy than of manipulation; that it is a process of arraying logical forces so that people themselves decide to do what you want them to, rather than of actually changing people's minds; and that any effort to get action by tampering with people's emotions not only runs up against the psychological limitations of resistance but also can be prohibitively time-consuming and expensive.

The way a seller deploys his forces depends of course on the buyer's forces, which include his motives. So the seller needs to take the buyer's motives into account in order to outmaneuver him and get him to move in the desired direction. Here is where the opportunities are; and, ironically, they will not be realized until the new motivation research knowledge which makes them such opportunities is reduced to its proper, limited role. I feel it is important to make this crystal-clear before going on to tackle the problem of constructing strategies.

Decision vs. diagnosis

It is always a temptation for managers to abdicate the functions of analysis and decision making when some "magical" technique promises to do the work for them. The new techniques we are learning from the mathematical and behavioral sciences do provide a stronger basis of information for understanding situations on which action is to be taken, and more accurate devices for measuring the results of action once it has been taken; but they cannot prescribe action. Moreover, even for those purposes, management itself must think through its problems, formulate its specific needs, and make explicit its purposes; otherwise the techniques are likely to be pointless, and only fruitful by accident. So it is good to be reminded that motivation research, with all its ballyhoo, is far from providing the "answers" to everything.

The very existence of limitations adds a positive opportunity. Managers should be glad that they must work with imperfect tools—for then other managers, in competing companies, will face the same impossibility of securing perfect results, and the premium will be to those who use the tools more skillfully. Indeed, it is the essence of aggressive management to take up imperfect tools and *make* them work! And the fact that the availability of new techniques may reduce the range of decision making simply means that, in the narrowing area where judgment and initiative *are* still needed, the effect of relative degree of skill is magnified: the more costly are the mistakes, and the greater is the edge over competitors gained by correct decisions.

So, as we now turn our attention to the *opportunities* for persuasion, the clue is that, however valuable the new research techniques may be for purposes of diagnosis, they are inept for decision making. It is management that must do the creative part of the selling job. This applies both to products and to ideas; but I shall carry the discussion forward in terms of products, since this area not only is important in its own right but serves to illustrate more concretely the principles that are involved.

Lessons of experience

I do not think you can discount the lessons of experience. There are certain things that any man who has done much selling knows; he may not understand the reasons, but he can tell you what works. The points that I intend to make are drawn from observation of many salesmen's activities, including my own for a number of years. I have found that the advertising men who have been most successful in *selling* products (in the sense of building consumer demand or brand preference) also subscribe to the same general philosophy.

The fact that consumer motivation experts often disagree violently among themselves (particularly when it comes to recommending action based on their findings) does not make them wrong, but it certainly does not make me wrong in advocating a more direct and realistic view of selling, either. Indeed, it is because I recognize motives as being both so important and so difficult to deal with that I believe we need to approach selling from the practical viewpoint of strategy.

In short, I am convinced that the best way to sell is along the following lines:

> It is normal and healthy for people to like to buy, just as it is abnormal and unhealthy for them to dislike to buy; and in selling we should deal with people as if we expected them to be normal and healthy rather than in need of mental hygiene—or at least predominantly on that side of the balance, so they have it *in their own power* to resolve any emotional conflict over buying.
>
> Whether the urge to buy is realized and/or any resistance is overcome depends on management's selling efforts (both on the broad economic scale and for individual companies); and more effort—just plain effort—may be almost as important as new skill.
>
> The way for management to secure the desired results is to employ a strategy that makes use of our best understanding of the psychology of the selling-buying relationship—both as to specific motivations in

different situations and, even more important, as to the general phenomenon of people wanting to buy, yet being wary of pressure or trickery, which applies in all situations.

The essence of such a strategy would be to minimize resistance and maximize the urge to buy through selling conducted on the *rational* level—namely, planning and presenting rational goals for people which will lead them to the particular product or brand, in such a way that they satisfy their motivations and even act as their own psychiatrists in the event of any conflict.

Selling of this kind is more effective than deliberate attempts at psychological influencing because it is more in line with the needs and capacities of salesmen, advertising copy writers, and top management; it is more likely to be psychologically sound for the mass of people on the buying end of the relationship; and so secures greater results at less expense.

Apart from the efficiency of the strategy, intensification of selling efforts along lines like these furthers the long-run objectives of both business and society; for it both serves to keep the economy dynamic and contributes to the standard of living of normal, healthy people.

If these concepts hold—and I think those people who have had much firsthand experience in selling would heartily agree—then it is possible to construct a simple (but intensive) strategy for a particular product in a particular market which will handle the complexity and subtlety of the particular motivations involved. In trying to "sell" my ideas in this article I shall make use of some of the same kind of direct, enthusiastic drive.

Urge and Resistance

It hardly needs to be demonstrated that people like to buy. There is a sheer enjoyment in acquiring things, which goes far back to primitive roots. The act of buying is an expression of power, of mastery. Also, people generally like to be nice to people; and if the other person is a salesman, then the inclination is to be nice to him—and the way to be nice to a salesman is to buy from him.

Now, as I understand it, the person who is normal and healthy-minded tends to do what society approves of. The purchase of goods and services—not just food and clothing but education, and not just *a* car but a car *of modern fashion*—is part and parcel of our way of life. And it is not only socially right to buy certain kinds of individual products and services; it also is right to buy lots of things in general. Indeed, this is how people's success is usually measured—as individuals or as families, in their own self-opinion or in the eyes of society. Or, at least, this is how *most* people feel, which is what counts.

So there is a positive urge to buy—to buy in general and to buy specific products. But there is also a negative counterforce that can cause resistance—resistance in general and resistance to specific purchases. Right now we are concerned with the general dimensions—with the underlying strategy (which of course then has to be adapted to more specific motivations).

Underlying strategy

Just as it is socially acceptable to buy, so it is *not* socially acceptable to *overbuy*, that is, to the point where a person appears reckless, improvident, a poor manager of his finances; or to buy *unwisely*, that is, without due regard for price and quality. Admittedly, these are vague terms; in fact they shift with time, and at any one time mean different things to different people. But the idea that there is a point beyond which it is not right to buy is nonetheless very real in every individual's mind, and people are uneasy lest they go beyond it without realizing they are doing so. As far as sellers are concerned, it is the existence of the resistance that is important, not the particular shading of individual buyers' ideas. It will always be operative, and strategy must be pointed to overcome it regardless of how strong it is.

Thus, no matter what that shading, there is the one, single, and over-all fact that for every selling situation the buyer must have some self-approved reason for saying *yes*—whether the affirmation is in terms of handing over the money or signing on the dotted line, or just feeling agreement with an advertising message. For example, a man may want to buy a new car because it is new and sleek and shiny, but he also needs some rationalization like "I'll get a better trade-in if I buy now." Or a woman may want a particular brand of soap because she thinks it will make her seductive to all mankind, but she also must be able to think something like: "If I look prettier, my husband will be pleased"; or more simply, "It will protect my skin"; or still more simply, "It cleans."

This is why it sometimes is difficult for a salesman to close a sale, even though the prospect may seem favorably disposed: the right kind of rationalization has not been offered, even though the actual motivation for buying may have been amply satisfied. The same thing is true in direct mail selling; a man may want to subscribe to a magazine because it makes him feel important, but the promotional piece must also assure him that by filling out and mailing the subscription order form he will receive some practical help in improving his professional skills or solving his business problems.

I am convinced this is also true in advertising; that of two ads, both of which apply to a product mainly bought for *irrational* reasons, the one that provides in addition some cogent *rational* reason should produce a stronger reaction than the one that does not. I suspect that one explanation of why the combination of an advertising appeal to the image of masculinity *and* a new crush-proof box worked so well for Marlboro cigarettes is that the box offered a generally acceptable rationalization.

Rational vs. irrational

I should like to rescue the terms *rational* and *irrational* from the confusion they seem to have fallen into. If applied carefully, they pose a distinction that can be very useful for selling and advertising:

> *Rational* applies to reasons for buying (or not buying) which are *self-approved*—that is, which the buyer feels to be right and reasonable because they are in line with his own expectations of himself as a thinking man and/or his understanding of what other people (society) would consider to be right and reasonable on the part of a thinking man.
>
> By the same token, *irrational* applies to reasons for buying (or for not buying) which are *not* self-approved and socially acceptable, as just defined.

Not that a buyer thinks this all out, or ever formulates it explicitly, but as a result of all his experiences and the current mores of society he just feels some reasons are "all right" for him, and others are not. Completely independent of this distinction is the distinction between conscious and unconscious, or between economic and noneconomic. The trouble is that the terms do sometimes coincide—e.g., *irrational* with *unconscious*, *economic* with *rational*, and so on—and that is why a careless tendency to equate them has developed.

True, rational reasons are more *likely* to be conscious than reasons which are not self-approved, because there is no cause for shame or anxiety about them and hence no tendency to push them into the unconscious. This is fortunate, because it means that rational motives are that much easier to identify for selling strategy. However, the fact remains that rational motives *can* be unconscious, particularly when conflicting motives toward a purchase are involved, as in this example:

> A man may want to buy a new labor-saving device for his wife, but be very concerned about the money outlay. Prudence in spending money is a rational motive, but the man also likes to think of himself as being good to his wife. So what does he do? He finds fault with the machinery of the proposed new washing machine (or whatever it

is)—and does not admit to his wife *or to himself* that a technical defect is *not* the real reason, and he is simply holding back because he doesn't feel right about spending the money.

Even more important, a rational motive may apply also to non-economic or intangible values, *if* it is self-approved. Most men would consider it reasonable that a man should buy helpful things for his wife, as in the example just cited; the fact that he and society think that it is one of his responsibilities make it reasonable—even though it may be a self-pleasure, too. Similarly, in this sense, it is rational to want to live in a good neighborhood, to have a modern-style car, to own a television set.

In fact, one of the great buying phenomena of modern times is the way it became almost obligatory to buy a television set so the children of a family could hold their own in their relationships with other children—an intangible but very rational reason. My interpretation is that people already strongly desired TV sets for unapproved, selfish reasons, and it was the overwhelming availability of a good rational reason for justifying the purchase which triggered the buying wave. (Note that the same combination of circumstances does not apply to *color* TV, which has of course not swept in anywhere nearly so readily.)

It is because of the overlapping of terms that it is absolutely essential to have a separate concept, like rationality, which makes a clear-cut distinction between what is approved and what is not approved, and thus pinpoints the crucial factor in selling strategy. To illustrate:

Suppose a man honestly wants to buy a small car for the sake of economy, but he is afraid he will look like an odd-ball. So he pretends, to the rest of the world *and to himself*, that he is thinking of how easy it will be for his wife to park. Being kind to the weaker sex is his only course; he cannot follow the economic motive because it is not self-approved. At this time and in this neighborhood there is something wrong with a man who doesn't have a big car like everybody else's.

But what is socially acceptable is always changing, and we will do well to keep this in mind as market researchers report "changing" consumer preferences. In fact, I wonder if some of the "changes" recently reported may not simply be due to differences in the freedom with which consumers feel they can *talk* about specific products and advertisements. Thus, in certain regions of the country it now is beginning to be popular to *boast* about the economies offered by small cars.

This does not mean that economy is becoming a more important motive than it used to be. It only means that here and there economy is becoming an accepted or self-approved reason for buying a small car. And the key to understanding the difference between the new and the old situation is not in whether motives have become more or less conscious or more or less economic, but in that change of rationality.

Cause and effect

We must recognize, too, that a rationalization often is nothing more than a convenient reason for action that actually reflects other motives. To illustrate:

> I would agree that it is rational for a woman to patronize a supermarket or a discount house for the sake of economy, but I would argue that this is not altogether her real reason. Certainly she is also influenced by her desire to *appear* (to herself and to the world) as a careful buyer or a shrewd bargainer—perhaps even more so than by her desire for actual money savings. And if she does *not* patronize such outlets, she can always find equally rational reasons—"The meats are so much better where I shop"; or, "They stand back of their products at my store."

There is no doubt that, no matter how rational people pretend to be, very often they buy (or do not buy) things for irrational reasons. But it does not follow that the best way to sell them is by appeals to those irrational motives. The very fact that people insist on devising some rationalization for themselves suggests that it may be effective to supply them with a strong rational reason, so they can follow their irrational bent to the seller's product more surely and speedily. On the other hand, it may actually be ineffective to use irrational appeals because they have more difficulty in securing positive attention, rather than just momentary, vague reaction; or, if they do get across, only serve to point out motives the buyer cannot be proud of as the thinking man he wants to be.

There is much discussion these days about brand images and consumers' self-images. I am sure this is a useful way of *describing* relationships between product and buyer, but not necessarily of *creating* such relationships. Is a brand image the cause of buying, or just the effect of selling? Is a self-image a coherent unit, or just a bundle of unsorted, unweighed, and unweighable motivations? Whether behavioral scientists can answer these questions or not, a large part of the job of making the brand image fit the consumer's self-image can be done, and may have to be done, at the rational level. After all, one of the biggest components of a person's self-image is the picture of himself as a reasonable, thinking man.

I know I am doing injustice to the scope and subtlety of psychological analysis, but such oversimplification is basic to the construction of efficient selling strategy. I am convinced that, *no matter what else is done or what other motivations are involved,* to close a sale or make a telling advertising impression the buyer *must* be given a self-approved reason for purchasing the product or preferring the brand. And, as we shall see subsequently, there is still plenty of opportunity, and indeed need, for understanding just what the specific motivations are in specific situations, and whether they are in fact rational or irrational.

Out in the Open

It is on the score of the general dimensions of urge and resistance that I advocate more open selling. People are hard to fool—increasingly so. But there is not just the danger that sly selling will be detected and boomerang—thus ruining that particular attempt *and* impairing all other, more honest attempts. Rather, the trouble is that such selling may be inefficient because it does not make use of the *positive* effect of openly helping people to buy.

Certainly, any apprehension on the part of buyers that someone is trying to sell them something without letting them know it and giving them a fair chance to make their own buying decisions will create almost insurmountable resistance. By the same token, selling that does not try to hide itself or pretend to be something different is reassuring—so long, of course, as it does not go over to the opposite extreme of pushing people to buy through blatant high-pressure techniques, which again will make them feel they do not have a chance to make their own decisions *on the rational basis that is so necessary to them.* There is as much difference between high-pressure selling and good low-pressure selling [2]—open, purposeful, low-pressure selling—as there is between such open selling and hidden selling.

Positive selling

People expect that a seller who has something to sell will want to sell it; that is rooted in our culture. Further, they respect sellers who have enthusiasm for their products; that too is natural. Indeed it is cause for alarm, and thus for resistance, if a seller apparently is *not* convinced he has a good product. And since the essence of the low-pressure technique is to present the product as the solution to some problem or need of the buyer, the more purposeful the approach, the more the buyer feels he counts.

It is criminal waste of the buyer's own self-interest not to use it to lead him to the product or the brand. Actually, he is likely to be happier if he is so led. I have observed many selling situations where

[2] See Edward C. Bursk, "Low-Pressure Selling," HBR Winter 1947, p. 227; "Thinking Ahead: Drift to No-Pressure Selling," HBR September-October 1956, p. 25.

a hopeless seller lost sales while a hopeful buyer in fact wanted to be persuaded to buy. For example:

> A middle-aged couple came into an appliance store, asked about a color TV set, and in general showed by the models they looked at and the remarks they made that, without realizing it, they had already made up their minds to spend a large amount of money. But every time they raised a question about price, the salesman quickly exhibited a cheaper model, not realizing that what they were asking for was not a better bargain but some assurance there was a rational reason for them to pay the amount in question.
>
> At least three times they were on the verge of saying, "We'll take it." At least three times the salesman lost them by not trying to sell them. They left the store without buying. Although they said—and by this time perhaps thought—that they could not afford the money for one of the small sets, it was obvious that they were completely unhappy because they had not been sold the big set they really wanted.[3]

In advertising too

Again, I think this idea also applies to advertising. To illustrate from the extreme: off-beat copy themes which deprecate the product, or act coy or cute, have proved singularly ineffective. Sometimes they achieve some temporary success just because they attract attention by their oddity, but usually people resent the lack of dignity; sellers who take justifiable pride in their products could not possibly talk or think like that.

If anything, the need for open selling is even greater in advertising, which has to depend on fleeting impressions amid the competition of a multitude of sights and sounds. People have developed a defense mechanism against even noticing ads which do not bear on some problem or want they already have in some degree. Today a picture of a refrigerator and a headline of a new feature will attract the attention of those who are refrigerator-minded, while the John-loves-Mary theme where the refrigerator only comes in subsequently is literally passed by.[4] It makes sense that people will see or hear the message that speaks to them in the terms of their own specific everyday interests—and one of the most important of these is the buying of specific products or services. So why not at least try to make a definite selling impact?

The utmost in waste of good dollars and glossy paper would seem to be the *non*selling that is characteristic of much advertising of

[3] Reported in "Northeastern Distributors, Inc., Recording—Part II," a case prepared and copyrighted, 1954, by Harbridge House, Inc., Cambridge, Massachusetts.

[4] See Richard D. Crisp, "Thinking Ahead: Advertising Research," HBR March-April 1953, p. 30.

industrial products or servcies. It may be true that here the burden is on the salesman in the field; but even in the secondary role of seeking inquiries or paving the way for the salesman, the message will come through stronger if it has at least enough "sell" to be pointed specifically and purposefully to the prospective buyer's problems. Why waste the opportunity to do *some* selling, when that must have more meaning to the buyer than any dull "institutional" generalizations?

Increased effort

Even if sellers and advertisers do not sharpen their skills, just doing more selling can be effective because it is actually in line with the general psychology of the buying-selling situation. Indeed, many sellers may be so far short of utilizing the full potential of their present selling approaches that *initially* they can gain more by straightforward increase in effort than by putting the same amount of money and time into new skills. There is a *continuing* gain, too. Increased effort usually brings about a clearer focus on buyers' motivations; it helps the seller to seek the right course instinctively, and so to improve the skill of his selling.

In sum, when a seller approaches a buyer more purposefully, there are two results: (1) The effort itself has a general effect on the buyer's attitude that is favorable. (2) This in turn makes the buyer more receptive to sales strategy designed for the specific situation—and here is where increased skill has its greatest opportunity.

Singular Strategy

People's minds are complex, and every individual's self-image is different from every other individual's self-image. But selling must be a concentrated, focused action. One of the advantages of the open selling just discussed is that it provides a general setting in which the individual—any and every healthy individual—will tend to move himself toward the purchase—any and every approved purchase. Now, it is also possible to take another big step to lead the customer toward the purchase of specific goods and services. It is possible to devise a singular strategy which will be effective in a plural market—plural in the sense of many individuals, and also in the sense that each individual has multiple, varying, and even conflicting motives.

Not that all products or services will have the same strategy. Far from it; each will be different, and this is why it is so important to know what particular motives are involved. So it is wise to make the best possible use of consumer motivation experts. The only question is: "What is the best possible use?" and I do not intend to go into that.[5]

But let me note, just so it does not get left out of the picture, that a good common-sense analysis of consumer motives is much better than nothing, can be better sometimes than a *poor* expert approach, and always is a helpful check against the findings of the social scientists. Let me also note that beyond the *fairly elementary point* of identifying the major motives involved, further research is likely to be marginal for the purpose under discussion here; the essence of the singular strategy is a single, central motive (or core of closely related motives), and it therefore avails little to know all the subsidiary, marginal motives in detail.

However—and this is important—that "fairly elementary point" calls for *much more* analysis and investigation than the usual seller employs. It is all too easy to assume that consumers are logical rather than psychological—and especially that they are logical with the seller's identical logic. They just may happen to have their own way of thinking and feeling. So there is always danger that without the stimulus of an objective, inquiring point of view the seller can overlook some *important* motive that could make or break the whole strategy. In selling there must be nothing taken "for granted"—or somebody else will do the taking "for real," such as a competitor out after the same consumers' dollars.

Design for buying

Once the motivations are known, the design of the strategy is simple: the seller concentrates on the strongest (or most effectively communicable) *rational* buying motive for the particular consumers he plans to sell to. This is calculated to work in all possible combinations of urge and resistance, on the theory that in every instance where there are reasons both for buying and for not buying the most effective procedure is to maximize the urge and/or minimize the resistance. Thus:

> Suppose there is a rational buying motive in your favor and no real resistance beyond the routine desire to be sure to make a good buy—as, for example, when a man honestly wants a car that will provide the most economical transportation to work. You just plow ahead and sell—you just demonstrate to him that your car will give him that transportation, reinforcing his existing rational motive.

[5] See Joseph W. Newman, "Working With Behavioral Scientists," HBR July-August 1958, p. 67.

But suppose the prospect's buying urge is irrational—as, for example, in the case of the "sexy" convertible mentioned by Bauer.[6] You do not aim at the irrational motive. It is in your favor, so why tamper with it? Why run the danger of making the prospect aware of his irrationality (or wickedness, if a sexual drive is in fact operative here), stirring up a conflict in his mind, and actually causing resistance? You just give him a strong rational reason to latch onto—service, trade-in, or sunshine and health—and free his already existing urge to lead him to it.

If, however, there is a strong negative reason present, the problem becomes more subtle. Go back a few years in imagination to the days when the automatic washing machine was first introduced; and take the case of a woman who wants to buy one for the straightforward reason that it will make life easier for her, but for whom this is not a self-approved reason. Moreover, such motivation is sharply in conflict with her unconscious picture of herself as a martyr to drudgery. She hesitates to ask for the product—that is, to ask her husband for it and/or even to ask *herself* for it; hence, resistance.

There are two possible courses of action here: (1) You can present a rational reason that will give strength to her irrational desire for a joyful Monday—such as "washes clothes cleaner" or "less harmful to fabrics"—which will overcome the irrational resistance, and off she will go (with her husband) to buy it. This is just about what happened, and it happened quickly. (2) You also can try to change the non-self-approved to self-approved—in other words, to make it rational. This is a longer, slower process, yet by now I suspect that hundreds of advertisers promoting hundreds of appliances have actually made labor saving for the housewife quite respectable.

The difficulty is compounded when there is no strong motivation already existent and working for you. Negative reasons become correspondingly more significant. If the resistance is on the rational side, it can usually be met rationally. Most rational objections, if anticipated and met head-on, can be turned to advantage by a good salesman operating on the rational level.

This is particularly true in business selling. In the case of a storekeeper hesitating to buy because he has a heavy inventory, the strategy is to show him that the turnover rate of the new product will decrease his investment per dollar of sales. Or, in the case of industrial equipment purchases, the quality or service features that add to price can almost always be translated into long-run dollar savings.

The toughest situation of all is where the cause of resistance is irrational. Usually, it will be expressed rationally, and no amount of meeting the prospect on this ground will change the picture. Even if you win the argument, he simply will shift from one meaningless position to another.

The surest course is, again, the long-run one of changing the irrationality of the resistance to rationality—making it socially acceptable, and thus self-approved. Take this situation: people may hesitate to make more long-distance telephone calls because of a feeling of uneasiness engendered by association with sickness, death, emergency, delayed arrival, and other unpleasant news conveyed by such calls—

[6] Op. cit., p. 108.

although they usually explain their reluctance on the ground of expensiveness. This may be one of those situations where irrational resistance is unconscious just because it is irrational and hence at odds with a person's picture of himself.

But the telephone companies by their advertising over a period of time have begun to make the telephoning of friends and members of the family appear a friendly, natural, constructive process—just witness the ease with which today's young people pick up the phone and place a call (usually collect). For the new generation it *is* rational.

My hunch is that this telephone advertising would have been still more effective if all mention of cost had been omitted. Even the claim that "it costs less than you think" calls attention to the fact that there is such a convenient rationalization for having an irrational feeling about long-distance calls. If so, this is a situation where only a long-range rational approach will make a good strategy; and an immediate rational appeal may actually reduce effectiveness. The moral is obvious: even though the selling strategy does not incorporate an irrational appeal, it is necessary to know that a strong irrational motivation is at work against you in order to select the proper rational approach. In other words, here is one more demonstration that motivation research does provide a valuable service when used for diagnostic purposes.

Of course, the strategy will vary for different markets; and where the market is made up of quite varied segments, each segment may have to have its own singular strategy. But, in general, there will be only one rational motive big enough to dominate the other forces involved. The appeals which are built around it may be manifold, but they represent the creative job of translating the motive into selling language, which is another question entirely.

Design for selling

Note that in all the above examples a rational motive turns out to be the best vehicle for carrying the prospect to the purchase. It is assumed that the prospect will provide some exertion himself, but of course something has to be done to get him started. Now I want to show why basing appeals on a rational motive also provides the best mechanism for the salesman's *action,* so necessary to get the prospect off dead center and actually moving toward the purchase.

For one thing, the salesman can use the rational approach more easily. It is more simple for him to understand, more natural for him to plan, more direct for him to follow. Further, by concentrating on one goal for the prospect and moving toward it purposely, he is likely to end up with an attractive presentation. Since he is thinking in terms of a need or want, rather than a product feature or advantage, he is necessarily concentrating on the prospect as a human being with thoughts and feelings, and will therefore instinctively tend to act so as to *please* the prospect. (That may well be a safer way to get the help of irrational appeals than by deliberately trying to use them; if appropriate, they will come through in gestures, in choice of words, in art work, without undermining the rationality of the approach.)

The fact that the goal is a rational need or want is even more helpful. Since it is acceptable, it gives the salesman the self-respect and confidence he must have if he is to keep on selling. Since it makes sense, he does not become embarrassed or confused. Not being a trained psychologist, he can be very wrong if he tries to figure out all the nuances of irrational motivations; and, even if by chance he is right, he will act self-consciously, and spoil the sincerity that is so essential for good low-pressure selling.

Some of the same demands prevail in mass selling programs and advertising. Sales managers and advertising executives are likely to function more effectively—more spontaneously and more aggressively—if they set out to sell on the basis of the best rational motive and do not get all tangled up with hidden persuaders. The straightforward effort to sell will stimulate their thinking processes, and will add punch to their messages. For example:

> The advertising firm of Doyle Dane Bernbach has been attracting much attention lately. It has built its billings to $20 million in less than ten years, eschewing research and emphasizing copy. According to the agency president, William Bernbach, "We get people to look and listen by being good artists and writers. We don't expect of research what it is unable to do. It won't give you a great idea."
>
> The agency stresses a simple but striking idea, a specific selling point. For bread: pictures of nibbled slices, and the message that "New York is eating it up." For an airline: a map of the Atlantic Ocean one-fifth torn away, and the message that "Starting Dec. 23, the Atlantic Ocean will be 20% smaller." And apparently clients have had big increases in sales.[7]

But there is an even more fundamental reason for depending on rational appeals if one is aiming for a plural market—as most sellers are, whether it be a specialized group or the mass market. Everybody's self-images or bundles of motives are a little different, and the trick is to pick an appeal that will best cover the particular market being sought—that will have great positive strength for most of the individuals, moderate to little weight for the balance (it is too much to expect 100% aim), and no deterring effect on any. For these purposes a rational motivation usually serves best. Irrational wants and feelings are diverse and subtle, but rational desires are neces-

[7] See *Time*, March 31, 1958, p. 78.

sarily shared by a large part of the market since they reflect the norms and customs of society. By the same token, they are unlikely to restrict the market by any deterrent of embarrassment or confusion.

Conclusion

Most people have healthy minds; they like to buy. There is no need to dig into their subconscious to free them from blocks and tensions before they buy. (Indeed, such an effort may be dangerous—may stir up conflict without enough time or skill to remove it—something even psychiatrists worry about.) Irrational resistances, even if in the subconscious, can be handled by the healthy prospect himself—and *will* be, if he is provided with a sufficient *rational* motive as incentive.

But selling is not just satisfying present wants or playing up to old desires. Selling is a process of increasing wants or, even better, creating new wants. This is what keeps our economy dynamic. Further, the more business gets consumers to consider the pursuit of noneconomic values as approved and rational, the more it is building people's potential for a higher, less materialistic way of life. And it is up to education to see to it that consumers say *no* to the more meretricious forms of satisfaction.

The danger of consumer motivation research is that business may rely on "scientific" techniques and forget to go out and sell. As far as getting buying action is concerned, the actual psychological subtleties may just be too tenuous for the hit-and-run of daily life. But we can use our understanding of how people buy to build a lot of little strategies for persuading people to want specific products and services, and one grand strategy of giving people continually bigger and better goals for themselves.

In either case, there is one big, uncomplex psychology at work—the interaction of enthusiastic seller and eager buyer, out in the open where they belong. And whatever irrational forces there are will be released if they are in your favor, contained if they are against you. Such selling is not manipulating people behind their backs; it is giving them rational motives for doing what is in their own best interests as individuals and as society-at-large.

36. SUBLIMINAL ADVERTISING *

Steuart Henderson Britt

Not new in labs

Subliminal stimulation is not something new. Psychologists have known about it for a long time, and the phenomenon has been demonstrated many times in the psychological laboratory.

Since subliminal *stimulation* is not something new, subliminal *advertising* is within the realms of possibility. However, subliminal advertising has not as yet, from a scientific standpoint, been completely demonstrated. Nor have the results reported been experimentally verified.

It will be recalled that *subliminal* stimulation refers to stimuli that are sub (below) the limen (threshold) of consciousness or awareness. This might be contrasted with *supraliminal* stimulation, where the stimuli are supra (above) the threshold of consciousness or awareness.

We might assume that the developers of subliminal advertising are stating as accurately as possible the results they believe they obtained. However, even with the most truthful intentions, it is possible that they may not have exercised proper scientific control of all variables, and so may not have interpreted their results correctly.

The real questions concern whether a complete "jump" can be made from the results in the psychological laboratory to the results reported for a movie theater by the proponents of subliminal advertising; and also whether the experimental design of their work was adequate.

Results of experiments

As to the first question, most of the experiments in the laboratory situation have been with individuals, not with groups; and the environment is quite different from that in movie theaters. Further-

* Reprinted by permission from *Advertising Agency Magazine*, Vol. 51, No. 11 (May 23, 1958).

Steuart Henderson Britt, Professor of Marketing, School of Business, Northwestern University; Editor, *Journal of Marketing*.

more, in most of the laboratory experiments, the individuals serving as subjects have known *what* they were supposed to be discriminating, but have not known *that* they were discriminating.

Also, for the most part, the laboratory experiments have demonstrated that *perception* can be produced from relatively simple subliminal stimuli; but there is little experimental evidence that *overt action* has resulted from subliminal stimuli. And there is no evidence that subliminal stimuli will cause a person to do something he does not want to do or that is not natural for him to do.

The figures reported by Subliminal Project Co., Inc., that popcorn sales increased over 57 per cent and sales of Coca-Cola by 18 per cent as a result of subliminal advertising in movie theaters, seem astoundingly high. Where the tests actually took place has been dubbed by some "one of 1957's best kept secrets." (It wasn't really, as the tests took place in the Fort Lee theater, Fort Lee, N. J.) What needs to be demonstrated is whether the experiments can be repeated, under the same conditions and with proper experimental control of all variables, and with similar results being obtained.

Design of experiments

This leads to the second question: The basic design of the experiments. Subliminal Projection officials have stated that complete facts about their work cannot be released until after their application for a patent has been acted upon. (A number of psychologists have questioned what there is to patent, other than the purely mechanical aspects of using S.P. in a theater.) Anyhow, experiments of the same general sort need to be carried out in the meantime, using five different groups of people:

Group 1. Subliminal adverising used—people *not told* it is in use.

Group 2. Subliminal advertising used—people *told in advance* that it will be used.

Group 3. Supraliminal (regular) advertising used.

Group 4. Both subliminal and supraliminal advertising used.

Group 5. No advertising used.

These five groups should then be compared as to any differences in sales results. It would be necessary, of course, to have the five groups matched with respect to such control factors as age, sex, buying habits, etc., and to have the tests carried out under comparable conditions, on the same days of the week and same hours of the day, and with identical entertainment features.

This experimental work should then be repeated by others, using five similar groups, to determine whether comparable results are obtained. Until this basic work is done and until the complete design of the experiment and specific results are made public, subliminal advertising is not likely to engulf us.

Ethical, practical considerations

Advertisers, agencies and media are certainly holding off on this whole matter. Most advertising men fear something that seems to them almost like "mesmerism," and are convinced that its use would bring serious damage to the whole field of advertising.

Questions concerning the ethics of the technique are by no means limited to the literati and "eggheads." The attitude of most network officials and of leading advertising men seems to be one of great caution, and the three major U. S. networks and the Canadian Broadcasting Corporation have adopted rules against use of the technique during network shows. The public probably will continue to be protected against what many would call invisible "thought control."

There is also a natural degree of skepticism among advertising men until further factual data are forthcoming. In addition to ethical considerations, the basic practical question is this: From a strictly commercial standpoint, can it be demonstrated that *subliminal* advertising is more effective than *supraliminal* advertising? A related question is: What is the cost per thousand commercial minutes, "subliminally" as compared with "supraliminally"?

Incidentally, experiments show that what is subliminal advertising for some people turns out to be supraliminal for others. After all, we differ considerably from each other in our abilities to play golf or hit a target. Likewise, we differ considerably in our abilities to perceive. There are great differences not only among individuals, but even for individuals at different times; what you or I perceive when hungry differs from what we perceive when not.

The logical answer would be for subliminal advertising to be so far below the threshold of consciousness that it would be impossible for even the keenest individual to perceive it. But then how effective would such stimulation be in producing action; in other words, what would be the most effective "levels" of subliminal advertising.

Finally, the technique may be impractical because it would probably provoke considerable feelings of anxiety among radio or TV listeners or viewers. The proponents of subliminal advertising have indicated that an announcement could be made at the beginning of any program employing the technique, stating that subliminal advertising is going to be used. But this could readily produce real anxiety about what kinds of additional unseen and unheard stimuli might be employed. People might become quite uneasy about the whole program and even turn off their sets.

In any case, there is one thing sure. People will continue to complain about commercials, whether subliminal or supraliminal. As all advertising men know, a favorite topic in many social gatherings is how "annoying" some radio and TV commercials are thought to be. If subliminal advertising ever does get used, you can be sure that people will then complain about the commercials they can't see or hear . . . as well as those they do see and hear.

37. SELECTING TRANSPORTATION SERVICES *

Richard M. Boyd

Those of you who have studied journalism will recall the requisite for the lead sentence of a news article. The same elements may also be appropriate in our consideration of the subject, "Selecting Transportation Services." The WHO or WHAT, WHERE, WHEN, WHY, and sometimes HOW applied in journalistic teaching can well serve as a guide in the selection of transportation services.

WHO would involve only passenger transportation. This phase of an industrial traffic department is often termed an evil and a headache, but it is a most important part. The importance stems largely from who is involved. It is only natural that as people rise higher on the ladder of success their personal comfort becomes a more important desire; and unless it is satisfied, those who are responsible often must suffer the consequences. The president of an industrial corporation often measures his traffic manager's effectiveness on the basis of what type of Pullman space he is able to secure for him. Accordingly, the WHO must be given special attention, and the type of transportation most suitable to the journey must be

* Reprinted by permission from *Carroll Business Bulletin*, Vol. II, No. 3 (August, 1958), pp. 83-89.

Richard M. Boyd, General Traffic Manager, Pittsburgh Plate Glass Company.

selected. Today, choice is usually between rail and air, with water and highway only occasionally to be considered.

In selecting commercial transportation, the individual's preference usually governs whether rail or air is used. The preference is often influenced by weather considerations, particularly in the wintertime. The industrial traffic department must make known to the individual how and on what schedule he can travel to the desired destination. He can then make the decision as to which will suit his requirements and afford comfort in keeping with his liking. Although first-class rail travel has tended to become more expensive than air in recent years, the difference in cost is not often a consideration in business travel. Arrival at destination at the time required and reasonable comfort enroute are more often the deciding factors.

International travel has become a choice between water and air. Only in recent years has the latter been considered dependable. But it is now generally accepted; and it becomes a question of whether time is available for water movement, with accompanying comfort, or whether the speed of air travel is required. Cost sometimes becomes a consideration because in such travel the slower means, water, is more expensive. The additional housing and meals enroute are responsible rather than the cost of operation.

With increased feasibility of air transportation, privately owned and operated aircraft have come into much greater use by industry and some individuals. Most of the larger companies today operate at least one plane for the use of executives, and many companies operate fleets of planes to accommodate their varying travel requirements. These private aircraft can be justified only on the basis of convenience and comfort. Their operation is always more expensive than the cost of buying commercial transportation.

For shorter trips, highway travel is preferable; and much of this is being done in "You-Drive-It" equipment. It has become common practice for people traveling on company business to engage rental automobiles at rail or air terminals in order to accomplish various missions—such as visiting plants, calling on customers, and the like. Industry practice of maintaining numerous chauffeur-operated automobiles has been abandoned to a considerable extent in favor of the lesser cost involved in the hire of "You-Drive-It" equipment. The cost of labor has been the primary factor influencing this change of policy. The user of the rental equipment does the work instead of a chauffeur who not only must be paid but who also often involves overtime.

Commercial bus transportation finds very limited use in industrial transportation requirements largely because of the convenience of "You-Drive-It's." In the past few years an advertising campaign by our largest bus operating company has provoked some consideration of bus transportation for industrial travel, but it is still on a very limited basis.

WHAT is to be moved falls into three general types: bulk, liquid, and merchandise. This quickly ties WHAT in with HOW, because the first two categories often require special-type equipment and sometimes the merchandise category dictates the use of special rail or truck equipment.

Bulk commodities may be shipped either in open cars, trucks, or barges or in closed equipment—depending upon whether protection from the weather is required. Formerly, bulk commodities were moved in the standard box car made tight by use of paper or other lining in order to prevent leakage at the doors or other openings. When trucks first came into the picture, standard box-car-type vans were utilized for movement of bulk commodities by this form of transportation. Today, however, an increasing number of commodities are being moved in covered hopper cars and trucks—even foodstuffs which require special lining of the equipment. Elimination of handling is the primary objective because of the resultant saving in labor cost. Covered barges have always been available for bulk movement, and their design has been changed little other than by addition of protective linings.

Movement of liquid commodities must necessarily be confined to tank cars, tank trucks, or tank barges. There has been a marked increase in special equipment for transportation of chemicals and other corrosive materials in recent years. We find tank cars lined with glass and various types of metal in order to protect against the action of the liquid lading.

The merchandise category covers a variety of commodities which may be moved either in open or closed equipment—that is, gondolas, flat cars, flat-bed or stake trucks, box cars, closed vans, open-top trucks with tarpaulins, and closed or open barges. For items of extreme height, sometimes depressed flat or well-type cars and underslung or depressed-frame trailers are required.

WHERE involves the origin, the destination, and any special requirements enroute. There are some important considerations involved here, particularly in the selection of the mode of transportation. If the origin and destination are on water, the marine type of transportation may be considered. If rail facilities are available at both origin and destination, then rail transportation may be used. In the absence of water or rail facilities, truck may be the only feasible type of transportation. Occasionally, a combination of water and truck or rail and truck is appropriate.

WHERE also involves distance, and this fact will often influence our considerations of HOW. Prior to World War II there were some rather well-propounded theories on truck transportation being practical only for distances up to, say, 200 to 400 miles. These have been dispelled in recent years, and now we find trucks being used for transcontinental movement of various commodities. Water transportation was sometimes considered practical only for the greater distances; but today we find it being used for some rather short hauls, particularly where bulk or liquid commodities lend themselves to easy loading and unloading.

The ability to cover distance with great speed has brought consideration of air transportation increasingly into the picture; but the cost factor, which will be discussed later, has limited the growth of air freight.

WHEN will always be an important part in our selection of transportation service. It involves not only the time required at destination but the time the material will be ready for movement from origin. If speed is a factor, usually the time required at destination is more important; but we are often influenced by nonavailability of material until a certain time, particularly when it is in the process of manufacture. Speed in shipping, consequently, may play a very important part in our selecting the mode of transportation and the individual carrier to be utilized.

Sometimes the industrial traffic manager is apt to be guided by the old saying, "Ours is not to reason why; ours is but to do and die." To the credit of the occupation, however, those engaged in industrial traffic work are becoming curious as to the reason for movement of a particular commodity from a particular place at a particular time, required at a particular place at a particular time. In some instances more than curiosity is involved—the traffic manager as a part of the distribution operation exercises responsibility in deciding whether material should be moved as well as actually arranging for the transportation.

WHY is also helpful in determining what transportation is to be utilized, particularly in instances where speed is a factor. If the exact requirements for the movement can be given, and the reason for its being needed at destination at a certain time explained, the buyer of transportation is often better able to figure an answer to the problem. If he is simply told the material must be at destination 8:00 A.M. on August 31, the situation leaves little room for the exercise of imaginative initiative. It does not present the urgency which would be apparent if he were told that a production line will be forced to shut down unless an additional quantity of material is ready for use at 8:00 A.M., August 31. In such a situation, there would be considerable difference between providing rail arrival at 8:00 A.M., truck arrival at that time, or arrival at the production line at that instant. Accordingly, WHY may be very important in a given situation, and a much more intelligent job of selecting transportation may be done if such information is available.

The most important element is HOW. Even after proper consideration of the other elements, we are still often left with a final choice of the mode of transportation. Seldom are we able to select from all types—other requirements usually narrow the choice down considerably.

If we have met all the basic requirements involved in the WHAT, WHERE, WHEN, and WHY categories, our consideration of HOW becomes largely one of cost. In the final analysis, a shipper must use the mode of transportation and the carrier within that mode which will do a satisfactory job at the least cost.

The term cost is sometimes a misleading one. It is necessary that the following aspects of cost be given complete consideration:

UNIT COST. The rate should be determined in terms of cents per 100 pounds or ton. For example, suppose we were to assume that the rate by rail, water, and truck is the same. In such a situation, we would quickly say that it is a choice between rail or truck because water is obviously too slow to compete. Upon further consideration, however, we might find that the tariff rate is not the only thing to be considered.

COST OF PACKING. Packing cost for movement by various means of transportation may vary considerably. Generally, there is more vibration and possible shock involved in rail movement; and often greater packing expense is involved in preparing for rail movement than is included in similar preparation for truck movement. When shipments are made by water, waterproofing to protect against the elements of weather is often necessary; and this may be a major item of expense. Although the cost in cents per 100 pounds of air freight and air express will always be greater, the reduction in the tare weight (because less packing is required for protection) may bring the over-all cost to a figure less than that applicable for rail or truck movement. This is particularly evident when comparison is made with the cost for railway express, since this type of movement usually requires the same packing as is necessary for rail freight shipment.

COST OF LOADING. In many situations, although the rail and truck rates may be the same, extensive blocking and bracing may be required for movement by rail with only nominal securing needed for movement by truck. In order to arrive at a true cost-per-100-pounds figure, this loading cost must be so calculated and added to the line haul rate.

Some bulk and liquid commodities can be loaded into barges by conveyors or pumps, whereas such transfer is not feasible for rail or truck movement. In such instances, even if the line haul rates are the same, water transportation may be preferred.

Package freight weighing less than 300 pounds is normally loaded from the platform into trucks by the motor carriers. Such service is not available for rail shipment, and this factor must be taken into consideration. Possible demurrage on rail cars or detention charges on trucks also must be considered.

It may be easier to load cars than trucks or vice versa. In our operations, we often find that it is easier to load by rail because a string of rail cars can be loaded in orderly fashion, whereas trucks must be loaded as they arrive at the plant. The difference in cost may depend on whether the material is adjacent to the particular loading dock or is at a distant point in the plant or warehouse area. In such situations, the cost of labor may vary considerably and may become a factor in influencing the mode of transportation.

When the terms of sale are f.o.b. factory, the buyer normally is given the option of specifying whatever form of transportation and carrier he prefers. Because of the cost-of-loading factor, it may make a difference in the manufacturer's profit. For this reason, the industrial traffic manager must endeavor to equalize rates by the various modes of transportation in order to compensate for differences in the cost of loading.

COST OF UNLOADING. Usually the ramifications are not so numerous as those involved in loading, but this factor must be given due consideration. One of the things to watch is whether the cost of removing dunnage from rail cars is greater than that involved in unloading trucks. In certain instances it may be more convenient to unload rail shipments—orderly procedure versus unloading of trucks on arrival. The rail spot may be adjacent to where the material is needed; or, on the other hand, split drop delivery by truck may be required.

MAINTENANCE-OF-INVENTORY COST. The availability of faster transportation facilities has materially changed the inventory system. Ability to obtain overnight delivery (or, on some items, delivery within a few hours), in many instances has eliminated the costly maintenance of inventories. Thus, even though it is inherently more expensive, air transportation is often economical because inventories can be reduced.

Transportation cost cannot be separated from all the other factors involved in receipt or forwarding of raw materials and finished products. Common labor comes high today and has become a major consideration in any transport operation. In selecting the mode of transportation, we must consider whether more labor is needed by one mode than another—for preparing for shipment, for loading, for unloading, or for handling after unloading. Each and all of these parts in the cost pattern will influence movement by one means in preference to another.

Because it is difficult to appraise the import of all these factors, they are sometimes disregarded by regulatory bodies in rendering decisions on rate adjustments made by one mode of transportation designed to meet the competition of another. It is becoming increasingly important that the deficiencies or advantages of modes be effectively pointed out to the regulatory bodies, so that real equality may be achieved and selection on individual merit rather than over-all cost advantage can be made.

Aside from strict cost considerations, there are many other elements. Often a shipment is routed by a particular mode of transportation or carrier because it offers the most accommodating service. Included in this arrangement are such factors as tracing, making pickups when required, good and prompt switching, accurate billing, and the like. The reputation of the carrier, the availability and flexibility of his service, his adjustment policy, and his attitude toward reciprocity are also important.

Sometimes the selection of the mode of transportation or particular carrier is dictated by a regulatory body. Such instances arise through denial of operating authority applications or refusal of the regulatory body to permit one mode of transportation to meet the rates of another.

Assistance or willingness to negotiate necessary and justifiable adjustments of rates is often a strong influencing factor. Carriers that are helpful in working out such situations usually profit from services rendered. Cost is so important that the shipper naturally is inclined to favor carriers that help him with his problems.

Establishment of transit privileges channels the selection of the type of transportation and the particular carrier to be used. In any transit operation, the shipper faces a penalty of higher transportation costs if he fails to use the same type of transportation and the same carrier within that form of transportation both to and from the transit point. For this reason, it is often said that establishment of transit privileges "ties the business" to a particular carrier.

Industrial development work often plays a major part in influencing the selection of transportation services. Assistance in plant location, installation of side-track facilities, orientation in the community, and other help which may be given by a good industrial development program to the location of a new plant undoubtedly influence traffic to be routed by that carrier.

Availability of warehouse facilities is often a determining factor in selecting transportation. Storage at reasonable rates with proper distribution facilities can influence the use of a particular carrier.

Sometimes initial selection commits the movement of traffic to a certain type of transportation, particularly when it is necessary to purchase or lease specialized equipment. Once an investment is made in barges, pipe lines, tank cars, or tank trucks, industry must continue to use the form of transportation for which such equipment is suited until it is amortized. Very often this is a long-range program; and with the supplementary facilities which are often necessary to accommodate such equipment, it can easily entail permanent commitment to the use of one form of transportation.

Among the miscellaneous elements, we cannot overlook personalities. "Joe is a nice fellow—I'll give him the business" quite often is a strongly influencing factor. Selling an intangible is difficult, and much depends on the individual personality and temperament of the salesman. The salesman who adequately describes the services of the company he represents, and how that company can be helpful in solving the problems of industry, is surely an influence in the selection of transportation services.

The determination of when transportation is to be used has been an important part in the process of selection. Occasionally it is impossible to secure common-carrier transportation adequate to the requirements and the job must be done with industry's own trucks. More often, the possibility of savings in cost is the motivating factor. Sometimes such savings are imaginary in that reduction in cost for one movement may result in increased cost for others. Any common-carrier operation must depend on averages; and if the more-remunerative traffic is removed, the cost of the less-desirable traffic may well rise. In any major industrial operation certain movements which could be handled at less cost by private transportation can be singled out, but consideration must be given to the ramifications of such action. Whether or not such savings are real is often clouded by the difficulty of charging to the operation a proper amount of overhead expense for supervision and coordination. Unless additional personnel are added to supervise or coordinate a private transportation project, there is a tendency to disregard the cost of supervision or what it takes to make the operation work. Unfortunately, once the decision to use private transportation is made, there is usually no turning back. Investment in equipment or commitments to long-term leases dictate the continuing use of this form. Accordingly, such efforts to make the operation pay are usually made by those responsible for the decision. This sometimes results in use of equipment for movements which could be more efficiently and economically handled by commercial transportation. Sometimes commodities which are wholly unsuited to the equipment are handled in back-haul movement in order to cover gasoline and driver expense.

In conclusion, the selection of transportation services has become a complex one—quite different from the days when there was no choice of modes. Today we enjoy the world's greatest transportation network, and it is becoming increasingly important that we use it intelligently and in the most efficient manner. The systematic, if not scientific, selection of the means of transportation and the best carrier within that means is a basic requirement to any successful manufacturing or distributing operation.

38. PATTERN OF U. S. FREIGHT TRAFFIC CHANGING FAST *

Stanley Ferguson

Sweeping changes, both technological and economic, in national freight traffic patterns are producing changes no less sweeping in the meaning of that favorite barometer of American traffic trends known as "revenue carloadings."

In some respects carloadings have lost much of their significance as an index of general traffic volume. In others—especially when used for long-term purposes of comparison—they tend to paint the railroad freight picture in hues darker than it really is.

These changes have been coming for some time. But they have been especially evident during the past decade and will probably become even more so in the future. Basically they are two:

First, railroads have lost so much potential traffic to other modes of transport—not only to trucks and private carriage generally, but to water carriers and pipelines—that weekly tabulations on revenue carloadings now apply to only about one-half the freight moving in this country. Thirty, and even 20 years ago, most freight moving any distance was hauled by rail.

Second, today's freight cars are larger, they are moved faster, loaded more heavily and travel further on the average than those in use 10, 20, 30 and 40 years ago. A single carloading today thus represents, in relative as well as absolute terms, a bigger movement.

Dropped in '59

In 1959 carloadings amounted only to 30.9 million, as against 38.9 million in 1950 and 45.8 million in 1930, the 1930 figure marking the highest point achieved by carloadings in the past three decades. The 1959 figures, of course, were depressed by the long steel strike and were regarded throughout the rail industry as disappointing in the extreme.

Reprinted by permission of the *Journal of Commerce,* Vol. 266 (November 28, 1960), p. 1.

Stanley Ferguson, Editor, *Journal of Commerce.*

But the sharp drop in revenue carloading figures, which are made available weekly, is not reflected in the much more significant figures showing how many revenue tons of freight were carried by the railroads for one mile. These figures only become available much later.

The 45.8 million carloadings in 1930 worked out to 383.5 million ton miles. The 38.9 million carloadings in 1950 represented 588.5 million tons miles. An 8 million drop in annual carloadings from 1950 to 1959 was accompanied by a decline in revenue ton-miles, but only from 588.5 to 575.5 million.

Several causes

The reasons behind this are several. For the one thing, the average freight tonnage loaded per car has been climbing slowly ever since the early 'thirties. There have been interruptions and occasional backslidings in this trend, notably in the war years and then in the early 'fifties, but it has held above 33 tons for the past four years, as against 27.6 tons in 1940 and 26.7 tons in 1930.

More significant, however, is the lengthening of the distance over which the loaded cars are hauled—a factor that makes a good deal of difference in the revenue each haul produces. In 1930 this averaged out to 185.9 miles, 10 years later to 202.5 miles. In 1940 it reached 229 miles, and last year it hit 250.7 miles—a record second only to that of 1958 when the average was 251.3 miles.

The fact that a number of large railroads, especially in the East, have been scrapping large numbers of ancient freight cars and replacing them with new, faster and larger units is expected to accelerate in some degree the discrepancies between carloadings and ton-mile figures.

Piggyback an offset

But the rapid growth of piggy-backing could provide a partial offset. Piggy-back cars, although traveling at high speeds and usually for fairly long distances, are seldom loaded beyond 14 tons, even though regarded as good revenue producers.

On the other hand, railroads get a degree of utilization out of their fast, roller-bearing piggy-back flats that they have found impossible to achieve with many other types of freight cars, especially the boxcar.

Over the past 40 years the average speed of American freight trains has been pushed from a little over 10 to just under 20 miles per hour. It has nearly doubled. But the average number of miles recorded by the average freight car per day has gone up only from 27 to just under 46 miles.

This reflects the fact that in 40 years there has been no improvement whatever in the detention of freight cars at terminal points.

Detention rate high

In 1920 the average freight car spent over 21 of the 24 hours of each day either standing or moving in terminals. Last year, and the year before that and, for that matter, during every year as far back as 1948 it spent more than 21 hours doing the same thing.

There have been a few years in the past 40 when the terminal detention period has been pushed slightly below 20 hours in 24 and when the average car actually spent more than 3 hours in 24 moving in trains. But far from showing any improvement, the figures actually show a slight slippage, for while the average terminal time in 1920 worked out to 21.36 hours, in 1959 it was put at 21.59 hours, and in 1958 at 21.62.

Durability doubtful

This is one factor tending to maintain the validity of carloading figures as a short if not long-range barometer of freight traffic trends. But how long it will be able to resist the onslaught of piggybacking and the growing number of elaborate electronic classification yards—both of them devoted to the objective of keeping the cars moving—is problematical.

There is a good deal of feeling among railroad executives that the next few years will see a strong upturn in the efficiency of car utilization. When this begins, economists will have to take another look at the true meaning of carloading figures.

39. HOW FIELD WAREHOUSING CONCERNS HELP SMALL BUSINESS *

Prepared by Technical Specialists in Private Business

There are two principal ways in which field warehousing can be of assistance to small businesses in the solution of financing and marketing problems:

(1) By making it possible to obtain a secured loan on inventory from a bank, finance company, or other lending agency;

(2) By making it possible—if the business is a manufacturer or processor with national or regional distribution—to place a full stock of products with distributors at little or no credit risk.

Field warehousing for loan purposes

Field warehousing may be defined as the legal and actual custodianship of inventory for the purpose of creating collateral. Basically it involves transferring some of the important functions of a public storage terminal out into the "field," onto the premises of a manufacturer, processor, or distributor.

If you're seeking additional working capital for your business and want to enter into a field warehouse arrangement, first determine whether or not your bank, finance company, or other regularly-used lending institution will advance funds against the particular inventory involved. When the lending agency has been decided upon, and a definite loan commitment made on the basis of warehouse receipts as the collateral security, one of the leading field warehouse concerns should then be called in for installation of the service. The names of these companies may be found in the classified telephone directory or may be obtained from a bank, finance company, or other lending agency, or from the Regional Offices of the Small Business Administration.

A representative of the warehouse company will inspect your premises to determine their suitability for a field warehouse opera-

* Reprinted by permission from *Management Aids for Small Business*, Annual No. 3 (1957). Edited by Edward L. Anthony.
Originally published as No. 60 in *Management Aids for Small Manufacturers.*

tion, and make recommendations as to the erection of any fences or partitions that may be necessary. In general, however, most indoor and outdoor storage areas are acceptable for field warehousing without change. Examples of storage areas now being successfully used for this purpose are:

(1) An entire warehouse building adjacent to a fruit cannery.

(2) A portion of an appliance distributor's warehouse room, separated from display space by frame and wire partitions.

(3) An entire loft above a textile manufacturer's plant.

(4) A storage tank system at a petroleum refinery.

(5) A grain elevator adjacent to a feed manufacturer's mill.

(6) An open lumber drying yard adjacent to a sawmill.

(7) A fenced yard for the storage of steel beams, angles, and shapes.

(8) An office filing case holding instrument parts.

When you, as a prospective borrower, have received your loan commitment from the lending agency, and your premises have been approved, you then enter into a storage agreement with the field warehouse company. That agreement sets forth the rates and charges for the service, and the period of time during which it will operate. Such contracts vary in length from 1 to 3 years; however, those for periods longer than a year are written to eliminate the accrual of charges in any year in which you don't use the service.

Under the contract, the warehouse company leases (for, say, a dollar a year) the room or area in which the pledged inventory is to be stored. A warehouse manager and any needed assistants are appointed—usually from among your regular employees. The field warehouse company "covers" the manager and his assistants with fidelity bonds. These employees continue to perform their usual duties when not engaged in field warehousing activities. Although their salaries will be paid by the field warehousing company, the full amounts of those salaries will normally be rebilled to you.

The field warehouse company next affixes locks to the leased room, or encloses the leased area and posts signs telling of its possession of the area and control of the merchandise or materials stored inside. Keys to the locked area are held by the field warehouse employees. The stored inventory is counted and warehouse receipts issued to the bank, finance company, or agency making the loan. From time to time, additional merchandise or materials may be placed in the leased premises for loan purposes, and warehouse receipts issued for it.

When you need some of the stored inventory, you pay the receipt holder for it, and get an order authorizing the warehouse manager to deliver the goods to you. In many cases—particularly those where the movement of your inventory is rapid—the receipt holder will permit the warehouse manager to deliver specified amounts of inventory without first obtaining a release. In such cases, the warehouse manager notifies the receipt holder periodically of the deliveries made, and the receipt holder then obtains payment from you.

The leading field warehouse concerns maintain running inventory-control records on electronic business machines. These records cover all deliveries to, and shipments from the warehouse location. Monthly collateral and inventory reports are provided both for the warehouse receipt holder, and for the depositor of the goods, so that both will be informed of all warehouse transactions.

Field Warehousing on Distributors' Premises

One type of arrangement which has been referred to above provides a way in which you as a manufacturer or processor with national or regional distribution, can place your products in the hands of your distributors without credit risk. The goods remain in the custody of the field warehouse company—an independent and responsible third party—until paid for or until released as provided in delivery instructions worked out with your knowledge and agreement.

In the event of financial difficulties on the part of a distributor, you can reclaim your goods, since you have not relinquished title to them.

When you use field warehousing in this way, the storage agreement covering the transaction is usually *between the distributor and the warehouse company*; however, in some cases currently in operation, manufacturers have entered into a master contract for the servicing of a large number of distributors on a nationwide basis. In any setup, the bonded warehouse personnel is provided by the distributor and the warehouse location is on his premises.

With this procedure, the warehouse receipts covering the stored goods are issued to you, the manufacturer; and you, thereby, retain control over the movement of the inventory as well as title to the goods. When your distributor wants to make a withdrawal against the inventory he may do so by following any one of a number of procedures which are arranged in advance. Some of the releasing procedures now being used at such warehouses are:

Delivery from the warehouses upon receipt by the field warehousing company's bonded representative of distributor's check, certified check, or cashier's check.

Delivery upon receipt by the field warehousing company's bonded representative of distributor's note, trust receipt, trade acceptance, or any other form of commercial paper stipulated in advance by the manufacturer.

Delivery upon receipt by the field warehousing company of an order for warehouse release, executed by authorized officials of the manufacturer.

Delivery upon distributor's request of goods up to a certain dollar-value limit set by the manufacturer—such deliveries being reported to the manufacturer either as made, or at stated intervals.

This particular aspect of field warehousing is extremely flexible and may be utilized in many ways which are advantageous for both the manufacturer and distributor. Three brief real-life examples illustrating this point are described below:

Case I: The Williamson Company,[1] a manufacturer of household appliances, is located in a heavily industrialized community. There is virtually no possibility of plant or warehouse expansion at its plant site. Williamson's business doubled in annual sales volume over a 5-year period, and it became imperative that completed units be moved out of the plant as soon as they came off the assembly lines. This situation was a constant headache. As a solution to the problem, field warehouses were set up on the premises of the company's major distributors, and the finished products were shipped to these locations. The goods were held by the warehouse company for Williamson's account until the normal selling season started. Then they were delivered on an orderly basis to the distributors. Thus, for the necessary holding period, the distributor's premises became an extension of the company's own warehouse. Both sides benefited by the arrangement.

Case II: The Jasmine Co., a young but growing firm of manufacturing chemists, needed a substantial inventory of high-cost raw chemicals. But their financial statement would not support the line of credit needed to place the required amount of goods in their plant. So Jasmine's president arranged with a field warehouse company to receive shipments direct from one of the major oil companies which

[1] All company names have been disguised.

produced the needed raw material. Soon shipments of the chemical were flowing to the warehouse in the necessary amounts. Thereupon, Jasmine was able to manufacture its product in large batches with greatly reduced costs; at the same time, the oil company doubled its sales to this customer.

Case III: The highly seasonal demand for the products of Vorassi and Sons, a building materials company, forced it to increase production during certain times of the year and curtail operations at other times. Vorassi knew that if he could level out production over the entire year, and employ an experienced working force on a permanent basis, a more efficient operation and consequently greater profits could be attained. Vorassi asked his banker for advice on the problem; the banker suggested that the company finance inventories of its products on the premises of distributors, and referred the company to a field warehouse firm. In due course, arrangements were made to field warehouse shipments of building materials on distributor's premises. Currently, company is giving distributors a discount to offset the field warehousing costs, but is gaining the privilege of shipping to them throughout the year. Vorassi can either hold the warehouse receipts as security for the building materials, or discount them at his bank in order to recover immediately the funds invested in the inventory. Or it can be arranged to have the receipts issued to distributor's banks, with the banks making funds available to the distributor.

Cost of field warehousing

A field warehouse company gets its income from the rates and charges set forth in the storage agreement mentioned earlier. Basically it sells a service and is paid by customers who use it. The rates are generally nominal, and are divided into two parts. First, there is usually a fixed yearly charge to cover the cost of locks and signs, bonding the warehouse manager and any assistants, and making periodic audits. Second, the warehouse company charges a monthly rate based on the value of the goods under warehouse receipt. When figured against the total amount of inventory put through the warehouse in any one year, the charges for the field warehouse service rarely amount to more than a fraction of 1 per cent.

Loans of almost any size can be obtained through the medium of field warehousing, but $10,000 is about the minimum amount which is considered economically practical for a warehousing company to handle. An inventory which is placed on the premises of a distributor by a manufacturer should be at about the same value level. In the latter instance, the manufacturer sometimes pays all or a part of the cost of warehousing.

The bank, finance company, or other lending agency which actually makes the loan based on warehouse receipts will make its regular interest charge, normally applying the prevailing interest rate. However, the individual situation, the reputation and business experience of the borrower, the marketability of the commodity, the period of the loan, and the size of the inventory all influence the rate charged by the lender.

Examples of field warehousing at work

Here are typical examples of ways in which manufacturers and distributors can use field warehousing.

Case IV: A large part of the current assets of the American Manufacturing Co. were tied up in its inventory of industrial equipment. The company needed more cash with which to move the goods into industrial channels. American's banker suggested that the company's inventory of raw materials be pledged as security for a loan. American arranged to have a field warehouseman establish a field warehouse at the plant and issue to the bank warehouse receipts for the stored inventory. The bank then made the needed loan to American.

Case V: The Supreme Oil Co. operates a six-tank bulk storage plant. Because of seasonal requirements, it must stock up in the summer for its winter sales, paying for and storing the fuel oil and gasoline far in advance of actual sale to its customers. This strains the company's working capital. As a solution to the problem, the company's banker suggested that its inventories of fuel oil, and gasoline be field warehoused as security for a loan. Subsequently, the services of a field warehouse company were obtained. It leases the storage tanks, controls the inventory in them, and issues warehouse receipts to the bank as security for its loan to Supreme.

Case VI: The Sunnyside Canning Co. operates a vegetable cannery in the Midwest. During the harvest season, Sunnyside has to pay out large cash sums to the farmers in the area, as the produce is delivered to the plant. As the vegetables are canned, they are placed on pallets and moved to the field warehouse which has been installed adjacent to the cannery. Warehouse receipts are issued on each day's pack, taken to the local bank, and a loan obtained on a prearranged basis. In this way, Sunnyside's working capital is kept current, in the face of unusually high seasonal demands. When the season is over, and the merchandise is sold, each carload lot is released from the warehouse by repayment to the bank of that portion of the loan represented by the goods being shipped. By the time a major portion of the cannery's pack has been shipped, the bank's loan has been completely liquidated, and the warehouse operation placed in temporary suspension until the next season.

Commodities commonly field warehoused

To get an idea of the scope of field warehousing and the possibilities lying in it, consider the following partial list of commodities which have been successfully field warehoused:

Agricultural Products

Alfalfa
Butter
Cotton and products
Feeds
Fertilizer
Grains
Hay
Honey
Livestock and by-products
Meals
Oils—edible and essential
Seeds

Appliances

Heaters—oil and gas
Home Freezers
Radios
Ranges
Refrigerators
Stoves
Television sets

Building Materials

Asphalt
Brick
Cement
Fencing
Flooring material
Insulation
Lumber
Nails

Chemical Products

Acids
Chemicals, raw
Drugs
Technical oils

Foods and Beverages

Beer
Canned foods
Cheese
Coffee
Distilled spirits
Eggs
Fish
Frozen foods
Fruit juices
Groceries
Nuts
Preserves
Wines

Fuels and Distillates

Alcohol
Coal
Crude oil
Fuel oils
Gasoline
Lubricating oils

Metals

Aluminum
Brass
Castings
Corrugated iron
Ore concentrates
Pipe
Scrap metal
Sheet and tubing
Steel
Wires

Textiles

Blankets
Clothing
Cotton cloth
Wool-cloth
Wool, raw

Miscellaneous

Agricultural implements
Air conditioning units
Airplane parts
Automobiles
Automobile parts
Bags and bagging
Containers:
  Bottles
  Cans
  Fiber cartons
Electrical equipment
Electronic parts
Engines
Furniture
Glass
Hardware
Machinery
Motors
Paints
Power mowers
Rubber
Tires and tubes
Toys

40. INDUSTRIAL FINANCING— ITS ROLE IN DISTRIBUTION *

Sydney D. Maddock

To me, and, I'm sure, to anyone who thinks about it, this is something of a miracle in the effectiveness of modern processing and distribution. For instance, it hardly seems possible that shrimp taken from the cool deeps 800 miles or more from some Gulf fishing port can show up on the plate of someone a thousand miles inland, a mile above sea level, and still be almost ocean fresh, even though weeks or months may have intervened.

This miracle of modern distribution becomes even more impressive when I trace the journey made by the shrimp from sea to consumer. It isn't a simple journey. To be a successful journey at all it involves nice timing, some intricate meshing of new machines and money. To bring a low-priced package of frozen shrimp to your table means the employment of a good bit of skill and experience and a big outlay of expensive machinery and equipment.

Almost every piece of equipment involved can be—and usually is—financed for the buyer in some way. The use of sound instalment financing makes the distribution of fresh shrimp from ocean to your table more economical and more efficient. To borrow a phrase from the war days: the industrial financing organization is the indispensable man behind the man behind the gun.

Let's use this example of frozen shrimp as a case history and see at how many points its journey is hastened or made more economical and efficient by time-financed equipment.

No more than a decade ago, the average Gulf shrimper was operating profitably with vessels some 50 feet in length, with an 800 gallon fuel capacity and space for maybe 15 tons of ice. The vessel cost about $15,000, on the average. The fishing grounds were nearby —25 to 50 miles from port—and the shrimper could return to base every night: at the most, within the week.

* Reprinted by permission from *Advanced Management*, Vol. 22, No. 1 (February, 1957).

Sydney D. Maddock, President, C.I.T. Corporation, New York.

During the past decade great changes have come to the fishing industry. For one thing, fishermen have been forced to travel to more distant grounds and to take their catches from greater depths, and the development of modern electronic equipment also has added to the expense of competing.

Today a successful shrimper in the Gulf is operating a vessel of 75 feet or more in length, with horsepower up to 200 and more and with fuel capacity of 1,000 to 6,000 gallons. These far-ranging vessels are working hundreds of miles from port and may stay out for many days, in fair weather and foul.

These modern trawlers carry electronic depth recorders that can be used in locating catches. They carry radio compasses, automatic pilots and expensive refrigeration equipment. These vessels cost from $10,000 to $100,000.

Shrimping is profitable for a skilled captain, but few are able to afford cash for vessels in this price range. Even those who can wouldn't want to tie up their capital to such an extent. Money must be employed just as wisely and as skillfully as are men and machines, otherwise profits are curtailed.

So right here, before the average captain even puts to sea, an industrial financing company is able to speed his trip, conserve his capital. With proper financing, geared to his own exact needs, he is able to acquire a modern vessel that will pay for itself as it earns.

Industrial financing companies have for years financed many kinds of income-producing vessels, including fishing vessels. We also finance the installation of machinery and equipment in vessels—new engines, radios, navigational aids, refrigeration equipment.

Usually the terms on a shrimp trawler call for a down payment, with the balance to be paid in three years in equal instalments. Naturally, this is not an invariable rule and contracts on some of the larger boats have been written with terms of five years.

I would like to remark here that one of the important items to be checked in financing a trawler is the experience and skill of the captain. Many of these remarkable men can neither read nor write. In some cases we have furnished them envelopes for each instalment with the amount of each payment written in. I remember one captain who took his envelope to the bank every month, listened while a teller read him the amount of the payment and then casually peeled off $100 bills from a truly astounding roll of cash. The bank would then mail us a draft for the payment. This captain, however, and his fellow captains—regardless of their lack of formal education are men of integrity and great skill. They are excellent credit risks.

An important part of this financing—the major portion of it—is done through the engine dealers or yards. They ordinarily are not so capitalized as to be able to carry large quantities of notes with their own funds. We discount completed transactions for them in order to replenish the dealers' or yards' supply of cash. In helping the yard attain a better profit, of course, this financing also benefits the fisherman, and the benefits extend, step by step, to the ultimate consumer.

When the successful shrimper returns to port with his refrigerated catch, the shrimp must be skillfully unloaded, washed, graded for quality, and headed and graded for size. This was a tedious hand operation until just a few years ago. But today, with a one dollar-an-hour minimum wage, heading and grading is done with a newly-developed machine at a lower cost per barrel.

If the shrimp are to be frozen they must be properly packed for the operation, frozen, glazed, and properly stored at just the right temperature. Perhaps, in addition, the frozen shrimp may be breaded. Close to half of all shrimp production is now going through breading plants. And they must be packaged for the consumer and prepared for shipment.

All in all, whether the shrimp or any other product is to be frozen or canned, or sold fresh, equipment is necessary to maintain quality, avoid waste and increase profits. Proper equipment is becoming more and more important in this type industry and the slower methods of processing and packing by hand are disappearing.

Many of these processing and packing companies are small operations. Proper financing is very important to most of these businessmen if they are to operate efficiently and profitably. They must have the proper machinery and equipment without weakening their working capital position. They are working with highly perishable products that must be processed and packed correctly and quickly.

The important thing to these packers is to obtain terms that are geared to their needs, terms that fit the pattern of their income. So again we find that sound, flexible financing from an industrial financing firm can permit these packers to modernize their operations to increase efficiency and profits, while reducing the price to the consumer.

The terms they can get on equipment vary because there is a wide variety of equipment involved. And there are other variable factors such as the amounts involved and the standing of the buyer. In any event, terms are set that suit the need. On some of the equipment used by these packers, terms may run to 10 years and payments can be geared to the new, faster depreciation allowed under the 1954 tax schedules.

On its trip to the consumer outlets the product will encounter materials handling equipment, one of the biggest categories of equipment financed by our firm. It will travel in refrigerated trucks, probably financed by an industrial finance company. And it will travel over highways built more economically because contractors were able to buy modern construction equipment on long terms geared to depreciation and to their income. Every hour trimmed from this trip by better highways, every factor speeding up the shipment, results in savings to the sellers and to the consumers.

As final steps, the consumer package is placed in a supermarket, safely frozen in a refrigerated display case. When it leaves the market it is checked out over a modern check-out counter and cash register. And here again we have pieces of equipment often financed for the market operator by the industrial firm.

I suspect the percentage of housewives who ever heard of an industrial financing company is a very small fraction of 1 per cent. But all of them—and all of us—have been indirectly affected by this relatively new source of industrial credit. In a competitive economy, the consumer is the beneficiary of any improvement in financing production, processing and distribution.

I have traced just one consumer product. Similar stories could be told of thousands of other products. C.I.T. Corporation alone handles the instalment financing of industrial and professional equipment used in practically every field of endeavor. Growth, particularly since World War II, has been amazing. I must use our own firm as an example, but growth is typical of the entire field. Since the war, C.I.T. Corporation's volume of financing has multiplied several times. In construction equipment, for example, it has more than tripled just in the past five years. And this year, overall volume is running some 60 per cent ahead of the record 1955 level.

Now, something must have been lacking in the sources of credit available to users of machinery and equipment to make such growth possible. Industry, competing for the consumer's dollar, striving for wider distribution of goods, wanted a certain kind of credit. More than anything else, I think, the older credit sources lacked flexibility.

Of course, there have been other factors in the growth of the industrial finance company. We have been aggressive in seeking business. We have offices and field representatives throughout the nation. The economy has been growing rapidly. But mostly we have grown because we have created for machinery users finance plans tailored to their precise needs. We have created finance plans for individual manufacturers and distributors—plans that have given them powerful new sales tools.

There are, actually, only a few basic ways a buyer can pay for machinery or equipment, whether it's a shrimp trawler, a fork-life truck, a dairy or a bakery or a giant earth-mover. He can pay cash. He can get a short-term bank loan. He can arrange a capital issue. He can get limited credit from the manufacturer or distributor of the equipment. Or he can use an industrial financing company.

A straight cash purchase, often thought of as the cheapest way to buy, can be the most expensive. A cash purchase can be ruinous when it depletes working capital and the buyer later has to pass up favorable cash purchases of inventory or winds up short of operating funds to meet regular or unforeseen demands.

Generally, a bank loan is used for working capital loans rather than for the purchase of equipment. The usual term is too short for any substantial purchase. Also, the use of bank credit for machinery purchases draws down the borrower's open line of credit, which should be kept for current requirements. And, in addition, it is hazardous to fund capital requirements so that the borrower is dependent on short-term renewals.

There are also certain advantages and disadvantages in the financing of capital investment by bonds, debentures, preferred or common stock. Usually, machinery and equipment purchases do not involve amounts large enough to make this form of financing economical. The smaller the amount involved, the higher the coupon or dividend rate will be. And the larger the underwriting commissions and expenses will be in proportion to the money obtained. Total financing expenses of a small issue may amount to 10 or 15 per cent, or more, of the amount of net proceeds.

The next source—credit from the manufacturer or distributor of the equipment—is sometimes used when equipment purchases are in limited amounts. However, manufacturers and distributors generally feel that it is not their function to serve as banker for their customers. Many can't afford to. Many others don't want to be burdened with the necessary credit-checking and bookkeeping. Most of them are turning all credit sales over to industrial financing firms. And an increasing number of buyers are turning to the financing firms on their own. This is particularly true when they want to buy from several sources and pay for all the purchases on one contract.

The usual instalment deal is a simple conditional sales contract. Buyer furnishes the seller, or the finance firm, with the details of the proposed purchase and gives him the customary financial data about himself or his company. When his credit is cleared, he makes a downpayment and completes the documents provided by the industrial finance company. The financing company pays the seller the balance due on the equipment. The buyer subsequently makes monthly payments to the financing firm.

The cost of the financing varies and terms vary to suit the individual situation. Sometimes monthly payments are skipped altogether during off-seasons—such as the winter months for payments on soft drink vending machines or slack seasons on canning and packaging machinery.

Earlier, I mentioned that some instalment contracts gear the payments to the new depreciation schedules. That is, payments are larger in the early years when depreciation allowances are large and taper off as depreciation allowances taper off in later years. In effect, the buyer pays for his new equipment by means of its own depreciation, without digging deeply into his working capital.

This type of financing—called Pay-As-You-Depreciate financing—was developed by C.I.T. to permit buyers to take advantage of the faster depreciation schedules. It answers just about all the needs of a machinery buyer and I consider it one of the most important developments ever made in industrial financing.

Under this kind of plan, the purchaser can pay for new machinery at substantially the same rate it can be depreciated instead of in equal monthly instalments. This makes the relationship between his depreciation reserves and expenditures for capital equipment much more realistic.

Terms on this type of financing generally are longer, stretched out to more nearly match the depreciable life of most machinery. Ten years on machine tools, bakery equipment, textile machinery, packaging machinery, printing and wood-working machinery and dairy equipment. Six to eight years on lift trucks. Six years on construction equipment and so on.

This financing program has been an important factor in the conduct of many an industrial firm. It is designed strictly for industry and some of the professions and bears no relation to consumer instalment credit. In fact, most consumers never heard of industrial financing firms. But, as I pointed out earlier, in a competitive economy any improvement in the methods of production and distribution of goods benefits the consumer brings him a higher standard of living at a lower cost.

The use of industrial instalment credit, to be sure, benefits the consumer indirectly; he is the beneficiary once removed. The first benefits go to the sellers and buyers of the machinery used to create consumer goods.

Now what are these benefits exactly? What does proper financing do for industry that makes it possible for industry to pass along better products and better services to the nation's consumers?

Flexible instalment financing helps the buyer of machinery and equipment because: it gives him longer, more realistic terms; it adjusts his payments for the equipment to the pattern of his income; it preserves his working capital and improves his financial statement; and it provides him with a reliable new source of credit; it helps him modernize to maintain his competitive position.

Sound instalment financing benefits the distributor, the seller of equipment because: it frees his salesmen from time-consuming credit and collection jobs and makes that time available for customer coverage; it improves customer relations; it makes more sales and larger sales; it turns all sales into cash for the seller and frees him of credit responsibility; it frees bank lines for inventory and operating uses; and it gives him the benefit of help from a national organization familiar with his field and his customers.

These benefits speed the distribution of goods just as the invention of a new conveyor system or machine tool makes life fuller and more enjoyable for the average American family.

But a new lathe or drill that will improve automobiles or electric fans, tractors or television, cannot improve anything until it has been put to work. A new process for packing food or paving highways or displaying merchandise will bring no benefits to anyone until the equipment necessary is produced, sold and put to work.

I like to believe that the role of the industrial financing company in helping men put these machines to work has been an important role in the development of our unprecedented standard of living. Being able to enjoy a fresh shrimp cocktail in Wichita or Denver may not be very important. But the story of how it became possible is important. And it's indicative of our growing economy. It illustrates how the fantasic growth of industrial instalment financing is influencing American business.

Most important to me is the fact that the industrial finance company is still a virtual infant. It has just begun to grow. "What is past is prologue."

41. FLOOR PLANNING *

Floor planning—the industry's term for wholesale financing—is big business, but it has never been looked upon as a major source of profit for sales finance companies. Without proper controls and with the greater amounts of money involved, wholesale financing presents an opportunity for larger individual losses than any other type of financing.

Actually floor planning is the basic foundation of the sales finance industry and provides benefits for both the dealer and his financing source. It is the final component of the complete financing service given the dealer in exchange for his retail business. It permits him to have an adequate stock of goods on hand for maximum selling effort, and because of the close alliance between company and the dealer, the sales finance company can act as an advisor and counsellor to the dealer.

Wholesale financing as it is done today really began with the start of mass production in the automobile industry. The limited financial resources of the early manufacturers made it essential for them to operate on a cash basis—and few dealers had money enough for any quantity of stock. Without wholesale financing they would have had to operate on a hand-to-mouth basis. Sales finance companies, however, solved the dealers' problem by paying the factory in cash for the needed inventory. The entire concept and procedure of floor planning has been developed, polished and simplified throughout the years, but the end result is still the same. The automobile industry still operates on a cash basis: cars come off the assembly line scheduled for delivery to dealers—and almost simultaneously they are paid for *by* the sales finance company *for* the dealer who ordered them.

In a typical wholesale arrangement for new automobiles, the dealer signs an application for floor plan accommodation which outlines the rights and the obligations of both the dealer and the sales

* Reprinted by permission of *Time Sales Financing*, Vol. 24, No. 1 (January-February, 1960), p. 3.

finance company. He also signs a document which authorizes the finance company to buy cars for him at the factory and sign the necessary papers (usually Trust Receipts) for him. This wholesale plan, pretty well standardized throughout the auto industry, provides a low cost, valuable financing service for dealers—and with maximum simplicity.

With some minor variations, this is pretty much the same procedure for the wholesale financing of appliances, boats, mobile homes, and other big ticket items floor planned by sales finance companies for their dealers.

Vital Need for Wholesale Credit

The vital need for flooring credit has increased steadily with the ever-expanding model lines of manufacturers. Whether they are shopping for cars, appliances or other major items, consumers expect to see a wide variety of styles, sizes and models from which to choose. Obviously dealers of some of today's products couldn't possibly display all of the variations in a line—but they still need a workable representative selection for a proper sales position. A Ford dealer in 1960 for instance, would need to show 41 cars to display one of each model in each of his lines. It would take 572 cars to have one sample of each with variations of optional equipment. Project this to include all of the possible combinations of colors and equipment, and his inventory would run well over 10,000. (In prewar days the entire line included only some half dozen models, six or seven colors—no two tones—one engine—one transmission, and so on.)

Automobile manufacturers today conduct extensive research based on dealers' experience records, 10-day dealer reports, purchase registrations, etc., and say they can accurately estimate the proper size and mix of inventory best suited to each dealership. For production planning they prefer to have dealers place basic stock orders regularly for inventory needs for perhaps 45 to 60 days ahead. Many finance companies, however, feel that a dealer's new car inventory should not exceed a 45-day supply based upon his current rate; and in areas where deliveries can be quickly made, a 20 to 30 day supply is sufficient.

How Much Wholesale Credit?

Some finance companies have set up a credit committee to determine the amount of wholesale credit to be extended to dealers. A number of factors are taken in consideration in establishing the dealer's line of credit: his rate of travel (turn-over); his investment; his character and his experience in the business; his profit potential.

A credit line equal to the 100 percent wholesale cost of a 45-day inventory is almost a standard today. In any event, finance companies rarely extend wholesale credit lines greater than two to two-and-one-half times the dealer's net worth.

An automobile manufacturer asked for his opinion on the amount of wholesale credit that should be extended in the best interests of the dealer and the finance company suggested the finance company base its credit extensions on the following: First, an estimate of the day's supply needed (considering the size of the dealership, distance from the factory, and amount of fleet business); second, the number of models the dealer is stocking and plans to stock, and then relate this to the dealer's sales experience record as well as his net worth.

Floor planning only supplements the dealer's cash requirements for his operation and he, of course, should have capital of his own invested.

Larger sums of money may be extended by sales finance companies for dealers' wholesale requirements than for retail financing, during the relatively brief periods of inventory buildup such as at the beginning of a new model year. However, because wholesale notes are scheduled to be paid off within six to eight weeks, more money is outstanding in retail instalment contracts, which may run from two to three years in the case of automobiles, to five to seven years for mobile homes. In many sales finance companies the normal ratio of retail outstandings to wholesale runs from about six or eight to one.

Rates for Wholesale

Automobiles—new

In automobile floor planning the financing institution pays the manufacturer for the dealer's supply of cars as soon as they are shipped. This credit is extended to the dealer for an initial period of three months—with the provision, of course, that each car as it is sold is immediately paid for by the dealer.

Insurance—fire, theft, and limited in-transit coverage—is provided for each car. Frequently this is handled by the finance company, however, many dealers provide their own insurance with appropriate loss payable clauses. Coverage is from the time of shipment until the car is sold at retail. If any cars remain unsold at the end of the first

90-day period, credit is usually renewed for another 90 days with another flat charge and continuing daily interest charges. If there is any renewal or extension beyond this first six months period, the finance company usually requires a substantial reduction—generally 10 percent—each month.

Over the years, rates for automobile wholesale financing were gradually lowered and fees became fairly well standardized. Usually the fee is composed of two parts—a flat charge and a percent per annum charge. By 1951 many financing institutions were charging a flat rate of one-eighth of one percent plus a 4 percent per year charge for the actual days involved. The flat charge varied sometimes: some companies waived the flat charge; some charged $1 for the first 90 days, and nothing for renewal, while others charged $1 for the first 90 days and $1 for each succeeding 90 days or portion thereof. In recent years because of the tight money market, floor plan rates have been slowly keeping pace with rising interest costs. Last September after the prime rate was raised to 5 percent—a 28-year high—many sales finance companies found it necessary to increase floor plan rates one-half of one percent. The new rate in most cases became 5½ percent.

At the same time one realistic bank has urged bank wholesale financing departments to re-appraise their wholesale financing rates:

"Wholesale financing does not warrant a prime rate and bankers should be realistic and at least equal the rate charged by sales finance companies. With the amounts involved, the risk, the cost of accounting, and periodic audits, a low rate or a prime rate is not realistic even though retail paper is obtained because of this accommodation. If retail instalment paper is subsidizing the wholesale accommodation, then you must consider this as a cost of acquisition. There is no better time than now to make sure that your charges are competitive and are such that you can continue to render at a profit, an Instalment Financing Service needed by the customers in your community.

"It is ironical, when we consider that most bankers are conscious at all times of the net yield received on their bond portfolios down to the last 32nd but have no idea of their net yields on instalment credit which they extend every day."

An article in a trade paper announcing this increase in flooring credit rates added that according to a recent study, changes in floor plan charges have little effect on the cost of the individual cars, even if the increases are passed on to the buyer since, the study showed, "an increase of one-half of one percent in the floor plan charge would cost the dealer an average of $1.68 per new car sold."

Used cars

Rates for floor planning for used car dealers are higher and no insurance coverage is furnished by the financing institution. Credit advances are not as large as for new cars and are rarely permitted in excess of a figure well under that listed in the standard used car books. Maximum extensions will probably be 50 percent of the high value listed in the book, or 90 percent of the low book-value.

Appliance wholesale rates

Appliance merchandising differs from that of automobiles in that usually the appliance manufacturer works through his national (but often independent) distributing organization, and it is the distributor who works with the dealer. Financing institutions floor planning for appliance dealers have little contact with the factory, but cooperate closely with the distributor.

Wholesale financing rates for appliances run about 2 to 2½ percent. As in automobile wholesale, the fee is usually composed of two parts: a flat charge of one percent plus a one-half of one percent for 90 days. Often too, there is a minimum charge for each Trust Receipt or wholesale mortgage. Maturity of initial credit is 90 days and normally an extension is permitted. This may be for another 90 days after a 10 percent curtailment for the remaining appliances plus one percent per month extension charge, or there may be three 30-day renewals with three 10 percent reductions. All-risk insurance on unpaid units on the dealer's floor is normally provided by the finance company from the wholesale fees.

Another variation in handling this type of wholesale paper is that frequently national appliance manufacturers will absorb their dealers' floor plan costs—sometimes entirely, sometimes in cooperation with the distributor.

Further, some of the manufacturers have developed plans to make flooring more attractive to the financing institution. These range from a purchase agreement on wholesale, to a guarantee on wholesale and perhaps partial guarantee on retail. Some sales finance companies insist on a repurchase agreement with the distributor and manufacturer on wholesale. Others prefer not to have such an agreement in order to have greater flexibility in working with the dealers.

Marine wholesale

Floor planning of dealers handling marine equipment is a somewhat more recent development than the other types of paper mentioned. In fact manufacturers claim it is inadequate in many areas and therefore handicapping retail marketing. For this reason some of them are working with local financing institutions and offering repurchase agreements to encourage more wholesale credit for their dealers. A few larger firms are providing direct dealer financing from the factory.

Seasonal Needs

Boats and marine equipment are a more seasonal type of inventory than other consumer durables. Yet dealers need adequate stocks for consumer selection in peak selling seasons; off-season sales are unusually slow.

A recent sampling of independent finance companies handling marine instalment sales contracts revealed that 73 percent of them are extending wholesale credit to the dealer. Security instruments can be either a trust receipt or chattel mortgage depending upon the legal restriction of the state involved. In some cases both are used.

The majority of companies extend wholesale credit to cover 90 percent of the factory cost. Reduction schedules are similar to those for mobile homes, requiring 10 percent reduction at the end of 60 or 90 days with 10 percent each 60 or 90 days thereafter, and full payment, in most cases, at the end of 180 days.

Thomas E. Courtney, president of the Northern Illinois Corp., of DeKalb, which handles quite a bit of marine floor planning says: "We floor plan new boats from the manufacturer to the established agencies in the same manner we handle cars, but boats are expected to be cleaned up by September. Occasionally we permit a good volume dealer to carry boats over the winter with an additional down payment in October, November and December. However, this practice is discouraged and the few exceptions have been good volume dealers."

Mobile home wholesale

Because of the relatively high unit cost, lengthy terms, and some bank restrictions on borrowing leveled against firms handling mobile home paper, sales finance companies generally did not get into this type of financing as early as banks. The importance of their participation today, however, is reflected in these statistics from the 8th annual (1959) report on Consumer Financing of Mobile Homes, compiled by the Mobile Home Manufacturers Association.

Some $274,809,586 worth of mobile home paper was held by 35 reporting sales finance companies; at the same time, 241 banks held only $218,316,034. Further the 35 companies held 92,112 retail contracts, while the 241 banks held only 87,225 contracts. (The report was estimated as covering 40 percent of the outstanding paper.)

Mobile home floor planning is similar to automobile wholesaling in that the financing institution pays the manufacturer and holds legal title to the homes on display until the dealer pays the finance company as the models are sold. One difference, however, is that some mobile home manufacturers, like some appliance manufacturers, provide a repurchase agreement.

Floor planning usually covers 90 percent of the factory cost (which sometimes includes the freight). If used models are floor planned, credit is generally extended for 75 percent of the price listed in the official Mobile Home Market Report. Inventory turnover is encouraged by requiring curtailments at 60 or 90 days and every 30 days thereafter, until final cleanup at 180 days. Because of the high unit cost the number of models dealers have on display is generally somewhat limited.

Some finance companies recommend that the amount of wholesale credit extended to the mobile home dealer be based on the amount of his working capital. However, the amount should be large enough to adequately cover the dealer's needs and avoid the possibility of his obtaining floor planning from more than one lending source—a special hazard in this type of paper.

Mobile home financing is a specialized field and thorough investigation of the dealer is vital. Unlike auto dealers, the trailer dealer is not ordinarily required to invest substantial sums in physical properties, sales rooms, parts departments etc., in order to obtain a franchise. Since it is thus comparatively easy to obtain a mobile home dealership, the investigation of the dealer, his experience, background, financial condition, and character, must be very thorough and accurate. One sales finance company handling mobile home floor planning, recommends a close scrutiny of the notes receivables when checking the dealer's balance sheet, since they might be down payment notes.

A sampling of 20 AFC member companies floor planning mobile homes shows that the lowest percentage of advance is 80 percent, the highest, 100 percent; some plans are secured by trust receipt, some by chattel mortgage, and some by a combination of both.

The most common reduction schedule reported by AFC members was 10 percent—90 days and the balance in full in six months. Financing rates reported ranged from 5 to 7 percent with six percent the most common. Some of the firms reported using a flat charge plus the percentage. Combination plans include 6 percent per year plus a flat charge of 1/8 of one percent; 6 percent plus a $5 to $20 flat charge; and $10.00 flat charge plus 5 percent.

A 1958 survey of 74 banks handling mobile home wholesale revealed that while none of them were floor planning 100 percent of factory cost, most of them handled 90 percent. Fifty-one percent did not require a manufacturer's repurchase agreement, but those banks which were carrying a large volume of such paper did require the agreement. Original maturity terms of 90 days were reported by 55 percent of the banks and 63 percent reported they required a 10 percent curtailment for extension. Almost all listed 180 days from date of original note for maximum maturity.

The Risk Element in Wholesale

The risk element in wholesale financing stems of course from the large sums of money involved and the liquid nature of the receivables.

The periodic audit or floor plan check is a costly item in wholesaling but a vital factor in preventing losses. Equally important is the selection of the dealer to whom wholesale credit is granted. A thorough and careful investigation of the dealer is an absolute "must." And Ernest A. Thompsen, executive vice president of Securities Acceptance Corp., Omaha, advises giving a second, and hard look at the dealer who takes the initiative and offers the finance company his business. It need not mean that he is unworthy of credit, or that he is finding it difficult to obtain flooring credit—but it is *not* the usual procedure.

Investigation of a dealer usually covers three areas—his financial condition, business experience record and his character. E. L. Maffett, executive vice president of A.S.C. Corp., Marion, Ind., has described procedures used by his firm in selecting dealers for wholesale financing:

First A.S.C. provides the dealer with an application form that includes his current balance sheet as well as figures for his sales, gross profit, overhead and net profit for the current and two previous years; names of banks and bankers he deals with; salary and drawing accounts of the dealership principals; a breakdown of the valuation of used cars shown on the balance sheet by year model and make. Other companies also insist on the dealer's furnishing them with the factory-approved forms including operating results for the year past, and on the dealer's supplying an aging of his receivables and payables.

The signed application is then *mailed* to A.S.C.'s credit department. Maffett says A.S.C. managers are not permitted to assist the dealer in preparation of the application.

The existence of mortgages, tax liens, suits, etc. are determined by a check of the county records.

Speaking of the dealer's business experience, Maffett says that his company's highest casualty experience has come from auto dealers who started with insufficient working capital and who lacked adequate experience in the management of an automobile business.

The character investigation is *always* made by independent, outside agencies. However, thorough investigation in local circles—the rumor mill—is also extremely important.

Maffett points out that obviously if any other financing institution has provided, or is providing wholesale, contact should be established to determine the amount outstanding as well as their experience. Also the name of that firm together with the name of the dealer should be on the payoff check.

Sometimes a new car dealer feels he needs additional working capital and requests his financing source to floor plan his used cars. While some finance companies feel a proof of assignment on the title and cancellation of any prior lien is required, most do not since they hold title to the used cars.

Wholesale credit should never be granted by two financing institutions to the same auto dealer without a clear understanding between the two financing agencies—and with no overlapping on the type of units each one finances. Many sales finance companies which provide floor planning for dealers with multiple lines feel that the proper approach is for them to allocate the wholesale credit by the different lines. A continuous check of the filing of statements of trust receipt financing at the office of that state's secretary will show whether a dealer has approached another financing agent for floor planning, Maffett says.

Every grantor of wholesale credit depends on a system of floor checks or periodic inventory audit to guard against dealer-default. Frequency of the check depends upon the financing agency's appraisal of the individual dealer—and no dealer should ever object to this necessary policing of wholesale outstandings.

Customarily a representative of the finance company visits the dealer's place of business once or twice a month to locate, inspect and personally verify the numbers—serial and/or motor—of every unit on hand, checking it against his master list of floor planned merchandise. (Flooring credit is rarely granted for any merchandise unless the individual unit is identifiable by permanently affixed serial numbers.) Of utmost importance, too, is a complete report on the physical condition of each item under floor plan.

Probably more material has been published on the procedures of floor checking than on any other phase of wholesale financing. Yet in spite of observing all the recommended precautions—varying the times of audit and identity of the checker; tracking down and verifying the numbers on every unit on the same day no matter *where* some may have been moved; examining titles; verifying names, addresses and dates of recent sales—finance companies still suffer periodic losses.

Perhaps one of the most unusual cases of a dealer coverup was that of the appliance dealer with a wonderful memory. A lax checker permitted this dealer to read numbers aloud from units, and he would read in order from the list a missing number to the dealer. Few dealers have as excellent a memory as this one, fortunately, for he was able to remember—and "read"—the missing numbers later in the audit from units which had been checked earlier. So in auditing floor planned units, *nothing* must be taken for granted and *nothing* left to chance.

Wayne D. Whiteman, vice president of the discount division of General Finance Corp., sums it up succinctly:

"The extension of wholesale credit is a very valuable tool for securing retail business—but eternal vigilance is the price of handling it successfully."

SECTION 4. COMMODITY MARKETING

The marketing of industrial and agricultural products comprises a crucially important segment of the nation's economy.

Section 4-A
Industrial Marketing

Industrial goods and services are sold to business and institutional buyers for use in their operations of these markets. The business firms within the manufacturing group represent the most important class of buyers. The United States Census of Manufacturers of 1958 reported about 327,000 manufacturing establishments.

Francis E. Hummel stimulates thinking on marketing research in the machine tool industry in his article, "Market Potentials in the Machine Tool Industry—A Case Study."

S. George Walters, Morris L. Sweet and Max D. Snider explore the impact of interurbia on industrial marketing in their article, "When Industry Moves To Interurbia."

Some 8,500 manufacturers' agents perform a vital role in the marketing of industrial and capital goods; yet too little is known about their operations. This gap in marketing knowledge is filled by the results of Dr. Stuart W. McFarland's survey, which are provided in his article, "Manufacturers' Agents."

Section 4-B
Agricultural Marketing

From a marketing standpoint an important characteristic of farm products is that they are produced on a small scale and must be concentrated to be marketed. This concentration process necessitates large numbers of middlemen.

Holbrook Working in his article, "Whose Markets?," evaluates recent occurrences in futures trading in wheat at Kansas City to answer the questions as to why futures trading exists and what groups are chiefly served by a futures market.

In "The Farmer and the Food Industries," Herrell DeGraff challenges Engel's Law on food expenditures. He points out that our economy has changed in ways that Engel or few others could hardly have foreseen. Two factors—the upgrading of diet and the increase in services built into a unit of food—have greatly expanded the food market in recent years.

Joseph G. Knapp poses the question "Are Cooperatives Good Business?," concluding that the cooperative form of enterprise both complements and supplements the services performed by other forms of private business, thus giving our system even greater flexibility and strength.

42. MARKET POTENTIALS IN THE MACHINE TOOL INDUSTRY—A CASE STUDY *

Francis E. Hummel

The purpose of this article is to stimulate thinking on marketing research in the machine tool industry by describing the approach used by the Bryant Chucking Grinder Company of Springfield, Vermont, in establishing a market potential for its line of machine tools.

Machine tools

Machine tools are the power-driven machines which cut or press metal into the forms desired. There are over two hundred types, each manufactured in a variety of sizes with different work or tool-holding attachments. The major groups of machine tools are drilling and boring machines, grinding machines, turning machines (including lathes), milling machines, planers and presses (including shears and forging machines). The major feature of the machine tool is the precision with which it can remove or form metal, with dimensional limits of error frequently measured in one-tenth of one-thousandth of an inch or less. This precision allows the industry to work with interchangeable parts and also makes possible the manufacture of the intricate mechanisms of our modern technology.[1]

Need for establishment of market potentials

The establishment of market potentials for each state and industrial area in the country is a prerequisite for sound selling in the machine tool industry. Market potentials can be used for a wide variety of purposes. The major uses are to:

1. Determine the areas of greatest potential for direct coverage by company salesmen for these areas.
2. Determine the number of salesmen needed to cover the field adequately.
3. Determine the boundaries of sales territories and districts.

* From *The Journal of Marketing*, Vol. XIX, No. 1 (July, 1954), pp. 34-41. Reprinted with permission from *The Journal of Marketing*, published quarterly by the American Marketing Association.

Francis E. Hummel, Manager of Marketing, Bassick Company, a Division of Stewart-Warner Corporation.

[1] See "Machine Tools Today" (Cleveland, Ohio: National Machine Tool Builders' Association, 1953).

4. Establish quotas for salesmen and districts.
5. Check advertising coverage.

Factors making market for machine tools

In establishing a market potential for any product, one must first consider all the factors which make a market for that product. There are a number of basic reasons why metalworking shops purchase machine tools:

1. To expand present production.
2. To manufacture a new product.
3. To reduce manufacturing costs by replacing present equipment with machines of new design.
4. To secure increased output per man-hour or higher standards of quality of product, or both.
5. To use because of a change in manufacturing methods.

These factors permit the inference that the market for machine tools includes:

1. Companies which do metalworking manufacturing and can utilize the equipment in question.
2. Companies seeing a need to utilize this equipment for regular production and/or as a tool room machine.[2] (Such needs are to increase output, reduce costs, etc. as indicated in the previous listing.)
3. Companies with sufficient funds to purchase new machines.[3]
4. Companies with a willingness to invest in new equipment.

In developing a market index for machine tools, one must consider all of these factors.

Problems in establishing market potentials

There are a number of special problems encountered in establishing market potentials for machine tools. The major problem arises because the industry experiences a widely fluctuating demand for its products and is affected measurably by defense appropriations and general business conditions. The cyclical sales fluctuations of machine tool manufacturers have historically been much higher in times of prosperity and lower in times of depression than those of most industry in the United States. The basic reasons for this widely

[2] These groups include those who need machine tools for their tool rooms. Accurate machines there are indispensable to metalworking manufacturing.

[3] Purchase through outright sale, chattel mortgage, or lease agreement.

fluctuating sales volume are: (1) the nature of the product—the product is high priced and is susceptible to long life through maintenance and repairs;[4] (2) the demand is derived from the demand for capital goods and for consumer goods—thus, buyers may postpone or accelerate their purchases of machine tools according to the outlook for their profitable use; (3) in recent years the defense and war efforts have created an additional strain upon the industry—during World War II, the industry expanded its dollar output considerably, only to fall back to extremely low levels between 1946 and 1949, owing in large degree to government sales of surplus equipment. After 1949, it experienced another great expansion due to the Korean situation. For example, the industry figures for metal-cutting machine tool shipments covering selected years of this period are:

1939	$ 200,000,000[5]
1942	1,320,000,000
1947	306,000,000
1952	1,125,000,000

(4) The depreciation policies established by the Bureau of Internal Revenue for taxation purposes—most companies are required to depreciate their equipment over long periods of time, even though these small depreciation allowances do not provide sufficient funds so that the companies can reinvest in new and improved machinery in the short run. In addition, the government did allow accelerated depreciation for tax purposes for the defense emergency but only to companies who secured "Certificates of Necessity." These factors have combined to create widely fluctuating sales volumes for the manufacturers in the machine tool industry.

Secondly, technological developments in machine tools and new processing methods of manufacturing metal are constantly occurring. This means that one is dealing with both a product and a market with change over time. The result is that one must follow these changing conditions and anticipate future developments in order to establish accurate market potentials.

Thirdly, one is dealing with relatively small numbers of customers and units, which makes the degree of error of any statistical findings large. The problem encountered is that, since a small number of units account for the total sales volume, the decision to purchase or not to purchase by one or a few large customers will vitally affect the results obtained. For example, in 1947 one customer accounted for

[4] Although it may be obsolete from a production or tolerance standpoint.
[5] Source—National Machine Tool Builders' Association.

26.9 per cent of Bryant's domestic output. This high percentage of sales made to one company was due to the small total number of units of new machines which were sold.

Fourthly, there is a lack of complete, current statistical data for measuring all the factors which theoretically affect the market for machine tools.

Method of Establishing Market Potentials by Bryant

In establishing market potentials for Bryant's precision internal grinding machines and precision boring machines, the following steps were taken:

1. Product list and industry classification

A list of products which could be manufactured on each machine under study was developed—separate lists of parts for both grinding and boring machines. This list was gathered from a review of job specifications on which past quotations and sales had been made by the company and from consultations with the company's sales and engineering executives. These product lists were then classified by industries and the U. S. Standard Industrial Classification numbers placed on each item. For example, one product finished on Bryant Internal Grinders is "raceways—industry, ball and roller bearings," classification number 3593.

2. Collection of basic data

The next step was to determine and collect basic data which could be used to measure the market for the foregoing types of machines. Each type of machine required a separate analysis of the market conditions affecting its purchase because it is used in part by different segments of the metalworking industry and because of different metalworking manufacturing methods used by the various industries.

Some of the basic data which were examined in studying the potential market for internal grinding and boring machines were:

A. Number and Size of Metalworking Plants Using above Equipment. This was the basic information needed—data on the number and size of metal working plants in the various industries which use grinding and boring machines were collected for each state and industrial area. This information pointed up the geographical location of the markets for these machines. An approximation of the size of these markets was made for each area by examining for each industry the number of production workers employed.

Some of the major sources of data used were: *U. S. Census of Manufacturers,* 1947; *Annual Survey of Manufacturers,* Bureau of Census, 1951, 1950, 1949; *Basic Marketing Data, Iron Age,* 1953; *County Business Patterns* (based on Social Security Reports), U. S. Department of Commerce, 1951; *Analysis of U. S. Metalworking,* Steel, 1952; *Market Data Book,* McGraw-Hill Publishing Company, 1949.

B. Need for New Original Equipment. An attempt was made to estimate the amount of new boring and grinding machines each industry would need in the period ahead because of increased business activity. A separate economic analysis was made for each major industry in which these machine tools are used in order to determine business trends and new technological developments in metalworking manufacturing. The object was to evaluate possible industry rates of business and capital expansion and to estimate the resulting effects on the sales of the boring and grinding machines. In this connection, correlations of past Bryant sales with business conditions and capital expenditures by industries were helpful in projection for the future. Of course, a major limitation to this analysis is that the past historical relationships may not apply to the future. Also, published data such as *Business' Plants and Equipment 1953-56,* McGraw-Hill Publishing Company, were helpful in attempting to evaluate future overall capital expansion programs.

C. Need for Replacement Equipment. An attempt was also made to estimate the amount of new boring and grinding machines each industry would need in the period ahead to replace old or obsolete equipment. Measures of the amount of obsolete boring and grinding machines held by the various metalworking industries were estimated from American Machinist's *Inventory of Metalworking Production Equipment,* November, 1953, which lists the number and age of these and other machine tools by major industries. In addition, there were field reports by Bryant salesmen covering a number of specific potential customers who had stated their replacement policies and programs. The above data were analyzed and an approximation made by industries for future replacement rates of boring and grinding machines.

D. Funds for New Equipment. Additional data were needed to obtain some measure of the relative industries' willingness to invest in new production equipment, since there is a large difference in the amount of funds available for the purchase of machine tools by the various industries. A number of sources of information were used to give partial indications along these lines, such as: (1) U. S. census statistics on value added by manufacture and expenditures for new machinery and equipment classified by industries, (2) capital ratings of a sampling of various firms, (3) information from sales force, and (4) future predictions of capital expenditures of business as published by the Department of Commerce and McGraw-Hill.

In addition, it was decided to include in the final calculation of the market index only concerns employing over fifty production workers, on the theory that companies employing less than this number of employees would not be likely to need these special production tools and would not spend the money for new machines even if they had such a need.

3. Calculation of index

The third step was to determine the best method of calculating the market index. Decisions were necessary regarding the type of index and the weighting to be used.

A. USE OF SINGLE INDEX. The first question was whether a single or multiple index should be used. A single index means using one set of data weighted by industry importance; a multiple index means combining two or more series of weighted data by industries.

For a single index, the common practice in establishing industrial goods market potentials is to use the number of production workers as the statistical series of data on the theory that industrial purchases within an industry vary approximately in relation to the size of the companies as measured by the number of workers they employ. If this is done, one must then attach subjectively weights to the various industries to take into consideration the factors of usage and need for the new equipment, along with sufficiency of funds and willingness to spend these funds for new equipment. The resulting effect is that the conclusions can be only as accurate as the judgment used in establishing such weights.

In using a multiple index, a number of statistical series should be used in an attempt to incorporate all or most of the factors which make a market for the particular machine tool under question. For example, the researcher might examine the following data by industries for their relevance in developing a multiple index:

1. Metalworking companies—number of plants and/or number of production workers.

2. Funds—either value added by manufacture or capital ratings.
3. Willingness to spend—past expenditures for new machines and equipment.

Naturally, the above data do not consider the usage and need for new equipment or the application of available funds for the *particular* machine tools under study. Therefore, these factors must be included by subjectively attaching weights to each industry, and then combining the above data into one index. In order to combine the various series, one must also weight each of the series in relation to one another.

After considerable experimentation with single and multiple indexes as applied to Bryant's grinding and boring machines, it was concluded that, because these machines were largely single-purpose tools,[6] a single index should be used in order to relate properly the importance in usage, need and availability of funds for a few industries which could not be measured by combining statistical series. The number of production workers was chosen as the series of data to be used.

B. ATTACHING WEIGHTS TO INDUSTRIES. In the case of both a single and multiple index, weights must be attached to the various industries constituting markets. These weights must be established for each industry in order to consider properly the differences in usage of the machines under study by the various industries, in addition to considering the other factors which affect the market for these machine tools in the various segments of the metalworking market.

A subjective judgment method was used in arriving at weights. These weights reflected the combined judgment of a number of individuals within the company's departments of sales, engineering and research. For example, in applying this judgment, some of the following factors considered were:

1. The amount of use each industry has for internal grinders and precision boring machines. For example, manufacturers of sewing machines have much less use for internal grinders than do manufacturers of aircraft engines because of the nature of the product and materials used.
2. The trend in general business conditions and the resulting effects on each industry's need for new equipment. The eco-

[6] Engineered and designed to preform specific operations on long production runs in contrast to general purpose tools designed to do multiple operations on a variety of parts in relatively short production runs.

nomic analysis previously referred to was useful here. For example, it was estimated that the proportion of internal grinding machines going to the automotive industry would increase in 1954 due to the trend toward more power steering and automatic transmissions.

3. The effect of the defense program on industrial purchases and governmental purchases of machine tools for stock piling. For example, assuming that the future will bring no new "hot" war, the proportion of machines sold for tank production was estimated for 1954 to be considerably lower than in the previous two years.
4. The capacities of one's machines in relation to competitors' machines. For example, it was estimated that Bryant internal grinders would find an increasing market in the ball bearing industry due to technological developments in machine design.
5. The sufficiency of funds and willingness to spend these funds for new equipment. The analysis along these lines previously referred to was useful in determining the relative differences among industries with regard to capital expenditures. For example, the McGraw-Hill study of *Business Plans for New Plants and Equipment, 1953-1956* stated that the biggest expansion in capacity "is planned in the electrical machinery, transportation equipment, and chemical industries. Automobile and machinery makers expect to expand faster than the average of all industry over the long pull, 1953-1956."

Thus weights were applied to each industry by considering the factors which affect the future sales of machine tools to them. These weights were attached by combined judgment of a number of individuals in the firm who were in a position to visualize the problems involved.

Consideration was also given to two other methods of arriving at a weighting system for various industries. One possibility would be to use a sample survey approach among the industries under study—a survey to discover what machines are held, their condition, and the future capital replacement and expansion policies of the firms. These findings could be correlated with the size and industries reporting, and the result used to determine weights. This method has many limitations. The major drawback is the necessity of soliciting the information from a number of men in an organization, since the questions cut across departmental responsibilities. Nevertheless, under some circumstances the cost might well justify a limited survey of this type among the firm's main customers and large potential customers.

A second possible approach to establishing weights would be to correlate the company's past sales to each industry with an economic measure of that industry's volume of sales or production over a period of years. Then, by estimating what the industry's volume will be in the future, a prediction of relative sales to each industry can be made. This method has severe disadvantages, too. The major limitation is that the past historical relationship may not apply to the future because the methods of metalworking processing change over a period of time as new types of machine tools are introduced on the market.

C. CALCULATION OF INDEX BY STATES AND INDUSTRIAL AREAS. After determining weights as described above, the next step was to calculate the market potential index for each state in the United States and all the major industrial areas. A separate index was calculated for these two types of machine tools—grinders and boring machines.

TABLE 1

EXAMPLE OF MARKET POTENTIAL CALCULATION FOR INTERNAL GRINDING MACHINES STATE OF ILLINOIS 1954

Standard Classification [1]	Industries [1]	Number of Production workers [2]	Proportion of U. S. Workers [3]	Weights for Industries [4]	Weighted Proportion U. S. Workers [5]
3541	Machine Tools	4117	.05013	3	.15039
3521	Tractors	41153	.53410	1	.53410
3531	Mining Equipment	8079	.10330	2	.20660
3532	Oil Well Equipment	157	.00541	1	.00541
etc.	etc.	etc.	etc.	etc.	etc.
		Totals		100	= 7.58446
				100	÷ 7.58446
					= 7.6
					Market Potential for Illinois [6]

[1] Industries having use for internal grinding machines.
[2] Number of production workers for each industry—source, *Iron Age*.
[3] The proportion of U.S. Workers in each industry found in the State of Illinois—Example, the total number of production workers in the U.S. machine tool industry are 82,130. There are 4117 production workers in the machine tool industry in the State of Illinois. 4117 ÷ 82130 = .05013. Each industry is thus figured separately as a proportion of the total workers in the U.S. for that industry.
[4] Each industry is weighted according to the method described. These weights are associated with the industry involved and are the same for each state.
[5] The proportion of U.S. Workers multiplied by the weights for each industry. Example, for the machine tool industry—.05013 × 3 = .15039.
[6] The weighted proportion of U.S. Workers divided by the sum of the weights for industries.

Table 1 gives an example of how the market potential index was calculated for internal grinding machines for the State of Illinois. Similar procedures were used for all other forty-seven states. The number of production workers in the various industries was used as the basic component,[7] with the weights attached for each industry. The market potential figure for Illinois (7.6 per cent) represents the proportion of the total U. S. market for internal grinding machines existing in that state. It is believed that the index has considered all the factors which make a market for this machine tool.

Conclusion

Utilizing the above statistical procedure, we calculated the proportion of the total United States market for precision internal grinding and boring machines for each state and industrial area. Our findings show that over 80 per cent of the United States market for precision boring machines and over 85 per cent of the United States market for precision internal grinding machines is concentrated in only ten states in the country.

The company's policy established at the end of World War II, designed to achieve maximum efficiency and economy in distribution, is to have its own salesmen cover the large market areas and to have agents handle the territories with small market potential and long distances to cover. Bryant's 1954 study pointed out some new areas of sufficiently large market potential for our machines to justify a change from the use of agents to direct representation by our own salesforce.

Bryant also plans to use these new market potential figures to check the effectiveness of our salesmen and agents. This calls for extreme caution owing to the nature of the market and the product. In the short run—one or two years—the indexes will be used only as general guideposts because machine tools, unlike many categories of products, are not purchased with any predictable degree of regularity. However, over a period of a few years, purchases tend to be made in accordance with potential demand within areas and, therefore, the index figures arrived at in this study are likely to provide an effective check of the efficiency of coverage of the company's sales districts.

In addition, the company has utilized the market potential statistics to establish new sales districts and to regroup individual salesmen within the areas of direct coverage.

Even though absolute accuracy is obviously impossible of attainment in trying to establish the relative market potential of sales territories in the machine tool field, we believe research efforts can provide highly useful sales management tools.

[7] Source: *Iron Age* (four digit breakdown for *Basic Marketing Data* supplied by *Iron Age*).

43. WHEN INDUSTRY MOVES TO INTERURBIA *

S. George Walters
Morris L. Sweet
Max D. Snider

Marketing management must reshape its policies and strategy in the light of a new concept of industrial location. This concept, whether called interurbia, megalopolis, or regional urbanization, has to date been considered primarily from the standpoint of the marketing of consumer goods, yet the impact of interurbia will have equal importance for the marketing of industrial goods.

Interurbia has been defined by the J. Walter Thompson Co.—Yale University study—as containing two or more adjacent metropolitan areas with either two cities of 100,000 or more, or one city of 100,000 and three cities of 25,000 or more plus adjacent counties with less than 25% farm population and more than 100 people per square mile. Actually, it is a combination of conventional standard metropolitan areas merging with adjoining areas to become a new type of urban region. For example, the Twentieth Century Fund has studied the area running from a line north of Boston to south of Washington.

It is not only the consumer who has migrated from the metropolitan area; industry too has dispersed, even beyond existing suburbs into a different type of area. Land that was previously marginal for industry use is now the site of factories.

This dispersion has a two-fold relationship to interurbia: First, factories in order to secure certain economies like horizontal plant layout, massive parking lots, etc., have leap-frogged into rural areas and then attracted labor; second, other plants have located near untapped sources of labor in interurbia.

Railroads were once a prerequisite for industrial activity; however, today highways play a comparable role in the growth of industrial activity in interurbia. Plants will locate along super highways and the labor force drawn to them will form new communities.

Interurbia is not an abstract or nebulous concept about which academicians speculate. The idea holds practical meaning for planning the marketing strategy of industrial goods. It is serving as the basis for new markets for both industrial and consumer goods.

* Reprinted by permission from *Sales Management*, Vol. 82, No. 4 (February 20, 1959).

S. George Walters, Developments Projects Manager, Mobil Oil Company; Morris L. Sweet, Research Assistant Professor of Business, and Max D. Snider, Assistant Professor of Marketing, Lehigh University.

The factors discussed above indicate that a much greater degree of flexibility in plant location becomes possible. Industry is no longer limited to sites on the outskirts of large cities or to established communities. The potential magnitude of this movement is its most striking characteristic.

What impact would a recession have on industrial interurbia? It could mean a temporary slowing up in the rate of plant construction. But an important anti-recession measure is likely to be highway construction which will set the stage after business recovery for an even greater rate of interurban plant development.

Any rapid increase in industrial interurbia would make present territorial data obsolete. Thus any index of sales potential which is based on census data should be considered in the light of the significant increase in industrial scatteration. This necessitates obtaining even more current data which may not always be easily accessible. While these changes may not affect methods of sales forecasting, greater ingenuity in gathering and interpreting the data upon which to base the forecast will be required. You will find up-dated data in Sales Management's July Survey of Industrial Buying Power.

Salesmen in interurbia will spend more time traveling to and from customers. There is a considerable range in the proportion of time devoted to traveling. In 1954 one authority estimated that about 40% of salesmen's time is spent in traveling. Assuming that the salesman works an 8-hour day, approximately 3.2 hours per day is spent traveling. If the new interurban salesman spends an extra hour per day in traveling, which is a conservative estimate, he would be spending 52.5% of his time in travel, and increase of 12½%. Hence, one new salesman for every eight present salesmen will be required in order to insure the same degree of customer coverage.

Not only will transportation costs be up, but there will be changes in the types of transportation used by salesmen. Private planes and chartered planes will become important means of transportation for those suppliers whose customers are widely scattered. As an adjunct to commercial air travel, and a substitute for inadequate bus and train service, car rentals will take on added importance.

Interurbia is likely to mean fewer accounts per salesman and a change in the character of his accounts and amount of earnings. If the salesman is required to spend more time traveling and less time selling, his present compensation plan will mean less income. With compensation closely correlated to changes in sales volume, the likelihood is that the present compensation plan will have to re-evaluated, perhaps with greater emphasis on straight salary.

When a company moves to the outer fringes, it does so because it has outgrown its present facilities. In its new location it may become a better customer; hence the supplier's salesman in the new territory may experience a windfall. In any event industrial interurbia demands a re-evaluation of quotas and all other standards of performance based on past data to assure an equitable system of compensation.

Management will eventually develop a sales force well suited to the requirements of interurbia. What qualities should receive greater emphasis? Emotional stability on the part of the salesman looms large. He will be working in areas without the conveniences and comforts of the city—away from his family for longer periods of time. Adapting to an entirely new mode of living—"motel living"—may be difficult for a salesman. (Evenings in a motel can be pretty dull.) Physical stamina, always critical in salesmen, becomes more important for the interurban salesman because of the extra strain of additional travel.

A greater degree of self-sufficiency will be a prime requisite. As part of his regular sales call, the salesman should be capable of inspecting equipment to see whether it is functioning properly. The new type of salesman will be less able to call upon the home office for instructions, and thus will probably be required to route himself. The scarcity of market data which reflects industry scatteration demands that the salesman be capable of channeling trade information to the sales manager.

Purchasers located in interurbia will have to recognize the difficulties faced by salesmen calling on them. The salesman traveling great distances should make advance preparations and in turn should not be kept waiting unnecessarily. Where facilities for eating, sleeping, and transportation are unavailable, the salesman may have to be given assistance. Location in isolated areas means trade information will be more difficult to obtain; thus visiting salesmen become an important source, not to be lost by too brusque treatment.

With the greater distance between buyers and sellers, trade exhibits may help both parties. The value of these trade shows to the buyer is determined by the number of competing suppliers who participate. Under favorable circumstances, the seller obtains a more effective method of reaching new prospective buyers.

The difficulties facing purchasing agents in interurbia may be partially offset by attendance at trade shows. The trade show can provide trade information, and uncover new sources of supply and new products.

A trend may develop toward the delegation of certain buying activities to outside purchasing services. While this service has always been available for hard-to-get items, the number of such items may be increased to interurbia. There may then be a comparable growth in the industrial field of the resident buying office which is a major factor in obtaining many types of consumer goods.

* * * * * * * *

Ethicon in Interurbia

What about interurbia from the viewpoint of the buyer in his performance of the purchasing function? Vincent Huether, chief purchasing agent of Ethicon, Inc., freely discussed the changes which have resulted from his company's move from the New Brunswick, N. J., area to Bridgewater Township, N. J., a distances of some 20 miles. Though the move has not caused any extreme changes in the company's operations, it does serve to point up some effects of interurban movement. Mr. Huether believes ". . . that the impact of industrial scatteration is something which must very soon be reckoned with by industrial management not only in the field of sales and purchasing, but from other important aspects of industry as well, such as personnel, traffic, finance, etc."

Ethicon, Inc., though a subsidiary of Johnson & Johnson, operates almost entirely autonomously; 95% of its output consists of surgical sutures in which field it is the dominant concern. In 1956, it moved from six scattered buildings in the New Brunswick area to a striking new building of 200,000 square feet in Bridgewater Township on U. S. Route 22. The move actually was spread out over a period of several months. It began around April 1, 1956, when the Shipping and Warehousing Departments were moved. Each major division was then scheduled over the next four or five months with the Research Department being the last to move in September 1956. The Purchasing Department moved to the new location on June 22, 1956. At the present time Ethicon employs approximately 700 people at the Bridgewater Township operation. In the new location there is almost complete reliance on truck transportation.

Before making the move, Ethicon notified all of its regular suppliers. The letter mentioned the date of the move with the approximate schedule for each division and mailing and delivery address. A map of the new location was enclosed.

Buying at Ethicon falls into two categories: raw materials and non-raw materials.

Raw materials include all items which are further processed for use in the end product, e.g., suture materials, chemicals, packaging components, etc. There has been little change in the procurement of raw materials. These are usually bought on the basis of specifications from a limited number of sources selected by purchasing.

With non-raw materials or MRO (maintenance, repair and operating equipment), there has been a greater change. The Johnson & Johnson policy is to buy locally whenever possible, consistent with price, service, and availability. Before leaving New Brunswick, Huether checked with his local suppliers to get their reaction, and most were happy to continue their business relationship with Ethicon, Inc. At the same time he checked with Ortho Pharmaceutical Corp. which has been located in the new area for seven or eight years. Ortho's purchasing agent was able to give information about local MRO suppliers and several were selected.

The move placed Ethicon in somewhat of a predicament. As previously mentioned, it is company policy whenever possible to buy from local suppliers. A problem arose of reconciling this policy with consideration to the many years of faithful service given by a number of suppliers in the New Brunswick area. The solution has come with the passage of time. Some of the former suppliers have dropped out because they lack adequate delivery facilities and personnel; and there's been a gradual shift toward those local suppliers who can provide the necessary equipment immediately.

Surprisingly, there has been a sharp increase in the number of salesmen calling on Ethicon since the move. Many salesmen driving on U. S. Route 22 are attracted by the building and decide to make a call. These salesmen usually represent firms located within a radius of about 50 miles.

	Salesmen's Calls
1952	900
1953	1160
1954	1438
1955	1518
1956	2407
1957	3360

Salesmen who call regularly have come to be expected at a particular hour and/or a particular day. Unless they come from long distances, they generally give no advance notice. Because of the more isolated locality, Heuther has re-emphasized to his buyers the company policy of seeing all salesmen promptly. No special time has been scheduled for interviewing salesmen.

Salesmen coming from distant points do not usually stay overnight in the vicinity, but prefer to return to New York. Those who don't drive come to Somerville by rail or bus, and then by taxi to Ethicon offices. With the return trip this is a distance of about 100 miles. Present rail or bus schedules might thus limit the salesmen to one call a day. One salesman has solved this problem by flying (a distance of approximately 40 miles) from Lodi, N. J., to an airport which is ten minutes from the Ethicon plant.

Servicing of equipment can be a problem to Ethicon. The greater distance from established service centers means a longer wait for the technical serviceman.

From Ethicon's limited experience, it can be concluded that even with an extremely cooperative customer, the performance of the selling function is going to change. The impact will be even greater with customer movement into more isolated interurban areas.

This study of Ethicon in interurbia indicates that more attention should be given to a number of factors, some of which are scheduling of salesmen, servicing, and channels of distribution.

The vendor offering the quickest or most readily available service will be in a more favorable position than his competitors. With the increasing use of more complex equipment, service will be an even more important factor.

In the past a marginal distributor might have been adequate for those areas which showed little sales potential. However, the increasing scatteration of industry means that today no alert supplier can consider any part of interurbia permanently marginal.

The efficiency of the purchasing and sales management functions will be seriously impaired if no consideration is given to present and future changes generated by interurbia. Many firms will, of course, continue to operate in their traditional manner and location. Thus management will be confronted with the need to develop appropriate policies for each situation.

44. MANUFACTURERS' AGENTS *

Stuart W. McFarland

The Role of the Manufacturers' Agent

Marketing, in the minds of many, is synonymous with the distribution of consumer goods, simply because this type of good—food, clothing, drugs, hardware—is most familiar. However, frequently overlooked are the billions of dollars of industrial or capital goods marketed annually. Overlooked also are the specialists who market them. Little has been written by students of marketing regarding these specialists, who are known as manufacturers' sales agents.

Industrial goods are those bought to facilitate production or to be used in the production of other goods. Equipment, parts, fabricated materials, and industrial supplies are examples. The national sales total for these industrial goods in 1958 involved $200 billion and concerned 25,000 manufacturers' sales branch outlets, 27,000 manufacturers' agents and brokers, and 110,000 wholesalers and distributors.[1] Also, for our purposes here, approximately 8,500 of the agent-broker classification were actually manufacturers' agents. Agents and brokers together sold a reported $45 billion in 1958, of which it is estimated that $8½ billion of goods were sold by the manufacturers' agents themselves.

A commonly accepted definition of a manufacturer's agent is:

> An agent who generally operates on an extended contractual basis; often sells within an exclusive territory; handles noncompeting but related lines of goods; and possesses limited authority with regard to prices and terms of sale. He may be authorized to sell a definite portion of his principal's output.

* Reprinted by permission of the *Atlanta Economic Review*, Vol. 11, No. 12 (December, 1961), p. 15.

Stuart E. McFarland, Professor and Chairman, Department of Marketing, School of Business Administration, Jacksonville University, Jacksonville, Florida. This study was done when Dr. McFarland was with the School of Business Administration of Georgia State College of Business Administration.

[1] *1958 Census of Business, Wholesale Trade, Preliminary.* These are wholesale trade figures less consumer good data—foods, household furnishings, beverages, and farm products.

> The term "Manufacturers Representative" is sometimes applied to this agent. Since this term is also used to designate a salesman in the employ of a manufacturer, its use as a synonym for "Manufacturers Agent" is discouraged.[2]

By contrast, the broker, with whom the agent is usually confused, may represent buyer or seller, but does *not* maintain a continuous relationship with his principal and is less concerned with capital goods. Brokers are especially active in foods and dry goods (large volume commodities). When concerned with buying for clients, they carry the well-known title of "buying brokers."

The increase in number of manufacturers' agents and in their activities during the period 1929-1958 is shown in Table 1.

Marketing activities of agents

HOW THEY START. After perhaps ten years' experience as a salesman for an industrial distributor or in a branch office of some large equipment firm, the salesman may garner four or five accounts and go into business for himself, as a manufacturers' agent. As such, he will perhaps eventually have five or six active and as many inactive accounts in an exclusive territory for the principal's particular brands. He will not handle a principal's entire line but perhaps only one or two related items, say a drill press and a grinder from the line. His territory, from which all sales are credited to him on a commission basis, might be two states, or some other carefully described political boundary—ten counties, two cities, etc. He proceeds to cover his designated market as he sees fit, but is sent sales leads by his principal. The better the territory, the more demands on his agent the principal usually feels justified in making.

TABLE 1

MANUFACTURERS' AGENTS IN THE UNITED STATES
ESTABLISHMENTS, SALES, PAYROLLS, STOCKS, AND PROPRIETORSHIPS
1929-1958

Year	Establishments	Sales for Entire Year	Proprietorships	Payroll Entire Year	Stocks on Hand at Cost, End of Year
1958	8,500*	$8,584,953,000*	6,900*	$185,625,000*	$26,071,000*
1954	8,720	7,154,144,000	7,323	159,125,000	22,491,000
1948	9,048	4,209,234,000	8,474	85,184,000	12,919,000
1939	9,778	1,397,017,000	8,800	37,129,000	11,894,000
1935	7,548	768,619,000	6,557	23,995,000	12,902,000
1929	6,987	1,775,355,000	n.a.	65,835,000	49,504,000

* Estimated by the author.
Source: *Census of Business.*

[2] American Marketing Association definition.

THEIR RELATION TO THE MANUFACTURER. Sales promotion and sales calls are handled by the agent for the principal, and sales reports are prepared by him. Because he is usually paid on a straight commission basis, he tends to work less with small accounts, understandably concentrating on the big buyers to earn big commissions. Thus, if the manufacturer is interested in intensive coverage of a market, he may supplement his agent with a sales office in major markets. The agent calls on the larger accounts where he has the most acceptability; and the manufacturer's sales force, paid on a salary and commission, spends its time working with smaller accounts that have big-account potential. The agent understands and accepts this, and if the relationship is carefully handled by the manufacturer the arrangement is usually satisfactory.

HOW THEY SERVE THE MANUFACTURER. Agents offer two extremely important services to the manufacturer—contacts and personal services.

Contacts. Inasmuch as the agent has spent perhaps ten years in the industrial market as a salesman, he will have the acquaintanceships and contacts needed to be effective in a complicated market or to reach an otherwise unapproachable prospect. Many of the agent's prospects do their buying routinely and loyally from the same sources and the same individuals if good service and quality of product have been maintained. Thus an Eastern chemical manufacturer wishing to enter the Pacific Coast market may well find an agent on the Coast who will give the manufacturer the "in" that is needed. The alternative may be to start at scratch with one's own traveling or resident salesman who must find and build up his own contacts, a costly and time-consuming work. Agents also have the technical background and know-how needed to assist engineers with knotty problems. Many an agent has donned overalls and entered a factory to find the answer to the reasons why given machines had too high a spoilage rate or became overheated unnecessarily. His recommendations may not call for his own product at all, but his assistance will not be forgotten when he does make a sales call later on.

Personal Services. Traveling as they do from one factory to another or from one distributor or dealer to another, agents are carriers of news and trends in an industry. They are in a position to say, "X Co. over in St. Louis had much the same problem and solved it this way. . . ." The agent thus is of service to another customer. To many a small manufacturer wishing to get his distribution program under way the agent is indispensable for he costs the manufacturer little or nothing until a sale is made. When this happens, the manufacturer then has the funds with which to pay the agent. Obviously this is important to those manufacturers with limited capital—and their number is legion.

Limitations of agents

Any broad discussion of agents should necessarily include the limitations of manufacturers' agents in the marketing activity.

THEIR TIME IS DIVIDED. It appears obvious that if the agent has five active accounts, the share of his time each account can depend on is perhaps twenty per cent. Similarly, if he has eight active accounts, this share can shrink to twelve per cent, hardly enough to satisfy most manufacturers unless demand creation is handled largely by industrial advertising. The ads generate sales leads, which then are sent to the agent for sales prospecting.

A manufacturer who wants intensive coverage of every possible account regardless of size may find that a sales force of his own employees, dedicated to his company and working full time for him and his product, is better suited to his needs.

THEY DO NOT CARRY STOCKS. Since most manufacturers' agents do not carry stocks and do not warehouse, it is apparent that an agent's services are limited under market conditions that require local servicing and fast delivery of parts from stocks. There are ways to compensate for such a weakness, including the use of public warehouse services, air shipments, the handling of custom-made products that would come direct from the factory to the user in any case, and compensatory inducements, such as low price.

If the product is highly technical, requiring considerable servicing and stocking of many complicated components, the agent will not be as useful as a local sales office which will have technical specialists and facilities to handle many small parts.

METROPOLITAN ATLANTA'S MANUFACTURERS' AGENTS

In order to get a clear view of certain phases of sales agents operations, a survey was conducted by this author among Atlanta based manufacturers' agents. Of course, the question arises whether the survey findings for one city will be typical of other regions. The author believes that they will. Nevertheless, he does acknowledge some difference in the make-up in the sales agents group. Thus, the proportion of such agents in Atlanta who fall in the "machinery, equipment and supplies" category is somewhat higher than for the nation as a whole (Table 2). As for the "electrical goods" group, the proportion is about the same for Atlanta and the nation.

TABLE 2

NUMERICAL COMPARISON OF MANUFACTURERS' AENTS IN METROPOLITAN ATLANTA AND THE UNITED STATES
1958

Lines Handled	U. S. Agency Establishments in the Category*	All Atlanta Agents in this Category**		Atlanta Agents Reporting in this Study
	%	No.	%	No.
Machinery Equipment and Supplies	23.0	118	42.0	48
Electrical Goods	12.3	35	12.0	15
Hardware, Plumbing, and Heating	11.2	28	10.0	5
Drugs, Chemicals, and Allied Products	3.7	11	3.5	2

* From *Census of Business* data.
** Based upon an Atlanta Chamber of Commerce Listing.

Despite the differences in the group make-up as stated above, the author is of the opinion (based on his personal knowledge of the field) that the survey findings presented below, based on the practices of Atlanta manufacturers' sales agents in two fields—"machinery, equipment and supplies" and "electrical goods"—are generally typical of sales agents.

Form of business organization

Of the forty-six machinery agencies reporting on their form of organization, twenty-eight are proprietorships, fourteen are corporations, and four are partnerships. The same organizational proportions hold true with the electrical goods agents.

The large number of agencies not taking advantage of the limited liability features of incorporation is surprising. There are two factors which may contribute to the number of proprietorships—the fact that so many of the agencies are one-man operations, thus limiting acts involving liability to one man anyway, and a natural reluctance to be burdened with the many governmental reports, records, and expense which incorporation entails.

Commissions earned

Machinery agents reported commissions averaging ten to fifteen per cent of sales. The fifteen per cent figure was common with sales of machine tools, materials handling equipment, and farm equipment. A lesser commission of ten per cent was mentioned in the sale of milling machines, blowers, filters, laboratory and air conditioning equipment.

Electrical goods agents average eight per cent commission for appliances and electronic components. Ten per cent is realized on the sale of electrical supplies and temperature controls. Heaters and switches, which are popular inventory items, bring five per cent. The smaller average commission realized by this group is understandable in view of the much larger total dollar volume sold.

Number of employees

Machinery agents generally employ three, four, or five salesmen, and the figure most often mentioned was three men. They also employ one person in a nonselling capacity, usually clerical or secretarial. Electrical goods agents commonly employ four salesmen, although the numerical dispersion is broader, with some reporting ten and twelve salesmen and others a one-man operation. They usually have two or three nonsales personnel.

Payroll

Dollar payrolls for agents customarily range from $15,000 to $100,000, with only a few exceptions on the higher side of these figures. Electrical goods agents have the larger payrolls, which is consistent with the fact that their staffs are also larger.

Warehousing

Sixty per cent of the reporting machinery agents have no warehouse facilities; those possessing or renting warehouse space have less than five thousand square feet in use. As for the electrical goods agents, about one half report warehouse facilities in use, and those reporting warehouses find it necessary to have ten thousand square feet or more of space.

Office space

Machinery agents tend to have small offices, most reporting their facilities as limited to five hundred square feet or less. Electrical goods agents, however, report larger office space than do machinery agents, with most of their facilities exceeding five hundred square feet of space. (These figures do not include display space, which only twenty per cent of the machinery agents report having in use. When display space is mentioned, it is described as being less than one hundred square feet of space.)

Geographic area served

The most frequently mentioned geographic territory served by both machinery and electrical goods agents working out of Metropolitan Atlanta was the "Southeast," identified as the area including Georgia, Alabama, Tennessee, Florida, North Carolina, and South Carolina. Next in mention was the area which might be described as the "entire South," or the ten southern states from Virginia in the Northeast down to Texas in the Southwest. Twenty-five to thirty per cent of the agents contacted mentioned these two areas. The next area in importance, mentioned by ten per cent of all agents interviewed, was the single state of Georgia. There is a high degree of geographic similarity in territories covered by both machinery and electrical goods agents.

The large territories assigned to most of the manufacturers' agents might be explained in terms of the South's more recent emergence from an agricultural to an industrial economy. Industrial centers in the area, like Tampa in the South, Charlotte in the East, and Memphis in the West, are widely scattered, tending to encourage the assignment of a larger area to one agent than otherwise would be the case.

Executive in charge of sales

Normally, these agents do not have an organized sales department or staff. The actual sales manager is probably the "president" or "owner." Only twelve per cent of the respondents mention the title "sales manager," as against fifty per cent mentioning either of the other two titles. Agencies which are one-man or two-man operations obviously are not in a position to have a "sales force" management program. However, it is surprising as to the number of agents staffing five, six, and seven salesmen and having no organized recruiting, selection, training, or compensation-motivation programs.

Most of the owners report that their sales leadership activities are limited to "general supervision and selling in the field." There is a slight but not a significant tendency among electrical goods agents to have a more organized sales management program.

Sales management functions

The majority—some fifty to sixty per cent of the agents reporting—do nothing in the way of organized training for their salesmen. Agents expending effort in this direction limit it to "on-the-job training" or training "under the supervision of an experienced salesman." Ten per cent of the agents mention their training program as two weeks at the principal's factory and an infrequent sales meeting with the principal's executives. Occasionally the principal's sales training staff will visit the agent's place of business. There is a definite impression that the agents rely heavily on the factory to train the agent's men, certainly in regard to product knowledge.

Recruiting of new salesmen is done through word-of-mouth advertising and by means of personal contacts in the industry. Some newspaper advertising is done and some personal applications are made to an agent, but most agents either have no system of recruiting and hiring or do not have to recruit because of a very low turnover of sales staff. The vast majority of agents report almost no turnover of staff because the sales staff is usually small and each man is "cared for" so that he remains happily on the job. University placement offices are preferred over private employment agencies as sources for new salesmen, and sometimes local chambers of commerce are consulted.

Salesmen's performance is evaluated almost entirely by the dollar sales they produce ranked against the sales potential of their territories. Some few agents do attempt to evaluate the per cent of calls that result in sales, e.g., a relationship between the number of prospects contacted and those that resulted as customers. Apparently there is little effort among machinery agents to evaluate the men in terms of the development of new accounts, keeping customers satisfied, closing ability, leadership in the field, or extraordinary territory coverage and development. And, as for the electrical goods agents, this survey found no apparent evidence pointing to the development and refinement of techniques to measure salesmen's effectiveness adequately.

Compensation and educational background of salesmen

Monthly compensation, usually on straight commission, amounts to about $600-$750 for a salesman in his late twenties with up to five years' experience. Ten machinery agents reported possible incomes of $1,000 to $1,500 a month for a good salesman of this age and experience! Any figure below $450 a month is rare.

Approximately one-fourth of the agents reporting, or eighteen agents, indicated that a college education is not essential to enter the field or to succeed in it. However, as might be expected, the more technical the line handled, the more desirable is an engineering degree, or a business administration degree with engineering experience.

Half of the machinery agents prefer a salesman candidate who has an engineering degree; twenty-five per cent prefer a man with a degree in business administration; and the rest, no degree at all. The same proportion holds true for electrical goods agents. There is no significant difference by lines handled in terms of agents' preferences as regards their recruits' preparation. The fact remains that a surprising number of agents (sixteen firms) would like to employ a salesman with a business administration degree and then train him in product knowledge and elementary engineering.

Policies as to advancement and promotion run to extremes. Either the young man can go "as high as President" if he has the ability, or he will remain indefinitely as a salesman, but earn more income. Several agents reported theirs to be a one-man business with no heir-apparent in sight, expressing the wish that a "good man would show up to take over when I retire." No agent mentioned as a possible future the opportunity to leave his firm and start a competitive business!

Management practices

Although most firms do require reports from their salesman, a required attendance at weekly sales meetings is not too common. Agents report that they do travel occasionally with their salesmen and do get them to attend annual sales meetings.

Commission payments are relied on heavily to motivate salesmen, although bonus payments and participation in profits are in use as motivation devices by six agents. One firm makes company stock available and another uses contests to stimulate its salesmen to better sales volume. But either increasing financial rewards or doing a good job of supervision is relied upon by the vast majority of agents as motivation techniques.

Pricing and sales promotion by agents

Almost half of the agents contacted report that their principals do the pricing at the factory, sending the agents the necessary price lists to use. However, ten agents do have complete price authority, especially in the machinery line. Seven machinery agents and five electrical goods agents report that they do have some flexibility in pricing to meet competition in the market.

Sales promotion activities of agents are limited to training distributor salesmen, following up on mailing lists of prospects, training service personnel, working with engineers, attending sales conventions, and making personal contact with prospects whenever possible. Sales quotas are sometimes used by principals—twenty-one agents mention quotas levied on them in some degree. Usually each line or account represented has its own quota. Marketing research is utilized very little as a part of the sales promotion activities except as occasional new product or competitor activity reports are required (mentioned by three agents). Usually the principal's staff at the factory takes care of the marketing research, if any is done.

Agents' advice to those entering the field

The advice of manufacturers' agents to college men considering entering the field is to take some engineering work or get engineering experience (twenty mentions), psychology (twelve mentions), salesmanship (ten mentions), English (nine mentions), mathematics (eight mentions), marketing (seven mentions), and accounting, public speaking, and general business administration.

Agents gave diverse answers as to the type of sales experience that would be especially helpful in the manufacturers' agent field, but they seemed to agree generally that meeting people anywhere and working with dealers or jobbers were especially helpful. Retail or door-to-door sales experience was thought helpful by six agents. Developing a good personality, being self-sufficient, a self-starter, and getting along with people were emphasized again and again as indispensable.

The manufacturers' agent has been called one of the glamour jobs in marketing—an opportunity in which the individual can be independent though he does not own the business, managerial though it means self-managing and motivating, and can some day open his own business merely by changing the title of his stationery. But if the person wishing to be a manufacturers' agent does not have the drive and self-motivation this job demands, success in the field seems quite remote. For those manufacturers' agents who, through sales ability and impeccable reputation, reach success, incomes can soar well above $30,000 a year in personal compensation.

45. WHOSE MARKETS? *

Holbrook Working

Recent occurrences in connection with futures trading in wheat at Kansas City give new and striking evidence on two questions that appear to be closely related. Why does futures trading exist? And what are the groups chiefly served by a futures market? The answers help to explain why futures trading in any commodity tends to concentrate in some one market—why, for example, futures trading in wheat has vanished from numerous exchanges in the United States where it existed half a century ago, and has remained most active in Chicago, though that market is no longer in the first rank as a handler of wheat; and how smaller futures markets can sometimes hold their own, or expand, in the face of this tendency toward concentration of futures trading.

Background

In the summer of 1953 a sharp conflict of opinion developed in the Kansas City Board of Trade. Kansas City is pre-eminently a market for hard winter wheat, and for many years [1] permitted delivery of only that class of wheat on its futures contracts. In 1940, however, the contract was changed to allow delivery, at the seller's option, of soft winter wheat.[2] The latter is more commonly referred to as "red wheat," though the hard winter is also a red wheat. The

* From *The Journal of Marketing,* Vol. XIX, No. 1 (July, 1954), pp. 1-11. Reprinted with permission from *The Journal of Marketing,* published quarterly by the American Marketing Association.

Holbrook Working, Associate Director, Food Research Institute, Stanford University.

[1] Apparently from the beginning of trading in futures at Kansas City, in 1876. Though futures trading began so early at Kansas City, it was at first sporadic. A clearing house for futures transactions was not established until 1899, and the Chicago *Daily Trade Bulletin* first saw fit to include Kansas City price quotations with those from other markets in 1902. (*Cf.* Federal Trade Commission, *Report on the Grain Trade,* Vol. II (1920), pp. 159, 164; Vol. V (1920), pp. 38, 191; Chicago *Daily Trade Bulletin* (February 11, 1920).

[2] The change was approved by a narrow margin, in April, to be effective for deliveries in December 1940 and subsequently. (*Cf.* Kansas City *Grain Market Review* April 15, 1940.)

change had little practical effect until 1953, because red wheat—soft red—is raised in quantity only to the east of Kansas City and has ordinarily been priced too high in Kansas City to be profitably delivered on futures contracts there.

During the last few years, prices of soft wheats throughout the country have tended to be depressed relative to the prices of hard wheats. A reason commonly cited has been the tendency for producers of red wheat to take less full advantage of the governmental price-support program than did producers of hard wheats; red wheat is commonly raised on small acreages per farm, in connection with diversified agriculture, while hard wheats are grown mainly on larger acreages and as the principal or only crop. There may have been other contributing influences. In any case, the price depression of red wheat relative to hard wheat increased to such an extent in the spring and summer of 1953 that the Kansas City future became in effect a red wheat future.

Prices of different classes of wheat tend to move somewhat differently. Consequently the change in effective character of the Kansas City future made it less effective than before as a hedging medium for millers of hard wheat and dealers in such wheat. Millers were the ones who suffered most from the particular disparities in price movement that occurred in the spring of 1953, and they promptly petitioned the Kansas City Board of Trade for a change in delivery provisions that would make the Kansas City future again a hard winter wheat contract.

A committee was appointed in early June to consider the question, and it invited expressions of opinion from the membership of the exchange. This produced a record of arguments pro and con to which we shall turn in a moment. After prolonged discussion, a vote was taken in late August at which the proposed change was rejected[3] by a majority of 92 to 79—a decisive rejection in view of the fact that a two-thirds majority was required for its adoption. The millers, however, returned to the attack with a proposal that a separate hard wheat contract be introduced for use as an alternative to the existing contract. To minimize objection, proponents of this change agreed to having it take effect only for delivery months in which trading had not already started; that is, to having trading in the new contract restricted to deliveries for July 1954 and later.

[3] Kansas City *Grain Market Review* August 24, 1953.

This meant foregoing any substantial benefit from the proposed change during the 1953-54 crop year, but it left little ground for opposition to the change because, if the new contract should be little used for July delivery it could be abandoned after a few months with minimum inconvenience from having tried it. This proposal was approved in October by a vote of 120 to 43.[4]

Contemporary Arguments and Historical Evidence

The original proposal that the Kansas City future be made again a strictly hard wheat future was apparently rejected because of majority opinion that the existing contract would attract more trading than a contract which restricted deliveries to hard winter wheat. The letters received in June by the committee considering the proposal advanced a variety of arguments,[5] but the two most often used were that one or the other contract—whichever the writer favored—would better promote the "liquidity of the market," and that one or the other would better meet the obligations of the exchange. If some exchange members found these two considerations in conflict (none of the letter-writers so expressed themselves), I judge that they were mainly people who thought that the exchange had an obligation to serve especially the interests of hedgers of hard winter wheat, by providing a hard wheat contract, even though it might draw less trade than the existing contract.

What appears most clearly from the letters is absence of agreement on essential facts. The argument of obligation was used on both sides; some holding that Kansas City had a special obligation to serve hedgers of hard wheat, others maintained that it should serve hedgers of soft wheat as well as hedgers of hard wheat. Liquidity of the market, according to some writers, could best be promoted by a hard wheat contract; according to other writers, liquidity would be better promoted by the "broad base" of the contract that allowed delivery of either hard or soft wheat. Even the less common arguments were used on both sides. Some writers held that the existing contract gave the better protection against manipulation; others argued that it favored manipulation. One writer advocated a hard wheat contract on the ground that it would favor

[4] *Ibid.*, October 13, 1953.

[5] Thirty-nine letters were received, of which one was from a non-member who asked to be heard as an interested user of the market. Apparently those who wanted a change were more inclined to express themselves than those who were satisfied, for 23 writers advocated the change while 16 opposed it. I am indebted to Mr. W. R. Scott, Executive Vice-President of the Kansas City Board of Trade, for making this correspondence available for study.

use of futures as a means of acquiring wheat; another favored the existing contract because it gave opportunity also for users of red wheat to acquire it through delivery; and a third writer maintained that promoting delivery was not a proper aim of a futures contract.

In view of what actually happened to futures trading at Kansas City, it is perhaps most remarkable that almost no one indicated both recognition of the importance of the issue under discussion and awareness of pertinent facts in the history of futures trading. There was one member, however, who wrote: "If we . . . continue to sanction soft red wheat deliveries our futures trading will, without any doubt, dwindle to the vanishing point, . . . as happened at St. Louis many years ago."

Three facts that could have been used to predict what happened to futures trading at Kansas City last summer appear clearly from the history of futures trading. These are that: (1) In the case of products in which there is much public interest, such as wheat, the volume of business on a futures market depends primarily on the amount of *hedging* business that it attracts; (2) In the absence of some important special influence, hedging business tends to concentrate in a single futures market; and (3) It is possible for a smaller independent futures market to survive and prosper in the face of competition from a larger neighbor, but it can do so *only* by offering hedgers some advantage that outweighs the lower cost of hedging in a larger market.

It is odd that the first and most important of these facts escaped recognition for so long as it did. During the earlier history of futures trading there was much excuse for believing superficial indications that futures markets were supported primarily by speculators; but for at least twenty-five years now there has been evidence available to show rather clearly that in fact the size of a futures market, at least in the United States and among the more prominent commodities, has depended on the amount of hedging business available. Almost every year of the last twenty-five has brought new evidence of the importance of hedging in determining the amount of futures trading on a market. Much of this evidence has been known all the while to the present writer and he is not proud of his own failure to notice, until a year or two ago, that the accumulating evidence required revising old ideas.

In the present connection it would be especially pertinent, if space were available, to trace year by year since World War I the fluctuations in amount of business done in wheat futures on each futures exchange in the United States.[6] The facts come out most clearly if the data used are those on open contracts. All of the larger changes in open contracts through the thirty years for which data are available[7] can be explained in terms of influences affecting the amount of hedging that would naturally have been done. When the data are studied for each market separately, obvious explanation is found for most of the year-to-year fluctuations in open contracts. In Kansas City, they varied with the size of the hard-winter-wheat crop; in Minneapolis, with the size of the spring-wheat crop; in Duluth, where the trading was chiefly in a durum wheat future, the amount of open contracts varied with the size of the durum wheat crop. When surplus stocks of wheat accumulated in the late 1920's, leading to increased hedging, open contracts rose on all markets. When the Grain Stabilization Corporation took over much of this surplus in 1930-31, so that the stocks were no longer hedged, open contracts dropped. When a new surplus appeared at the end of the 1930's, federal loans and direct holding by the Commodity Credit Corporation created an actual shortage of wheat supplies in commercial hands, and hedging and open contracts in wheat futures dropped sharply.

It remains not wholly clear why the total volume of open contracts should vary so closely with the amount of hedging as it does, in spite of the fact that a large fraction of the contracts are made and held by speculators. But if one accepts the fact that the total volume of open contracts *does* vary closely with the amount of hedging, then it becomes quite clear why futures trading in a commodity tends to concentrate in a single market. As between two futures exchanges of substantially different size, the larger one always offers hedgers an advantage of economy. This is why hedgers attach so much importance to "liquidity" of a market. In the large, liquid, market they can place or remove hedges with little "price effect."

What is commonly referred to as the "price effect" of hedging transactions may be better understood if looked at in another way. There is nothing inherently peculiar about hedging orders in a futures market, but they do have the characteristic that they are usually placed for immediate execution. Though speculators may often buy

[6] Other evidence leading to the same conclusion is discussed in Holbrook Working, "Futures Trading and Hedging," *The American Economic Review*, pp. 318-320. My thinking was first turned in this direction by an early draft of a manuscript by H. S. Irwin on the history of futures trading in eggs; see Irwin, *Evolution of Futures Trading* (Mimir Publishers, Madison, Wisconsin. In Press).

[7] *Cf. Grain Futures Statistics*, 1921-1951, U. S. Department of Agriculture Statistical Bulletin No. 131 (July 1953), p. 16.

or sell only if the price reaches some particular level, the purposes of hedging usually dictate buying or selling futures promptly after marking a purchase or sale in a "cash" market. In any competitive market, whether for wheat futures, for houses, or for used cars, the urgent buyer must expect usually to pay a higher price than he would have to pay if he shopped around; the urgent seller must expect usually to sell at a lower price than he would get if he took the time and trouble to seek out someone who was eager to buy.

In markets where there are frequent purchases and sales for whatever the market will bring, some people make a more or less regular business of buying from urgent sellers in order to sell to urgent buyers. The more of such business there is to be done, and the shorter the expected interval between purchase and resale, other things equal, the narrower is the usual margin between "buyer's price" and "seller's price." On wheat futures markets, this margin between buyer's price and seller's price is usually only a fraction of a cent per bushel, but whereas it is usually only 1/8 cent or 1/4 cent at Chicago, it may be two or three times that large at a smaller market.

Whether one gives as explanation the "price effect" of hedging orders, or the existence concurrently of differing prices for urgent buyers and urgent sellers, the fact that the larger of two futures markets tends to provide the cheaper hedging is well known to experienced hedgers. The importance of this difference in cost has increased over the years. Half a century ago a small futures market could count on getting much of the hedging business that originated in its locality; there was futures trading in wheat not only on the familiar exchanges of today, but also at St. Louis, Detroit, Toledo, Buffalo, New York City, and Baltimore.[8] Improving communications thereafter, and decline in the proportion of business done by small firms, probably both tended to promote shift of hedging business to the more economical hedging market at Chicago. All of these smaller futures exchanges except that at St. Louis either had closed by 1917 or failed to reopen after World War I. St. Louis reopened, but steadily lost business, and discontinued futures trading in 1938.

[8] There was futures trading also at Milwaukee and on the "Open Board of Trade" at Chicago; but these trading boards, which continue to operate, are unwelcome appendages of the Chicago Board of Trade rather than independent exchanges. They function through arrangements by which their contracts may be exchanged for contracts of the Chicago Board of Trade for purposes of making or receiving delivery. (*Cf.* Federal Trade Commission, *Report on the Grain Trade*, II, 128-29, 138-39; Washington, 1920.)

Yet it is possible for a small futures market to hold its own in competition with a larger neighbor, as is shown by the experiences of Kansas City, Minneapolis, and Duluth. Each of these exchanges had a distinctive futures contract that offered advantages for which a substantial group of hedgers were willing to pay. At Kansas City, until 1953, the future represented hard winter wheat. At Minneapolis the contract was for hard spring wheat. Duluth did its principal business in a durum wheat future.

At Duluth even a distinctive contract eventually proved insufficient to support futures trading. At its highest level, in 1928, durum wheat production was less than half that of hard spring wheat. The highest level of open contracts at Duluth, reached in 1928 and 1929, was similarly less than half the volume of open contracts at Minneapolis. Then a succession of virtual failures of the durum wheat crop and a great decline in durum acreage so curtailed durum hedging and futures trading that Duluth became a very unsatisfactory hedging market. Further declines in its business when durum stocks fell very low in 1944 and 1945 left Duluth unable to attract much hedging of even durum wheat, and futures trading there was discontinued in 1946.

At Minneapolis, on the other hand, and at Kansas City until 1953, maintenance of a distinctive futures contract kept for those markets the business of hedgers who valued a "close" hedge for the class of wheat represented by the contract.

The history of futures trading gives also some ground for a fourth conclusion pertinent to interpreting what happened at Kansas City in 1953. Apparently the wheat-hedging business that a smaller futures market can most successfully attract, through a distinctive contract, is the business of millers. Operators of large storage elevators seem to give less weight than millers to the advantages of a "close" hedge. This is indicated by the fact that when storage elevator stocks have declined sharply, and much more than mill stocks (as happened when the Grain Stabilization Corporation accumulated its stocks in 1930-31 and when the loan program and CCC holding took such strong effect at the end of the 1930's) open contracts fell off more at Chicago than at either Kansas City or Minneapolis.

Causes and Consequences of Hedger's Dissatisfaction

The reasons for dissatisfaction of millers with the Kansas City futures contract may be seen from Chart 1. The "premiums" which it shows are differences between the quoted spot price of the cheapest

CHART 1

PREMIUMS ON NO. 2 HARD AND NO. 2 SOFT RED WINTER WHEAT AT KANSAS CITY, TUESDAYS AND FRIDAYS OF MARCH-SEPTEMBER, 1953 *

(Cents per bushel)

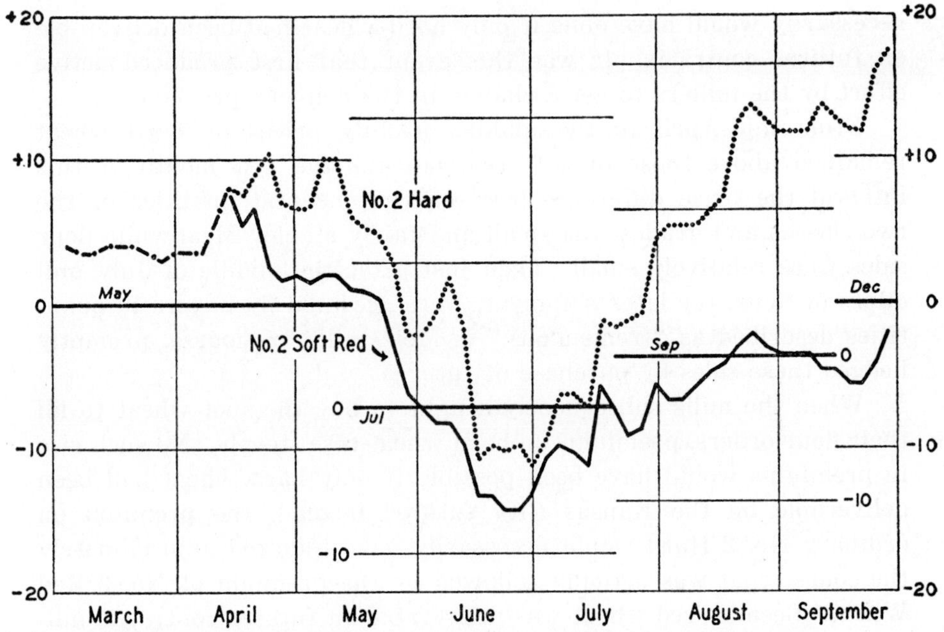

* Quotations from Kansas City *Grain Market Review*, for cheapest quality of each grade.

qualities of No. 2 Hard and No. 2 Soft Red Winter wheat, on the one hand, and the price of the near future on the other hand.[9] Because a hedger gains or loses as a result of changes in the relation between cash and futures prices, it is such changes in premiums that concern him rather than the price changes themselves. The zero lines used for plotting premiums on the chart are shifted with each change in the delivery month used as a basis for quoting the premiums, and their levels are so placed that the curves reflecting premiums may properly be drawn as continuous curves. The conformation of the curves is nevertheless influenced to some extent by the choice of dates at which the shifts were made.

In mid-April a rise in premiums of both hard and soft winter wheat was followed by further rise in the hard-wheat premium, while the soft-wheat premium turned down. This was the point at which the Kansas City futures contract became effectively a soft red wheat

[9] The spot quotations as originally published are in fact obtained by *adding* quoted premiums to the closing price of the future, so the chart was based directly on the quoted premiums.

contract. Millers who had hedged forward sales of hard wheat flour and thereafter had to buy the wheat at high premiums, lost money because the flour sales had been priced on the reasonable assumption that the hard-wheat premium would fall close to zero in May, as it necessarily would have done if only hard wheat had been deliverable on futures contracts. It was this event that first produced active effort by the millers to get a change in the delivery provisions.

From mid-April to the middle of July prices of hard wheat remained above those of soft red, but for the last month of this interval the price difference between the cheapest qualities of the two classes and grades was small and fairly stable. Meanwhile flour sales were relatively small. Then just after the middle of July mill offers of flour, for later shipment, were accepted by buyers in quantities described as "tremendous."[10] Most mills, of course, promptly hedged these sales by purchase of futures.

When the mills subsequently sought to buy the spot wheat to fill their flour orders, premiums on hard wheat rose steeply. No such rise in premiums would have been possible if only hard wheat had been deliverable on the Kansas City future; instead, the premium on ordinary No. 2 Hard would necessarily have followed approximately the course that was actually followed by the premium of No. 2 Red Wheat. Because red wheat was deliverable on futures contracts, millers lost heavily.

It should be noticed that the hedging losses incurred because Kansas City allowed delivery of either of two classes of wheat fell on hedgers who had a long position in futures. The same events brought unexpected profits to those who happened to hold short positions in futures as hedges against wheat stocks. This illustrates what may be a general tendency that could explain the indications of historical experience, mentioned earlier, that operators of storage elevators tend to hedge at Chicago while mills tend to favor markets where the future represents a specific class of wheat. Multiplicity of deliverable classes of a commodity, as for Chicago wheat, creates a sort of bias in favor of hedgers of stocks (short hedgers) and against hedgers of forward orders (long hedgers).[11]

Even prior to July, dissatisfaction with the Kansas City future had led some millers in the Kansas City area to use other markets for

[10] *Cf. Southwestern Miller*, July 21, 1953.

[11] After a rise in spot premiums such as that in July and August (Chart 1), there will eventually be a corresponding decline, in which holders of stocks will incur losses on their hedges; but the decline tends to come from a high level of premiums caused by shortage of supplies, so losses on the small hedged stocks are correspondingly small in total.

hedging. A few had chosen to hedge at Minneapolis, expecting to get the best available hedging protection there because the Minneapolis contract was for hard wheat, though for hard spring.[12] Presumably more had shifted their hedging to Chicago. The Chicago futures contract was also effectively a red wheat contract, but hedging could be done more economically there than at Kansas City because it was a broader and more liquid market. Still it was not until July, when millers began to incur still heavier losses than before on their Kansas City hedges, that large numbers of millers withdrew their hedging business from Kansas City. Probably many dealers in hard wheat also withdrew hedging business from Kansas City; the letters received in June had expressed dissatisfaction with the Kansas City contract on the part of a number of dealers, as well as of all the hard wheat millers who expressed opinions.

The consequences of further withdrawal of hedging business from Kansas City that began in July are shown in Table 1 and Chart 2. Total open contracts at Kansas City dropped rapidly from 30 million bushels on July 15 to 10 million bushels in November. Volume of trading (average daily sales) dropped similarly. Because volume of trading fluctuates so much from day to day and from week to week, under influences that tend to affect different wheat futures markets similarly, the effect of the special influence operating at Kansas City is reflected better by the ratios shown in the last column of Table 1 and in Chart 2 than by the absolute figures. Average daily sales of wheat futures at Kansas City during the first two weeks of July were nearly 23 per cent of the volume at Chicago. During November, Kansas City sales averaged less than 8 per cent of Chicago sales.

The table and chart show also annual data for seven earlier years, to provide a base for comparison. The most noteworthy feature of the record for earlier years is the steep rise in relative volume of trading at Kansas City between 1946-47 and 1952-53. The low level of the sales curve in the first two years reflects existence of a relatively small amount of speculative and scalping trade at Kansas City, and a good deal of dependence on arbitrage ("spreading") against Chicago to maintain reasonable liquidity of the Kansas City market. A similar condition had existed in earlier years. By 1952-53 Kansas City had built up its volume of trading to nearly the same position relative to open contracts as prevailed at Chicago; in that year daily

[12] Two of the letters received in June by the committee considering possible change in the Kansas City contract were from millers who reported having turned to Minneapolis for their hedging.

TABLE 1

OPEN CONTRACTS AND TRADING IN WHEAT FUTURES AT CHICAGO AND KANSAS CITY AND RATIOS, ANNUALLY, 1946-47 TO 1952-53 AND SEMI-MONTHLY FROM JULY 1953 [1]

(*Million Bushels: Per Cent*)

Periods (Years are June-July)	Open Contracts [2]		Daily Average Sales		Ratio (Per Cent) Kansas City to Chicago [3]	
	Chicago	Kansas City	Chicago	Kansas City	Contracts	Sales
1946–47	27.6	7.8	6.2	.4	28.3	5.6
1947–48	69.4	16.6	14.4	1.4	23.9	9.7
1948–49	61.4	20.9	10.9	1.5	34.0	13.8
1949–50	62.7	12.9	10.8	1.2	20.6	11.4
1950–51	65.1	19.8	11.8	2.0	30.4	17.2
1951–52	74.2	18.0	10.2	2.2	24.2	21.6
1952–53	76.1	18.6	10.4	2.5	24.4	24.0
1953–54 [4]						
July 15	86.4	29.6	31.6	7.2	34.3	22.9
July 31	97.8	25.6	17.7	2.8	26.2	16.0
Aug. 14	101.0	21.8	29.7	3.0	21.6	10.1
Aug. 31	99.4	18.3	23.9	2.4	18.4	10.0
Sept. 14	95.3	16.0	19.5	1.9	16.8	8.8
Sept. 30	92.5	13.7	16.6	1.4	14.8	8.3
Oct. 15	94.5	12.2	11.1	1.1	12.9	9.5
Oct. 30	98.0	12.1	11.7	1.3	12.3	11.5
Nov. 13	92.0	10.9	16.7	1.2	11.8	6.9
Nov. 30	83.3	9.9	15.5	1.3	11.8	8.4
Dec. 15	76.9	9.1	14.5	1.1	11.8	7.4

[1] Compiled from reports of the Commodity Exchange Authority and from the Kansas City *Grain Market Review*.
[2] Averages of month-end open contracts, except as noted below.
[3] Calculated from figures carried to more places than are shown to the left.
[4] Open contracts for the dates shown; sales averaged for the half-month ending on that date.

sales at Chicago averaged 13.6 per cent of open contracts and daily sales at Kansas City, 13.4 per cent of open contracts there.

Such a drop in futures business as occurred at Kansas City in the last half of 1953 is only what should reasonably have been expected in view of conclusions drawn above from the earlier history of futures trading.[13] If the amount of business done on a futures exchange depends primarily on the amount of hedging that it attracts, and if a relatively small futures market in competition with a larger one can obtain a substantial amount of hedging business only by offering hedging facilities of superior quality, then it was only natural that when Kansas City hedges lost their quality advantage, futures trading there should have dropped off rapidly.

Even so, I find it surprising that the loss of business at Kansas City was so abrupt as it was. Open contracts declined by one-half, in terms of the ratio to Chicago open contracts, in a space of only

[13] The conclusions were in fact published shortly in advance of the Kansas City experience, in the paper cited earlier in footnote 6.

CHART 2

AVERAGE OPEN CONTRACTS AND TRADING IN WHEAT FUTURES AT KANSAS CITY AS A PERCENTAGE OF CHICAGO, JULY 1946 TO DECEMBER 1953 *

(Percentages; Logarithmic Scale)

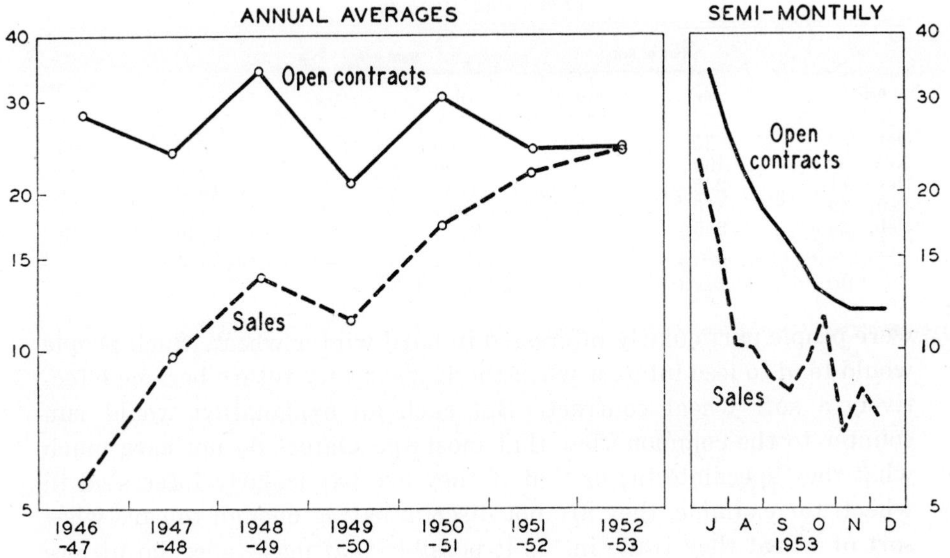

* The sharp relative decline in open contracts and in sales at Kansas City from June 30, 1953 reflects dissatisfaction of hedgers with the Kansas City futures contract. Provision for new contract terms, made on October 13, did little to check the decline because the new terms were applicable only to contracts for delivery in July 1954 or later. Data from Table 1.

two months. Volume of trading at Kansas City, expressed also as a percentage of the corresponding figure at Chicago, dropped by one-half in a single month—from 22.9 per cent of the Chicago volume in the first half of July to 10.1 per cent in the first half of August. It is hard to say whether such rapid drops are reasonably attributable solely to loss of hedging business, since we do not know just *why* speculative trade in futures tends to increase and to decrease as it does in response to changes in hedging trade. If the connection between hedging trade and speculative trade tends to be a rather loose one, as I incline to suppose, the sharpness of the decline in total futures business at Kansas City is not fully explained by dissatisfaction of hedgers with the futures contract there.

If some supplementary explanation is needed to account fully for what happened to futures trading at Kansas City, it must be an explanation that involves discouragement to speculative trade—some special discouragement at Kansas City that depressed trading there *relative* to trading at Chicago. The most obvious possible explanation is that perhaps a good many speculators in Kansas City wheat

TABLE 2

MONTH-END OPEN CONTRACTS IN KANSAS CITY NEW-CROP FUTURES AND PERCENTAGE IN HARD WHEAT CONTRACTS, OCTOBER 1953 TO FEBRUARY 1954 *

(*Thousand Bushels*)

Date	Hard or Red		Hard Only			
	July	Sept.	July	Sept.	Total	Per Cent Hard
Oct. 30	35	—	860	—	895	96
Nov. 30	195	—	1590	—	1785	89
Dec. 31	235	—	1708	—	1943	88
Jan. 29	375	5	2010	26	2416	84
Feb. 26	565	5	2153	37	2760	79

* Data from Kansas City *Grain Market Review.*

were people particularly interested in hard winter wheat. Such people would tend to lose interest when the Kansas City future became effectively a soft wheat contract. But such an explanation would run counter to the common view that most speculators do not care much what they speculate in; or that if they are particularly interested in wheat, for example, they are not discriminating enough to care what sort of wheat they trade in. Is it possible that many speculators are more discriminating than is commonly supposed?

RESULTS OF THE EXPERIMENT

Decision of the Kansas City exchange to try a hard wheat contract, along with the old one, opened the way to finding out which would be the more popular contract in actual use, and by how wide a margin. But because trading in hard wheat futures was restricted to deliveries in July 1954 or later, the two forms of contract did not compete on an equal basis. Table 2 compares the amounts of old-style contracts and of hard wheat contracts in effect for July and September delivery at the end of each month from October through February. The heavy predominance of hard wheat contracts at first reflects abnormal forcing of hard wheat trading into the July delivery because it could not be done for earlier delivery months. This effect diminished as time passed, but was undoubtedly still present at the end of February. At that time it was reasonable to think that the percentages in the final column of Table 2 might possibly continue their evident downward trend as the volume of contracts for May delivery declined to extinction in late May, with the result that when all outstanding contracts were for new-crop delivery months, no more than about 70 per cent of their volume might be in the hard wheat contract.[14]

Such an outcome appeared possible only on the assumption that hedgers who preferred the old contract terms might hold that preference strongly enough to overcome their aversion to use of a relatively inactive contract. That proved not to be the case. By the time the last contracts for May delivery were closed out, on May 24, the volume of contracts for July delivery stood at 5,597 thousand bushels, of which 91 per cent were in the hard wheat contract; and trading for deliveries after July was confined entirely to the hard wheat contract.

Though a relatively small futures market that competes for hedging business with a larger one can lose ground very quickly if its contract ceases to offer some special advantage to hedgers, it cannot so quickly regain lost ground by restoring that advantage. Once business has fallen off, such a market suffers aggravated disadvantage from its small volume of business. Thus by the end of May, when Kansas City was once again using a hard wheat contract for all delivery months, its volume of open contracts had recovered only to 16.5 per cent of the volume at Chicago, and its volume of trading still averaged only about 7 per cent of the volume at Chicago. Further recovery of business in wheat futures at Kansas City may nevertheless be fairly rapid. The gain in volume of open contracts from 11.8 to 16.5 per cent of the total at Chicago, between December and late May, is an impressive one—a gain of 40 per cent—and it has been attained at a time of year when Kansas City open contracts tend to be near their lowest level. And one may confidently expect the relative volume of trading at Kansas City to respond soon to the increase in relative volume of open contracts, aiding the further recovery of hedging business that will be stimulated by movement to markets of the 1954 crop of hard winter wheat.

[14] When the final draft of this paper went to the Editor, suggestion of this possibility was followed by speculation on the further possibility that at Kansas City, contrary to nearly all other experience with futures trading, it might prove feasible and desirable to maintain trading in two futures contracts. Subsequent events have shown that conditions at Kansas City did not allow emergence of such an interesting exception to the general rule. The paragraphs that follow have been added in galley proof.

46. THE FARMER AND THE FOOD INDUSTRIES *

Herrell DeGraff

I

I am honored and privileged to share this platform and thus to meet with the many of you who are deeply involved, wholly involved, with food—the food that is indeed the Life Line of America. Though my interest could be called merely academic, and thus remote from the complexities of your operating problems, nevertheless I too, live and work and eat and sleep the food business. My job, if I fulfill its opportunities, gives me little chance to do anything else. I was reared in agriculture, and in addition to having been a one-time farmer, have also worked in food processing and in food distribution. These have been experiences which I now cherish.

Perhaps because of these experiences, I can see the interrelated problems, and the interdependent nature, of all parts of the food business a little more clearly. The farmers with whom I long have worked need you, as you need them—and as both you and they need the food distributors who stand between you and the final consumer.

If there can be said to be three major groups in the food business —producers, processors and distributors—certainly each one is quite completely dependent on the other two. And if anyone cares to break the total Life Line into more and still smaller pieces, the consequence is only more interdependencies. However self-important and self-impressed any one group may come to feel about its own contributions to society, it still is true that interdependence with all others in the food field far outweighs any independence.

In recent years, mainly because of my academic post, I have had the rare privilege of trying to explain each group within the food business to the others, and also the total food business to the consuming public. I certainly consider this a great privilege because of my

* Reprinted by permission of Herrell DeGraff from a talk presented at the Golden Anniversary Meeting, Grocery Manufacturers of America, New York City (November 10, 1958).

Herrell DeGraff, Former Babcock Professor of Food Economics, Graduate School of Nutrition, Cornell University, now Executive Vice-President, American Meat Institute.

respect for the people who have contributed so magnificently to the great progress of food production, food processing, and food distribution. But it is also a sobering challenge. This is so because anyone can discuss the total industry, or its parts, only as he sees it. Who could come before you and speak for the farmer—that is, for all the diverse interests and points of view within agriculture—from a background of full understanding and total objectivity? It seems to me there is no such person, anymore than one person could speak for all retail or all processor interests. I welcome this chance to speak about "the farmer and the food industries" (which properly should be called "the farmer and the *rest* of the food industries") even though what I say can be only one man's point of view. Some of the things I say you may not like. But I have a purpose, so please hear me out.

You need hardly be told that food processors, along with food distributors, are often regarded as organizations which buy cheap from farmers and sell high to consumers. Food marketing, meaning everything that happens to food beyond the farm, now absorbs considerably more of the food dollar than goes back to farmers. That this is because of justified and wholly desirable services built into our food—and that it will always be true under anything approximating "normal" economic conditions—does not change the criticism of the price-spread or the "farmers' shrinking share of the food dollar." It is not an idle matter in my thinking that food marketing—both processing and distribution—is widely regarded as "big business." This view is widespread in spite of the fact that, numerically speaking, the great majority of food handling firms beyond the farms actually are small business. We live with a prevalent public attitude, however unfortunate, that "big" is synonomous with "bad." Recent events indicate that we no longer attach the attitude to certain family names, but still retain the attitude itself. This seems to me highly significant, both to an agriculture in which producing units are getting bigger, and to processing and distributing industries in which certain trends are tending to emphasize the factor of bigness. I make this point because it is on my mind this second week of November, and also because it has some meaning in connnection with other things I wish to discuss.

II

This nation's food no longer is the product of a simple economic organization. Rather, it is a complex and continuous flow of services, from the farmer—and behind the farmer, from his supplier industries—all the way through to the consumer. It is a food supply without season or geography, and the most processed, packaged, and highly-serviced food supply ever known. The sum of the services that have made it what it is have built and held a total market for food materially greater than anyone who might reason from traditional economic doctrine could have expected it to be. A century ago a German economist named Ernst Engel stated a principle, that has come down to us as Engel's Law, and that has been a road block to a good deal of thinking about food. Briefly, Engel's Law states that as income rises a family spends for food a smaller proportion of its increased income. If this principle still applied to our economy as Engel stated it, and as it long was thought to apply, the dollar volume of our food business today would be some 25 to 30 per cent less than it actually is.

But our economy has changed, in ways that Engel or few others could hardly have foreseen. Women no longer are confined to the home and the kitchen. They have employment or other interests outside the home, which mean that many millions of them, in essence, are carrying two jobs. Maid service is essential to them to lighten the burdens of homemaking—yet they cannot hire domestic servants. Much of the maid service they require is furnished in the food they buy. Our food business today is geared to serving the needs of homemakers—both those who are gainfully employed and those who are not—who neither can nor will spend long kitchen hours in food preparation. We have a food supply almost unbelievably changed from the bulk-ingredient supply of a generation ago—the food supply Engel knew, and in terms of which he stated his doctrine.

There are two points on which Engel went wrong. First, consumers with increased knowledge of the health values of proper eating will upgrade the nutritive quality of the family diet out of increased purchasing power. This means, basically, an increased proportion of the "protective" foods furnishing an abundance of protein, vitamins, and minerals. Knowledge of these more subtle factors in food and health was, of course, grossly lacking in Engel's day.

Second, Engel did not know about convenience foods, and the kinds of services that make them possible. And not knowing about them, he could not know that the market for food services is enormously expandable, and that it behaves very differently than does food-quantity in an environment of high purchasing power and rising income. In other words, there is no Engel's Law for food services.

It is these two factors alone—the upgrading of diet, and the increase in services built into a unit of food—that have enormously expanded the food market in recent years beyond what would have been anticipated from the growth of population.

III

How have farmers contributed to these trends?

First of all, they have produced the abundance on which the high volume of processors and retailers has been built. Whatever else anyone may say about agriculture, it surely cannot be accused of lack of volume.

Secondly, they have produced diversity. Few products adaptable to the wide climatic range of the country have to be obtained from any other part of the world.

Third, they have produced quality—and this is not only high quality in itself, but more importantly, it is uniform high quality. And the importance of the uniformity is hard to overemphasize.

In today's food distribution—the retail end of the Life Line—based as it is on self-service and impersonal selling, uniformity has become an essential of successful operation. The consumer who has found a product she likes wants it to be the same tomorrow as it was today, the same every time she takes it off the shelf. Some of this uniformity comes from advances in your processing techniques. But in large part also it is a new characteristic of the products delivered to you by the producers.

The origin of high uniform quality of farm products actually is the science now being applied in agricultural production. A fruit crop may be sprayed 20 times during the growing season, in consequence of which you get a highly desirable product delivered to your plants. But the real advance is not the spraying. It is the work of plant pathologists, and entymologists, and chemists, and engineers, who studied the life cycles of pests, who learned how to control them, who devised chemicals to do the job and machines to apply the chemicals.

Agriculture today is not confined to the farm. Much of it does not even begin on the farm. It begins in the laboratory, the experimental plot, and in testing stations. It is the physicist and the chemist, the geneticist, the physiologist, and the pathologist. It is their research findings taken over by industrial concerns and incorporated into more effective production supplies for use by a farmer who may never have heard of the underlying science that made the improved supplies possible. These include feed, seed, fertilizer, pesticides, medicines, machines, fuels, and many other things, the end product of which is an abundance and quality and uniformity of product never before achieved. In other words, agriculture is a partnership of science, industry, and farmers—that now has arrived at amazing achievements after decades of development.

This emerging partnership has by no means run its course, for the simple reason that the science in which it has been generated can actually be no more than in its infancy. The post-war decade has brought an amazing growth of population. And only a foolhardy person would now guess what the eventual population of the country will be or when we will achieve it. We only know that it will be much bigger than it is now and that the increased numbers of people will have to eat from no more crop land than the approximate acreage we are now using. Time may prove that statement to be wrong, but it is the present prospect. And yet, as I see it, there is no cause for concern however big the population may become. One need only let his imagination range across the potentials yet to be realized in agronomic and biologic science to come up with many things as startling as anything Jules Verne dreamed up at his best.

I find more which occupies my thinking with the immediate future than I do in that which is far distant. I find myself bothered, for example, about two fundamental, but opposing characteristics of the American people. One of these is that we worship at the shrine of technological progress. The other is that we do not want to pay a major part of the price of the same technology. In terms of agriculture, we want the advancing technology, the production potential, the abundance, and the new high quality of food that goes with it. But then, I judge from the national temperament, we want to keep the historic relationship of costs and prices, and the sociologic and economic balances in our rural economy that prevailed before the technology developed. No more clear-cut nor impossible example of wanting to "have the cake and to eat it too" ever existed.

Where we are today in the agriculture which is your source of supply is at best a partial adjustment to present technology, and necessary further adjustment which we are both forcing and blocking at the same time.

The applications of mechanical power to farming have enormously increased the number of acres and animals that can be handled by one man. The use of fertilizers, pesticides, better varieties and better livestock have contributed large increases in production from each acre and animal. In consequence, agriculture has become a business of shrinking employment opportunity. Capital requirements have increased, and perhaps most important of all, the complexities of management have intensified to a new high level, and continue to rise.

Some farms have been brought into adjustment with the new technology. They are the ones with the requisite land, capital, and management skill to be successful commercial operations. They may be thought of as the leaders in an amazingly dynamic agriculture. Their unit costs of production are sufficiently low to stimulate them to keep on expanding production even at prices which cause less-adjusted farmers to go into the red. Never in history have our farms or farmers been all alike, but in the dynamics of today's agriculture they are becoming increasingly more unlike.

A million and a quarter farms, out of some 4.75 million enumerated by the Census produce 80 per cent of the total sales of farm products. This comparatively small number of high-volume producers are your suppliers. Most of the complexities of national farm policy are centered within the other 3½ million—but this topic, vital as it is, we should not try to get into here.

IV

Farm production today is much more market-oriented than it has been in the past. This is reflected in increased direct selling from the farm to the processor or distributor, and a decreasing use of central market terminals. Central terminals traditionally have been places of assembly, where large quantities of products can be brought together so that buyers could "inspect all the offerings." With greater scientific control over production methods and production hazards on the farm, the variability of products is reduced and production-to-specification has become increasingly possible. It is basically this fact that has been sharply increasing the amount of direct selling from food producers to food handlers.

Of course, the shift has been most pronounced on farms where a fuller degree of adjustment has been made to the scientific potentials. There has been much less shift from the farms which lag far behind in production methods.

We are currently living with a phenomenon called "integration." Integration is essentially a drive towards still greater market orientation in farm production. It represents primarily a formalization of contractual relations between the different groups in food producing and handling, with the object of greater competitive success in the market place. Integration recognizes that farming no longer is an art. Science can control production hazards in increasing degree. Science can improve the quality as well as the quantity of products. Science can contribute in many ways to greater efficiency in farming and food industries. The vertical integration of agriculture with which we are now living is basically a recognition of these facts and a drive for their fuller realization.

I suggested that integration is primarily market-oriented. I think that even in those aspects directed toward improving production practices on the farm, the deeper motivation actually is more successful competition in the final-product market. It is part of the almost universal drive today to compete more successfully for the consumers' dollar.

Among farmers, just as among food processors, there is increasing competition between one food product and another. The family who ate chicken for dinner bypassed pork or beef. If they used frozen potatoes, they did not use minute rice. If the dessert was ice cream, they probably did not use a prepared pudding.

Agriculture is a competitive business, not one aggregate of producers who all have the same interests. It never has been a one-unit business, even though some people, notably government officials and college professors, often treat it as though it is. Today it is less a one-unit business than ever. More correctly, it must be seen as a large number of sub-group interests—product sub-groups—each trying to build the largest possible market for its own product. Unless and until we are willing to see our agriculture in this setting, it is impossible to understand the highly dynamic food production and marketing developments with which we are living. How successful each product-group of producers may be hinges not alone on their own efforts, but also on the processors who handle their product and who strive along with them to build their own market. Thus the total food market is a highly competitive situation, with product pitted against product, and producer-processor teams each working to get there first with the most.

The product specifications written by food distributors or food processors have only one purpose. It is to assure that characteristics which the farmer-processor team is capable of building into a product will actually be achieved, so that consumers will find the product more attractive and will buy it in competition with alternatives. The "integration" of production, processing, and distribution—whether it is informal or contractual—has basically the same purpose. It is a natural, logical development growing out of improvements in production, processing, and marketing technology, and stimulated by the competitive nature of the market.

There are strong reasons why producers, or processors, or even food distributors may decide to encourage the advance of integration in the food business. For producers, the rapidly expanding capital needs of agriculture, or the increasingly complex management requirements, or possibly an increased control of risk, may be factors fostering integration from their point of view—if through the integration device they might help solve their problems in these areas. Processors, likewise, may try to solve their volume of supply, or season of supply, or quality of supply problems by the device of contractual integration. Food distributors may seek closer compliance with their product specifications through contractual relationships with producers and suppliers. At every step the contractual integration may result in fuller realization of the potentials for improved product at points where current practice may be lagging behind full realization of technological advances.

How fast integration may advance and how far it may go certainly are questions to which no one now can give answers. There are indeed strong reasons for more of it to develop, and many students of food and agriculture believe it will be much more widely used in the years ahead.

But I want to suggest one reason why we should hope that integration should not proceed too fast or go too far too quickly.

The broiler industry is by far the most highly integrated part of agriculture to date. In considerable part because of its integrated character it has advanced amazingly fast. Currently we are producing about 1.5 billion broilers a year, compared to only a few million 20 years ago. But over 90 per cent of our enormous broiler production now is raised by about 28,000 growers. It has been calculated that if hog production were to reach a comparable stage of integration to what we now have in broilers, as few as 60,000 producers maintaining 100 sows each could produce our total pork supply. Or similarly, 200,000 dairy farmers keeping 100 cows each could supply the total market for milk. Each of these possibilities—and they are distinctly possible—would represent decreases in numbers of producers to small fractions of the number of farmers who now raise hogs or produce milk.

My question is whether anyone could believe—given our present political climate—that we could go in this direction and have anything less than parallel regulation by government in proportion as production might be concentrated in so few hands?

In fact, would not the integrated unit, large in size and few in number, come to be looked upon as the producing unit? And given the political climate of our time, should we not expect government to move in on the regulation of margins in these integrated food operations? And where could such regulation lead, except to make food a public utility?

The advance of technology in agriculture has led to this impasse. A relatively few producers, large in size and highly efficient in their operations, can produce all the food we need at far below currently prevailing production costs among large numbers of farmers, who for any of many reasons have not been able to come into adjustment with the technological potentials. This is our real farm problem. Moreover, the technology continues to go forward, and the lack of adjustment to it among a very large proportion of all farm families becomes more pronounced. The political battle over those often referred to as the "big and oppressive" versus those who are called the "small and unprotected" will become increasingly intense. You will continue to get your supplies, in volume and in quality. I see only improving conditions for you in this direction. But you are not remote from the political battle over agriculture—a battle that is an anomaly. We believe in technology, in efficiency, and in progress. But I am forced to the conclusion that we do not believe in the adjustments in the sociologic and economic characteristics of our rural economy that are inseparable from putting the technology into practice. You may think you are remote from this dilemma, but I doubt that you are.

Yet, however, the policy battle turns out, I believe you will get the farm products you need, in both quantity and quality, to continue to build the food business to the great volume that is its potential. This will be because the technology will not, and indeed cannot, be stopped. I expect the food business to continue to go forward in volume, far beyond what the traditionalism of Engel and others would indicate. This is because I expect you to continue to compete, strongly and successfully, for a continuing increased share of rising consumer purchasing power.

47. ARE COOPERATIVES GOOD BUSINESS?

Joseph G. Knapp

Since 1752, when Ben Franklin helped to establish a mutual insurance company, cooperatives have grown in size and scope, until today they include many different types of organizations performing many varied functions:

> 3,000,000 farmers have nearly $2,000,000,000 invested in marketing and purchasing cooperatives, which do an annual business of $10,000,000,000.
>
> 62% of independent grocery sales and 42% of the total food volume are accounted for by retailer cooperatives and voluntary chains.
>
> 7,000,000 people belong to some 15,000 credit unions, with over $2,000,000,000 of combined assets.

The cooperative form of organization is well established and growing in many fields. There are forest and fishery, irrigation, and electrification cooperatives. Mutual insurance companies employ this principle. College students use it to obtain their books, equipment, board and room as cheaply as possible. There are cooperative housing units and medical care associations. Newspapers make use of a cooperative, the Associated Press; and the Railway Express Agency is operated jointly as a cooperative by the railways. CARE—the Cooperative for American Remittances to Everywhere—has supplied many needy people in some 50 countries with materials worth $165,000,000.

Each of these organizations is different; each has its own peculiar problems and sphere of operation; yet all have a similar effect on the economy. It is the purpose of this article to discuss the position of such cooperatives in our private enterprise system—their principles and purposes, their differences from other forms of business enterprise, their weaknesses, their achievements, the adjustments they must make, and their role in the future of our economy.

Principles and Purpose

A cooperative is an organization set up by a group of persons or firms to perform services for themselves. Their object is to secure *better* services, in terms of quality and cost, than they could otherwise obtain. Their chief instrument for achieving this purpose is

* Reprinted by permission from *Harvard Business Review*, Vol. 35, No. 1 (January-February, 1957), pp. 57-64.

Joseph G. Knapp, Administrator of the Farmer Cooperative Service, United States Department of Agriculture.

group integration, which is a source both of bargaining power and of efficiency. For example:

> A group of farmers, faced by low-quality, high-cost feed, fertilizer, and other basic supplies, may realize that if they join together, their volume of requirements will be high enough to enable them to buy supplies of the quality they desire at the lowest possible costs.
>
> They may also feel that they can get better distribution and better prices for the commodities they produce if they have an organization through which their joint output can be marketed.
>
> Many farmers would attribute great importance to the advice as well as the help that they receive from cooperatives, both in procuring the raw materials necessary to produce the best results and in obtaining more satisfactory market outlets than they would otherwise have. Cooperatives often perform educational activities that promote the efficiency of the industry.

Cooperatives, in short, aim to provide for other groups in the economy some of the economic benefits enjoyed by large businesses, and they seek to accomplish this aim through economies of scale and organization.

Private enterprises

A distinction is frequently made between cooperatives and private business, but this distinction is highly questionable. Dr. Edwin G. Nourse has pointed out that the real distinction between cooperatives and other private firms lies in the performance of the entrepreneurial function. He includes cooperatives in the private-enterprise system, but he stresses that the direct participants in the cooperative form of business supply both the exploratory and directional functions and the capital, and so dispense with the entrepreneur in the usual sense.

Dr. Nourse is right; cooperatives are a distinctive form of private business. They are set up by individuals or by business firms; their object is to serve their members at cost; their members are primarily interested in improving their own incomes; they are financed by those who benefit from them. These are certainly characteristics in keeping with our private-enterprise system. Obviously cooperatives are not formed and do not distribute financial benefits along the same lines as other private business enterprises. But most certainly they are private as distinct from public enterprises, which are operated by the people through a government agency. And they are private as distinct from socialistic enterprises, which are state-controlled, state-financed, and state-directed.

Indeed, it is difficult to find terms to distinguish cooperatives from other types of business organization. Some writers refer to companies in the latter group as private, proprietary, and independent; but a cooperative is also private, proprietary, and independent. The difference is not between "profit" and "nonprofit" enterprises because, although cooperatives as such are not formed for profit, the members are motivated by a desire to improve their economic position.

Again, the distinction cannot be made between "cooperative" and "noncooperative" forms of business, for cooperation must be present in all business. It seems to me that the comparison can most easily be made by distinguishing cooperative from "general business" enterprises. Since only a small fraction of all business is done by cooperatives, it seems reasonable to call the part not done by them the "general" part of the private-enterprise system.

Distinctive aims

While there is no rational foundation whatsoever for arguing that cooperatives are not private enterprises, there are at least four important ways in which a cooperative does differ from general business. When a group of individuals or firms establish a cooperative, they have in mind certain distinctive purposes, as follows:

(1) They seek to obtain services for themselves at cost—not to obtain profit from rendering services to others.

(2) They try to render the greatest financial benefit to their members as users—not to maximize profit for owners as distinct from users.

(3) They distribute amounts remaining after payment of the costs of doing business among those who are served by the cooperative in proportion to their use of its services—not in proportion to their investment in the enterprise.

(4) They plan to have an organization that will be controlled by its patron-members (each of whom ordinarily is allowed a single vote) —not by the owners in proportion to capital contributed.

These distinctions do not imply superiority to either the cooperative or the general form of private enterprise. Each provides an alternative way of doing business, and each contributes to the vitality of what we are pleased to call our American competitive economy.

Although cooperatives are not less "private" than other forms of business enterprise, they do appear to be more democratic. The arrangement of giving each shareholder one vote regardless of his stake in the enterprise makes the cooperative business more subject to popular control than most economic institutions.

Public acceptance

In view of the fact that cooperatives are private enterprises, democratically run, it seems somewhat perplexing to find that large sectors of public opinion regard them unfavorably.

Probably one of the main reasons why cooperatives are misunderstood is that in the eyes of many people they enjoy undue advantage under the federal income tax laws. It is impossible in this brief article to explain fully the cooperative position with regard to the federal income tax, but the substance of it is this:

> The cooperative operation does not result in the formation of net income by the cooperative subject to tax. Should any firm elect to forego the making of income and operate according to cooperative principles on a cost-of-service basis, it likewise would have little or no net income subject to tax. Any business can enter into a contractual agreement with those that it serves to return to them savings resulting from their patronage and free itself from income tax on those amounts. In other words, our tax laws at the present time provide no general advantages to cooperatives that are not available to any other organization which elects to operate so as not to accumulate income.
>
> One way of looking at this problem is to realize that only individuals or firms that earn an income incur the burden of paying tax on it. Except in a strict legal sense, cooperatives are not business entities in themselves but are, in the last analysis, the member individuals or firms who comprise them. Accordingly, net margins derived through a cooperative belong to the patron-owners; if their net incomes are increased by virtue of belonging to the organization, then they are the ones to pay the income taxes.

To some extent, the difficulty faced by cooperatives in justifying themselves before the public is explained by the fact that most channels of communication are dominated by the more prevalent types of business organization. Sometimes, unfortunately, a great deal of misunderstanding is fomented by those with special axes to grind.

On the other hand, cooperatives themselves have been responsible for much of the public's ignorance of their purposes and principles, for they have not concerned themselves enough with the problem of clarifying the misconceptions that many people entertain about them. In some cases, cooperatives have met opposition by preaching cooperation to the converted, rather than by searching out their natural allies and widening their circle of acceptance.

It is today more necessary than ever that cooperatives exhibit values which will tend to make them well regarded, for (thanks partly to the success of their own efforts) they now have a tougher competitive situation to meet than formerly, and the need for their services in many areas is not so obvious as it used to be.

However, this problem is at last being recognized. Cooperative leaders are now generally aware that they must show themselves to be up-to-date and efficient if they are to obtain and hold the respect of the business community. More and more cooperatives are emphasizing the constructive viewpoint that they do not aim to compete with general business except on the basis of efficiency; their contracts with their members, which result in cooperative margins not being taxed at the corporate level, are an essential, legal part of their form of organization—not a device to secure a tax advantage.

Trials and Errors

All businesses make mistakes, and cooperatives are no exceptions. They may be poorly organized. They may be inadequately provided with capital. They may not retain good management. In addition, a cooperative has special problems stemming from a form of organization that emphasizes authority from beneath:

> Granted, cooperatives are not so democratically run as Quaker meetings. It is true that the members elect boards of directors, who establish the policies, select managerial employees, check up on performance; who assume, in fact, the duties of the directors of a general business enterprise. The cooperative managers, as in other forms of business, are delegated certain rights. But the fact remains that the *entire structure is responsible to the members.* The patron is the ultimate boss, and the operating control is, in the final analysis, vested in him.

The weaknesses of this administrative structure are apparent; they are the weaknesses of all democratic organizations. To have a strong cooperative it is imperative that the members have a clear understanding of the nature of the enterprise and of their responsibilities to it. When this understanding is lacking, there are many things that may go wrong:

> A cooperative may be swayed by an emotional leader.
>
> Extraneous issues may interfere with basic business objectives; there may be a confusion of social and economic philosophies.
>
> It may be difficult to develop sound business procedures supported by strong boards of directors and capable executive personnel.
>
> Managers and other employees may be hired on a personality basis instead of for their capabilities.

Strange to say, one of the weaknesses of cooperatives has been a lack of cooperation among cooperatives. This is really not so surprising, for each cooperative is an economic and social organism. It takes time to federate and amalgamate in order to achieve maximum operating efficiency, just as it does with school districts or national states. Cooperatives, like large buildings, have to be built a brick at a time.

Positive Achievements

In spite of their shortcomings, cooperatives have many positive achievements to which they may point with pride. Although the cooperative system is by no means the panacea for all economic ills, it has an excellent record of social usefulness in several fields:

(1) The farmer has been the greatest single beneficiary of the American cooperative, for it has given him a form of economic organization adapted to the peculiar conditions of his industry. Farmers individually have little power in the market place. Organized in cooperatives they can meet power with power. Without such organizations they would have to rest content with whatever service they could get; they would have no choice. Cooperatives have secured for them the benefits of other organized groups while preserving for them their status as individual concerns.

(2) The cooperative has performed a similar service for the individual and the small business firm. It has given them the advantages of big business—volume economies, access to managerial skills, and sufficient capital for research and development. It has thus helped to perpetuate small enterprise with all its opportunities for individual expression and satisfaction, so valuable in an economy of increasingly large business firms.

(3) Perhaps the most important accomplishments of cooperatives have been their educational activities. There are millions of individuals who feel that they have a stake in the private enterprise system of this country because they are members of various kinds of cooperative organizations. They not only are served by these organizations but also take part in their management through membership meetings and through elected boards of directors. Several hundred thousand individuals are getting direct business training and management experience through being members of cooperative boards of directors. These organizations are, therefore, training schools in democratic and business procedure.

Cooperatives can also take credit for spreading economic literacy through their educational programs, informative annual reports, membership meetings, and periodic publications for members, with a total circulation running into the millions.

(4) Cooperatives have made information regarding methods of marketing and costs of various operations and functions generally available. Without cooperatives we would lack much detailed information regarding the working of our business institutions, for other forms of business can maintain a high degree of secrecy while cooperatives must operate "in a glass house." This free dissemination of operating figures by cooperatives might be thought of as their yardstick function.

(5) Cooperatives have helped to keep the competitive system competitive. By setting certain standards of business service and performance they have spread the benefits of their operations to those served by their competitors. For example, the value of cooperatives to all farmers in the form of better competitive terms made possible by their presence in the agricultural industries amounts to millions of dollars annually. This statement can be substantiated in many areas by the decline of margins taken for marketing and purchasing services when cooperatives began to provide effective competition.

(6) It is sometimes maintained that cooperatives can copy but cannot innovate; actually, they can be proud of their record as innovators. Dissatisfaction with old practices has often led to the formation of a cooperative to do something in a better way. For example, the cooperatives inaugurated both the open-formula principle in selling feed and fertilizer and the method through which farmers buy their supplies

on specifications. They pioneered in establishing quality grades for fruits, eggs, and other products. Their methods of revolving fund financing represent a definite departure from tradition.

Program for Expansion

The achievements of cooperatives are socially valuable enough to warrant further expansion both in the fields where they operate already and perhaps also into new fields. But growth will call for well-directed programs to overcome defects and to meet the problems of a constantly changing competitive environment. Probably the most challenging task of cooperatives is to become big enough to get the advantage of large-scale operation and thus maintain their position in a world of increasingly larger business enterprises. This means that:

(1) Cooperatives must increase their organizational and operating flexibility. They must become strong enough to meet the competition of large, aggressive business concerns which have greater freedom of action because they are not so responsible to large numbers of members. Members must select directors and officers who can provide as keen direction and as much drive as is characteristic of more autocratically organized concerns.

(2) The quality of managerial personnel must be raised. Cooperatives have a serious problem of recruiting, training, and keeping the kind of experts and managers that they require. Because they are not so well endowed financially as many other large business firms, they must hold their employees by making their work and job opportunities attractive. I anticipate that cooperatives are going to give increasing attention to management development and incentive payment plans in the next few years.

(3) They must find ways of obtaining the capital necessary not only for large-scale operations but also for undertaking new activities. Under present high-cost conditions it is difficult to organize cooperatives in many fields where there is a need for such enterprise. The need may exist, but the development of an organization strong enough to meet the need may call for rare promotional ability.

(4) Cooperatives must learn to cooperate, to work together. Because of obligations inherent in serving their members, cooperatives are not able to employ the device of merger to spread out into new market areas and diversify their operations to the same extent as other business firms. However, they can achieve many of the advantages of large-scale operations through various forms of regional federation while retaining strong *esprit de corps.* In other words, cooperatives must learn how to *integrate.* To a great extent, this involves subordination of local and personal interests for the good of a larger whole.

(5) Questions of business policy must be thoroughly analyzed, to see if new ways of doing business might bring a larger following without the sacrifice of safety or basic principle.

Take, for example, the question of installment credit. Cooperatives have to decide if and how far they should depart from the traditional cash-trading rule in order to attract patronage. Similarly, some farmer cooperatives are finding that the traditional one-price policy cannot be uniformly maintained without driving away some of the larger patrons who could get special concessions because of their size from other business firms. Cooperatives have the problem of giving such patrons price incentives to reflect lower cost in serving them without letting this disrupt the basic cooperative concept.

(6) Cooperatives must become even more conscious of the need for research and modern business methods. With the huge sums being spent today by large corporations for research, there is a danger that some cooperatives will be researched out of the market. However, many are responding to this challenge by taking advantage of research findings from the agricultural experiment stations and other agencies or by performing research services for themselves. The same is true in regard to other modern advances that are going on in the business world, such as management development, job evaluation, mechanization, automation, and motivation research; cooperatives are not lagging far behind in making use of them.

In the process of expansion, however, cooperatives must remember their limitations. Members are often so pleased with the achievements of their cooperative that they keep on demanding more and more. Distant fields look green, and there is the constant temptation to overreach. For example, experience in the past has indicated that farmer cooperatives cannot set up monopolies and control prices, but it seems that this lesson must be learned over and over again.

There is also the internal problem of maintaining membership support for a limited number of business objectives. In the case of cooperative associations with large numbers of people involved, it is difficult to keep their attention centered on the basic economic purposes. There is the danger that the organization will be pulled into political, religious, racial, or other divisive controversies.

Focus on education

If the problems involved in growth are to be met successfully, the fundamental need is for an educational program which will assure that the cooperative membership wields its authority on behalf of progress.

Although cooperation is a natural impulse, it has to be trained. People have to learn how to cooperate, how to work together. A certain element of self-discipline is called for. Cooperative business is not something that can be built upon spontaneous impulses. It is easy enough to get people to cooperate under the great stress of emergency, but to get them to work together over a period of time calls for organization. However, much cooperative experience has demonstrated that people can be taught to be good cooperators. Even the most individualistic type of person will work with others when he knows that it is to his advantage. The logic of cooperation must be understood and accepted, and there must be confidence in the receipt of benefits from the cooperation.

Future Role

If cooperative leaders are successful in instituting growth programs to overcome defects and to meet problems, then opportunities for achievement by this form of business are many. The cooperative is exceedingly well designed for combating a number of economic problems in our community, and for dealing with some of our future social problems as well. However, only when cooperatives are operating efficiently for themselves can they effectively perform the functions potentially theirs in our economy.

Economic functions

There are a number of important economic problems that the cooperative will be able to help solve:

> Cooperatives can integrate farms with markets and with sources of supply, and thus make agriculture a stronger segment of our society. Many farmers already belong to cooperatives which give them efficiency in procurement and in marketing. If such organizations are extended and combined, they can make farms the control center of a business system designed to meet their needs. Farming under these circumstances ceases to be isolated and becomes the heart of an integrated farm-enterprise system with the advantages of integration, including a better adjustment of supplies to markets. This process has already gone further than many realize, and has great promise in building a stabilized agricultural community.
>
> Cooperatives can also help to keep the economy in balance. Because of the large numbers of people investing in them, cooperatives are conservative organizations. Farmer marketing and purchasing cooperatives alone represent the investment interests of 3 million farmers. This is a stabilizing factor in our economy, and as cooperatives grow in membership and strength, it may prove of increasing importance in times of stress.
>
> Cooperatives may also serve as a check against higher costs of distribution. Because cooperatives provide services at cost, farmers and other individuals tend to join them to make ends meet when the costs of distribution go up. Even if cooperatives are not able to achieve significant savings for their members, they may be able to strengthen competition and reduce the margins taken by others.
>
> Cooperatives can help to maintain competition, which may well be a problem in future years, because in many fields the number of effective competitive firms is declining. Through their principle of returning margins to patrons, cooperatives can keep other forms of enterprise on their toes by demonstrating price advantages to those served. Many cooperative leaders hold that this function is of the greatest importance in assuring a good standard of service for all. If service or price is unsatisfactory, the cooperative route will be taken.

Social functions

In an increasingly organized and mechanized world, where it is becoming more and more difficult to maintain one's individuality, membership in a cooperative will provide individuals or small-scale firms with a choice of alternative ways in which they can be served, and thus will retain for them some of the old-time satisfactions of "consumer sovereignty." In other words, cooperatives will help to prevent the individual from becoming a mere unit of response in a standardized world of mass production, mass distribution, mass communication.

The threatened loss of individuality is not strictly an economic problem but a social problem arising from economic conditions. With continued economic progress, however, it is anticipated that more and more consideration will be given by all firms to the satisfaction of the individual in terms of things other than price. Economic growth will assuredly have a great impact on the lives of our people. With ever-growing abundance, competitive pressures may be blunted. As Paul T. Homan has stated:

> "It appears to me, as I suggested earlier, that the curve of growth is bound to flatten off. As this occurs, the economic apparatus of the country—geared to innovation, enterprise, and rapid growth—will become increasingly obsolete. The most critical economic goals ahead are therefore likely to be institutional in character, testing our ability to reshape our scheme of cooperative working relationships amicably, sensibly, and with due regard to the higher aspirations of man." [1]

Thomas C. Cochran was also subscribing to this point of view when he said that "the modern corporation has inevitably become more than an economic institution and its managers have more than material responsibilities." [2]

These quotations do not refer particularly to cooperatives, but they do reflect a realization that indistinct but powerful forces are transforming our society and that our business institutions will have to take these forces into account. Organizations must adapt their procedures to meet these psychological probings. The whole area of motivation research indicates that business is becoming more and more concerned with what people really want, which often differs from their conditioned response.

[1] "The Social Goals of Economic Growth in the United States," *American Economic Review*, May 1956 (Papers and Proceedings of the Sixty-Eighth Annual Meeting of the American Economic Association, New York City, December 28-30, 1955), p. 34.

[2] "Business and the Democratic Tradition," HBR (March-April 1956), p. 39.

Thus it is possible that the cooperative form of organization may be much more attuned to the times 50 years from now than it is today in that it gives the individual a voice in the business that serves him. There is also the interesting question of whether, in the search for recognizing the individual, the large corporations of today will not take on more and more features that we think of as associated with cooperative enterprise.

The Prospects

Where will cooperatives be in 20 years? I remember that this question was asked me a couple of decades ago with regard to the farm cooperatives. I then optimistically estimated that they would double in volume of business. They have more than done this, and there has been a corresponding growth in the number of members involved.

With the good start that farmer cooperatives have and with the strong cooperatives now operating, continued growth can be reasonably assumed. These organizations are, on the whole, well managed. They are suited to the needs of farmers and are aided by an excellent system of research and education through federal and state agencies.[3] Already they have done much to ameliorate the cost-price squeeze confronting farmers, and in the future they can be expected to assume a larger part of the job of economic stabilization.

Retail prospects

Other forms of cooperative enterprise will also undoubtedly continue to grow. According to Robert W. Mueller, editor of the *Progressive Grocer*, the retailer cooperatives and voluntary chains "have made enormous gains in recent years."[4] That this movement has been a force strong enough to limit the gathering of stores into chain systems seems to be an especially striking accomplishment.

Although the rate of expansion of such firms will probably decline somewhat, the field does not seem to be saturated. How far the development will go will depend on the management skills available and the adaptability of this form of enterprise to changing conditions. Success breeds success, and as achievements grow, support for cooperatives will follow.

[3] See John H. Davis, "From Agriculture to Agribusiness," HBR (January-February 1956), p. 107.

[4] "The New Look in Grocery Wholesaling—What It Means to the Retailer," *Progressive Grocer* (May, 1956), Section I, p. 59.

Consumer cooperatives

Just as cooperation among retailers may be a means of preserving competitive opportunity, cooperation among consumers may be the means of obtaining superior retail service. It has long been the belief in business circles that consumer cooperation—the operation of retail businesses by consumers—is impractical. There is much in our business history to support this view, but it is pertinent to point out that in a number of localities some very interesting and significant experiments in consumer cooperation are being carried on. For example:

> The Consumers Cooperative Society of Palo Alto, California, boasts some 21 years of continuous growth. As of January 1956, it had 3,741 members, and its sales in 1955 were $4,262,159. The annual report of this organization reveals its extensive operations in providing supermarket and many other services through several centers.

While special circumstances and able leadership have helped this business, its future, like the future of all such cooperatives, looks brighter than it has for years.

Conclusion

As people and firms become better acquainted with the adaptability of the cooperative form of enterprise to their needs, its use can be expected to spread, though it need not and should not ever completely supplant other forms of business. The cooperative form of enterprise both complements and supplements the services performed by other forms of private business, thus giving our system even greater flexibility and strength.

By providing a self-help mechanism through which people and business firms can serve themselves according to their needs, the cooperative can also democratize and decentralize parts of our economic life, provide pace-setting competition for other forms of business, and give the individual a sense of belonging. It can act as a balance wheel—or a safety valve—in our economy by providing an alternative type of business organization within the free-enterprise system that we value so highly.

SECTION 5. CHANNELS OF DISTRIBUTION

Channels of distribution are key factors in determining the producer's operating policies and the profitability of his business. Retailers and wholesalers who want to retain or improve their competitive market position must be familiar with the changing pattern of distribution and the reasons for change. For many consumer products it is unlikely that retailing middlemen can be replaced by a direct producer-to-ultimate-consumer channel. A continuing problem to the producer is the selection of the most efficient retail channel or channels, and those which best adapt to changing consumer behavior. In contrast to the selection of retail channels, the producer more frequently must decide whether to use wholesaling middlemen or to deal directly with buyers of his product. If he does decide to use wholesaling middlemen, what groups should be used?

Increasing movement of both consumers and industry is an inescapable aspect of today's United States economy, with a decided impact on marketing. Those firms who constantly study location trends can select channels of distribution that are in the forefront rather than the rear guard of the rapidly changing location picture. Perhaps they themselves must relocate.

Distribution cost analysis can be valuable to the producer in determining whether to perform the marketing functions himself or have middlemen perform all or some of these functions. Cost analysis also enables both producer and middlemen to ascertain which segments of their business are profitable or unprofitable.

Section 5-A
Distribution Cost Analysis

The increase in distribution costs presents a challenge to marketing executives. In "Eleven Approaches to the Problem of Distribution Costs" Professor Donald R. G. Cowan comments on distribution costs, not from the aspect of their complete elimination, but from the elimination of inefficiencies.

Charles H. Sevin in "Analytical Approach to Channel Policies—Marketing Cost Analysis" stresses the need for adequate cost information, and by the use of case studies indicates that the selection of the most profitable channel is likely to be done individually.

Section 5-B
Wholesalers

According to Dr. Herman C. Nolen in "The Modern Wholesaler and His Adjustment to a Changing Economy," the wholesaler has not received sufficient credit for keeping pace with changing conditions and for his contribution to economic progress.

"A New Type of Middleman—Rack Jobbers" by James A. Slater provides an understanding of a category of wholesalers who have established their usefulness.

Another study of food distribution points up the difficulties in separating production and marketing, and reveals the changes in the American economy that are illustrated by developments in the food industries. The main sectors involved in Professor George L. Mehren's article, "The Changing Structure of the Food Market," are consumers, retailers, wholesalers, processors, and producers.

Section 5-C
Retail Organizations

Although William Snaith's talk, "Retail Competition as It Affects the Department Store," was originally given before an audience of department store executives, his incisive analysis is valuable not only to retailers but also to all who are interested in the marketing of consumer goods.

Norris Willatt's penetrating analysis in "Convenience Markets" of the bantam drive-in store concept contradicts the wide spread belief that the small store is obsolete. Since the number of these stores is still relatively small, about 1,500, the impact on retailing, particularly for food and drugs, is still to be realized. But the likelihood of their rapid increase in number of stores must be considered in any long range market planning.

An overall picture of non-food merchandising by food stores is presented in "Non-Foods Merchandising"—a pioneering study by Professor Milton Alexander.

Professor Alexander's study is followed by Donald Bruce Reynold's current analysis, "Non-Foods Are Big Business," of a national survey of seven basic non-food lines.

The consumer has shown less desire to spend time for shopping and greater receptivity to innovations which will provide additional leisure time. E. B. Weiss in "The Coming Era of In-Home Retailing" discusses how in-home retailing transcends such traditional channels as mail order, house to house canvassing, club plans, and wagon distributors. He predicts a revolution in methods of reaching the consumer at home through the use of electronic equipment and instrumentation.

Are "Tenant-Selection Policies of Regional Shopping Centers" likely to contribute to the longevity of shopping centers? Are they in the best interests of consumers, retailers and manufacturers? Morris L. Sweet considers the possible results of present policies.

Not to be confused with the tenant in a controlled shopping center, the retailer in a solo highway location is becoming the recipient of closer scrutiny by competitive retailers and manufacturers. E. B. Weiss points out some of the ramifications of this new form in "Highway Retailing—The Next Great Retail Revolution."

Section 5-D
Retail Policy Considerations

What factors have brought about consumer acceptance of one-stop shopping in supermarkets? Where can the line be drawn as to what will or what won't be eventually sold in one store? Provocative answers based upon many years of experience with one of America's leading and progressive food chains are provided by Thomas C. Butler in his article, "The Supermarket Invades the General Merchandise Field."

Dr. James S. Cross in his talk, "Motor Product Marketing," presents a broad brush treatment of strategies and concepts in motor products marketing. His analysis of the future position of the service station underscores again the importance of segmented merchandising as a vital component of marketing strategy.

Professor Stanley C. Hollander's article, "The American Retailer —Subservient to the Public," draws upon a number of historical, sociological, and psychological studies in comparing the shopper of today with those of previous periods. He relates how shoppers are attracted by different types of store service, as well as different types of merchandise. The article should be of special interest to students considering retailing as a career.

Urban planning has become a major concern of all segments of society in the United States and throughout the world. The complex ramifications, both domestic and foreign pertinent to industry and commerce, are discussed by Professors Morris L. Sweet and Finn B. Jensen in "The Planned Community." Urban planners are faced with making decisions on matters that have long been of concern to those in the marketing field. Just as urban planners must become aware of the vast body of marketing knowledge so must those in the marketing field explore and become conversant with developments in urban planning.

48. ELEVEN APPROACHES TO THE PROBLEM OF DISTRIBUTION COSTS *

Donald R. G. Cowan

Once again, business managements are turning their attention to distribution costs. Distribution costs include all the outlays for effort required in the process of bringing to consumers and industrial users the products of factories, farms, forests, and mines. They cover many vital services such as buying, selling, transportation, storage, risk-taking, financing, market information, and market management—at manufacturing, wholesaling, and retail levels.

For many products, the expenditures involved in their distribution exceed those required in production, and account for more than half of the price paid. Since these expenditures are usually made by many independent—and often competing—managements, they are frequently more complex, more subject to uncertainty as to their effectiveness, and more difficult to control than production costs.

Business interest in this subject always rises when declines in sales volume are in prospect or in progress. The period of the 1930's was the heyday of distribution cost analysis, while during World War II when production rather than distribution was the all-engrossing problem, attention was given it by a mere handful of companies mainly because of misgivings about their postwar sales volume and their desire to find the most effective channels and methods of distributing old and new product lines.

This lack of concern continued through the prosperous postwar period except for the brief hesitancy in business in 1949 and 1954 when again a few companies gave temporary attention to the costs involved in their distributive systems, especially when they were obviously out of line with those of their competitors. In addition, a small number have felt it necessary to examine their distribution costs for the special purpose of defending their pricing policies. The recent business decline has revived interest in distribution costs.

* Reprinted by permission from *Michigan Business Review,* Vol. X, No. 3 (May, 1958), pp. 23-29.
Donald R. G. Cowan, Professor of Marketing, University of Michigan.

A Growing Problem

There are several reasons why many business executives are as yet not fully aware that distribution costs are an increasingly serious problem.

Consumers have been willing to pay prices which cover all costs and yield satisfactory profit margins. Radically new labor-saving devices in production and expanding volume have helped to keep costs and selling prices from rising as much as wages. Very frequently the successive wage increases obtained by plant employees during the past decade were automatically given to distributive employees on a blanket basis without much regard to the efficiencies of the individual receiving them. It was taken for granted that the higher level of distributive expenses would be offset by the expanded physical and inflated dollar volume. The result has been that marketing and selling expense ratios to dollar sales volume have not seemed out of line, and comparatively little attention has been given to the cost and effectiveness of all sorts of distributive practices.

But the situation is changing rapidly. Marketing and selling expense ratios have been rising in many companies. Volume has declined in some industries, and there is the widespread necessity to meet competition by expanding and training the marketing staff as well as by stepping up expenditures for advertising, promotion, delivery, and technical services to buyers.

Efficiency of Distribution Costs the Test

Management, of course, does not expect to eliminate distribution costs. In fact, it would not be surprising if expenditures for distribution services tend to rise, in view of the widening markets for many products which are not prime necessities of life. Millions of consumers, in using their increasing purchasing power, are free to choose not only between different brands of the same product but also between entirely different products and services—between a new house, car, washing machine, television set, insurance policy, stocks, bonds, or a bank savings account.

Management would be derelict in its duty if, in the competitive race, it did not strive to maintain and expand the market for its product or product line. Hence, its problem is not the complete elimination of distribution costs but rather the elimination of inefficiencies. The test questions are what expenditures are effective enough to bring a profitable return for the effort, and how different efforts may be made more effective. In other words, it is a matter of the ratio of efficiency to expense.

No magic formula exists for meeting this problem. Management must tackle many phases of distribution cost and efficiency with various tools and remedies at its command. The first step is a many-sided diagnosis, similar to the use of an analyzer in finding out what is making your automobile engine inefficient and costly to operate. Having found the difficulties, management can apply the proper tools and methods to bring improvement. Distribution's complexity necessitates a many-sided diagnosis, and a variety of remedies involving resourceful management. Hence, there are many approaches to distribution efficiency and its accomplishment. A number of these may be outlined briefly.

I. The Product Approach

Since how many can be sold for a given expenditure of time and effort is one important measure of efficiency, it is of prime importance to see that the right product is being offered for sale. People buy, primarily, on the *merits* of competing products, and the easiest and most profitable product to sell is the one which most nearly satisfies the requirements of its particular market. A food may be made of the finest ingredients, clothing may contain the best yarn and workmanship, a washing machine may have the most durable parts, a watch may contain ever so many expensive jewels, and an electric stove or car may have many extra gadgets—nevertheless, they must meet the taste, pattern, style, price range, and other requirements of a selected segment of the market in order to be sold profitably.

To better satisfy demand, new products are continually being invented, and existing products improved. We have forgotten the makers of bicycles, automobiles, soap, furniture, and ham who have passed into limbo because they thought that consumer tastes stood still; conversely, the growth and profits of many existing companies have resulted from their keeping up with changing product preferences.

To do this, not only is physical research necessary, but also marketing research is very desirable in determining the product characteristics which people like and dislike in competing products. Moreover, buyers' reactions to both new and improved products may be determined by consumer product tests. In one of many such experiments, the tests showed that improvements were necessary in the color, texture, and flavor of food; these improvements not only reduced the product's raw material costs, but also caused rapid increases in the sales of the new product, reduced selling expenses proportionately, and increased profits.

Sometimes the preference of wholesalers and retailers from the standpoint of product gross margin, volume, and handling costs may also be very important.

Product improvements, geared to market requirements, increase the effectiveness of all kinds of selling, advertising, and other kinds of distribution expense.

II. The Product-Line Approach

The distribution of a product-line rather than of a single product will frequently reduce marketing costs—when certain conditions are met. Briefly, products suitable for a line should be sold in the same market, and should be distributed through the same channels without involving very different methods and problems. Food stores, for example, handle very wide lines of goods for the convenience of all consumers, but wholesalers tend to restrict their lines to products having common requirements in wholesaling. The meat line requires refrigeration, and the vegetable line needs fast transportation.

One frequent mistake is to assume that products made by the same plant department may be sold by the same salesman. For example, a company manufacturing and marketing a line of metal office furniture and lockers found that it could also make kitchen cabinets with the same materials and machines. Its salesmen could not sell kitchen cabinets through office furniture houses, however, and had to take time to call on other types of retail outlets, thereby causing office furniture sales to decline. In the end, a seperate sales force had to be established.

Even when the products in the lines are distributed together, there is a limit to the number of products in the line set by the limited time and ability of the salesmen to sell them all and the tendency of some buyers to purchase individual products from different suppliers. Within limits, however, widening the line of products with common standards of quality and uniform branding tends to economize in selling, advertising and other distribution expenses.

III. The Channels Approach

Many alternative marketing channels are available, and the choice made will greatly affect distribution costs and efficiency. Many conditions govern the choice of channels such as the marketing of a single product or a related product group, the volume of output, the size and breadth of the market, the practices of competitors, the relative advantages and disadvantages of using manufacturers' agents, brokers, wholesale merchants, owned sales offices and warehouses, retail outlets of different types, a partially or completely integrated system, direct selling to industrial users compared with warehouse selling, direct selling from plant by salesmen or mail order catalogs, and the like. Moreover, as a firm's output grows, it is necessary to reconsider what channels may provide more efficient distribution and to revamp the structure of price discounts.

IV. The Engineering Approach

Distribution involves many physical activities in the moving and storing of goods so they will be available in proper quantities where and when wanted by the ultimate buyers. This involves both transportation and space utilization between and within various establishments.

There are many opportunities for studying the use of various kinds of handling equipment, the arrangement of physical layout, and the systematizing of many activities through time and motion analysis, sometimes leading to a sufficient degree and standardization to make possible the use of automatic or semi-automatic machines in place of labor.

Several reasons for the rapid expansion of motor truck transportation have been the savings in handling and deterioration of goods, time involved, and flexibility of movement for medium length hauls. One firm, for example, is studying the possibility of obtaining convenient return loads from others so as to give it more control of the transportation to and from its plants and warehouses on an economical basis.

Time and motion studies have been applied to salemen's activities with startling results to show how much time is devoted to travel, selling, order and report writing, and miscellaneous duties.

V. The Operations Research Approach

The operations research approach, which is very new and closely allied to engineering, offers many possibilities.

It offers opportunities for the comparison of alternatives in minimizing effort in accomplishing a given end. For example, it may help in choosing the location of a warehouse, a jobbing center, a sales office, or a salesmen's headquarters which will minimize the physical operations of salesmen and deliveries of goods. It may be extended to the choice of store locations which will maximize consumer convenience in shopping.

Many selling organizations have kept records of salesmen's calls on customers. When they consider how territories may be revamped to increase the number of calls and call-time and to reduce time devoted to travel, waiting, and miscellaneous activities, they are, in effect, applying operations research to a phase of distribution costs, and usually with very beneficial effects through increasing salesmen's selling time and hence his productivity at little or no additional cost.

VI. The Accounting Approach

The accounting approach is more familiar to sales executives, but it has not been exploited fully in distribution. Typically, it involves the classification of a firm's distribution expenses, volume, and earnings, by salesmen's territories, by general line and specialty salesmen, by departments and products, by activities performed, and the like. The resulting comparisons of expenses, volume, and earnings have been helpful in indicating which classified segments of distribution have been more or less profitable.

Some firms have profit and loss statements for branch houses, many individual salesmen, product departments, and sales departments, and ask each responsible person to operate each unit as profitably as possible.

All of these applications of accounting are beneficial and it is regrettable that some sales executives try to get along without them or make insufficient use of them in budgeting and planning their selling operations. Very frequently, the accounting records are partly to blame because they combine profitable and unprofitable situations together, thereby failing to spotlight them for attention.

Many records of expenditures, volume, and earnings need to be extended so as to relate them to the actual physical operations of distribution. For instance, most sales executives need to know more than total expenditures in each sales territory. They want the cost per call and the total cost of the salesmen's calls, time spent on each customer and prospect, the cost of telephoning different customers including payments for telephone service and the employee's time in doing so, the cost per delivery and the total cost of making deliveries to each customer and the cost of correspondence, bookkeeping and special services for each customer.

Sometimes the special selling services cost more than regular selling. For example, the practice of assigning engineers and chemists to industrial customers for short or long periods of time is very costly and is no less a selling expense because these men may be on a plant payroll.

The analysis and comparison of costs and the development of standard costs as guides are insufficient in themselves. They must be compared with volume and earnings in order to determine whether or not they are justified.

For many purposes in controlled selling it is very helpful to divide costs into fixed and variable categories, according to different degrees of variability. For example, over reasonably short periods, salesmen's calls and truck deliveries are to be viewed as direct costs which may vary in number by area, by size, and type of customer, and by product. If the earnings are not sufficient to cover even the direct costs of these efforts at the wholesale or retail level, there is nothing contributed towards offsetting the overhead costs of sales supervision, sales office, warehouse, and general expense, or towards paying dividends, although in some instances the volume may be desirable in keeping a plant in operation, compared with the cost of shutting it down.

From the longer range viewpoint of general management, many distribution costs such as those for branches, sales officers, and the like which seem fixed at a given time, are variable; and, after study of adequate records of expenses and earnings, may be changed to bring about higher net profits. There is, indeed, a great opportunity for the accountant to help in making distribution more efficient and profitable.

VII. The Economic Approach

The economic approach takes up where accounting leaves off. It is concerned with changing marketing conditions, sales forecasting, sales potentials by markets, areas and customers, buying habits, competition, pricing, and the application of selling, advertising, and other kinds of effort under conditions of diminishing returns to the point of marginal balance between expenditure and income and further to the point of maximum total profit or minimum loss.

In all these fields, the tools of analysis most frequently used by the marketing economist in making measurements useful to management in improving distribution efficiency are statistical facts and methods. For example, the expansion of public and private debt has been a powerful influence in expanding the buying of most kinds of both capital goods and consumers' durable goods. The economist may examine the effect of debt expansion on a company's sales and analyze the outlook.

The economic analyst may aid in measuring area and company potentials and in allocating different kinds of selling and advertising effort to these potentials with a view to maximizing profit. He may analyze the income and expenditures of different consuming classes and aid in determining prices and price spreads on products of differing quality so as to maximize sales volume and profits. Further, he may give advice on the appropriateness of borrowing funds and long-range investment commitments for distribution facilities of all kinds under various conditions.

Shifts in the population, industry, the rise of supermarket retailing, the integration of various stages in the marketing channels both vertically and horizontally, foreign trade and monetary conditions, and many other economic phenomena fall within the purview of the marketing economist, and provide a vast opportunity for him to be helpful in improving distribution efficiency.

VIII. The Personnel Approach

The personnel approach to distribution efficiency is somewhat different from those already described. In the long run, the ability of its distributive employees is a powerful influence in determining the firm's growth and competitive standing. Many aspects of distribution, especially the customer selling function, cannot be reduced to the impersonal and uniform activities of a machine. Hence, the selection, training, and compensation of distributive personnel, and the fitting of the employee to the task are very important long-run factors influencing distribution costs, yet the opportunities for improvement are far from exhausted in a multitude of companies.

In training, for instance, much time is devoted to familiarizing salesmen with the characteristics and advantages of products compared with those of competitors. This is necessary, but so also is the generally neglected field of training the salesman to do a more effective job by organizing his activities and using the most productive selling methods.

Has the salesman been told how to increase his selling time and reduce his travel and waiting time; how much a call costs and how large an order must be to cover the direct expenses of obtaining and handling it; how to find out what a customer needs; when to let the prospect talk instead of himself; how to prolong the call so as to have time to sell the whole line; when to show a sample so it will increase the order and not reduce it as frequently happens; and what appeals to use in given circumstances?

Such training requires careful, competent study of the effective and ineffective methods used by a company's own salesmen and competitors in the same field, and no general book on selling techniques will meet the peculiar needs of the particular selling task.

Selection, compensation, and training of distribution people are very important current problems not only because new recruits are being added to the organization, but also because a majority of distributive employees have never had a test of selling in a real buyer's market.

IX. The Organizational Approach

The organizational approach is much wider than that of personnel. In order to bring about a hard-hitting organization, there must be clear perception and definition of the tasks to be performed at each level of management, both line and staff. Smooth-working relationships and communication between these tasks must be worked out; authority commensurate with responsibility must be delegated; procedures and inducements for stimulating maximum effort must be applied, and regular evaluations of performance must be made at all levels in order to eliminate ineffective personnel or unprofitable activities.

Since marketing conditions are continually changing, the organization must be flexible enough to allow tasks to be eliminated or added as distribution needs change. Otherwise, what was once a hard-hitting organization soon becomes petrified and ineffectual. Effective organization is a prime requisite in accomplishing efficient distribution.

X. The Standardization Approach

Distribution comprises a multitude of activities in which the human element looms large and in which, therefore, there is much variation in performance. The difficulties of bringing about standardization in these human activities are at bottom the reason for lack of machine mechanization in many phases of distribution, especially in buying and selling. Nevertheless, there are important opportunities for increasing efficiency through standardization.

It has been pointed out already that employee tasks may be carefully defined as a step towards organization efficiency and that the effective methods to use in face-to-face selling may be determined through which training of salemen may be applied more uniformly with very beneficial results. Through product testing and marketing surveys the effective product selling appeals may be determined and more uniform use of them may be brought about. Brands are the symbols of certain standardized product characteristics. A few motives dominate the buyer's choice of brands. If these are determined, the salesmen's appeals may be standardized. To the extent that such standardization can be accomplished, advertising of various kinds may be used to convey a standardized selling message which may accomplish economies not possible in personal selling, thus making more advertising a step towards more economical distribution to the mass market. Hence, within limits, standardization of various activities may be an important contribution to economical distribution.

XI. The Management Approach

The management approach includes and employs all the other approaches just outlined, but there is always something more, a priceless ingredient, which makes its contribution distinctive. It is not alone management's comprehension of all the different avenues by which distribution may be made more efficient and less costly, but also its open-minded, imaginative, and rational approach to the use of new methods under conditions of continual change in distribution.

It must consider which alternative combinations of machines, personal effort, advertising, channels, products, and the like, will yield the largest distributive return in the future. Sometimes, for example, more advertising expense and less personal selling expense will increase volume and at the same time reduce expenses.

It must use the previously outlined approaches and methods in analyzing the results of its past plans and programs in order to decide what to continue to do in the future.

But it must also go beyond the analysis of past experience in deciding upon future ventures. This does not mean that it should gamble in the ordinary sense. Rather, progressive management uses test-tube experiments in distribution. The following example shows the usefulness of conducting an experiment. A large firm, well-known everywhere, more than twenty years ago, developed a line of hard-frozen branded meat cuts which were to be distributed along with fresh meats and which were well adapted to modern retail self-serve selling. This firm spent large amounts of money in providing hard-freezing equipment in its own wholesale units and launched the entire venture in distribution on a wide scale. The venture was an unexpected failure because it had overlooked the then total absence of hard-freezing display cases in retail shops, the consumer prejudice, now past, against anything frozen, the necessity of educational advertising to explain the charging of what seemed to be a higher price for a trimmed meat cut of branded quality as compared with an untrimmed and unbranded fresh meat cut, and above all, the opposition of the powerful union of retail meat cutters. Some surveys of conditions and opinions of retailers, or an experiment in distribution on a very limited scale simulating the conditions to be encountered on a national scale would have saved millions of dollars for investment in the project at some future time when market conditions were more favorable.

More recently, another large firm, well-known everywhere, developed a line of insecticides which obviously could not be distributed through its regular channels. It decided to set up distribution through grocery stores, and developed a national distribution for doing so. It failed. Besides studies of where people buy insecticides, and what women buy in grocery stores, a limited experiment under conditions simulating those to be encountered nationally, might have helped to avoid a costly mistake in distribution.

The management approach to accomplishing new distribution efficiency includes a willingness to venture on new paths with risks minimized by a maximum of knowledge gained not only by the analysis of past experience, but also by scientifically conducted experiments showing how improved distribution may be successfully attained. Open-minded, imaginative, and rationally venturesome management is indeed a priceless ingredient in accomplishing efficient, profitable distribution.

In summary, the current need of attention to distribution efficiency has been emphasized. Eleven different approaches to the problem have been outlined, namely, the product, the product-line, the channels, engineering, operations research, accounting, economic analysis, personnel, organization, standardization, and management. There are others, too, if time permitted. Nevertheless, these approaches constitute a challenge to marketing executives to tackle a vast and relatively unexplored opportunity for reducing distribution costs by increasing distribution efficiency.

49. ANALYTICAL APPROACH TO CHANNEL POLICIES—MARKETING COST ANALYSIS *

Charles H. Sevin

"When we talk of channels of distribution, we often picture mentally a sort of Old Man River who justs keeps rolling along; a broad and placid current down which all merchandise flows to its ultimate destination. Of course, we admit it will be a bit muddy and disorderly at times, but regard it as essentially changeless. In the long perspective, this just isn't so. Channels have shifted and always will." [1]

On the other hand, when we consider the shifts in channels, and, when we talk of channels from the point of view of management, we often picture mentally a businessman sitting at his desk and going over a list of factors on the basis of which he "selects" the best channels through which his products are to be distributed to their ultimate consumers. The marketing literature is replete with lists and analyses of these factors—factors to be considered in the initial selection of channels, factors to be used in evaluating alternative channels when a change in distribution policy is being weighed, and factors which explain why certain channels are more likely to be prevalent for certain types of goods.

Of course, the truth is not likely to be found at the extremes; channels are neither like an Old Man River which just keeps rolling along nor are they selected on the basis of a list of factors which are subject to the analysis, control, and decision of management. Channels are sometimes thrust upon a businessman by the specific circumstances and enviroment with which he has to deal, and they are sometimes rationally selected by him; but frequently the situation is more complex than either of these simple extremes.

* C. H. Sevin, "Analytical Approach to Channel Policies—Marketing Cost Analysis" in Richard M. Clewett, *Marketing Channels* (Homewood, Illinois: Richard D. Irwin, Inc., 1954), pp. 433-469. Reprinted by permission of the publisher.

Charles H. Sevin, Consultant.

[1] Walter Mitchell, Jr., "The Changing Channels of Distribution," *Dun's Review and Modern Industry*, (November, 1946), p. 17.

Additionally, a study of the decision-making process in marketing leads one to suspect that the neat listings and analyses of the criteria determining the selection of channels may often be somewhat academic. One researcher, for example, in reporting on decisions with regard to marketing expenditures generally, arrived at the following conclusion based on a series of interviews with marketing executives:

> Specific questions such as these [which might well include the selection of channels] are the ones which puzzle the typical business executive. They are also the questions which he has to do something about. He must act. He cannot postpone decisions until the "best" method of arriving at answers is devised. Consequently, he does act. By methods which he himself admits are not perfect, he arrives at decisions which, even when they prove to be workable, he cannot be sure are good. He . . . wishes that he knew more about how to make the decisions and how to appraise the results.[2]

If the above is a valid picture, then management is more deserving of sympathy than of criticism. The brief difficulty in making sound decisions regarding channels of distribution has been a lack of adequate information. And in view of the complexities of the decisions which have to be made, it is easier to set forth the kinds of information that are needed than to obtain the data.

Most problems with regard to channels arise out of the general drive for continued expansion of sales volume which is such a vital and valuable factor in our business thinking, or out of the related dissatisfaction with the selling and other services of middlemen. Although there is no conflict at all between the urge for expansion and the necessity of cost control and the ultimate profit results, sales coverage is often extended to many different channels without much information on relative costs and profits.

It is axiomatic, of course, that a particular business should use those channels or combinations of channels which will contribute most to the securing and maintaining, not simply of the greatest attainable sales volume, but of that combination of sales volume and cost which will yield the maximum amount of profit, both in the short run and in the long run. Thus, in resolving any problem regarding channels, ideally, the ultimate decision will go to that method which is *believed* to promise the greatest net profit. Obviously, making such a decision is no simple or easy task.

When analyzing the comparative advantages of different channels, many businessmen give primary consideration to the factors related

[2] James W. Culliton, *The Management of Marketing Costs* (Boston: Harvard University, Graduate School of Business Administration, 1948), p. 2.

to sales volume, without giving sufficient consideration to the relative marketing costs involved in obtaining that volume or to the comparative net profits. One likely explanation for the difficulty in making sound decisions regarding problems in connection with channels is the lack of adequate cost information.

Where a business is already using several different channels, then a customer cost analysis (with customers grouped by class of trade) will show the relative costs and profits by channels. More usually, however, the problem is to compare actual costs and profits of present classes of trade with estimated costs and profits of alternative channels under consideration. In this case, the problem is not so simple, and it may not always be possible to determine what the results will be until an experiment has been tried.

The actual cost analyses and experiments of those businesses whose experiences are described in the following Cases show that the choice of the most profitable channels is a problem to be solved individually. What is the most profitable channel for one firm may not be for another competitor. The cases do show, however, that there is considerable opportunity for business generally to increase volume, reduce costs, and increase profits through analyses of relative costs and profits by channels.[3]

Case No. 1

A distribution cost analysis showed that 95 per cent of all the customers sold direct in one small area were unprofitable. By applying the results of this analysis to the over-all company picture, two thirds of the direct customers were estimated to be unprofitable. As a result of these studies, the company is in the process of changing its channels of distribution by transferring unprofitable small accounts, served direct, to its dealer organization. Based on accomplishments so far, the company expects to achieve lower inventory, overhead and break-even points, a 15 to 30 per cent net reduction in marketing costs, and a 20 per cent increase in net profits.

Our company distributes its industrial products direct to users and through dealers. We sell direct to a large number of small accounts. For example, an analysis of the direct sales of one of our major products for an entire year showed the following break-down by customer-volume groups:

[3] The three cases that follow are taken from Charles H. Sevin, *How Manufacturers Reduce Their Distribution Costs*, U. S. Department of Commerce (Washington, D. C.: U. S. Government Printing Office, 1948), chap. iii. As nearly as possible, the cases are expressed in the words of the executives interviewed.

Customer-Volume Groups, Number of Units of Product Purchased	Number of Accounts, Per Cent of Total	Sales in Physical Units, Per Cent of Total
Under 1,000	78.18	2.34
1,000- 5,000	14.63	3.99
5,000-15,000	3.72	4.10
Over 15,000	3.47	89.57
Total	100.00	100.00

This analysis showed that 78 per cent of the accounts—those buying less than 1,000 units—were responsible for only slightly more than 2 per cent of the sales. (On the other hand, the customers in the largest volume group, while only 3.7 per cent of the number of accounts, brought in almost 90 per cent of the direct sales of this major product.) In short, many customers served direct, important numerically, are just a drop in the bucket where physical volume is concerned.

We made a detailed analysis of one area in one district, the results of which are shown in Table 1. Those customers served direct who buy only $20 or less per month constitute 90 per cent of the total number of customers. They receive 74 per cent of the service calls, are responsible for 57 per cent of the invoices, and yet give us only 35 per cent of the total dollar sales volume in the area. This analysis showed us that a great amount of effort was being devoted to a large number of customers whose business was very small in the aggregate. We decided to investigate what this means in terms of cost, and profit or loss.

TABLE 1

CUSTOMERS, CALLS, INVOICES, AND SALES BY CUSTOMER-VOLUME GROUPS *
(Percentages of Totals)

Customer-Volume Group, Amount of Monthly Purchases †	Number of Customers	Number of Calls	Number of Invoices ‡	Sales Volume ‡
$ 0.00	52	48	8	9
$ 0.01–$ 3.00	16	10	13	9
$ 3.01–$ 5.00	9	3	9	3
$ 5.01–$ 10.00	8	7	15	8
$ 10.01–$ 20.00	5	6	12	6
$ 20.01–$ 40.00	5	12	18	10
$ 40.01–$100.00	4	6	17	18
$100.01 and over	1	8	8	37
Total	100	100	100	100

* Data cover one area.
† Classification based on purchases of major products only.
‡ Data refer to purchases of all products, both major and minor.

We surveyed the daily activity of our entire sales force in this district and found that half of the salesmen's time is spent in other than face-to-face (or telephone) contact with customers. Traveling, waiting, and administrative time account for the other half and are most costly. Although on the average the salesmen normally spend less time with the little customer than with the bigger customer, yet the length of time of the call does not vary too significantly with the size of the customer, because on each call there are a certain number of operations which have to be performed. It was also found that approximately 88 per cent of the salesmen's travel expenses are fixed regardless of the distance traveled; that is, their expenses are not variable with mileage. We figured that the average sales call costs about $5.00.

An invoice represents a transaction. A customer's order is received, handled, and filled. The clerical paper work alone for this transaction is expensive. We followed it through from start to finish in one district and here is what happens to the order:

> Telephone operator to order clerk to addressograph operator to shipping-order typist to computer to distribution clerk to hectograph operator to accounts receivable bookkeeper or cashier—with side trips to several files and equipment records—to the customer, to accounting clerks and some to sales clerks, and to credit.

This paperwork routine means that the names of our customers have to be listed in most or all of the following: (*a*) customer card file, (*b*) correspondence file, (*c*) specification file, (*d*) price card file, (*e*) name plate file, (*f*) accounts receivable ledger file, (*g*) customer code number file, (*h*) credit file, (*i*) equipment records file, and some other places, too.

Per transaction—per invoice—that is a lot of work. The direct cost of clerical time comes to about $1.50 per transaction.

There are a number of variations and complications on this theme, which cover such points as the physical storage, handling, and movement of goods, and additional paperwork in physical distribution. For example, it was found that delivery time per delivery did not vary significantly with the volume of goods delivered. It was also found that distance traveled was a minor factor compared to the stopping time or labor costs; two thirds of the delivery cost was labor and only one third was truck operation, maintenance, and depreciation. It was found that the direct costs per delivery comes to about $1.50 on the average.

It was obvious that we could not make a profit on small customers served direct with our necessarily wholesale methods of selling, record keeping, and physical distribution which cost us at least $3.00 per transaction on the average.

Translating the factors discussed above (along with a number of other factors) into dollars and cents, we found a profit-and-loss picture for one area for customers served direct. (See Table 2.)

TABLE 2

GROSS PROFITS, MARKETING EXPENSES, AND NET PROFIT OR LOSS BY CUSTOMER-VOLUME GROUPS *
(Percentages of Sales)

Customer-Volume Group, Amount of Monthly Purchases †	Gross Profit ‡	Marketing Expenses ‡				Net Profit or Loss ‡
		Selling	Physical Distribution	Field Administration	Total	
$ 0.00	43	93	20	16	129	—86
$ 0.01–$ 3.00	51	21	32	26	79	—28
$ 3.01–$ 5.00	74	15	57	67	139	—65
$ 5.01–$ 10.00	59	16	37	34	87	—28
$ 10.01–$ 20.00	68	18	43	36	97	—29
$ 20.01–$ 40.00	70	21	43	32	96	—26
$ 40.01–$100.00	67	6	37	18	61	6
$100.01 and over	61	4	42	4	50	11
Averages for area ..	61	18	38	19	75	—14

* Data cover one area.
† Classification based on purchases of major products only.
‡ Data refer to purchases of all products, both major and minor.

In making this cost analysis by customer-volume classifications our marketing expenses were divided into three groups. Each of these functional cost groups included both direct expenses for the area and a share of the overhead for the district, but not for the company as a whole. The three groups were as follows:

1. *Selling expense.*—This group included salesmen's salaries and travel expense, and was allocated to customers on the basis of number of sales calls.

2. *Office expense.*—This group included the salaries and other direct costs of all the paper work and related operations, and was allocated to customers on the basis of number of invoices.

3. *Physical distribution.*—This group included such items as warehouse rent, warehouse labor, truck or delivery costs, and cost of shipment of goods to warehouse. Eighty per cent of the delivery costs were allocated to customers on the basis of number of deliveries made (to which a weight of 4 is given), and 20 per cent of the basis of airline distance of customer from warehouse (to which a weight of 1 is given). Warehouse labor, rent, taxes, and so forth were allocated to customers on the basis of cost of sales. Parcel post charges and wrapping charges were also allocated on the basis of cost of sales.

The results show, as well expected, that the little customer with his little order is too small to be served direct. (See Table 2.) Our wholesale machinery bogs down from a profit standpoint. For each dollar of sales, $1.29 of marketing expense is poured into the little customer in the smallest group (those buying minor products only). At the other end of the scale, only 50 cents of the sales dollar is used for marketing expense, despite the much higher call and delivery frequency on these bigger customers. The big customer buys enough for us to justify direct sales coverage. The little customer buys so little from us that no direct coverage at all is warranted. In between are customers who are getting too much sales attention. They are not big enough to justify so many calls and deliveries.

The profit and loss picture for these customers shows that we lost 86 cents on each dollar of sales to the customers in the smallest volume group; for each dollar of sales we took in, we spent $1.86. Ninety-five per cent of all the customers served direct in this area were unprofitable. (See Table 1.) The losses on these unprofitable customers more than offset the profit on the profitable customers, so that the area as a whole was in the red to the extent of 14 per cent of sales.

Our small customers were unprofitable in spite of the fact that we obtained higher prices from them because of our quantity-discount schedules. In fact, as can be seen from the figures below, it turned out that the higher the price the higher the loss; the higher prices obtained from the small customers were much more than offset by the still higher costs of selling, physical distribution, and billing:

Customer-Volume Group, Amount of Monthly Purchases *	Index of Average Price Paid for Product A	Index of Average Price Paid for Product B	Net Profit or Loss on Total Sales, Per Cent of Sales
$ 0.01–$ 3.00	100	100	—28
$ 3.01–$ 5.00	99	100	—65
$ 5.01–$ 10.00	95	100	—28
$10.01–$ 20.00	85	92	—29
$20.01–$ 40.00	75	84	—26
$40.00–$100.00	84	92	6
Over $100.00	51	76	11

* Classification based on purchases of major products only.

This study of profit and loss by size of customer showed us why we were operating in that area at an annual net loss of $6,000. Our remedy was to change our channels of distribution. Since we had no dealer in this area, we set up our local salesman as the dealer. The discount to our new dealer will cost us about $16,000 a year in gross profit (assuming no change in physical volume), but there will also be a savings in the district of some $25,000 a year in marketing expenses for a net gain of $9,000. That changes the picture in the area from a $6,000 net loss into a $3,000 net profit.

This change in methods of distribution also liquated about $4,500 of inventories (warehoused in the area) ; our delivery truck was sold to our dealer; and it contributed to a reduction in district overhead of at least $1,000 annually. Since the entire investment and operating expenses are now the dealer's own, our break-even point in the area is now zero. In short, the results of this change were lower inventory, lower overhead, lower break-even point, lower costs, and higher profits.

After the success of this experiment on a small scale, we extended our studies, area by area, to our three largest districts. The application of our cost analysis indicates that about two thirds of the customers served direct in these districts are unprofitable. Our solution is to transfer to our dealer organization those customers to whom it is unprofitable to sell direct. If, in any particular area, there are some profitable customers left after this transfer, we then weigh the advantage of also turning over these profitable customers to the leaders in order to save trucking, warehousing, office, and other expenses by the elimination of all direct sales in that area.

Specific decisions and actions are being taken to reduce our marketing expenses in the areas where we are in the process of changing our channels of distribution. For example, we plan to consolidate or eliminate the routes of many of our salesmen. We also plan to eliminate or consolidate many truck routes. This means a reduction in the number of trucks (some of which may be sold to dealers), in mechanics, and in garage space. We are in the process of getting rid of 5 out of 19 warehouses in one district.

We will also consolidate our field office space and reduce office personnel. We are now able to use consolidated billing which can be done only with large customers. Those techniques cannot be used with small customers because their credit is apt to be poor and their purchases are infrequent. This change will reduce overtime in the office because of elimination of peak work at the end of each month. We also are extending these economies of consolidated billing to some of our dealers because their volume has sufficiently picked up to justify these short cuts. Finally, the smaller size of our field office staff means that it will be more easily supervised.

At the same time that we are putting this cost-reduction program into effect in three of our largest districts, we are submitting yardsticks for the guidance of the managers of our remaining districts, since we believe there are similar cost-reduction opportunities in many areas across the country. We have furnished them five clues for the detection of unprofitable direct customers:

1. A high price.
2. Low physical volume per invoice.
3. Low dollar sales per invoice.
4. Low average dollar sales per sales call.
5. Low average sales per month.

In order to help our managers apply these yardsticks we have shown them how to determine the following factors for their own districts:

1. Average billing per invoice—for each customer-volume group.
2. Average dollar sales per call—for each customer-volume group.
3. Average monthly sales per call—for each customer-volume group.

In order to help them appreciate the costs involved in servicing their small direct customers, they are shown how to compute two rough averages:

1. Cost per sales.
2. Cost per invoice.

We have told our district managers that, if a customer buys less than $20 a month of our major products, he is practically bound to fall in the unprofitable small customer class—that is, unprofitable to be served direct. In a memorandum to our district managers, we have also made the following suggestions:

> By making this analysis on a customer basis by salesman's territory, you have a realistic, functional picture of the composition of your business. You will be able to determine what customers should be turned over to dealers. You will see what business is left in the territory for the salesmen. You will be able to see where reorganization of sales territories will be necessary.
>
> The first thing you can do is to minimize sales coverage on the small direct accounts, and that applies to prospects as well as customers. There is no sense in pitching up your profit pipeline by converting unprofitable direct accounts into dealer accounts, while at the same time your salesmen are puncturing your profit pipeline with more small direct business.
>
> Because of the many accounts affected, it appears desirable to initiate a gradual weeding out of unprofitable small customers, starting at the level of under $5.00 worth of major products per month or else you can proceeed sales territory by sales territory, studying the areas within each sales territory. A systematic continuous transfer to dealers over a 6-month period should enable a district to clean out all the unprofitable small customers with a minimum of confusion.

We do not believe that we will lose any physical sales volume because of the transfer of our small customers to dealers. Our dealers are organized to handle the small business. Our dealers will be able to give our small customers more frequent delivery and other services than we have been able to give them by selling them direct. Dealers' truck drivers are combination salesmen, deliverymen, servicemen, and credit-and-collection men. Consequently, our dealer can accomplish with one person those functions which it takes four people in our company to perform. In short, our dealers can do a more efficient, as well as a better, job than we can in serving our small customers.

In order to be conservative, our planning has been based on the assumption that our physical volume remain about the same as a result of this change in channels, although we would lose some dollar sales volume and some gross profit because of dealer discounts. However, because of the reasons outlined in the preceding paragraph (and because of generally favorable business conditions) we have experienced rising trends in both physical and dollar sales volume in those areas where we have changed our channels of distribution. Moreover, in spite of the loss in gross profits because of dealer discounts, the potential savings in marketing expense in our three largest districts alone are so great that there will be a substantial addition to our net profits.

We expect that our dealer discounts in the long run probably will go down because they will handle a much larger volume, whereas their overhead will not be greatly affected, so that they will get an increased net profit. We have already discussed this possibility with some of our larger dealers, and they have agreed that both the company and the dealer organization will be on a better competitive basis, as well as a better net profit position, if this should come about.

We also expect to set up a dealer sales organization by transferring some of our better salesmen who have been calling on direct accounts. Thus, we will have one sales force which will handle direct sales to large industrial accounts and another sales force which will call on our dealer organization. We plan to get these latter salesman to teach our dealers better methods of merchandising, inventory control, credit extension, and so forth.

While on the one hand we are expanding our dealer organization because of this change in channels, on the other hand we expect to have fewer and better dealers. We are weeding out our so-called sit-down dealers—those small dealers who carry our line, but do not promote it. We are going to drop those small dealers who are unprofitable customers to us, as well as transfer industrial accounts which are unprofitable as direct customers.

For example, we made an analysis of order size by channel of distribution. Here is what we discovered in one of our largest districts:

Order-Size Group	Direct Sales		Dealers	
	Number of Invoices, Per Cent of Total	Sales, Per Cent of Total	Number of Invoices, Per Cent of Total	Sales, Per Cent of Total
$ 0.01–$ 5.00	25	2	23	1
$ 5.01–$10.00	21	3	15	1
$10.01–$20.00	20	6	18	3
$20.01–$50.00	18	13	21	8
$50.01 and over	16	76	23	87
Total	100	100	100	100

Thus, even though the average order from our dealers is almost twice as large as that from our direct customers, the former are as apt to place a small order as the latter. The first order-size group ($0.01-$5.00) is unprofitable, and the second size group is marginal. Since we are undertaking a mass transfer of small accounts to dealers, this analysis posed a question: If the small order (normally received from small direct customers) is unprofitable, why transfer it to the dealer, who won't do any better and who in addition gets a discount?

Education of dealers is the approach we are presently using, with emphasis on larger orders, less paper work, and a complete well-balanced stock. At the same time, we have established a policy of weeding out those minor dealer outlets which are doing a poor merchandising job, and continue to use our own warehouse inventories for filling their orders.

Based on the accomplishments so far in our three largest districts, we anticipate the following results from changing our channels of distribution: Approximately two thirds of our direct customers will be transferred to dealers. Although there may be as much as a 2 per cent decline in dollars sales volume because of dealer discounts, we expect that physical volume will be maintained and probably increased. Fixed marketing expenses, inventory investments, and break-even points will be lower. There may be a net reduction in our marketing personnel of as high as 40 per cent, a 15 to 30 per cent reduction in our total marketing costs, and as much as a 20 per cent increase in our net profits.

Case No. 2: Unprofitable Channels

A somewhat unique graphic method of cost analysis was used to seperate the variable from the fixed element of each category of marketing cost and for getting costs at different levels of sales volume. Variable costs were allocated to four different channels of distribution. As a result of these analyses, one entire channel of distribution was discontinued, as were small customers in another channel, while sales pressure on the remaining profitable customers was increased. In one postwar year, net profits doubled from $150,000 to $300,000.

Our methods of analyzing and controlling our distribution costs are a part of our control of over-all costs and profits. Because of the difficulties of predicting our sales volume, we do not set up a planned cost at any one fixed volume of sales. Instead, we establish a plan for unit costs and profits at all expected volumes of sales. Of course, on low volume, the results will not be as satisfactory as on high volume, but at least, under a plan made in advance, we have greater assurance that our costs and profits are the best possible for the sales conditions with which we have to contend.

Our first step is to determine how our profits and how all of our costs—both manufacturing and distribution costs—vary with changes in sales volume. This, of course, is not a simple job, because there are always other factors besides changes in output—such as changes in wage rates, and cost of materials, and changes in efficiency—which affect our unit costs and total profits. However, we have been able to make approximate adjustments for these factors (accurate enough for our purposes) and to chart month-to-month changes in our profits and costs as related to corresponding changes in our volume.

Chart 1

Relation between Profit Margin and Sales Volume

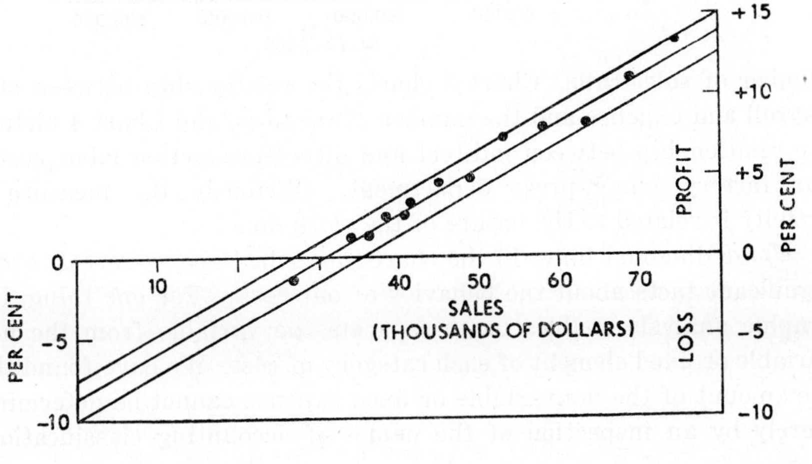

Of course, increasing sales generally bring increasing profits and decreasing sales bring decreasing profits. Chart 1 is a picture of this fact. Sales are measured on the horizontal scale, profit margins after variable costs (but before deducting fixed costs) are measured on the vertical scale. Each dot on the chart represents the profit margin at the sales volume of 1 month. After having adjusted for other factors (such as changes in wage rates) these dots follow a definite pattern and are grouped pretty closely to the diagonal line which we call our "normal" profits margin for any given sales volume.

Likewise, we have been able to draw a graphic picture of the "normal" relationship of each important category of cost to some measure of output (not necessarily sales) to which it is related. For example, Chart 2 shows the relationship of total field selling expense to total

CHART 2

RELATION BETWEEN NUMBER OF SALES CALLS AND SELLING EXPENSE

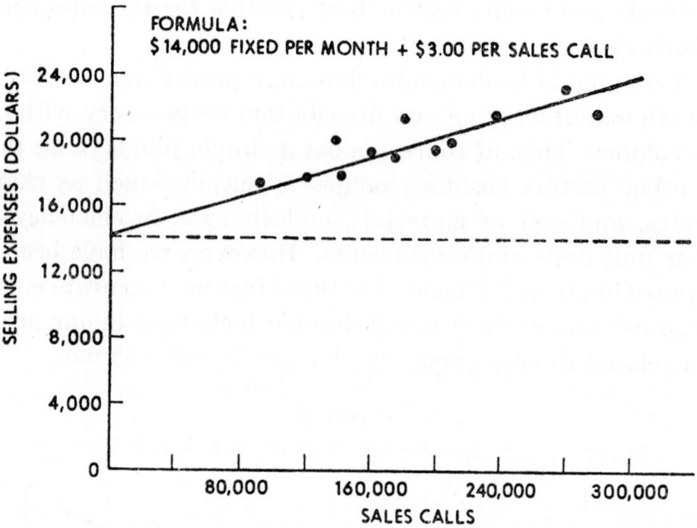

number of sales calls. Chart 3 charts the relationship between office payroll and expense and the number of invoices, and Chart 4 pictures the relationship between indirect and direct production labor cost in our factory punch-press department. Obviously the measure of activity is related to the nature of the work done.

These diagonal lines, in the charts described above, reveal several significant facts about the behavior of our costs. For one thing, this graphic analysis enables us to separate the variable from the nonvariable or fixed element of each category of cost. We have found that the amount of the nonvariable or fixed expense cannot be determined merely by an inspection of the names of accounting classifications,

CHART 3

RELATION BETWEEN NUMBER OF INVOICES AND OFFICE PAYROLL AND EXPENSES

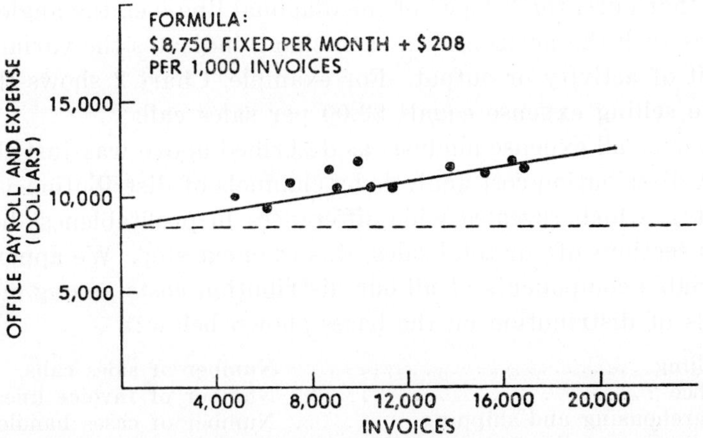

with some costs being labeled variable and others labeled fixed. Many of our expense accounts contain unexpected amounts of nonvariable expense which can be discovered only by analysis. The charts enable us to separate the fixed from the variable expense components.

The point at which the diagonal line cuts the vertical scale shows the approximate amount of the fixed or nonvariable element contained in each expense, because this point indicates the amount of the expense when the amount of the output or activity to which the expense is related is zero. Thus, in Chart 2, the nonvariable selling expense is $14,000 per month. That is, even though not a single sales call was

CHART 4

RELATION BETWEEN DIRECT AND INDIRECT PRODUCTION LABOR COST, PUNCH PRESS DEPARTMENT

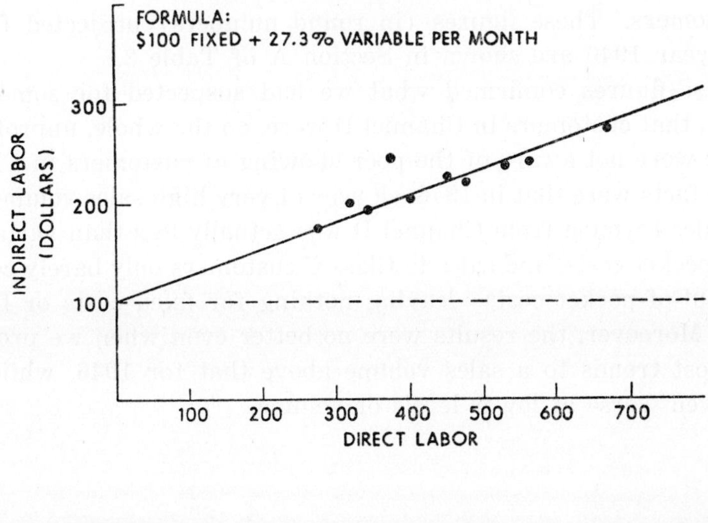

made, our stand-by or fixed selling expense would normally approximate $14,000 per month.

Furthermore, the "slope" of the diagonal line, i.e., the angle which it makes with the horizontal in each chart, indicates the variable cost per unit of activity or output. For example, Chart 2 shows that the variable selling expense equals $3.00 per sales call.

The over-all expense analysis as described above was just the first step. A distribution cost analysis by channels of distribution (and by products), which revealed wide differences in profitableness between various sections of our total sales, was the next step. We apportioned the variable components of all our distribution costs among our four channels of distribution on the bases shown below:

Selling	Number of sales calls.
Office	Number of invoice lines.
Warehousing and shipping..........	Number of cases handled.
Delivery (trucks)	Number of deliveries.

Of course, these bases are the same as the factors with which we had related the totals of the various distribution costs in order to separate their variable and nonvariable components and to get the variable unit costs. Next, by adding up the distribution costs allocated as above, we obtained the total variable costs by channels of distribution. (We assumed that there were no differences in our variable manufacturing costs by channels of distribution, since all classes of customers generally purchase the same proportions of all our products.)

Our next step was to analyze sales by channels of distribution and to deduct total variable costs by channels (production plus allocated distribution costs) from these sales. Of course, in this way, we determined the differences in profitableness between our different classes of customers. These figures (in round numbers) projected for the entire year 1946 are shown in Section A of Table 3.

These figures confirmed what we had suspected for some time, namely, that customers in Channel D were, on the whole, unprofitable. But we were not aware of the poor showing of customers in Channel C. The facts were that in 1946—a year of very high sales volume—the total sales revenue from Channel D was actually less than variable or out-of-pocket costs, and sales to Class C customers only barely covered these out-of-pocket costs—leaving nothing for fixed costs or for net profit. Moreover, the results were no better even when we projected these cost trends to a sales volume above that for 1946, while they were even worse at lower levels of volume.

TABLE 3

SALES, VARIABLE COSTS, AND PROFIT MARGINS BY CHANNELS OF DISTRIBUTION

A. BEFORE CHANGES IN CHANNELS, 1946

Channels of Distribution	Sales	Variable Costs *	Profit Margin	Per Cent of Sales
A	$ 750,000	$ 400,000	$350,000	47
B	250,000	100,000	150,000	60
C	300,000	300,000	....	.....
D	200,000	250,000	†— 50,000	†—25
Total	$1,500,000	$1,050,000	$450,000	30
Less: Nonvariable expense	....	....	300,000	.....
Net profit	....	....	$150,000	10

B. ESTIMATED EFFECT OF CHANGES IN CHANNELS

Channels of Distribution	Sales	Variable Costs *	Net Profit
C	‡—$150,000	—$205,000	$ 55,000
D	‡— 200,000	— 250,000	50,000
A and B	§100,000	85,000	15,000
Total	—$250,000	—$370,000	$120,000

C. AFTER CHANGES IN CHANNELS, 1947

Channels of Distribution	Sales	Variable Costs *	Profit Margin	Per Cent of Sales
A	$ 825,000	$415,000	$410,000	50
B	315,000	130,000	185,000	59
C	120,000	110,000	10,000	8
Total	$1,260,000	$655,000	$605,000	48
Less: Nonvariable expense	....	....	310,000	....
Net profit	....	....	$295,000	23

* Production plus distribution costs.
† Loss.
‡ Eliminated.
§ Added.

We turned our attention to customers in Channel D first. An extensive study, including a similar distribution cost analysis by customer-volume groups within this channel, convinced us that there was nothing we could do to make these customers profitable. Even the larger customers in this channel were unprofitable. Therefore, we decided to eliminate this entire channel of distribution, since it was responsible for an actual out-of-pocket loss at any anticipated level of sales volume. By dropping this channel we figured to save $250,000 in out-of-pocket variable costs, while losing only $200,000 in sales—thereby adding $50,000 to our net profits at 1946 levels of business.

Next we turned our attention to customers in Channel C. We classified them into groups according to the amount of their purchases in 1946, and by allocating the variable costs to each group, we found that the large customers were earning a profit margin over their variable costs. The results are shown in Table 4. This analysis indicated that Class C customers purchasing under $10,000 were the ones who caused the unfavorable showing for the entire group. They were responsible for an out-of-pocket loss of $58,900. On the other hand, customers in Channel C buying over $10,000 in 1946 turned in a profit margin (before nonvariable costs) of $58,680.

The next step was to review with our salesmen every single Class C account in the under-$10,000-annual-volume group and to cull out all those whose future potential did not promise to make them profitable. This review called for the elimination of about $150,000 in sales and approximately $205,000 in out-of-pocket or variable costs, thereby adding $55,000 to net profits on an annual basis.

TABLE 4

SALES, VARIABLE COSTS, AND PROFITS MARGINS, BY CUSTOMER-VOLUME GROUPS, CHANNEL C, 1946

(Dollars)

Customer-Volume Group, Annual Sales per Customer	Sales	Variable Costs	Profit Margin
$20,000 and over	63,980	23,050	40,930
$10,000–$20,000	73,600	55,850	17,750
$ 1,000–$10,000	131,900	164,000	*—32,100
$ 1–$ 1,000	32,100	58,900	*—26,800
Total	301,580	301,800	*— 220

* Loss.

These planned changes in our channels of distribution called for an increase in our net profits by eliminating losses. But they would also leave us with the same dollar fixed cost which would be larger relative to a smaller total sales volume. In other words, the elimination of $350,000 of unprofitable sales would leave us with idle manufacturing and distributing capacity.

Therefore, our next step was to plan to utilize this idle capacity by increasing our sales pressure on the profitable accounts in Channels A, B, and C. Of course, we realized that this increase in sales could not be accomplished in 1 year, and it could not be obtained without added out-of-pocket expenditure for sales promotion. Accordingly, in order to increase the number of calls on profitable customers and prospects in our remaining channels of distribution, our plan for the first year called for the retention of two of the salesmen who had been calling on unprofitable customers in Channels C and D. We planned to obtain during the first an increase of $100,000 in sales in Channels A and B with a profit margin of $50,000 and added expenditures of $35,000 for sales promotion, leaving an increase of $15,000 in net profit.

Our plan of eliminating unprofitable channels of distribution and concentrating on profitable channels, of course, involved much more than has been outlined above. For example, we had to draw up specific plans for dropping certain salesmen and reorganizing remaining salesmen's territories. Similar plans for our office, warehousing, shipping, and delivery operations were also necessary.

As a result of all these changes, we planned that there would be an addition of $120,000 in our net profits in the first year, as summarized in Section B of Table 3. The results of our actual operations in 1947, of course, varied somewhat from this plan, since there were many other factors operating to influence the results, some favorable, such as the rising price level, and some unfavorable. However, the net results as shown in Section C of Table 3 were even better than we expected; our net profits were approximately doubled from $150,000 in 1946 to $295,000 in 1947.

Case No. 3

Three comparable test areas were chosen in each of which a different channel of distribution was used for a trial period of 1 year. This was thought to be the only sure way to find out what would happen to sales, costs, and profits, if new sales channels should be adopted. As a result of these tests, far-reaching changes in marketing methods are being made by this company. Distribution costs at the factory are being cut by approximately 50 per cent, and profits are rising correspondingly, while prices have been reduced.

During the war, when production and sale of our entire line to the civilian market was at a standstill, we made a thorough analysis of our distribution channels. This preliminary analysis narrowed the field down to three different channels—our prewar sales channels and two others which we had been considering and debating for a number of years. Briefly, the pros and cons of these methods were as follows:

1. We had been selling to wholesalers who in turn sold to retailers. Supplementing the efforts of the wholesaler's salesmen, however, we had a large staff of our own salesmen who took orders from retailers to be filled and delivered by our wholesalers. Our salesmen also arranged for point-of-sale display material and for payment of cooperative advertising allowances to qualifying retailers. The principal

argument for this method was that our men provided the supplementary selling effort necessary to get a high volume of sales in view of the competitive situation. Of course, this added to our distribution costs.

2. The second method considered was to continue to sell to wholesalers, but to discontinue calls on retailers by our company sales staff, relying on wholesalers' salesmen to undertake the promotion and display of our products. This proposed change had been debated endlessly. The proponents claimed that it was essentially wasteful and costly to have a large and expensive sales force duplicate the efforts of the wholesalers and that we could save more than we would lose in sales. Those opposed to this method argued that it would result in lower sales, higher costs, and lower profits.

3. The third method proposed was diametrically opposed to the second—to eliminate the wholesaler entirely by selling "direct" to the retailer. This meant the continuation and expansion of our retail sales force, plus the opening up of a sizable number of our own wholesale branches to carry stocks and make deliveries. Those in favor of this method believed that our continued use of retail salesmen was absolutely essential—otherwise our competitors would take business away from us—and that, therefore, it would be cheaper to take over the entire job of distribution. Of course, the other side stated that this would be the most expensive and least profitable of all the methods proposed.

Actually, after we made these preliminary analyses, we were still far from a solution, although the issues involved were clarified and the essential factors were brought into sharper focus. We saw that, theoretically, the problem boiled down to the following factors which we had to consider in choosing the "best" method of distribution: (1) sales volume; (2) costs involved in obtaining that volume; and (3) the resultant profit, both in the short run and the long run.

Of course, we were interested in determining the channel or combination of channels which would produce that combination of sales volume and cost which would yield us the maximum amount of profit. This did not necessarily mean either the greatest attainable sales volume or the lowest possible cost, but the "best" relationship between the two. Moreover, we had to consider the long-run point of view—that is, the relative stability of sales and profits by using different methods of distribution.

We finally decided that we could not determine the best plan of marketing by any theoretical analysis of the above factors or by any weighing of the relative advantages and disadvantages of each method. The only way to find out what would happen to our sales, costs, and profits would be to try out each method of distribution under actual operating conditions. Moreover, the problem was important enough to warrant this approach. Accordingly, three comparable test areas were chosen in each of which a different channel of distribution was used. These three channels were as follows:

1. Our prewar method of selling through wholesalers plus company salesmen calling on retailers. This was a "control" area, in a sense, since we kept a record of what happened to sales during the test period.

2. Sold to wholesalers only. Company salesmen did not call on retailers in this area.

3. Sold direct to retailers only. Wholesalers were discontinued in this area. We did not build our own wholesale branches in this area, but, instead, rented storage and office space in public warehouses and arranged for public warehousemen's staffs to deliver our orders. Our own staff handled the office work.

Naturally, we were interested in what would happen to direct marketing costs in each of these three test areas. But in order to get a true picture of relative costs and profits we would also have to measure the effects of each of these methods of marketing on our indirect marketing costs, i.e., marketing costs at the home office. Accordingly, both direct costs and those indirect marketing costs which would be affected by changes in our channels of distribution were charged to the three test territories. The methods which we used in apportioning these cost groups are shown in Table 5.

The results of the test for a period of 1 year are shown in Table 6. Selling to wholesalers only without sending our salesmen to call on retailers (Column A) proved to be the cheapest of the three methods of marketing, with costs of 3.91 per cent (Item 9). It was also the channel that provided us with the biggest profit margin at the factory, 13.09 per cent of sales (Item 11).

Selling through wholesalers plus sending our salesmen to call on retailers (Column B) was, as expected, the most expensive method of distribution. Total distribution costs at the factory for this channel were 9.92 per cent of sales, compared with 3.91 per cent for selling through wholesalers only and 5.51 per cent for selling through company-operated wholesale branches (Item 9). Consequently, the operating profit at the factory was only 7.08 per cent of sales as compared with 13.09 per cent for wholesalers only and 11.49 per cent for company branches (Item 11).

TABLE 5

FUNCTIONAL CLASSIFICATION OF EXPENSES AND BASES OF ALLOCATION TO CHANNELS OF DISTRIBUTION

Distribution Cost Group	Bases of Allocation To— Wholesalers Only (Col. A)	Wholesalers Plus Retail Salesmen (Col. B)	Company Branches Plus Retail Salesmen (Col. C)
Factory distribution costs			
1. Inventory control of finished goods ..	Number of invoice lines	Number of invoice lines	Number of invoice lines.
2. Assembling shipments	Number of cases shipped	Number of cases shipped	Number of cases shipped.
3. Transportation ...	Direct	Direct	Direct.
4. Selling expense:			
a. Wholesale ...	Number of sales calls	Number of sales calls	Not allocated.
b. Retail	Not allocated ...	Direct	Direct.
5. Sales supervision:			
a. Wholesale ...	Estimated cost per salesman	Estimated cost per salesman	Not allocated.
b. Retail	Not allocated	Direct	Direct.
6. Point-of-sale advertising material .	Number of pieces of advertising material	Number of pieces of advertising material	Number of pieces of advertising material.
7. Branch supervision	Not allocated	Not allocated	Direct.
8. Billing and accounts receivable	Number of billing lines	Number of billing lines	Number of billing lines.
Branch distribution costs			
12. Storage	....	....	Direct.
13. Assembling shipments	....	....	Do.
14. Packing and shipping	....	....	Do.
15. Transportation to retailers	....	....	Do.
16. Selling	....	....	Do.
17. Billing	....	....	Do.
18. Accounts receivable	....	....	Do.
19. Credit	....	....	Do.
20. Branch supervision	....	....	Do.

Selling through company branches (Column C) was found to have an effect on the indirect factory distribution costs. Thus, the cost of supervising a larger retail sales force was 1.47 per cent as compared with only 0.79 per cent for this expense when selling through wholesalers plus retail salesmen (Item 5b). Also, there was an expense of 1.23 per cent for supervision of branches (Item 7) which was not incurred under the other two channels. Of course, these indirect costs may have been temporarily higher than "normal" because of the newness to us of this channel of distribution.

Under Channel C, our direct branch distribution costs of 20.51 per cent (Item 21) were barely covered by the regular wholesale gross margin of 22 per cent (Item 22) which we gave to our independent

TABLE 6

DISTRIBUTION COSTS, GROSS MARGINS, AND PROFITS FOR THREE CHANNELS OF DISTRIBUTION

(Percentages of Sales)

Distribution Costs	Wholesalers Only (Col. A)	Wholesalers Plus Retail Salesmen (Col. B)	Company Branches Plus Retail Salesmen (Col. C)
Factory distribution costs			
1. Inventory control of finished goods	0.01	0.01	0.04
2. Assembling shipments	.85	.86	.87
3. Transportation	.76	.76	.75
4. Selling expense:			
a. Wholesale	1.41	1.39	
b. Retail		4.71	
5. Sales supervision:			
a. Wholesale salesmen	.34	.33	
b. Retail salesmen		.79	1.47
6. Point-of-sale advertising	.30	.83	.94
7. Supervision of branches			1.23
8. Billing and accounts receivable	.24	.24	.21
9. Total factory distribution costs *	3.91	9.92	5.51
10. Gross margin at factory	17.00	17.00	17.00
11. Operating profit at factory (10 − 9) †	13.09	7.08	11.49
Branch distribution costs ‡			
12. Storage			1.94
13. Assembling shipments			2.20
14. Packing and shipping			.84
15. Transportation			1.70
16. Selling			7.59
17. Billing			1.73
18. Accounts receivable			1.56
19. Credit			1.62
20. Branch supervision			1.33
21. Total branch distribution costs			20.51
22. Gross margin at branches			22.00
23. Operating profit at branches (22 − 21)			1.49
24. Total operating profit (11 + 23)	13.09	7.08	12.98
25. Index of change in sales volume	124	129	131
26. Index of total dollar operating profit (24 × 25)	1,623	913	1,700

* Does not include national advertising and other distribution costs at the factory which were the same for all channels of distribution.

† General and administrative expenses are not deducted.

‡ In order to make the ratios in this column comparable with those of the other channels, branch distribution costs, margins, and profits are expressed as percentages of sales volume at factory selling prices (at prices billed by company to branches, which were the same as prices billed to independent wholesalers), rather than at branch selling prices (prices billed by branches to retailers).

distributors.[4] This left an operating profit of only 1.49 per cent at the branches (Item 23) which, when added to the operating profit of 11.49 at the factory (Item 11), amounted to a total of 12.98 per cent (Item 24). This was less than the profit ratio of 13.09 per cent when

[4] For comparability, these percentages (Items 12 through 23), are expressed as ratios of sales at factory prices to both wholesalers and company branches, rather than at prices of wholesalers and branches to retailers. The ratios would, of course, be lower if expressed as percentages of branch sales volume at prices to retailers.

selling through independent wholesalers (Column A), but more than the profit ratio of 7.08 per cent when selling through wholesalers plus company-paid retail salesmen (Column B).

We then compared our branch distribution costs with the operating cost ratios of our independent wholesalers, and found that in non-metropolitan areas, our wholesale distributors probably could do the job at an appreciably lower cost. This was even after allowing for the possibility that a permanent operation from company-owned warehouses might be cheaper than using public warehousing space and facilities. However, in one metropolitan district where there was a high sales concentration, we found that our company branch probably could do the job at about the same cost as an independent wholesaler. Also, having our own branches in large metropolitan areas provided certain "strategic" advantages, such as more direct control and flexibility in adjusting to company policies.

Next, in order to evaluate the effect of the three channels on our sales volume, we set up an index of the change in sales for each channel for the test year, compared with the preceding year (Item 25). The sales index for the "control" area in which we continued to use our previous methods of distribution (Column B) was 129, contrasted to 124 in the territory where we stopped sending salesmen to call on retailers (Column A) and 131 in the territory where we operated our own branches (Column C).

Our salesmen and sales executives made spot checks by visiting retailers in the areas where we discontinued our retail salesmen to see whether the wholesalers' salesmen were doing a good job in merchandising our products, arranging displays, and so forth. Although there were exceptions, the reports on the whole indicated that wholesaler's salesmen were not doing as satisfactory a job as had been done previously by our own men.

Many of our sales executives were naturally enough inclined to credit the relatively smaller increase in volume in this area (Column A) to this factor, and to state that it proved the need for supplementary selling effort. The fact that the sales increase was the greatest in the area where company salesmen did all the retail selling was also cited to suggest this viewpoint. On the other hand, it was pointed out that the differences in sales increase between the three test areas were probably not great enough to be "significant" and could be due to any one of a number of other factors.

In order to evaluate the effect of both differences in sales volume and differences in cost associated with the three channels, we set up a measure of comparative total dollar operating profit. This was done by multiplying the total operating profit per dollar of sales for each channel (Item 24) by the index of sales volume (Item 25).

This index of total dollar operating profit is shown as Item 26 in Table 6; it is 1,623 for selling through wholesalers only (Column A), as compared with only 913 for selling through wholesalers and having our salesmen call on retailers (Column B). Thus, even if we should have to forego the profit on about 5 per cent of our attainable sales volume (see Item 25, Columns A and B), yet the savings in distribution costs would be so much greater that our final dollar operating profit would be increased by 78 per cent.[5]

In short, this analysis indicated that, as between selling through wholesalers without retail salesmen and selling through wholesalers with retail salesmen, the former would be the more profitabe channel of distribution. Of course, this was a short-run analysis only; there was the possibility, over a longer period of time and under different business conditions, of a greater cumulative loss of sales to our competitors, as a consequence of not having our own sales staff to call on retailers.

On the other hand, the relatively high distribution costs, both in the home office and in the field, which were incurred when selling through company branches (Column C), apparently were offset by the higher sales volume, so that this channel's index of total dollar profit —1,700—was the greatest (Item 26). Because of this and the other advantages of company branches outlined previously, it appeared that in metropolitan districts our own branches would be a more profitable channel of distribution than independent wholesalers. In nonmetropolitan areas, however, it appeared that independent wholesalers would be a more profitable channel of distribution than our own branches, because of their appreciably lower operating costs.

Based on the results of these test areas we are making far-reaching changes in our channels of distribution. We are establishing company branches in several metropolitan areas where we do a major portion of our business. In all other areas, however, we are strengthening our relations with our independent wholesalers, even though we are withdrawing our retail salesmen from all their territories (with only a few exceptions). This latter may be a short-run solution, but we feel that we will be able to meet the possibly more stringent competition of the future by other means than through the essentially high-cost method of supplementary retail selling.

[5] 1,623 − 913 = 710 (Item 26, Columns A and B); 710 ÷ 913 = 78 per cent.

We are constantly working with our wholesalers in helping them to improve the efficiency of their operations and get their costs down, based on the first-hand experience obtained in operating our own branches. We also have a training program for wholesalers and retailers. to increase the selling effectiveness of their salesmen.

We believe that it is even more important to get reductions in our wholesalers' and retailers' costs than it is in our own distribution costs. Although our own distribution costs, including national advertising, will probably be less than 5 per cent of our sales, after we have completed changing our channels of distribution, our wholesalers' margins (prewar) were around 20 per cent of their sales and retailers' margins for our products approximated 30 per cent of the retail price. With the adding of new lines by our company and the high level of national income, our total sales volume per wholesaler on our products has more than doubled and the average retailer's volume on our products has also increased substantially. We believe that all of these factors will make it possible for our distributors—both wholesale and retail—to operate profitably on smaller unit costs and margins.

We expect an over-all savings in our own distribution cost at the factory of around 5 percentage points and we have reduced the prices of our products accordingly. We believe that this price reduction will more than offset the possible loss of selling pressures from withdrawing our own retail men from most of our independent wholesalers' areas and that, under existing circumstances at least, we stand to gain more than we lose competitively.

The results, to date, of the changes in our channels of distribution have been even better than expected. Although it is difficult to separate the influence of the high level of business activity generally from the effects of our new channels, our sales volume has increased greatly. Our distribution costs at the factory are dropping fast to the desired less-than-5-per cent ratio, while the operating costs of our branches and independent wholesalers are also being reduced. Our net profits are correspondingly increasing.

Distribution Cost Analysis Techniques [6]

The usefulness of distribution cost analysis is emphasized by the fact that all of the companies whose experiences were highlighted in preceding sections were able to accomplish striking cost reductions and striking increases in profits. The cost reductions and profit in-

[6] See Appendix to this article, pp. 530-532, for definition of cost terms.

creases were accomplished because the misdirection of marketing efforts were of such large proportions and, therefore, the opportunities for improvement were so great. It is probable that any company which has been operating for many years on a program based on drift plus intuition, likewise has a marketing operation which can be improved substantially by the adoption of policies based on even relatively simple techniques of distribution cost analysis.

An extended discussion of the principles and methods of distribution cost analysis is beyond the scope of this chapter. However, the basic procedures or steps involved, which will be discussed later, are summarized here:

1. The separable, or direct, expenses are measured and assigned direct to customers or commodities.

2. The common, or indirect, expenses are allocated or assigned to functional-cost groups.

3. The factors which measure the variable activity of the various functions are identified, and the amounts of these factors, in the aggregate, are determined.

4. A measurement is made of the share of the variable activity of each of these functional-cost groups which is utilized by the segment of sales whose cost is being measured.

5. The ratio of the share of the activity of the function that is being utilized by a segment of sales (Step 4) to the total quantity of the activity of that function (Step 3) indicates the portion of the cost of that function which is allocated to that segment of sales.

6. The excess of dollar gross margin over the sum of the direct expenses and the shares of the various functional-cost groups allocated to a commodity or customer or other segment of sales indicates its relative profitability or unprofitability.

Functional classification [7]

Although the proportion of direct marketing costs may frequently be significant, the greater part of a firm's distribution costs are likely to be indirect. To facilitate their allocation, as well as for purposes of expense control, these indirect expenses are classified into functional groups.

The basis of the functional classification which would be used by any given firm is a study of the marketing activities performed by

[7] A functional classification puts together all the expense items that have been incurred for the same activity. A functional classification, therefore, permits the allocation of an entire cost group by means of a single factor.

that company. It is important that the functional classification be sufficiently detailed so that the work performed in any one function will be of the same general kind. Such homogeneity facilitates the assignment of an entire functional-cost group by the use of a single factor of allocation, as will be described hereafter.

Assignment of natural expenses to functions

It is usually necessary to apportion many natural expense items among several functional-cost groups since they relate to more than one functional activity. They are distributed by means of time study, space measurements, counts, managerial estimates, and other methods. The increased cost and effort of preparing functional-cost classifications may be much more than offset by the advantages of improved cost control, as well as by the advantages of cost analysis.

Illustrative functional classification

Most companies, especially those serving wide markets and producing and selling a number of products, have complex organizations and engage in a wide range of marketing activities. Consequently, it is difficult to set forth a widely representative functional classification of distribution expenses. Each company would have to set up its own classification to reflect its own marketing activities. For illustrative purposes, however, the following example of a functional classification of distribution expenses for a rubber manufacturer is shown.

Functional Classification of Distribution Expenses for a Rubber Manufacturer [8]

1. Investment in finished goods:
   - Taxes on stock
   - Insurance on stock
2. Storage of finished goods (portions of following expenses applying to factory, branch and district warehouses):
   - Rental expense, or
   - Maintenance and repairs to buildings
   - Taxes on buildings
   - Insurance on buildings
   - Depreciation on buildings
   - Heat, light, and power
   - Outside storage space

[8] The functions and the primary expense accounts are based, in part, on those suggested by the *Uniform Accounting Manual for the Rubber Manufacturing Industry* (Commercial Expense Division) (Rubber Manufacturers' Association Inc., 1933).

3. Inventory control, finished goods:
   - Salaries—stock-record clerks
   - Salaries—merchandise distribution (allocation of stock to district and branch warehouses and preparation of orders on factory)
   - Overhead—space, equipment, supplies, and supervision charges
4. Order assembly (physical handling):
   - Salaries—warehouse labor
   - Overhead—space, equipment, supplies, and supervision charges
5. Packing and shipping:
   - Material
   - Labor
   - Overhead
6. Transportation (on merchandise shipped from factory or branch to customer and from branch to branch, and on returned goods):
   - Freight
   - Truck
   - Express
   - Parcel post
   - Transportation on consigned merchandise, factory to branch
7. Sales solicitation (special commodity or customer subdepartments or subfunctions will be set up according to the operating organization of the company, each with the following primary expense accounts):
   - Salaries—salesmen
   - Commissions—salesmen
   - Commissions—agents
   - Commissions—brokers
   - Traveling expenses—salesmen
   - Entertainment—salesmen

   Overhead (except for the second account below, these overhead accounts would not, of course, be set up by commodity or customer subdepartments):
   - Salaries—sales executives
   - Salaries—merchandise-department managers
   - Salaries—district branch managers
   - Sales employment and personnel
   - Sales training
   - Sales research
   - Sales engineering service
   - Adjustment
   - Sales records
   - Space and equipment charges
8. Advertising:
   - Advertising space:
     - Newspapers
     - Magazines
     - Posters
     - Outdoor signs
     - Electric signs
     - Advertising agency services
     - Art work—outside
     - Radio
     - Displays
     - Motion pictures
     - Electros

Overhead:
Salaries—advertising managers and assistants
Advertising expenses
Space and equipment charges
9. Order entry:
Salaries—clerical (allocated portion)
Overhead—space, equipment, supplies, and supervision charges
10. Billing:
Salaries—clerical (allocated portion)
Overhead—space, equipment, supplies, and supervision charges
11. Credit extension:
Salaries—clerical (allocated portion)
Overhead—space, equipment, supplies, and supervision charges
12. Accounts receivable:
Salaries—clerical (allocated portion)
Overhead—space, equipment, supplies, and supervision charges

Allocation procedures

After the indirect costs have been classified by functions, they are allocated on the basis of utilization by channels, products, customers, and so forth, of the variable activities giving rise to those costs. The principle followed is to charge the channel or customer (or other segment of sales) with the cost of its share of the variable activity of each functional-cost group; that is, the cost of the portion of the variable marketing and administrative effort for which it is responsible.

Variable functional activity

The identification of the variable activity which is involved in each functional-cost group and the broad relationship between the functional costs and the characteristics of products and channels are often evident merely from study. Some functional activities vary according to certain characteristics of the commodity and are not greatly affected by channel or customer characteristics. Others vary primarily according to certain channel or customer characteristics regardless of what product is being purchased.

For example, the variable activity involved in the storage and investment functions depends almost solely on the bulk, weight, perishability, and inventory value of the product stored, and is affected but little by the customer who buys the product. Similarly, the credit function will vary according to the financial integrity and other credit characteristics of customers with little regard to the nature of the commodity on which credit was extended.

As regards still other functional-cost groups, the broad relationship between these costs and product and customer characteristics is more complicated. For there is every shade of combination of customer responsibility and commodity responsibility for the variable activity and, therefore, the amount of expense, within the different functional-cost groups.

Partial allocation

It is neither feasible nor useful to attempt a full allocation of all distribution costs in most businesses, although there are many who make such an attempt. That is, those functional activities which vary entirely with customer or channel characteristics should not be allocated to commodities, and, conversely, those related solely to commodity characteristics should not be allocated to customers or channels or territories. However, some functional-cost groups would usually be allocated to both customers and commodities.

In addition to the difficulty of tracing a direct connection between the variable activity of some functions and product or customer characteristics, there is another reason for not making a full allocation of distribution costs. For the control uses of these cost data which we are discussing, namely, to determine relative costs and profits by channels and to determine the appropriate action to be taken in regard to these channels, little would be gained by making a full allocation.

A full allocation may involve the assignment of some indirect expenses which represent functions not being used to capacity,[9] on the basis of an arbitrary factor such as sales volume. This may have the effect of making some commodities, customers, channels, territories, etc., with large sales volume and low percentages of gross margin, appear to be relatively unprofitable. Actually, since these functions are not being used to capacity, these indirect expenses would not be affected by substitution, elimination, or an increase of sales in the short run.

For example, storage and investment costs usually would not be allocated to customers, because these activities are not usually related to customer characteristics and because they would not be affected by short-run changes in the number of customers. Likewise, credit costs usually would not be allocated to commodities since they would not be affected by addition or elimination of products "at the margin."

[9] Such evidence as is available indicates that important distribution and administrative facilities or functions may, in normal times, be rather consistently underutilized in the typical business.

Furthermore, a desire for a full cost allocation may involve an erroneous conception of the use of distribution cost analysis in connection with pricing policy. It appears to some that, if they know the total or "real" unit distribution cost plus the total unit production cost, they can then arrive at the proper price merely by adding the desired unit net profit. If, however, such a pricing procedure gives insufficient recognition to demand, it may be worse than one which is not based on any knowledge of unit costs at all. If prices determined on this total unit cost-plus basis are too high, in the light of demand and competition, sales volume may be lower than before, so that total costs per unit will be higher than calculated, and may not be covered even at the higher prices. Or if cost-plus prices are too low, then profits are sacrified.

Summary of procedure

Table 7 summarizes the preceding discussion of distribution

TABLE 7

Functional-Cost Groups	Bases of Allocation	
	To Commodities	To Channels
1. Investment in finished goods	Average inventory value	(Not allocated)
2. Storage of finished goods	Floor space occupied	(Not allocated)
3. Inventory control, finished goods	Number of invoice lines	(Not allocated)
4. Order assembly (handling)	Number of standard handling units	Number of invoice lines
5. Packing and shipping	Weight or number of shipping units	Weight or number of shipping units
6. Transportation	Weight or number of shipping units	Weight or number of shipping units
7. Selling	Time studies	Number of sales calls
8. Advertising	Cost of space, etc. of specific product advertising	Cost of space, etc. of specific customer advertising
9. Order entry	Number of invoice lines	Number of orders
10. Billing	Number of invoice lines	Number of invoice lines
11. Credit extension	(Not allocated)	Average amount outstanding
12. Accounts receivable	(Not allocated)	Number of invoices posted

cost analysis techniques, showing some illustrative functional cost groups and bases of allocation to commodities and to channels.

COST ANALYSIS AS A BASIS FOR POLICY

Sometimes, as a last resort, and after investigating all other alternatives, the decision is made by the executives to eliminate the unprofitable channels which have been revealed by a distribution cost analysis.

A decision to eliminate unprofitable channels is, of course, far-reaching, affecting every aspect of the business. A decision to eliminate an unprofitable segment of sales because its "savable" distribution costs exceeds its net revenue, for example, would need to be reviewed in the light of the fact that smaller production runs and a reduced scale of production with the same amount of fixed costs might increase the unit manufacturing cost. Thus, further cost analyses are necessary if the business executive, after studying all of the alternative courses of action, seeks to determine the effects of eliminating those unprofitable segments of sales that cannot be turned into sources of profit. These further analyses involve the following steps:

In the first place, it is necessary to make a forecast of just what will happen to sales volume over a period of time, after the business changes from a policy of indiscriminately covering the entire market to a policy of selective distribution. This, of course, is an analysis to be made by the marketing executives.

Secondly, it is necessary to estimate the decrease in total expense that would result from eliminating the unprofitable sales. This is not an easy matter since the distribution costs which were allocated to sales to discover the unprofitable segments would not provide the answer, for some of these costs could not be saved and would continue after the sales were dropped. Therefore, it is necessary to separate the nonsavable (or fixed) costs from the savable costs. The total savable costs less the net revenue that will be given up, shows, of course, the net savings, or the addition to the net profits of the business that will result from dropping the unprofitable sales. (Of course, if the net revenue that will be given up exceeds the expenses that will be saved, the net profits in the short run will be greater with, than without, the relatively unprofitable sales.)

Thirdly, it is necessary to make definite plans to get expenses down when unprofitable sales are to be cut off. The experiences of several businesses have shown that projected savings in distribution costs often are never realized because of failure to make and execute definite plans for expense reduction.

It should be emphasized, however, that to curtail sales volume by eliminating an unprofitable channel is only *one* way, and not the only way to make use of cost results. While it is true that profits made from one segment of the business are often largely dissipated through losses on unprofitable customers and commodities and while it is true that cost results sometimes lead to the lopping off of obviously unprofitable business, the main application is in another direction.

Effective use of distribution cost analysis findings consists in shifting the allocation of sales and advertising effort so as to secure a greater return in sales volume and profits. Salesmen may discontinue calling on unproductive types of customers in a certain channel, for example, primarily in order to give them more time for adequate cultivation of the more profitable prospects. Shifting effort to the points where it counts most is the keynote of the use of cost analysis in connection with channels.

Thus, there is no conflict at all between the use of distribution cost analysis in connection with problems of channel policy and the urge for expansion of sales volume. On the contrary, since sales cultivation either of old markets or of new markets requires expenditure of time and money, the resources devoted to marketing in any channel will accomplish greater results if applied with maximum efficiency.

Appendix: Definition of Cost Terms [10]

Direct vs. Indirect. A large portion of marketing costs are indirect rather than direct costs. Direct costs are those which are incurred for and benefit a single segment of sales and therefore can be traced direct to specific customers, commodities, or other sales components. Indirect costs are those which are incurred for and benefit more than one segment of sales and therefore cannot be traced directly to specific products or customers.

Common vs. Separable. Common costs are those which cannot, *as a practical matter,* be traced direct to specific customers, commodities, or other sales components. Separable costs are those which can readily be traced to customers, commodities, and so on.

Whether a given outlay is a common or separable cost may depend on the circumstances of the business and on the segment of sales for which cost is being measured. If salesmen are paid on a salary basis, for example, the outlay for their wages is a common cost so far as individual commodities are concerned. On the other hand, if the salesmen work on a commission basis, the commissions paid are a seperable cost of selling individual commodities, and they also are separable in regard to the cost of selling to individual customers.

In general, the greater proportion of marketing expenses are common costs, either because the process of tracing such costs to specific units of sales may be too expensive or, in some cases, because there may be no available method of making a practical and reasonably accurate separation.

[10] This appendix is taken from Charles H. Sevin, *Distribution Cost Analysis,* U. S. Department of Commerce, Economic Series, No. 50 (1946), p. 52.

Fixed vs. Variable. The distinction between common and separable costs is related to another twofold classification of marketing expenses, namely, fixed and variable costs. Fixed costs may be defined as those which do not change in total amount when the sales volume is varied. Variable costs, on the other hand, are those which change in total amount when the sales volume is varied. The distinction between fixed and variable costs thus depends on the behavior of costs in relation to changes in sales volume. The distinction between fixed and variable costs is not a hard and fast one, but depends on the circumstances of the individual business and the particular segment of sales for which costs are being analyzed.

Thus, some fixed costs arise from a lack of flexibility in certain of the circumstances or factors under which the business operates. This lack of flexibility may be owing to sunk or irrecoverable expenditures, or it may be the result of contractual obligations assumed by the business. In other words, the amount of marketing activity or effort for which the cost is incurred may vary with changes in sales volume, but, owing to contractual obligations, the businessman cannot immediately make adjustments in the amount of the expense.

For example, the amount of delivery activity will vary with changes in sales volume, but if a distributor who delivers by truck owns the trucks and pays his drivers on a weekly basis, most of his delivery expenses will be fixed costs in relation to changes in sales volume that do not necessitate changes in the number of trucks or drivers. On the other hand, if the distributor contracts with an outside firm for delivery on a zone-tonnage, package, or similar basis, his delivery expenses are a variable cost.

Similarly, if the distributor rents his warehouse or store on the usual basis of a fixed amount per annum, his rent is a fixed cost. However, if the distributor should have a percentage lease—in which the rental is a stated percentage of sales volume—his rent would be a variable expense.

Furthermore, practically all costs are fixed only within a certain range of sales volume and become variable when greater changes occur. If sales drop to a very low level, for example, branches may be closed or a smaller warehouse or store building rented, delivery trucks and other equipment may be sold, and policies with respect to retaining key workers and executives in the organization may be revised.

The permanency, as well as the range of change in sales volume, affects the distinction between fixed and variable costs. When a curtailment in sales is expected to be brief, the building, equipment, and organization will be kept intact, but when a long period of depression appears to have set in, expenses will be pared down. Conversely, when a sufficiently large gain in sales is expected to continue more or less permanently, an expansion of the scale of plant and organization to take care of this increased business will result in a rise in fixed costs.

This suggests that the proportions of fixed and variable costs in a given firm may change according to the time interval and the size of the segment of sales under analysis. In the long run and with respect to a large segment of sales, practically all costs may be classified as variable.

In the short run, however—as long as the "scale of plant" for making sales remains unchanged—and with reference to small changes in sales volume, most marketing expenses are in the nature of fixed costs. That is, small changes in sales volume can occur without appreciably affecting the aggregate amount of the distributor's expenses. For example, the net addition to the aggregate operating costs of a wholesaler or retailer as the result of making an additional sale are usually insignificant in amount.

The relationship between common and separable costs on the one hand and fixed and variable costs on the other can be readily seen. In the short run, and in relation to a small segment of sales volume, the separable, or direct, costs are most variable, while the common or indirect costs are, in general, fixed. In the longer run, the common or indirect, costs tend to become variable.

Average vs. Marginal. Another classification of costs is based on a distinction between marginal and average costs. Narrowly defined, the marginal unit cost is the increase in aggregates costs as output, that is, sales, is increased by one unit. The amount by which the aggregate costs increases is the cost of the additional unit. The average unit cost of any given output, on the other hand, is the aggregate cost divided by the number of units produced or sold. For example:

Number of Units	Aggregate Costs	Average Cost per Unit	Marginal Cost per Unit
10	$100.00	$10.00	....
11	104.50	9.50	$4.50
12	108.00	9.00	3.50

Escapable vs. Nonescapable. A somewhat similar twofold classification distinguishes between escapable expenses. For example, if a single department in a department store were shut down, the expenses which could be saved would be escapable, while the remaining expenses of the store would be nonescapable. Thus, the escapable costs would be the same as the marginal costs, while the nonescapable costs would be equal to the aggregate costs after the department had been eliminated.

Imputed vs. Outlay. For certain kinds of analysis, it is necessary to consider imputed costs as well as actual outlays. For example, a theoretical interest or rent might be charged to a commodity, even though no actual expenditures were made for these expenses. Such costs would be imputed costs as contrasted with actual outlays or expenditures.

Natural vs. Functional. The ordinary expenses of a business (actual outlays) may be classified in several ways. The more usual method is on a so-called natural or object-of-expenditure basis. For example, rent and wages are natural expense items. For purposes of analyzing distribution costs, it is found useful to reclassify the natural expense items into functional-cost groups.

A functional-cost group is the cost of a single activity; thus a functional classification puts together all the expense items that have been incurred for the same activity. A functional classification of expense facilitates the allocation of the common, or indirect, expense items, and permits distribution of an entire cost group by means of a single factor or basis of allocation.

50. THE MODERN WHOLESALER AND HIS ADJUSTMENT TO A CHANGING ECONOMY *

Herman C. Nolen

New and exciting things are taking place in our present economy, not the least of which is the emergence of the wholesaler as a dynamic force in our business and cultural progress. Today's wholesaler is no longer the passive order taker for producers or the simple purchasing agent for retailers. He is a vital element in the distributive chain which is so necessary to the orderly marketing of the huge output of our vast industrial, agricultural, and mining organizations. The wholesaler is deserving of great credit for his contributions to our economic progress but unfortunately he so seldom receives that credit.

Many of us think of wholesalers as outmoded middlemen who have been and are cluttering up the pathways of economic expansion. We think of them at times as institutions which are adding to the growing costs of getting merchandise from producer to consumer without contributing worthwhile services in return. In the next few minutes I hope to demonstrate to you that today's wholesaler is keeping pace with the rapidly changing developments in our economy and, in many ways, is actually showing the way to other units. Do not underestimate the ability, the influence, and the power of today's wholesaler. He may not have surrounded himself with a battery of publicity agents who are singing his praises to the multitude, but he is silently, steadily, and effectively doing his part to enable our economy to grow and bring prosperity and higher living standards to our people.

Who is this wholesaler who is doing so much to broaden the market for the huge quantities of new products which are flowing out of our vast productive empire? He is a specialist—a specialist in distribution and this is an age of specialization. And, we must remember that the benefits of specialization are not confined to our industrial operations. These benefits are equally applicable to the

* Reprinted by permission of Herman C. Nolen from a talk given before the American Marketing Association Conference, Harvard University School of Business, June 25, 1958.

Herman C. Nolen, Chairman of the Board, McKesson & Robbins, Inc.

field of distribution, and today's wholesaler is proving himself to be a most efficient factor in our marketing mechanism.

The mere fact that buyers and sellers are constantly attempting to undertake to do the wholesaling job themselves keeps wholesalers efficient. Whenever a buyer or a seller feels that he can perform wholesaling services more efficiently, cheaper, or better than the wholesaler, he is very likely to assume those services. The result is that the wholesaler is constantly under pressure to do his job effectively. He also is more responsive to changes in our economy than other agencies as he cannot afford to lag behind modern developments or he finds himself no longer being used. He must adapt himself quickly and continually to changes.

Before reviewing the changes which are taking place in wholesaling today, and the factors responsible for them, let us just briefly mention some of the functions which wholesalers are performing for their customers, the wholesaler:

1. anticipates customer requirements
2. assembles goods from a multitude of sources
3. buys in economical quantities
4. maintains a reservoir of goods
5. delivers promptly
6. grants credit
7. provides informational and advisory services.

and for the manufacturers, the wholesaler:

1. establishes connections with the whole field of retail outlets
2. furnishes advice as a distribution specialist
3. reduces costs of physical distribution
4. reduces manufacturers' capital requirements
5. simplifies accounting and credit problems.

Not all wholesalers perform all these services full-line, full-service wholesalers do—others render one or more of the services mentioned. Retailers and producers will find it possible today to utilize from wholesalers just the services they desire to use. In the wholesale field there are many types of specialized distributors available and the list of wholesaler types seems to be growing larger all the time.

Before discussing in detail the various types of adjustments wholesalers have made and are making to meet the constantly changing factors in our modern economy, let us review some of the more important economic changes which are affecting the operation of wholesalers.

Most of the changes in our economy which are vitally affecting wholesalers today center around three basic elements—advertising, distribution costs, and mass distribution.

All of us are aware of the growing importance of advertising in our economy—not only in terms of money spent, media used, but in influence on producers, consumers, and particularly on distributors. No single agency is more affected by the growth in advertising than is the wholesaler. How is advertising influencing wholesaling?

First of all, wholesalers are feeling the influence of advertising on consumers. Consumers have become brand conscious. Wholesalers find it difficult to find a market for unbranded or unknown merchandise brands, and that is especially true of goods marketed through self-service. Advertising, too, is making consumers much more intellegent purchasers and vastly more style conscious.

Another advertising factor affecting wholesalers is that of its high cost and the necessity for manufacturers to make huge initial outlays for advertising. This is particularly true of television advertising today. The fact that a manufacturer may have to commit himself for expenditures running into millions of dollars for a comparatively short TV schedule, forces him to utilize wholesalers to get maximum distribution for him prior to the appearance of his commercials. Not many manufacturers have selling organizations capable of assuming this responsibility and you cannot finance TV network programs with gradually expanding or spotty distribution. The job must be done prior to the appearance of the ads or much of the advertising value may be dissipated.

The fact that distribution costs both absolutely and relatively appear to be rising is affecting wholesalers as well as other marketeers. Producers and distributors are checking their costs more carefully than formerly. Labor and transportation costs particularly are rising. The demand for more services on the part of buyers is causing distribution costs to inch upward. The shorter work week with expanding fringe benefits are also squeezing profit margins.

Another important economic factor affecting wholesale distribution is the continued growth of large scale retail outlets. The supermarket, the chain store, and more recently the shopping center developments, are changing our distribution patterns. Meeting the requirements for capital for expansion is a real problem for the newer and less well established operators. Inventory turnover is assuming added meaning for these people. Large scale retailing has brought with it wide spread unionization in retail outlets.

The post war retailing phenomenon—the discount house—is altering merchandising patterns. So is the continued expansion of self-service, self-selection, and open display of merchandise.

In the past few months the recession has brought with it intense competition and in markets hard hit by labor layoffs, savage price competition. Detroit, Pittsburgh, Seattle, and other such centers have been particularly hard hit by this movement.

The economic changes I have mentioned are not the only ones which are affecting wholesaling in the United States today, but I believe they are the most important. The growing influence of advertising, the continued upward trend of costs, the growing importance of large scale distributors, and the development of suburban shopping areas are causing wholesalers to re-adapt their methods, their policies, their plans and their practices to these new conditions.

How the wholesaler is adjusting himself to changing economic conditions is a credit to him and also to American business know-how. He is adapting himself most promptly and continually to the constant flood of changes in our economy. His close margin of profit makes it necessary for him to be most responsive to even minor variations in the economic climate in which he works.

Let's first discuss his adjustment to the growing importance of advertising to manufacturers, to retailers, to consumers, and the need for speed in attaining that adjustment. Wholesalers today are concentrating on the well advertised national brands and particularly those which move rapidly over the retailers' counters. In many instances they are providing for automatic distribution for manufacturers. In many fields wholesalers accept automatic distribution from manufacturers and, in turn, provide retailers with automatic distribution of products in advance of advertising programs. This is enabling advertisers to secure a much better return on their advertising dollars. They are encouraging retailers to recognize brand ratios in their merchandising and to provide display areas in proportion to sales.

In many instances wholesalers today are providing display services including window, in-store, counter, and bin display services for advertised goods. Manufacturers today can engage in advertising activities with confidence that the merchandise they promote will be available for sale and properly displayed in retail outlets. Wholesalers today are offering cooperative advertising assistance to groups of retailers. They are assisting the manufacturer in merchandising his advertising to the retailers and in that way greatly increase its effectiveness. Few manufacturers today can get a full return from their investment in advertising without the assistance of the wholesalers, particularly if the goods are sold in a large number of outlets.

The wholesalers' adjustment to rising costs in distribution is less dramatic but, I believe, even more effective. Like all businessmen, wholesalers have a constant battle to keep their costs in line and I think they are doing a good job in pursuing the majority of the conventional methods of keeping down expenses, such as increasing merchandise turnover, eliminating waste, and the like. However, there are certain areas in cost cutting in which the wholesalers have made great progress in the last few years. One has been in the simplification of warehouse and office jobs. Wholesalers, as experts in distribution, have done an outstanding job in eliminating wasted motion and effort. For example, if you will pardon the reference to my own company, in the past three years we are handling one third more tonnage with 9 per cent fewer people in our offices and warehouses. In my opinion, that is quite an achievement in an industry that is not highly mechanized. That increase in production has been achieved largely by getting people to do their jobs better and not by the introduction of labor saving machinery.

A very large percentage of wholesalers are now using labor saving devices in their accounting and general office departments. Recently, a wholesale druggist on the West Coast has developed and installed a mechanical warehouse for storing, picking, and packing merchandise. This revolutionary idea is still in the development stage but it may provide an entry for the introduction of mechanization to our basic distribution problems. Tabulating cards are fed into the machine at one end and thousands of individual items are picked by the machine and fed through a belt to the shipping platform. The fact that this machine was developed by a wholesaler and by the cooperative efforts of a number of wholesalers I think is indicative of the kind of thinking which is present today in many of our wholesale establishments.

Another program for cutting costs, which wholesalers are following aggressively, is selectivity—and especially selective selling and selective servicing of customers. Wholesalers have learned that not all customers are entitled to all services—only those customers who will concentrate their purchases with a wholesaler are entitled to his red carpet services. Selective selling and servicing of customers is being practiced by practically every wholesaler in the country.

Wholesalers also are concentrating on increasing order size, on high line extension and on promoting fast selling merchandise. These practices bring down costs.

Earlier I stated that one of our problems has been increased transportation and delivery costs. Wholesalers have been quick to adjust their operations to these increased costs by making use of the delivery services not normally used for servicing their customers. Many wholesalers are giving rapid service to their customers through the use of newspaper trucks, especially those returning after delivering newspapers. They are using buses extensively. They are having florists and milk delivery companies work for them. In our business we have made extensive use of Western Union delivery service. For example, in the city of Portland, Oregon, we can provide our downtown customers with eleven deliveries a day. In the city of Detroit, Michigan, we are providing five deliveries a day to our customers and at a cost which, percentagewise, is no greater than our cost of 15 years ago when we offered one delivery every three days to our customers.

In those industries where it is necessary to provide merchandise to customers at the very lowest cost possible, some wholesalers make available the basic service at a minimum cost. An example is the grocery field where the basic cost of servicing a store may be provided to a customer at 3½ or 4 per cent. If the customer desires additional services, such as display help in a store, advertising assistance, store design, etc., he pays extra for those services. In any event, he can get merchandise from the wholesale warehouse to his establishment at a cost which is phenomenally low. It might interest you to know that in one large city in the United States there is a single wholesale establishment that does over $300 million annually in that one area on that basis. That is a volume of business I believe that is unmatched in any field in so small an area.

One area of cost which is proving very stubborn to reduction is that of selling. Selling costs have not been as susceptible to expense control as have other costs in wholesale establishments. It has been very difficult to greatly increase the productivity of salesmen. Every wholesale establishment, probably more so than other business firms, has used telephone and mail services extensively. They are also using sales contracts and group selling techniques to cut costs in this area. Progress is being made, but it is slow. And wholesale sales managers are very much aware of the value of their salesmen's time.

A third major area of adjustment for wholesalers to changing economic conditions has been in the field of customer relations. I feel that wholesalers, more than any other sellers, realize how important it is to keep their customers strong and fortunately they are doing just that. Wholesalers have long realized that a prosperous business cannot be built on weak customers, so wholesalers today are making every effort to keep their customers strong.

Let me go over some of the means by which wholesalers are assisting their customers, the retailers. Today most any individual retailer can go to his wholesaler for assistance on location analysis. Wholesalers have developed programs and means for evaluating the amount of business that can be done in an area. They know about the growth trends in cities and suburbs and their judgment in this regard is widely sought by individual retailers.

A second service which is being widely utilized is that of store design and modernization. If you will pardon further reference to an individual company—to illustrate a point—our company has helped modernize one out of every five drug stores in this country in the past five years. We have provided store design service, traffic flow analysis, and, in most instances, we have actually provided the store fixtures. If the retailer needs assistance in financing that modernization program he is planning he can get help through his wholesaler. Depending upon his credit standing he may be able to buy the fixtures and pay for them over a period of years, with or without a down payment, and in many instances the fixtures can be leased through the wholesaler.

Many retailers are finding today that taking a new location presents certain problems with the lease, which did not confront them a few years back. In shopping centers and other large scale developments the leases are pretty complicated arrangements and many wholesalers today provide legal assistance on new leases and adjustments in old leases for their customers. This is something which a wholesaler can provide better than anyone else because of his intimate knowledge of the business and its problems, which is not possessed by financial institutions or manufacturers.

Most wholesalers today provide store opening services and I have known of instances where retailers open a new store and the opening was handled completely by the wholesaler. He selected merchandise for the store, he put it on the shelves, he priced it, he prepared the advertisements, he made arrangements with local newspapers, radio and TV stations, trained the help, provided all the gimmicks for the gala store opening, and then turned over to the retailer a thriving retail business.

Sales training and merchandising assistance have been widely provided by wholesalers. Large chain organizations may be able to do their own training of personnel and may provide merchandising assistance but the smaller retailer looks to his wholesaler for that service and he is being provided a service which is on par with that available to the chain stores.

Advertising services are being provided to retailers, cooperative advertising, monthly mat services, and special event advertising is available to retailers in most fields through their wholesalers.

Store management counseling is available to retailers—not only are manuals and courses in management provided, but also experts from the wholesale establishments can be called upon for assistance on individual problems. Accounting systems are commonly made available as well as income and other tax advice.

Some wholesalers are providing many special services to retailers. For example, rack jobbers will select, price-mark, shelve, inventory, and advertise merchandise for their retail customers. They will even provide fixtures—all the retailer has to do is provide space, collect the money, pay for the merchandise that disappears—the rest is all done by the wholesaler.

Whenever customers need special service, wholesalers in most cases will provide the service required. Wholesalers are constantly studying the need for new types of service required by their customers.

In order to keep the smaller retailers competitive with the large mercantile groups, wholesalers today will provide merchandising leaders and specials. In many instances these specials are provided at prices well below those which the chain stores have obtained.

The instances I have cited are not the only adjustments which wholesalers are making to the ever changing economic patterns in this country but they are some which I thought would be of interest to you and they are the types of adaptations that are proving extremely helpful to customers, to retailers and to manufacturers. Today's wholesalers are not old fashioned, outmoded, antique operators. They are moving just as rapidly as our other business institutions and, I believe, they are adjusting themselves to changing conditions with greater speed than most others. In my opinion, there is no doubt that the wholesaler is making his full contribution to better living in this country through making available to our people the merchandise they need at the lowest possible cost. To accomplish this the wholesaler is extremely sensitive to those changes and his adjustment to those changes is being made continually.

The fact that the wholesaler's relative position in our economy is about the same as it was twenty or thirty years ago shows that he has done a successful job of adjusting his operations to changing conditions. Of course, it is true that some types of wholesalers are not as important, yet on the other hand other types are considerably more so today. Wholesalers follow pretty much the same course as other institutions, some do a careful skillful job, others slip because of certain inadequacies. Those who have learned to roll with the punches and counter aggressively are enjoying success. Those who do not find that the parade has passed them by. Fortunately, wholesaling has attracted to its arena its share of good men. As a result we can come to only one sound conclusion—the wholesaler will continue to occupy his niche in our American economy and continue to expand in service, in value, and in prosperity, along with the other essential elements—the producers and the retailers—to bring better living to American consumers.

51. A NEW TYPE OF MIDDLEMEN —RACK JOBBERS *

James A. Slater

What is a Rack Jobber? He has been called a multiplicity of names: rack distributor, rack merchandiser, housewares distributor or merchandiser, service distributor or merchandiser, drug and toiletry distributor or merchandiser, rack service salesman, jobber, rack operator, distributor and merchandiser. The term "rack jobber" has been used throughout this report because of its general acceptance among marketing people.

Much confusion has been associated with rack jobbers and the type of middlemen they represent; even many super market operators need an explanation of the term. Hence the purpose of my research was to gather data about rack jobbers: who they are, why and where they operate, and how they do so.

A rack jobber is a type of wholesaler who warehouses and delivers goods, sets up displays within an area provided by the retailer, and takes full responsibility for reordering stock on his own authority, usually with little or no help from store personnel. Although rack jobbers exist outside the grocery field, this presentation will be directed primarily at their relationships with the food industry.

Background on food store operations

Many problems have confronted the grocery store entrepreneur during evolution from the old time general store to the beautiful super market of today. The advent of the super market, with its self-service type of operation brought problems in regard to display techniques, packaging, pricing methods, pilferage control, advertising, purchasing, profit margins and many other areas. As cash register tapes grew longer and turnover more rapid, competition increased and profit margins shrank. As far as the super market operator was concerned, the first two points pleased him immensely, but the competition and low margin considerations caused him many headaches.

* Reprinted by permission from *Research Reports*, East Lansing, Michigan: Bureau of Business Research, Michigan State University (November, 1956).

James A. Slater, Bureau of Business Research, Michigan State University.

A great many operators managed to keep their doors open through the darkest periods; others were not so fortunate.

SALVATION THROUGH NON-FOODS. Those who stayed in business still had a dilemma to solve. Many learned the hard way to cope with their packaging, displaying and price problems. The problem of low profit margins was often met by the introduction of non-foods into the markets. These items, with a gross profit of 25 to 35 per cent, looked good in a field where gross profits ranged around 17 per cent. Futhermore, non-foods were a natural for the super market. One important factor favoring their sale in grocery stores was the change which has taken place in consumer buying habits. The housewife who makes two or three trips to the food store in an average week finds it simple to purchase her non-food necessities where she sees them displayed. Thus convenience of purchase and the possibility of impulse buying are big factors in the sale of this merchandise.

The life-saver had been thrown to the super market operators; but the majority was not familiar with the particular problems of non-food merchandising. In addition many learned that their warehousing, delivering and stocking facilities were not adequate for such items as housewares, toys, health and beauty aids, soft goods, school supplies and phonograph records.

ENTER THE RACK JOBBER. While super market operators saw the potentialities of non-foods in their stores, many realized they would achieve little or no success in merchandising these unfamiliar items themselves. Although a bit leery at first, they began to see the advantages of turning their non-food departments over to an expert, the rack jobber.

In effect, the rack jobber has given the super market another department, non-foods. He maintains this department without troubling the store's personnel. The store manager is relieved of a responsibility. Furthermore, the profit margin offered the retailer is very attractive. As a rule the store provides two things: store space and collection of the customer's money.

FUNCTIONS AND SERVICES PERFORMED. The rack jobber is performing a great service for the retailer when he purchases goods from diverse manufacturers of all types of products. Discretion in selection is of utmost importance if the goods that are bought are to have successful sales through the super market. Rack merchandisers, to succeed, must make every effort to provide goods that catch the consumers' fancy. They are assuming a risk when they guarantee the store that in the event of poor sales performance the unsalable merchandise will be replaced by something more attractive.

After the goods have been bought they are stored temporarily in the jobber's warehouse until such time as they are used to fill an order. Frequently the price is marked on the merchandise before it leaves the warehouse. However, the manufacturer usually establishes the price of a product either through Fair Trade or through his suggested price lists. Warehouse chores include division of large shipments into one or two dozen units, stock control, salvage of returned merchandise, and preparation for shipment.

Transporting the goods from the warehouse to the store is another of the jobber's functions. It is not uncommon for him to have a fleet of trucks which service the stores anywhere from three times a week to once a month. Most jobbers extend their service further by putting the goods on the racks themselves. These racks are, in many instances, loaned for the purpose. In addition, special display fixtures are frequently provided for the stores. Dump, table, and shelf extension displays have gained wide-spread popularity as types of special display fixtures.

Rack jobbers have taken an active part in supplying manufacturers with market information. Likewise, much help is given the store operators in this respect. Package specifications, size and nature of consumer demand, promotional advice, and pricing suggestions are included in the service which the jobber gives both suppliers and customers. The two associations of rack jobbers, the American Rack Merchandisers Institute and the Toiletry Merchandisers Association, have acted as clearinghouses for market information.

If one rack jobbing service can be singled out as most valuable, it is probably stock rotation. When a product does not sell in one locale, a jobber replaces it with another one. The poor seller may then, surprisingly, turn out to be a good seller when placed in another store.

Other services which may be offered by jobbers include: filing of excise tax reports with the government; advertising; seasonal promotions; sprucing up shelves and merchandise; complete handling of all records on shipments and receipts.

Types of Merchandise Handled. Rack jobbing is not limited to non-foods. Soft drinks, bakery products and potato chips are placed in many grocery stores by rack jobbers. However, this study has been limited to non-food merchandise. The most popular non-foods in which rack jobbers specialize are drugs, housewares, toys, paper products, magazines and books, records, appliances, soft goods, greeting cards, jewelry, pet supplies, tobacco products, and garden utensils.

The individual items which are selected for display must sell themselves. Impulse buying plays a dominant role, as do national advertising and brand name. The products receive little or no sales push from the store personnel; such merchandise, as many writers have noted, must be *presold.*

PROBLEMS ENCOUNTERED. One of the main problems which rack jobbers have to meet is that of compensation. The rack jobber maintains he should receive larger discounts than regular drug or houseware distributors because of the services he performs for his suppliers. The suppliers, usually manufacturers, contend that they would be discriminating unduly if special concessions were given.

On his part, the jobber claims the manufacturers are putting a great deal of pressure on him to carry complete lines. Some say they cannot depend on the manufacturers' shipping schedules. Others report that some manufacturers refuse to deal with their concerns because of possible repercussions from druggists, department stores and hardware retailers.

On the selling side of the picture there are also many problems. Retailer demands for extended credit, larger percentages, increased deliveries, less space, more products, lower prices, immediate success of an item, and faster turnover are not only contradictory but frequently outright impossible. Other perplexing problems have to do with pilferage, space allotment, promotion, pricing, returns, and store managers' lack of concern.

Competition has been a problem to many jobbers. Some chains are buying direct from manufacturers. Others are purchasing their non-foods from regular drug or housewares wholesalers who offer only a few services. Others have joined coperative buying organizations. Some buy from their food salesmen who handle non-foods as incidentals to their food products.

EFFECT UPON OTHER OUTLETS. The retail druggists have felt the effects of the sale of drugs in super markets. To rid themselves of the super market hex they have tried several means including legal action, various forms of pressure on manufacturers, and inflammatory advertising methods. Undoubtedly the druggists' sales volume in this merchandise has declined proportionately to their other sales.

Although department, hardware, variety and tobacco stores have not voiced their disaffection publicly, they have suffered in sales volume since the incursion of cigarettes, toasters, and kitchenwares into super markets.

DOES THE RACK JOBBER OFFER ENOUGH? The answer to this question can be approached from two points of view: margins and services. It is between these two tensions that a rack jobber must establish some balance. He has the choice of offering the retailer more services and lower gross margin percentages or offering larger percentages and fewer services. If the rack merchandiser attempts to give both, he will find he is operating in the red or is out of business entirely.

It would be desirable for some retailers to receive larger percentages in lieu of services. Some feel that they can provide most of the services such as self restocking, pricing, displaying, etc., cheaper and better than their jobbers. Others may maximize their total net profits from non-foods by having the rack jobbers perform more services and reduce the retailers' take accordingly.

If one were to submit a general admonition for rack jobbers, it would be that these distributors should offer more services to the smaller grocery establishments, even though necessitating a decrease in the amount of discount given them. The converse should be true for large chain organizations.

The problem is not simply one of offering more or less; it is a question of the proper combination of two factors. The rack jobber must realize that he is dealing with a heterogenous group of customers and that there is considerable variation in the needs of these retailers. It is imperative that the jobber look upon his customers as individuals rather than masses. Only thus will both the profits of the jobber and the profits of the retailer be maximized.

52. THE CHANGING STRUCTURE OF THE FOOD MARKET *

George L. Mehren

Major Questions

The common practice is to classify the food industry into the following stages:

1. Consumers
2. Retailers
3. Wholesalers
4. Processors
5. Producers

From any viewpoint, however, production and marketing of foods are integral parts of a single economic process. Some element of this process has always been in ferment. Large-scale production and nationwide distribution of foods were firmly established decades ago. In general, however, until some thirty years ago, large-scale processors along with some small ones procured supplies and made sales through small firms with no effective procurement, price, product, or promotion policies and with no wholesaling facilities.

The changes

Two broad changes have since occurred. First, drastic shifts in scale and technology at retail have been associated with dramatic changes in all other segments of the food industry. Now, many small-scale processors—along with some large ones—sell increasingly on a direct price-specification basis to large retailers with their own price, brand, and promotion policies, wholesaling production facilities and captive supply agencies. Firms in several segments now attempt to extend the scope of their profit policies through manipulation of product, demand, and price. The instruments of firm policy have not changed, but they can now be used at different levels of the production process.

* Reprinted by permission from *The Journal of Farm Economics*, Vol. XXXIX, No. 2 (May, 1957), pp. 339-353.

George L. Mehren, Professor of Agricultural Economics and Chairman, Department of Agricultural Economics, University of California.

Second, marketing has come to mean a systematic integration of product, planning, procurement, manufacturing, and merchandising. Enterprise organization is shifting accordingly. Technology has changed at all levels. New management devices have emerged. These seem to be the really new developments.

The analytical framework

The two sets of change are motivated essentially by enterprise profit objectives. They are achieved in part by shifting market structure. They can, therefore, be described, analyzed, and appraised in terms of shifts in five interrelated catagories, which together can specify the profit policy of a firm:

(1) scale and method of production;
(2) scale and method of procurement;
(3) merchandising—including nature and number of products, volume control, variation of product, and demand control;
(4) market structure manipulation; and
(5) internal organization and operations of the various types of enterprises at the several levels of production.

The Retailers

No major change occurs in any one segment alone. Recent changes in retailing are the most spectacular and the closest to consumers. However, there has not been a unique line from retailing back to farm production free of general-economy influences. Even so, specification of retail changes in terms of the profit determinants set out above provides a frame for description and appraisal of the entire food market structure.

Production Scale and Methods

The food store exemplifies a pattern now general in all retailing. One-stop, automobile shopping has been associated with new scale and type, both of stores and companies and methods of operation.

Sales—size distribution

Stores doing $375,000 sales or more annually comprise about 7 per cent of grocery and combination stores. They do about 60 per cent of total business. Retailers grossing from $75,000 to $375,000 yearly comprise less than 20 per cent of stores and do more than 25 per cent of total volume. The remaining 75 per cent of all stores do less than 15 per cent of all business. This concentration in large outlets has increased about equally in chains and independents and in all regions and types of neighborhoods. Sales volume has been increasing fastest in the larger outlets, although most of the increased total sales is from new stores. Suppliers thus sell more than four fifths of their volume to outlets large enough to establish their own procurement, wholesaling, and merchandising policies and often their own manufacturing facilities.

Nearly 40 per cent of the stores affiliated with a supermarket association gross more than $2 million annually, about 12 per cent do more than $3 million, and the average is nearly $1.75 million annually. Supermarket sales have increased tenfold since 1940. Almost two thirds of the large markets gross more than $30,000 weekly per outlet, which is the typical minimum target for a new store. About 45 per cent of new supermarkets are grossing more than $50,000 weekly. About 5,000 small stores close annually. Nearly 90 per cent of sales volume in 1960 will be done by stores large enough to develop an enterprise profit policy. They will not primarily handle products differentiated by others. They will be able to use most available physical efficiencies and to perform processing, packaging, and labeling functions. Larger companies will have either absorbed or eliminated the wholesaling function in some commodities.

Physical operations

Size of retail selling, stocking, parking, and total store areas is increasing in all regions. More than 2,250 new supermarkets are built per year, averaging at least $1 million annual gross. Some 300 old supers are renovated yearly. Sale of self-service meat products, packaged produce, and frozen products is accelerating. The large food store is the key unit in shopping centers, where more than half the new starts are made. New markets are still becoming more elaborate and mechanized. Hours of operation per day have been extended. Customers per store and sale per transaction are both still increasing. Clerk service, credit, and delivery have virtually disappeared. Housewares, drugs, cosmetics, magazines, stationery, toys, and hardware are still being introduced into new departments. There are still regional differences in size of outlet, but the pattern of concentration soon will be general throughout the country.

Items handled

The increase in sales and size per store is paralleled by changes in physical operations. The average number of items per store has gone from about 800 in 1930 to more than 5,000. There should be about 6,000 by 1960, with the increase mainly in convenience food items and nonfood products. This increase is not all in new products. The average number of items in each old-line brand is also up sharply. For every three new items, two old ones disappear in the bitter struggle for stocking, reordering, shelf space, facing, and promotion. Household supplies, drugs, toiletries, and baby foods are the major new items. The number of units sold per week for most products is very low. Increased gross and tonnage, therefore, reflect increased number of items. Problems of out-of-stock, ordering, stocking, space allocation, departmental spacing, and promotion have been serious. New products account for about 20 per cent of all sales and nearly 45 per cent of grocery department sales. Many new items are just now catching on.

Tonnage and inventories

Tonnage sold has increased about 25 per cent since 1948 with no increase in inventory tonnage. The average retailer inventory for 40 grocery items is 1.1 month, down from 1.4 in 1948. Nonavailable items average about 5 per cent by number, with about 3 per cent out of stock and some 2 per cent in stock but out of shelf. Changes in pack and package have decreased out-of-shelf rates.

Store organization

Packaging of perishables is general, with half the average sales floor used for them. Expansion of frozen foods has been limited by lack of cabinet space. More than half the new markets operate complete bakery departments. Large stores allocate 15 per cent of merchandise area to produce, nearly as much to meat products, 5 per cent to dairy foods, and the remainder to grocery and other departments. The potential for precooked foods is yet untapped.

Measures of efficiency

Gains in physical efficiency appear to have been captured about equally by all types of large retailers. As measured by sales per employee, which have been rising for a decade, labor efficiency does not seem to increase indefinitely with sales per store. Sales per customer and per check out apparently increase indefinitely with number of check outs and with sales volume. Sales per square foot increase up to the very large sizes and then decline. There is no simple measure of relative physical efficiency by size groups. However, motorized check outs, express lanes, parcel-pickup stations, and carry-out belts and conveyors are generally found only in large outlets with different methods of operation in smaller stores.

Layout is changing constantly. Back-room price marking is general. Larger stores do much stocking after closing hours. Sales volume is heavily concentrated in all regions on Fridays and Saturdays. Nearly all major companies and affiliated groups have specialists in physical operating methods for each major department. Personnel selection and training programs are general.

Increasing mechanization

New convenience foods and nonfood items may yield further engineering advantage to larger units. Automation is already under way in warehousing, item selection, ordering, billing, inventory control, display building, and carry out. Experimental units have been built for automatic shelf stocking, price marking, and the complete card-punch store. In sum, available data indicate substantial physical advantage in cost as volume increases. However, rising expense ratios indicate that enhanced physical efficiency has not fully offset rising factor prices. Declining percentage profit margins have partly offset increases in operating expense ratios. Thus, the modern food store differs from its small-scale parent not merely in size of unit and number of items. In terms of physical operations, it is a completely different creature. The prospect, as well as it can be guessed, is for somewhat larger scale and perhaps for drastically different operating methods. There will be still greater sales per store, more spacious layout, even more luxurious appointments and facilities, more room for new products—especially pre-cooked foods, more parking space, mitigation of the check out and bundling bottleneck, and increased mechanization of stocking and prepricing.

Concentration in retailing

New stores have not been heavily concentrated in the largest companies. There has been an accelerated merger movement, but the percentage of total business done by companies with more than 25 units has not increased. The revolution in size per outlet and operating methods is common to large chains and independents alike.

These are the compelling facts: About 45,000 large stores out of some 350,000 do about 7 per cent of the retail food business. Large retailers are increasing their share of the total business volume. Wholesalers, processors, and producers will probably be unable to reverse this trend. Thus, they must adjust their own methods to the requirements of this new retail trade. The final impact of changes in retailing upon other segments is not clear. Procurement policies impinge directly on producers as well as on processors and distributors. New retail merchandising policies directly affect processor and distributors and ultimately affect producers.

Procurement

Two major changes have occurred in procurement by retailers. First, they have required suppliers of some products to sell on a straight price-specification basis. Second, they have required suppliers to adjust their services to the new types of retailing. Failure to adjust involves loss of a major fraction of business. There appear to be dominant buyers in most markets. The terms accorded dominant buyers seem to be extended immediately to all other large buyers. Some retailers are sensitive of the implications of large-scale buying, just as large processors once feared the implications of large-scale selling. Violent controversy has frequently emerged, but the results implied in small-number theory do not seem to be appearing.

In procurement of perishables on a specification price basis, retailers specify physical standards, volume, and delivery terms. Then, they receive price offers from suppliers. Most large retailers require direct delivery. Branch houses and old-line wholesalers are thus foreclosed from this trade. Scope of merchandising policy by processors diminishes and their margins decline. Large retailers in general do not affect prices and margins. Firm price lists are increasingly used. Retailers seem to spread purchases systematically to avoid dependence on suppliers and further to avoid establishment of consumer attachment to particular brands. Nonprice ties are infrequent.

Retailers justify integrated production units as means to save selling costs, maintain quality control, and provide a yardstick on other suppliers. Some control over procurement price may sometimes be attained. Retailer labeling of items bought in bulk is common. In many cases, specialized suppliers have developed and service large retailers almost as if they were integrated departments of the retailer. There is some cooperative processing among large retailers.

The change in scale at retail leads to direct procurement of specification items on a cordwood basis, without selling expense, and often at a minimum margin. In consequence, the status of many old-line firms and markets has deteriorated.

Physical scale and methods of procurement by retailers have also changed. Market-supply areas have also shifted. Nationwide suppliers seem to hold an advantage over local processors primarily in highly differentiated products. Transportation methods shift drastically in patterns not clearly understood even by the trade. The wholesale selling function is disappearing. Large retailers cannot be serviced by street salesmen. The wholesaling function in general is being taken over by retailers or is in some cases being eliminated. Channels to retail often approximate the straight-line specification channels into government and large institutional outlets. The declining franchise of many wholesaler or processor brands precludes effective resistance by many suppliers.

Voluntary and cooperative procurement by independent markets is still confined largely to groceries but is spreading rapidly to other products. Affiliated retailers do more than 60 per cent of total independent grocery business, although less than one third of independent marks are so affiliated. About 80 per cent of large independents own warehouses, but some 45 per cent of such companies participate in group wholesaling. The typical affiliated procurement agent operates for practical purposes almost exactly as does the centrally owned purchasing unit. In the voluntary group, an old-line wholesaler sponsors independent grocers and provides merchandise, advice, promotional material, management aids, and usually a group label. The cooperative groups are retailers who jointly own and operate a wholesale unit. These voluntary and cooperative stores are estimated to do slightly more business than the chains. They operate almost exactly like the chains, with preprint order books and what amounts to cash terms. Wholesale margins are very low. Processors must first get on the books of such wholesalers in order to get their products on the retail shelves.

Thus, there are two major types of procurement agencies now: the direct buying chains and the direct buying associated groups. Both types are extending into the perishable fields. Even drop shipments generally pass through the wholesaler. The wholesale function is, therefore, effectively integrated with the retail function.

Merchandising

Retail merchandising policy can be described in terms of (1) the commodity mix, (2) product differentiation, (3) promotion, and (4) price policy. Processors and retailers are integrating all four into a coordinated total profit policy. Both market structure and enterprise organization have changed in consequence.

Product mix

The commodity mix seems to be governed by two broad objectives: (1) to facilitate one-stop, total household shopping and (2) to shift kitchen operations into the food industry through convenience items. Demand for new product lines followed a sequence of fresh-frozen products, including entire meals; more than 600 other prepared items; kitchen and other household appliances along with push-button food and bathroom items; a series of specialized products for different age groups; and now experimental methods of preservation. The optimum size and operation of the retail store will change with techniques and new products mixes.

New items

Increases in volume have been concentrated in really new convenience products with constant or decreasing price. Sales have also increased for nonconvenience products which are new in terms of flavor, color, size, package, or other attribute—often introduced in a combination deal. Consumers seem willing quickly to shift to new products, and mass media can make new products known quickly. Apparently, promotion is most effective for new products introduced at the outset of development of the line. Convenience-items tonnage has increased by about 300 per cent since 1950, largely as a net addition to total volume, of which such items are now more than 40 per cent. Frozen foods, soaps and detergents, drugs, cosmetics, beauty aids, toiletries, and household supplies have contributed most heavily to the increase. Changes seem to catch hold in the Southwest, but they spread quickly.

Nonfoods

Recent gains are greatest in housewares, dishes, toys, and stationery and moderate in health and beauty aids, cooking utensils, kitchen tools, magazines, and outdoor and picinic supplies. Sales of paper, hardware, and soft-goods items have not been increasing much. Most retailers push the high-profit items. Optimum measures of preselling, minimum turnover or gross margins, inventory control, and clean-up sales are yet unsettled. Rack jobbers will probably be used until retailers acquire know-how. Essentially the same physical procedures are used as for foods. Costs of handling and selling are not precisely known. Nonfoods are probably a plus in volume, with far better margins than on foods.

Brand battle

Retailers push their own labels because they consider that (1) their own names are a better consumer pull than packer names; (2) their shelves, bins, and cases should be used mainly to promote their own products; (3) margins are usually better on their own labels; and (4) they avoid being underpriced by a competitor. Accordingly, they push only packer brands which are difficult to duplicate or with strong consumer pull.

Packers without strong brands are reduced to bulk suppliers of specification items with no real merchandising policy. Nearly every major retailer either processes or acquires products for their own labels. Packers state that if they refuse proffered private-label business, they thereby foreclose volume and sale of their own products. If they accept, they lose merchandising control and have no long-run assurance of volume. Some packers accept private-label business and increase promotion of their own brands. Retailers state that very few brands have a compelling franchise. Retailer brands are common in meat, dairy, delicatessen, bakery, and frozen-food departments. While they carry many packer brands in groceries, they say that no single brand must be carried.

Packers claim that retail display and pricing depreciate brands. Retailers reply that many branded items are really undifferentiated. New products, effectively differentiated, enable processors to build a product image and to control selling them, advertising, pricing, packaging, display, store position, and point of purchase promotion. Once the product is duplicated, these means of profit policy are gone. Thus, the battle of brands is a major focus of the pattern of change.

Retailers and packers agree that there are well-established consumer loyalties to stores. However, packer brands which are effectively differentiated and promoted must be carried to maintain store loyalty. Unchanged branded products have gained about 10 per cent in sales over the last decade. New or improved products gained 500 per cent. Real differences among many brands have diminished. The retailer can control impulse buying, but packer promotion of a strong brand often forces him to give effective display. Crude data indicate that no national brands have truly national distribution; their rates of change in position are about the same in all regions; about one fifth of them are exposed to less than half the total food store traffic; the average exposure percentage is declining; and they lose position mainly because they lose differentiation. Major advertised brands still dominate grocery volume, but packer merchandising policy may still be narrowing. Specifications procurement by large retailers has also required drastic adjustments in farm production.

Retail advertising and promotion

Retailers large enough to affect procurement practices and margins and to differentiate product can also use virtually every device for advertising and promotion within their own regions. As retailers control more determinants of profit, such control decreases in other segments. Consumer promotion does not seem generally fruitful for old-line established products. Use seems most profitable with new and actually different products. The entire battery of advertising media and methods is increasingly used by large retailers. In many states, fairly small retailers advertise on a cooperative basis. In-store promotions are general. There is now a bandwagon movement to trading stamp plans and other continuing premium plans. Retailers engage research units also, just as processors do. Advertising and retail promotion are carefully planned and tested but, as elsewhere, no precise appraisal appears possible. Most important, retailers can now compete effectively with any other segment of the food industry in this second major component of merchandising policy. Retail sales methods and organization have changed drastically but less so than the changes imposed upon processors and distributors. Even if processor brands are presold, sales methods must be geared to the new scale of retail buyers and procedures. "Selling" of cordwood products is useless or even damaging. Sales methods are identical with those in the governmental or institutional trade. Processing and distributive margins for such goods have been substantially reduced. Price competition among many large retailers is brutal. But the merchandising program of the large seller of any item at any level is a combination of any and all means by which demand can be manipulated favorably—the product mix, quality, wrap, pack, package, style, brand, advertising, and other promotion. Any successful manipulation is almost immediately duplicated by competitors. Some retailers seem sensitive of statutory limitations on methods of merchandising and procurement.

Retail margins

Retail margins have drifted downward. Margins have been flexible and have been applied on a commodity-class basis, with relatively simple bookkeeping. Large retailers do not confuse size of margin with size of contribution to net receipts. They have not supported resale price maintenance, unfair practices, or minimum markup laws. Price wars are not frequent. Only rarely will large retailers meet local competition item by item and day by day.

Market Structure

Market structure has shifted, with mergers as a major instrument. In 36 mergers reported for the first nine months of 1955, 6,100 stores were involved. More than 50 important mergers occurred in the whole year. About half of the deals involved companies with less than 25 units. Reasons offered include difficulty in finding locations, offers are high—about 5 per cent of the merged stores were acquired by non-food companies, and tax laws. Mergers accelerate private-brand development. New capacity, scale, and techniques from mergers have broken old distributive channels, eroded old price protection and methods, stimulated pressure for volume by processors, broadened the product mix in food stores, heightened entry into nonfood items, depreciated old brands, eliminated the old pricing principle of the high margin, and slowly seem to be putting most foodstuffs on the fast-turnover basis common to products lacking firm consumer attachment.

The total United States position of major chains has not greatly improved. Regional chains are growing and many develop comprehensive merchandising programs, as do many single-outlet units. Increases in size per unit and in size of company mean that retailers will not again be subordinate in methods or precision of merchandising. Changes in both processing and production will largely reflect retail changes. Similar operations are appearing in the institutional trade, which in some areas accounts for nearly a third of total food business. Again, older types of distributors must either adjust to the new requirements of retailers or defeat them in the battle of brands. A price-leadership structure, both in procurement and in merchandising, exists in many regions. Independent retailers are closely organized and can now use many policies developed by larger companies. Nearly all retail groups in all regions now have a price policy; elasticity is limited both in buying and in selling. When services are differentiated, cross-elasticities also diminish. As scale and method of operation change, entry elasticity falls. Market structure can be defined in these terms. As the retail component moves away from the atomistic classification, other components move toward the structure.

Enterprise Organization

Food retailers are no longer untrained general merchants who sell bulk items or branded products with no real differentiation, promotion, or price policies. These are large businesses, with high average income and investment and staffed by carefully selected and trained officers. Company executives carry broad responsibility. The store manager is also a major executive, often with 100 subordinates and occasionally 250. Changes in firm structure, policies, and procedures are general, but few governing principles are discussed in formal academic literature. Yet, changes in scale and methods of production, procurement, and merchandising could not have occurred without correlative management changes, especially for older firms and often as a matter of survival. Here, one principle emerges—most of the activities of the firm are interrelated. Activities jointly related to the enterprise profit account must be subject to a single authoriy, with a single results stream and a parallel report structure. Activities not so related must be decentralized.

Marketing broader than selling

Marketing now seems to encompass coordination of product, package and label, promotion, sales methods and organization, practices, and market testing. Enterprise management is emphasizing leadership, coordination, and planning rather than specific technical know-how. The general trend toward market orientation is evidenced by new structuring of companies, status for marketing jobs, titles, policies, procedures, and corporate alignments, and new marketing functions—especially in research. Where the firm is large and can vary its product or promotion, marketing departments exend far beyond selling. Where a competitive market structure exists at transfer points and where bulk products are sold, no market policy can exist and the enterprise should be organized accordingly.

Decentralization

Decision making is being decentralized. Some decisions cannot in fact be made above a particular level. In other cases, there is no scale advantage in central decisions or central staff or service functions. Again, what seems to be the governing rule is slowly emerging: If at any administrative level a decision of one unit constrains the decisions of others, joint profit maximization requires an authority and folding of results. If the decisions are practically independent, then a coordinating authority may be fatal to profit maximization. This principle seems to affect control and appraisal of products, of line and staff functions of all types, and of both market and administrative territories. Management is beginning to center around product lines rather than market functions. The integration into marketing of all related functions has created a complex of unsolved difficulties and devices for solution.

Old-line wholesale selling facilities and methods are virtually obsolete in some trades. Internal transfer pricing among functional departments is ineffective and correlative profit centers seem to be disappearing except where atomistic competition exists at transfer points. Otherwise, transfer prices neither measure nor induce departmental efficiency and may be hostile to combined profit maximization. Companies, therefore, try to create the required conditions or eliminate functional organization. Thus, rigid departmentalization by functions and the exclusive sales franchise are also disappearing. With differentiated products, actions taken by one functional unit in fact limit actions open to related units. Separate departmental profit targets are only by accident consistent with maximum total profits for all related functions. Both authority and results, therefore, center around commodities.

Many staff and line services are clearly interrelated among all units of larger companies—budgets, large or volatile inventories, long-run investment, governmental and labor relations, law, credit and banking policy, overhead allocation, product and processing standards on differentiated products, brands and labels, some types of promotion, auditing, results analysis, and performance appraisal. Even so, central units are yielding nominal control over decisions actually beyond their capacity or offering no scale advantages or other interrelationship.

Sales organization

Processors and wholesalers are adjusting sales organization and methods to the new requirements of retail and institutional outlets. These outlets procure on a bid basis and by direct channels. Thus, *sales* departments are being integrated into *marketing* departments often including product development and engineering; manufacturing, inventory planning, and control; promotion and advertising; sales administration, planning, and management; and market research. There is not yet agreement on proper organization for marketing many different food products from many areas to many different classes of buyers in many different markets. Preoccupation with sales volume and margins is yielding to concern for total profit. Postwar competitive pressures for new products and for full-line selling has shifted product and sales planning to top management, including the controller. Effective reorganization reflecting the new marketing concept is not easy. Primary departments owning inventories and making sales must be coordinated with such operating functions as commission selling, purchasing, transportation, insurance, or construction. Both must be integrated with staff units. Decentralization requires formulation of policy delegations and effects a change in profit centers. Related decisions among units at the same administrative level must be coordinated. The two major problems are (1) specification of decision-making units with a parallel stream of results and (2) integration with service units. Analysis of these changes is almost nonexistent.

Other Segments

The fabric of recent change is such that none of the major shifts in any firm or segment could easily occur without the others. Thus, in treating changes at retail, many of the related adjustments in other sectors have been touched. Management adjustments are general. Therefore, only few observations relevant to other functions are offered.

Wholesaling

Wholesale sales have increased sixfold since before the war, labor productivity has risen, and both margins and expense ratios have fallen sharply. Cash-and-carry, self-service wholesaling through affiliated warehouses is now nearly universal. In the business of 20 years ago, warehouses were multistoried, with hand operations, traveling salesmen, credit, wagon and rail delivery, small orders from many wholesalers, wholesaler brands, and high expense ratios for assembly, packing and invoicing. To survive, independent retailers had to buy cheaply and operate at low cost. Some 280 retailer-owned wholesalers serving more than 35,000 stores operate without salesmen, deliver on schedule, and finance themselves through cash sales. Merchandising and store-operation counsel are provided systematically. Profits are mainly returned as dividends. Average expense is often lower than in chain operations. Through some 450 voluntary wholesalers with nearly 90,000 affiliates, the retailer may buy from the sponsor, use a chain name, and receive supervision in store layout, operation, and merchandising.

With increased lines and limited brands in each, both classes of wholesalers have made large independent retailers fully competitive with chains through highly efficient plants. The preprint weekly order form virtually eliminates sales expense, a cash basis, and drop shipment. Self-service procurement by retailers probably depreciates most wholesaler brands. It also accelerates consumer advertising and in-store promotion. Larger retailers are rapidly turning to direct procurement from their own warehouses, although some 45 per cent of the largest companies are affiliated with wholesalers. Rack wholesaling for nonfood and specialty items may be taken over after experience is gained by retailers. Affiliated groups are increasingly oriented to retailer profit. They are moving from their own labels and long-margin items toward those yielding highest profit to retailers. In a sense, wholesaling is becoming an integrated department of retailers rather than a self-contained set of independent, profit-seeking units.

Processors

Processors selling differentiated products have had to change operations and policies in order to conform to retail trade requirements. Many established products and merchandising methods are no longer acceptable to retailers. Many retailers can specify product and require price offers. Consumer control by processors has generally diminished. Even so, the battle is not over. Many processors have altered enterprise structure both to adjust to changes and perhaps to control some of them. They have developed direct-sales merchandising, especially for bulk or specification items. High-speed and full-capacity operations are being built. The crucial importance of effective differentiation and promotion is being recognized. Product planning, new product development, and engineering have become major functions closely coordinated with manufacturing, procurement, and sales. Processors seek so to develop, promote, and price their own products that retailers will find it profitable to give them space within a fairly road price range and reasonaly free of variation from small changes in product, price, or promotion by competitors. Generally, there are few merchandising advantages from national operation in handling most cordwood foods.

Some old companies recognize that some scale advantages will permit price competition that retailers cannot meet by other channels. Actually, differentiated products can acquire and hold shelf space. Accordingly, they seek new products and new methods of preservation which cannot easily be duplicated either by retailers or by specialized processors satisfied to sell to retailer specifications. And they are also integrating their management structure for the purpose of coordinating the entire process of planning, production, and sale of effectively differentiated items. Promotions of all sorts have been accelerated. Processors of all types still provide a lively competition which is different but no less active.

Producers

The basic changes in retailing, wholesaling, and processing are reflected in major changes in product, scale, and method of operation of growers in livestock, poultry, fruits, and vegetables. Cooperative producers who process wholesale branded commodities have also been affected. The nature of the changes, their causes, interrelationships, effects, and possibilities for control do not seem to be fully explored.

Summary

The sweeping changes general to the American economy have been most marked in the food industries. The changes are closely interrelated with respect to the various functions of a given firm and to the functions of firms in different segments of the production process. One way to classify this flux is suggested by the outline of this report. The main sectors involved are consumers, retailers, wholesalers and other distributors, processors, and producers along with operating and service groups. For each enterprise, the profit account can be specified in terms of production, procurement, and merchandising policy; firm structure; and market structure. Any combination of these two sets of attributes would provide a reasonable basis for study. I would like to know what the changes have been and are—their causes, interrelationships, effects, and susceptibility to control. These questions are not presently answered.

53. RETAIL COMPETITION AS IT AFFECTS THE DEPARTMENT STORE *

William Snaith

Eighteen years have passed since I talked to this group although in the interim I have been involved in many of your individual problems. The very fact that they were individual problems placed a boundary on the solution with little or no opportunity to take a long objective look at the future from an industry point of view.

During this period, as the head of a service organization serving the manufacturer as well as the retailer, we have worked for other retail groups such as Newberry's and now Penney's, and pending, an over-all study for the Super Market Institute. In this project we are to develop ideas for the increased sale of perishable and nonfood categories working with a selected committee of industry leaders.

I believe my most important discovery eighteen years ago was that department store retailing was an art rather than a science; an art that used science to reinforce an opinion. I have not changed my mind in those eighteen years. It would be difficult to bring together more confirmed and divergent opinion than is represented in this room. In normal circumstances one can justify this phenomenon by classifying the opinions as right or wrong. In this case, you all seem to be right, and you have your success to prove it. This does not make the analysis of the future of the department store any easier, since it becomes difficult to apply general conclusions to a particular store. Your cities have separate problems. I have heard seemingly rock hard statistical evidence rough handled by many of you men to the end that you destroy the conclusions that seemed incontrovertible at the outset.

And so this morning I will talk to you as an artist to fellow artists with a minimum of statistics and a lot of belly hunch about feelings and opinions that I have been formulating through the years by exposure to your industry and other forms of retailing.

I believe there to be urgency for action, because it is my considered opinion that the next ten years for retailing will be more

* Reprinted by permission of William Snaith from a talk, October 1, 1958. William Snaith, President, Loewy Snaith Corporation.

revolutionary than the last ten. The program for action which I will discuss this morning is an integrated approach by the downtown store, the branch unit and the convenience store toward increasing the total share of the market.

Revolution in the market place

To say that there is a revolution in the market place is a cliche. If we hear it often enough we get used to it and live with it out of boredom. One of the important points being overlooked is that we have not one revolution but two. They interact, one on the other.

1. On the one hand there is the struggle for an increased share of the market by different forms of retailing;
2. On the other, the manufacturer's struggle for a greater share of the market carried directly to the consumer.

In the first part of the revolution we have seen the emergence of large groups of chain stores, in a vast geographical expansion, taking an ever-increasing share of the market, perhaps not through individual excellence of a single store but rather by the sheer weight of numbers.

We have seen these chains retaining their mobility and flexibility and taking advantage of two important merchandising considerations; the ability to dramatize themselves through price and through the offering of geographical convenience. Because of the requirements set by your downtown store for location of its branches this kind of geographical convenience has not been as available. And so, small retailing mushrooms all around you.

The evidence from the other revolution is not as obvious. Its effects are just beginning to be felt. This revolution is centered around the gradual ascendancy of national brands. The past few decades have fostered a direct producer to consumer relationship. Through massive advertising, some manufacturers have been able to displace the retailer as the principal selector and guarantor of merchandise and to place the retailer in the position of being a distributor of presold merchandise.

The most flagrant and obvious example is in the appliance field, large and small. The supermarkets, newcomers to the field with no previous reputation in the nonfood categories, have recently made huge advances in drugs, hosiery, garden supply and such lines of merchandise—based on the reputation of national brands. The central fact about both these revolutions is that so far the dynamics are against the department store.

Nature of the market place

This two-headed revolution is made possible by the changing nature of our market place; in its economics, in its social composition.

1. Our economy has come to have an extraordinary dependence on consumer goods. Some 40 per cent of all consumer goods purchases have no functional necessity.
2. Retailing has undergone geographical fragmentation through the dispersal of population.
3. Specific kinds of retailers have lost identification with specific kinds of merchandise,
   - (a) through the availability of merchandise of national reputation to many more stores,
   - (b) through the loss of character and individuality on the part of older forms of retailing, and
   - (c) through the anonymity of shopping centers.

Present state of retail competition as it affects the department store

There has been a great deal of discussion regarding the impact on the department store of the metamorphosis of the variety store into the junior department store and the emergence of the discount house and its use of national brands as a device to dramatize itself. The significance of these two phenomena in relation to the department store is generally attuned to the private conviction of whatever men discuss the subject.

However, there is an inexorable quality to some of the march of change. In some instances, change will be forced upon types of retailing in spite of the convictions of those who presently run the businesses. For instance, take the case of the supermarket. The changes it faces are written on the wall. These changes will undoubtedly have an effect on department stores. The supermarket will have to increase its efforts in the nonfood lines, not so much from the desire for volume or adventure but because they have neared maturation in terms of primary geographical expansion.

1. The average supermarket, which in 1940 used to serve 5,500 families, now serves 1,800.

2. In 1956 a single supermarket competed with two other stores in its franchise area. In 1957, it was competing with three.
3. In one year, 1956-1957, the number of supermarkets that had no direct competition in their trading areas dropped from 47 per cent to 11 per cent of the total.

In the inevitable search for volume in this thinner market, supermarkets have been slowly expanding their lines so that now the industry average, for nonfood lines, is 8 per cent, with more near the 20 per cent than the 8 per cent indicates.

They are now in an exploratory period of testing categories and methods. By sheer weight of numbers they will make their presence felt in the total market in several merchandise categories in which the department store as well as the variety-junior department store have vested interests. Soft-line staples and houseware items, drugs, stationery, toys, etc., are the immediate items.

As it becomes less important where an item is purchased, supermarkets have the advantage of ultimate convenience. The problem they must solve is to adapt a list of permanent items to their present method of doing business. Their industry reports indicate that continuing progress in this effort is being made.

From this very brief look at a section threatening retailing, let me turn to the department store in particular.

The department store is a sick or healthy industry depending on how you look at the figures. It has grown in absolute terms if not in relative terms. Proof is available to anyone with a particular ax to grind. Most statistics agree that the department store has been able to stablize itself in many of the items it considers central to its existence. It has gained in some. It has lost in others. In overall terms in relation to its past history, it has grown.

On the other hand, its growth has not kept pace with the economy. In cutting up the larger consumer dollar, other retail agencies have taken a greater share than the department store. Often its growth has been achieved at the expense of a fellow department store. It does not have mobility and flexibility, and its moves are so often dictated by defensive needs as by aggressive desires.

It is constantly open to potential new attack in any of its attractive categories by agencies that enjoy some managerial genius and finance in addition to their inherent mobility and flexibility.

The point I would like to make today is that whatever the interpretation of the future of the department store (that is, whether it is considered as doing a pretty good job and merely needs some improvement or that the department store must recognize its failure to maintain its pace in the economy), the same basic kind of program will have to be employed with an extra effort on maintaining pace.

I base this on an assumption that the department store has strength, and, therefore, can consider only a program that leads from strength and not from weakness. In talking about strengths, I will not dwell on the classic requirement of assortments or depth. First, this subject has been beaten to death by experts, and I am certainly not the man nor is this the occasion for talking on this subject. Let me, rather, talk about some other aspects of the problem.

First, I would like to go back to a statement I made earlier: that approximately 40 per cent of all merchandise is bought for no functional necessity. When that information is digested only a limited interpretation is possible.

Urgency to buy

An urgency to buy has been given to the consumer.

It is not enough to say that this urgency to buy has been created by advertising. Advertising may stimulate the awareness of goods, but something must create the basic desire to own goods. Since the purchases exceed functional need, low price cannot do it. Price can only establish a preference. The same holds true for availability and convenience. They only make it easier to buy. What creates the desire to buy? I maintain that goods are the principal symbols of status in this country. We live in a nation of unusual social mobility. A generation is not frozen in a social stratum. It moves through the levels, generally upward. Goods are one of the simplest forms of indicating a real or imaginary position in society: The house one lives in, the neighborhood, the car one drives, how one's wife dresses, the school the children go to, and others.

Our advertisers make us aware of this every day of the week. They trade on the longing for status. They identify us with a product. They picture us as being in a position of wealth—or of power or of everlasting youth, of sexual attractiveness and invincibility.

The status of goods is lodged in many things:

> It is a value symbol for money and position. It establishes fashion leadership, i.e. keeping up or ahead of the Jones. It has sociological implications. It can indicate our taste or discernment or create individuality. It sometimes has snob value, one example being foreign cars.

Through the goods we own it is possible to indicate all these things. As a matter of fact, we have very little else, no uniforms, no titles, no standard forms of public recognition as they exist in some European countries.

The important thing to consider in the dynamics of status is that while there is only one direction anyone is interested in—upward, status operates at many different levels.

We have high, middle, and low needs as well as brows. In the work of our office in merchandise design we design for the mass market, which means we design for the middle, but we find that we must include a style leader for the high to reflect acceptance downward. The Ford Company designs a Thunderbird for a particular market and then advertises all of its cars as having Thunderbird styling. It is interesting to note that the discount house is successful where it can use the status symbol established by the manufacturer and is weaker in the lines where the value and status are questionable.

The supermarket in the sale of food alone has the same kind of problem. Its greatest potential source of profit lies in the perishable category, and still this is the part of the business that shows the least amount of development because here the presold value-status of the manufacturer is absent.

My thesis, therefore, is that the department store must project as the underlying psychological motivation for any of its moves in the future the idea that it is the best projector of the status symbol for the broadest part of the consuming public. The department store must work to offset a trend which today makes the merchandise the important thing and the place where it is bought relatively unimportant. To offset the idea that it is only necessary to buy General Electric or a Hathaway shirt or a Lionel train and that it makes no difference where you buy it, the heart and core of a program directed to such an end will have to be built around the differentness of the department store and the specialness of its merchandise. This is the present strength of the department store, and I suggest you lead from your strength. In addition, the so-called cheaper stores have been conscious of their inferior presentation and are rapidly trying to close the gap.

The downtown store

I think that in not too many years we will see a stabilization of the city, not a massive return perhaps, but a significant change in the pattern. The flight from the city was inevitable when the cities failed to meet the needs of an erupting population in terms of housing, schools, transportation, open space. However, the city never lost certain qualities. It is still the cultural center of its areas. It contains the museums, the theaters and opera, zoos, botanical gardens, etc., and, if it doesn't, it should.

We are the project directors of the new Cultural Center in Montreal. In our preliminary study we developed the requirements of the city and defined its requirements in terms of opera, concert, theater, etc. As the planners of the Montreal Cultural Center, we have convinced the Committee that the Center belongs downtown and not out in an outlying park.

The city contains the yeasty ferment and excitement that comes with masses of people and many ideas. The city is a large arena for gregarious people with social instincts. The city is a symbol of status. After years of soul-searching and painful deliberation, we now see through-way projects, parking projects, cultural and recreational facilities being built in every large city, along with apartment house projects and these apartment houses are not exclusively designed for low income groups. Some cities are more advanced in this work than others, but the trend is developing. Before long we will see a stabilized population in the cities. Some of our social thinkers envisage the future on the eastern seaboard, for instance, as an almost continuous dwelling area with centers around the major cities.

Conversely, many small towns and suburban areas have felt the shock of too rapid expansion and are now faced with problems as severe as the cities with one additional strike against them. They haven't the tax base. Consequently, we find town after town with inadequate schools, water and sewage disposal facilities, road and highway problems, and no money to meet the needs. These conditions are being met by discouraging rises in taxes for which, in return, the citizens get little or no services, depending on state police protection, volunteer fire departments and self-drilled wells in a falling water table.

I suggest, therefore, that the long term dynamics are not necessarily against the city if the cities can rise to the occasion and meet the needs of the people. As I see it, the downtown store must hold the line in the city in its present condition and prepare for the renaissance. The downtown department store has a two-fold function:

1. It is designed to meet the merchandise needs of its immediate area.
2. It is the communication and style center of its community of stores, the sun of its solar system.

We live in an era of communication. The downtown store must be used as a pace setter for all its satellites. The department store must develop some new techniques in communication.

It must make fashion and the way of life its core. It is the show case of the American standard of living. It is the show piece of its satellites. To represent this position, these ideas must be held foremost:

1. A department store is different from other forms of retailing. If it must go in for self-service it must do it in a different way. It establishes its difference at every level.
2. The department store brings specialness to merchandise. It must create the desire to buy beyond just putting out merchandise on a come-and-get-it basis. In effect, the store must become the place where people can see the idea they hear about and have the differences in merchandise defined by occasion, price-line, function or what-have-you.
3. The store must supply excitement by design, by idea and by event, by atmosphere.

A great deal of the department store energy has gone into meeting competition by operating method, and this certainly must continue. But I suggest you also lead from your strength. You are different. You are "higher-class." You do appeal to the status requirements of your community. Certainly, if you did not have this strength anyone who could offer lower prices would have slaughtered you by now.

4. You must take direct action to improve the status of your label. Look at the money industry invests in corporate identity, in packaging, in advertising to give its goods greater status. Don't trade on the increase of the manufacturers and diminish yourself. Give yourself a kind of brand identification.
5. There is not just one way to do this. You must analyze your potential consumers. What do they need in the way of status symbols? Are they sophisticated and want high style? Then you give them a high-style store. Do they need security and reassurance in taste? Are they afraid of sophistication? Then

> they need the kind of store that reassures them. In the AMC we see two brilliant examples of analysis in the same city: A & S and Bloomingdale's, serving different segments of the same population.
>
> Look at your present downtown stores. What kind of character do they have? Or, are they anonymous and indiscriminate? You ought to do the kind of image study on yourselves that we do for industry.

It is not necessary to have any particular kind of character. It is necessary to have one. As a fashion leader in your community, you must stand for something. The closer a store comes to satisfying the status needs of a community, the better it will be. Your store needs a character that you can carry over to your branches and to all other units in order to integrate your total program of effectiveness. In essence, I am saying that you still retain one enormous strength, your status in the community. Identify your consumer's status needs in terms of merchandise with your reputation. Make the place where merchandise is bought equal in importance to the goods that are advertised.

I can give you a mysterious example. We have been designing restaurants for the Stouffer chain. The sale of meals is weird and wonderful, since value is established on the most tenuous and unrecognizable grounds.

The Stouffer group has no "21's" or Colony's or Perino's or any such snob units. It sells right down the middle to a mass market.

In a recent unit on Fifth Avenue, we designed a restaurant to seat 790 people. Since you cannot seat so many people together and stay in business, it was obviously necessary to divide the restaurant into separate rooms, five in all. All the rooms serve from the same menu; waitresses dress alike and offer the same service. People are generally seated as places in the various rooms open up, so there is a minimum of regular patronage by room.

Now here is the kicker. Each room has a different consistent average check directly traceable to its atmosphere and decor. They go from $4.00 in the dark wood room to $2.75 in the wall paper room. The middle room is $3.00. In one room people take an extra drink and order from the other side of the menu. The room moves them to this. In the other room people are more conservative. We cannot make all rooms into the dark wood room, because this is a mass restaurant and must serve a broader public. The restaurant has a consistent character with these definable differences. And I think an important demonstration as to how people react to status symbols. You must strive to exert this same kind of influence on your consuming public.

I will not attempt to discuss any details of layout or fixturing. If you have questions that you feel I may be able to help, I will gladly answer them during the question period.

The branch unit

Enough branch units have been built so that now most of the basic questions can be answered. The value of a branch need no longer be proved. In the first great flurry of building branches the immediate requirement, that of meeting some local competition in terms of geographical convenience, has been met. Several important questions remain unanswered. They are part of the larger problem. Namely; What is the best way to take a greater share of an increasing market?

Short of going into a pattern of total decentralization (a solution I think unlikely anytime I think of the size of the downtown investment), the branch unit should only be expected to perform a definite and specified task. Unlike Sears or any of the variety chains the problem for the department store is not national expansion but rather local penetration without weakening any of its existing units. Therefore, the function of the branch store should be re-examined.

Its purpose, simply stated, is:

1. to increase its total share of the market through convenience;
2. to offset competition by other department stores and other forms of retailing;
3. to do these with a maximum throw off of profit for the total enterprise.

Inevitably, when the problem of how to get more business without hurting the business you have is considered, you wind up asking yourself: where and how big? This question is not so pressing for branch units that do not impinge on the primary shopping area. Around large metropolitan centers there are suburban developments at great distances from primary areas. Stores that go into these areas are a clear gain, as are stores in remote towns. Therefore, we need not consider them as problems to the downtown store.

But in the branch adjacent or within the primary district, one fact is increasingly apparent: that these branch units draw from a limited franchise area. The draw is the same whether the store is moderate size or a super branch. The difference in volume from moderate to big size is made up by the share it takes out of its immediate market. Everyone has his own method of determining this franchise area. The affecting factors are driving time, competition, and geographical conditions. As a rule of thumb, we use a six mile radius, adjusted to conditions, as optimum penetration. Anything in business drawn beyond this six mile radius is occasional. Some 75 per cent of the branch store business is obtained from this inner circle. However you arrive at your conclusions it seems reasonable to discard the branch as an originator of business from great distances. If it is, therefore, considered as getting its business within a definite area adjacent to or within the orbit of the downtown unit, it is certain that at some point size becomes a critical factor in the continued health of the downtown unit. And unless management looks toward eventual reduction in or disengagement from downtown, this is the increasingly serious aspect of the branch problem.

Another element enters consideration of the size of branch units in their effect on the downtown. No new retail area is sacrosanct. A powerful store creates powerful neighbors. They either build along side of you or are invited into your shopping center. They fatten on the traffic you create. Therefore, it is not only the business you yourself take out of an area but the scale of the retail opportunity you give your competition and the total impact on the downtown.

In speaking of competition, it seems difficult for me to escape the conclusion that the present pattern of shopping center development can only be harmful to the department store. If we recognize the fact that a revolution which places the manufacturer and consumer in an increasingly closer relationship is going forward, and that the retailer is slowly losing some of his hold on the consumer, then anything which aids and abets this anonymity of the retailer can only hurt the department store.

In the average center so much emphasis is placed on the center itself by its architecture, signing and promotional devices that an overall aura of value is placed on everyone within the center. And in this era of increasing availability of goods to all sorts of retailers as opposed to emphasizing the special qualities of the department stores, the center seems to say: "We really don't care at what store you buy your goods. The important thing is to buy it at the center."

The big center is built:

1. as a real estate investment;
2. to lower the rental percentage for the branch store;
3. to choke off other centers;
4. to develop big traffic to be enjoyed by the branch unit.

1. As a real estate investment I have very little to say on that point, except that I am talking today to retailers, and retailing is my first consideration, as it should be yours.
2. As for lower rental, this may amount to 1 per cent or 1½ per cent—no inconsiderable amount. But how much business is lost downtown by the impact of the total center, and how will you reduce your rent there?
3. A big center may choke off other big centers, but it does not slow down the isolated, competing branch store inside your circle nor the mushrooming convenience centers.
4. While there is no doubt that a big center normally develops big traffic, the traffic-builder is the branch department store which gets only a little help from its neighbor.

It is my belief that if a department store goes into a center it should do so with competition carefully selected and held to a reasonable minimum. The department store should avoid creating a great retail opportunity for competition. It should be jealous of its own identity, increasing its apartness rather than its conformity.

Composition of volume in branch units

The composition of volume in the moderate and larger units is approximately the same. In other words, the basic volume is built around the most wanted categories in either case. In addition, a regular habit pattern of purchase seems evident. These purchases can be typed as:

1. Convenience buying, where the most needed goods are closest at hand;
2. Fashion-convenience buying, where wanted goods in the fashion-convenience category, having a slower cycle of repurchase, will draw customers within six miles to your branches;
3. High unit purchasing, which demands the full shopping experience and excitement that only your downtown store can provide.

In considering this buying pattern, a method of deployment of stores should be considered that would take advantage of the first two types by getting a larger unit or units.

If one accepts the validity of the downtown store, an integrated approach to the market must be undertaken. More flexibility by type and location in branch expansion should be considered so that a greater penetration of the total market can be achieved. This must be done within a pattern of distribution that the department store can control rather than in an exploding jungle of retailing.

I submit that it makes sense for the department store to fragment the retail market geographically even more rather than to attempt reconcentration. By this I mean that more, smaller stores should be built rather than new, strong retail centers. I propose this for your consideration for the following reasons:

(a) Small units do not create new, glamorous competition for downtown.

(b) They do not create large retail opportunities for your other downtown merchants.

(c) Reconcentration does not stop the growth of convenience centers. Multiple units fight for a share of the market on the basis of geographical convenience.

I propose that for the total envelopment of its trading area in order to get a larger share of the market and greater profit the department store deploy the following kind of units:

A. At the core of your strategic complex is the revitalized, reglamorized downtown store in an exciting city. The merchant will have to push for civic development downtown.

B. Located around it, at approximately twelve mile intervals, more or less (depending on the population and geographical characteristics of the area), branch units should be built of a size warranted by the densities of the population within the area and the purchasing power of the residents they are to serve.

These stores would have a twofold purpose: to get greater penetration by convenience, and to project the overall status quality of the total store group.

C. Among these branches and in selected areas within the primary area, smaller units should be started which are twigs rather than branches. The purpose of this latter group is to offer most wanted goods on a convenience basis. Since this plan for expansion is relatively new and concerns an invasion by department store retailers of an area subject to the greatest attack by other forms of retailing, I have left it to the end for exploration.

Several experiments using this system are now under way, and several suggestions have been made. The idea has been supported and attacked with equal enthusiasm. I wish to go back to my earlier statement that this "twig" should not be something apart. It should be integrated into a total system of penetration of the market place built around the status position of the department store.

Some of the current ideas are:

That the small unit become part of the convenience complex with other kinds of merchants;

That it form an association with food merchants and/or others to offer department store goods on a solely convenience basis.

The only portion of this plan that is attractive is, that since food is the most wanted goods on a convenience basis the store would be a stronger convenience attraction with such goods on hand.

This does not make it compulsory to join the food merchants. You can settle for being neighbors. I presume locations can be developed which would include room for a supermarket and other convenience stores.

What I find unattractive is the sacrifice of character on the part of the department store if it should try to do a coordinated program with food stores. Because of its small size the "twig" must be more assertive in its specialness of character.

It must support its more limited assortments with the status of the total operation. In addition supermarkets are now competing in trading areas with such small numbers of family units that it is relatively impossible for a twig store to function on 1,800 families.

A second idea is the development of basement branches. I do not believe this to be the area of major development. Its success is dependent on finding proper communities willing to accept this kind of store without the attendant loss of face.

Department store management has always tended to invest its divisional separations with far more importance than its customers do. Department store operation is notorious for making its customers adapt themselves to the store's management structure.

To what degree can the department store divorce its basement from its total projection? Is the basement important because it is part of the total status symbol of the store, or does it exist on its offering of abstract value such as price? Because of my experience in the design and development of merchandise with its subsequent marketing problems, I believe that status of the total store plays an enormous role in the strength of the basement and that the projection of that status would be weakened if the basement were isolated and promoted separately away from its relationship to the total store.

In addition, I think an importance has been given to price that is not wholly consistent with its power as a merchandising tool. Unquestionably a need for low price appeal exists in sections of our community because of low income. However, price has assumed its importance because it was the most dramatic and useful tool for new retailing enterprises which had no other. Price has not demonstrated its effectiveness for merchandise that cannot establish other values. Price becomes most powerful where it is used to compare established merchandise against a fictitious list price or with prices offered by another retail agency. In the downtown store price operates under the status of the store, and the basement compares itself to upstairs in the same status. One of the reasons given for using basement organizations is that until now strong buying groups which have been built by the stores have not been used to any degree in branch expansion. What I cannot understand is why it is necessary to stratify them or codify them to the degree you find important. If an area needs basement merchandise, then why not use it in part of your total projection? Why must you leave out basement stores simply because you cannot turn the whole show over to them in one way or another?

Another reason given is that in building a smaller store you cannot adequately represent yourself as a capsule of the total downtown store. On the other hand, since the basement store is merely a segment of the total store, a smaller representation can be made acceptable. I think this is specious reasoning designed more to explain your position to a fellow merchant than to your public. A store is a store, and a size is size.

I have made it plain that I believe the strength of the department store lies, in great part, in its status position. To relinquish this, is to depart from a position of strength.

The reason for building small units is to pick up a share of the market which goes to others mainly on a convenience basis. The others are doing it on a basis of price. Why should you throw away your weapons and operate in their arena by their rules? Either you say it is impossible to do it at all, as some merchants have said to me, or you do it with your best foot forward.

To make a small unit acceptable is a problem in communication. I propose that a name such as "convenience" or "neighborhood store" be given the small unit and that it be offered as a customer service in most wanted department store merchandise, closest at hand and adjacent to a larger unit a few miles off.

The merchandise assortment and price line will be adapted to each neighborhood. Its effects will not be greatly felt outside of that particular neighborhood. When I started to develop this thesis I talked to a great many merchants in and out of the department store field. Consistently, when I talked of this small unit, merchants in the nondepartment store field felt it could be a big money maker. Department store merchants went from "maybe" to "it is impossible" which generally resolved itself into "we don't know."

When the elements of cost of operating a small unit are examined, the area of unknowns is greater than the known. Department store experience has tended to put expensive management into its branches. This may be necessary when a store is driving for a larger volume. But the retail scene is filled with examples of successful medium size units run by streamline branch management; Saks Fifth Avenue and Lord & Taylor, to name two. You ought to find out.

When it comes to services, how much of the service you offer is actually used by your customers in your branches? In a convenience store with a take-with stock, how much delivery would be used even if offered? As to credit, more of your low price competition is coming to it. J. C. Penney is experimenting with such a plan. Sales help can be cut down without going to the check out. Ohrbach's is a good example of what I mean. Ohrbach's is no service store, still, as a fashion store, it does not suffer from the stigma of a supermarket.

I submit that the facts about the cost of operation of a small unit can only be known when such a unit is developed and costs are tailored to its needs.

The other big questions raised about such a unit are: What is the composition of the store? What do you propose to sell? How big should it be and will it represent you adequately? Is it a valid unit?

I wish I could offer you pat answers to all of these questions at this time. But concise figures still do not exist. I have looked at various studies made by several groups. They come near an answer but still require the affirmative "belly hunch" to bring them into being.

I told you in the beginning that I would use a minimum of science and a maximum of my background and experience and "belly hunch" as my basis for analysis.

Let's take the last question first. Is this "twig" a valid unit? In essence, if you could assemble a series of neighborhoods, you would bring a branch unit to them. What I suggest is to figuratively break up some unattainable branch and take the pieces to individual neighborhoods.

Branch units do not now halt the growth of convenience centers, which means that there is room in the neighborhoods for your kind of goods. If there is room and need for your goods, the unit is valid. What seems to make it less valid in your eyes is only that you bring less of your kind of goods in one place to your public. The fear is not that you won't sell, but what will be the effect of such small stores on the reputation of your total enterprise. I think we come back to a problem of communication. A device and format can be developed. Others make a go of such stores. Why can't you, who have more experience in the field?

When I attempt to answer what you should sell in these stores, I can only recommend that you analyze the consistency of the average convenience center which grows in many cities despite branch units and regional centers. Leaving out stores not carrying department store merchandise, the average convenience center will contain:

	Sq. ft.
General Merchandise Category (Made up usually of a Penney, Grant's, Woolworth, if a small department store is contained then it is larger)	75,000
Women's Apparel—about	15 to 15,000
Men's stores	7 to 12,000
Children's stores	3 to 7,000
Shoe store	16,000
Furniture	15 to 20,000
Hardware store	5 to 15,000
Misc. made up of Yarns, Fabrics, Toys, Sporting goods, Jewelry	5 on up.

Anywhere from 120,000 to 180,000.

Fifty per cent to sixty per cent of the business of these convenience centers comes from a radius within three miles; approximately 75 per cent comes from one within five miles. It has been said that the existing retailing in this area represents maturation. However, this does not stop additional units from opening, and all areas are not equally well developed. In addition, department store status and quality merchandise is not offered.

However, let us consider the convenience unit not so much as a defensive weapon as an instrument for gathering an increased share of the market. Therefore, in an attempt to establish a size, let us see what is available for the department store in terms of existing business in their various convenience units.

Recognizing that the department store "twig" unit cannot offer a broad selection in all of its merchandise and that a representative selection in major Ready-To-Wear and Furniture would be imposible, let us see what it can show without embarrassment and then edge up from there. Perhaps then we can arrive at some kind of composition of volume on a very modest basis.

	Sq. ft.
Accessories, including Hosiery, Cosmetics	2,000 plus
Corsets, Lingerie	2,000
Hats, Millinery	400
Sportswear	2,500
Children's	3,000 plus
Men's and Boy's Furnishings, Sports, Slacks, Jr.	3,000
Shoes—all	2,500
	15,400
Apparel	3,500
Robes—House dresses	1,000
Sporting goods, toys	1,500
Home store—curtains, drapes, domestics, blankets, linens, lamps, houseware	10,000

This gives us a store of 31,000 square feet of selling space, capable of producing on a modest basis: $2 million a year, with services and building utilizing a gross area of perhaps 40,000 square feet.

A 31,000 square foot store represents only about 20 per cent of the average downtown store merchandise in convenience goods center, and, therefore, does not require that the other stores go out of existence in order to make room for itself.

(By talking about the convenience goods center, I do not imply that the department store twig unit should go into a center. "Center" in this context, simply means the stores in the trading area.)

I believe 31,000 square feet to be a modest size store. Perhaps 50,000 square feet gross would be possible with the consequent increase in volume. It would also be possible to get a greater production out of a small unit. (Many of the existing branches have more square footage than they need for the volume they are doing.)

I propose that such small units installed in areas that are a No-Man's Land between your downtown and branches or between branch and branch will secure for you the greatest share of the market in those areas of merchandising which have been open to the greatest attack by other forms of retailing. With such units you would take a minimum chance. You would have mobility, flexibility. They would not require a major investment. They could be opened, closed, moved or added to. You could move with your public.

In summary, therefore, let me say that:

1. the department store must take steps to reassert the importance of the place where merchandise is bought to offset prevalent emphasis on national branding;
2. it must use its status position to a greater degree and work toward making that position stronger;
3. it should approach the exploitation of its trading area in a total manner.

The emphasis should be placed, firstly, on the downtown and branch and, when it is demonstrated as useful, secondly, on the convenience or community twig.

In spite of the Cassandra cries, the department store has demonstrated a hardiness in the face of competition. It has been fighting with one hand tied behind its back. It has not used all the tools at its command.

54. CONVENIENCE MARKETS *

Norris Willatt

Towards the close of the old year, members of the National Association of Convenience Stores, Inc., assembled in Dallas, Texas, for their first annual meeting. The delegates were the owners of what are otherwise known as bantam or drive-in stores, a modern, streamlined version of the fastest growing branches of U. S. retailing. Indeed, the representatives of this mushrooming industry have been so busy minding their stores that they had had no time to get together until the session at Dallas, where they made plans for the first official census of the business.

The convenience market, then, is a fairly new phenomenon in the U. S. Essentially, it is a small store, where a limited range of brand merchandise can be bought in a hurry. Most such outlets are open from 7 a.m. to 11 p.m., including Sunday, normally their busiest day. The average customer drops in for only a few minutes, and picks up perhaps two or three items, with a combined value of a dollar or so. Because of the quick turnover, such a store can get by with a relatively small parking lot. Its staff usually consists of two fulltime employees, and one or more part-time helpers. The former may be either a day and night manager, splitting shifts, or a husband and wife, taking turns.

Typical layout

According to a survey by the marketing research department of the National Cash Register Co., the typical layout of a drive-in market varies from 1,200 to 2,800 square feet. If offers practically all types of merchandise found in larger markets, but scales down the number of items (to between 1,800 and 3,500, from the 6,000 or more in a typical supermarket) by offering fewer competing brands, sizes and assortments. The basic inventory is canned goods, produce and

* Reprinted by permission of *Barron's*, Vol. XLII, No. 2 (January 8, 1962), p. 11.

Norris Willatt, contributor to *Barron's*; United States Correspondent for London Financial Journals.

dairy items; most stores also carry beer, soft drinks, ice cream, lunch meats, frozen foods, health and beauty aids. Some sell toys, housewares and soft goods. So far, most do not handle fresh meats. According to the same survey, gross profit in the business averages 21% of sales, compared to some 18% for the supermarkets.

Just how many convenience, bantam or drive-in markets are in business in the U. S. today is an unanswerable riddle. Some 30 companies, representing 2,000 stores, signed up as founder-members of the new trade association, and there may be 1,000-1,500 in operation. As recently as the mid-1950s, only a handful existed from coast to coast. Equally uncertain is current annual dollar volume. However, on the basis of a Progressive Grocer estimate that the average bantam store grosses $175,000 a year, $500 million would appear a conservative guess.

Growth of the chains

The business consists in large part of individual stores, on the mom-and-pop pattern. The rapid growth in the past five years or so, however, has come from the chains, which have established standardized outlets under their own guidance. Some of the largest are privately-owned, such as 7-Eleven, Inc., of Dallas, which has close to 700 stores; Convenient Food Mart, of Chicago, with several hundred; Pak-A-Sak Service Stores, Inc., of Shreveport, La.; and Circle K. Food Stores, Inc., Phoenix, Arizona.

Publicly-owned chains include Jackson's Minit Markets, Jacksonville, Fla.; Pik-Quik, Inc., Tampa, Fla.; U-Tote'm, Inc., Bellaire, Texas; Speedee Mart, Inc., San Diego, Calif.; and Speed-Way Food Stores, Inc., Brooklyn, N. Y. Also in the business are American Service Co. and the Atlantic Co., both of Atlanta, Ga., the latter through its E-Z Food Shops division. Finally, Rexall, through its Owl Drug Co. subsidiary, is a part owner (with private interests) of the Pronto chain in the Los Angeles area.

RECENT RESULT OF SELECTED CONVENIENCE STORE CHAINS

Company	Period	Net Sales (In Thousands) 1961	1960	Net Per Share 1961	1960
Jackson's Minit	6 months to Oct. 28	$7,515.2	$4,254.8	$0.15	$0.11
Speedee Mart	6 months to Oct. 1	550.5	276.2	0.21	0.12
U-Tote'm	6 months to Sept. 30	[a] 213.7	[a] 166.4	0.34	0.28
Atlantic Co.	6 months to June 30	9,466.2	9,990.1	1.01	1.18
American Service Co.	6 months to June 30	3,499.3	4,366.0	[d] 2.08	[d] 2.24

[a] Net before taxes. [d] Deficit.

Up to now, stores of the type have been concentrated largely in the South. The reasons are that the mild climate there favors a small, open-front, walk-in type of store; that Southerners, because of their small-town populations and large rural areas, are used to patronizing small stores; and that the pioneer chain, 7-Eleven, was located in that region. Lower wages below the Mason-Dixon Line also may have been an influence.

At the start, the factor of climate may have been highly important, as the early stores did a large business in such warm-weather items as beer, soft drinks and ice cream. Participation of such firms as American Service and the Atlantic Co. is closely related to their operations in refrigeration, and Rexall-Owl reportedly entered the field as an offshoot of its ice cream distribution. While the majority of chain stores are company-owned, lately a shift towards the franchise-type store has developed.

Fiscal results mixed

Financially, the industry's recent results have been mixed (see table). Some stores, apparently suffering from growing pains, have slipped into the red. The latest published figures on Pik-Quik for six months ended April 30, 1961, showed a deficit of $139,877, on the heels of a loss of $130,294 a year earlier, despite an almost three-fold increase in sales, to $2.7 million. For the same six months, American Service Co. reported a loss of $190,235, as sales fell by nearly 18%, to $3.5 million. The company also reported deficits for calendar 1960 and 1959. Inasmuch as American Service also sells coal and ice, operates cold storage warehouses and rents refrigerated space to others, the losses do not stem wholly from its 64 convenience stores.

For the six months ended June 30, 1961, net of the Atlantic Co. declined slightly, to $1.01 per share, from $1.18 a year earlier, as sales slipped to $9.5 million, from $9.9 million. The company, however, says it is relying greatly on the 120 stores in its E-Z Food Shops chain as a vehicle for future investment and expansion, to compensate for the deterioration of its traditional ice business. (Last March, incidentally, Atlantic Co. raised the dividend on its common stock to 25 cents a quarter, from 15 cents.)

Other companies, however, have been ringing up more favorable results. For six months ended September 30, 1961, U-Tote'm reported unaudited net of $112,215, or 34 cents a common share, up 18% from $94,455, equal to 28 cents a share (of which 10% represented capital gains). The concern looks for a sizable increase in net for the full fiscal year, ending March 31, 1962. While it releases no interim figures on sales, for the year ended March 31, 1961, volume ran to $9.5 million. At the end of 1961, the U-Tote'm chain consisted of 175 convenience stores, about two-thirds of them company-owned outlets.

For the six months ended October 1, 1961, Speedee Mart reported net of $61,905, or 21 cents a share compared to $37,628 a year earlier, or 12 cents a share, on the basis of 300,932 common shares currently outstanding. Operating revenues rose to $550,541, from $267,250, as sales by franchised stores more than doubled, to over $6.6 million.

For the full fiscal year, which will end April 1, Speedee expects sales by stores in its chain to increase to $14.3 million, nearly double the $7.6 million reported for fiscal 1961. Per-share net should top the 48 cents reported last year, when considerably fewer common shares were outstanding. By the end of the fiscal period, the company expects to have increased its chain to 115 convenience markets, from 74 at the start of the year.

Jackson's Minit Markets, for its part, lately has shown a sharp jump in profits, aided by its several stores in Brevard County, site of Cape Canaveral. For the six months ended October 28, 1961, the company reported a 38% increase in net, to $100,086, or 15 cents a share, from $72,685, or 11 cents a share, a year earlier. Volume increased more than 75%, to $7.5 million, from $4.2 million.

Sales and profits are being boosted further in the second half of the fiscal period, reports President Julian E. Jackson, owing in part to the Government's selection of Merritt Island, deep in company territory, for the $20 billion project to put a man in space. The concern, which operates both drive-in Minit Markets and regular supermarkets, now has a total of 85 stores.

Growth in prospect

Everybody in the bantam market business—even those chains which have had a setback in earnings—is talking in terms of growth. Pronto's management, for example, is weighing expansion beyond the Los Angeles area. American Service Co., which today has stores in Georgia and Tennessee, plans ten additional outlets in 1962.

Atlantic Co., with operations now confined to the Southeast, also expects to open ten new stores this year. At the same time, the company is upgrading many of its existing stores, converting them from cracker-barrel-type operations to model markets, designed by the Raymond Loewy organization. Atlantic has just completed 13 such renovations, and intends to give a similar face-lifting to 50 more in the chain during the next six months.

Jackson's Minit Markets, already blanketing most of Florida, is expanding into the more highly populated southern section of the state. U-Tote'm, now located in Texas, Arkansas, Florida, Arizona and Southern California, will add several stores before the close of the current fiscal year, including its first outlets in Virginia, Colorado and Northern California.

In December, Speedee Mart opened six stores, including two in San Jose and two in Sacramento. For the present, the company expects to stay in the Golden State, but plans later to expand elsewhere in the West. The tentative schedule calls for opening 50 more franchised stores during fiscal 1963.

For the industry as a whole, at least in theory, expansion opportunities are without limit, since most of the country still is virgin territory. According to the philosophy behind the bantam store, every neighborhood could support at least one, where the housewife could pick up any staples needed between trips to the supermarket.

Growing pains

Over the longer term, then, the industry looks for substantial further growth. On some estimates, the number of units may top 5,000 by 1965. Such a blueprint for the future looks promising enough. However, as the industry already has discovered, growth is not always without pain. In some cases, the chains, in their eagerness to expand, have picked poor locations, with the melancholy consequence of ultimately being forced to shut down stores. In certain areas, convenience markets have located too close together, and have found that there was not enough business to go around.

Then, too, although convenience markets supposedly complement, rather than compete with, supermarkets, things do not always work out so neatly. For example, such stores have done pretty well in San Diego, where the supermarkets follow a conservative policy on hours of operation. However, they have found the going much tougher in Los Angeles, where the supermarkets are more aggressive, some staying open 24 hours a day.

Labor, too, has proved a burden in some areas. While a comparatively low wage scale has favored hiring in the South, in high-wage areas, such as California, the cost often has proved prohibitive. A solution is being sought through franchising. Thus, Speedee Mart, a pioneer in this type of operation, sponsors man-and-wife teams as store owner-operators. The company chooses locations, buys, plans and develops the real estate, sometimes blueprinting a whole convenience center, with coin laundries, dry cleaners and similar outlets.

School for operators

Preferably, Speedee sells the center to a private investor, leases it back, and then sub-leases to the operator, who buys his own inventory and puts up a security deposit. Speedee even runs a school, in which the operator is taught the essentials of the business. The company also provides centralized purchasing, management, accounting, advertising and inventory supervision and banking service.

Total investment in a Speedee Mart Store averages about $13,700. However, it is possible to go into business with a cash down payment of $4,000, the balance to be paid out of profits from the store. Speedee collects a 13.9% service fee, based on annual gross sales. The company advertises that it expects franchisees to net between $9,000 and $20,000 annually, provided gross profits are as high and expenses as low as they should be.

Naturally, these bright hopes are not always fulfilled. Indeed, failure to achieve the anticipated volume has led to a quick turnover of some franchised stores, disputes between store operators and franchising firms and even a few lawsuits. Originally, franchises were written with a short-term cancellation clause available to both parties. Nowadays, however, the trend is toward binding franchisees to longer periods. For example, Speedee Mart requires its store operators to sign on for a minimum of one year.

Industry consolidation

As noted, a good many of the headaches of the convenience store firms stem from rapid growth. Most will be cured by more experience, as the industry enters a period of more moderate but more orderly expansion. Already a process of consolidation, through merger and acquisition is under way. For example, in April, 1961, Pik-Quik merged with L'il General Stores, Inc., another Florida chain. The result was a combined operation of 79 stores, with a total volume in excess of $5.5 million. Besides the many units built by the company's own real estate division, Speedee Mart has grown by the acquisition of seven Min-A-Mart stores in the Oakland area, 11 Handy Pantry stores in San Diego, and two Minit Marts in the Los Angeles area.

55. NON-FOODS MERCHANDISING *

Milton Alexander

To the grocers of America, non-foods are the "wonder drugs" for ailing profits. It has still to be determined, however, which of these new non-foods are here to stay; and under what conditions they are to be most effectively sold.

Oddly enough—at least, to the younger generation of grocers—non-foods have a long history in food stores. Thus, 30 years ago, grocers quite commonly sold headache remedies, "galvanized ware," and work gloves—just as they do today. But what sets the "new" and the "old" apart are these fundamental distinctions:

1. The growth of non-food acceptance is unparalleled in the history of American food stores.

2. Non-foods have won a full-time place in grocers' inventories. Since the end of World War II, they have outgrown their traditional role as sporadic "fillers;" and (excepting seasonal items) they are available the year 'round. Furthermore, the tendency is away from isolated items, and toward a rounded assortment of products within lines handled.

3. Non-foods are gravitating farther and farther from mere kitchen use, and toward the more inclusive sphere of "household necessities." Such "new" non-foods as flashlights, bath towels, children's wear, and phonograph records illustrate the drift, which has been naturally coupled with a marked diversification of lines and items.

In current terms, therefore, non-foods may be defined as: those non-edibles which are being widely and regularly adopted for sale in food stores; but which items have been, by previous tradition, sold in other types of retail outlets.

Unfortunately, definitions seldom "stick" in a dynamic business like food retailing. Witness the complete integration of such old non-foods as soaps, cleansers, waxes, polishes, and cigarettes. In each

* Reprinted by permission of the *Progressive Grocer* Vol. 31, No. 10 (October, 1952), p. 197.
Milton Alexander, Associate Professor of Marketing, Fordham University.

instance the pliable word, "groceries," was stretched to accommodate the newcomer. So it will be, very likely, with the current crop of non-foods.

Grocers like their high margins

Almost to a man, grocers trace their enthusiasm for non-foods to shrinking profit margins in food products—behind which stand such relentless economic facts as inflation, price control, and bitter competition. No wonder that most grocers, including the chains, are found to espouse fair trade regulation in non-foods. Price cutting would probably spell the doom of such lines in food stores.

On the minus side, meanwhile, are other thorny problems that give pause to non-food enthusiasts. Who is to supply them with non-foods, the manufacturer, wholesaler, or rack jobber? On what basis shall they be awarded display space? What about reprisals from non-grocery competitors? How will the new items be accommodated, what kinds of fixtures displayed, and where?

But at least one thing is certain as of now: the opportunities for profit-making, presented by non-foods, are being grasped by increasing numbers of self-service grocers. . . .

Let us return, now, to the issues raised earlier in this article—first, to examine at closer range the motives behind the acceptance of non-foods.

First in importance is the quest for higher margins. . . .

Squeezed by steadily rising overhead and direct costs on the one hand, and reduced percentage margins on the other, the grocer naturally seeks out these greener profit pastures.

Shortages of various foods, which prevailed during World War II, also served to rouse the grocer's interest in non-foods. As an inspection of representative wholesaler catalogues reveals, there was a sudden spurt in such items as glassware, sanitary napkins, and saccharin tablets. A change in reference from "drugs" to "drug department" is also significant. Many of these earlybirds ultimately won acceptance, and so cleared the way for still newer products.

High margin just one test

Evidently, however, higher margin cannot—by itself—assure the successful sales of non-foods in food stores. It must be hooked up with certain other merchandising characteristics such as rapid turnover, low unit price, clear identification (of product and brand), standard reordering procedure, and relatively high sales per square foot. . . .

Self-service merchandising may, of course, speed up some of the turnover of some lines particularly by boosting consumption of low-priced, convenience items. For instance, self-service has promoted impulse buying of items that are quickly consumed like health and beauty aids. It is doubtful, however, whether the rate on certain other items like durable household articles can be altered. For in many products the pattern of consumption is set; and only the brightest kind of profit opportunities could induce a grocer to tie up capital in slow movers. . . .

A self-service operation demands items that are easily identified by the consumer. Therefore, those fare best which are nationally advertised, and standardized in quality and packaging; and which do not require special instructions for use. Lacking these advantages, a non-food item could slow up traffic, and thus aggravate congestion in the aisles and checkout areas, in addition to complicating the problems of stock supervision. Despite the recent trend toward more informative labeling, many non-foods (particularly in textiles) have still to meet this objection. . . .

Must lend itself to re-ordering

To be declared eligible, an aspiring non-food must posses one other basic feature: it must lend itself to simple re-ordering. No style and fashion cycle for the food merchant! And it must be an item that is regularly stocked by suppliers; and one, so uniform in quality, and so restricted in variety (e.g. of size and color) as to be readily identified by the grocer-buyer. While considerable advances have been scored in the standardization of housewares (and, of course, health and beauty aids), such is not the case with many types of soft goods and toys. To cope with the fickle tastes of consumers, manufacturers are almost constantly changing specifications, which tends to rule out routine re-ordering. Further, inasmuch as non-foods are accepted on the strength of their sales, this lack of uniformity tends to becloud the grocer's records. It is important for non-food manufacturers to realize that responsibility for buying their lines—even in large chains—is usually shifted to buyers of traditional items who usually have neither the experience nor time to evaluate subtle changes in unfamiliar merchandise.

Problems to be solved

These six tests for acceptance underline the problems in developing of non-food sales.

First, as has been noted, grocers are handicapped by a lack of skill in buying and merchandising non-foods. Hence their dependence, in some lines, on rack jobbers.

In his search of non-food suppliers, the grocer is often caught between a yearning for lower cost and a desire for service. Rack jobbers, it is generally agreed, have done an admirable job in pioneering new items. Even large chains sometimes prefer to let jobbers tackle new problems of stock turnover, rotation, display. Obviously, however, their service entails a cost.

Meanwhile, there is still a critical need for *realistic* promotional help from suppliers. Increasingly, the latter are expected to furnish point-of-sale helps which grocers are now often obliged to improvise.

Another still-to-be-solved puzzle concerns the optimum method of promoting and displaying non-foods. Unless manufacturers do more pre-selling, many non-foods will require a personal sales push; and may have to be merchandised at least, temporarily, on a service basis. In this connection, grocers would also welcome improvements in packaging to spur eye appeal (and so increase impulse sales); and curb soilage, breakage, pilferage, and pricing mistakes.

Of all problems confronting grocers in the sale of non-foods, none is tougher than the chronic shortage of display space. As a "Johnny Come Lately," each non-food must pass a rigid test of profitability; and space tends to be allocated on the basis of *present* sales performance. Of necessity, therefore, the most eligible non-foods are those which score high in absolute profit yield. Ideally, these are the items that combine high turnover, high sales per square foot, and better-than-average markup; and preferably plus sales.

Sufficient space—a big obstacle

Non-foods have appropriated gondolas and gondola ends, as well as space in the checkout areas. Still, more room is urgently required. It is probably fair to say that space limitations will prove to be the most persistent stumbling-block to non-food expansion; and this may oblige grocers to limit lines and varieties of acceptable non-foods.

The policy of some to "sprinkle" non-foods among related foods and groceries may "spread" space; but it will scarcely make a dent in the problem. After all is said and done, however, space limitations may be a blessing in disguise. For otherwise, grocers might not weight acceptance so carefully, and might recklessly take on items without proper pre-testing.

One final set of typical non-food problems remains to be considered—restrictive leases and/or competition with neighboring non-grocery outlets. Neither appears to be as significant as it was once thought to be; and certainly, the public-relations angle predominates over legal considerations.

Less trouble with leases

Restrictive leases, it is true, often limit the lines that grocers may handle. But the word "groceries," on the other hand, is amazingly elastic (witness the migration of soaps, polishes, tobacco, paper products etc. into food stores!). It is quite certain that landlords will be helpless to halt the new drift of non-foods once they have been fully integrated within food store operations.

By virtue of basic changes in food and grocery retailing, however, non-foods have become a "natural" in food stores. . . .

Given a fully departmentized food store, it becomes rather easy to add new product lines. It is also natural for grocers to want to exploit the highest traffic density in the entire retail field.

Self service is the second major development to provide an impetus for non-foods. Were it not for the rise of self-service merchandising, non-foods would have been stymied. For few grocers are prepared to offer continuing clerk service on such items as soft goods, hosiery, housewares, etc. Certainly, too, self-service, with its minimal sales cost per employee, prods grocers to take on new lines—and so spread sales costs still thinner. Finally, as will be stressed below, the open-display character of self-service enables grocers to merchandise non-foods as they have never been merchandised before.

Price cutting added impetus

A third major impetus to non-foods came from the grocers' concern about price cutting, so perennial in food and grocery retailing. This, of course, heightened their interest in items which seemed to be immune. As has been noted, independent and chain grocers hope to keep it that way—to achieve a 30% (or better) margin on non-foods. Whether they can is debatable, however. If non-foods should eventually fall prey to runaway price cutting, it would cancel one chief motives for their initial acceptance. And that could very easily slow the trend.

The merchandising climate fostered by these basic changes has obviously helped the cause of non-foods. Here are some specific considerations that deserve most of the credit for non-food success in food stores:

• *Highest Shopper Traffic* This is the grocer's principal drawing card for non-foods, and with good reason. In no other type of retail outlet does an item enjoy so high a rate of customer frequency; and, consequently, so long an exposure to buying impulses. . . .

• *Open Display* This opens up vast new sales opportunities for non-foods. Exposed to customer inspection and free choice, they tend to ignite buying impulses—as they seldom can within glass cases or inaccessible shelving. This advantage would seem to be restricted, however, to the more standardized, "staple" non-foods like health and beauty aids, and hosiery. There, too, product advertising and informative labeling are essential in providing basic buying facts. The best has yet to come in open display of non-foods—with the perfection of display.

• *Relative Inefficiency of Non-Grocery Outlets* This has long been an open secret; but a torrent of self-criticism by merchandising executives has made it all but official. As countless surveys have shown, the sales personnel of these other types of retail outlets do not know enough about the merchandise they are supposed to sell, and are often out of step with promotions and advertising. As a result, many of these stores have begun to experiment with "self-selection" (which is the highbrow equivalent of self-service). Many other time-honored retail practices—credit, returns, and delivery—are also under fire. In any event, bungling "salesmanship" has helped knock the props from under the claims of personal selling advocates.

• *More Family Shopping* This, too, has broadened the market for "household necessities." As is common knowledge, male shoppers often comprise roughly one third of the self-service food store's week-end trade. Their free-spending habits, diversified product interest, and helping hand at the distaff side all have promoted acceptance for non-foods.

The grocer's verdict on non-foods is just about in, now. And in the light of retailing history, it leads the writer to these conclusions:

Within the framework of a departmentized self-service food store, non-foods are here to stay, and to enjoy a period of continued, if cautious, advances. With few exceptions, only these will be finally integrated which pass the six merchandising tests of rapid turnover, low unit price, routine reordering procedure, adequate margin, quick identification, and high sales per square foot.

Sales tests (probably on a continuing basis) have still to determine which items are going to stay, and how they will be sold.

Within limits suggested above, there will be a diversification of non-food lines and items, aiming toward more rounded assortments and an expansion of related-item merchandising techniques, so dear to the heart of self-service operators.

Increased competition in store

There will be increased competition among foods and non-foods. There is some danger that under the stress of competition and the profit squeeze, some grocers will plunge headlong into lines they cannot profitably handle thus risking losses in money and customer good will, and neglecting their food and grocery operations.

Non-foods have ushered in a Golden Age in mass retailing—one in which the grocers' unique brand of self-service merchandising has been found to apply in new, high-profit product areas, hitherto deemed off-limits to food stores. And in so doing, food dealers have strengthened still more the most efficient and dynamic retailing system the world has ever known.

56. NON-FOODS ARE BIG BUSINESS *

Donald Bruce Reynolds

Non-foods, one of the most widely discussed topics in the food industry today, are presently accounting for 5.2% of total sales and are progressing in an orderly manner as additional products are selectively added to inventories. This optimistic appraisal of the overall contribution of non-foods is based on the results of a comprehensive nationwide survey conducted by *Progressive Grocer.*

The non-foods analysis rates the seven basic classifications of merchandise that have been generally introduced into supermarkets on a large scale since World War II. These seven departments are health and beauty aids, housewares, magazines, soft goods, toys, phonograph records, and stationery.

The survey examines these departments in terms of source of supply, total sales, profit margins, performance in terms of space occupied, number of items offered to shoppers, where and how they are displayed, future plans, and what operators say to the query, "How's business?"

This article will confine itself to the total non-foods picture. Subsequent articles in the non-foods series will provide detailed studies of each of these seven departments.

Experience teaches best

Operators in the non-foods business, whose experiences we are presenting, unanimously agree the main reason they sell non-foods is to satisfy the demands of their customers!

Most non-foods volume (3.8%) is provided by the three departments that have been offered the longest by food stores—health and beauty aids (2.3%), housewares (.92%), and magazines (.58%). Based on experience gained over years of merchandising health and beauty aids, most store operators point to soft goods (.53%) of total sales as the "most likely to succeed" non-food line of the future.

* Reprinted by permission from the *Progressive Grocer* Vols. 11, 12, 1; Nos. 37, 38 (November, 1958, December, 1958, and January, 1959). Later published as a three-part special report on non-foods.

Donald Bruce Reynolds, Marketing Associate, J. Walter Thompson Company, New York, New York.

With probably the least distribution of any of the seven basic departments, soft goods has, during the period of less than a year, shaken off early industry estimates of "high risk, low profit" and is now receiving select treatment from rack jobbers and direct buying retail organizations alike.

Coming most often in small packages, non-foods have been merchandised in food stores by persons who have foreseen a gradual and evolutionary growth as food store customers have come to realize that they are being provided with *truly* one stop shopping.

Outstanding in an area of merchandising foreign to food store men has been the rack jobber. He has assumed the task of purchasing, warehousing, servicing, and guaranteeing the sale of this merchandise in food stores that have been placed under his supervision.

The penalty of shrinkage and returns, generally estimated between 3% and 10% of sales, depending on the line, is shouldered by the service wholesaler. This is the most disheartening aspect of his entire service role in that there is little or no possibility to reclaim any of this loss through salvage.

The rack jobber is most firmly entrenched as a basic source of supply of phonograph records, toys, stationery, soft goods, and housewares. He continues to be a leading factor in the health and beauty aid business and now services about half of the nation's markets. Magazines are in the hands of specialized magazine wholesalers.

Chain and independent retail organizations have for some time been employing non-foods merchandisers who have drawn their experience from the variety and department store field. The reason for this is a twofold approach to direct buying. First, the margin of profit normally taken by the service wholesaler becomes the property of these enlightened retailers; and secondly, specialists can eliminate the risk of direct buying.

The particular talents of the rack jobber, which include his ability to absorb all of the unpleasant aspects of selling non-foods, however, have often resulted in his resecuring business that had been taken from him during such experiments.

According to survey respondents, a near average U. S. supermarket turning in a volume of $18,500 each week produces sales of $943 from non-foods departments.

The overall gross margin of 31% represents merchandise purchased from rack jobbers, manufacturers, wholesale grocers, and all other sources, and brings a weekly $292 gross margin on sales.

The near million dollar a year supermarket devotes 83 linear floor feet to all non-foods and offers an assortment of 1046 different items in this space. Space limitations have hampered full non-foods development, but this handicap may also have served a useful purpose since operators and wholesalers alike are forced to be highly critical in their choice of merchandise when new items are being put to test.

Retailers participating in this survey report a net gain in sales of all non-foods of 16% over last year. However, 61% indicate that business is to some extent better than a year ago in these departments.

Complete optimism is evident in the attitudes toward expansion in the immediate future. Phonograph records spark the least optimism with 7% of respondents saying they will expand space for this line. A substantial 31% of operators profess confidence enough in the success of soft goods to justify a solid expansion program.

The strength of non-foods is best evaluated in terms of profits. Combined non-foods volume represents 11% of total grocery sales (including non-foods), but by a sharp contrast, provides 18% of grocery dollar margin (including non-foods).

How All Non-Foods Compare With Top Ten Gross Profit Producers in Super Valu Grocery Department

(Survey Figures)	% Margin	$ Weekly Margin
All non-foods	31%	$292
Household supplies	28.3%	$136
Beverages	12.1%	$118
Crackers, cookies	25.3%	$103
Canned vegetables	21.4%	$ 98
Paper products	23.4%	$ 92
Candy	25.5%	$ 87
Canned fruit	21.6%	$ 72
Cigarette	6.0%	$ 55
Cereals	18.1%	$ 49

Again, these Super Valu dollar gross margin figures were adjusted to an $18,500 weekly supermarket volume so they would be directly proportional to the non-food figures.

The significance of these dollar gross profit comparisons is that non-foods sales are generally made in addition to regular grocery sales, and that much of the non-foods volume is supplied by rack jobbers who absorb all risk and expenses while guaranteeing sale. Merchandise that is purchased through other sources will, of course, bring a greater profit, which tends to offset any increase in operating expenses.

Sales of these rapidly turning toiletries are accounting for 2.3% of total food store volume where they are stocked. Of all seven non-foods departments, this one is the most easily managed since nearly all items are presold, branded, and widely advertised making them familiar to both store operator and customer. This fact makes health and beauty aids the most logical choice of operators for self-management. Rack jobbers service more than half of stores selling health and beauty aids.

An all store average weekly sale of $408 at 32.5% gross margin provides a dollar margin of $133 weekly to store owners. A typical health and beauty aid rack occupies 20.1 linear floor ft. and contains 381 items. The large store ($32,000 weekly sales) offers 486 items in 29 linear floor ft.

Houseware-household items in food stores have advanced to nearly 1% of total sales (.92%) and are being supplied predominantly by rack jobbers. Ranking second only to health and beauty aids as a department, housewares produce an average 33% gross profit on sales. This is an average figure representing purchases made from other sources as well as service wholesalers.

Average weekly housewares sales of $158 contribute a dollar profit to operators of $52. The average housewares department occupies 19.5 linear floor ft. and contains 167 different items. The influence of pegboard is most easily detected in this department since the multiplicity of items necessary to the successful housewares section requires extra square footage from an area already curtailed on total linear floor feet. Simply stated, if housewares cannot be merchandised outward, they must go "up."

Also, many housewares items are designed for easy hanging in home kitchen walls and handles and other naturally shaped openings present an easy target for pegboard hooks which have become synonymous with housewares.

Magazines are not recent arrivals in food stores, and in the opinion of many operators are actually considered more nearly "traditional" grocery items than the remaining six departments.

Magazines distribution is estimated to have reached 11,900 supermarkets, a figure that gives them 41% distribution in the 28,800 supers. These supers are very evenly divided between chains and independents, 14,500 to 14,300. Special magazine wholesalers supply this department in food stores, and since total U. S. distribution is limited by the locations of these wholesalers, magazines cannot be made equally available to all stores.

Combined sales of magazines, comics, children's books, and adult pocketbooks in the average store represent $110 a week or .58% of total store sales. Publications other than magazines account for more than 72% of the total of 188 titles in a typical department that measures 12.3 linear floor ft. The average gross margin on sales in this line amounts to 26%.

The wooden display generally used for magazines and comics occupies 10 linear floor ft. in the average store. Children's books and pocketbooks are most often placed on rotating wire racks that utilize the remaining 2.3 floor ft. devoted for the department.

Many operators are most emphatic in their recommendation that store owners and managers pay close attention to type of magazines being left by distributors. Magazines of a non-family nature usually draw the most complaints from retailers while the exposé or confession publications often turn out to be good library material but relatively poor sale material.

Operators are about evenly divided on the subject of the magazine and book department as a "built-in baby sitting service while Mother shops." There are as many retailers who dislike magazines for this reason as there are who favor them because they allow adult customers to give their undivided attention to selection of merchandise while their offspring lounge with reading material.

The case for soft goods, a department that has developed to better than one-half per cent of total store sales while being represented in the fewest stores of all, is a very strong one. Developing very slowly, soft goods have benefited from the alert supervision retailers have given the department. Food dealers as well as their suppliers are most careful in their scrutiny of new items.

Most operators and rack jobbers believe that soft goods sales will increase in future years in direct proportion to the number of well-known and branded items the customer is able to recognize on the rack. Convenience is a big factor in favor of selling soft goods in food stores, but until a shopper recognizes either a brand, or, specific quality (which takes longer) customers and operators alike will continue to appraise soft goods with a certain feeling of reservation.

Soft goods distribution lies heavily in the hands of the rack jobber except for the promotion of "in and out" merchandise which groups and chains have been successful in rotating on a limited scale. Departments of depth continue to be serviced primarily by service wholesalers.

The typical soft goods department does weekly sales of $99 at an overall gross margin of 31.9% to produce a gross profit of $32 weekly.

The previously mentioned promotional items that have been successfully merchandised by retailers buying direct have been responsible for raising the gross profit to a near 32% average. Rack jobber soft goods carry a 25% margin.

The average soft goods department occupies 9.8 linear floor ft., and this dimension increases only slightly as the size of the store increases. The over-$1-million markets surveyed average 10.5 linear floor ft. of soft goods display and the remaining respondents (stores under $1 million in sales) present an average rack of 9.4 linear ft. In any case, the prevailing attitude is a favorable one to soft goods since the number of items handled changes only slightly in various size stores with the average store offering 76 items.

Supermarkets have been estimated to sell 10% of all phonograph records today. Combined children's records, populars, and LP-albums are providing .30% of total store sales in the average supermarket. Records are displayed for the most part away from the grocery gondola or shelving and special rotating vertical wire racks are most frequently used. While this method does provide maximum utilization of floor space, and complete flexibility so that the line can be situated in traffic locations that respond best, record manufacturers question the effect of piling different titles in stacks that are hard to shop. Stores with outstanding record departments are using gondola shelving and end display locations in place of wire racks. The average record department in stores surveyed occupies 5.3 linear floor ft., and stocks 94 titles.

Rack jobbers are the dominant suppliers of records to food stores today. Record sales in the average store amount to $64 per week and the 28.4% margin on sales presents store operators with $18 weekly margin.

The peculiarities of record selling are great and they vary within almost every store. For this reason the rack jobber experiences little competition in supplying stores with this category of merchandise whose sale is so dependent upon trends and public appeal.

Key toy manufacturers estimate that 65% to 75% of food markets are stocking toys to some degree. Our survey reveals that toy sales amount to .35% of total store sales. Toy volume in food stores has risen in recent years as departments have been enlarged from the strict pre-school appeal to the broader lines that include hobby kits, playground games, and sporting goods. Thus expansion of the line has created greater interest and at the same time broadened the market for toys in food stores.

Most food store toy items sell for under $1. Thus, the normal surge in sales at Christmas time is not as great in food stores as it is in department, specialty, or discount outlets. Quite evenly balanced throughout the year, the food store toy business generally will not fall lower than 3% of total yearly sales in any month with a December maximum of about 15% of total.

Until food stores take on the larger ticket items that traditionally sit beneath Christmas trees—bicycles, electric trains, and hobby horses, etc.,—toys will continue to be sold without extreme fluctuation due to season or holidays.

Toy sales account presently for $63 weekly in the $17,000 a week store and a 33% gross margin supplies $21 weekly dollar profit. While the linear floor footage devoted to display of toys ranges from an 8.2 ft. average in stores doing under $1 million sales, to 12 ft. in stores over the $1 million mark there is little difference in the number of items stocked in the departments. The average 9.6 linear ft. department contains 93 items, including toys, hobby kits, playground games, and sporting goods. Larger markets claim 96 items and smaller markets, 91.

Stationery departments in food stores generally include school supplies, pens and pencils, writing paper and envelopes, gift wraps and ribbons, and crayons. Nearly half of our respondents included playing cards and greeting cards as part of their overall stationery inventory.

Sales of these items represent .23% of total store volume, and their 41% margin brings a $16.80 weekly margin.

The average department occupies 6.3 linear floor ft. and includes 47 items.

While many operators merchandise their stationery department and school supplies most widely at the Labor Day weekend, the rack jobbers who supply most of this merchandise point out the practicality of prolonging these promotions throughout the first several weeks of school when students are getting a better line on the equipment they will need for their classes.

How strong is the influence exerted over non-foods by health and beauty aids and housewares? *Progressive Grocer's* recent study, which includes magazines, soft goods, toys, phonograph records, and stationery as well, indicates health and beauty aids and housewares are by far the two hardest working and most active non-foods departments in the U. S. food store.

Combined non-foods sales measured up to 5.2% of total store volume, and these two popular departments contribute 60% of all non-foods sales. Health and beauty aids, 2.3% of total volume, and housewares with nearly 1% (.92%) of sales are clearly the leaders in these seven non-grocery product categories. A good industry-wide estimate is health and beauty aid sales up 14% and housewares sales 16% better than last year.

Respondents told us their drug and housewares departments measure about 20 linear floor ft. each, and when this footage is added together, these two non-foods sections are occupying nearly half of all floor feet allocated to non-foods. They account for 52% of all non-foods items.

From the more productive dollar standpoint, health and beauty aids and housewares quite obviously have earned this extra footage along with the recent increase in number of items. These departments ring up 60% of non-foods sales, and are contributing 63% of all dollar margin earned by the seven non-foods departments.

	Beauty Aids	+	Housewares	=	Total		All Non-Foods
Items stocked	381	+	167	=	548	(52% of total)	1,046
Lin. floor ft.	20.1	+	19.5	=	39.6	(48% of total)	82.9
Weekly $ sales	$408	+	$158	=	$566	(60% of total)	$943
Weekly $ margin	$133	+	$ 52	=	$185	(63% of total)	$292

The figures presented for health and beauty aids, housewares, and total non-foods, above, are based upon all store average of $17,000 a week. For purposes of self-analysis within these two departments, an operator can adjust his own store volume and the sales of his individual departments to see how he compares with the all store average.

Later in this article, there will be three separate groups of figures presented. In addition to the previously noted $17,000 weekly average, the "over $1 million" bracket of stores studied will represent a $32,000 weekly effort, and the "under $1 million" grouping will have stores averaging weekly $11,500 volume.

Health and beauty aids sales through food stores have exceeded the $1 billion mark with the 1957 total of $925 million being increased by 14% this year.

The successful selling of these popular toiletries and remedies has provided valuable experience for all stores. Operators have been able to use this merchandising background as a guide to expansion into other non-foods lines, and customers have taken the opportunity to let food stores know they like, and will demand, the convenience of truly one-stop shopping.

Principles of stocking, ordering, displaying, and evaluation of merchandise necessary for the sale of health and beauty aids have served as valuable tools while stores have progressed with more non-foods departments.

Health and beauty aids have established a "pattern," which is something other infant non-foods departments lack. These drug items are bought on demand, they are widely advertised, and are easily recognized by shoppers. Unlike many housewares, soft goods, or toys, they are usually consumed within a specific period. For this reason, ordering falls into a routine similar to replacement of groceries.

Even though they represent the non-foods department that is most easily operator-managed, health and beauty aids are still much the responsibility of the rack jobber. Rack jobbers service over half of the stores selling health and beauty aids, a department with a distribution in food stores estimated at 95%.

Increasing his share of the health and beauty aids market appreciably last year, the rack jobber now supplies about 52% of merchandise, while the wholesale grocers' and manufacturers' direct sales each account for 24% shares of this business.

Manufacturers' direct sales, according to respondents, jump to 28% in larger stores (over $1 million) and the wholesale grocers' share climbs to a similar peak in the "under $1 million" stores.

The average store in our study reported weekly health and beauty aid sales of $408 at an average 33% margin with a weekly $133 margin. In stores with a weekly $17,000 volume this profit performance would set the pace for most popular grocery categories.

Health and beauty aids have sold rapidly enough to raise their share of total store sales to 2.3%. In terms of space occupied this business has proved an eye-opener. With size and number of items growing rapidly each year, one may seek to analyze this department in terms of actual results. Has all of this growth been profitable for these operators who have enlarged their drug departments?

Comparing health and beauty aids with the twelve leading producers of gross profit per linear foot of floor space in the grocery department as revealed by *Progressive Grocer's* Super Valu Study, we find this non-foods leader challenged seriously only by one grocery category.

Canned fish, with a $6.34 margin performance per linear floor foot is the only product group that approaches the $6.62 figure turned in by the average health and beauty aids department. These Super Valu grocery averages are based upon a store with $24,000 weekly volume.

Comparing the profitability of the drug department in terms of space occupied, we find it outdistances all of the following grocery categories: canned fish, baking needs, jams and jellies, candy, household and laundry supplies, salt and spices, canned fruit, salad dressing, shortenings, canned vegetables, dried fruit, and canned prepared foods.

The average supermarket in the study reported a health and beauty aids department of 20.1 linear floor ft., with an item count of 381, or 19 items per floor ft.

Weekly sales per floor foot are $20.30. The average item in the drug department provides sales of $1.07 and a penny profit of 34.9¢ per week.

Merchandise purchased from all sources of supply combined brings an average 33% gross profit. Purchases from the rack jobber alone carry a lower 30% profit for respondents.

"Future still rosy"

Nearly 80% of stores reported sales were up over last year for health and beauty aids. The increase was 16% and it was accompanied by cheery estimates for the future. Better than 25% will enlarge their departments either by re-arranging the present shelving or gaining additional shelf space from store remodeling.

Gondola shelving is still the preferred display spot for these profitable toiletries, with nearly 80% of stores voting for this conventional merchandising method. More than 85% said they favored a "midway to late" location for their health and beauty aids.

U. S. food stores sales of varied household-hardware type merchandise increased by an industry figure of 16% during 1958 and have now reached $350 million. Our respondents' estimates closely paralleled this sales improvement picture as they indicated this volume to be 15% better than a year ago.

The housewares department has been a vehicle for the introduction of the widest varieties of new merchandise to non-foods sections. As the scope of this department widens, housewares will continue to offer a great potential for increased sales in food stores.

Selecting the proper items and keeping these housewares departments new looking and appealing are two conditions that exert a strong influence on sales.

Great has been the opportunity for related item selling of housewares, or, mixed merchandising within the regular food sections.

Many operators have cashed in on the natural sales appeal of many housewares articles and frequently merchandised them next to their grocery counterparts.

For brief but profitable periods, supers have successfully sold can openers in the canned fruits and vegetables sections; egg slicers in the egg section of the dairy department; cereal bowls with breakfast foods; soup bowls with canned soups. Each of these examples of mixed merchandising illustrates the built-in strengths of one-stop shopping.

Sales of housewares items as reported have advanced to nearly 1% (.92%) of store volume. As with health and beauty aids, housewares growth has been steady and selective. The number of items and linear floor feet allotted this department have increased while bringing financial reward to supplier and food store alike.

Presently, the average housewares department in a market with a weekly $17,000 volume measures 19.5 linear floor ft. and offers 167 different items. This department produces weekly sales of $158 at 33% profit on sales for weekly $52 margin.

Since the average housewares article is larger than most non-foods items, there are eight different items displayed within each linear floor foot. This figure also indicates the orderly approach to housewares merchandising being followed by service wholesalers and operators alike who generally refuse to overload the department and make it complicated for shoppers.

Weekly housewares sales average $8.10 per linear floor ft. with a resulting $2.67 profit per foot.

Each item on the housewares rack brings 95¢ a week in sales and a penny profit of 31.1¢ as well. Again, the margin realized from rack jobber-supplied merchandise (30%) is lower than the 33% overall profit reported.

The rack jobber wins this contest hands down. He supplies housewares to 62% of our respondents. In stores exceeding $1 million yearly volume, the service wholesaler was named 69% of the time as the man who brought in the housewares. Fewer stores under $1 million yearly average ($11,500 a week) said they relied upon the rack jobber for housewares. Of these supers, 59% said the rack jobber was their source of supply. However, the non-foods wholesaler does not loosen his grip appreciably even on these under $1 million stores.

The combined strength of skilled purchasing, ability to warehouse for long periods of time, an active service force, and guaranteed sale of merchandise foreign to food men, enables the service wholesaler to dominate the supermarket housewares business.

Again, as with health and beauty aids, operators reported housewares business uniformly better than a year ago. Business was better than a similar period in 1957 according to 64% of stores. Operators indicated these sales were 15% stronger than 1957.

Housewares departments were entirely new to 3% of respondents, a fact that illustrates the steady development of this profitable department.

A bright future for housewares is clearly evidenced by the fact that 24% of stores declared they would devote extra space to this department. They plan to get this footage by re-allocating existing store space, or, by physically expanding present sales area.

Gondola shelving is favored for display of housewares by 63% of respondents, but, the influence of pegboard as an aid in the space squeeze is clearly explained by the 38% of stores that indicated they displayed housewares on "special equipment elsewhere."

Many supermarket men have overcome the space handicap by placing long rows of housewares pegboard immediately above perishables departments.

The tops of low-built sales fixtures are pressed into service for display of bulky items like dinnerware. These flat surfaces become useful sales areas due to their location in the heavy traffic pattern produced by the presence of the perishables within these cases.

There are two areas of display most frequently cited as "best" by operators. Slightly more than half, 53%, said they preferred to locate housewares departments in the middle of the shopping trip. A "late" department is the choice of 31% of stores participating in the study.

The trend in housewares display practically reverses the pattern within health and beauty aids, where 57% preferred a late spot and 31% found a middle location the best. In both cases operators leaned heavily away from an "early" location for these non-food lines.

Promises of highly profitable returns from the sale of non-foods have not prompted supermarket operators to rush conversions to variety or general department type stores. In fact, *Progressive Grocer's* non-foods study indicates that food stores continue to absorb the seven lines of non-foods without surrendering their basic identity as food markets or disturbing the desirable flow of traffic throughout the store.

Survey data on health and beauty aids and housewares, the two most active non-foods sections, have been presented. This third article of the non-foods series takes a closer look at magazines, soft goods, toys, phonograph records, and stationery. While each of these five departments falls generally within the range of ¼ to ½ of 1% of total store sales, collectively they account for 2% of volume. These non-foods are sold at gross margins that far exceed the average on grocery products.

These departments represent the younger element in non-foods merchandising, yet they supply regular and substantial profit stimulants when handled with imagination and common sense.

Magazine sales of $110 per week in a supermarket that averages $18,800 account for better than ½ of 1% of total store sales. This sales volume is made at an overall gross margin of 26% and produces $28.60 weekly margin.

The average supermarket magazine department presents 188 different titles that include magazines, comics, youth books, and adult paper backs. Only 52 titles or 28% of the total are magazines. Most supermarkets, in gaining an exemplary department performance, have limited themselves to preferred magazine titles and rounded out a variety assortment with other publications. This gross margin is strengthened by the sale of higher profit books.

The average department occupies 12.3 linear floor ft., with about 10 ft. utilized for magazine display and the remainder for the special racks that house comics and other books. Magazine racks are generally multi-shelved wooden gondolas and more than half of stores said they located these departments late in the traffic flow. Another 36% recommended a location early in the shopping pattern and the remaining 13% indicated they displayed magazines and books around the middle of the store.

As in the case with most non-foods, the size of the magazine department varies little from the smaller to the larger supermarket.

Display of publications in good traffic spots other than the permanent rack location is a practice of magazine merchandisers who supply smaller combination racks with the top section intended for their own magazines and the lower area at the store manager's disposal. These portable subdepartments are found most frequently at the checkout, but also are often seen in wide aisles of the perishable departments.

In most supermarkets where efforts to sell magazines have been intensified by publishers and their representatives there is frequently one and in many cases two special wire holders attached to permanent positions on cash registers.

Magazines are supplied by special distributors who bring most magazines to supermarkets and handle servicing duties which include returns. These wholesalers are limited in the U. S. and for this reason it is estimated only 41% of supermarkets have magazine departments. A recent count by a leading publishers' representative placed magazines in 11,900 supermarkets. The only factor holding back these sales nationally is lack of equal availability to all stores.

More than half of our respondents said magazine and book sales were on the upgrade. They place this improvement at 14% better than 1957. The fact that another 14% said they had taken on the department for the first time this year indicates efforts are being made to make this department available to all food stores.

Even though 15% said they will devote more space to magazines, "watch and wait" seems the password since 71% intend to stand pat with the magazine and book footage they now have.

Magazine items are displayed either on gondola ends or within existing grocery shelving in 40% of stores. Special supplemental display equipment holds popular publications for 60% of respondents. Efforts to place limited sized racks in spots of heavy traffic have obviously been successful.

The second non-foods department in this report to exceed ½ of 1% of total store sales is soft goods. This news represents a near-spectacular success story because many operators recall the handicaps of only a year ago (minimum profit and quality) that limited all soft goods selling in food stores.

Increasing in numbers are manufacturers who are willing to be represented in food stores. This desire is indicated either by selling their major brand name to the supermarket or supplying a second label of equal quality. Both of these steps have helped raise the quality of soft goods in food stores and at the same time make operator and shopper more susceptible to repeat purchases.

A Detroit consumer study this year conducted in conjunction with Wayne State University indicated a strong shopper preference for stores with soft goods. Of 1150 families interviewed, 83% said they preferred to buy nationally branded soft goods when they make super market purchases!

Weekly soft goods sales of $100 at an average gross margin of 32% brings $32 gross margin to the average supermarket. The margin of profit, of course, varies with the source of supply—but so does the risk. Rack jobbers were reported as supplying 73% of soft goods at a 25% profit to operators. Groups and chains, however, realize there are preferred items of soft goods that can be quickly sold with little or no risk involved. Direct purchases of these items are sufficient to raise the gross margin to 32% for all soft goods.

Usually included on this favored direct purchase list are hosiery-socks, bras, sportswear in season, baby pants, crib sheets, briefs, etc. A major reason for this success has been the operators themselves giving promoted items a grocery-style advertising and display campaign.

An average 9.8 linear floor ft. is devoted to soft goods, and a highly selective 76 items are placed in the average department. An outstanding $1.30 sales per item leads all non-foods and another winner, a 42.1¢ margin per item, is a further advantage of strict handling.

Only eight items are offered per linear floor ft. in the average soft goods department. This fact has helped maintain order within the department. Pegboard is frequently utilized as more and more items are being transparently packaged for easy hook display.

Soft goods are displayed on regular gondola ends and shelving by 66% of respondents. Special fixtures elsewhere are used by 31% and 13% said they use tables to display soft goods.

Nearly half of stores agree sales are up, and the gain over 1957 is a rousing 23%. Another high for all non-foods is the 31% who said they intend to press more space into use for this department.

Operators divide opinions nearly equally when asked whether they prefer soft goods departments at a middle or late location.

Toy departments ($63 weekly) accounted for better than 1/3 of 1% of store volume and returned an average 33% margin, or $21 each week.

Respondents indicate departments average 9.6 linear floor ft. and contain 93 items. Each different toy produces 68¢ weekly sales with a per item profit of 22.6¢. There are ten items per linear floor foot in the stores of respondents.

Plans for expansion of the toy department are expressed by 15% of stores, and 61% indicated sales were 13% stronger than a year ago. Toys were newly stocked by 12% of stores during 1958.

The many methods of display utilized were apparent when stores answered the question, "how do you display them?" The large number of combination answers indicates how easily toys adapt themselves to supermarket impulse selling techniques.

End of gondola is a method employed by 40% of stores, and 45% also say they displayed toys within regular gondola shelving. Nearly a third of respondents place toys on special display equipment. Merchandisers are obviously duplicating toy displays in hopes of catching the adult or juvenile eye at one spot or another.

A middle to late location for toys is the choice of 87% of stores. Multiple answers again in this category raised the total to more than 100%.

Most popular toy items are bagged in transparent wrap and prepared for peg hanging. Peg-toy departments hold articles that usually sell for less than 69¢ and most of them are quickly unserviceable once in the hands of children. This fact may induce replacement sales, but it also runs the risk of parental displeasure.

Toy department shelves have expanded considerably. Many of them now include more expensive games, hobby kits, and sporting goods. "Toys" themselves, which must be interpreted as film bagged items are the leader in this non-foods section. Following in order are indoor games, hobby equipment and kits, outdoor games, and sporting goods.

Two facts learned from our study effectively describe the distribution pattern for records:

First, the service wholesaler accounts for better than 90% of this merchandise. Second, weekly volume of stores surveyed jumped from an average of $17,100 for stores selling toys to nearly $21,500 average volume for stores selling records.

Since the larger supermarkets are presently selling records, the per cent of total sales figure is apt to suffer by comparison to a lower volume market that is selling other non-foods. It is noted average record sales of $64 weekly were realized in stores with $21,500 volume. This performance is $1 better than toy sales, but, the lower volume of super markets stocking toys ($17,100) helped strengthen the per cent of total sales figure for toys.

Weekly $64 sales of records at 28% brings an $18 gross margin. These profits are obtained from a rack that measures 5.3 linear floor ft. and contains 94 different titles.

Popular discs and other singles dominate the display in the typical record department with 40 titles. The remaining titles consist of 34 long-play albums, and 20 records for children. In larger volume stores, the size of the department fails to change much, but the kind of records stocked does.

The higher profit long plays take first place with 38 titles (items) in stores with weekly volumes in excess of $30,000. Populars and other singles supply 36 titles. A five ft. rack is most popular in $12,000 weekly markets and stores averaging $31,000 report departments one half foot longer.

Phonograph records distribution took a long step in food stores during 1958. The total of stores that added this line was 35% of respondents! Records, therefore, made the greatest non-foods distribution gains for the year.

Non-foods conscious operators lean toward good space management when it comes to selling phonograph records, too. Many super market owners warn against going too heavily into records that require special equipment in the home before this special equipment has been generally purchased by their customers.

As more of this equipment is placed in U. S. homes, the market for the "new sound" recordings will expand. For the present, however, food stores are devoting most space to the bread-and-butter items in records.

Records are displayed frequently at both ends of the shopping trip. One third of stores said they locate the record department at the beginning of traffic flow and 44% indicated they prefer a late placement of records. Even though many stores said they can sell leading popular discs from a checkstand rack, most manufacturers indicate this is no place to sell a $3.98 long play.

While they may appear in the less than ½ of 1% of total sales category, phonograph records place second only to champion health and beauty aids in two performances.

Records attain $12.08 sales per linear floor ft. each week. They also rank second in the all-non-foods picture by bringing $3.40 dollar margin per linear foot.

Stores stocking phonograph records say sales of these entertainment items are up 11%, and 7% of these stores will allocate more footage to this department in the future.

Writing paper and envelopes, pens and pencils, notebooks, gift wrap, greeting cards, and playing cards are grouped in stationery departments. Glues and paper mending tapes have been brought from the housewares department and sensibly situated with other desk accessories for use in the home and classrooms.

Stationery carries a 41% profit, the greatest of all non-food margins. The top margin applied to weekly $41 sales brings $16.80 weekly profits.

Supermarkets are giving stationery an average 6.3 linear floor ft., and have filled these shelves with 47 different items. In this way, shoppers see an entire department. Each item supplies 87¢ weekly sales and 35.7¢ profit.

Most stores indicate special seasonal Christmas displays of gift wrapping, tags, and ribbon, as well as greeting cards, bring extra impulse sales and very encouraging profits during the final month of the year.

Operators generally agree stationery is a good department when kept within logical space boundaries. Departments in excess of the footage reported by respondents, except in unusual cases, will fail to provide sales and profits proportionate to space actually occupied.

Rack jobbers are servicing 57% of all respondents' stationery departments who report a margin of 39% from this source of supply. Certain select items of stationery carry little risk and such a healthy profit margin that many large chain and group organizations are buying basic envelope and writing tablet lines direct from manufacturers. These direct purchases pull the profit margin to 41% for stores studied.

"Better than last year" stationery sales were reported by 62% of stores, with the net gain at 10%. New departments are in 13% of supermarkets.

The gondola end is the prevailing display spot, with nearly 50% of stores indicating an end position, and 32% saying they used special equipment elsewhere. Where should stationery be located? Operators are evenly divided on this question, and a slight edge is given to mid-store.

57. THE COMING ERA OF IN-HOME RETAILING *

E. B. Weiss

Before I am charged with predicting the demise of the retail store, I had better state that there will always be a retail store. Moreover, I doubt that—in our time—retail volume, done away from the retail store, will ever challenge the volume done on the floor of retail outlets.

However, there is plenty of evidence indicating that the percentage of total retail sold away from the retail floor has been mounting for the last decade. Clearly, mail order retailing has been on the rise for ten years. Equally clearly, telephone retailing has shown sufficient growth potentials to encourage AT&T to go all out in encouraging more retailers to cultivate telephone volume. And there is no room to doubt that in-home retailing has moved ahead on an enormous scale; the variety of merchandise, as well as total volume, retailed this way has broadened in a remarkable way.

But shopping from home—as differentiated from shopping in the retail store—is destined for even greater growth during the 1960's than was recorded during the 1950's. I believe this will take place for two sets of reasons, one set involving some traditional factors and the second set involving novel factors.

The first group would include the following reasons:

1. Most shopping long ago lost its lure as fun; as entertainment; as diversion. With the exception of some shopping for big-ticket merchandise, most shopping today is a chore—a bore. This encourages shopping from the home.

2. Shoppers are being subjected to more inconvenience (as in the modern food super); more hazards (as in parking and in traffic); more physical problems (as in toting merchandise to the car, up into the home, etc.). Shopping from the home can be much more convenient, involve fewer hazards, fewer physical problems.

3. The time factor is also involved. In-store shopping involves considerable time, when every step of the shopping expedition is

* Reprinted by permission from *Advertising Age*, Vol. 31, No. 34 (August 22, 1960), p. 66.

E. B. Weiss, Director of Merchandising, Doyle-Dane-Bernbach, Inc.; Columnist, *Advertising Age*.

clocked. Shoppers want to shop fast—in split seconds. The very fact that so many millions of shoppers have time to shop only at night spotlights the time problem. Shopping at home can save time.

4. In-store shopping involves many costs to the shopper. These include car costs, baby-sitter costs, wear-and-tear on garments (as well as on patience). In-home shopping can be a real economy.

5. The presold brand, the standardization of merchandise, the reliability both of brands and retailers, all combine to encourage shopping from the home.

The second group of factors includes the more exciting developments. These would take in:

1. The eventual use of the home TV set as a shopping facility. This has been predicted for some years. We may be slightly closer to it today than we were a decade ago. Ultimately, it will play at least as much of a role as shopping via the telephone—indeed, it will be tied into telephone ordering from the home. Since AT&T has shown such a keen interest in exploiting the potentials of telephone shopping, it is probable that the vast facilities of this great communications system will be employed to accelerate the advent of the eventual era of shopping via the telephone and home TV screen.

2. The use by large retailers of electronic data processing and shopping.

3. The use by large retailers of electronic data processing and handling equipment will also make the various forms of in-home selling more economical to handle and therefore more feasible. The data processing equipment can record orders from the home (mail, telephone, etc.) and can also be hooked into the electronic handling equipment that sorts out and assembles the order. And, of course, this equipment can work round-the-clock—a considerable advantage in view of the great trend toward nocturnal shopping and Sunday shopping.

As a matter of fact, since some manufacturers are beginning to show an interest in going into retailing, it may be that some experiments will be made by manufacturers involving in-home retailing.

Centuries ago, a substantial percentage of retailing was done right in the home. The Yankee tin peddler typified this era. Then for decades the trend was toward doing less shopping from the home, a trend that was only temporarily decelerated by the appearance of the great mail order houses.

But now, for at least a full decade, there has been mounting evidence of a strong ground swell involving a return to shopping from the home. Modern social conditions (the working wife, etc.), modern technology (the whole spectrum of electronic communications) and modern marketing (the presold brand plus universal credit) all combine to make in-home shopping (by mail, by telephone, by T.V. screen, by the in-home salesperson) thoroughly logical.

In-home shopping, plus the vending machine (which, in big apartment houses, will permit shopping from within the building) promise to be two of the fascinating marketing developments of this decade. I think further evidence supporting this prophecy is found in the fact that, in 1960, more mail order catalogs will be distributed than ever before. And Sears reports that its mail order business is once again in a true growth situation.

58. TENANT-SELECTION POLICIES OF REGIONAL SHOPPING CENTERS *

Morris L. Sweet

The current development of regional shopping centers and their prospects for future growth raise critical questions about policies that determine the selection of retailers as tenants. What is the effect of present tenant-selection policies on distribution costs? Are present tenant-selection policies likely to contribute to the longevity of these new retailing institutions? Do their current selection policies assist or hamper the distribution of consumer goods? Do they expand or limit consumer choice? Can excluded retailers survive outside regional centers? The importance of these questions is enhanced by the possible application of selection criteria developed in regional centers to the planned redevelopment of downtown shopping areas.

Tenant-Selection Policy

This article is concerned with selection criteria related to the merchandising character and practices of retail tenants—that is,

* From *The Journal of Marketing*, Vol. 23, No. 4 (April, 1959), pp. 399-404. Reprinted with permission from *The Journal of Marketing*, published quarterly by the American Marketing Association.

Morris L. Sweet, Research Assistant Professor of Business, Lehigh University.

mass retailers, rather than merchants selling luxury goods of limited appeal. It assumed that the basis of unacceptability is not lack of financial stability or managerial competence and integrity.

The present policy

An important factor in current tenant-selection programs is the emphasis on planned or limited competition, protection against undue competition from new tenants, and limitation of the introduction of new merchandise lines by existing tenants. Retailers who are too aggressive or unorthodox in their merchandising policies are not wanted. The common result of such tenant-selection procedures is the exclusion of successful low-margin mass retailers from regional shopping centers. If possible, a buffer zone is established around the center to keep these retailers at a distance.

This policy stems from the procedure followed in planning a center. When a desirable site is found, the developer obtains an option to buy the land. He then attempts to secure long-term leases from prospective tenants as a basis for financing the construction of the center. Leases with "prestige" tenants facilitate his efforts to secure the necessary funds. The most desirable "prestige" tenant is a large traditional department store. The next most desirable tenant is a national chain.

Thus the department store and the national chain are in a strong bargaining position, and they can hold out until the developer accedes to their demands. Tight money-market conditions have made it even more necessary for the developer to grant concessions to those retailers considered blue-ribbon tenants by the lending agency. One result is the more favorable rental arrangements given to the department store. These arrangements are such that "most department store deals are of the loss leader type." [1] The reason for the preferential treatment is the drawing power of the favored retailer from which other less favored tenants benefit.

An extremely important concession to be observed in tenant-selection policy is the creation of "certain types of restrictive covenants protecting the tenant against certain types of competition." [2] This gives selected retailers the right to veto any prospective tenant.

Gimbel Bros. has the right to approve all prospective tenants at

[1] A. L. Alcorn, "Problems of Tenant Selection and Rental Determination in Shopping Centers," *Journal of Property Management* (Fall, 1956), pp. 29-35, at p. 33.

[2] "CAUGHT IN TIGHT MONEY PINCH Independents Lost in Shuffle as Centers Seek Big Names," *Women's Wear Daily* (October 19, 1956), pp. 1, 29.

the Cross County Center, Yonkers, N. Y. Macy's was unable to take over the John Wanamaker store at this center. The rental asked may have been too high, or key tenants in the center may have disapproved of Macy's as a fellow retailer. If Macy's was vetoed, the action is paradoxical in the light of later developments at the Roosevelt Field Shopping Center in Long Island.

In addition to getting free land upon which to erect its own building, Macy's was also given a veto privilege over other tenants at the Roosevelt Field Shopping Center. All other stores were to be leased on a minimum guarantee and percentage basis.[3] The poor showing of this center, one of the country's largest, has been well publicized.[4] A major factor appears to have been too much dependence on the department store. When Macy's did not provide sufficient drawing power at the center, the developer and other tenants wanted an additional heavy-traffic pulling retailer, preferably Ohrbach's. The success of a nearby discount department store made this type of retailer the logical tenant. But Macy's is believed to have demanded additional concessions before surrendering its veto against an Ohrbach type tenant.

Effects of present policy

The poor earnings record of many shopping centers has encouraged investors to re-examine the potential of shopping centers.[5] Against this skepticism should be noted the optimism of such statements as the following. According to Theodore Berenson, a leading shopping-center developer, "our centers are planned for a fifty-year business cycle, and once a regional gets in they are suicide to compete with." An Urban Land Institute Report states: "Even those regional centers without the best locations or stores will nevertheless be successful because their heavy capital investment will deter any competitor from attempting to set up a better designed center in the same trading area." [6]

But does the present tenant-selection policy warrant any such confidence in the future of the regional shopping center? Is the

[3] Eugene J. Kelley, "SHOPPING CENTERS Locating Controlled Regional Centers," *Eno Foundation for Highway Traffic Control* (Saugatuck, Connecticut, 1956), pp. 107-108.

[4] "WEAKNESSES POP UP Roosevelt Field Misses First Year Sales Goals," *Women's Wear Daily* (September 27, 1957), pp. 1, 26.

[5] David Hoddeson, "CRACKED FACADE Shopping Centers Have Lost Their Glamor for Investors," *Barron's* (August 12, 1957), p. 17.

[6] "Shopping Centers Here En Masse," *New York Times* (October 21, 1956), Section 3, pp. 1, 11.

regional center strengthening its competitive position by linking its future development to that of the department store and other traditional retailers? In the years since World War II many department stores have experienced difficulty in adapting to changing conditions and to new forms of competition. As a result of conventional merchandising methods, many national chains have also found themselves in a vulnerable position.[7]

The innovator

Historically the innovating entrepreneur has been considered a disturbing element by those whose equilibrium he upsets. Within the center the customary resistance exists toward innovative competition. This type of competition is a "dynamic which threatens the status quo, puts all known goods and methods potentially out of date, and makes hazardous all investment in specific production equipment and distribution alignments. It is the antithesis of handicap competition which aims deliberately to preserve existing channels of distribution and to give security to competitors rather than to maintain competition." [8]

If the center is successful in freezing local retailing into a mold which is immune to change, new retailing forms or concepts will probably develop outside the center. Such changes are socially desirable since they result from increased efficiency which generally brings merchandise to consumers at lower prices.

However, the established retailer is reluctant to adopt changes which disturb his smoothly functioning organization. For example, starting on a self-service basis differs from conversion to a self-service basis because it does not involve the discharge of employees or changing the physical layout of the store. The innovator does not have the problem of preserving what may have taken years to build; he utilizes innovation without concern for existing methods. Retailers of this type have enjoyed the greatest growth since World War II. Their thinking has consistently been in terms of a high turnover-low margin policy and not in terms of higher markups.

If regional centers follow a policy of excluding such retailers, their competition will only be intensified. Competition not only emanates from other regional centers, and it does not knock at the

[7] Faye Henle, "NEW LOOK IN WOMEN'S WEAR Self-Service, Discount Merchandising Pay Off for Apparel Chains," *Barron's* (October 7, 1957), pp. 5, 6.

[8] Edward M. Barnet, "Showdown in the Market Place," *Harvard Business Review* (July-August 1956), pp. 85-95, at p. 89.

center gate and wait to be admitted. Outside retailers will have to compensate the shopper for giving up the conveniences of the center. They can do this and survive only by performing the retailing function more efficiently. In this rivalry the center merchant may find himself at a disadvantage, with higher costs than the excluded retailer who is not subject to center controls and higher rents.

The degree of control a center can exercise over a particular trading area is limited by the automobile and the availability of alternative retailing facilities. These facilities are rapidly coming into existence in the form of farmers' markets, mill outlets, smaller shopping centers dominated by discount houses and supermarkets, and retailers in free standing locations. Certain of these retailers using austere or primitive facilities seem to have gauged consumer preferences better than the developers of many elaborate shopping centers.[9]

The Public Interest

Does the regional shopping center have any responsibility to the public in its selection of tenants? The answer would seem to depend upon its economic importance as a regional retailing center. The center attempts to reach its goal of becoming the area's major retailing institution by developing into the civic, cultural, and social center for the region—as integral a part of modern life as were the Greek, Roman, and medieval markets and fairs. If the center reaches this goal, it might find itself vested with substantial public responsibility and subject to some degree of public control. Thus present tenant selection procedures could play an important role in determining the extent of public responsibility.

Legal aspects

Much of the common law affecting trade emanated from the medieval markets which later developed into retail centers and were most influential from the twelfth to the fifteenth centuries. Legislation derived from these markets may become even more meaningful when applied to their lineal descendants, today's shopping centers.

> . . . But when persons hold themselves out as dealing with the public, when persons desire to enter a trade or calling of their own choice, and when exchange (trading) is publicy conducted, property and persons become subject to the overriding law of the market. Under Anglo-Saxon

[9] Morris L. Sweet, "Will Today's Farmers' Markets Become Tomorrow's Super-Market?" *Printers' Ink* (October 12, 1956), pp. 28-31.

> law (which is the basis for the Sherman Act), everyone has of common right the liberty of coming to market to buy in competition with others. Everyone has of common right the liberty of access to the market, to buy or to sell, without monopoly control, concerted action or other restraints on competition. . . .[10]

Power of exclusion

Does the shopping center begin to assume the characteristics, importance, and responsibility of the medieval market if it is the civic, cultural, and social center of the community? Its economic importance may be the result of municipal assistance in rezoning, which enables the center to occupy the most strategic location in the region. Does an excluded retailer then have grounds for demanding admission to the center on the basis of common or statutory law? Obviously, physical limitations preclude the acceptance of all who might wish to become tenants. But does the center have the unilateral right to select and exclude prospective tenants? Several decisions, although not directly concerned with the shopping center as such, suggest the difficulties that could arise from arbitrary use of such a power. These rulings also point out the need for continued administrative review of tenant-selection procedures by the center management.

The Sherman Act

In *Gamco, Inc.* v. *Providence Fruit & Produce Building, Inc.* (194 F.2d 484, 1952), the Providence Fruit and Produce Building controlled the building and surrounding land where retail buyers habitually congregated and which had the best shipping facilities in Providence. Gamco, a wholesaler, leased space in the Produce Building, and upon affiliation with a Boston wholesale fruit and produce dealer was refused renewal of its lease. The State Supreme Court upheld a suit for trespass and ejectment, but the U.S. Circuit Court overruled the decision; the Supreme Court (97 L. Ed. 636) upheld the Circuit Court ruling.

The defendants contended that the availability of alternative sites precluded any charge of monopoly, but the court held that the availability of substitute sites was not an adequate defense. It was only at the Produce Building at which buyers gathered and which had the most economical transportation facilities; it was thus a

[10] Report prepared by Dr. Vernon A. Mund for the Select Committee on Small Business, U. S. Senate, 85th Congress, 1st Session, *The Right to Buy and Its Denial to Small Business*, Document No. 32 (1957), p. 74.

monopolist's advantage to impose upon the plaintiff the work of developing another site.

The court further stated:

> Admittedly the finite limitations of the building itself thrust monopoly power upon the defendants, and they are not required to do the impossible in accepting indiscriminately all who would apply. Reasonable criteria of selection, therefore, such as lack of available space, financial unsoundness, or possibly low business or ethical standards would not violate the standards of the Sherman Antitrust Act. But the latent monopolist must justify the exclusion of a competitor from a market which he controls. . . . The conjunction of power and motive to exclude with an exclusion not immediately and patently justified by reasonable business requirements established a prima facie case of the purpose to monopolize. . . . (pp. 487, 488)

The final judgment in this case *United States* v. *Providence Fruit & Produce, Inc.*, C. A. 1533, District of Rhode Island, February 6, 1953) contained the following provision with implications for the limitation of center control over the operations of existing tenants.

IV. The company is enjoined and restrained from: . . .

(B) Interfering with or restricting any tenant in the conduct of its business; provided, however, that the Company shall have the right to promulgate reasonable, uniform and non-discriminatory rules and regulations relating to the physical operation of the Produce Building.

Another pertinent case is *American Federation of Tobacco Growers, Inc.* v. *Neal* (183 F.2d 869, 1950). The plaintiff, a farmers' cooperative, was refused selling time at tobacco auctions controlled by the defendant, a tobacco board of trade, and which was a prerequisite to doing business in the Danville, Virginia, market. The court held that the Sherman Act had been violated.

> . . . A restraint of trade involving the elimination of a competitor is to be deemed reasonable or unreasonable on the basis of matters affecting the trade itself, not on the relative cost of doing business of the persons engaged in competition. One of the great values of competition is that it encourages those who compete to reduce costs and lower prices and thus pass on the saving to the public; and the bane of monopoly is that it perpetuates high costs and uneconomic practice at the expense of the public. (p. 872)

Another legal factor which might be considered is that of the state interest involved. Federal legislation may not necessarily apply to an intrastate shopping center, but most states have legislation comparable in many respects to the federal Sherman and Clayton Acts. "Some twenty-seven states have adopted constitutional provisions which condemn monopoly, restraint of trade, restraint of competition, price fixing, and in some cases, concerted action to limit output. . . . Some forty-one states, moreover, have enacted statutory provisions against such offenses."[11] There has been limited activity under the provisions of this type of legislation. Since there is no need for new legislation to be enacted, they may serve to facilitate action by interested parties.

Conclusions

The pertinent question at this point is what would occur if the philosophy of the regional shopping center were to change, and if those tenants now considered marginal were admitted to the center. The need for such change is foreshadowed by the incipient development of a new type of retailer, a combination of the supermarket and discount house. Supermarkets are expanding even further into nonfood lines to the extent of duplicating the merchandise lines of the discount house, and discount houses are expanding into food lines. The competitive problems of the regional shopping center would be accentuated because the combined supermarket and discount house offer more intense competition in all merchandise lines. The merchants in the center, besides being subject to higher costs which limit their competitive ability, were selected on the basis of a center philosophy of limited or planned competition. This orientation would contribute little in a struggle for survival.

The advantages of admitting presently unacceptable tenants are demonstrated by the increase in the shopper appeal of downtown areas when these retailers have moved into buildings formerly occupied by traditional department stores. Further proof is suggested by the consideration given to such retailers when the regional shopping center fails to meet its sales goal. If these tenants were admitted to the regional center at its inception, its drawing power would be strengthened by providing the shopper with a more representative and desirable selection of merchandise and prices.

There would be a favorable reaction on marketing costs as other center tenants are stimulated to reduce costs and are prevented from becoming complacent. The center could then absorb and utilize innovation instead of being threatened by it. Problems could arise for the developer, with the likelihood of retailers questioning the

[11] Vernon A. Mund, *Government and Business* (New York: Harper and Bros., 1955), 2nd edition, p. 446.

suitability of present rental arrangements which are based on the costs of building and operating the center.

The absence of the low-margin mass retailers makes the center attractive largely to the shopper seeking goods of limited appeal or regarding the center as a showplace. With the passage of time another type of regional shopping center may be planned without frills for the low-cost retailer, or some of the existing centers under pressure may be reoriented toward the low-cost retailer. The use of the automobile and the increased availability of comparative price information limit the power derived from location and distance. If the center is successful, outside retailers will demand changes in admission policies; and legal controls are a possible concomitant of a closed door policy.

A modified open-door policy that gives equal consideration to those retailers now considered unacceptable or marginal is necessary; the center cannot thrive as the citadel of the *status quo*. The regional shopping center can assure itself of a healthy and continued existence and make a contribution toward lowering distribution costs by encouraging the innovating entrepreneur.

59. HIGHWAY RETAILING—THE NEXT GREAT RETAIL REVOLUTION *

E. B. Weiss

The next great retail revolution—retailing on the highways!

And, like every major change in retailing, the highway location will leave a deep imprint on the total marketing programs of manufacturers in every merchandise category.

The highway retail location is not to be confused with the shopping center. The shopping center is a retail community—the highway location is a solo operation.

The retail members of a shopping center are controlled in many facets of their operation by lease provisions and tend to act cooperatively in certain functions including promotion. The retailer on the highway functions with total independence—even his parking lot is his own.

Store architecture in the shopping center is rigidly controlled, and of course conforms to the requirements of the shopper in that particular physical environment. On the highway, store architecture enjoys a total freedom—and, as one consequence, highway stores are developing new physical concepts to meet the unique requirements of the highway shopper. Inasmuch as store architecture is premised on merchandising considerations, it follows that the new store architectural plans emerging on the highways will, through this factor alone, compel new merchandising plans by manufacturers.

It is hugely significant to note that even the food super is showing a keen interest in the solo location out on the highways. As a new type of department store, the food super apparently is concluding that it is quite capable—entirely by itself—of drawing all the traffic it requires for a profitable food plus nonfood operation. Another reason for this interest by the food super in the solo highway location may be that its newest arch rival, the newer discount house chain units—located out on the highways and which now include a food

* Reprinted by permission from *Highway Retailing—The Next Great Retail Revolution*, 1958, pp. 5-7. Copyright by Doyle-Dane-Bernbach, Inc.

E. B. Weiss, Director of Merchandising, Doyle-Dane-Bernbach, Inc.; Columnist, *Advertising Age*.

section occupying 30,000 square feet and more—have proved that they can compete on a solo basis with the strongest shopping centers. The discount house (and the modern gas station) are really sparking the retail revolution out on the highway.

There is no question that the marketing map is destined to be totally revised by the $70-billion-plus road-building plan of Uncle Sam—plus other major developments in transportation, communications, and the social aspirations and habits of our shopulation. What is the marketing significance of these developments? Let's see:

It means that the present geographical limits of commutation (from 20 to 35 miles) are to be extended—considerably.

It means that new techniques of commutation will develop—including "reverse" commutation (from the city to the outlying sections) and including a growing army of workers who travel up to 50 miles each way every day by "pooled" car to their place of employment. And the helibus, the vertical rise plane, the monorail, the "regional mass transportation system" concept will still further crash through present commutation limitations and encourage people to move still farther out.

It means that "time" and not mileage will be the factor in determining both where a family lives and where a family shops—time and *convenience*. And the new highways will shrivel time and add enormously to travel convenience. They will double the mileage covered in ten minutes, 20 minutes, 30 minutes, an hour.

It means that shopping hours will go still more nocturnal—and that peak hours will be still fewer and still more peaked. Saturday may stage a comeback.

It means that drive-in shopping will become still more common.

It means that shopping will become still more of a split-second affair.

It means more shopping by the family—more shopping by men.

It means more shopping on Sunday—and a return to more "fun" in shopping.

It means a flattening out of the shopping center development—the next great dynamic retail location development is out on the highways.

It means that the automobile, which has already changed the face of marketing, will once again make obsolete existing marketing maps—the automobile and the new highways.

It means still larger store units—the food super is thinking, for its highway locations, of units as large as 200,000 square feet all on one floor (with perhaps a mezzanine or basement). Not 20 per cent of downtown department stores can boast of 200,000 square foot units!

It means that the old concept calling for a *grouping* of stores (as in downtown and shopping center areas) will be dropped—the new *mobility* of the shopper will bring the required traffic to solo locations and limited strip locations on the highways and this has already been amply demonstrated.

It means new concepts in self-service—and just as self-service developments of the last ten years compelled major changes in manufacturers' programs, so will the new versions of self-service applied to every conceivable kind of merchandise out on the highways necessitate new thinking in packages, in pricing, in fixturing, etc.

It means new developments in warehousing—the more far-flung retailing becomes, the more important the marketing role of warehousing.

And it means—as it did in shopping centers—a greater demand for certain merchandise categories and a lessened demand for others. (Note: "Outer space" living means a growing popularity for riding horses—a trend that is right now strongly in evidence. It also means that houses will ultimately be traded in like cars, as is the case right now in the Los Angeles area. A house is no longer forever.)

Yes—the new highway location means many new marketing developments. What is more, these developments are for the near-term—not for the long term. Highway retailing is not a vision of a remote future; it is here today and growing with remarkable rapidity.

60. THE SUPERMARKET INVADES THE GENERAL MERCHANDISE FIELD *

Thomas C. Butler

Selling food and general merchandise under the same roof is not new in American retailing. However, the practice has received greater attention in recent years because of the spectacular advances which have been made in promoting this sales technique.

Salesmanship deliberately designed to catch the eye and to excite consumer interest is not new. In an earlier era of American merchandising, the General Store performed much the same function. Admittedly, the General Store didn't stock refrigerators. It offered an inventory restricted to basic, staple items which its rural clientele regarded as necessities. Its appeal, nevertheless, was exactly the same as today's super-market: a wide variety of household necessities in one location, saving valuable time for its customers.

During the early years of supermarket development in the 1930's, food stores concentrated on selling groceries, meats, produce. Gradually, nonfood selections were added to the supermarket line. Early ventures into nonfoods usually had a direct relationship to the kitchen —pots and pans and similar household products.

The picture had changed radically by 1949. The Supermarket Institute compiled statistics among the major chains at that time and revealed the following information about American supermarkets: 64 per cent of the stores were selling health and beauty aids, 10 per cent had housewares, 6 per cent had electrical appliances, 2 per cent had dry goods, 1 per cent had florist shops and—perhaps most indicative of all—one-half of 1 per cent of the supermarkets had begun to sell shoes.

These percentages increased steadily during the next ten years. From 1950, when nonfoods represented $200 million in supermarket sales, the figure rose to more than $2 billion in 1959. Nonfood sales now stand at approximately 5 per cent of total supermarket sales. In the single year 1958-59, suppliers of nonfood merchandise reported

* Reprinted by permission of the *Atlanta Economic Review*, Vol. XII, No. 2 (February, 1962), p. 10.
Thomas C. Butler, President of The Grand Union Company.

these percentage increases among supermarkets contracting for their goods: health and beauty aids, 8.7 per cent; toys, 16.4 per cent; housewares, 7.4 per cent, and phonograph records, 39.4 per cent.

Such statistics demonstrate that the traditional "food only" concept of the supermarket has been replaced by a new image in the buying public's mind. Why this image has assumed new dimensions, and to what extent, is a fundamental aspect of food retailing today.

Suburbanity, automobiles, and leisure time

At the close of World War II, there were 31 million automobiles on the American roads. Five years later, the number had increased to 49 million. In 1961, our highways were straining under the record number of more than 70 million motor vehicles.

The mobility which these automobiles provided led directly to the opening of districts outside the crowded metropolitan centers for desperately needed new home construction. An America-on-wheels became a suburban society, with approximately 70 per cent of the millions of new homes constructed since the end of the war built in areas surrounding central cities. The consumer who is buying these new automobiles and homes is working about 20 hours less per week than his grandfather did at the beginning of the century and has an income representing almost three times the buying power.

Here, then, we have the major factors underlying swift public acceptance of the one-stop shopping concept: mobility, suburban living, and an increase in leisure time. With demands of family, home ownership, and community activity all competing for the consumer's extra hours, there has been a constantly increasing tendency in recent years to buy as much as possible in a central location.

The One-Stop Shopping Concept

Supermarketing is a prime example of consumer acceptance of this one-stop trend. One of the basic appeals of the supermarket is its concentration under one roof of the services and merchandise of perhaps a dozen smaller stores. Variety of merchandise is expanded and prices go lower, a difficult combination to beat. In 1946, the average U. S. supermarket was stocking 3,000 items. By 1950, this total had grown to 3,750 items, and today it stands between 6,000 and 8,000 items. Today there are approximately 30,000 supermarkets in the country, with an additional 6,000 predicted in the next five years.

If the consumer hadn't supported one-stop shopping, the number of items offered for sale in supermarkets wouldn't have increased by almost 100 per cent in 15 years.

By what yardstick, then, might we conclude that the one-stop shopping concept must draw the line at food? I submit that there is no hard and fast rule governing what people will and won't buy in a single store. With that in mind, my own company, Grand Union, developed what we call the Grand-Way idea of selling. Merchandise lines were expanded to include not only items related directly to kitchen use, but to embrace virtually everything needed in the home. We then applied time-proven supermarket methods to merchandise this expanded inventory: self-service, wide selection, low prices through high volume. This is our company's philosophy.

We are well aware that there are those in the supermarket industry who contend that nonfood sales have only a limited future in the supermarket picture. They are entitled to their opinions, of course. We feel, however, that such a contention ignores the facts of present-day economic life. If nonfood sales in American supermarkets can rise from $200 million to more than $2 billion annually during a decade in which a minimum of professional attention was being given by supermarket management to nonfood development, then how much greater is the potential with proper management? I submit that the potential for general merchandise sales by supermarkets has not even been calculated, let alone reached.

Like it or not, even those supermarket operators who see dark days for the nonfood end of the business have had to get their feet wet to survive. Health and beauty aids and a magazine rack are as common in supermarkets today as baked beans. Kitchen aids, paper products, plastics, floor polishes, and a hundred other items are now included in the basic inventory of a supermarket.

Marketing of foods by department and chain stores

Marketing foods and general merchandise together has by no means been confined to the supermarket operator. Often it has been the nonfood merchant who has added a food line to his inventory to attract business. Many of the nation's largest department stores now have bona fide grocery departments. These, in some cases, have been augmented by meat, gourmet foods, and other departments of supermarket dimensions. More recently, several of the larger discount chains, both those specializing in hard and in soft goods, have opened supermarket-sized food departments. So, also, have some of the large drug chains.

Each of these moves has been motivated by a desire to cater to the needs of the new postwar consumer; to provide for as many shopping needs as possible under one roof.

Some of these new food departments are concessions, others are self-owned and operated. Whatever the control, it means that many other retailers—the department and drug stores, the variety and apparel dealers, and the discount houses—recognize the pulling power of food. As a basic necessity, food provides customer traffic which is then exposed to the nonfood merchandise.

Competitive advantage of food retailers

With due respect for the sagacity of our growing competition, we in food retailing feel that we have two tremendous advantages in meeting it: first, long experience in the highly competitive, extremely low-profit field of food sales; second, a large and loyal customer following. This following has been carefully cultivated—in our case—for eighty-nine years.

Our experiment in large-scale general merchandising began in 1956. We had known for some time of the trends toward one-stop shopping, the increasing sales of nonfood items in supermarkets and, of course, were well aware of the basic customer attraction in food. We were also well aware that the merchandising of hard and soft goods would require marketing skills and techniques with which we were unfamiliar. We were willing to learn.

Problems involved in entering general merchandising

1. *Recruitment of specialized personnel.* An initial necessity was the recruiting of specialized personnel from the general merchandise field: buyers, store managers, salesmen, advertising and sales promotion men, and others. We recruited and screened carefully. We are still recruiting and screening as the Grand-Way operation enlarges. Our initial care in selection was well worth the effort, for it provided us with experienced personnel who were able to deal with problems peculiar to general merchandising.

2. *Contacting of new suppliers.* One of the problems was that of ascertaining new sources of supply. While rack jobbers and direct delivery organizations are essential to the operation we planned, a

larger proportion of total requirements had to be purchased direct from suppliers; and an experienced staff, familiar with the special requirements of nonfood retailing, was able to establish and maintain our contacts in the field.

3. *Use of different control procedures.* Accounting and inventory control practices could not be transferred intact from food retailing and applied to general merchandising. If we were to be successful in the nonfood field, we had to admit at the start that we had a lot to learn. Again, it was necessary to recruit people who had experience in these particular skills. We also set up a Grand-Way advertising and sales promotion department, staffed with people who knew general merchandise and how to sell it.

With the fundamental Grand-Way operation established and functioning within the framework of the company, we continued a program of establishing contact with new sources of supply. We had to educate manufacturers, brokers, and rack jobbers to the fact that Grand Union had entered the nonfood field, not in a haphazard or temporary fashion, but in earnest. We made it plain that we were staffed, had the stores and the know-how to buy and market a full line of general merchandise on a competitive basis.

High volume, quick turnover—low prices

Calling our new stores Grand-Way Discount Centers was a logical application of the supermarket theory which we intended to apply to nonfood selling. The supermarket's success in keeping prices low results from the theory of high volume sale of quick-turnover merchandise. The word "discount" carries a connotation which is particularly attractive to today's consumer, who is more price conscious than ever. Let's be candid: the manufacturer's list price which used to set the absolute retail standard is only a memory. Acknowledgment of this is found in the words "suggested list price" found on many price tags today. The discount house, almost entirely a post World War II phenomenon, is firmly established in the American market place. It would have been inconsistent for the supermarket, accepted by the buying public because of its ability to reduce food costs, to market general merchandise on any but a discount basis.

Modern General Merchandise Store in Operation

The first Grand-Way was opened in Keansburg, New Jersey, in June 1956. This was an existing Grand Union supermarket which had been doubled in size, to 40,000 square feet. The additional 20,000 square feet of space was stocked with hard and soft goods—dresses, major appliances, toys, sporting goods, phonograph records—a multi-thousand item display of general merchandise.

The Keansburg store was used as a merchandising laboratory for approximately a year and a half. Consumer preferences were determined, slow-moving items were replaced, seasonal buying was accommodated, displays were enlarged or made smaller.

We discovered a number of things: for instance, that the more open and available the merchandise is to the consumer, the greater is the impulse to buy. This should not have been a surprise. Supermarkets for years have allowed the consumer to examine the merchandise—to pinch and squeeze, to turn over and hold up to the light.

We also learned that the movement to the suburbs brought us many shoppers who wanted large and varied displays of merchandise. They had been accustomed to shopping in metropolitan department stores. Many stocks and selections had to be enlarged to provide the basis for comparison so dear to these shoppers.

Food and nonfood: reciprocal buying effects. We had been correct, happily, in theorizing that nonfood traffic would assist food and buying and vice versa. For example, in a later adaptation of the Keansburg experiment, we enlarged a conventional supermarket to 41,000 square feet and created a Grand-Way. The existing supermarket had been recording a volume of $18,000 a week. Soon after the market reopened as a Grand-Way, food sales had risen to $45,000 per week. Thus in the same food department, with not one square foot of space added, volume rose by 150 per cent because of additional traffic generated by the general merchandise section.

As of December 1961 there were 20 Grand-Way Discount Centers (some built as such and some from enlarged food markets), carrying an inventory of 30,000-plus nonfood general merchandise items.

Present plans call for construction of four or five additional Grand-Way units during the next year. At the same time, we have also turned our attention to another facet of the flexible Grand-Way idea of merchandising—converting existing supermarkets into Grand-Way Discount Centers through enlargement.

While this program seems similar to our initial Grand-Way development, there is a decided difference. Earlier enlarged supermarkets represented an experiment. Current adaptation of this nature are a means of bringing a now-successful concept to an area where we are sure that general merchandise and food under one roof will serve consumer needs.

The first of these "conversion" Grand-Ways will open early in 1962 in Manchester, Connecticut. The completed unit will total 72,000 square feet—18,000 square feet for the existing supermarket plus a 53,500 square foot addition.

In the Grand-Way Discount Centers it is now possible to buy the week's groceries, then step into another area of the store (which may occupy an area of 100,000 square feet) and buy a refrigerator in which to store those same groceries.

In four short years we feel that we have come a long way in this new kind of food and nonfood merchandising. Originally, appliances and other nonfood merchandise were displayed on conventional grocery gondolas; now we have fixtures especially designed for general merchandise display. The first store was operated on a strictly cash-and-carry basis. It soon became obvious that department store techniques of credit buying and lay-away plans were necessary, particularly with the more expensive appliances such as refrigerators, television and hi-fi sets. Grand-Ways are self-service as far as is practically possible, but a completely inflexible policy in this regard would be self-defeating. Cameras, for example, need the presence of qualified salesmen to advise, sell, and instruct.

Our business position

We are still basically a food chain. While operating 20 Grand-Ways, we also have more than 450 Grand Union supermarkets in ten eastern states, the District of Columbia, and Puerto Rico. We plan to open 33 conventional food markets during the current fiscal year. The supermarket is here to stay; there's no doubt about that. Hundreds of new communities have been created by the building boom since the war, and a continually rising population indicates that we're not going to run out of customers.

Nonfood development within the confines of the conventional supermarket is necessarily limited by the size of the store, the extent of nearby competition, and other factors. But the $2 billion in nonfood sales which supermarkets now register annually is significant. It shows a trend which the conventional supermarket operator must take into consideration if he is to realize the most profitable return on his investment.

Why the Supermarket Entered the General Merchandise Field

Several developments have placed television sets alongside canned tomatoes in our stores:

1. A steadily increasing volume of nonfood sales in conventional supermarkets justified a reappraisal of the role of general merchandise in food stores.

2. Consumers in recent years have evidenced a growing preference for one-stop shopping. The traditional supermarket proved this. We at Grand Union have proved to *our* satisfaction that the pattern does not stop with food.

3. Some discount houses, department stores, drug—even variety and apparel chains—have become direct competitors of the supermarket by the addition of food departments as adjuncts to their general merchandise sections.

4. Supermarket operators, like everyone else, have been caught in a rising spiral of the cost of doing business. Inflationary pressure, more costly stores, increased labor rates, and a host of other economic factors have contributed to this. Supermarkets, with their traditionally low net profit margin of less than 2 per cent, must exploit every means of profit increase. Today's well-run nonfood department can operate at substantially higher gross margins than can be generated in the food departments. Here is one way to keep costs low. It is only logical that a food chain should be interested in its development.

You might say we have come full circle; that Grand-Way is yesterday's General Store. So it is. The General Store served a specific need in its time. So does Grand-Way today. The population swing is away from the central city concept which dominated our life for the first half of this century. This is creating a buying pattern in many ways paralleling the social situation characteristic of an earlier time.

How far will we go in the general merchandise field? Only time, continued experimentation, and the housewife can answer that. We will expand or contract our inventories in response to consumer reaction. We have a flexible idea and will be learning for a long while to come. But we feel definitely that we are on the right road.

61. MOTOR PRODUCTS MARKETING *

James S. Cross

Several months ago our Marketing Management indicated that they would like to have some thought given to the question, "What kind of service stations are we likely to have in the United States ten years from now?" The purpose of this assignment was to help in establishing a framework within which certain future marketing decisions could be made.

In dealing with a question of this nature, there are basically two ways to proceed. First, one can examine the trends of the past for some guide as to what might be anticipated in the future. Second, a careful study can be made of the present marketing situation, the likelihood of change can be examined, and the alternative directions of the change can be postulated and analyzed.

In our thinking about the future course of motor products marketing, we used both of these approaches. We were able to identify a considerable number of distinct trends, including the following:

1. Early patterns in motor products marketing.
2. The split account.
3. Company owned and operated stations.
4. Large volume outlets.
5. Private brand competition.
6. Multi-grade marketing.
7. Trends in prices, taxes and margins.

Early patterns in motor products marketing

We date motor products marketing from around the turn of the century when the relatively light weight high speed gasoline engine was sufficiently developed to be practical for automotive transportation. The major product of the petroleum industry at that point

* Reprinted by permission from James E. Cross from a paper for presentation to a session of the Lubrication Committee, Division of Marketing, of the American Petroleum Institute at Detroit, Michigan, February 22, 1962.
James S. Cross, Manager, Economics Department of the Sun Oil Company.

was kerosine. It wasn't until 1911, in fact, that gasoline consumption overtook kerosine for the first time.

The tankwagon system that the industry had devised for the distribution of kerosine was well organized when gasoline came upon the scene. Initially, gasoline was distributed in this same manner. The early motorist could also obtain fuel for his automobile at grocery stores, hardware stores, implement dealers, feed merchants, livery stables, blacksmith shops, or bicycle shops, or even at the local apothecary store, as benzene. These same establishments generally carried lubricating oils and greases.

Servicing the motorist at this time was an adventure with a measuring can and funnel. To dispense gasoline a dealer would fill a five-gallon can from a barrel or 55-gallon drum stored in a small enclosure situated in back of his store, carry the can out to the curb, and then pour the fuel into the car's gas tank through a chamois-lined spout.

In those earlier days, most of the lubricants sold were lightly refined, high-viscosity products made from specific types of crude. Requirements were not severe, since engine speeds were low and clearances between moving parts were large. Combustion pressures did not impose excessive loads on rings, cylinder walls, or bearings. Engines were relatively simple in design; compression ratios were low by present day standards; octane requirements were minimal and fuel additives unnecessary.

It is recorded that there was a genuine doubt that the "horseless carriage movement" would ever be more than a fad. The need of every motorist, it was pointed out, to keep his car in an expensive "automobile house" equipped with complete repair facilities, drainage pits, washing apparatus, and turntable would be a deterrent to more widespread ownership of the automobile.

Proof of the lack of vision on the part of the early forecasters, however, was soon evident in the steady rise of automotive transportation. And as the number of motor vehicles in the country increased, so did the need for petroleum products. Garages were soon established, providing new outlets to satisfy the growing consumer demand for gasoline, lubricants, and greases. Other types of retailers, in the meantime, were finding that the distribution of petroleum products was becoming an increasingly important part of their business.

As the use of the automobile expanded, oil companies recognized the need to set up retail establishments that could serve the public more effectively. Thus, a new institution, the "filling station," was born, where a motorist could drive in and have his tank filled conveniently. There is a great dispute as to who built the first real station. Among the earlier stations was one built in 1907 by the Standard Oil Company of California. It consisted primarily of a main storage tank connected by a feed line to a 13-gallon tank, a glass gauge, a valve-controlled hose, and a display of oils and greases on two shelves.

The filling station concept spread rapidly as suppliers attempted to capture a larger share of the growing market. In the decade from 1910 to 1920, the number of stations increased at the rate of about 1,200 a year, and by 1920 there were 15,000 in operation. Competition among the oil companies for the automobile business was so strong that stations were built wherever there were motorists to be served.

During the period of the 1920's motor vehicle registrations increased at the rate of 13 per cent per year, while gasoline consumption increased at the rate of 16 per cent per year. In the meantime, due to the impetus given the industry during World War I and because of new discoveries of crude oil in the Southwest, supply increased at an even faster rate than demand, resulting in glutted markets.

Under these circumstances, the inevitable market disturbances occurred. Price cutting, secret rebates, and other concessions given by suppliers brought on waves of price wars. These were met by further price cutting or by giving away premiums, such as dishes, blankets, and flashlights. Even trading stamps were used as a competitive weapon in this area.

Despite turbulent marketing conditions the industry grew very rapidly and by 1929 there were in the United States 121,513 filling stations. In a short thirty-year period the industry had come of age.

The split account

Let us stop at this point and go back and pick up another trend—the rise and fall of split account marketing. The typical service station of today handles several brands of lubricating oil, and often sells competing brands of tires, batteries, and accessories. But it markets only one brand of gasoline, and in this respect is fairly unique among retailing institutions. It may be interesting to trace the development of this sales pattern.

During the early days the oil companies did not command sufficient capital to build their own stations. At the same time, the drive for gallonage among competing suppliers was so great that they were willing to consider any available outlet. Further, the so-called general store had historically sold competing brands of a wide variety of items. Thus, it was a natural development for an outlet to retail the motor fuel and lubricants of more than one supplier. At some locations as many as 20 pumps were installed to handle the numerous brands of gasoline on the market.

While reliable industry data on split accounts are not available, we have ascertained from our own records that in 1936 Sun Oil Company sold gasoline to over 9,000 dealers, of which 32 per cent were split accounts. Since that time split accounts have declined, until today we have only a few left. In fact, in our whole marketing territory less than 0.5 per cent of the stations are split accounts.

The factors which contributed to the demise of the multi-brand station are several. First, from the motorist's point of view, he soon learned to recognize and respond to the distinguishing characteristics of the single brand outlet which guaranteed him product quality. Also, he often found the split account station out of the particular brand he desired. From the dealer's point of view, by operating on a single brand basis it was found that the supplier relationship was much simpler and less costly. The dealer soon realized that most of his customers were purchasing one particular brand anyway and that he could, by suggestion, sell the others on the same brand. And most important, the dealer found that a single brand station developed larger volume and therefore greater profit.

Finally, the supplier found that undivided accounts were increasing his volume at a much faster rate than multi-brand stations. Also, by selling to undivided stations he was able to reduce selling and delivery costs, and since volumes were larger he was able to justify the greater capital investment required to provide more adequate facilities and service.

Company owned and operated stations

During the period of the 1920's and early 1930's one of the most significant developments in retailing was the growth of the chain store. This idea was embraced by the oil industry. It was felt that the advantages offered by vertical integration of operations from the well to the ultimate consumer, better choice of locations, and coordinated merchandising and promotion would serve to eliminate many of the inefficiencies which had inevitably crept into the dealer type operation. The chain store idea applied to service stations probably would have fallen of its own weight eventually, but in 1935, promoted by legislation which levied a special tax on chain stores, companies in many parts of the country acted to lease their stations to dealers. The key to successful service station operation was found to lie in the close contact between the dealer and his customers and between the dealer and his employees. Promoted by the profit motive, the independent businessman was in a better position to provide the service required while keeping operating and overhead costs at a minimum. Thus the lessor-lessee arrangement became the dominant factor in service station operation.

The drive toward high volume outlets

The importance of reducing unit overhead by means of high volume stations had been recognized early in the game. But the industry seemed more intent in building large numbers of stations in the 1920's and early 1930's rather than high volume outlets. Although there was some evidence of a reversal of this pattern in the late 1930's, the trend was choked off during the war years.

Significant changes began to emerge, however, in the service stations of the postwar era. The completely integrated building, which contained lube-bays, wash-bays, as well as a show room for tires, batteries and accessories and the dealer's office under one roof gained wide acceptance. Many of the more marginal outlets disappeared and much emphasis was placed on obtaining high throughput per account. The impetus toward high volume outlets came from the desire to reduce distribution costs as well as the desire to earn a fair return on the increasing investment required in land, building and equipment to establish a modern service station.

As a result of this drive toward high volume outlets, competition for the motorist's business intensified. Large sums were spent for advertising in an attempt to build customer loyalty to a particular brand, and suppliers promoted the use of consumer credit as a further means of increasing brand loyalty. When market studies emphasized that consumer purchasing patterns were influenced primarily by the station operator, more money and effort than ever before was spent on dealer training.

Another manifestation of the drive for volume was the revival of the use of trading stamps and premiums as a means of attracting and holding additional business.

Private brand competition

The decade of the fifties saw the emergence of the private brand outlet as a major force in motor products marketing. In Sun's marketing area, for example, the number of these outlets increased 67 per cent from 1954 to 1960. During this same period there was only a 2 per cent increase in the number of major brand outlets.

Prior to the fifties, the private brand outlet had not gained very much consumer acceptance. These stations often sold an inferior grade of gasoline, were unattractive in appearance, and provided very little service for the motorist. However, where competitive forces allowed this type of outlet to sell at a substantial discount from the market price, private branding flourished.

More recently, most private branders have been characterized by the large multi-pump type modernistic establishment. Further, competition for volume among suppliers has resulted in the ready availability of good quality gasoline. At the same time, the increasing costs incurred by typical branded service station operators resulted in a reluctance to engage in price competition with the high volume low margin operators. The motorist, in the meantime, with his growing concern for economy, found in the private brand marketer a means of lowering his automobile operating cost. These developments have enabled private brand outlets to gain a substantial share of the market.

In addition to the keen competition from within the oil industry, service station retailing is now faced with new and perhaps even stronger competition from other types of retail establishments. Food stores, mail-order chains, discount houses, and other outlets are expanding into discount oil marketing operations.

Multi-grade marketing

Another significant development has been the trend toward multi-grade marketing. Consumer preference during the 1950's for higher-compression engines resulted in higher octane requirements in motor fuel. This trend, coupled with the fact that older cars were still on the road, led to a growing spread in octane requirements within the passenger car fleet. In 1953, the approximate beginning of the so-called octane race, there was a spread of about seventeen research octane numbers between the lowest and highest requirement cars. By 1959 the spread had increased to about twenty-five research octane numbers. To meet this problem Sun Oil Company abandoned its traditional one grade policy and adopted custom blending. This multi-grade system has enabled us to cover the entire octane requirement spectrum. Other marketers met the problem by adding a third grade.

The present emphasis on economy cars has brought an end to the octane race, at least for the present, but not the problem of covering a wide range of octane requirements. Currently some marketers are introducing sub-regular grades to satisfy the demands of the economy buyer as well as to meet the growing competition of the discount operation.

Trends in prices, taxes and margins

Perhaps the most significant set of trends which we should examine are those which relate to prices, taxes and margins. We have observed that throughout the history of the industry the marketer has been periodically squeezed by depressed price levels, low margins, increasing costs, and higher taxes. I would like to focus your attention now upon the situation which has been developing since the end of World War II. This is shown on Chart I.

First, note that the price of regular grade gasoline increased from 23.71 cents per gallon in 1947 to 30.76 cents per gallon in 1961. It is significant, however, that most of the observed increase occurred prior to 1958. There has been little change in the average price since 1957.

Second, taxes during the period increased from 6.18 cents per gallon to 10.23 cents per gallon, an increase of 66 per cent.

Third, the dealer tankwagon, which represents the price that the dealer pays to his supplier, increased from 12.33 cents per gallon in 1947 to a peak of 16.69 cents per gallon in 1957 and has since declined to 15.80 cents per gallon.

Finally, the dealer margin, after increasing from 4.60 cents per gallon in 1947 to 5.42 cents per gallon in 1957, has since declined to 4.73 cents per gallon. This represents the lowest margin since 1948.

If you can picture a backdrop to this chart showing crude prices which have increased almost four cents a gallon during the period, hourly earnings which have almost doubled during the period, and a construction cost index which has more than doubled, this would serve to bring out in sharper focus the problems faced by the oil marketer.

So much for past trends. Some of these we may lay aside as having run their course, while others undoubtedly have enough momentum to carry them into the future.

CHART I

PRICES, TAXES AND DEALER MARGINS—REGULAR GRADE GASOLINE

(FIFTY-FIVE CITY SURVEY IN THE U. S.)

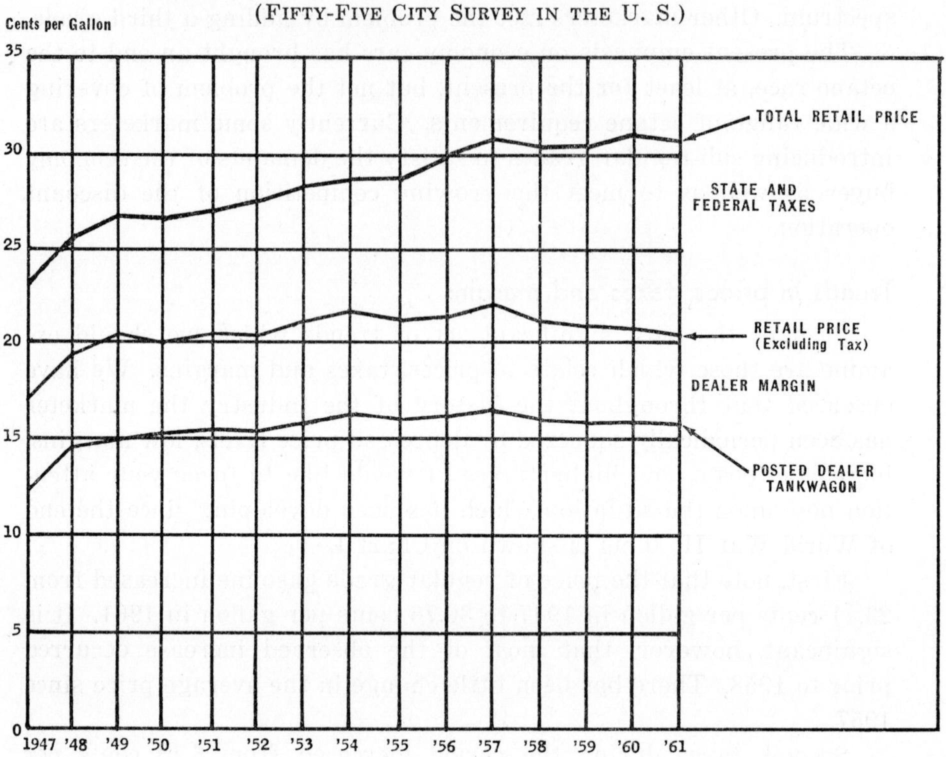

The Current Situation

Let us now take a look at the current marketing situation to see whether or not anything might be gleaned which would have predictive value for the future.

What elements are there in the current marketing picture which would lead one to say that changes are in the making? We might consider such factors as the changing role of the automobile, dealer turnover, the effect of taxes, and the effect of zoning and other locational problems.

The changing role of the automobile

While very meager quantitative data exists on the psychological relationship between the motorist and his car, we have evidence that subtle changes are taking place. We learn that today's automobile owner views his car on a functional basis and is no longer as emotionally involved with it as was true in the past. Automobile users of today—and this will probably be more true in the future—want and need a rather wide variety of highly specialized transportation vehicles. They appear to be more interested in the performance features of automobiles and less interested in styling and unneeded horsepower. Correspondingly, today's consumer appears less interested in purchasing gasoline which is higher in quality than that required by his car.

Thus it appears that the future motorist is likely to be less guided by emotional buying motives and more influenced by rational purchasing considerations.

Dealer turnover

The petroleum industry today is faced with a serious problem of attracting and holding qualified men in the service station business. On the one hand, the qualifications of a service station dealer are high. He should have substantial managerial ability, an attractive personality and temperament, and should be in a position to supply capital in the amount of several thousand dollars. On the other hand, due to increasing costs and decreasing revenue, his take home profits have not been keeping pace with renumeration in alternative occupations.

In spite of intensified efforts, the industry is losing approximately 28 per cent of its dealers each year. It is evident that dealer availability will be a key factor in shaping the course of future marketing developments.

The effect of taxes

Turning now to the tax problem, Table 1 indicates the effects of gasoline taxes in Sun Oil Company territory during the past four years. During this time taxes increased 2.10 cents per gallon. Concurrently, the price paid by the consumer increased 0.45 cents per gallon, equal to 21.4 per cent of the tax increase. At the same time, the dealer's margin declined by 0.54 cents per gallon, equal to 25.7 per cent of the tax increase. The suppliers' tankwagon price, in the meantime declined by 1.11 cents per gallon, equal to 52.9 per cent of the tax increase.

While the incidence of taxation is difficult to measure precisely, due to other factors which influence price, it is our contention that the burden of the tax increase was absorbed approximately as indicated by the ratios on the table. In other words, we would argue that, if the taxes had not been imposed, prices would not have been very much different than they actually turned out to be during the past four years.

Thus, the economic effects of high and increasing excise taxes must be borne in mind when considering possible restructuring of the industry in future years.

Zoning and other locational problems

Still another serious problem confronting the industry is the increasing number of unfavorable interpretations of local zoning ordinances. As a result, desirable service station sites are becoming

TABLE I

DISTRIBUTION OF GASOLINE TAX INCREASES IN SUN'S MARKETING AREA

1957-1961

Gasoline Taxes Have Increased	2.10¢ per gal.	100.0%
In the Meantime—		
The Price to the Consumer Increased	0.45¢ per gal.	21.4%
but		
Dealer Margins Have Declined	0.54¢ per gal.	25.7%
and		
The Posted Dealer Tankwagon Has Declined	1.11¢ per gal.	52.9%

(Source: Fifty-Five City Survey)

increasingly difficult to obtain. The arguments against a station at a given site usually include those of fire and traffic hazard despite impartial statistics which show the opposite to be true. Statements by city planners indicate that the real objection to service stations has been in terms of an "esthetic nuisance." The attention getting design and displays at stations have frequently been termed "garish." The prevailing attitude seems to be that service stations are fine—as long as they are in someone else's neighborhood. The cost of real estate has increased rapidly in recent years, particularly in areas experiencing high rates of population growth. This, in turn, has intensified the pressure to obtain high throughput per outlet.

Other locational problems result from the current highway construction program. The dislocation of established traffic flows will render many thriving stations in existence today unprofitable. Naturally the new highways also offer new market opportunities, and stations will have to be located not only along these roads but on feeder routes as well.

The Future of Motor Products Marketing

Let us return now to the question originally posed, "What kind of service stations are we likely to have in the United States ten years hence?" One assumption that might be made is that no change will occur—that motor products will be marketed ten years from now in much the same fashion as they are today. There are two good reasons for thinking this might be so. One is the normal resistance which everyone has to change. Simple lack of momentum may serve to maintain the status quo. The other reason has political and sociological implications. It may be felt that the status quo *should* be preserved, by legislative action if necessary, in order that people and property will not be adversely affected by the impersonal forces of the market place. For these reasons it can probably be safely said that much of our marketing structure which is in place today will still be here at the end of a decade.

But on the basis of the trends which we have studied and the key problems which affect the industry today, we would say that some fundamental change is inevitable. It appears to us that we shall depart, to a significant degree, from traditional marketing patterns, while at the same time incorporating the successful features of our present system into tomorrow's motor products marketing. For planning purposes we have assumed that three basic types of stations will emerge, modified and tailored to serve the needs of a particular situation:

1. High volume stations primarily offering motor fuel and oil.
2. Neighborhood "servicecenter" stations offering complete automotive servicing.
3. Horizontally integrated service stations offering diversified product and service lines in addition to complete automotive servicing.

High volume stations

Recognizing the needs of the transient and commuting segments of the motoring public, one of the basic station types of the future is expected to be the high volume station designed primarily to sell motor fuel and oil. This type of outlet would also handle a general line of standardized accessories and minor parts which would be sold but not installed.

The station site would be long rather than deep to allow fast moving traffic to enter and exit with minimum effort. The station building would be minimal, consisting primarily of office and storage space, and rest rooms. Pump islands would be organized for complete fast automotive service, and would be arranged so that a number of cars could be handled at the same time.

These stations would be strategically situated, primarily on highways handling commuter traffic or on feeder routes leading to super highways.

The key features of this type of station would be fast, efficient service, rapid customer turnover, high gallonage and low unit overhead. It would be anticipated that prices would be established which would be lower than those prevailing at neighborhood stations.

Neighborhood "servicecenter" stations

In view of the requirement of the American family to have automotive equipment readily available to meet basic transportation needs, a distinct station type of the future is likely to be one situated in or near community centers. We would foresee this type of station designed to offer complete automotive servicing facilities, in addition to providing motor fuel and lubricants, as well as a complete line of tires, batteries and accessories.

Personnel is likely to be one of the limiting factors to this type of operation. Dealers would be required who were well versed in retailing management, including such areas as the selection and utilization of manpower, merchandising techniques, and inventory control. In addition, well trained, highly skilled service personnel would be needed.

Another limiting factor is likely to be the availability of good sites. Where these are located close to prime residential districts there may be a requirement that they blend in with surrounding buildings. Heavy investment will undoubtedly be required for land and buildings, as well as for the equipment necessary for proper maintenance and repair of automotive equipment.

The key attributes of this type of station would be efficient service and convenience to nearby customers. It would be expected that prices would be established at such stations which would be higher than those prevailing at highway locations.

Horizontally integrated stations

Based upon the concept that the consumer of the future will be heavily oriented toward so-called "one stop marketing," we anticipate opportunities for motor products to be integrated with other merchandise lines. Under this type of arrangement service stations could operate independently within a complex of retail establishments, or could be integrated, more or less formally, in joint ventures with other retail institutions. The latter might include food supermarkets, restaurants, laundry, dry cleaning establishments, or even banks. The key marketing considerations involved in this idea would be the opportunities afforded to take advantage of high consumer traffic generated by the joint operations as well as the opportunity to spread the overhead of an extremely expensive piece of property. Thus, the horizontally integrated station would offer the fundamental advantages of conserving consumer time while increasing marketing efficiency within the limitations of an ever decreasing margin.

Conclusions

From the above analysis we can distill out the following significant conclusions:

1. It is evident that motor products marketers will be faced with the necessity, in the future, of improving efficiency and reducing unit costs in order to operate profitably within the marketing margins which are likely to be available.
2. A great many of the marketing problems which we see before us can be resolved into the common denominator of site selection and development.
3. Many of the remaining problems which we visualize are related in some way to the selection, training, development, and remuneration of qualified dealers. Highly qualified dealers are scarce.
4. Finally, we would emphasize the importance of anticipating the future requirements of the motoring public and of maintaining a position at the leading edge of prevailing trends in motor products marketing.

62. THE AMERICAN RETAILER—SUBSERVIENT TO THE PUBLIC? *

Stanley C. Hollander

Two thousand years ago retailers ranked at, or near, the bottom of the social scale. The Greek and Roman philosophers may have regarded retailing as a necessary evil, but they had little feeling, other than contempt, for the merchandiser. Plato, for example, felt retailing should be confined to "those weakest in bodily strength and, therefore, of little use for any other purpose," and ranked retailers as "servants little above the dullest class of hirelings." [1] During the Middle Ages the scholastic philosophers seemed to hold about the same views as did their Graeco-Roman predecessors and authorities. Public opinion of retailing probably exhibited a fairly close resemblance to the philosophers' views; certainly we know of few, if any, ancient or medieval retailers who were considered eminent citizens or leading figures in their day.

The humble origins of the retailing profession may be considered simply as an interesting fact without any particular modern significance. Or, the same origins may be viewed as a source of satisfactions to today's large-scale merchant who feels some sense of pride in the way the business has developed. But this humble historical background may also have some fairly important implications for contemporary merchandising. This article seeks to explore these implications with particular reference to the recruiting and training of retail personnel and to the conduct of retail businesses.

Is subservience necessary?

The basic questions are whether retailers are, or should be, subservient because of the historical degradation of the merchant

* From the *Journal of Retailing*, Vol. XXXIV, No. 3 (Fall, 1958), pp. 143-153, 175-176. Copyright 1958, New York University. Reprinted with permission of the author and the *Journal of Retailing*.

Stanley C. Hollander, Professor of Marketing, Michigan State University.

[1] *The Republic*, Book II. Interesting collections of similar views from ancient and some medieval writers can be found in such sources as Paul H. Nystrom, *Economics of Retailing* (3d ed.; New York: Ronald Press Company, 1930); Edmund Whitaker, *History of Economic Doctrines* (New York: Longmans, Green and Company, Inc., 1951); William F. Kelley, "The Development of Early Thought in Marketing and Promotion," *The Journal of Marketing*, July 1956, pp. 62-67.

and whether customers consequently expect a deferential or servile attitude. At least one modern sociologist seems to feel that the answers to these questions are affirmative, and we will be able to note reflections of the same thinking in many other writers. Caplow, discussing the fact that American retailers, unlike their European counterparts, often live some distance from their stores, comments:

> One basic motive for separation is that the norms of deference imposed on the shopkeeper prevent him from displaying a distinctly higher status than his customers, while his aspirations toward the role of businessman impel him to do so.[2]

Consequently, the retailer who wishes to live and enjoy himself in business-class surroundings and in the style to which his success has entitled him has to get out of the neighborhood and become anonymous, so far as his customers are concerned. In the store, however, according to this point of view, deference is still essential:

> . . . personal relations with cutomers are often the decisive factor in the history of a retail business. . . . The merchant is expected to minimize his status and exaggerate that of the customer by exaggerated forms of deference, by yielding in minor arguments, by expressing more interest in the customer's personal affairs than the customer is expected to show in his, and by small personal services. . . .[3]

A well-known study of one community within a large metropolis seems to provide a neatly corroborative example of this position:

> The storekeeper's status in the community depended in part on his type of store. Those who served the apartment population gained no local status thereby, whether they resided locally or kept their residence outside. Among the more prosperous of the old storekeepers, a number had moved to Brooklyn and commuted to work, while others had stayed, declaring that their property was not safe in the neighborhood unless they were there to watch it. On the whole, it was smaller, less pretentious of the shopkeepers who retained their local residence, and, with few exceptions, they were not distinguished from their neighbors by either their wealth or social position.[4]

[2] Theodore Caplow, *The Sociology of Work* (Minneapolis: University of Minnesota Press, 1954), pp. 128-29. Although the text is by no means clear on this point, Caplow possibly may be referring only, or especially, to smaller retailers. The tendency to lump all merchants together, both large and small, is a common characteristic of much of the literature.

[3] *Ibid*, p. 119.

[4] Caroline F. Ware, *Greenwich Village*, 1920-1930 (Boston: Houghton-Mifflin Company, 1935), p. 64. Miss Ware does not consider whether the successful storekeepers moved because of inability to retain trade while enjoying their prosperity or whether they were the only ones who could afford to move or whether there might have been other reasons for moving, such as the desire to be near friends or family.

Social status and shopping expectations

In an extremely interesting speech, to which we shall return later, the well-known marketing research director of the *Chicago Tribune,* Pierre D. Martineau, postulated a subservient relationship between salespeople and *some* customers: "The lower status shopper expects the clerks to be 'just people.' The upper middle-class woman expects them to be high-salaried servants." [5]

Certain patterns of marketing behavior seem to be associated with the view that extreme deference is the keynote of retailer-customer relations. The writer has heard one automotive executive state that his company, as a result of motivation studies, seeks dealers who are obviously substantial enough to stay in business and to reassure the customer that service will be available in future years, but who at the same time do not seem superior to, or removed from, the company's working-class customers. The firm avowedly shuns retailers who will advertise themselves as "the largest dealer in the community" or otherwise obviously display dominance and status. One of the editors of *Fortune* has observed that "What is really lacking in the salesperson is a sense of individual dignity." [6] Professor Beckley has pointed out the way in which failure to protect the status of the employee and to insist that "the customer is always right" has complicated the human relations problems of retail management.[7] The impact of status considerations upon recruiting, at both the clerical and executive levels, needs little elaboration.

If retailing really is a task for high or medium-grade servants and successful operation really is dependent upon obsequiousness, deference, and subordination, then retailers and retailing teachers should face up to the unpleasant truths. There is considerable evidence, however, that this is not the whole story.

Influence of industrial revolution

For instance, the historical argument for subservience based on the theory of a "humble origin" tends to ignore the influence of the industrial revolution on social status. An eminent British economic

[5] Robert L. Clewett (ed), "The Pattern of Social Classes," *Marketing's Role in Scientific Management* (Chicago: American Marketing Association, 1957), p. 242.

[6] William H. Whyte, Jr., "What's Wrong with Retail Salesmanship," in *Why Do People Buy?: A Close Look at Selling* (New York: McGraw-Hill Book Company, 1953), p. 59.

[7] Donald K. Beckley, "Identifying Problems of Human Relations in Retailing," *The Journal of Marketing,* July 1955, pp. 51-53.

historian has maintained that retailing became "middle class" with industrialization:

> This advancing middle-class group speedily produced its effects on other parts of the social structure. With its expanding consuming power and rising standards of living, it transformed the market for consumers' goods and services. It needed many more superior shop-keepers and master craftsmen to minister to its needs, and brought into being a host of shops which set out to do a predominantly middle-class trade. At the same time it required more attorneys and solicitors, more medical men a cut above the ordinary country surgeon or apothecary, more ministers of religion, especially in Great Britain of nonconformist persuasions, and presently more schoolmasters and schoolmistresses capable of giving its children a sound middle-class education. The professions and the superior tradesmen, hitherto mainly dependent on upper-class custom, came to provide more and more for middle-class needs and became therewith themselves more and more "middle class." [8]

We can also turn to studies of consumer attitudes, motivation, and behavior to see what we can learn about customer expectations of store service. The literature on store selection is amazingly sparse, and what does exist provides contradictory evidence.

Undoubtedly many more studies have been made than have been published, since private research is often considered confidential. Undoubtedly, also, the enormous difficulties of truly ascertaining *why* people patronize particular stores have, or should have, deterred some of the studies. Blankertz has shown how the expressed rankings of Philadelphia stores, made by a very carefully selected sample of charge account customers, failed to correspond at all meaningfully with the shopping behavior of the universe from which that sample was drawn. He concluded that expressed explanations for store preferences are often simply pleasant rationalizations for past behavior.[9]

Nevertheless it seems that neither merchants nor students of retailing have gathered as much information as they should on who shops where, and why. This lack has been noted many times without very much response, although the recent surge of interest in motivation research seems finally to have evoked some stimulating work on the problem.

[8] G. D. H. Cole, "The Conception of the Middle-Class." *British Journal of Sociology*, 1950, pp. 279-80.

[9] Donald F. Blankertz, "Motivation and Rationalization in Retail Buying," *Public Opinion Quarterly*, Winter 1949-1950, pp. 659-68. The value scales on which the sample was requested to rate the stores apparently did not include location, which seemed to be crucial when actual behavior was measured, since customers seemed to concentrate their shopping in one of the two clusters that characterize Philadelphia's downtown department stores.

Psychological studies

To some psychologists and psychiatrists, apparently, the retailer-consumer relationship often seems a contest from which the customer wishes to emerge with a feeling of triumph (according to Thorndike)[10] or sometimes a masochistic feeling of defeat (according to Bergler).[11] Thorndike argues that the "flattery and servility of the old-time shopkeeper" has been replaced by discounts, bargain offers, trading stamps, and added services, all of which appeal to the customer's "great pride . . . in a laborious astuteness in [petty] bargaining." Economists and morialists may scorn "that miserable ingenuity," but:

> . . . we shall not get rid of it by scorning it. We must either cure people of the cravings to which it appeals, or satisfy those cravings in some better way. One better way, though doubtless not the best, is for the buyer to have illusory feelings of sagacity, power, and victory by choosing from several mail-order catalogues, or from the offerings of several shops, even though he gets no economic advantage from the use of his time."[12]

The act of buying is for the bargain hunter not a rational situation but a battle of wits. He tries to outsmart the seller who, on the other hand, seeks to give him, the involuntary "sucker," the narcissistic illusion of triumph. That many people buy for the sake of a bargain and not because of need is intuitively known to every merchandiser; he bases his "sales" on that fact.[13]

Study of English customers

Others, while not going as far as Thorndike and Bergler, still see the retail salesman supporting the customer's ego. When she first came to England in the 1930's, Marie Jahoda, eminent European psychologist, conducted an extensive marketing research study for Messers, P. E. Gane Ltd., large-scale manufacturing retailers of furniture in Bristol and Newport, England. Her study, which is filled with rich detail on consumer reactions to the stores and their merchandise, was released for publication after the war and appeared as Section III of *The Sociological Review* (a British journal) for

[10] E. L. Thorndike, *Human Nature and the Social Order* (New York: The Macmillan Company, 1940), pp. 626-28.

[11] Edmund Bergler, "Psychopathology of 'Bargain Hunters,'" *Journal of Psychopathology*, April 1947.

[12] Cf., Gilbert Burck, "What Makes Women Buy?" *Fortune*, August 1956, pp. 93 f. Donald F. Blankertz, "Mr. Retailer, What Do You Know About Your Customers?", JOURNAL OF RETAILING, Spring 1950, pp. 28 ff.

[13] Bergler, *op. cit.*, p. 623.

1946, under the title, "The Consumer's Attitude Towards Furniture." The report is filled with references to an "atmosphere of personal service and personal interest in every customer" as one of the firm's strong points in competing with other local shops and with the major London outlets. However, she also notes that many customers are affected by a fear of seeming inferior or unknowledgeable or tasteless to the salespeople, which is rather different thing from a desire to be superior:

> There are a number of stories which illustrate something that could be called "the inferiority complex of the customer." Salesmen have to realize that such a thing exists and take it into account in dealing with customers.[14]

Several American studies

Joseph H. Newman has reported motivational studies made for the Jewel Tea Company that emphasized the housewife's "need to feel important, to feel that she was in control of the sales visit, and to feel that she was an efficient shopper. . . ."[15] Burleigh Garner has also mentioned a house-to-house firm (not identified) which learned that attempts on the part of salesmen to increase sales merely alienated customers and that "it was necessary to emphasize the role of the salesman in serving the customer."[16] Ernest Dichter, another well-known figure in motivation research, has announced somewhat similar results from a study of shopping behavior, although many details are hazy in his account of the study:

> Actually proximity had very little to do with store selection. We found stores convenient to apartment houses and residential neighborhoods which were "isolated," that were shunned by the neighborhood, although they were clean and carried standard merchandise. They were avoided because the owners or sales personnel were considered intruders, they had failed to establish a sympathetic relationship with their neighbors.[17]

On the other hand, considerable evidence exists that such "rational" factors as convenience of location, merchandise assortment, and prices will exert tremendous influence on shopping behavior. Such studies tend to support the view that shopping is instrumental

[14] *Op. cit.*, p. 31. Martineau reported the same attitude among Chicago shoppers, pp. 234-41.

[15] Joseph H. Newman, "New Insights, New Progress, for Marketing," *Harvard Business Review*, November-December 1957, p. 101.

[16] "How the Social Sciences Are Used in Advertising," *Printer's Ink*, December 11, 1953, p. 60.

[17] "The Real Reasons Why People Buy," *Advertising and Selling*, July 1948, p. 560.

behavior, carried on to accomplish the job of assembling a collection of merchandise with a minimum expenditure of time and money, rather than an end, pursued for the sheer joy of the activity itself:

> While shopping is still a pleasure to some consumers, there is evidence that, with the multiplication of alternative activities, there is mounting distaste on the part of both men and women for the labor of buying things, a desire to simplify and to expedite the process as much as possible.[18]

Retail gravitation studies and the whole literature that has grown out of "Reilly's Law" indicate that simple unwillingness to travel "excessive" distances sets important limits upon store selection. These studies, it is true, do not indicate which individual stores will be patronized and which ones rejected in any particular shopping district, but they do indicate that "a fairly convenient" location is usually a prerequisite to patronage.

Alderson Associates, Inc., a Philadelphia marketing research firm, created an ingenious shopping game that was played by the housewives on its continuing family outlook panel. The game seemed to indicate that women preferred to shop in stores having either a very wide or a very deep selection of merchandise and very few or very many price lines, and tended to avoid stores of an "in-between" or indeterminate character. The actual purchasing activities recorded by panel members seemed to substantiate the experimental results.[19] The conclusion drawn from the experiment and from discussions with the panel seemed to be that women disliked most shopping work and tried to patronize the stores they felt were likely to supply them upon the first visit. Thus, these shoppers were seeking to minimize the time and labor input given to the shopping activity. Alderson concluded:

> The instrumental skill of the American household involves rational foresight and skill in problem solving. The realization that buyers come into the market to solve problems is more reliable than the notion

[18] Robert S. Lynd, "The People as Consumers," *Recent Social Trends* (Report on the President's Research Committee on Social Trends [New York: McGraw-Hill Book Company, 1933]), Vol. II, p. 910.

[19] This experiment has been reported in a number of sources, an indication perhaps both of the experiment's ingenuity and of the dearth of reportable studies in this field. See, "When a Woman Shops, What's on Her Mind?", *Printers' Ink*, January 20, 1956, pp. 20 ff.; Gilbert Burck, "What Makes Women Buy?" *Fortune*, August 1956, pp. 176-77; "Getting Inside the Shopper's Mind," *Business Week*, November 12, 1955, pp. 58 ff.; Wroe Alderson, *Marketing Behavior and Executive Action* (Homewood, Illinois: Richard D. Irwin, Inc., 1957), p. 183. However, the fullest discussion available appears in the firm's house organ, *Cost and Profit Outlook*, February 1956, under the title, "Experimental Research in Consumer Behavior."

that selling is simply a matter of implanting habits or taking advantage of impulses in passive and muddleheaded consumers. A product, a service, or a retail store must function to survive the test of the market.[20]

None of the studies described above or below, however, seems to take into account *all* the variables which *may*, and which often are, credited with affecting the retailer-customer relationship. The factors that have seemed significant to at least some students include such matters as community size, customer class, and customer attitudes and personality. Probably other factors, such as merchandise category and size of purchase, are equally relevant.

Influence of community

The size of the relevant community, and the extent to which social and business relationships are intertwined, seem to have impressed a number of writers. According to this view, the small-town retailer must arrange his life to suit his customers.

It is of no small importance that the people not only like him [the small town merchant] and his clerks and delivery men but his wife and relatives as well. So necessary is the required personal relationship that he and his family must deliberately try to cultivate pleasant, if not intimate, relationships with everyone and tactfully avoid any relationships which might cause personal differences. It is due to this need to understand their customers as persons that the business men become among the most thorough students of the life of the town. For they must know a good deal about the private affairs and the whims of the people in order to know what is likely to please and what will probably offend.[21]

City life, on the other hand, is seen as depersonalizing contacts and as inducing a completely different value scale. The city dweller, in this view, shops where he gets the best deal.

American urban society is characterized by a value system which allows people's behavior, particularly with regard to economic relations, to be governed by rationalistic bargaining. Other factors such as sentiment and kinship decline in importance in the interaction process. Findings that neighborhood loyalty or sentiment in no way influence shopping orientation illustrate this point. Thus, retail stores are unfettered by sentimental, personal, or kinship considerations and may locate wherever various factors combine to produce the maximum profit. . . . This is the place where most people believe they can achieve

[20] *Marketing Behavior and Executive Action*, p. 184.
[21] Albert Blumenthal, "Life in the Small Town," in Don Calhoun, Arthur Naptalin, *et al.*, editors, *Introduction to Social Science* (rev. ed.; Chicago: J. P. Lippincott, 1957), p. iii-193. See also, Svend Riemer, "Villagers in Metropolis," *British Journal of Sociology*, 1951, pp. 31-43.

the maximum in their exchange relationships. That the majority of respondents of the three cities [studied] felt that they could get the best results there for the lowest cost in money and at a tolerable cost of time and inconvenience reflects these relationships.[22]

How rigid is class structure?

Many contemporary sociologists entertain considerable doubt about the validity of the rigid class structure studies that became so popular some years ago after Warner published his "Yankee City" series, They doubt that people can be very neatly divided into six categories (or any other given number) ranging from upper-upper to lower-lower, and that any given individual's position will appear the same, at any one time, to all viewers and for all purposes. C. Wright Mill's study of the "middle class," for example, included a considerable number of small merchants (those employing relatively few people). He found two groups of high-status people in the community who looked down on this mercantile group; one a sort of local "aristocracy" that considered the merchants' family connections and educational background as inferior, and the other a very aggressive group of rising business and professional people who felt the small merchants occupied a lower status because their business and contacts were primarily *local.* On the other hand, many of the people whom Mills assigned to the lower groups tended to look up (erroneously, in his view) at the retailers as part of a business class that controlled community affairs. " 'Shopkeepers,' says a lower class woman, "they go in the higher brackets . . . they don't humble themselves to the poor.' "[23]

Others have found so much variance between different studies of occupational rankings that they seem to have little confidence in such research except as a gross and consequently relatively useless tool.[24] Moreover, it may be argued that what may be a valid "class" or "power" structure for one purpose (e.g., who is elected to the country club) has only limited relevancy to other questions (e.g., who patronizes what stores). When Blankertz and his marketing research students studied the customer records of Philadelphia department stores, they found much more heterogeneity in clienteles than they had anticipated, and much less of a dichotomy between "shawl trade"

[22] C. T. Jonassen, *The Shopping Center versus Downtown* (Columbus, Ohio: Bureau of Business Research, Ohio State University, 1955), p. 95.
[23] C. Wright Mills, "The Middle Class in the Medium-Sized City," *American Sociological Review*, October 1946, p. 522.
[24] Cf., Caploy, *op. cit.*

and "carriage trade" stores than had been expected. To a considerable extent, the large department stores seemed to be universal shopping centers. They reported a strong inference that the "reputed appeal of certain stores for certain (income) groups has been greatly exaggerated. Regardless of reputation, each seems to secure the same composition of patrons." [25]

Two examples of disagreement with this view may be of some interest. As part of his doctoral work at Yale, Lloyd Saxon Graham queried a panel of 150 New Haven families, drawn equally from six occupational categories, on their rate and method of acceptance of a number of new activities and services. He found a high rate (about 80 per cent) of acceptance of supermarkets as a source of food supplies among two categories, one of which included the business proprietors, semiprofessional people, and managers, while the other consisted of skilled workers. Much lower rates existed among professionals, clerical and sales workers, semiskilled and unskilled labor, ranging from 48 to 56 per cent. He noted a number of problems, however, such as small sample size, difficulties of classifying individual respondents, and uneven dispersion of supermarkets throughout all neighborhoods in the city, which tended to weaken the strength of his conclusions. [26]

Martineau, in the paper already cited, placed considerable reliance upon class categories as determinants of store clientele:

> I have found that the typical big retailer, in a rough sense, feels that he sells everybody. But nothing could be farther from actuality. The social class profiles of each store, even of the chain grocery supermarkets that conceivably have universal appeal, indicate that the shopper senses instinctively whether this is a lower lower-class store or an upper middle-class store. She isn't going to take a chance of feeling out of place in a store where she doesn't fit . . . .
>
> The shopper is intimidated by some stores, she feels that some are considerably beneath her. She is looking for the ones where she feels comfortable and where her goals are understood and respected. All of this has nothing to do with economics. The very shouting of bargains and sales . . . conveys to the high status shopper that she doesn't belong in that kind of establishment. She avoids any milling mobs.[27]

However, he also notices that discount houses and bargain appliance stores are patronized by many middle-class customers and others relatively high on the status scale (a fact observed in many other

[25] "Shopping Habits and Income," *The Journal of Marketing*, January 1950, p. 577.

[26] *Selection and Social Stratification*, (Doctoral dissertation, Yale University, *1951*).

[27] *Op. cit.*, pp. 241-42.

studies), which seems to involve some contradiction of the position taken above.

One seldom-noted possibility is that the two stores, radically different in nature, may draw from the same general population by virtue of radically different appeals to the different individual interests and tastes scattered throughout any population segment. Ross Cunningham has suggested, for example, that just as there are brand-loyal and brand-disloyal families, there may well be store-loyal and store-disloyal ones.[28]

A particularly interesting typology of consumers has been advanced by a Chicago sociologist, Gregory P. Stone. Studying a group of consumers to learn their reactions to a new department-store branch, Stone found four types of individuals. The largest single category was composed of economic shoppers," who adopted a cold-blooded and rational attitude to shopping, were interested in price, quality, and variety, and had "an unfavorable evaluation of practices and relationships with personnel which impede the quick, efficient sale of merchandise." A much smaller group of "apathetic shoppers" had little or no interest in shopping and simply patronized the nearest or most convenient outlet.

Somewhat less than half of his sample consisted of two other groups. "Personalizing shoppers" had a tendency to personalize and individualize their role in the stores, rated stores in terms of closeness of relationship between customers and personnel, and often would refer to stores they patronized as "my . . . store." "Ethical shoppers," on the other hand, seemed to feel a moral obligation to patronize particular types of outlets, usually neighborhood stores or small shops.[29] Presumably a certain amount of subservience would be an appropriate tactic for handling the "personalizing shoppers"; it seems less necessary to the "ethical shoppers"; of no significance to the "apathetic shoppers"; and actually distasteful to the "economic shoppers."

Survey evidence, in short, merely suggests that many, but not all, customers may be satisfied without subservience. The empirical evidence of retail successes seems to provide a somewhat stronger contradiction of the concept of the necessarily subservient merchant. If we take, for example, the retailing firms cited in the American Institute of Management's list of "excellently managed companies,"

[28] "Brand Loyalty—What, Where, How Much?" *Harvard Business Review*, January-February 1956, p. 116.

[29] Gregory P. Stone, "City Shoppers and Urban Identification: Observations on the Social Psychology of City Life," *American Journal of Sociology*, July 1954, pp. 36-45.

we find such organizations as The Great Atlantic & Pacific Tea Company, The Kroger Company, American Stores Company, Food Fairs Stores, Inc., Federated Department Stores, W. T. Grant Company, J. C. Penney Company, S. S. Kresge Company, McCrory Stores Company, Melville Shoe Company, Sears, Roebuck and Company, Inc.[30] All these organizations have, quite obviously, found ways to satisfy and please substantial numbers of consumers. But even a considerable stretch of the imagination fails to picture any of these institutions standing hat in hand, tugging at the forelock, and displaying servility (or even very much deference) toward the consumer.

In fact, we do not have to look to the giants to find an impersonal and undeferential air. At least one writer has noted this as characteristic of department-store retailing:

> Today department stores are offering a galaxy of "special services" (gift wrapping, fur storage, layaway plans, etc.) as counterfeit for the genuine spirit of customer services which dominated their operation twenty years ago. True customer service, a pervading interest in the personal welfare of each individual customer, has been replaced by a depersonalized and almost callous attitude toward the customer family.[31]

The growth of some modern discount retailers, who offer little service and provide few amenities, is also a case in point.

The obvious conclusion is reiteration of our need for much more information on what constitutes the attracting power of individual stores in drawing individual customers. We ought to know more about the patronage motives of different individuals and groups, and we need to learn how these motives cause differences in selection between specialty stores and one-stop shopping emporia, between discount stores and fashion leaders, between large and small outlets. We ought to ask whether different judgment scales are used in appraising food, clothing, appliance, automobile, and other kinds of dealers. In short, we need to know more about the retailer-customer relationship.

However, the evidence does suggest certain observations. One concerns the extent to which, in recruiting and in personnel matters, the large-scale retailers would be well advised to try to disassociate

[30] *Manual of Excellent Managements 1957* (New York: American Institute of Management, 1957). The A.I.M. selection methods have been subjected to considerable discussion and criticism of late, and undoubtedly there are excellently managed retail firms omitted or overlooked even in the total A.I.M. list from which the above names were cited. But this is not relevant to the present discussion. Many or most of the other firms that either the readers or the author might add to the list certainly resemble the firms cited in behavior and customer attitudes.

[31] Robert D. Loken, *What's Wrong with Department Stores* (Urbana, Illinois: University of Illinois, n.d.), p. 3.

themselves from small-scale stores. In occupational prestige studies, in which the broad and misleading category "retail proprietorship" has been reported as low-ranking, for example, the explanation often seems to lie in the supposed small-scale, low-income, and restricted contacts of the business. These are very often characteristic aspects of the "Momma, Poppa, and Rosie" store, but they do not apply to the retail giants. Second, it seems clear that substantial numbers of successful retailers can operate without subservience. Nevertheless, it may also be true that some so-called "quality" or "prestige" stores are, wisely or unwisely, frightening away some potential trade.

Finally, we should note that both retailers and retailing teachers are fond of talking about a rather mystical quality called "store personality" or "institutional character." By this we may merely mean that all parts of the firm's operations ought to be consistent with each other, that advertising, pricing, merchandise selection, and service ought all to reinforce each other. Personality, in this sense, accords perfectly with the idea that shoppers have expectations of stores, and that consequently stores should be conducted to develop and reinforce favorable expectations, rather than confuse or disappoint prospective customers. Often, however, we seem to use "personality" in a different sense, to imply an anthropomorphic quality, and to suggest uniqueness, distinctiveness, flair and flamboyance, and the development of interest in the store itself, as distinct from its merchandise and its services. We can all think of some very successful stores that have all, or many, of these characteristics; it is much harder to remember all the "quaint" and "cute" shops that have failed to make money. But if in many instances shopping is simply operational behavior through which fairly rational individuals seek to gather bundles of desired goods without excessive expenditure of money, time, or effort, then our beloved concept of "personality" is less important than such mundane aspects of retailing as merchandising, pricing, and customer service.

63. THE PLANNED COMMUNITY *

Morris L. Sweet
Finn B. Jensen

The solution to urban problems proposed by many planners has long been establishment of a planned or balanced community. The community would be more nearly self-sufficient and, in turn, less reliant for its existence on the large city centers; in effect, a multi-core city of comparatively independent units is the goal. The question, which is the theme of this study, is the desirability of this goal in relation to the performance of the industrial and commercial functions that are so integral a part of urban life in the United States. The analysis is to a large extent based on first-hand observation of the new Swedish communities by one of the writers.

In recent times the theoretical and practical impetus for the balanced community, the New Town or Garden City, comes from the work of the Englishman, Ebenezer Howard who, at the beginning of the twentieth century, developed the concept of the Garden City. This concept called for all land to be owned by the community; homes were to be placed around a large central court which would contain the public buildings, and retail facilities and industry would be located on the perimeter. The town area of 1,000 acres would encompass some 30,000 people and the town would be encircled by a 5,000-acre permanent green belt. The specific approach taken by Howard is not as germane to this paper as is his concept of the integration of residential, social, cultural, industrial and commercial facilities within and into the life of the community.

The heritage left by Howard still engenders bitter controversy as to whether or not the balanced community is a suitable means of preventing or solving the critical problems facing urban areas or is likely to place additional burdens on urban life. The timeliness of the

* Reprinted by permission of the *National Civic Review*, Vol. LI, No. 5 (May, 1962), pp. 251-256.
Morris L. Sweet, Research Assistant Professor of Business, Lehigh University.
Finn B. Jensen, Professor of Economics, College of Business Administration, Lehigh University.

issue is pointed up by the diverse positions taken by two well known observers of the American city.

Lewis Mumford is of the opinion that:

> Howard's emphasis on unity and balance and self-containment remains a salutary contribution to every kind of urban renewal; and it is no accident that the finest examples of civic design in the twentieth century have been in cities like Amsterdam, Frankfurt-am-Main and Stockholm, where the medieval tradition of corporate responsibility has not been completely overthrown by the speculative scramble and ideological *laissez faire* of the nineteenth century. It was perhaps only by proposing to build a new city that all the functions, activities and purposes of a fully developed city could be recognized, since many of these had lapsed, while others had become grossly overemphasized in the undirected growth of existing cities.[1]

Whereas Mumford advocates decentralization somewhat along the lines advocated by Howard, Jane Jacobs takes the viewpoint that the Garden City and its varied mutations are harmful to the best interests of urban development:

> Howard set spinning powerful and city-destroying ideas. . . . He conceived of good planning as a settling of things once for all; in each case the plan must anticipate all that is needed and be protected, after it is executed, against any but the most minor subsequent changes. He conceived of planning also as essentially paternalistic, if not authoritarian. He was uninterested in those aspects of the city which could not be abstracted to serve his Utopia. In particular, he simply wrote off the intricate, many-faceted, cultural life of the metropolis. He was uninterested in such problems as the way great cities unofficially police themselves, or allow for the exchange of ideas, or operate politically, or invent new economic arrangements. In short, he was not designing for city life at all.[2]

The evaluation of the balanced community that follows stems from an analysis of the Swedish experience which is in terms of the 1960s, rather than of Howard's English community of 1900, and attempts to discover the pertinence to U. S. governmental urban planning policies. Sweden has pursued a policy of fostering the balanced community and Stockholm is, in fact, a laboratory where these communities can be observed and the appropriate results utilized in the United States. The Swedish integrated community is unlike the typical U. S. suburban residential community, which is more geographically isolated from employment and major cultural areas.

A prime objective of the New Town is to minimize travel and traffic congestion by decreasing the distance to and from working

[1] *The City in History* (Harcourt, Brace and World, 1961), pp. 521-522.

[2] "Modern City Planning: The Victory Over Vitality," *Columbia University Forum* (Fall 1961), p. 21.

and shopping areas through provision in the initial community plans for such areas near residences. In addition to covering the objective of minimizing travel, this analysis is also concerned with other substantive questions that arise from plans for permanently integrating industry and commerce into the community. Half the population of the Swedish New Town of Vallingby is estimated to have neighboring places of employment.

Industry

Planning must, of course, be concerned with more than just housing and, in 1947, the Swedish government began an investigation into business location which involved an evaluation of population growth, population movement and industrial growth. The objectives were to find the best possible distribution of population and industry in the light of social welfare, economic growth and national defense. A by-product of this investigation has been increased awareness of the need for greater knowledge as a prerequisite to planning which, in turn, cannot be centered entirely in the national government. But central planning, if developed with care and there is recognition of the limitations, can be helpful to business, labor and urban planners.

A major limitation of the planning being discussed is too great reliance on expectations that industry will remain within the confines of the New Town. Industry does not function in a static world from which the impact of changing economic forces can be excluded and there are many obstacles to making places of employment and residence contiguous.

The obstacles to integrating industry are compounded in those communities that, by virtue of distance from alternative or supporting economic opportunities, become economically dependent on one industry. Even in communities not greatly dependent on one major industry, permanency of employment or adequate matching of the labor supply with employer demand may not exist within the balanced community. From the standpoint of the demand for labor, there is likely to be too limited a need within the balanced community, both in terms of quantity and range of skills. Adequate professional opportunities can exist only within a larger framework than that of the small integrated town. Analagous is the situation whereby children growing up in New Towns must be given sufficient scope to develop in diverse ways rather than be limited to eventual employment in the New Town industries.

Further limitations on minimizing the distance from home to work are the increasing number of families with workers of dissimilar skills who, consequently, are likely to be employed in different localities. Another complicating factor is the greater ease of changing the place of work than of changing residences.

The tendency of planners to favor light industry poses an additional problem because it increases the susceptibility of movement from a community. The preference for light industry may be due to the greater flexibility allowed the architect or the difficulties in adapting site characteristics to construction of a factory with heavy equipment and specialized transportation facilities.

In contrast to these influences making for greater dispersion of work sites, a situation peculiar to the United States may have the result of insuring a greater degree of permanency in employer-employee relationships with a stabilizing effect on workers' places of residence. In the past an employer had practically unlimited freedom to relocate his business anywhere, subject only to the voluntary surrender of this right to the union and no attempt on his part to subvert employee rights protected by federal labor legislation.

Several legal decisions, however, now being appealed to the U. S. Supreme Court, have ruled that employee seniority and re-employment rights are maintained even after the union contract has expired, the employment terminated and the plant closed and moved.[3] The impact of such decisions could be that the movement of industry, when necessary for expansion or other reasons, will take place within a shorter distance to enable the employer to avoid being subject to the costs of compensating or re-employing displaced employees. Instead of interregional, intraregional industrial movement may take place which will require improved intraregional transportation facilities. The movement of industry, even though for relatively short distances, does over a period of time bring changes in residences.[4]

Another factor limiting dispersion of industry is the need for proximity to a broad variety of repair and service agencies, subcontractors, suppliers of materials and component parts, warehouses and banks, necessary for uninterrupted and efficient operation, particularly with the spread of automation. A location too distant from the central city can involve excessive costs for the manufacturer. Con-

[3] Herbert Burstein, "Plant Moves Limited by New Court Ruling," *The Journal of Commerce* (November 15, 1961), p. 1A; "Seniority Struggle," *The Wall Street Journal* (July 21, 1961), p. 1.

[4] S. George Walters, Morris L. Sweet, and Max D. Snider, "When Industry Moves to Interurbia," *Sales Management* (February 20, 1959), p. 65.

versely, the suppliers of specialized services cannot survive in an isolated New Town. Activities that are of interest to a particular type of business can exist only where the total number of prospective users is of sufficient magnitude.

The disadvantages of decentralizing industry are mitigated by establishing the New Towns on the outskirts of cities. Thus the New Towns surrounding Stockholm have the advantage of location in an urban area with both a diversified industrial structure and a large pool of skilled labor. This can be interpreted in terms of industry being able to draw upon a wide range of services and labor skills, and there are sufficient and varied job opportunities to give workers job mobility and thus avoid the perils of the one-industry town. The decentralization of the New Towns on the periphery of Stockholm enables industry to take advantage of the economies accruing from decreased production costs yet remain in proximity to metropolitan services. Workers can benefit from the availability of a wider market for their services and not reman completely dependent upon one employer.

Commerce

The objective of self-sufficiency within a new community is more easily developed in the initial planning for retail, as contrasted to industrial, facilities. The relationship between population and consumer demand is a more obvious one, e.g., the demand for food, clothing, automobiles, etc., than is the relationship between population and industry, that is, determining what type of industry would be suitable and the lack of certainty as to the availability or desire of these firms to locate in the community. The result has been that planners have been influential in determining the Swedish retail pattern.

In Sweden the decision as to the establishment of a center has to be integrated with other decisions for the location of residences, industry, offices, mass transit, and cultural and social facilities. This integration does not extend to the point where public ownership is a necessary concomitant of Swedish governmental policy, however; there are both publicly and privately operated centers.

Before establishing major shopping centers, close study is made of U. S. centers and, among the various European countries, U. S. centers have had the greatest influence in Sweden. Despite this close study, there are different objectives and practices in establishing and operating commercial facilities as between Sweden and the United States. In the U. S. private enterprise takes the initiative in deciding to open a center; the key goal is to obtain maximum return on the investment. Subject only to local zoning laws, the developer in the U. S. usually has great freedom in determining the size and location of the center, whereas the Swedish planning mechanism, by taking many factors into consideration, insures that coordination with other urban facilities is not left to the desires of the developer. The greater coordination results in less risk for the merchant in the Swedish center than for his American counterpart, where there is less direction of the growth of an area. The projections of population, housing, etc., have a greater likelihood of coming to fruition in Sweden and the businessman can make decisions accordingly.

To plan for the number, kind and size of stores required, town planners and retailers' associations prepare estimates. Says the Stockholm Chamber of Commerce:

> On the basis of statistical material concerning the annual purchases of different goods by the average household and of the known relationship between the number of store employees and the population in already existing communities, and knowing the turnover and the costs estimated by retailers in different fields for shops of certain sizes, we have tried to determine certain average figures for the consumer base required by different kinds of shops.[5]

Complete reliance cannot be placed by government and business on these estimates of commercial activity. It is difficult to forecast the type and number of stores that will be needed and still provide a return sufficient to cover costs and a return on capital. The statistical data is not necessarily applicable to every community; there are differences in population characteristics and in proximity to alternative shopping facilities.

In the tightly planned community, provision for space that will be needed at a later date has to be made on the basis of statistical projections. The larger the community, the greater the likelihood of error in the forecast; there are more categories of goods for which estimates must be made and there is a greater impact from changes in consumer demand or the development of new types of retailing institutions. In contrast, the relationship between store space and turnover has been fairly well developed for food retailing in Sweden.

Over-all community planning is likely to result in some inflexibility for which complete preparation cannot be made. If the existing

[5] *Some Facts About Town Planning for Retail Distribution in the Suburban Areas of Stockholm*, The Stockhold Chamber of Commerce, Stockholm (June 16, 1954), p. 9.

stores do not satisfy customer needs, there follows additional but unplanned travel to other shopping areas for which there may be inadequate roads or transit. With a set amount of space set aside, there is less opportunity for the entry of new firms and existing merchants tend to obtain some degree of monopoly control.

An examination of retailing in the United States indicates the limited value of long range forecasts for specific types and locations of stores, i.e., the change in the competitive position of traditional retailers and the reversal in practices of selection of store location. The greater control of land use in Sweden, however, leaves less flexibility in site selection than is enjoyed by U. S. retailers, e.g., downtown or highway.

A comparable change may be imminent in Sweden because of the greater than anticipated increase in automobile ownership. Plans for the New Towns predicated upon a particular shopping pattern will have to be revised in light of the decreased necessity to patronize the New Town shops. There is a less predictable shopping pattern as the consumer, by use of the auto, has a wider range of choice. Swedish town plans, which have been based largely on movement by means other than the private auto (a study showed 77 per cent of the women who shopped at Vallingby came by foot and mass transit from within a distance of five kilometers),[6] must be readjusted.

Conclusions

Following Howard's line of reasoning, housing, the industrial park and the shopping center each functioning independently can only result in chaos. Planners must take into consideration the degree of instability that is endemic in an era of rapid technological change, and there is limited basis for expecting industry and commerce to remain within the confines of a specified locality or unaffected by innovation. If much of this change is on an intraregional basis, projections for housing will be more reliable than those for manufacturing and retailing.

Today's critical urban problems require a re-examination of the age-old concept of the planned community from the standpoint of its usefulness for the United States. The examination would have to be concerned with the newer integrated communities, since the planning which might have been feasible for Ebenezer Howard's Garden City

[6] Lars Persson, *Kunderna I Vallingby,* K. L. Beckmans Boktryckeri, Stockholm (1960), p. 203.

is no longer as pertinent in an era of rapid economic and social change. The goal of the New Town to attain a high degree of self-sufficiency and thus keep travel to a minimum is of questionable value; the effect of attempting to maintain a closed economy in the 1960s is likely to be stagnation.

Despite the limitations inherent in planning programs, there is recognition also of the difficulties that arise from having the growth of a city determined by the unilateral action of landowners, builders, manufacturers, merchants and government. The climate of opinion today is no longer unalterably opposed to any consideration whatsoever of the planned community; there is an increasing willingness to have unilateral decisions tempered and coordinated by planning that no longer permits the unbridled temporary maximization of economic gain at the expense of desirable community growth. Thus coordination of efforts by these groups can provide the greatest social and economic benefits for all segments of the community.

SECTION 6. GOVERNMENT AND MARKETING

What is the role of government in marketing? This controversial issue seems ever to be unresolved. The ideal balance between the freedom of business to organize and the controlling government power needed for general welfare is a delicate balance indeed.

The Chairman of the Federal Trade Commission, the Honorable Paul Rand Dixon in his talk, "Lets Take a Hard Look at Promotions," indicates that the government is not an abstract force in the market place. He dramatically illustrates the influence of the regulatory agencies viz a viz the Robinson Patman Act in shaping the entire pattern of doing business. Thus marketing decisions must be made within the framework set by the external environment.

Professor George W. Stocking and Willard F. Mueller in their article, "The Cellophane Case and The New Competition," explore the criteria by which economists can determine the existence of monopoly and attempt to apply relevant criteria to duPont's cellophane operations.

Friedrich Kessler, Newton D. Brenner, and Richard H. Stern writing in "Automobile Dealer Franchises: Vertical Integration by Contract" conclude that manufacturer-dealer relations have been marked by a continuous conflict of interest. They point out that it would seem wise to let the market place determine which elements are most efficient rather than use legislation to support the existing distribution pattern.

Former Chairman John W. Gwynne of the Federal Trade Commission in his statement before the United States Senate Subcommittee on Retailing, Distribution, and Fair Trade Practices discusses the merchandising practices of discount houses, resale price maintenance, loss leader selling, and deceptive practices.

Former Assistant Attorney General Victor R. Hansen in his address, "Federal Policy on Antitrust Matters," points out that market structure in itself is not the only subject of inquiry in monopolization cases because market behavior or market conduct still plays a part in cases brought under the Sherman Act.

64. LET'S TAKE A HARD LOOK AT PROMOTIONS *

Paul Rand Dixon

Recently published figures remind me again of the size of your industry. Food stores sales were just under $50 billion in 1961. That was almost 10% of gross national product. You are indeed very important people.

But you wholesalers have your problems, as do also all of the other segments of your industry. In fact, I suppose, each segment is itself the problem of one or more of the others.

All of you, however, are faced with the same challenge—the challenge of change. Among the many facets of that problem are changes in channels and methods of distribution. Some bits of more or less relevant information in this connection have come to my attention recently. Here are a few of them.

U. S. Steel has closed the last of its company stores. In 1920 it had about 100.

Discounters now retail about $2 billion worth of food annually. That is about 4% of the total. Five years ago they were not around. One forecast is that their sales will quadruple in four years.

Trading stamps in 1961 cost an 80-store Ohio grocery chain over $2 million. This was more than it paid in taxes and nearly as much as it spent for rent, light, heat and utilities in that year.

And, finally let me quote from an article about franchising in Dun's Review:

> . . . In one noteable case . . . franchising has bolstered an entire industry. This has happened in the food industry, where the old-line wholesaler has steadily lost ground to the supermarket chains. Into the temporary vacuum have moved jobbers who, working through the franchise system, have been doing a hefty business in sponsoring so-called voluntary chains of food store operators.

In this turmoil of change, with its accompanying struggles for supremacy and for survival, many practices have been used which have necessitated rather frequent interventions by the Federal Trade Commission. Among these are allowances for advertising and other promotional services and facilities which discriminate between competing customers.

* Reprinted by permission of Paul Rand Dixon from an address before National Wholesale Grocers, Bal Harbor, Florida, April 16, 1962.
Paul Rand Dixon, Chairman, Federal Trade Commission.

In the food industry, characterized as it is by low profit margins, such discriminations are especially destructive of the kind of economic system which we must have and which the Commission is charged with promoting—an economic system which is both competitive and fair. So let's take a hard look at some of these promotions.

Under Section 2(d) of the Clayton Act, as amended by the Robinson-Patman Act, payments for advertising and other promotional schemes are unlawful unless they are available on proportionally equal terms to all competing customers.[1]

Even after twenty-five years of interpretation by the Commission and the courts, there are some people, even some lawyers, who purport to have great difficulty in understanding these words. They are represented as being a vast legal swamp. But they are not so complicated that he who has the will cannot find a way to conform to their mandate.

This is neither the time nor the place for me to embark upon a comprehensive dissertation in complete exposition of all aspects of Section 2(d) but I thought it might be helpful if I touched on some of those that appear to be most timely.

I shall concern myself principally with some of the problems involved in making advertising and promotional allowances "available" to competing customers, as that term is used in the statute, with emphasis on the necessity of a supplier making his "terms" known to his customers.

Although the word "available" is used in the statute instead of the word "offer," the Commission has consistently held that an allowance is not "available" within the meaning of Section 2(d) if it has not been offered or otherwise made known to all competing customers.[2]

The law does not compel a seller to give advertising or promotional allowances on all of his products if he elects to give them on some.[3]

[1] Section 2(d) of the Clayton Act, as amended by the Robinson-Patman Act, reads as follows:

"That it shall be unlawful for any person engaged in commerce to pay or contract for the payment of anything of value to or for the benefit of a customer of such person in the course of such commerce as compensation or in consideration for any services or facilities furnished by or through such customer in connection with the processing, handling, sale, or offering for sale of any products or commodities manufactured, sold, or offered for sale by such person, unless such payment or consideration is available on proportionately equal terms to all other customers competing in the distribution of such products or commodities."

[2] Vanity Fair Paper Mills, Inc., Docket 7720 (March 21, 1962); Liggett & Myers Tobacco Company, Inc., Docket 6642 (September 9, 1959); Chestnut Farms Chevy Chase Dairy, 53 F.T.C. 1050 (1957); Henry Rosenfeld, Inc., et al., 52 F.T.C. 1535 (1956); Kay Windsor Frocks, Inc., et al., 51 F.T.C. 89 (1954).

[3] Atalanta Trading Corporation v. F.T.C., 258 F.2d 365 (C.A. 2, 1958).

But when he grants an allowance on any product, the law requires that he make it "available" on proportionally equal terms to all competing resellers of the product. This means that the seller must make his proposition known to every competing customer. Whether a customer participates is a decision for him to make, and he obviously must know the specific terms of the plan before he can determine whether he is interested.[4]

The development of a plan is probably the most important step a supplier should take in preparing to grant advertising and promotional allowances. This plan should include the terms of the allowance, stated as precisely and as clearly as possible. All customers can then be made aware of the acts they must perform, or the services or facilities they must provide the seller, to be eligible for the allowance. The Commission's Guides speak clearly on this subject.[5] Plans were lacking in several cases where the Commission has found violations of Section 2(d).[6]

Although it is not necessary for a plan to be formal and in writing, it probably should be, particularly where there are many competing customers or where the plan is at all complex. It must not be tailored to favor a customer or class of customers; instead it must present something which is reasonably suitable to and usable by all competing customers. Clearly, if you offer a customer something he cannot reasonably use, it is not "available" to him.[7] This may necessitate offering all customers more than one way to participate in the promotion. The plan cannot expressly, or by the way it operates, eliminate some competing customers. Where the seller has alternative plans, his customers must be given the opportunity to choose among them.

The statute prescribes no way to proportion payments or allowances, and properly so. Just as the small customer may have to be protected by having alternative plans available to him, so each supplier should be allowed to make allowances in any lawful manner that suits his business. Generally, payments can be proportioned most easily by basing them on either dollar volume or physical quantity of goods purchased.

[4] Chestnut Farms Chevy Chase Dairy, *supra*.

[5] Guides for Advertising Allowances and Other Merchandising Payments and Services, issued May 19, 1960.

[6] Vanity Fair Paper Mills, Inc., *supra*; Liggett & Myers Tobacco Company, Inc., Docket 6642 (September 9, 1959); Chestnut Farms Chevy Chase Dairy, *supra*; Henry Rosenfeld, Inc., et al., *supra*.

[7] See Lever Brothers Company, 50 F.T.C. 494 (1953); Liggett & Myers Tobacco Company, Inc., *supra*.

Similarly, the statute does not specify how to make payments or allowances "available" to customers, but a seller has a wide variety of ways of communicating with them. Probably the seller is in a better position if he makes his offer in writing. His instructions to salesmen, brokers, or other representatives, in and of themselves, are not considered as offers to his customers. These representatives, in turn, must actually transmit the message to the customers. Several cases decided by the Commission make this point.

In the case against Chestnut Farms Chevy Chase Dairy [8] officials of the company testified that driver salesmen had always been instructed to inform every customer of the availability of promotional allowances, but a number of small customers testified that they had not received any such information. The Commission held that, in these circumstances, there had been no proof of an offer and that, therefore, the allowances were not "available."

In the recently decided Vanity Fair case,[9] a similar issue was raised. Here the supplier instructed its sales representatives to inform its customers concerning its promotional policy. It was argued that this instruction satisfied the availability requirement because it adequately supported an inference that all customers were offered the allowance. The Commission rejected this contention, stating that it could not infer an offer from these facts.

To be on the safe side, then, suppliers should make offers of all advertising and promotional allowances affirmatively and directly to all competing customers.

The Vanity Fair case is also illustrative of what I had in mind when I spoke a few moments ago about the desirability of having a promotional plan with specific terms. This supplier also had a policy of considering customers' invitations to participate in their one-time special promotions, such as anniversary sales. Additionally, it was the practice of the supplier to respond to these solicitations "if payment requested for the services rendered was in an amount reasonably related to the cost of the services to the customer." In rejecting the contention that allowances on this basis were granted to all competing customers on proportionally equal terms, the opinion stated:

> The Commission is additionally of the view that even if the evidence were adequate to support a finding that all competitors knew of respondent's promotion policy, respondent's payments for promotional allowances would nevertheless violate Section 2(d) because they were not granted on proportionally equal terms. There was no provision for

[8] 53 F.T.C. 1050 (1957).
[9] Vanity Fair Paper Mills, Inc., Docket 7720 (March 21, 1962).

> graduating these allowances to the amounts of goods purchased during a given period, nor were the allowances based on any other guiding factor. Respondent, in its brief, concedes that the special payments to Weingarten were given as a result of individual negotiation. Respondent's plan, if indeed it was a plan at all, was to make payments, in an amount reasonably related to the cost of the services, for one-time special promotions where the customer requested the allowance. Such an arrangement requires individual negotiation in each case, and necessarily results in a failure to proportionalize in accordance with the requirements of Section 2(d). . . . Any policy which is no more than a general offer to grant allowances, and which requires the customer to seek the allowance and to bargain as to the terms thereof, is not an adequate basis for compliance with the requirements of Section 2(d).

One feature of the "anniversary" sale type of promotion sets it apart from ordinary ones. It is planned and operated according to the customer's specifications and desires. Suppliers participate on the customer's terms. The customer, in this situation, is not satisfied with the allowances he receives under the terms of the supplier's "regular" agreement, he wants something more, and is actively soliciting more. Often he gets more and knows it.

Of course, if the supplier does not make the special allowances available to others in the required manner, he has violated Section 2(d). But, has the customer violated any law?

Under Section 2(f) of the amended Clayton Act, a customer may not knowingly induce or receive the benefit of an unlawful price discrimination. There is no similar provision of this statute, however, with respect to knowingly inducing or receiving the benefit of an unlawful promotional allowance.

The Commission, fortunately, has more than one weapon in its arsenal. Section 5 of the Federal Trade Commission Act prohibits unfair methods of competition. Since the activities of some large buyers in connection with soliciting special allowances seemed clearly to qualify for treatment under this section, the Commission issued formal complaints on that theory, and, after a hearing, decided that the practices were unlawful.

Many members of the Antitrust Bar expressed grave doubt that these solicitations were illegal under Section 5, as the Commission had decided, and results of a judicial review were eagerly awaited. Naturally I am pleased to be able to report that, in the recently decided Grand Union case [10] a Federal court of appeals upheld the Commission.

So far, in this hard look at unlawful promotions, I have done little more than describe some aspects of some of them. Now, I shall con-

[10] The Grand Union Company v. F.T.C., (2d Cir. 1962).

tinue this hard look by examining how, in certain cases, it should be possible to act to cure not only serious troubles in this area but also in others. First, I shall tell you about a lawsuit out in California.

The case is *Dooley* v. *The Big A Stores.* Big A published an 8-page advertisement offering nylon stockings at nine cents a pair, with a limit of 2 pairs to a customer; ironing board pads with covers for 38 cents, with a limit of one to a customer; and a well-known brand of coffee as a gift, with a limit of a pound to a family.

Dooley, the small merchant, saw a frightening similarity between this ad and his business obituary. So, he got his lawyer to sue Big A.

The basis of the suit was a California statute making it unlawful to sell below cost when the effect was to divert trade or otherwise injure competition. The statute also provided that an intent to injure or destroy competition would be presumed where the price was below cost of acquisition or replacement, which ever was lower, and where the quantity available to any one consumer was limited to less than the entire supply offered.

Now, of course, Mr. Dooley's lawyer asked for damages and also for a permanent injunction if, after what might be extended litigation, the court found in Mr. Dooley's favor. But Mr. Dooley's lawyer, being a good one, didn't stop there. In addition, he asked that Big A be enjoined from selling at these prices while the case was being tried —that is, he asked for a temporary or preliminary injunction—because a permanent injunction at the close of the litigation might come too late.

At a hearing Mr. Dooley's lawyer showed the court that there was no dispute about Big A's prices being below the lower of its costs of acquisition and its costs of replacement. He then pointed to the statutory presumption of injury to competition that arose when such prices were combined with a limitation on quantity. Thereupon the court granted the preliminary injunction and ordered the trial to proceed.

This is how the law can operate to prevent small retailers—and their wholesale suppliers—from becoming mere statistics in Dun & Bradstreet's tables of business fatalities.

Unfortunately the Commission cannot now operate so effectively as the California court can to protect small businessmen. We can issue only permanent injunctive orders to cease and desist. Except in certain cases, such as some involving food, drug, and cosmetic advertising, where the Commission may apply to Federal district courts for temporary injunctions, we lack the power to protect firms from injury, no matter how great it is, while the case is being tried.

Immediately after I assumed office, the Commission revised its procedures and organization in an earnest and much-needed effort to do a better job and to get it done with all the speed consistent with the fairness required by due process of law. We have made some progress and we are going to make much more.

But despite all the Commission has done and all it can do to hasten the day of permanent relief in all cases, there will always be some situations in which the continuation of the allegedly unlawful acts during the course of the litigation will result in irreparable injury. Yet, as I have said, except in certain cases, the Commission is now powerless to give immediate relief.

Pending legislation would remedy this grave deficiency in the administrative process at the Commission. It would authorize the Commission itself, in appropriate cases, to issue temporary cease-and-desist orders against the continuance of allegedly unfair practices while cases concerned with permanent relief from such practices are pending before the Commission.

Of the several bills that have been introduced in the House of Representatives, the principal ones being considered at this time are H.R. 8830 and H.R. 8831 which are identical. One of them was introduced by Congressman Patman and the other by Congressman Steed of Oklahoma.

Not only has the White House Committee on Small Business studied and recommended approval of the proposed legislation, but so also has President Kennedy himself. In a letter of August 28, 1961, to the Honorable Oren Harris, Chairman of the House Committee on Interstate and Foreign Commerce, the President, after concluding "that such legislation will provide essential protection for small businessmen and thus strengthen competition throughout the Nation's economy," stated that he was "hopeful that Congressional action on behalf of the objectives of this legislation will be both expeditious and favorable." In an especially forceful paragraph in this letter the President stated the case for the proposed legislation as follows:

> Effective law enforcement by the Federal Trade Commission has long been hampered by delays in litigation and an increasing backlog of cases. Despite a concerted effort to decrease these delays through recent revision of the Commission's organization and procedures, the basic difficulty requires additional remedies. At present, the Commission is powerless to halt allegedly illegal practices until the termination of

> frequently protracted proceedings. As a consequence, small businessmen who are so often the target of discriminatory and monopolistic activities are often irreparably injured or destroyed long before the lengthy process of adjudication has been completed. The proposed legislation will provide means to prevent such injury during that interim period. It will thus provide important protection for the small business community and, indeed, all those who are confronted by violations of the laws which seek to sustain our competitive economy. Such orders should, of course, be subject to the protection of appropriate due process, including the safeguards of judicial review.

Again on March 15, 1962, in his Special Message on Protecting the Consumer Interest, President Kennedy urged the enactment of legislation granting to the Commission the authority to issue these temporary orders. On this occasion he said:

> The Federal Trade Commission should be empowered to issue temporary cease-and-desist orders against the continuance of unfair competitive practices while cases concerned with permanent relief from such practices are pending before the Commission. Under the present law, smaller competitors may be driven into bankruptcy or forced to accept merger on adverse terms long before present remedies become effective, thus reducing the competitive safeguards vital for the consumer. Similarly, deceptive trade practices in consumer goods may do their damage long before the Commission can 'lock the barn door.' I, therefore, reiterate my previous recommendation that the Congress give prompt consideration to effective legislation to accomplish this purpose.

Of course, the proposal to authorize the Federal Trade Commission to issue temporary cease-and-desist orders has brought forth cries of anguish and alarm, especially from certain modern-day common scolds who one week excoriate us for being ineffectual and the next week lambaste us because we are not.

Of these critics, there are some who, almost fifty years after the event, have not yet wholly recovered from the shock occurring as a result of the Commission having been given the power to issue cease-and-desist orders even after a full trial. Naturally they are extremely agitated by the suggestion that we should now be given authority to issue temporary orders; but let them not misrepresent the nature of the orders or the procedure under which they would be issued.

Injunctions, even temporary ones, are not the weapons of a police state. In the English judicial system, which we have borrowed, injunctions were first issued a great many years ago as an equitable remedy by the Chancellor, who was sometimes referred to as the Keeper of the King's Conscience, in cases where the ancient writs of the common law were too rigid to accomplish justice.

Temporary orders to cease and desist will not be issued routinely or as a matter of course. They will be used only in circumstances comparable to those where, under traditional and well-established legal principles, temporary injunctions have been appropriate in judicial proceedings.

The traditional requirements for the issuance of a temporary injunctive order are, first, a *prima facie* showing that, as alleged in the complaint, the law has been violated, and, second, a showing that irreparable injury will result if the temporary order is not issued.

The Commission will have the burden of establishing these two matters at a hearing of which the respondent—the party proceeded against—will have notice and the right to appear and show cause why the temporary order should not issue.

If the Commission, after this hearing, decides that a temporary order to cease and desist is required in the public interest to prevent irreparable injury, it will issue such an order in writing with an accompanying statement of its findings and reasons. No respondent will be required to comply with this order by the Commission; he can only be compelled, after judicial review, to obey an order of the court enforcing the Commission's order.

Judicial review of the Commission's temporary order will be before Federal courts of appeals, the same courts which review the Commission's final orders to cease and desist. This review will be available either upon a petition by the respondent to vacate the order or upon the application of the Commission to enforce it.

In order to prevent unnecessary hardship, the Commission will place on a special calendar or docket every case in which it issues a temporary cease-and-desist order. Cases on this docket will be expedited in every possible way consistent with fairness and justice. You may be sure that the temporary order will be vacated in every case which the Commission does not carry through with due dispatch.

Temporary cease-and-desist orders, then, are not a devilish device of dictators but an ancient instrument for achieving justice. There will be a hearing and there will be judicial review, all in the best tradition of our system. It could not be otherwise.

Not long ago a business columnist stated that the "antitrust laws apparently are not strong enough to insure the continued existence of small business as it is known in the country today." Perhaps he could be persuaded to modify his view if the Commission had the power to issue temporary orders to cease and desist.

65. THE CELLOPHANE CASE AND THE NEW COMPETITION *

George W. Stocking
Willard F. Mueller

On December 13, 1947 the Department of Justice instituted civil proceedings against E. I. du Pont de Nemours & Company, charging du Pont with having monopolized, attempted to monopolize, and conspired to monopolize the manufacture and sale of cellophane and cellulose caps and bands in the United States in violation of Section 2 of the Sherman Act. Almost precisely six years later Paul Leahy, Chief Judge of the United States District Court for the District of Delaware, rendered a decision in the matter.[1] He pointed out that the charge against du Pont of having monopolized cellophane involved two questions: "1. does du Pont possess monopoly powers; and 2., if so has it achieved such powers by 'monopolizing' within the meaning of the Act and under *United States* v. *Aluminum Company of America* [?]" He concluded that "unless the first is decided against defendant, the second is not reached." [2] Judge Leahy did not need to reach the second question for he found the defendant not guilty. In doing so he concluded that "[f]acts, in large part uncontested, demonstrate du Pont cellophane is sold under such intense competitive conditions acquisition of market control or monopoly power is a practical impossibility." [3] In reaching this conclusion Judge Leahy reviewed at length evidence introduced by the defendant to show that du Pont

* Reprinted with permission from *The American Economic Review*, Vol. XLV, No. 1 (March, 1955), pp. 29-63. Copyright 1955 by the American Economic Association.

George W. Stocking, Professor of Economics, Vanderbilt University; Former President, American Economic Association.

Willard F. Mueller, Chief Economist and Director of the Bureau of Economics of the Federal Trade Commission.

1 *United States* v. *E. I. du Pont de Nemours & Co.*, 118 F. Supp. 41 (D. Del. 1953). This study is based largely on the testimony and exhibits in this case, but it does not consider cellulose caps and bands. Du Pont discontinued making caps before the government filed its complaint, and the district court, as with cellophane, found no monopolizing of bands. The Supreme Court has indicated that it will review this decision. References to the government's exhibits will be designated as GX, to the defendant's exhibits as DX, and to the transcript of testimony as T.

2 118 F. Supp. at 54.

3 *Ibid.*, pp. 197-98.

behaved like a competitor, not like a monopolist. The court found that du Pont conducted research to improve manufacturing efficiency, to reduce cost of production, and to improve the quality and develop new types of cellophane. It promoted the development and use of packaging machinery that could handle both cellophane and other flexible wrapping materials. In doing so it not only helped to increase cellophane sales but stimulated improvement in rival flexible wrapping materials. It supplied customers with technical services to help them solve problems created by the use of cellophane. It developed over fifty types of cellophane tailored to meet the special wrapping needs of particular products. It studied the buying habits of the public. It conducted market studies to determine the effect on sales of packaging a product in cellophane. It promoted sales by educating potential cellophane users to the sales appeal of a transparent wrapping material. It reduced prices to get into new and broader markets. The court found that in response to price and quality changes buyers at times shifted from cellophane to competing products and back again. The court concluded that "[t]he record reflects not the dead hand of monopoly but rapidly declining prices, expanding production, intense competition stimulated by creative research, the development of new products and uses and other benefits of a free economy." [4]

This conclusion, based as it is on 7,500 pages of testimony and 7,000 exhibits, cannot easily be dismissed. Many economists relying on the logic of the "new competition" will find in it support for their theories. One has already pronounced Judge Leahy's opinion as a victory for our profession.

Such an optimistic conclusion so lightly reached by an economist and such high praise so extravagantly given by a judge warrant, first, a brief statement of the criteria by which economists can determine the existence of monopoly and, second, an application of the relevant criteria to du Pont's cellophane operations in an effort to answer the question, has du Pont had monopoly power in making and selling cellophane?

Detecting monopoly is simpler than measuring it.[5] While economists recognize that few if any industrial markets are free entirely from the influence of monopoly, by studying the structure and be-

[4] *Ibid.*, p. 233.

[5] Fritz Machlup is probably correct in concluding that "so many different elements enter into what is called a monopolistic position and so complex are their combined effects that a measurement of 'the' degree of monopoly is even conceptually impossible." *The Political Economy of Monopoly* (Baltimore, 1952), p. 527.

havior of markets they can generally isolate characteristics which taken together will permit them to classify markets as effectively competitive or noncompetitive. In trying to classify du Pont's market for cellophane, we shall rely primarily on three criteria: (1) What role has business strategy played in du Pont's production and sales policies? (2) Is cellophane sufficiently differentiated from rival products to have a distinct market, or is its market that of all flexible wrapping materials? (3) Do the trend and level of its earnings reflect monopoly power or competition?[6]

I. Business Strategy as Evidence of Monopoly

Economists have said a good deal about the role which strategy plays among oligopolists jockeying for market position. They have said less about the significance of business strategy as a basis for classifying an industry as monopolistic or workably competitive. We believe it is an important criterion. Purely competitive markets do not generally confront buyers and sellers in the business world. Frequently sellers are few, products are differentiated, knowledge is imperfect, obstacles to the movement of factors exist. Business firms from time to time make deliberate adjustments in both their price and production policies; they resort to strategy to improve their lot. Strategy may be directed to other than price and production policies. Business executives are constantly alert for any business advantage that will make their market position more secure or isolate them from the impact of competitive forces. They seek control of the sources of the best raw materials and the richest natural resources. They try to improve their products and processes or to discover and develop new and better ones. They try to protect their accumulated know-how as business secrets or, where they can, to obtain patents that legalize monopoly.

[6] Clair Wilcox uses the following criteria in classifying markets in his TNEC study, *Competition and Monopoly in American Industry* (1940): (1) the number of producers and the extent of industrial concentration, (2) uniformity of price quotations, (3) degree of price flexibility, (4) volume of production and extent of utilization of capacity, (5) rate of profit, and (6) rate of business mortality. Alone no one of these is a satisfactory index, and together they may be misleading unless perchance there is a consistency among the several indexes. We place considerable emphasis on two factors not included in Wilcox's list, business strategy and product differentiation, and we consider only incidentally if at all most of the factors on which Wilcox relied. Applying Wilcox's criteria to our conception of the cellophane market, we find that producers are few, concentration is high, profits are high, turnover of producing units is low, business mortality is low. These criteria suggest monopoly power. On the other hand, cellophane prices have been flexible and surplus capacity has been negligible. These characteristics suggest competition. Whether or not the factors we have chosen are adequate to answer the question we have raised we leave to the reader.

Economists recognize these practices as manifestations of business rivalry, as aspects of the sort of competition that characterizes modern industrial markets. Business rivalry is itself a symptom of the absence of pure competition. Farmers who, lacking government aid, sell in competitive markets do not regard each other as business rivals but as neighbors. But even when businessmen forego active price competition, they generally do not abandon all rivalry. Correctly, economists have concluded that this rivalry may protect the public interest. It leads to technological innovation and to economic progress. Although economists recognize that business strategy may lead to monopoly, some economists believe that in a dynamic capitalistic society monopoly is inevitably short-lived. It is continually being undermined by the rivalry of other firms. The better product, the better process of today gives way to the better product, the better process of tomorrow. Only the imperfections and mortality of monopoly make it tolerable. Businessmen striving for monopoly promote the public welfare by failing to achieve their goal. Where they achieve it, either by independent business strategy or by collusive action, the public interest may not be served.

With these principles in mind, let us examine du Pont's strategy in developing the cellophane business in the United States. In doing this we do not mean to suggest that its strategy was immoral or unlawful. As Knauth has so well said:

> The contracts and arrangements which businessmen make from day to day seem to them wise, prudent, sound, and inherent in the nature of modern business. When their practices receive legislative interpretation and are denounced as monopolistic, they are puzzled. What has hitherto been deemed eminently proper and ethical now subjects them to unexpected critism and opprobrium.[7]

No opprobrium is intended in this analysis.

Du Pont became acquainted with cellophane through its production of artificial silk. In 1920 it had entered into a contract with the Comptoir des Textiles Artificiels, a French corporation, which through its affiliates was then an important manufacturer of rayon in France, Switzerland, Belgium, and Italy, for the joint operation of an American rayon company using the viscose process. The viscose solution for making rayon was practically identical with that used in making cellophane.[8] The Comptoir had made about 970,000 pounds of cello-

[7] Oswald Knauth, *Managerial Enterprise* (New York, 1948), p. 11.

[8] Report of Dr. Fin Sparre, head of du Pont's development department, April 14, 1923, GX 392, pp. 5431-32.

phane in 1922, nearly 40 per cent of which it sold in the American market as a transparent wrapping material. Aware of the affinity of rayon and cellophane processes and impressed by the prospects of large cellophane sales in the American market, du Pont in 1923 signed an option contract with Arena Trading Corporation,[9] a Delaware corporation which was acting for itself and its associates, including La Cellophane, Société Anonyme, the Comptoir's affiliate which made cellophane. Under the option Arena provided du Pont with all relevant economic and technical information to enable it to decide within four months whether it wished to make and sell cellophane in North and Central America through a corporation jointly owned by it and La Cellophane. If du Pont decided affirmatively, Arena agreed to transfer to the new corporation its technical knowledge, patent rights, trade marks, and good will and the exclusive right to make and sell cellophane in the North and Central American markets. This arrangement apparently contemplated the new corporation's becoming the sole producer of cellophane in these markets. At that time only the French Comptoir through its affiliates made cellophane any place in the world.

On June 9, 1923 du Pont entered into an organizational agreement providing for the transfer to the new company, Du Pont Cellophane Company, Inc., of "an unqualified, unrestricted and exclusive right to use all and every process now owned" by Arena "or which may hereafter be acquired by it . . . in connection with the manufacture of cellophane . . ." [10]

Before entering into this agreement du Pont had made an intensive study of the market possibilities of cellophane and of its production problems and decided that Arena could not deliver all the protection from competition that it had promised. About the patents du Pont's development department had said: "[T]he patent protection at present is exceedingly inadequate not to say worthless, and the future patent protection is problematical because it is based on applications for patents, the issuance of which may not be determined for a matter of two years or more." [11] The development department had concluded that it was "by no means certain that the American Cellophane

[9] Agreement of January 6, 1923, GX 1458, pp. 5999-6008.

[10] GX 1001, p. 992. The agreement specifically excluded processes which might subsequently be acquired by Arena from third parties, but it gave du Pont an option to purchase such rights for the North and Central American markets. Although Arena did not guarantee the validity of the patents to be licensed (*ibid.*, p. 989), it specifically promised to give the new company "the exclusive right to manufacture cellophane in North and Central America to be used for any purpose whatsoever." *Ibid.*, p. 993. Arena and Du Pont Cellophane signed their license agreement December 26, 1923. GX 1002, pp. 998-1001.

[11] GX 392, p. 5433.

Company could *maintain* a monopoly on the strength of either present or prospective patents."[12] Du Pont accordingly insisted on a provision in the organizational agreement that should the patent protection prove inadequate, Arena was to forfeit ten thousand shares of common stock in the new company.[13]

Du Pont apparently recognized that La Cellophane's trade secrets promised a protection from competition that the patents did not, and that as the first domestic producer of a differentiated if not unique product[14] it could for some time at any rate anticipate monopoly revenue in making and selling cellophane. It calculated that with an investment of $2,000,000, at current domestic prices for imported cellophane it could earn $631,832, an annual rate of 31.6 per cent.[15] This it regarded as sufficiently attractive to justify the venture.

Du Pont the sole domestic producer

Du Pont became the sole domestic producer of cellophane and thereby a monopolist in its sale. The Department of Justice contended that it was an unlawful monopoly from the outset,[16] but the district court decided otherwise. Whether lawful or not, du Pont was a monopolist in producing cellophane, and it anticipated and in fact earned monopoly profits from the outset.

This is a characteristic of any successful innovation. As Knight has pointed out,

> There is . . . no clear distinction in practice between profit and monopoly gain. . . . New products . . . must also yield enough temporary monopoly revenue to make such activities attractive.[17]

But as Knight has also pointed out, we must distinguish between justifiable monopoly revenue—returns to the innovator—and what Knight calls monopoly gains. Monopoly gains according to Knight are monopoly revenues that are "too large or last too long." What is too long or too large Knight does not say, but he clearly implies that the procedure by which they are made large and perpetuated may

[12] *Ibid.*, p. 5434. Emphasis supplied.

[13] GX 1001, pp. 989-90.

[14] Du Pont's development department concluded that glassine, sheet gelatin, and tin foil, cellophane's closest rival products, offered no serious competition because of price or quality differences. GX 392, pp. 5437-38.

[15] *Ibid.*, p. 5451.

[16] Brief for the United States of America, pp. 150-56, *United States* v. *E. I. du Pont de Nemours & Co.*, 118 F. Supp. 41 (D. Del. 1953).

[17] F. H. Knight, "An Appraisal of Economic Change—Discussion," Proceedings of the American Economic Association, *American Economic Review* (May 1954), XLIV, p. 65.

convert justifiable monopoly revenue into socially unjustifiable monopoly gains.

Having achieved at the outset a monopoly in producing and selling cellophane in the American market, du Pont took steps to protect its position.

One of its first strategic moves was to obtain an increase in the tariff. This became urgent in 1925, when Société Industrielle de la Cellulose (SIDAC) completed a cellophane plant in Belgium and began exporting cellophane to the American market at cut-rate prices. Du Pont first considered a patent infringement suit against Birn & Wachenheim, SIDAC's American distributors, but fearful that it would lose such a suit decided against it and in favor of a try for higher duties.[18] Its first step in getting the tariff raised was to request the United States Commissioner of Customs to reclassify cellophane as a "cellulose compound" instead of as a "gelatin compound." When the Commissioner refused, du Pont appealed to the United States Customs Court. Its appeal was successful; the court ordered a reclassification and on February 24, 1929 the duty increased from 25 to 60 per cent ad valorem.[19] Apparently this was enough to prevent price cutting by importers. At any rate du Pont's quarterly competitive report for the second quarter of 1929 stated:

> The present tariff rate (.40 per pound) as fixed by the United States Customs Court, has increased the cost of importing Transparent Cellulose Sheeting to such an extent that the competitors are adhering more rigidly to their published price list. Their selling policy in the past has been to obtain preference with the manufacturer by offering special price concessions.[20]

Du Pont won the field so completely from imported cellophane that its cellophane sales for 1929 represented 91.6 per cent of the total business in the United States,[21] whereas importers had had 21 per

[18] About the suit Dr. Sparre of du Pont wrote W. C. Spruance, du Pont vice president, on August 3, 1925: "My belief is that it would cost a whole lot of money and that we would lose in the end, that is if the other side would be willing to fight." GX 1069, p. 1153. About du Pont's effort to get higher duties on cellophane, L. A. Yerkes, president of Du Pont Cellophane, had written Spruance on July 25: "In order that you shall be entirely familiar with the Cellophane status, I want to let you know that we are endeavoring to have the duty on Cellophane raised from 25% to 45%, and Curie, Lane and Wallace are of the opinion that we have a fair chance of getting this through." GX 1068, p. 1142.

[19] The district court appropriately characterized du Pont's protest against what du Pont regarded as an improper classification of cellophane as "the normal act of a business concern engaged in active competition with importers of foreign products." 118 F. Supp. at 167. The court also recognized that the tariff readjustment eventually shut out foreign competition. *Ibid.*, p. 221 .

[20] GX 432, p. 5690.

[21] Du Pont Cellophane's quarterly competitive report, fourth quarter 1929, GX 434, p. 5714.

cent in 1927 and 24 per cent in 1928.[22] The Tariff Act of 1930 fixed the duty on imported cellophane at 45 per cent ad valorem,[23] and cellophane imports were never again significant. In no year between 1930 and 1947 did they amount to 1 per cent of cellophane consumption in the United States.[24]

Division of world markets

La Cellophane's plan to develop the American market through a single company jointly owned by it and a domestic firm was not unique. Before transferring to Du Pont Cellophane Company, Inc., its rights to the American market, La Cellophane had made a similar agreement with Kalle & Company (hereinafter Kalle) covering the German market. Ultimately Kalle obtained exclusive rights to La Cellophane's process and patents for the manufacture and sale of cellophane in Germany, Austria, Hungary, Czechoslovakia, Yugoslavia, Poland, Russia, Romania, China, Denmark, Sweden, Norway, and Finland.[25]

Although La Cellophane had agreed to furnish du Pont with such technological information and patent rights as it might later acquire from its other licensees, du Pont sought to fortify its market position through a direct agreement with Kalle.[26] On May 7, 1929 both parties agreed to exchange free of charge except for patent fees all patent rights and technical data covering cellophane that they then had or might later get.[27] This agreement did not specifically recognize a division of markets, but on October 30, 1929, C. M. Albright, Du Pont

[22] *Ibid.*, first quarter 1929, GX 431, p. 5677.

[23] 19 U.S.C.A. sec. 1001, par. 31(c). In 1951 the tariff was reduced to 22½ per cent ad valorem. *United States* v. *E. I. du Pont de Nemours & Co.*, 118 F. Supp. 41, 167 (D. Del. 1953).

[24] GX 182A, p. 515A; GX 182, p. 515.

[25] Letter of October 30, 1929 from C. M. Albright, Du Pont Cellophane vice president, to the Buffalo office, GX 1091, p. 1195.

[26] As early as September 1925, J. E. Crane, du Pont's European manager, had written H. G. Haskell, du Pont vice president, of talks with Dr. Duttenhofer of Kalle & Company on the desirability of cooperation between du Pont and Kalle. Crane wrote: "Dr. Duttenhofer stated that as we were to cooperate in other matters it would be a pity to compete in artificial silk and cellophane." GX 1393, p. 1800.

[27] GX 1087, pp. 1183-86. Perhaps another reason for du Pont's wishing to deal directly with Kalle is that on April 1, 1929 Du Pont Cellophane became du Pont's wholly owned subsidiary by an exchange of stock. Du Pont organized a new corporation, also named Du Pont Cellophane Co., Inc., La Cellophane to sit on its board as long as du Pont considered this in the new company's best interest. The 1923 agreements remained in force. Agreement of March 18, 1929 between du Pont and La Cellophane, GX 1003, p. 1005. On July 1, 1936, du Pont dissolved Du Pont Cellophane Co., Inc., and replaced it with a cellophane division in its rayon department. Memorandum dated February 17, 1944, on the history of du Pont cellophane, prepared in du Pont's cellophane division, GX 1, p. 8.

Cellophane vice president, listed for the Buffalo office the countries to which Kalle had exclusive rights. About the agreement Albright wrote: "The agreement, for obvious reasons, does not include the territorial limits, and it is suggested that this letter be attached to the copy of agreement for our future guidance." [28] By the summer of 1930 du Pont had patents on its moistureproof cellophane in the United States and possessions, Belgium, France, and Italy and had applications pending in Great Britain, Canada, Japan, the European countries in Kalle's exclusive territory, and eight South American countries.[29] Du Pont assigned its moistureproof patent rights in the countries in Kalle's territory to Kalle or gave it implied licenses under which Kalle took out patents in its own name.[30]

Five years later du Pont entered a technical exchange and license agreement with British Cellophane Limited (herinafter BCL), a La Cellophane licensee, which specifically delineated the territories within which each party would operate.[31] Under this agreement du Pont was to assign its British patents on moistureproof cellophane to BCL. Du Pont also assigned its French patents on moistureproof cellophane to La Cellophane [32] and its Canadian patents to Canadian Industries Limited.[33]

Meanwhile all the world's leading cellophane producers except du Pont had tried to establish an international cartel to assign territories and fix quotas among themselves. Du Pont representatives attended the first day of the cartel conferences in Paris February 11-12, 1930 as "guests and observers" but did not sign the "official report" (agreement).[34] The district court found that they were not authorized to make commitments for du Pont and made none. Nevertheless the agreement recognized the North American market as belonging to du Pont and Sylvania.[35] It did not cover moistureproof or photographic cellophane. SIDAC and La Cellophane agreed to study the possibility

[28] GX 1091, p. 1195.

[29] Memorandum dated August 26, 1930, from Du Pont Cellophane's cellophane department to W. S. Carpenter, Jr., chairman of its board of directors, GX 2469, p. 3164.

[30] Du Pont Cellophane memorandum dated March 17, 1933, GX 1098, p. 1205; letter to Kalle dated March 20, 1933, GX 1099, p. 1206; memorandum dated April 27, 1934, Review of the du Pont-Kalle Relations, prepared by du Pont's patent service, GX 1102, pp. 1210-12.

[31] Agreement of May 3, 1935, GX 1109, pp. 1229-34.

[32] GX 1102, pp. 1210-12.

[33] Letter dated February 12, 1942, transmitting patent assignments, GX 1187, pp. 1409-26.

[34] GX 1414, pp. 1841-44.

[35] Sylvania Industrial Corporation's entry into the American market is described in the following subsection.

of pooling their patents but with the understanding that this would not apply to du Pont patents.[36]

In 1934 du Pont relied on the 1930 cartel agreement in asserting its right to the West Indies as against BCL, to which La Cellophane had granted a license and with which du Pont was then negotiating its technical agreement. In a December 13, 1934 letter to La Cellophane [37] du Pont referred to the minutes of the February 11-12, 1930 meetings of cellophane producers and quoted La Cellophane's letter of April 1, 1932 [38] describing the cartel's division of the world and containing the phrases, "Cuba being situated north of the Panama Canal, belonging thus to your territory." By May 21, 1935 the du Pont-BCL agreement [39] had been signed and du Pont and La Cellophane had agreed that du Pont's territory included the West Indies except the possessions of European powers.[40]

The cartel's course was not an easy one. World depression and the pressure of totalitarian governments for foreign exchange turned members' eyes toward South American markets, and even with agreements and quotas South America prices were unstable. Du Pont's sales there under its 1930 agreement with La Cellophane (discussed in the following subsection) were particularly disturbing to cartel members.[41] On September 6, 1938 La Cellophane wrote du Pont that "it is apparently impossible to bring about a price accord for South

[36] The court was not impressed by the "official report" of the cartel agreement. It stated: "Failure to prove any effect from it, this cartel aspect of the case raises a straight issue of fact. Du Pont did not make such an agreement." 118 F.Supp. at 221. Moreover, the court found that the actual conduct of the producers implicated in the agreement was inconsistent with the existence of a cartel. In the court's inimitable language, "Intricate theories of a conspiratorial network is cast aside." *Loc. cit.*

[37] GX 1034, pp. 1064-65.

[38] GX 1022, p. 1044.

[39] Agreement of May 3, 1935, GX 1109, pp. 1229-34.

[40] Memorandum dated May 21, 1935, "to be attached to original contract between E. I. du Pont de Nemours & Co. and Arena Trading Corporation of June 9, 1923," GX 1040, pp. 1075-76.

[41] Du Pont's 1930 agreement with La Cellophane gave du Pont half of whatever rights La Cellophane got in South America and Japan. Early in 1932 du Pont wrote La Cellophane that "we have made our prices in South America on plain Cellophane to correspond with yours" (letter dated January 29, 1932, GX 1112, p. 1248), and it tried to find out what quotas for South America La Cellophane and the other producers had agreed on; but it became dissatisfied with the operation of the agreement and on June 2, 1932 informed La Cellophane that henceforth du Pont would "consider ourselves free to pursue our own policy of sales in South America, Japan and China." GX 1023, p. 1045. La Cellophane did not take this declaration of independence too seriously and continued to point out that du Pont sold more than La Cellophane did in South America and Japan. On December 27, 1934 du Pont, although reiterating its stand taken in 1932, expressed willingness to exchange figures on its sales in those markets for La Cellophane's and those "of the other members," GX 1037, p. 1070.

America in our Convention." [42] The second world war weakened still further agreements to divide markets. Du Pont's agreements with Kalle and BCL were to run twenty years, subject to renewal, but in 1940 du Pont disavowed all formal territorial limitations, not only with these companies but with Canadian Industries Limited and La Cellophane as well, "in the light of legal developments in this country." [43]

SIDAC completes with La Cellophane and with du Pont

Although La Cellophane had promised du Pont a monopoly in making and selling cellophane in the United States, it could not fulfill the promise. As du Pont feared, neither its patents nor its know-how was sufficient to protect it from competition. In 1925 two former employees of La Cellophane, using La Cellophane's trade secrets, helped establish SIDAC, which began to sell in the rich American market.[44] It made its first sales through Birn & Wachenheim, who had handled La Cellophane's business in the United States before the organization of Du Pont Cellophane. In 1929 SIDAC established an American subsidiary, the Sylvania Industrial Corporation of America, and quit exporting cellophane to the United States.[45] By this time it had subsidiaries in England and Italy and competed in La Cellophane's export markets. La Cellophane sued SIDAC for patent infringement and in settlement accepted a stock interest in SIDAC; thus indirectly it became through Sylvania du Pont's competitor in the American market, in violation of its 1923 agreements with du Pont.

Negotiations over this matter were prolonged. Du Pont conceived its problem to be how to "accept reparations and at the same time protect its future position without contravening American statutes." [46] In lieu of reparations La Cellophane lifted the 1923 restriction limiting du Pont to the North and Central American markets. La Cellophane granted it equal rights with itself in Japan and South America.[47] La Cellophane also agreed to keep technical information, patents, and

[42] GX 1445, p. 1920.

[43] Identical letters dated October 17, 1940, GX 1273, p. 1602, GX 1274, p. 1603, GX 1275, p. 1604, GX 1276, p. 1605.

[44] Memorandum dated February 17, 1944 on the history of du Pont cellophane, prepared in du Pont's cellophane division, GX 1, p. 12.

[45] Du Pont Cellophane's quarterly competitive report, third quarter 1929, GX 433, p. 5702.

[46] Memorandum of a November 14, 1929 discussion by du Pont officials, GX 1410, p. 1831.

[47] Letter dated March 6, 1930 from du Pont to La Cellophane, GX 1013, pp. 1027-29; excerpt from minutes of May 8, 1930 meeting of du Pont's board of directors, GX 1015, p. 1031.

other data which it received from du Pont from going directly or indirectly to SIDAC or Sylvania.

Du Pont seeks patent protection

When du Pont obtained its option to participate jointly with La Cellophane in developing the American market, it had not investigated the validity of La Cellophane's patent claims. The terms of the option had been "predicated on the practical absence of serious competition on the part of other manufacturers either in this country or other countries."[48] Shortly after its organization Du Pont Cellophane launched a research program designed to strengthen its market position by improving cellophane. One of its chief defects was its permeability to moisture. Du Pont promptly attacked this problem and by 1927 had developed a moistureproofing process and had applied for patents. Its basic patent covering moistureproof cellophane, Charch and Prindle patent No. 1,737,187 issued in 1929, was a product patent broad in scope and extensive in claims.[49] J. E. Hatt, general manager of Du Pont Cellophane's cellophane department, in summarizing du Pont's moistureproof cellophane patent situation in 1930 recognized its vulnerability and indicated that du Pont had taken steps to bulwark it. He described patent applications that du Pont had filed and quoted patent counsel's opinion that they promised "important and substantial additional protection."[50] Between 1930 and 1934 Du Pont Cellophane authorized a research project further to bolster its patent position. In reporting on the success of this project in 1934 President Yerkes said:

> This work was undertaken as a defensive program in connection with protecting broadly by patents the field of moistureproofing agents other than waxes which was the only class of material disclosed in our original Cellophane moistureproofing patents.

[48] Report dated April 14, 1923 by Dr. Fin Sparre, director of du Pont's development department, GX 392, p. 5455. See also pp. 5453-56.

[49] A problem arising during the second world war when the government needed more moistureproof laminated products than du Pont could supply directly, reflects the breadth of the patent claims. Hines of du Pont posed the problem in this way: "What is the best procedure to give the Government these laminated products necessary to win the war and, having decided on that, what can be done to preserve du Pont's position in a postwar economy?" Recognizing that the government's interest might best be served by allowing converters to make them, du Pont feared that the converters might "at the end of the war, be possessed of a great deal of information with respect to the preparation of moistureproofing compositions and the technique of moistureproofing film with them and would be disposed to continue in such a business on a peace-time basis to the detriment of the Company's interests." Memorandum dated January 26, 1942 from du Pont's patent service to du Pont's cellophane research section, GX 2497, pp. 3255-57.

[50] Memorandum of August 26, 1930, GX 2469, p. 3160.

> The investigations on this subject did, in fact, lead to the discovery of a number of classes of materials which could serve equally well for moistureproofing agents . . . Each of these classes has been made the subject of a patent . . . Altogether, 13 patent applications are being written as a result of the work done under this project, all in view of strengthening our Moistureproof Cellophane patent situation.[51]

These steps proved adequate to forestall other domestic competition [52] and to bring Sylvania Industrial Corporation to terms when it invaded the American market.

Syvania reaches accord with du Pont

Sylvania completed its Virginia plant for making cellophane in 1930. Apparently its early experimental research to develop a moistureproof cellophane rested, as did du Pont's, on the use of a nitrocellulose base to which gum, wax, and plasticizer were added. When du Pont's Church and Prindle patent covering moistureproof cellophane was issued, du Pont advised Sylvania informally of its claims and Sylvania after considering them "felt obliged to discard the work they had done up to that time, and approach the subject from a new angle." [53] The new angle substituted a vinyl resin base for the nitrocellulose base. Du Pont, regarding this as an infringement, advised Dr. Wallach, Sylvania's president, that "we would be obliged to enforce our patent" [54] and eventually filed an infringement suit against Sylvania.[55] In the antitrust proceedings against du Pont the government contended that the "entire infringement suit was nothing more than a harassing action designed to coerce Sylvania into entering

[51] December 1933 report to Du Pont Cellophane's board of directors, January 22, 1934, GX 488, p. 6478. Du Pont spent $19,503 on this research project. This compares with an expenditure of only between $5,000 and $10,000 authorized in October 1924 to hire a single chemist to develop the original moistureproofing process. DX 393 and DX 394. Total expenditures for "technical activities expenses," which included all types of technical work designed to improve cellophane production and processes, came to only $32,048 during 1925 and 1926. DX 387.

[52] Du Pont's strong patent position may not have been wholly responsible for the reluctance of other domestic companies to produce cellophane. Apparently Union Carbide & Carbon Corporation in the 1930's considered entering the cellophane field. It purchased rights to a process for making a transparent wrapping material similar to cellophane. Lammot du Pont in a letter of December 2, 1931 to L. A. Yerkes, president of Du Pont Cellophane, stated that in the course of an hour's conversation on this topic with Messrs. Jesse Ricks and Barrett of Union Carbide & Carbon "[t]hey assured me repeatedly they did not wish to rush into anything, most of all a competitive situation with du Pont. Their whole tone was most agreeable. . . . In the course of the conversation, various efforts at cooperation between Carbide and du Pont were referred to, and in every case assurances of their desire to work together, given." GX 4381, p. 4300.

[53] Memorandum dated February 18, 1931 from J. E. Hatt, Du Pont Cellophane's general manager, to its executive committee, GX 2482, p. 3204.

[54] *Loc cit.*

[55] The bill of complaint in *Du Pont Cellophane Company* v. *Sylvania Industrial Corporation* appears in the record of the Cellophane case as GX 2479, pp. 3183-90, and Sylvania's answer as GX 2480, pp. 3181-99.

a highly restrictive agreement." [56] The district court in finding for du Pont rejected this contention.[57] Since the court has spoken, we do not express judgment on this issue. But we wish to review briefly evidence that throws some light on du Pont's strategy.

The record indicates that (1) du Pont in negotiating for reparations following SIDAC's entry into the American market considered and rejected a proposal that it grant Sylvania a license which would restrict its output; (2) after warning Sylvania that it would defend its patents and learning that Sylvania challenged their validity, du Pont postponed action while entrenching its patent position; [58] (3) although professing confidence in its ability to establish its patents' validity, du Pont offered to settle the issue by granting a license limiting Sylvania's production of moistureproof cellophane to 10 per cent of the companies' combined output; [59] (4) on Sylvania's rejecting this offer du Pont formally notified Sylvania that it was infringing du Pont's moistureproofing patents and asked that it cease; [60] (5) upon its refusal to desist du Pont formally inaugurated infringement proceedings; and (6) before the proceedings were carried to completion du Pont and Sylvania settled the suit by a patent exchange and licensing agreement.[61]

[56] Statement to the court by J. L. Minicus, counsel for the government, T. 2472.

[57] Judge Leahy said: "Neither party dictated the terms of the license agreement by which the suit was settled." 118 F. Supp. at 151. He based this finding on testimony by L. A. Yerkes, president of Du Pont Cellophane. Although Judge Leahy had said that if he found that du Pont did not posses monopoly power it would be unnecessary for him to pass on whether it had monopolized cellophane under section 2 of the Sherman Act and the principles of *United States* v. *Aluminum Co. of America*, 148 F. 2d 416 (2d Cir. 1945), he nevertheless made a decision on that charge also. He ruled that du Pont's licensing and technology exchange agreements with La Cellophane did not unreasonably restrain trade and that their territorial limitations were ancillary to the acquisition of trade secrets. 118 F. Supp. at 219. He ruled that the circumstances under which du Pont acquired its patents failed to show that the "acquisitions affected its ability to exclude competition" (*ibid.*, p. 212), and that du Pont placed only "lawful and reasonable limitations on use" in its licenses (*ibid.*, p. 211). In any event, he ruled, du Pont had a lawful monopoly in its moistureproof cellophane patent. He said: "Evidence does not disclose combining of competing or independent process patents or efforts to control unpatented products" (*ibid.*, p. 214).

[58] A running memorandum of developments in the du Pont-Sylvania patent controversy between July 9, 1931 and April 6, 1933, in the du Pont files, contains the following statement: "At Board meeting on 8/21/31 . . . [i]t was felt by Mr. Pritchard [du Pont's patent counsel] that actual suit against Sylvania should not be instituted until we have these claims issued in form of actual patents. . . . L.A.Y. [Yerkes, Du Pont Cellophane's president] still felt it would be desirable for us to have Sylvania under a license agreement if possible." GX 2478, p. 3181.

[59] *Loc. cit.* On August 27, 1931 Yerkes wrote to Dr. Wallach confirming an oral offer made on or about July 9, 1931. A memorandum dated July 13, 1931 outlines the terms of the offer. GX 2483, p. 3206.

[60] GX 2478, p. 3181. The memorandum refers to a letter dated 11/19/31 which lists the patents du Pont claimed to be infringed.

[61] Agreement dated April 26, 1933, GX 2487, pp. 3212-33.

Both parties no doubt thought that they stood to gain by a settlement. If Sylvania lost the suit, it would be forced to stop producing moistureproof cellophane or to produce it on such terms as du Pont might offer. If it won, anyone with adequate resources could produce cellophane, and selling cellophane would become a competitive enterprise. After a discussion with Sylvania's general counsel du Pont's patent attorney summed up Sylvania's plight as follows:

> During the conference Mr. Menken stated that in his opinion the case should be settled. He said that they were very fearful of what the result would be to their company in the event they succeeded in having the claims of the patents which are involved in the litigation held invalid. He seemed to realize the old adage that the defendant can never win. . . . If the Du Pont Cellophane Company succeeds and the patents are held to be infringed, Sylvania Industrial Corporation will be under injunction and will be obliged to stop manufacturing moistureproof wrapping tissue. On the other hand, if they succeed in having the broad claims of the patents held invalid they will throw the art open, as far as the broad claims are concerned, to anyone and therefore will have additional competition. Sylvania . . . has plenty of ready cash but are hesitant about enlarging their plant facilities pending the litigation since, if successful, they will only invite further competition.[62]

With neither side ready to test the validity of du Pont's patents, the parties compromised. The compromise constituted no threat to du Pont's dominant market position.

Under the settlement reached April 26, 1933, Du Pont Cellophane granted Sylvania a nonexclusive license (made exclusive in 1938) of du Pont's five basic patents on moistureproof cellophane and agreed to license to it any patents within their scope which du Pont might get before October 16, 1948. Sylvania agreed to grant similar rights to Du Pont Cellophane under any patents which it might get. Sylvania agreed to pay du Pont a royalty of 2 per cent of its net cellophane sales for the use of du Pont's basic patents and an additional 2 per cent if Sylvania accepted licenses under future du Pont patents representing departures from the five basic patents. But the settlement went further than a mere cross-licensing of present and future patents. It provided that Sylvania's production be restricted to a fixed percentage of total moistureproof cellophane sales, beginning with 20 per cent in 1933 and increasing by 1 per cent until it reached 29 per cent in 1942. Should Sylvania exceed its share in a given year, it agreed to pay a penalty royalty of 20 cents a pound or 30 per cent of its net cellophane sales, whichever was higher. If du Pont used any of Sylvania's patents,

[62] Letter dated August 4, 1932 from W. S. Pritchard to B. M. May, GX 2811, pp. 6073-74.

it agreed to a similar penalty for exceeding its basic quota. But it never used them.

Until June 1951 du Pont and Sylvania were the only producers of cellophane in the American market.[63] Between 1933 and 1945 (when they contracted for smaller royalties and abandoned penalties for exceeding their quotas), with Sylvania's output geared to du Pont's, du Pont could determine how much cellophane should come on the market. Actually the penalty provision of the agreement never operated and its deletion from the 1945 agreement produced no marked effect on Sylvania's production. The court found that "[i]ts policies as to expansion in no way changed following the termination of the 1933 agreement in 1945." [64] Although their shares varied from time to time, du Pont supplied about 76 per cent and Sylvania 24 per cent of the market from 1933 to 1950.[65] But gearing Sylvania's production to du Pont's must have lessened Sylvania's incentive to independent, vigorous rivalry, price or nonprice, and the record indicates that until January 1, 1947 Sylvania's quoted prices were generally identical with du Pont's.[66]

Conclusion

Du Pont's moves and countermoves to protect its domestic market were the strategy of a producer operating in a monopolistic, not a competitive, market. Its agreements with foreign producers to license patents and exchange technical data, its domestic patent program, its effort to get higher tariffs, its restrictive market agreement with Sylvania, all reflect du Pont's effort to preserve what is apparently

[63] In June 1951 Olin Industries, Inc., began the production of cellophane at Pisgah Forest, North Carolina. Testimony of Fred Olsen, Olin vice president, T. 6829.

[64] 118 F. Supp. at 157.

[65] Data on production, 1933 to 1950, table in *United States*, v, *E. I. du Pont de Nemours & Co.*, 118 F. Supp. 41, 116 (D. Del. 1953). In the five years following the expiration of the 1933 agreement Sylvania's percentage of total domestic production was only 1 per cent higher than its percentage in the five years preceding the expiration of the agreement. American Viscose Corporation acquired Sylvania in 1946.

[66] Du Pont and Sylvania not only identical prices for their most important cellophane types, but their price changes almost always became effective on the same date. GX 549, pp. 7128-66. During the postwar period of short supplies and after the government had instituted its suit against du Pont, differences in Sylvania's and du Pont's prices appeared. DX 591, p. 1128. Judge Leahy was impressed not by the identity of quoted prices but by the fact that Sylvania at time made discounts from its list prices which du Pont did not match. In speaking of du Pont-Sylvania competition he declared that Sylvania "has continued to expand to the full extent of its financial resources" (118 F. Supp. at 212); and that although du Pont was superior in the services rendered to customers, in technology, in price, and in the development of special types of films, competition between the two companies has "flourished" (*loc. cit.*).

regarded as a monopoly market. That du Pont and Sylvania (whose production was geared to du Pont's and whose quoted prices were generally identical with du Pont's) together monopolized the market for cellophane seems scarcely debatable. That du Pont acted as though in its monopoly of cellophane it had a valuable property right which it sought to exploit is equally clear. But was du Pont mistaken? Were available substitutes so similar that du Pont's monopoly of cellophane was in reality a mirage or a phantasy? Is there in fact no distinct market for cellophane, but only a larger market for flexible wrapping materials with producers so numerous that none can make monopoly profits? Let us turn to that question.

II. Cellophane—A Differentiated Product?

For several years du Pont was the sole domestic producer of cellophane and for a quarter of a century Sylvania and du Pont were the only producers. But buyers of flexible wrapping material need not rely solely on these two suppliers. Several hundred rivals produced flexible wrapping materials, in many uses substitutes for cellophane. May not these have converted a monopolistic market into one of workable competition? Let us examine briefly the relevant theory and then the facts.

Price theory and product differentiation

Although others have made important contributions to an understanding of the significance of interproduct competition, Chamberlin, the pioneer, offers a good starting point for this discussion. Chamberlin has recognized that "[a]s long as the substitutes are to any degree imperfect, he [the seller] still has a monopoly of his own product and control over its price within the limits imposed upon any monopolist—those of the demand."[67] But Chamberlin also recognized that rival products, where entry is free and differentiation not marked, could eliminate excess profits even in the "monopolized" field. Expressing his findings diagrammatically, he concluded that the sloping demand curve facing the producer of a differentiated product may become tangent to the cost curve somewhere above lowest average cost. Chamberlin regarded this as a "sort of ideal" solution. As he put it, "With fewer establishments, larger scales of production, and lower prices it would always be true that buyers would be willing to pay more than it would cost to give them a greater diversity of product;

[67] E. H. Chamberlin, *The Theory of Monopolistic Competition*, (5th ed. Cambridge, Mass., 1947), p. 67.

and conversely, with more producers and smaller scales of production, the higher prices they would pay would be more than such gains were worth." [68]

Chamberlin's conclusion that the entry of producers of substitute products will eliminate monopoly profits is based upon two important assumptions: (1) his uniformity assumption—"both demand and cost curves for all the 'products' are uniform throughout the group"; [69] and (2) his symmetry assumption [70]—"any adjustment of price or of 'product' by a single producer spreads its influence over so many of his competitors that the impact felt by any one is negligible and does not lead him to any readjustment of his own situation." [71]

If cost and demand curves are not uniform, or if the "group" of firms producing the substitute products is sufficiently small to introduce the oligopoly problem, we may expect a divergence from the above solution. As for the uniformity assumption, Chamberlin says: "[I]n so far as substitutes of such a degree of effectiveness may not be produced, the conclusions are different—demand curves will lie to the right of the point of tangency with cost curves, and profits will be correspondingly higher. This is the explanation of *all* monopoly profits, of whatever sort." [72] Thus, unless effective substitutes exist, Chamberlin argues that monopoly profits may be "scattered throughout the group." [73] If Chamberlin's symmetry assumption is not fulfilled, an

[68] *Ibid.*, p. 94. This assumes, of course, that buyers know what they get and get what they want in buying a differentiated product. This is a dubious assumption. Years ago a well-known pharmaceutical company by its advertising endeavored to create a widespread fear of halitosis. "Not even your best friends will tell you." Having created a fear of halitosis, it provided a product to dissipate it, thereby rendering the buyer a service for which he was willing to pay.

[69] *Ibid.*, p. 82. To simplify his exposition Chamberlin first assumes uniformity in cost and demand curves. Later he abandons this assumption in the interest of reality. In abandoning it he reaches the conclusion indicated in the text: where sufficiently effective substitutes are not offered in the market, monopoly profits result.

[70] G. J. Stigler so describes this assumption. *Five Lectures on Economic Problems* (London, 1949), p. 17.

[71] Chamberlin, *op. cit.*, p. 83.

[72] *Ibid.*, p. 111. Emphasis in original. This statement of the problem seems to make it similar to if not identical with the conventional, neoclassical conception of monopoly. Richard T. Ely for example pointed out: "The use of substitutes is consistent with monopoly, and we nearly always have them. For almost anything we can think of, there is some sort of a substitute more or less perfect, and the use of substitutes furnishes one of the limits to the power of the monopolist. In the consideration of monopoly we have to ask, what are the substitutes, and how effective are they?" *Monopolies and Trusts* (New York, 1912), pp. 35-36.

[73] Chamberlin, *op. cit.*, p. 113. By the "group" Chamberlin apparently means firms making products which although differentiated are designed for the same use, *e.g.*, toothpaste manufacturers. In his "Monopolistic Competition Revisited," *Economica*, Nov. 1951, N.S. XVIII 352, 353, he abandons the group concept, arguing that "competition is always a matter of substitutes, and . . . substitutes

oligopoly solution may be expected.[74] In either case monopoly profits result.

In applying Chamberlin's theory to the flexible packaging materials market and to cellophane's position in it, the empirical issue revolves about (1) the degree of effectiveness of substitutes, and (2) the number of rival firms. If substitutes are not effective enough to eliminate monopoly profits, it is not necessary to consider the oligopoly problem.

Clark's analysis [75] leads to similar conclusions, viz., that competition among substitutes may eliminate monopoly profits; but Clark goes further than Chamberlin in finding these results salutary. According to Clark the high cross elasticity of demand tends to flatten the monopolist's demand curve. Moreover, the monopolist's fear of potential competition may lead him to behave as though potential competition had become a reality. These two restraining forces, rival substitute products and potential competition, may yield cost-price relationships similar to those of pure competition. They may make imperfect competition workable.

An increasing number of economists have come to believe this. Robertson develops the idea somewhat further. In reviewing the significance of interproduct and interindustry competition he concludes that we really need not worry about monopoly for "there is probably not much of it." There is not much of it because the "old-fashioned apparatus of competition works in new ways to save us." [76]

Moreover, this new apparatus of competition once more makes relevant a theory of competition based on large numbers.

> To assess the competitive situation of a firm we must still resort to counting numbers. We cannot do away with the group, for the group exists in the real world. Yet counting only those firms which are within the "industry" tells us very little. We must do our counting by taking categories of uses for the output of an industry, considering what products of other industries directly compete within these categories.[77]

---

are always a matter of degree." In abandoning the group concept he does not abandon the conclusion that where substitutes are similar enough and entry is free, monoply profits will disappear and the demand curve will be tangent to the cost curve at some point above minimum cost. But he also recognizes that the "isolated" monopolist, in spite of close substitutes, may find the demand for his own product strong enough to yield him "profits in excess of the minimum."

[74] *Monopolistic Competition*, p. 102.

[75] J. M. Clark, "Toward a Concept of Workable Competition," *American Economic Review* (June 1940), XXX, pp. 241-256.

[76] R. M. Robertson, "On the Changing Apparatus of Competition," Proceedings of the American Economic Association, *American Economic Review* (May 1954), XLIV, 61.

[77] *Ibid.*, pp. 53-54.

Since a monopolist's product may serve in a great variety of uses, a monopolist may find it "profitable to forego monopoly control in one use in order to push the commodity into many uses." [78] Thus monopoly serves the public by serving itself and in doing so loses its power over the market.

What Robertson has discovered for the economists, businessmen had already professed. David Lilienthal, writing about the "new competition," said:

> I am not saying that active competition between the producers of the same product is of no present consequence. It certainly is. My point is that under present-day conditions it is often the least significant form. The competition between alternative materials, or ways of satisfying human needs and desires, has become a new dimension of competition.[79]

It was on such principles that Judge Leahy relied in reaching his conclusions in the Cellophane case.

This calls for a more careful consideration of the uniqueness of cellophane, of du Pont's pricing policies in selling it, and of the rate of earnings realized in doing so. If cellophane is sufficiently differentiated from other flexible wrapping materials, its demand curve may "lie to the right of the point of tangency with its cost curve" and its producer may receive monopoly profits in making and selling it. If cellophane is a less highly differentiated product within Chamberlin's conception of the term and if entry to the manufacture of rival wrapping materials is not blocked, the maker of cellophane will be faced by a sloping demand curve; but the curve will be tangent to the cost curve at some point about lowest average cost, and the seller will not make a monopoly profit. If the differentiation is so slight and potential competition so imminent as to bring it within Clark's concept of the term, the seller's long-run demand curve will be close to the horizontal (his control over price will be slight) and prices will be close to lowest average cost. If the cellophane market conforms to Robertson's model, cellophane's differentiation will be too slight to count, monopoly profit will not exist, and its price will be competitive. To which of these models does the market for cellophane conform?

The market for cellophane

As a first step in answering this question we will examine briefly the flexible packaging materials market. The district court in deter-

[78] *Ibid.*, p. 57.
[79] D. E. Lilienthal, *Big Business: A New Era* (New York, 1953), p. 60.

mining whether du Pont monopolized the market for cellophane concluded that "the relevant market for determining the extent of du Pont's market control is the market for flexible packaging materials." [80] In this broad market the court found several hundred firms selling a variety of differentiated products for an even wider variety of uses. They sold either directly to packagers or to converters who prepared packaging materials for special uses. The court found that in 1949 du Pont cellophane accounted for only 17.9 per cent of the total square yardage of domestic output and imports of flexible packaging materials.[81] (Apparently this did not include kraft paper.) Such a small percentage scarcely demonstrates that du Pont had monopolized the *flexible packaging materials* market. Nor had it. But in passing judgment on the validity of the court's view that there is a single market for flexible packaging materials it may be helpful to classify the major contemporary materials according to their special qualities and major uses.

Cellophane is a thin, transparent, nonfibrous film of regenerated cellulose. It comes in two major types: plain and moistureproof. Moistureproof cellophane far outsells plain. In 1950 plain cellophane sales totalled $12,005,737; moistureproof cellophane sales, $116,660,-209.[82] Because moistureproof cellophane sales are over nine times those of plain, our analysis will give primary consideration to moistureproof. Moistureproof cellophane is highly transparent, tears readily but has high bursting strength, is highly impervious to moisture and gases, and is resistant to grease and oils. Heat sealable, printable, and adapted to use on wrapping machines, it makes an excellent packaging material for both display and protection of commodities.

Other flexible wrapping materials fall into four major categories: (1) opaque nonmoistureproof wrapping *paper* designed primarily for convenience and protection in handling packages; (2) moistureproof *films* of varying degrees of transparency designed primarily either to protect, or to display and protect, the products they encompass; (3) nonmoistureproof transparent *films* designed primarily to display and to some extent protect, but which obviously do a poor protecting job where exclusion or retention of moisture is important; and (4) moistureproof *materials* other than films of varying degrees of transparency (foils and paper products) designed to protect and display.

[80] 118 F.Supp at 60.
[81] *Ibid.*, p. 111.
[82] Table showing comparison of du Pont and Sylvania plain and moistureproof cellophane sales, 1924-1950, 118 F. Supp. at 123.

Kraft paper is the leading opaque nonmoistureproof wrapping paper. For general wrapping it has no equal. It is cheap, strong, and pliable and gives adequate protection. On a tonnage basis it easily tops all other packaging materials in total sales. But it is neither designed for nor adapted to the special uses for which cellophane was created and, as one market expert has put it, "in the true sense" does not compete with cellophane. More accurately, we think, cellophane does not compete with it. On a cost basis it cannot compete. At less than one cent per thousand square inches, kraft paper sells for less than cellophane's manufacturing cost.

The leading moistureproof *films* which might compete with cellophane include polyethylene, Saran, and Pliofilm. These are relatively late-comers in the packaging field. In some qualities they match or even excel cellophane. But we have it on the authority of du Pont market analysts that these films have offered little or no competition to cellophane in its major markets. According to du Pont's 1948 market analysis, prepared by its experts for company use in making decisions, although Saran was "superior in moisture protection, no significant commercial uses" had developed for it "due principally to its high price" and "no substantial cost reduction" was in sight.[83] In 1949 a thousand square inches of 100-guage Saran # 517 sold for about 2½ times as much as the same amount of moistureproof cellophane (see Table I). Du Pont experts found polyethylene lacking in transparency, "too limp to operate satisfactorily on wrapping machines, . . . difficult to heat seal, print and glue," with "poor surface slip and high static, and . . . permeable to volatile oils and flavorings." [84] Pliofilm, an older rival first marketed in the mid-thirties, has a rubber base and is particularly well adapted to packaging foods preserved in liquids, a relatively narrow market. Despite its superiority in this use, its high cost (in 1949 a thousand square inches of 120-guage Pliofilm N2 sold for about 1⅔ times as much as moistureproof cellophane) made it "an active competitor of Cellophane only in those fringe uses bordering markets that need greater moistureproof protection than Cellophane provides." [85] In 1939 Pliofilm sales were only 2 per cent of cellophane sales; by 1949 they had increased to only 4.4 per cent.[86]

[83] DX 595, p. 1156.

[84] *Ibid.*, pp. 1155-56. The court said of polyethylene: "Many of these deficiencies could be corrected through research, and were." 118 F. Supp. at 81.

[85] DX 595, p. 1153. In 1950 Goodyear developed a type satisfactory for fresh meats. 118 F. Supp. at 81.

[86] GX 531, p. 7101; GX 81, p. 309; DK 596, p. 1173.

TABLE I

COMPARISON OF AVERAGE WHOLESALE PRICES OF CELLOPHANE WITH PRICES OF OTHER FLEXIBLE PACKAGING MATERIALS IN 1949

Packaging Material	Price per 1,000 sq. in. (cents)	Per Cent of Cellophane Prices		Price per lb. (cents)	Per Cent of Cellophane Prices	
		Moistureproof	Plain		Moistureproof	Plain
Saran 100 gauge #517	6.1	265.2	290.5	99.0	207.1	221.0
Cellulose Acetate .00088″	3.3	143.5	157.1	82.0	171.5	183.0
Polyethylene .002″—18″ flat width	5.4	234.8	257.1	81.0	169.4	180.8
Pliofilm 120 gauge N2	3.8	165.2	181.0	80.8	169.0	180.4
Aluminum Foil .00035″	1.8	78.3	85.7	52.2	109.2	165.2
Moistureproof Cellophane 300 MST-51	2.3	100.0	109.5	47.8	100.0	106.7
Plain Cellophane 300 PT	2.1	91.3	100.0	44.8	93.7	100.0
Vegetable Parchment 27#	1.4	60.9	66.7	22.3	46.7	49.8
Bleached Glassine 25#	1.0	43.4	47.6	17.8	37.2	39.7
Bleached Greaseproof 25#	.9	39.1	42.9	15.8	33.1	35.3
Plain Waxed Sulphite 25# self-sealing	1.1	47.8	52.4	15.2	31.8	33.9
Plain Waxed Sulphite 25# coated opaque	.7	30.4	33.3	11.9	24.9	26.6

Source: Prices per thousand square inches and per pound, *United States v. E. I. du Pont de Nemours & Company*, 118 F. Supp. 41, 83 (D.Del. 1953). Robert Heller & Associates, management consultants, conducted the price survey for du Pont on which DX 995, the original source of these data, is based. G. W. Bricker, who personally supervised the survey, testified that "each of these materials is a principal standard material of that type." T. 4497. In selecting a particular grade Bricker relied on the device of the Bureau of Labor Statistics. American Pulp and Paper Association economists, and the individual companies from which he got his data.

Cellulose acetate, a nonmoistureproof transparent *film,* is an old cellophane rival. First appearing in 1931, by 1939 its sales were only 3 per cent of cellophane's. Ten years later they were only 3.7 per cent.[87] Its chief quality disadvantage is that it is not moistureproof. It compares in quality with plain cellophane, but its 57 per cent higher price in 1949 placed it at a serious competitive disadvantage.

About these several films du Pont in its 1948 market analysis concluded:

> The principal markets for non-viscose films have been competitive with Cellophane only to a very minor degree up to this time. Some are used very little or not at all in the packaging field—others are employed principally for specialty uses where Cellophane is not well adapted—none have been successfully introduced into any of Cellophane's main markets due to their inherent shortcomings.[88]

[87] Comparison of total du Pont and United States production of cellophane and imports of selected flexible packaging materials, 1925-1949, DX 981, p. 1.

[88] DX 595, p. 1147.

On the superiority of cellophane as compared with other films for most of cellophane's uses, the experts apparently agreed. Olin Industries, Inc., later to become the third domestic cellophane producer, after investigation reported: "According to du Pont, Cellophane is considered the only all purpose film, and any product to be *truly competitive* with Cellophane must have the following attributes: (1) low cost, (2) transparency, (3) operate with a high efficiency on mechanical equipment, (4) print well both as to speed and appearance."[89] Olin concluded:

> There are no films currently marketed which are potentially competitive to any substantial degree in Cellophane's major markets when measured by the above attributes necessary for wide usage. Other transparent films will find their place for those low volumes uses which can absorb the additional cost of the film and which necessitate certain physical properties not possessed by Cellophane.[90]

Consumer decisions confirmed the judgment of the experts. In 1949 converters used roughly fourteen times as much cellophane as all other packaging films.[91]

Apparently cellophane has no effective rival in another segment of the flexible packaging material market, the outer wrapping of packaged cigarettes. Clear as plate glass, flexible, easily ripped open, moistureproof, it displays and protects with such perfection that except when they can't get it cigarette makers use no other overwrap.[92] The court recognized this, noting however that makers of Pliofilm, glassine, and aluminum foil keep trying to break into this market. They have not succeeded.

The court to the contrary notwithstanding, the market in which cellophane meets the "competition" of other wrappers is narrower than the market for all flexible packaging materials. Cellophane dominates the market for cigarette overwraps, it does not compete with kraft paper for general wrapping, and in its more specialized markets the nonviscose films do not compete with cellophane except in fringe uses.

[89] Report on "the evidence in support of entry by Olin Industries into the Cellophane business, based on the purchase of patent license and 'know-how' from du Pont," December 15, 1948, GX 566, p. 7575.

[90] *Loc. cit.*

[91] DX 985. This is a market analysis prepared for du Pont by Robert Heller & Associates.

[92] A shortage of cellophane in the mid-'forties forced some cigarette makers to use other materials. Brown and Williamson Tobacco Company once experimented with selling Kools and Raleigh cigarettes in a one-piece foil package. 118 F. Supp. at 108.

Food packaging

In 1949, 80 per cent of du Pont's cellophane sales were for packaging food products; here cellophane encounters its most vigorous rivalry, "competing" with vegetable parchment, greaseproof paper, glassine, wax paper, and aluminum foil. Each of these wrapping materials is a differentiated bundle of qualities, competing in a wide variety of uses. Users attach a different importance to the several qualities. Many value transparency highly, a quality in which cellophane is outstanding. Some, however, regard transparency as a disadvantage. All are likely to rate moisture protection as important, but wax paper, aluminum foil, and some types of glassine are about as good as cellophane in this. Food packagers in selecting wrapping material no doubt consider carefully the unique combination of qualities represented by each of these materials. They resell the product they wrap and they are cost-conscious. Presumably they try to select the material that, quality considered, will give the greatest value. In determining values they must consider consumer response to the several materials. In any event, some buyers of packaging materials changed from one kind to another in trying to get their money's worth. Some candy makers and some bread bakers, for example, operating on narrow margins in the mid-'thirties switched from cellophane to a less costly wrapper when their other production costs mounted. The court concluded from the evidence that "shifts of business between du Pont cellophane and other flexible packaging materials have been frequent, continuing and contested." [93] In no one of the more important uses for packaging foods did cellophane in 1949 supply as much as 50 per cent of the total quantity (in square inches) of wrapping materials used (see Table II).[94] Only in the packaging of fresh produce did cellophane sales top the list. Its percentage of total sales varied from 6.8 per cent for packaging bakery products to 47.2 per cent for fresh produce. Like du Pont's percentage of total sales of all flexible wrapping materials, these specific figures scarcely demonstrate that du Pont has monopolized the sale of flexible packaging material to food packagers.

[93] *Ibid.*, p. 91.

[94] Table II is based on evidence which the court reproduced in the opinion. In less important uses not included in the court's tabulation cellophane accounted for the following percentages of total quantities of the selected flexible wrapping materials used: dry beverages, 6.4 per cent; breakfast cereals, 12.6 per cent; dry fruits and vegetables, 63.7 per cent; frozen dairy products, 1.1 per cent; flour, meal, and dry baking mixes, .5 per cent; nuts, 77.3 per cent; paste goods, 97.4 per cent; paper products, 38 per cent; and textile products, 62.3 per cent. DX 984.

TABLE II

COMPARISON BY PERCENTAGES OF TOTAL QUANTITY OF SELECTED FLEXIBLE PACKAGING MATERIALS, CLASSIFIED BY END USES *

Type of Material	Bakery Products	Candy	Snacks	Meat and Poultry	Crackers and Biscuits	Fresh Produce	Frozen Food Excluding Dairy Products
Cellophane	6.8	24.4	31.9	34.9	26.6	47.2	33.6
Foil	.2	32.5	.8	.1	.2	.1	.7
Glassine	4.4	21.4	62.8	2.7	10.0	.1	2.1
Papers	88.6	21.6	4.4	57.5	63.2	45.6	60.3
Films	.0	.1	.1	4.8	.0	7.0	3.3
Total	100.0	100.0	100.0	100.0	100.0	100.0	100.0

* Based on 1949 sales (in millions of square inches) of nineteen major converters "representing a substantial segment" of the converting industry, *United States* v. *E. I. du Pont de Nemours & Company*, 118 F.Supp. 41, 113 (D.Del. 1953). G. W. Bricker of Robert Heller and Associates, management consultants employed by du Pont, testified that the above data covered two-thirds of du Pont's and Sylvania's cellophane. T. 4474.

Such facts apparently led the court to conclude that du Pont, although selling about 76 per cent of the cellophane and together with Sylvania—whose production was geared to du Pont's—selling all of it, had not monopolized the market for *all* flexible wrapping materials. No one is likely to quarrel with this finding. But in an economic sense a firm may have a monopoly of a differentiated product, that is, it may behave like a monopolist and enjoy the fruits of monopoly in selling it, even though it meets the rivalry of substitutes. That is the economic issue here. Is cellophane so highly differentiated that du Pont in selling it can follow an independent pricing policy, that is, is the cross elasticity of demand for cellophane so low that du Pont, while pricing it independently, can enjoy a monopoly profit in its sale? Let us examine this issue.

When du Pont first marketed cellophane, it apparently thought cellophane had unique qualities and it adopted a strategy designed to prevent competition from any other producer, in short, to protect its monopoly.[95] It also priced cellophane from the outset to yield monopoly revenue. Its long-run aim in selling cellophane was apparently that of any monopolist, viz., to maximize revenues. But the maximizing of revenues over time even by a monopolist may call for a farsighted and vigorous policy in exploiting a product. Monopolists, although they

[95] If cellophane had encountered the effective competition of rival wrapping materials, du Pont would have had nothing to gain by impeding entry. That is to say, if cellophane were merely one of many substitutable products among which effective competition prevails, the price of each would be driven down to a competitive (cost-remunerative) level and it should be a matter of indifference to du Pont whether this results from rival products or from new producers of cellophane.

can restrict output and charge relatively high prices, may not find it profitable to do so. Du Pont argued and the court concluded that the test of monopoly is the power to exclude competition and the power to raise prices. A more logical test is the power to exclude competition and the power to *control* prices. That a monopolist may find it profitable to lower prices, increase sales, and reduce costs, even though the public benefits, does not necessarily mean, as Robertson suggests, that he has relinquished monopoly power. To use monopoly power rationally is not to forego it.

President Yerkes of the Du Pont Cellophane Company, Inc., concluded as early as 1924 that to maximize earnings du Pont should reduce cellophane prices. On this issue he said:

> I am in favor of lowering the price. . . . [I] think it will undoubtedly increase sales and widen distribution. . . . Our price I think is too high based purely on manufacturing cost and too high in comparison with other wrapping papers on the market, and while we cannot approach the price of glassine or other oil papers, if we make a substantial reduction we will in some cases get somewhere near there.[96]

Walter S. Carpenter, Jr., chairman of du Pont's board of directors, expressed a similar idea when he testified in the Cellophane case:

> . . . the purpose of reducing our price and also improving our quality was to broaden our market. . . . As a general philosophy I was always in favor of the reduction of the price as we were able to do so by the reduced costs, and I think that I consistently urged that on the management.[97]

The Yerkes-Carpenter philosophy apparently prevailed. The price of cellophane, which averaged $2.508 a pound in 1924, was reduced in every year until 1936, when it averaged 41.3 a pound. With minor interruptions the decline continued until cellophane sold for an average price of 38 cents a pound in 1940. Inflation accompanying the second world war reversed the trend. With few exceptions cellophane prices moved upward until 1950, when they averaged 49 cents a pound.[98] But despite the reductions moistureproof cellophane (300 MST-51, the principal type) sold at from two to seven times the price of 25# bleached glassine and from two to four and a half times the price of 30# waxed paper, its most important rivals.[99]

[96] Memorandum of some remarks made at a meeting of the board of directors, Du Pont Cellophane Company, Inc., December 11, 1924, DX 337, p. 643.

[97] T. 6278-79.

[98] Table of annual average prices from 1924 to 1950, *United States* v. *E. I. du Pont de Nemours & Co.*, 118 F. Supp. 41, 82 (D.Del. 1953).

[99] Defendant's Brief on the Facts and the Law, Appendix A (graph based on prices per 1,000 sq. in.), *United States* v. *E. I. du Pont de Nemours & Co.*, 118 F. Supp. 41 (D. Del. 1953).

Du Pont's independent pricing policy

On its face du Pont's pricing policy was consistent with that of a monpolist. Other evidence supports this conclusion. Had cellophane's major rival wrapping materials completed with it effectively (*i.e.*, had the cross elasticity of demand between cellophane and other wrappers been high), the prices of such wrapping materials would have moved concurrently to prevent, as Chamberlin says, "incursions by one seller, through a price cut, upon the markets of others." [100] In fact, however, while du Pont was "broadening its market" by reducing cellophane prices, the prices of other wrappers did not follow a similar pattern. Bleached glassine prices were constant from 1924 until 1933 and again from 1934 to 1938. They rose in 1939 and again in 1940. Waxed paper prices fluctuated between .5 and .52 cent per thousand square inches from 1933 through 1939 and in 1940 increased to .62 cent. Vegetable parchment prices declined from 1.3 cents to 1.0 cent per thousand square inches between 1924 and 1928 and thereafter fluctuated between .95 cent and 1.05 cents. Bleached greaseproof prices rose from .45 cent per thousand square inches in 1933 to about .55 cent in 1940.[101] But du Pont's cellulose acetate film dropped in price from 59.3 cents a pound in 1935 to 53.6 cents in 1940,[102] and aluminum foil prices dropped from 2.45 cents to 1.65 cents per thousand square inches between 1928 and 1940. The prices of these rival products and of cellophane followed the same trend, but cellophane and cellulose acetate film sold for substantially more than aluminum foil; and it seems likely that the cross elasticity of demand between the cellulose films and aluminum foil is even less than between them and the other products compared.

Under inflation wrapping material prices have increased since 1940, but not similarly. Average cellophane prices increased by about 20 per cent between 1940 and 1949, but the prices of most other wrappers increased more rapidly: vegetable parchment, about 40 per cent; bleached glassine, 40 per cent; cellulose acetate, 50 per cent; waxed paper, 75 per cent; and bleached greaseproof, 80 per cent. The only two wrappers to increase less in price than cellophane were Pliofilm, 13 per cent, and aluminum foil, 9 per cent.[103] These price patterns

[100] Chamberlin, *Monopolistic Competition*, p. 90.

[101] DX 994-A. These price comparisons, like those for 1949 in Table I, rest on data collected for du Pont by Robert Heller & Associates and are based on the prices of one principal standard material of each type named.

[102] GX 490, p. 6507; GX 495, p. 6665.

[103] DX 994-A.

indicate that cellophane continued to decrease in price relative to most other wrapping materials.

The above facts demonstrating cellophane's independence of other wrapping material prices strongly suggest that du Pont was not selling cellophane in an effectively competitive market. Either cellophane's rival products were not close enough substitutes to feel the effect of cellophane price decreases (*i.e.*, the cross elasticity of demand between cellophane and these products was low) or they were already selling at cost and could not prevent cellophane's invasion of their markets. In either event they did not constitute sufficiently close substitutes to insure effective competition.

Although du Pont lowered its cellophane prices from time to time as it re-examined its demand and cost functions, at no time did it compete with its most popular rivals on a price basis. As H. O. Ladd, director of du Pont's trade analysis division, put it:

> The main competitive materials . . . against which Cellophane competes are waxed paper, glassine, greaseproof and vegetable parchment paper, all of which are lower in price than Cellophane. We do not meet this price competition. Rather, we compete with these materials on the basis of establishing the value of our own as a factor in better packaging and cheaper distribution costs and classify as our logical markets those fields where the properties of Cellophane in relationship to its price can do a better job for the user.[104]

But while du Pont resorted to aggressive selling, emphasizing the superiority of its product and extending its services,[105] the evidence does not indicate that at any time it carried quality competition so far as to equalize average cost and selling price. Price differences no doubt reflected at the margin the customers' evaluation of differences in quality, but the record does not indicate that they reflected differences in cost. If they had, with as many firms as are selling flexible wrapping materials, monopoly profits would have disappeared and the market would have become effectively competitive. Let us turn then to du Pont's earning record.

[104] GX 589, p. 7530.

[105] Du Pont showed great ingenuity and aggression in developing new uses for cellophane and expanding old ones. R. R. Smith, assistant director of sales of du Pont's film department, testified that in 1934, when white bread regularly sold for 10 cents a loaf and its profit margin was small, he and other salesmen actually created the specialty breads industry—new varieties of bread which could be sold at a price large enough to cover the higher cost of wrapping them in cellophane. T. 5704-5. In 1936 Smith studied the sales methods of door-to-door bakery salesmen and du Pont made a sales training film "which had nothing to do with packaging" (T. 5721) but showed the way to higher profits even when using cellophane. "The promotion was extremely successful." T. 5705. In 1951 du Pont had about 45 per cent of the variety bread-wrapping business. T. 5721.

III. Has Du Pont Earned Monopoly Profits?

As du Pont reduced cellophane prices, output and sales expanded rapidly. In 1924 du Pont produced only 361,000 pounds of cellophane and sold $1,307,000 worth. A decade later it produced $39,358,000 pounds and sold $18,818,000 worth. In 1940 when cellophane sold at 38 cents a pound, its all-time low, du Pont produced 81,677,000 pounds and sold $31,049,000 worth.[106] Such increases in output and sales had called for a continuous expansion in investment. In 1925 du Pont's fixed and working capital in producing cellophane was $2,122,000. In 1934 it was $24,008,000 and a decade later $41,133,000 (see Table III).

Du Pont's production and pricing policies paid off. In 1925 it earned, before taxes (operating earnings),[107] $779,000 on its cello-

[106] See comparisons of du Pont and Sylvania production and sales, 1924-1950, *United States* v. *E. I. du Pont de Nemours & Co.*, 118 F. Supp. at 116, 123 (D. Del. 1953).

[107] Du Pont computes operating earnings for each operating division by deducting all of the expenses directly related to its operations from its sales. Among these expenses are production, selling, administration, and research expenditures conducted within and for the particular division. Du Pont calculates its rate of operating earnings on the basis of its working and fixed investment allocated to its cellophane operations.

Net cellophane earnings are calculated by allowing for federal income taxes, capital stock tax, franchise, state income, and foreign taxes, "B" bonus, and fundamental research by the chemicals department. Federal income and other taxes constituted the great bulk of these deductions: 90 per cent as early as 1935 (GX 490, p. 6506) and during the second world war parctically all, when the company was paying large excess profits taxes. Consequently, cellophane operating earnings may be thought of as primarily representing earnings on total cellophane investment before taxes, and cellophane net earnings as earnings after taxes.

The problem of empirically determining profit rates is subject to many pitfalls. However, the procedure used by du Pont to determine cellophane earnings is subject to fewer criticisms than are usually encountered in profit estimates. It is true that earnings may be understated somewhat because of expenditures not directly related to cellophane manufacture and sales as noted above. On the other hand, some might argue that actual earnings are overstated in some years and understated in others because operating investment is necessarily based in part on historical rather than replacement costs. This error is reduced by the fact that du Pont has increased its capacity periodically by substantial amounts, so that of its historical costs a substantial portion is always recent history. However, some of the most frequent and important shortcomings of profit estimates are not involved in our calculations; operating investment does not include assets capitalized in expectation of excess profits, nor has overcapacity broadened the investment base. Probably the most convincing argument as to the credibility of these earnings is that du Pont has no reason to delude itself as to what it is earning in making cellophane. The investment base which du Pont uses to calculate its rates of operating and net earnings is its estimate of the actual total investment involved in its cellophane operations. Such an investment base is considerably larger than that used by the Federal Trade Commission in its study, *Rates of Return (after Taxes) for 516 Identical Companies in 25 Selected Manufacturing Industries, 1940, 1947-52* (Washington, D. C., 1954), which uses stockholders' investment as its base. If this base were used in calculating rates of cellophane earnings they would undoubtedly be greater for all years. For example, in 1935, the year before Du Pont Cellophane was consolidated with du Pont, the latter's equity in Du Pont Cellophane was only $9,696,000. GX 490, p. 6504. If this were used as a base upon which to calculate du Pont's rate of earnings in that year, instead of that actually used in Table III, its rate of operating earnings would be about 60 per cent instead of 24.6 per cent.

phane operating investment. In 1934 it earned $6,000,000 and in 1940, $12,000,000. Although its annual rate of earnings before taxes declined somewhat from a high of 62.4 per cent in 1928, in only two years between 1923 and 1950 inclusive did the rate fall below 20 per cent (see Table III).

Du Pont's cellophane pricing policy is consistent with the economists' assumption that a rational monopolist aims to maximize profits. This did not always call for a price reduction. In 1947 du Pont earned only 19.1 per cent before taxes and only 11.2 per cent after taxes on its cellophane investment [108]—the postwar low. Raising the average price of cellophane from 41.9 cents a pound in 1947 to 46 cents a pound in 1948 paid off. By May 1948 du Pont's operative earnings had increased to 31 per cent. At that time its division manager announced that "if operative earnings of 31 per cent is [*sic*] considered inadequate, then an upward revision in prices will be necessary to improve the return." [109] He suggested a schedule of prices which would increase operative earnings to about 40 per cent.[110] This was not put into effect until August 1948. Operative earnings for 1948 averaged only 27.2 per cent; but by 1949 they had increased to 35.2 per cent and by 1950 to 45.3 per cent. Operative earnings after taxes yielded 20 per cent on du Pont's investment in 1950.

Du Pont's pricing policy in the postwar inflation is also consistent with the theory of monopolistic behavior, but the record indicates that profit maximization was not the sole factor affecting price decisions. The division manager in suggesting price increases called attention to other relevant factors:

> 2. What effect, if any, will a price increase have on our case when it is heard before the Federal Judge? I have not covered this with our Legal Department but in view of the position they took last July and August, prior to the October increase, I am inclined to think they should be brought in for a discussion on this matter.
>
> 3. The du Pont Company may get some undesirable publicity from the press. A price increase on Cellophane could be looked upon as added fuel to the present recent spurt in the inflationary spiral and add to the present pressure for an increase in wages. This question is currently a live one at several of our Cellophane plants. Probably it would be in order to discuss this with Mr. Brayman.[111]

[108] One reason for the relatively low earnings in 1947 was du Pont's inability to put its new capacity at Clinton, Iowa, into production as early as predicted. DX 372.

[109] GX 591, p. 7539.

[110] *Ibid.*, p. 7540.

[111] *Loc. cit.* Mr. Brayman was the director of du Pont's public relations department.

TABLE III

DU PONT'S OPERATING INVESTMENT, OPERATING EARNINGS, AND NET EARNINGS ON CELLOPHANE, 1925-1950 *

Year	Operating Investment (000)	Operating Earnings (000)	Rate of Operating Earnings (per cent)	Net Earnings (000)	Rate of Net Earnings (per cent)
1924	$ 2,000				
1925	2,122[b]	$ 779[a]	36.7[b]	$ 650[b]	30.6[a]
1926	2,482	1,447	58.3	1,191[c]	48.0
1927	2,464	1,104	44.8	906[d]	36.8
1928	2,559	1,597	62.4	1,318[e]	51.5
1929	5,099[a]	2,845[f]	55.8[f]	2,645[f]	51.9
1930	11,178	4,460[g]	39.9[g]	4,273[g]	38.2
1931	18,163	5,431[h]	29.9[h]	5,196[h]	28.6
1932	21,600	3,888[i]	18.0[i]	3,882[i]	17.9
1933	23,277	4,958[j]	21.3[j]	4,800[j]	20.6
1934	24,008	5,978[l]	24.9[k]	4,325[l]	18.0
1935	24,598	6,051[k]	24.6[k]	4,934[k]	20.1
1936	26,262[m]	7,642[m]	29.1[m]	6,119[a]	23.3[m]
1937	27,284[o]	6,876	25.2[n]	5,293	19.4[n]
1938	30,655[a]	8,430[p]	27.5	6,867	22.4
1939	31,837	11,833	36.8	9,137	28.7
1940	33,737	12,179	36.1	6,882	20.4
1941	40,995	16,234	39.6	6,231	15.2
1942	43,482	11,566[q]	26.6	3,652	8.4
1943	42,449	14,263	33.6	3,821	9.0
1944	41,133	13,903	33.8	3,990	9.7
1945	40,431	13,868	34.3	5,620	13.9
1946	41,495	12,241[r]	29.5	6,929	16.7
1947	53,424	10,204	19.1	5,983	11.2
1948	64,800[s]	17,600[s]	27.2	n.a.	n.a.
1949	n.a.	n.a.	35.2[t]	n.a.	n.a.
1950	67,532	30,592[t]	45.3[t]	13,506	20.0[t]
	Average Rate of Return......		34.4		24.2

* For definition of operating investment, operating earnings, and net earnings see footnote 107. Before 1937, investment and earnings figures include cellulose caps and bands, cellulose acetate, and adhesives, for some years. On the whole this inclusion decreases the rate of return figures for cellophane slightly, since some of these items were actually sold at a loss at times. The net effect is insignificant, however, since they represent such a small proportion of total earnings and investment—less than 5 per cent in 1935. GX 490, p. 6507.

a Derived from relevant colunms
b 1925-1928, GX 483, pp. 6409, 6410
c GX 481, p. 6375
d GX 482, p. 6396
e GX 483, p. 6418
f GX 484, pp. 6431, 6433
g GX 485, pp. 6441, 6443
h GX 486, pp. 6453, 6455
i GX 487, pp. 6464, 6466
j GX 488, pp. 6479, 6481
k GX 490, p. 6503
l GX 489, p. 6493
m GX 384, p. 969
n 1937-1947, GX 591, p. 7539
o GX 492, p. 6571
p 1938-1941, GX 495-A, p. 6716
q 1942-1945, GX 499, p. 6839
r 1946-1947, GX 501, p. 690
s GX 577, p. 7323

t GX 573 (I), p. 8. Exhibit impounded by court, cited in government's Proposed Findings of Fact, p. 48, and Brief for the United States, pp. 144, 145, *United States* v. *E. I. du Pont de Nemours & Company*, 118 F.Supp. 41 (D.Del. 1953)

Sources: The exhibits referred to are annual profit and loss statements of Du Pont Cellophane Company or the cellophane division of E. I. du Pont de Nemours & Company.

After considering these questions du Pont executives decided on the price increase.[112]

[112] In considering the probable effect of a price increase on cellophane earnings, the division manager stated the matter as follows: "Can we sell the capacity output of our plants? . . . The District Managers are divided in their opinion. . . . However, the majority of the District Managers, the Director and Assistant Director of Sales are of the opinion, barring a recession, the tonnage can be sold." *Ibid.*, p. 7539. Although this reasoning is consistent with that of a mono-

Cellophane's earnings record offers persuasive if not convincing evidence that du Pont has had monopoly power in selling cellophane. A comparison of du Pont's earnings from cellophane with its earnings from rayon lends force to this conclusion.[113] Despite the dissimilarity of the end products, several factors justify the comparison. Cellophane and rayon stem from the same basic raw materials. Both are radical innovations. Both were initially manufactured under noncompetitive conditions and both enjoyed substantial tariff protection. The same business management produced both products. The French Comptoir shared in the management of both Du Pont Cellophane and Du Pont Rayon until 1929. Yerkes, president of Du Pont Cellophane, was also president of Du Pont Rayon. Presumably du Pont in controlling business policy for both companies was actuated by similar business motives.[114] Both products have had several reasonably close substitutes. The production and consumption of both increased phenomenally.[115] Cellophane and rayon have been similarly characterized by rapidly developing technology, rapid reduction in costs, and rapid decline in prices.[116] The chief difference in the manufacture and sale of the two products significant to the course of profits apparently lies in the structure of the rayon and cellophane industries. Although rayon manufacture began in this country as a monopoly, rival firms came into the industry promptly. American Viscose Corporation began as the sole domestic producer of rayon shortly before the first world war and du Pont followed in 1920. By 1930 these concerns had eighteen rivals. As late as 1949 fifteen firms occupied the field. Although the four largest firms in recent years have usually accounted for

polist interested in maximizing profits, Judge Leahy cited it as evidence that du Pont did not have the power to raise prices arbitrarily. *United States* v. *E. I. du Pont de Nemours & Co.*, 118 F. Supp. 41, 179 (D. Del. 1953).

113 Data are not available to compare du Pont's earnings from cellophane with the earnings of producers of other wrapping materials. These are without exception diversified firms producing a variety of products. However, the record discloses that in every year from 1935 through 1942 du Pont failed to cover costs in selling cellulose acetate film, which it sold in competition with two other concerns (GX 490 through GX 497).

114 The district court found: "Same individuals were the principal du Pont executives in du Pont Rayon Co. and du Pont Cellophane Co. Same policies of improving quality, lowering cost of production, and reducing unit price to gain greater volume of sales were followed as to both companies"; and that du Pont's "price policy for rayon was the same as for cellophane." 118 F. Supp. at 86.

115 United States consumption of rayon increased by about 320,000,000 pounds between 1920 and 1938. Jesse W. Markham, *Competition in the Rayon Industry* (Cambridge, Mass., 1952), p. 230. Cellophane consumption grew by about 80,000,000 pounds between 1924 and 1938. DX 600, p. 1216.

116 Rayon prices dropped from $6.00 a pound on February 1, 1920 to $0.51 a pound on July 29, 1938. Federal Trade Commission, *Investments, Profits, and Rates of Return for Selected Industries* (a special report prepared for the Temporary National Economic Committee, 76th Cong., 3d Sess.), 1941, p. 17985. Cellophane prices dropped from $2.51 in 1924 to $0.42 in 1938. DX 336, p. 642.

about 70 per cent of the total output and although most of the firms have generally followed a price leader, Markham from his painstaking and exhaustive study concludes that freedom of entry and the pressure of substitute products have made the rayon industry workably or effectively competitive.[117] The course of both du Pont's and the industry's rate of earnings supports this conclusion (see Table IV). Federal Trade Commission data reveal that in 1920, when du Pont first produced rayon, American Viscose Corporation, until then the country's sole producer, realized 64.2 per cent on its investment.[118] Although du Pont showed a loss in 1921, its rate of earnings rose to 38.9 per cent by 1923. Thereafter its rate of earnings and those of the industry declined until by 1929 they had fallen to 19.0 and 18.1 per cent, respectively. When six more firms entered the industry in

TABLE IV

INVESTMENT OF PRINCIPAL COMPANIES IN RAYON, INVESTMENT OF DU PONT IN RAYON, INVESTMENT OF DU PONT IN CELLOPHANE, AND ANNUAL RATE OF RETURN BEFORE TAXES ON THESE INVESTMENTS, 1920-1938

Year	Total Rayon Investment of Principal Rayon Companies	Du Pont's Rayon Investment (millions of dollars)	Du Pont's Cellophane Investment	Average Rate of Return of Principal Rayon Companies (per cent)	Du Pont's Rate of Return on Rayon Investment (per cent)	Du Pont's Rate of Return on Cellophane Investment (per cent)
1920	$ 40.7			64.2		
1921	51.2	$ 2.9		42.0	(—2.1)	
1922	66.0	4.0		50.1	34.1	
1923	89.1	6.3		43.2	38.9	
1924	110.6	8.9		26.7	27.9	
1925	141.7	14.0	$ 2.1	30.6	34.2	36.7
1926	159.3	20.2	2.5	20.1	15.2	58.3
1927	166.7	24.4	2.7	25.8	27.0	44.8
1928	199.1	29.6	2.6	24.5	26.6	62.4
1929	228.0	38.4	5.1	18.1	19.0	55.8
1930	244.6	41.1	11.2	5.0	(—0.9)	39.9
1931	234.5	37.0	18.2	3.4	4.5	29.9
1932	223.2	33.5	21.6	1.5	1.2	18.0
1933	238.3	32.4	23.3	12.2	12.7	21.3
1934	249.9	38.7	24.0	6.9	8.6	24.9
1935	255.4	46.0	24.6	6.7	5.3	24.6
1936	267.0	50.0	26.3	11.5	11.0	29.1
1937	281.3	54.6	27.3	12.1	13.1	25.2
1938	296.6	61.7	30.7	2.5	4.2	27.5
Average Rate of Return				21.4	15.6	35.6

Sources: Rayon investment and earnings, Federal Trade Commission, *Investments, Profits, and Rates of Return for Selected Industries* (a special report prepared for the Temporary National Economic Committee, 76th Cong., 3d Sess.), 1941, pp. 17988, 17990, 17998. Cellophane investment and earnings based on Table III. Comparable data on total rayon investment and earnings are not available beyond 1938.

[117] Markham, *op. cit.*, pp. 181, 206, 208.

[118] Federal Trade Commission, *op. cit. supra note* 116, p. 17644. In this report the Commission's method of estimating rates of earnings on the basis of total investment is apparently similar to du Pont's method of calculating its operating earnings for its various divisions. See note 107 *supra*.

1930,[119] average industry earnings fell to 5.0 per cent and du Pont suffered a loss of 0.9 per cent. During the following eight years du Pont averaged only 7.5 per cent on its rayon investment, and the industry as a whole put in a similar performance.

In striking contrast, du Pont with only a single rival in producing cellophane (and that rival's output closely geared to du Pont's) earned less than 20 per cent on its cellophane investment in only one depression year. From the beginning of the depression in 1929 through the succeeding recovery and the 1938 recession du Pont averaged 29.6 per cent before taxes on its cellophane investment. On its rayon investment it averaged only 6.3 per cent.

IV. Conclusions

Apparently the cellophane market does not conform to the Chamberlinian model in which substitutes are so close that no producer may long enjoy monopoly returns—a "sort of ideal" equilibrium adjustment with the demand curve tangent to the cost curve at some point above lowest average cost. It does not conform to Clark's model of workable competition wherein rival products and potential competition reduce the slope of the demand curve, or to Robertson's model wherein substitutes are so close as to result in a competitive price. Rather, cellophane is so differentiated from other flexible wrapping materials that its cross elasticity of demand gives du Pont significant and continuing monopoly power.

Du Pont has used its power with foresight and wisdom. It has apparently recognized that it could increase its earnings by decreasing its costs and prices, by educating its potential customers to the benefits of wrapping their products in cellophane, by improving machinery for packaging, by helping converters and packagers solve their technical problems. It has built a better mousetrap and taught people how to use it.

But du Pont has not surrendered its monopoly power. Its strategy, cellophane's distinctive qualities, and the course of its prices and earnings indicate this. Du Pont's strategy was designed to protect a monopoly in the sale of a product it regarded as unique, and its pricing policies reflected the judgment of its executives on how best to maximize earnings. We think its earnings illustrate Knight's distinction between justifiable profits to the innovator and unjustifiable monopoly gains. They have been "too large" and have lasted "too long."

[119] Markham, *op. cit.*, p. 47.

66. AUTOMOBILE DEALER FRANCHISES: VERTICAL INTEGRATION BY CONTRACT *

Friedrich Kessler
Newton D. Brenner
Richard H. Stern

For reasons of space, much of the original footnote material has been omitted, but the interested reader should consult the original article for more complete documentation.

In preparing the article, the following materials were used; and where cited may be found in the form indicated in parenthesis: HEWITT, AUTOMOBILE DEALER FRANCHISES (1956) (HEWITT); PALAMOUNTAIN, THE POLITICS OF DISTRIBUTION (1955) (PALAMOUNTAIN); *Hearings Before the Antitrust Subcommittee of the House Committee on the Judiciary*, 84th Cong., 2d Sess. (1956) (*H.R. Hearings, Dealer Franchises*); *Hearings Before a Subcommittee of the House Committee on Interstate and Foreign Commerce*, 84th Cong., 1st Sess. (1955) (*H.R. Hearings, Marketing Legislation*); *Hearings Before a Subcommittee of the Senate Committee on Interstate and Foreign Commerce*, 84th Cong., 2d Sess. (1956) (*S. Hearings, Marketing Practices*); *Hearings Before the Subcommittee on Antitrust and Monopoly of the Senate Committee on the Judiciary*, 84th Cong., 1st Sess. (1955) (*S. Hearings, General Motors*); *Staff Report of the Subcommittee on Antitrust and Monopoly of the Senate Committee on the Judiciary*, 84th Cong., 2d Sess. (1956) (G.M. REP.); FTC, REPORT ON MOTOR VEHICLE INDUSTRY (1939) (1939 FTC REP.); FTC, REPORT ON DISTRIBUTION METHODS AND COSTS pt. IV (1944) (1944 FTC REP.); REPORT OF THE ATTORNEY GENERAL'S NATIONAL COMMITTEE TO STUDY THE ANTITRUST LAWS (1955) (ATT'Y GEN. REP.).

American business has developed three kinds of retail sales outlets. At one end of the scale is the independent retailer, exemplified by the general store or the corner grocery store. His independence is safeguarded: the manufacturer or wholesaler from whom he buys is only one of many possible sources supplying him with the goods he needs

* Reprinted by permission of *The Yale Law Journal*, Vol. 69 (1959), pp. 1-129.

Friedrich Kessler, Justus S. Hotchkiss Professor of Law, Yale Law School.
Newton D. Brenner, Member of the New York Bar.
Richard H. Stern, Trial Attorney, Antitrust Division, United States Department of Justice.
Edith Fine, Collaborator.

for resale. At the other end of the scale is the agent who may be a branch or subsidiary of the manufacturer. The franchised dealer occupies a position between the two extremes. Under the franchise system, distribution of the product is limited to chosen retailers in each community.

The unique advantage of franchising for the manufacturer lies in the considerable control over the process of distribution he may exercise without exposure to the burdens and responsibilities of an agency relationship. Ideally, the dealers are carefully chosen from among those of proven ability. Selected dealers, experience has shown, tend to be more aggressive in cultivating a market and servicing the product. They are generally "co-operative" in carrying out the manufacturer's suggested program of selling. And the franchises of dealers who do not prove their worth may be eliminated by cancellation or nonrenewal.

In return, the franchised dealer receives from the manufacturer added capacity to build and maintain a strong retail organization. Restriction of outlets tends to protect the dealer's inventory and plant investment. Moreover, the nature of the relationship fosters mutual dependence, and the dealer can expect the manufacturer to assist him in effective merchandising. The dealer also gains increased prestige through affiliation with a large organization, frequently of national extension.

Finally, the consumer, we are told, gets better service under the franchise system and is assured that the retailer carries a complete stock of the manufacturer's products.

However great these advantages, the franchise system is not free from shortcomings and frictions. The manufacturer may suffer because the dealer, sheltered by the restriction of outlets, does not exert his "best efforts." The "uncooperative" dealer may lose his franchise and, to the extent it is built around exclusive representation, his business. Again, due to lack of outlet competition the consumer may suffer from a high price level or be at the mercy of a dealer whose services are inadequate.

Retail distribution through franchise arrangements has grown significantly during the last forty years. It has become the principal market channel for such products as automobiles, electrical appliances, farm implements, radios, television, tires and wall paper. Because of the nature of the commodity involved, the franchise system has had its most spectacular development in the automobile industry. As the system exists today, the manufactured product is channelled through the manufacturer's own sales organization directly to selected retailers. With the industry's development of its own decentralized assembly plants, the independent distributor-wholesaler, once important in the distribution process, has largely disappeared, except in low-volume lines. Large manufacturers usually regard the distributor as an economic luxury. And direct sales by manufacturers to the consumer, always small in number, are limited to fleet vehicles or those that require special design or finish.

The economic significance of the franchise system in the automobile industry is illustrated by the following figures: in 1954, the industry turned out a total of 9,177,919 cars and trucks. Its investment amounted to 7⅓ billions of dollars; 780,000 persons were employed in the process of production. Distribution was handled by 42,000 franchised dealers, whose total investment amounted to nearly 5 billion dollars. The investment of the average dealer amounted to $118,000. The dealers in turn employed 660,800 persons or 9.7% of all employees engaged in retail selling. Thus, the cost of distributing cars, in labor and capital, is almost as great as the cost of manufacturing them.

A. The Automobile Franchise and the Evolution of Its Terms

The franchise system would seem eminently suited to the distribution of automobiles; in this field, each party obviously has a substantial interest in the other's conduct. President Harlow Curtice of General Motors, says of the dealer:

> "Legally he is not the agent of the manufacturer. Yet in his community he is looked upon as the manufacturer's representative. The degree of business success he is able to earn in his community depends importantly upon the quality and value of the product with which the manufacturer has provided him.
>
> "Conversely, the success the manufacturer enjoys in all markets, throughout the country, is determined in subtantial degree by how well his 'representatives' the dealers—perform their functions. An unusual mutuality of interests exists between the automobile manufacturer and the dealer." [1]

Although the franchise system had many staunch supporters among dealers even before recent modifications, it has been a source of conflicts and tensions. The number of law suits brought by franchised dealers against manufacturers, the 1939 Federal Trade Commission *Report on Motor Vehicle Industry*, recent congressional

[1] 1s. *Hearings, Marketing Practices* 685.

hearings culminating in federal legislation and the great number of state statutes reflecting dealer displeasure all demonstrate that the supposed mutuality of interests between manufacturers and franchised dealers did not prevent the franchise system from causing dissatisfaction. Its actual operation, the dealers complained, precluded them from attaining an independence as full as that of most merchants. In reality, the argument runs, automobile dealers have been in large measure the manufacturers' agents. Through their dominant economic position, the manufacturers have employed the franchise, a "one-sided document which is neither contract, license or agreement," to gain maximum control over the management of the dealers' business without corresponding "legal" responsibility. Under the terms of the franchise, the factories "give the orders while the dealer takes the losses."

The modern franchise indeed enables the manufacturer to wield great "vertical power" in the form of supervisory control over retail operations. The franchise is embodied in a detailed standardized contract presented by the manufacturer to the dealer. The master contract is frequently accompanied by printed addenda concerning such matters as capital requirements and succession. Modern franchise contracts show great similarity; the absence of complete uniformity may be ascribed to the competition for dealers among the five remaining manufacturers. This high degree of standardization is best illustrated by the "entire agreement" clauses. Patterned after provisions frequently found in insurance policies, the modern franchise states that it supersedes all prior agreements, that it constitutes the "entire agreement of the parties" and that only certain executives of the manufacturer, usually the Vice-President or Sales Manager, have authority to alter the written contract.

The terms of the franchise contract, however elaborate, do not give a complete picture of the dealership as an institution. "[They] do not show [that] 'priceless ingredient' of prime importance—namely, the manner in which the contract is administered." [2] The policies and practices of the manufacturer may be made relevant with the help of skillfully drafted clauses in the franchise agreement, but often the dealer must comply simply because of the economic power of the manufacturer. A prospective dealer, to be sure, is free to accept or reject a dealer franchise. Once he has committed his capital and entered the business, however, the power of the manufacturer comes into operation. The dealer must, on pain of cancella-

[2] 1939 FTC Rep. 139.

tion or non-renewal, accede to the demands which the manufacturer, in the interest of market penetration, deems necessary and reasonable. Thus the manufacturer has an assured market in his dealers. Of course, his power to terminate or not to renew is tempered by considerations of enlightened self-interest. The manufacturer gains nothing by destroying a valuable member of a sales organization developed over the years with his own assistance and financial contribution. On the other hand, cancellation or non-renewal are valuable means of replacing inefficient dealers with new ones, selected from the waiting list prepared by field representatives. This practice is common among the Big Three of the five major automobile manufacturers.

The franchise clauses and manufacturer practices about which dealers have most strongly complained are not of recent origin. In the earliest stages of the automotive industry's development, the manufacturers' principal concern was building enough machines to supply a constantly widening market. Expansion of plant facilities was, therefore, often regarded as more important than the development of a centrally controlled sales organization. But early in the history of car marketing, the relationship between dealer and manufacturer took on aspects of supervision and control. While the dealer between 1900 and 1920 did assume increasing responsibilities and perform successively greater functions, he did not become an independent merchant. Although manufacturers realized that labelling the dealer an "exclusive agent" might burden them with responsibilities they were unwilling to assume and ceased using that term, the dealer's position remained unchanged. Other methods of control already present in early franchise contracts, such as the much-litigated Peerless franchise dating back to 1902, could, with the help of freedom of contract, be refined to such a degree that resort to agency structure was unnecessary.

The movement toward greater control received strong impetus in the waning of the first seller's market in the 1920's. From then on, manufacturers were compelled to pay increasing attention to retailing problems. They learned that the dealer is a "principal competitive weapon." For through the dealer the manufacturer has contact with the public, and upon the sales of the dealer "rests the success or failure of the whole manufacturing process." And "since automobile sales usually require considerable service, demonstration, and post-sale service, manufacturers check on the performance of these tasks."

With the gradual development of the terms of the franchise, several unique features have become apparent. Today the dealer is required to develop his territory to the satisfaction of the manufacturer, a requirement buttressed by a host of ancillary provisions. Termination clauses are designed to assure adequate performance and attempt to insulate the manufacturer from liability. But franchises do not compensate the franchised dealer by giving him "territorial security," a protected sales area. Small wonder dealers complained that the modern franchise is "one-sided," "neither contract, license or agreement." In response to dealer complaints, adverse public opinion and new federal legislation, the terms of franchises have recently been considerably changed in the dealers' favor. A brief historical survey of the most important clauses, their changes and development is necessary to an understanding of the present franchise system.

Control over dealer's operations

Early in the history of automobile marketing, the manufacturer attempted to assure adequate territory development by the dealer, at that time called an exclusive agent. Two clauses were the subject of experiment: one imposed upon the dealer a duty to take a minimum number of cars, the other a duty to use his best efforts in the development of his territory. The first type was soon abandoned; it made for inelasticity and the manufacturer realized that the second type could provide sufficient protection. In fact the latter has proved to be of great importance, particularly since the dealer's efforts were tested by the manufacturer's "satisfaction."

Until recently, no objective criteria measuring satisfaction were provided. The manufacturer alone had discretion to determine the meaning of adequate development of territory: in substance the term means quotas. Telegrams sent out by factory representatives to dealers and later submitted in evidence at recent congressional hearings indicate that the manufacturer measured performance in terms of "percentages of price class" and "national average." Protected by satisfaction clauses, manufacturers pressured dealers for orders until these tests were met. In recently amending its development of territory clause, General Motors has made a beginning in spelling out objective criteria of satisfaction.

Nonetheless, manufacturers have retained considerable control due to the flexible nature of the satisfaction clauses. This practice points to a basic conflict of interests between manufacturer and dealer. For the dealer, the cost of selling an additional unit may be greater than the revenue derived from its sale. The dealer's operating capacity may be limited; handling extra cars may entail the purchase of new, or the costly crowding of old, facilities. Accordingly, it may be against the dealer's interest to push sales beyond this point. But the unit costs for the manufacturer tend to decrease with increased production. He will therefore pressure the dealer to increase his volume of sales.

To secure the goal of market penetration, franchises commonly contain many other provisions designed to ensure that the dealer performs to the manufacturer's satisfaction. Manufacturer control over the dealer's operation is not limited to supervision of the development of the dealer's territory. The judgment of the manufacturer has supplemented, if not replaced, that of the dealer on retail merchandising operations typically reserved to the retailer's judgment. The General Motors contract of 1955, for example, expressly stipulated that the dealer must devote his full time, attention and energy to the conduct of his business—a provision which was modified, however, in 1956. Similarly, by express provision, Packard and Nash contracts as late as 1948 attempted to make sure that other business interests of the leader did not interfere with his duties under the selling agreement. Furthermore, franchises contain detailed provisions dealing with the "operating requirements" of the dealer. Under this heading fall clauses defining satisfactory location of the dealer's place of business, as well as those regulating sales and servicing facilities, parts, accessory and used car sales, advertising and sales personnel.

In addition, the dealer, in the interest of establishing production schedules and evaluating current market trends, has to submit every month a "three months' estimate of requirements" and a "ten day report showing retail sales of both new and used cars made during said period, new and used car stocks, and unfilled orders on hand at the end of said period." All this information must be supplied on forms furnished by the manufacturer. Furthermore, dealers, however small, must adopt complex and uniform accounting systems. Finally and most important, the franchise contract gives the manufacturer power to determine the dealer's minimum capital requirements.

At first, automobile manufacturers' franchise contracts did not require the dealer to carry only the one manufacturer's products. Early in the history of automobile merchandising, however, exclusive representation clauses appeared, limiting the dealer's sources of supply to a single manufacturer. The dealer typically was required to handle only the vehicles covered by the franchise, and to stock and use factory parts and accessories exclusively.

Until 1956, the manufacturer was able to charge the dealer rail freight from Detroit, even when the automobile was assembled at a point nearer the dealer's place of business or was shipped by cheaper means of transportation. Thus, the manufacturer profited from phantom freight charges. In the most recent franchise agreements, the manufacturer still determines the mode of transportation in the interest of a smooth outflow of his products, since warehousing is not available to him. Phantom freight charges, however, were abolished in 1956 but not without price increases.

Resale price maintenance provisions became a feature of some franchises and, with the help of "that priceless ingredient" inherent in all franchises, namely, the administration of the contract, dealers were induced to finance their wholesale purchases and retail sales through finance companies chosen by or even affiliated with the manufacturer. By way of compensation, the dealer was given a large territory protected against raids by any outsiders, originally including even the manufacturer. Gradually, the latter reserved for himself the qualified right to sell directly within the dealer's territory and insisted on the right to appoint other dealers within a given territory. The resulting nonexclusive dealership was, however, still protected against raiding by outsiders, cross selling and bootlegging. Cross selling refers to selling to residents of another franchised dealer's territory. Bootlegging means selling to a nonfranchised dealer for resale.

During the forties, franchise provisions expressly tying the dealer to the manufacturer's products began to disappear. Still, the manufacturer successfully continued (and still continues) to insist, as a matter of practice, on "adequate representation" with regard to his products. The policy of manufacturers until quite recently did not favor dealerships combining their lines with those of any other manufacturer, such division of selling effort being considered to detract from the adequacy of representation. Where the dealer's territory was such that single line dealerships were not feasible, combination of the various lines produced by the manufacturer was preferred. This policy was, in large measure, reinforced by the dealer's self-interest; many dealers felt that they could not afford the additional costs attendant to the carrying of multiple lines. With regard to parts and accessories dealers were expected to adequately represent the manufacturer as his merchandiser. Financing through manufacturer sale and finance companies also seems to have continued to this day as a matter of practice to a substantial degree. Resale price maintenance, however, has altogether disappeared.

The benefits of a protected territory were lost for the dealer between 1949 and 1952. Territorial security was abandoned even as a practice and so were provisions and practices penalizing a dealer who sold cars to any one but a consumer or another franchised dealer. This change is attacked by dealers as having contributed to bootlegging—a practice criticised by many dealers and part of the industry.

Thus as a practical matter dealers, by and large, have continued to be exclusive representatives of their manufacturers without enjoying, however, the "benefits" of a protected territory. Small wonder that efforts have been constantly made to restore territorial security in one form or another. To date these efforts toward restoring exclusively in favor of the dealer have not succeeded.

Recent developments in automobile franchising, however, amount to a relaxation of the requirement of exclusive representation. Dual and multiple franchises have begun to emerge under which dealers desirous of widening their market may, with the consent or at least the acquiescence of the manufacturer, distribute the products of several different manufacturers. Big three dealers not only distribute foreign cars, but they have begun to handle small domestic automobiles also, for instance, those produced by American Motors. Whether dual lining will ever constitute a radical departure from the franchise system as we have known it remains to be seen. Until now the dual lining development seems to be restricted to makes which are not in competition with one another. The test of dual lining will come when the Big Three have developed their own small cars.

According to an address by Victor R. Hansen, Assistant Attorney General in charge of the Antitrust Division, before the Nov. 26, 1957 meeting of the National Independent Automobile Dealers Association, the Justice Department looked favorably on the practice. The then Assistant Attorney General stated: "I see in this trend a development which is likely to have favorable effects on competition in the automobile manufacturing industry as a whole and on the ability of automobile dealers to utilize their facilities more intensively and thereby to increase their profits without raising consumer prices."

Duration of franchises and cancellation terms

Early automobile franchise contracts reflected the seasonal fluctuation in demand for the product. Franchises typically provided for termination at the end of a model year. In addition, the manufacturer could cancel for cause. The growing financial strength of manufacturers was reflected by changes in duration clauses; the contract, though often providing for automatic extension if not canceled, terminated or superseded by a new agreement—thus giving the semblance of a permanent arrangement—could be terminated by either party on short notice, even without cause. The manufacturer alone profited from such clauses; for the dealer who had to protect his investment, the power to terminate was usually empty.

Over the protests of its dealers, General Motors in 1944 returned to a one-year franchise which could, however, be terminated only for cause. This modification may have been motivated by a desire to escape regulatory provisions enacted by state legislatures prohibiting the manufacturer to cancel "unfairly and without regard to the equities." Whatever its origin, the change enabled the manufacturer to accomplish by nonrenewal what he had been able to do before by cancellation, without fear of court intervention. Under this type of contract, General Motors has hardly ever needed to invoke the cancellation for cause provisions. By 1948, General Motors' example had been followed by three other manufacturers, though not by Ford or Chrysler. Under the pressure of public opinion, General Motors and Ford have recently changed their dealer franchises to run for five years if the dealer so wishes, but the five-year contract still contains a cancellation for cause provision. Most important, the cancellation for cause provision is expressly coupled with the satisfaction clauses. The manufacturer is entitled to cancel if the dealer fails to comply with any of the clauses geared to the manufacturer's satisfaction requirement. Cancellation has thus remained one of the chief sources of the manufacturer's power.

To alleviate the hardship of cancellation or nonrenewal, recent versions of franchises have made several important innovations. Franchises now contain elaborate provisions for the succession of a qualified person—generally the dealer's son-in-law, or a person nominated by the dealer—participation by the dealer's widow, protection of the premises in case of termination and ordinary liquidation and assistance to the estate in the event of death. Recent franchise terms also impose upon the manufacturer a duty to assist the dealer in protecting his investment even in cases of justifiable termination. In the General Motors franchise, for instance, the manufacturer not only must repurchase parts, but must also help the dealer to dispose of real estate, whether owned or leased. The manufacturer may even have a limited duty to purchase or lease the premises "at a fair and reasonable value to be determined by independent appraisal." The negotiations necessary to meeting these obligations must be conducted "with the utmost good faith." However, the dealer's right to claim the benefits of the provision for assistance is conditioned on his compliance with elaborate provisos and releases aimed at protection of the manufacturer. The new Ford franchise has parallel provisions, although seemingly of a more limited nature.

Obligations of the manufacturer to deliver and exculpation clauses

Early franchises were either silent or vague on the manufacturer's duty to deliver. By 1908, however, at least one contract contained a clause making the dealer's orders not binding on the manufacturer until accepted, and such a clause had come into general usage by 1939. Formerly, franchise contracts also contained iron-clad provisions relieving the manufacturer from liability in case of nondelivery, however caused. Present franchise contracts relieve the manufacturer from liability for failure or delay in filling orders only if nondelivery arises from reasons beyond his control. But the manufacturer is ultimately protected by clauses which date back as far as 1914 and provide that termination of the franchise contract cancels all unfilled orders.

Dealer relations boards

Recently attempts have been made by industry to answer dealers' grievances through utilization of dealer relations boards, consisting of top manufacturing executives. These efforts have not yet succeeded in solving the plight of the dealer. The boards have been criticized for combining the functions of prosecutor, judge and jury. To counter this criticism, General Motors in 1956 revised its grievance procedure by selecting an umpire chosen on the basis of special qualifications and experience. His function is to adjudicate appeals, at which the dealer may be represented by counsel. Moreover, several companies, following another innovation of General Motors, have appointed a vice-president to handle dealer relations.

B. The Franchise System and Common Law of Contracts

The case law on automobile dealer franchises, dating from the early history of the industry, dramatically reveals the unending attempts of the dealers to break the vertical power of the manufacturer, exercised through the franchise terms. Indeed, the case law on dealer franchises is in large measure composed of suits involving automobile franchises. These suits have been founded on a variety of alleged injuries. Many early cases involved claims for commissions lost through nondelivery or invasion of the dealer's territory by the manufacturer. Others sought return of deposits made by the dealer on cars which the manufacturer never shipped. Today these situations have given way to damage suits by dealers against manufacturers for "wrongful" termination of a franchise contract, failure to deliver cars ordered before the franchise was effectively cancelled or had expired, or failure to deliver in accordance with a separate agreement. In addition, actions have frequently been brought for breach of contracts to give, extend or renew a franchise. Dealers have even sued manufacturers for fraud and deceit in making oral promises which induced them to enter into a contract. The amount of litigation reflects the size of the stakes involved. A terminated dealer frequently is unable to get a franchise from another manufacturer. Since his capital investment is so specialized that it cannot easily be transferred to other kinds of business, termination has often been called an economic death sentence. And many dealers are large retailers, able to afford the cost of litigation at the appellate court level.

Manufacturers responded to the challenge of litigation by attempting to draft franchise clauses insulating them from liability and the risk of having a jury determine both liability and measure of damages. Although unsuccessful in eliminating litigation altogether, the draftsmen have prevented the dealers from winning a great percentage of their lawsuits. Like the draftsmen of insurance policies, the authors of dealer franchises have been engaged in a continuous process of rewriting, raising new obstacles to recovery whenever the old are surmounted.

Validity. An initial block confronting the dealers lay in the argument that a franchise, marked by the absence or indefiniteness of obligations, was not a valid and enforceable contract. Until recently, the validity issue was continuously raised in franchise litigation, the defendant manufacturer almost invariably arguing that the agreement lacked mutuality of "assent and obligation" and merely set "forth the basis on which orders were to be handled." This strategy arises naturally out of the institutional framework surrounding franchise agreements. After a dealer has committed his capital to a franchise, protection of the manufacturer's interest does not depend on the availability of legal sanctions. In fact, legal invalidity of the franchise, precluding court control, adds to the strength of the manufacturer's nonlegal sanctions.

For many decades, the invalidity argument may have been the most powerful weapon available to manufacturers in defending damage suits by dealers. It was honored by most courts, provided the manufacturer engaged in careful draftsmanship. If the contract gave each party the right to terminate on short notice, with or without cause, or for just cause—the meaning of the term was left open—it was unenforceable either for lack of definiteness or for lack of mutuality. The result followed even more readily when the franchise further granted the manufacturer the right to change prices or refuse requisitions and freedom from liability in case of cancellation or failure to deliver unaccepted orders. The lack of mutuality defense failed only if the right of the manufacturer to terminate was anchored in objective criteria, such as "violation of any of . . . [the] provisions [of the contract]" or "violation of any of the conditions." Thus General Motors was unsuccessful in arguing lack of mutuality in a suit for profits lost through nondelivery of cars; the "concession to sell" expressly provided for continuation unless cancelled or terminated for reasons spelled out in the contract.

In the late thirties, the attitude of the courts toward validity began to change, even with regard to franchises terminable at will. While lack of mutuality continued to be used as a defensive weapon, courts viewing franchise contracts found the "provisions and the acts of the parties are consistent only with the existence of a contract imposing some reciprocal conditions and at least binding upon the parties to some extent." [3] Still, dealers were usually unable to recover, since the manufacturer often had legitimately invoked a termination clause or because the damages claimed were not "within the contemplation of the parties" or because the manufacturer had successfully insulated himself by nonliability clauses.

TERMINATION CLAUSES. These clauses usually allowed either manufacturer or dealer to terminate at will or permitted the manu-

[3] *Kane* v. *Chrysler Corp.*, 80 F. Supp. 360, 362 (D. Del. 1948).

facturer to terminate for "cause"—the violation of a duty imposed upon the dealer by the franchise agreement. The relative importance of these alternatives has varied, their development and use geared to judicial decisions. In *Chevrolet Motor Co.* v. *Gladding,*[4] for example, the manufacturer, claiming that the dealer had violated his duty to give exclusive representation, invoked a ten-day cancellation clause. The court held that the jury should determine whether the dealer had broken his contract. To avoid the judicial risk created by this decision, termination clauses were changed. Provisions were made for termination at will upon short notice in addition to the existing clauses allowing termination for cause. For almost two decades following the Gladding case, manufacturers severed their relationships with dealers by invoking termination at will provisions or by failing to renew franchises after their expiration dates. This practice has been particularly rewarding, since courts, by and large, have been unwilling to enforce alleged oral promises to renew or not to cancel.

DAMAGES AND EXCULPATION CLAUSES. To further decrease the risk of liability, manufacturers turned to exculpation clauses which courts were usually unwilling to disregard. The courts honored not only clauses making all orders subject to acceptance, but also provisions expressly excluding liability for nondelivery. The manufacturer also escaped liability where the franchise contract provided that termination canceled all outstanding orders or gave the manufacturer an option to repurchase in case of termination. In addition, a provision insulating the manufacturer against claims for reimbursement based on "expenditures in preparation for performance or in performance of the dealer's obligation" has been honored. And manufacturers have frequently been successful in arguing either that the lost profits claimed were too speculative or that the reliance damages sought were not causally connected with definite assurances on their part.

GOOD FAITH. The case law on automobile franchises reflects a profound belief in freedom of contract, even though the courts are fully aware of the onesidedness of the terms of the franchise contract and the plight of the dealer. Thus, time and again, the courts have insisted that the dealer's predicament was of his own making. He had voluntarily signed the franchise contract with all its clauses insulating the manufacturer against liability:

[4] 42 F.2d 440 (4th. Cir. 1930).

It appears that the plaintiff has been disappointed in its expectations and has been dealt with none too generously by the defendant; but, while we sympathize with its plight, we cannot say from the evidence before us that there has been a breach of binding contract which would enable it to recover damages, While there is a natural impulse to be impatient with a form of contract which places the comparatively helpless dealer at the mercy of the manufacturer, we cannot make contracts for parties or protect them from the provisions of contracts which they have made for themselves. Dealers doubtless accept these one-sided contracts because they think that the right to deal in the product of the manufacturer, even on his terms, is valuable to them; but, after they have made such contracts, relying upon the good faith of the manufacturer for the protection which the contracts do not give, they cannot, when they get into trouble, expect the courts to place in the contracts the protection which they themselves have failed to insert.[5]

Similarly, the courts have been reluctant to read into the terms of the franchise a duty on the part of the manufacturer to exercise the power to cancel only in good faith. This attitude has prevailed even where the dealer claimed to have incurred large expenditures in reliance on an oral promise to renew or not to cancel. Manufacturers in general have been successful in persuading the courts that the official who made the oral agreement was unauthorized to do so, that the oral agreement was part of the written contract and thus subject to its limitations, or that it was too indefinite to be enforced. Moreover, the dealers have also failed in their attempts to rely on trade custom for establishing a manufacturer's duty to renew. Thus the courts have refused to apply the so-called Missouri doctrine under which "an 'agent' who has incurred expense induced by his appointment may recover it if he has not had sufficient opportunity to recoup it from his business." [6] This doctrine, frequently invoked in cases involving indefinite franchises concerning consumer goods other than automobiles, has been held inapplicable to contracts containing fixed duration terms or expressly terminable at will. The policy considerations behind this attitude have been forcefully summarized by Judge Clark in *Bushwick-Decatur Motors, Inc.* v. *Ford Motor Co.*:

With a power of termination at will here so unmistakably expressed, we certainly cannot assert that a limitation of good faith was anything the parties had in mind. Such a limitation can be read into the agreement only as an overriding requirement of public policy. This seems an extreme step for judges to take. . . . generally speaking, the situation

[5] *Ford Motor Co.* v. *Kirkmyer Motor Co.*, 65 F.2d 1006 (4th Cir. 1933).

[6] "A doctrine seemingly not applicable when the relationship has already endured for some time." *Bushwick-Decatur Motors, Inc.* v. *Ford Motor Co.*, 116 F.2d 675, 676 (2d Cir. 1940).

> arises from the strong bargaining position which economic factors give the great automobile manufacturing companies: the dealers are not misled or imposed upon, but accept as nonetheless advantageous an agreement in form bilateral, in fact one-sided. To attempt to redress this balance by judicial action without legislative authority appears to us a doubtful policy. We have not proper facilities to weigh economic factors, nor have we before us a showing of the supposed needs which may lead the manufacturers to require these seemingly harsh bargains.[7]

In the light of existing case law, it is not surprising that the general counsel of General Motors, when testifying before a Senate subcommittee, conceded that his company was able to defeat, on a motion for summary judgment, practically any effort by a dealer to recover damages.

C. The Impact of Antitrust Law

Until recently the impact of antitrust law on the power relationship between manufacturer and dealer has, on the whole, been as disappointing from the dealer's point of view as the influence of the common law of contracts. The hopes of dealers to become "independent businessmen" and obtain relief from onerous franchise arrangements either as a result of government intervention or private antitrust suits did not materialize. On the contrary, the antitrust laws in operation have tended to reinforce the existing power imbalance; restrictions in franchise contracts favoring the dealer have been removed while restrictive practices protecting the manufacturer have tenaciously survived.

Government intervention against integration systems

Determining the extent of antitrust violation was one objective of the 1939 Federal Trade Commission investigation of automobile distribution. Although the report did not conclude that the law was being violated in any particular instances, it focussed attention on two aspects of the franchise relationship: territorial security and exclusive representation. The Commission emphasized that evidence of antitrust violation could not be found from the express language of the franchise agreements alone, but that the practices under these agreements must be scrutinized to determine whether competition was being restrained in the industry.

[7] 116 F.2d 675, 677 (2d Cir. 1940).

Territorial security and other restrictions favoring dealers

Aspects of the franchise relationship which limit competition at the dealer level are an unmixed benefit to the dealer, since they provide him with security against loss of sales to competitors, giving him a degree of monopoly power enabling him to maximize profits. For the manufacturer, there are both advantages and disadvantages to giving the dealer the benefit of such restrictions. Insofar as the dealership is more sound because of an assured market, the manufacturer secures the advantage of a reliable distribution system and his task of building a strong dealer force is eased, but to the extent that retail price is raised, sales volume may suffer.

Two types of restrictive arrangements favoring dealers have received particular attention: anticross-selling and antibootlegging provisions. To the extent that restriction of these practices constitutes a restraint on alienation, it is void under the rationale of the Dr. Miles case,[8] not only under antitrust law principles but under contract law and property law principles as well. Thus, the Attorney General was successful in advising the industry to drop territorial limitation clauses from franchises,[9] even though a manufacturer's right to exercise some such control has been recognized.

Automobile manufacturers, in the past, have displayed ambivalent attitudes toward cross-selling and bootlegging. And they have not hesitated to appoint stimulator dealers in order to "encourage" greater sales efforts from their regular dealers, a practice hardly consistent with the maintenance of a protected market for the dealer. Moreover, enforcement of restrictions against cross-selling or bootlegging exposes manufacturers to the serious risk of treble damages suits by dealers whose business benefits from such transactions. As

[8] *Dr. Miles Medical Co.* v. *John D. Park & Sons Co.*, 220 U.S. 373, 404-05 (1911). See also *United States* v. *Bausch & Lomb Optical Co.*, 321 U.S. 707 (1944). In the former case, plaintiff was denied an injunction against defendant's inducing third parties to breach their contracts with plaintiff not to sell its goods to unaccredited dealers. In the latter case, the government secured an injunction against a similar arrangement. Moreover, in the Dr. Miles case, the court notes that the franchise contract was, in effect, the same as a horizontal conspiracy or combination among dealers to fix prices. "As to this, the complainant can fare no better with its plan of identical contracts than could the dealers themselves if they formed a combination and endeavored to establish the same restrictions, and thus to achieve the same result, by agreement with each other." Since price-fixing is illegal per se under the antitrust laws, this arrangement must be found unlawful. Allocation of territories is also illegal per se under the antitrust laws; hence, similar conclusions may be drawn about allocation of territories by franchise contracts.

[9] Statement of Assistant Attorney General Barnes, *H. R. Hearings, Marketing Legislation* 362. The Department of Justice has relied on Dr. Miles and Bausch & Lomb, *supra*, to challenge the GM proposal to restrict bootlegging. See *id.* at 359; 2 *S. Hearings, Marketing Practices* 1474.

far as the interests of the general public are concerned, it would appear that cross-selling and bootlegging facilitate better bargains for the consumer and that, to this extent, the interests of the franchised dealer pull in an opposite direction from those of the public. However, it has been suggested that the service provided by strong, reliable dealers in repair and replacement of car parts is of great value to the consumer, and that this service is possible only when dealers are given the ability and incentive to maintain it because their market is protected. Whether the benefit is worth the price is arguable.

Although, at present, restrictions in the franchise contract which favor the dealer seem to be unlawful, recent and proposed legislation may alter the situation drastically. An attempt to penalize cross-selling is found in the proposed Franchised Dealer Bill; essentially, this measure would require dealers who "poach" on another dealer's territory to pay a commission to the "rightful" dealer.[10] A more oblique approach toward protecting the dealer's market may be found in the recently passed Automobile Information Disclosure Act,[11] an attempt, ostensibly, to limit the practice of the dealer's "pack," *i.e.*, quoting an inflated list price for a car in order to make bargaining concessions easier. The act requires all new cars to display a sticker disclosing the price of the car and its accessories, identification information, and the name of the retail dealer to whom the car was originally consigned. The act has been bitterly attacked by nonfranchised dealers as an attempt to deprive them of their source of supply. They contend that overstocked franchised dealers will be unwilling to resell to nonfranchised dealers because of fear of manufacturer retaliation. Since this act does not attempt to amend the antitrust laws, it would appear that any manufacturer caught using information obtained from the mandatory sticker in order to prevent dealers from selling to bootleggers would be in serious antitrust difficulties. Nevertheless, the improved opportunity given for policing dealers is obvious.

Exclusive representation

His dealer organization is the manufacturer's sole outlet to the public, and for this reason he is vitally interested in the strength of the individual dealer. But, having built up this strength, the manu-

10 S. 4293, 85th Cong., 2d Sess. (1958).
11 Pub. L. No. 506, 85th Cong., 2d Sess. (July 7, 1958).

facturer wants to be repaid by having the dealer concentrate all his efforts on selling only the products of the manufacturer and no others.[12] This pressure for exclusive representation is directed primarily to automobiles, the product central to the franchise agreement, but it also extends to finance company arrangements, replacement parts and advertising matter. In studying this aspect of the franchise relationship, it is necessary to examine both express provisions of the franchise and established practices under it.

EXPRESS CONTRACTS. In the past, manufacturers have insisted on franchise provisions expressly requiring exclusive dealing. Sales of automobiles have been conditioned on the dealer's selling no automobiles made by competitors of the manufacturer, and on the purchase of replacement parts, financing, and the like from the manufacturer. But recent case law indicates that such express contractual arrangements would be unlawful.

In the leading case on exclusive dealing contracts, the Supreme Court declared such contracts unlawful under section 3 of the Clayton Act whenever "competition had been foreclosed in a substantial share of the line of commerce involved."[13] Economic justifications for exclusive dealing are declared irrelevant once the contracts are found to have the proscribed impact on the market. Thus, explicit provisions in franchises which require the dealer to sell the cars of only the manufacturer granting the franchise have been abandoned. Provisions requiring the dealer to purchase other products or services from the manufacturer are also discontinued. Such tie-ins have been strongly criticized as serving "hardly any purpose beyond the suppression of competition," and in a recent case on the point have been declared illegal per se in any but *de minimis* situations.[14]

PRACTICES. Hence, exclusive arrangements result not from express contractual provisions, but rather from informal practices rotating about the non-renewal sanction. Government intervention against such practices is faced by severe theoretical and evidentiary problems.

Section 3 of the Clayton Act, the government's most potent weapon against exclusive dealing contracts, forbids sales made on

[12] For an admirable account of the economic and antitrust problems presented by exclusive dealing arrangements, see Lockhart and Sacks, *The Relevance of Economic Factors in Determining Whether Exclusive Arrangements Violate Section 3 of the Clayton Act*, 65 HARV. L. REV. 913 (1952).

[13] *Standard Oil Co.* v. *United States*, 337 U.S. 293, 314 (1949). For a discussion of government action to force manufacturers to abandon tying clauses see 1 WHITNEY, ANTITRUST POLICIES, 438-450 (1958).

[14] *Northern Pacific R.R.* v. *United States*, 356 U.S. 1 (1958).

the agreement, condition, or understanding that the buyer not deal in the goods of a competitor of the seller, where the effect may be to lessen competition substantially. However, the courts have maintained that the law applies only to sales, *i.e.*, consummated sales, and not to offers to sell on restrictive terms or refusals to deal except on restrictive terms.[15] And cancellation or nonrenewal of a franchise is considered a refusal to sell, not a sale.[16] Thus, refusal to deal with a dealer who will not represent the manufacturer exclusively is not in itself a Section 3 violation.

Section 1 of the Sherman Act forbids contracts, combination and conspiracies in unreasonable restraint of trade. For the reasons given, *supra,* express contracts are no longer used. Hence, conspiracy or combination would have to be found, either between manufacturers and dealers or between the manufacturer, its officers, agents and subsidiaries. Agreements between a parent corporation and its subsidiaries which have the effect of restraining trade have been successfully attacked, but conspiracies between the agents of a corporation and one another or with the corporation itself have seldom been found by courts. Section 2 of the Sherman Act forbids monopolization, attempts to monopolize, and conspiracy to monopolize trade. Except insofar as proof of a conspiracy is not required, the test of illegality which the prosecution must meet is even more stringent than under Section 1.

The evidentiary problems involved in proving that the practices of automobile manufacturers meet the statutory standards of illegality are illustrated in three cases, GMAC, J. I. Case, and Richfield. In GMAC,[17] the Justice Department brought a criminal action under Section 1 charging that General Motors and its sales subsidiary had conspired with other General Motors subsidiaries, General Motors Acceptance Corporation and General Motors Acceptance Corporation of Indiana, to coerce dealers to do their financing through GMAC. The franchise contracts between the dealers and GM contained no clauses restricting the dealers' financing. But coercion was found to exist through manufacturer pressure during renewal conferences, cancellation of the franchises of uncooperative dealers, and shipment of wrong color or wrong model cars to such dealers. The corporate

[15] The leading case is *Nelson Radio & Supply Co.* v. *Motorola, Inc.*, 200 F.2d 911 (5th Cir. 1952), *cert. denied,* 345 U.S. 925 (1953); see Barber, *Refusals to Deal under the Federal Antitrust Laws*, 103 U. Pa. L. Rev. 847, 860 (1955).

[16] *Hudson Sales Corp.* v. *Waldrip*, 211 F.2d 268 (5th Cir.), *cert. denied,* 348 U.S. 821 (1954).

[17] *United States* v. *General Motors Corp.*, 121 F.2d 376 (7th Cir.), *cert. denied,* 314 U.S. 618 (1941).

defendants were each fined $5,000, at that time the maximum penalty under Section 1.

However, the Justice Department did not prevail in the suit for an injunction against J. I. Case, a farm equipment manufacturer, to prohibit the requirement of exclusive representation as an unwritten term of the franchise.[18] The government alleged that Case had maintained exclusive representation by forcing dealers to drop competing lines on pain of cancellation. Finding that the acts proved by the prosecution did not show any "pattern or policy on the part of Case to obtain an agreement or understanding from its dealers that they will not handle competing lines," the court explained that cancellation of a dealer who carried dual lines might be coincidental or merely in pursuance of a sound business policy of dealer selection. In addition, the court found the fact that many dealers handled Case exclusively not to constitute evidence of an understanding forced upon them, because such practice was frequently a matter of volition. Finally, the court drew attention to the fact that many Case dealers did in fact carry lines of other manufacturers. Thus, in GMAC, where the evidence of coercion was flagrant, the Justice Department had no difficulty in winning its case, but in J. I. Case, where the evidence was weaker, the Justice Department lost. Is coercion, then, essential to a finding of illegality? As we shall see, in examining the Auto Dealer's Day in Court Act, *infra*, this is a recurrent problem in the law of franchise relationships.

In the Richfield case,[19] given a situation intermediate between GMAC and J. I. Case, the Justice Department succeeded in making out its case for an injunction. In one set of its contracts, the oil company leased gasoline stations to the dealers with a right reserved to cancel the lease on 24-hour notice. The court found that such a power effectively compelled exclusive dealing from the station operators, in violation of Sctions 1 and 3. Perhaps similar reasoning might be used against an automobile distribution system using franchises terminable without cause on short notice, or perhaps even against a system relying on nonrenewal as the sanction to back up an understanding of exclusive dealing.

The practice of coercing dealers into a program of exclusive representation has also been attacked as an unfair method of com-

[18] *United States* v. *J. I. Case Co.*, 101 F. Supp. 856 (D. Minn. 1951). The suit was brought under § 1 and § 3.

[19] *United States* v. *Richfield Oil Corp.*, 99 F. Supp. 280 (S.D. Cal. 1951), *aff'd per curiam*, 343 U.S. 922 (1952).

petition or an unfair act or practice in commerce under Section 5 of the Federal Trade Commission Act. In the Timken case,[20] the Commission found a *prima facie* Section 3 case made out against a bearings manufacturer when evidence was introduced that he refused to deal with jobbers who dealt in the goods of his competitors. The Commission aggregated the refusals to deal into a concerted plan from which it could be inferred that those sales which were consummated were made on the understanding that the buyer would stop dealing in the goods of competitors of the seller. In other cases, Section 3 and Section 5 violations have been found when dealers received special discounts for dealing exclusively. Section 5 is a particularly potent weapon because under it the courts do not require the existence of a contract, combination or conspiracy. Moreover, certain practices may be attacked under Section 5 before they develop into fullblown Clayton or Sherman Act violations; this is the "incipiency" doctrine. And finally, there is authority that the scope of Section 5 reaches well out beyond that of the Clayton and Sherman Acts, striking down practices not even incipient violations of those acts, but which are merely "unfair" as determined by the specialized economic expertise of the Federal Trade Commission.

Thus, it is doubtful to what extent the exclusive representation practices are vulnerable to antitrust attack. Where the manufacturer's behavior can be shown to be coercive or to constitute a tie-in sale, illegality is relatively easy to establish. Where there is an exclusive dealing system maintained by gentlemanly behavior only, the question is open. Outside the franchise area, authority has it that absence of coercion does not insulate a seller from prosecution. It would appear that the same reasoning would be applied to automobile franchise contracts. Nevertheless, although coercion is probably illegal, and tie-ins have been declared illegal per se, exclusive dealing itself is not illegal per se.[21] The test is one of market foreclosure, a standard probably between the per se test and the customary Section 1 rule of reason test. Although the case law would seem to permit use of a looser standard by the Federal Trade Commission, the present Commission has not chosen to so extend the scope of its powers. And in any case, in all situations where the use of oral or even unvocalized understandings of exclusive dealing are the industry practice, the prosecutor faces severe evidentiary problems. Indeed,

[20] Timken Roller Bearing Co., CCH TRADE REG. REP. Paragraph 27,244 (FTC Dkt. 6504, 1958 (interlocutory appeal).

[21] *United States* v. *Columbia Steel Co.*, 334 U.S. 495, 523-24 (1948).

even learning of the existence of the restrictive practices may prove difficult.

Present and prospective impact of antitrust

In summary, the elimination of restrictive franchise clauses favoring dealers under the impact of antitrust pressure and the failure of manufacturers to control competition among dealers as a matter of practice has alerted dealers to the dangers to them of increased competition and made them increasingly aware of the powerful position of the manufacturer. The disappearance from franchises of restrictive clauses favoring the manufacturer has not necessarily affected restrictive practices. As a result, "remedial" legislation has been sought.

Should the government ever seriously undertake to prosecute automobile manufacturers for demanding exclusive representation, the franchise system might fall into decline. The dealer system might even be replaced by "supermarkets," or "dealers handling any or all makes of cars." Whether this would increase or decrease the existing barriers to entry in the industry is a moot question. Perhaps barriers would be raised at the marketing level while they were lowered at the manufacturing level. This would not necessarily mean an increase in retail prices. The contrary has occurred in the case of food supermarkets. Certainly, it is to be anticipated that such changes in the distribution structure of the industry would be resisted by those with a stake in the present structure. Thus, legislation carving out exceptions to the antiturst laws and seeking to preserve the status quo might be anticipated. Indeed, two statutes have been passed affecting the automobile industry which seek to impose a regime of status rather than contract in franchise relationships.[22] To some extent, both statutes contain elements hostile to antitrust philosophy.

Private antitrust suits by dealers

Dealers with operating franchise agreements are understandably reluctant to attempt to secure independence by suing their suppliers for violating the antitrust laws. Once a dealer has been canceled, however, his attitude often undergoes radical changes; unless he can predict voluntary renewal of his franchise, he has no relationship which might be jeopardized by bringing a law suit. Thus, private

[22] Day in Court Act, *infra*; Disclosure Act, *supra*, note 11; see also Franchised Dealer Bill, *supra*, note 12.

antitrust case law in the automobile industry is heavily weighted with actions involving canceled dealers. Although potentially the private antitrust suits may provide protection against "abuses" of cancellation, such actions have proved largely unsuccessful, judging by the reported opinions. There are major if not insurmountable obstacles to successful private antitrust action in the automobile industry.

Private damage suits are available to a party injured by a violation of the antitrust laws under Section 4 of the Clayton Act which allows treble damage recovery to "any person who shall be injured in his business or property by reason of anything forbidden in the antitrust laws." Thus, a cause of action under Section 4 has three essential ingredients: (1) a violation of the antitrust laws by defendant, (2) an injury to plaintiff, (3) proximate cause between factors (1) and (2). Some courts have read into the statute a fourth criterion: public injury caused by factor (1). Typically, dealers have proved unable to make out one or more of these ingredients of the cause of action under the statute.

The antitrust laws relevant in this context include Section 3 of the Clayton Act and Sections 1 and 2 of the Sherman Act. Section 3 of the Clayton Act forbids *sales* made on condition, agreement or understanding of exclusive dealing. A dealer who declines to deal exclusively with his manufacturer and who is disciplined by termination or nonrenewal cannot invoke this statute because no *sale* at all is made. The technical obstacles to recovery by terminated dealers under Sherman Act Section 1 appear equally serious. Section 1 requires a contract, combination or conspiracy which unreasonably restrains trade. Between the canceled dealer and the manufacturer no injurious contract, combination, or conspiracy exists of which complaint can be made. The dealer *may* allege a combination or conspiracy of which he is the victim, but lower courts have required a plurality of actors for this offense and they refuse to consider the possibility of conspiracy or combination between a corporation and its officers. Moreover, even when plurality of actors can be shown, as in an agreement between the manufacturer and a rival dealer, courts have considered such restraints of trade "reasonable" either because they are made for sound business reasons, or because the effect on commerce is not substantial since the elimination of one dealer has only a limited effect on the buying public.

Attack under Sherman Act Section 2 dispenses with the conspiracy problem, but monopolization has not been successfully proved in dealership cases because of the existence of reasonably close substitutes competing with defendant's product.

The existence of injury to the dealer has generally not been disputed. In most cases the plaintiff dealer has been driven completely out of business. But proof that this injury was proximately caused by a violation of the antitrust laws has been an unsurmountable obstacle. In the Clayton Act context, refusal to deal, as we have seen, is not a violation. The manufacturer's violation, if any, is considered to be in the sales to other dealers who submit to exclusive terms. But the courts regard these sales as causing no injury to the plaintiff. "[I]t is the absence of a contract with the plaintiff, not the presence of agreements with distributors in other parts of the country, of which the plaintiff must complain." [23] Again, under Section 1 of the Sherman Act the dealer may allege that the restrictive understandings between the integrating firm and the integrated dealers who submit to the exclusivity requirement are contracts, combinations or conspiracies which offend the act. But the reply is likely to be that the offense to the antitrust laws occasioned by illegal understandings with other dealers is no cause of injury to the canceled dealer.

Some lower courts have added a further obstacle to treble damage recovery by insisting that Section 4 of the Clayton Act is not satisfied by proof of a private injury caused by an antitrust violation. These courts have required dealer plaintiffs to establish that defendant violated the antitrust law in a manner which injured the public interest. Individual refusals to deal, even if they result in injury to the canceled dealers, are usually considered to entail no injury to the general public when substitute products are available. Injury to competition, *i.e.*, to the market, is said to be essential to recovery, and injury to competitors is not sufficient. However, the most recent case on this point has stated the problem in far more sophisticated terms. It abandons public injury as a requirement under Section 4, a statute whose literal text has no such requirement. Instead, the court takes the position that the public injury requirement is inherent in the antitrust laws themselves; absent a per se violation, no unlawful restraint of trade can be found unless there is a "restraint injurious to the public." The proposition may soon be evaluated by the Supreme Court on appellate review of the case.

[23] *Nelson Radio & Supply Co.* v. *Motorola, Inc.*, 200 F.2d 911, 915 (5th Cir. 1952), *cert. denied*, 345 U.S. 925 (1953).

In summary, canceled or unrenewed automobile dealers have not won antitrust relief. Perhaps the courts may recede from their present restrictive interpretation of the antitrust laws as applied to private damages actions. Impetus for such change may come from the Supreme Court, which had, until this year, denied review of dealer damage suits. The Supreme Court has in the past adopted a broad interpretation of the antitrust laws as the government intervention cases discussed, *supra,* reveal, and the same philosophy may influence future decisions on dealer suits. But until the present lower appellate court case law trend is reversed, dealers cannot look to the antitrust laws for relief from the power of the manufacturer or from the terms of their franchises. To be sure, dealers have been incidental beneficiaries of government intervention against certain restrictive arrangements which unlawfully foreclosed the market, but such intervention has not occurred against specific cancellations or instances of nonrenewal. Understandably, the dealer has sought relief elsewhere.

D. Reform Movement

The dealers, having suffered defeat before the courts in their struggle to attain the status of independent merchants, understandably have resorted to group action for combatting the manufacturer's vertical power and the attendant rigors of competition on the distribution level. Ever since its origin in the days of the depression, this movement has gained momentum. The chief spokesman for dealer demands is the National Automobile Dealers Association (NADA), founded in 1917. Three phases of development can be distinguished: the NRA, the period of state legislation and the phase of federal legislation. Playing an ever-increasing role, the Association has attempted, throughout each of these periods, to obtain better terms for its members by negotiating with the manufacturers. But its efforts to persuade the manufacturer to accept the Equitable Dealer Contract have been unsuccessful. And the manufacturers generally have refused to participate in contract negotiation with the NADA or groups formed by their own dealers.

The NRA

With the advent of the NRA and the introduction of a Code for dealers, group action had its first noticeable success: During this period, price competition among dealers was substantially eliminated by controlling used-car prices. The so-called Blue Book, which prescribed a ceiling on trade-in allowances, was introduced. Marked by the absence of vigorous competition, the NRA period often has been labelled the golden age of dealers. The manufacturers, on the other hand, suffered a reduction in market from the lack of aggressive dealer competition. Accordingly, manufacturer pressure defeated the dealers' attempts, after the demise of NRA, to preserve by self-regulation the benefits enjoyed during its life.

All other dealer group action has been aimed at mobilizing public opinion and enlisting the help of legislators. Appeals to the legislature were maintained on both state and federal levels. The philosophy behind these movements reflects the attitude of retailers generally in the post-depression era. Without the enactment of "fair trade laws," they argued, their existence as "small businessmen" is threatened by the evils of "cut-throat" competition and domination by "giant monopolists." Many dealers, the argument continues, have gone into bankruptcy or given up their dealerships. This reduction in dealerships has resulted in a "loss to the public of retail outlets and service facilities, which are essential to the automotive economy."

State legislation

Approximately twenty state statutes regulate the distribution of motor vehicles. Some states, for example Mississippi, which enacted the first regulatory statute in 1934, have an approval type of regulation. Like an insurance policy, the franchise contract must be approved by a governmental agency in order to be binding. Other state statutes control competition among dealers; some of this group prohibit nonfranchised dealers from selling "new cars." But the bulk of the regulatory statutes are aimed at the elimination of enumerated unfair practices inflicted by the manufacturer on the dealer. Unfair or inequitable termination of the franchise by the manufacturer is the chief target. The sanctions against violation vary greatly. Some legislatures have relied on the deterrent effect by utilizing penalties such as fines, loss of license or dissolution. Others attempt to give the injured dealer relief in the form of an action for damages or a suit in equity.

Of the state legislation regulating automobile merchandising, the Wisconsin and Colorado statutes are most interesting. The Wisconsin act, which has set a pattern for many state statutes, forbids a manufacturer to use threat of cancellation or nonrenewal as a means of forcing dealers to accept delivery of unordered goods. And it forbids cancellation of dealer franchises "unfairly, without due regard to the equities of said dealer" or nonrenewal "without just provocation." The statute does not expressly give the injured dealer a private remedy. The only sanctions provided are fines and the denial, suspension or revocation of the license required to do business.

On the other hand, the Colorado statute, while forbidding the practices proscribed by the Wisconsin act, makes express provision for dealer remedies. Cancellation or delayed renewal is not effective unless approved by a court, state or federal. Where the cancellation power has been invoked without such approval, the dealer is given the right to apply for injunctive relief staying the manufacturer's action. Should the court find the dealer injured, he can collect treble damages.

Although the Colorado statute has been declared invalid as an unconstitutional exercise of the police power, the constitutionality of the Wisconsin act has been upheld. Moreover, in interpreting the statute, the Wisconsin Supreme Court has strengthened the rights of the dealer by granting him injunctive relief against violation by the manufacturer.

Federal legislation

The dealers, acting through their collective body, the NADA, succeeded in obtaining legislation in only three states by 1937. Accordingly, they appealed to the congressmen of these three states for federal aid. Representative Withrow of Wisconsin introduced a resolution which authorized the FTC to investigate the motor vehicle industry. After lengthy hearings, the resolution was passed, authorizing the FTC to make an investigation on a scale far beyond that envisaged by the sponsor. The FTC issued the requested report, consisting of more than one thousand pages, in 1939.

The Commission found "that motor vehicle manufacturers, and, by reason of their great power, especially General Motors Corporation, Chrysler Corporation and Ford Motor Company have been, and still are, imposing on their respective dealers unfair and inequitable conditions of trade. But it also found that:

> Active competition among automobile manufacturers, although some of them made very large profits, gave to the public improved products, often at substantially reduced prices. In the automobile industry this has been especially true of those manufacturers who are able to obtain large volume of production through competitive improvement in motor-

> vehicle construction, style, performance, and safety, particularly in the low-priced class. Such competition has been the basis for the remarkable growth of the industry.
>
> Consumer benefits from competition in the automobile-manufacturing industry have probably been more substantial than in any other large industry studied by the Commission.

Concerning dealer practices, the Commission's report contained the following findings regarding attempts to restrain competition:

> The Commission finds that local associations of motor-vehicle dealers in various parts of the country have engaged in the following practices to fix or maintain prices: (1) Fixing minimum prices on new cars, often by means of uniform maximum discounts from the manufacturer resale prices in transactions where no trade-ins are involved; (2) establishing maximum purchase prices, or allowances, for used cars taken in trade; (3) regulating bidding on used cars taken in trade by means of uniform minimum increases on all bids subsequent to the original bid, or by requiring all bids subsequent to the original bids to be less than the original bid; and (4) adopting published used-car price guides as a basis for maximum allowances for used cars. . . . The Commission found that many local associations operate used-car valuation or appraisal bureaus that are essentially combinations of dealers in particular localities who are bound by agreements to restrict competition in used-car trading.

In light of these findings, it is not surprising that the remedy suggested by the Commission with respect to unfair manufacturer treatment of dealers was rather restrained.

> It is recommended that present unfair practices be abated to the end that dealers have (a) less restriction upon the management of their own enterprises; (b) quota requirements and shipments of cars based upon mutual agreement; (c) equitable liquidation in the event of contract termination by the manufacturer; (d) contracts definite as to the mutual rights and obligations of the manufacturers and the dealers, including specific provision that the contract will be continued for a definite term unless terminated by breach of reasonable conditions recited therein.

Disappointed with the FTC report, the NADA persuaded Congressman Patman to sponsor the Motor Vehicle Bill of 1940. The bill, which was to be administered by the FTC, required franchises to contain certain minimum provisions safeguarding the interests of the dealer. It met with a strange fate; replies to a questionnaire indicated that the majority of dealers was against the bill. This attitude might, at least in part, have stemmed from the dealers' fear that the Patman bill would portend more extensive federal regulation.

Attempts to introduce other federal legislation were interrupted by the outbreak of the war, but the movement was revitalized by the development of a buyer's market and the attendant great increase in dealer competition characterizing the post-war period. In response to demands made by the NADA, a constant flood of bills dealing with automobile merchandising has been introduced in the Congress. These bills led to a broad investigation culminating in hearings conducted by a Senate Subcommittee on Automobile Marketing Practice. The Senate Subcommittee on Antitrust and Monopoly, in examining General Motors, also devoted much study to manufacturer-dealer relations.

The purpose of the many bills introduced—more than thirty during the last session of the Congress—was to secure economic independence for the dealer by protecting him against the coercive power of the manufacturer and against competition from other, particularly nonfranchised, dealers. Various schemes were utilized to accomplish this goal. Following the techniques of the Patman bill of 1940 and state regulation of life insurance policies, some bills attempted to correct the unequal bargaining power of the parties to the franchise contract by "legislating the franchise terms"—establishing minimum provisions for all franchise contracts. Other bills exempted clauses and practices concerning territorial security, bootlegging and phantom freight from the reach of the antitrust laws. Still others aimed at "unfair methods of competition and unfair practices." However bills in this group may vary, they share one feature: arbitrary cancellation by the manufacturer is treated as an unfair practice. Finally, a more general approach is employed in the Day in Court Bill. Reasoning from the premise that cancellation was at the heart of the dealer's problem, the sponsors introduced a requirement of good faith dealing into the franchise contract, thus arming the courts with the weapon they had claimed in the past was not at their disposal.

As introduced in the Senate, the bill offered the dealer double damages and recovery of attorney's fees in an action based on "the failure . . . [of an] automobile manufacturer to act in good faith in performing or comply with any of the terms or provisions of the franchise, or in terminating, cancelling, or in renewing the franchise. . . ." "Good faith" was defined to impose upon the manufacturer, its officers, employees or agents a duty

> To act in a fair, equitable and non-arbitrary manner so as to guarantee the dealer freedom from coercion, intimidation, or threats of coercion or intimidation, and in order to preserve and to protect all the equities of the automobile dealer which are inherent in the nature of the relationship between the automobile dealer and automobile manufacturer.

As passed by the Senate, the bill allowed the dealer only compensatory damages and defined good faith to include the actions of both parties. But only the dealer was given a cause of action for violation of the duty to act in good faith. The manufacturer was limited to using lack of good faith as a defensive weapon in suits brought by the dealer.

As finally passed, the bill incorporates further amendments introduced in the House of Representatives.[24] The most important changes are an antitrust savings clause and a rewording of the good-faith provision. The latter reads as follows:

> The term 'good faith' shall mean the duty of each party to any franchise, and all officers, employees or agents thereof, to act in a fair and equitable manner toward each other so as to guarantee the one party freedom from coercion, intimidation, or threats of coercion or intimidation from the other party; *Provided*, That recommendation, enforcement, exposition, persuasion, urging or argument shall not be deemed to constitute a lack of good faith.

While the duty of good faith applies to existing franchise agreements, the dealer is given a cause of action only when the manufacturer's breach occurred after the passage of the act.

According to the House report, this legislation was necessary because:

> Concentration of economic power in the automobile manufacturing industry of the United States has developed to the point where legislation is required to remedy the manifest disparity in the ability of franchised dealers of automotive vehicles to bargain with their manufacturers. Investigations of the automobile industry, moreover, demonstrate a continuing trend toward greater concentration, as well as abuse by the manufacturers of their dominant position with respect to their dealers. These investigations have disclosed practices and conditions which require new legislative methods and a change in established concepts. The bill as amended proceeds from the conclusion that in the automobile industry concentration of economic power has increased to the degree that traditional contractual concepts are no longer adequate to protect the automobile dealers under their franchises.

And recent concessions made by manufacturers were deemed insufficient to overcome the necessity for legislation in the area.

> While it is true these developments in the automobile industry may diminish some of the abuses found to exist, this does not derogate from the necessity for legislation at this time. For one thing, the new General Motors selling agreements afford no guaranty against dealer coercion or intimidation or threats thereof by the manufacturer. Furthermore, what the automobile manufacturers do in response to congressional

[24] 70 Stat. 1125, 15 USCA § 1222 (1957 Supp.)

> investigation or in contemplation of pending legislation, they can readily undo. The record before the committee demonstrates that, in the past, gains made by dealers after investigation into market practices of the automobile manufacturers have not always been retained. This bill assures a minimum amount of protection for the dealer under the terms of any automobile franchise.

President Eisenhower, in signing the Day in Court Bill, recognized the existence of serious problems in manufacturer-dealer relations. But his statement indicated reservations on the wisdom of this legislation.

> The legislation represents a serious Congressional effort to deal with abuses Congress found to exist. At best I believe it constitutes only a partial solution to the problem. In addition, it presents legal problems, some of which could be of the most serious character.
>
> Ordinarily when parties enter into business agreement outside the realm of public utilities, legislative action which qualified their rights to terminate or renew the agreement in the manner provided by this legislation would be considered an unwarranted intrusion by the Federal Government into an area traditionally reserved to private enterprise. Therefore, this bill represents a new departure in the exercise of Federal authority, a point which will undoubtedly come to the attention of the courts. However, in view of the findings of Congress on the special conditions in the automobile industry, which may be of a temporary nature, I am approving the bill. At the same time I am directing the antitrust enforcement agencies of the Government to review the conditions in the industry which brought about the demand for the legislation, to determine whether they continue to exist, to study alternative or different solutions to the problem, and to make recommendations for appropriate action by next Congress.

E. The Day in Court Act as Law

The legislative history demonstrates that implementation of the Day in Court Act will entail difficult judicial interpretation. The courts will have to solve two basic issues: the meaning of good faith, and the "nature" of the remedy, including the question of damages. In addition, opponents of the Act will probably challenge its constitutionality. In this version of the article, only the problem of good faith will be taken up. It will be discussed both in the context of the statute and within the framework of the franchise system in practice.

Good faith and coercion

The basic problem under the act is determining the standard of behavior which is required of the parties of the franchise. In this connection, two phrases used by the statute are crucial: "good faith" and "coercion, intimidation, or threats of coercion or intimidation." Is the duty to act in good faith restricted to abstention from coercive practices, or does it have a wider scope? Moreover, what is "coercion"?

GOOD FAITH. When interpreting this elusive concept, the wording of the statute itself, its legislative history, including the changes Congress imposed and the versions it rejected, the Congressional reports, and finally, judicial canons of construction have to be taken into account.

Considering the wording of the act itself, Section 1(e) declares "good faith" to be the duty of each party to the franchise to act in a fair and equitable manner toward the other *so as* to guarantee him freedom from coercive practices.[25] The words "so as" may be read either as words of qualification, limiting the duty to act in good faith to only abstention from coercion, or else as words of illustration, exemplifying coercion as only one instance of bad faith. Thus, the statutory wording is inconclusive for determining the scope of the duty.

Does legislative history furnish a better answer? The original version passed by the Senate imposed on the manufacturer in the name of good faith a duty to act in a fair, equitable, and non-arbitrary manner toward the dealer in order to guarantee him freedom from manufacturer coercion and preserve all the equities of the dealer inherent in the franchise relationship. But the House changed the bill in two ways: the phrase about preserving all the equities was deleted and the duty to act in good faith was imposed upon the dealer as well as upon the manufacturer. The two changes suggest two contradictory interpretations of the scope of good faith. Insofar as the House deleted the phrase defining good faith in terms of preserving all the equities of the dealer, it would seem clear that it was found unnecessary to grant any protection further than guaranteeing freedom from coercion. However, imposition of the duty to act in good faith upon the dealer suggests a contrary interpretation. It seems hardly probable that Congress wished to protect automobile manufacturers from dealer coercion. Yet, if the duty to act in good faith which the act imposes on dealers is a duty limited to abstention from coercion, then this unrealistic conclusion follows as the legislative purpose. Thus it is necessary to probe still further to ascertain the scope of good faith under the act; the changes by Congress in the wording of the law do not help us.

[25] See text of act, Appendix, *infra*, ...

Turning to the House Report, we find much ambiguity again. However, one passage uses language which strongly suggests that coercion is necessary for there to be lack of good faith. In discussing 1(e), the report states that the term "fair and equitable manner . . ." is qualified by the requirement of coercion and that "in each case arising under the bill good faith must be determined in the context of coercion or intimidation or threats . . ." Moreover, we must reckon with the probability that, given a statute which derogates from common-law rights of freedom of contract, the courts are likely to interpret it restrictively, despite its self-declared remedial purpose. Thus, the House Report interpreted in the light of well established ideals should incline the weight of decision toward restricting the duty to act in good faith solely to the abstention from coercive practices.

COERCION. Hence the next question pressing for decision is: What is the meaning of "coercion"? Certainly, coercion is minimally intimidation and predatory behavior. Sending a dealer cars of the wrong quantity or color or threatening him that he will be driven out of business when he refuses to accede to manufacturer demands, in all probability, is coercion under the act; these are no longer acceptable means of persuasion of dealers to submit to manufacturer demands. Is such behavior the outer limit of "coercion" under the act?

As before, the wording of the statute itself is inconclusive. "Coercion" is not expressly defined in the act. However, the legislative history is very helpful in this connection. In discussing 2(e) the House Report emphasizes that "in each case arising under the bill good faith must be determined in the context of coercion or intimidation or threats of coercion and intimidation." The Report continues:

> The existence of coercion or intimidation depends upon the circumstances arising in each particular case and may be inferred from a course of conduct. For example, manufacture pressure, direct or indirect, upon a dealer to accept automobiles, parts, accessories, or supplies which the dealer does not need, want or feel the market is able to absorb, may . . . constitute coercion or intimidation. Similarly coercion or intimidation may be found where the manufacturer attempts to require the dealer to handle exclusively, or sell a specified quota of parts, accessories, and tools made or approved by the manufacturer.
>
> If the evidence discloses normal sales recommendation or persuasion the manufacturer would be liable. On the other hand, if the manufacturer goes beyond normal sales recommendation or persuasion . . . his activities could give rise to a cause of action under the bill. . . .

> Manufacturer coercion or intimidation or threats thereof is actionable by the dealer where it relates to performing or complying with any of the terms or provisions of the franchise, or where it relates to the termination, cancellation or renewal of the dealer's franchise. Thus, where a dealer's resistance to manufacturer pressure is related to cancellation or nonrenewal of his franchise a cause of action would arise.

The Report became even more explicit when it declares:

> The manufacturer's obligation to act in good faith extends to all of his franchised dealers, including: dealers who sell automobiles to other dealers, franchised or not, for resale to the public; dealers who sell outside of a 'zone of influence' or 'territory'; and dealers who sell automobiles at less than manufacturers' suggested resale prices. Contract provisions restricting an automobile dealer from transacting business with customers of his choice, or from selling outside a specified territory could violate the antitrust laws. Any restriction on a dealer's right to sue based on the fact that he is selling to another dealer, franchised or not, for resale to the public or based on the fact that he sells outside of a territory or sells at cut rates would contravene the Congressional purposes underlying Section 4 of this bill which provides that this measure shall not repeal, modify, or supersede, directly or indirectly, any provision of the antitrust laws.

In the light of the foregoing, the emphasis on coercion becomes understandable. The chief target of the Act is exclusive arrangements brought about by coercion, particularly those exclusive arrangements which do not appear in the franchise but which form a practice and are enforced and policed by cancellation or nonrenewal, or threats of cancellation or nonrenewal.

Such coercive practices already constituted violation of the antitrust laws, but they could be attacked only by court action in proceedings brought by the Department of Justice or by a cease and desist order of the Federal Trade Commission, and then only when they amounted to a substantial lessening of competition, an unreasonable restraint of trade, or an unfair trade practice or method of competition. The dealer injured by coercive cancellation or nonrenewal was given no effective private cause of action under the customary interpretation of Section 4 of the Clayton Act. Under the new act, an auto manufacturer who fails to renew a recalcitrant dealer can no longer find refuge in the doctrine that, by refusing to deal, he is merely invoking his unalienable right to trade with whom he pleases. In this respect the Dealer Act goes indeed beyond the existing antitrust law, supplementing it as the preamble asserts.

BARRIERS TO COMPETITION. At this point it may appear that one aspect of antitrust policy has been sacrificed at the expense of another; has the countervailing power of the dealer against the manufacturer been so built up as to create even more serious market problems than existed? Does the dealer enjoy a local monopoly, a little principality of his own, under the new act? This would not seem to be the intention of Congress. The House Report declares that the passage in the Senate bill which required the manufacturer to act so as to preserve all the equities of the dealer inherent in the franchise relationship was deleted by the House "to preclude any interpretation inconsistent with antitrust principles." And Section 4 of the act becomes even more meaningful in this connection when another passage of the report is considered:

> The bill . . . does not prohibit the manufacturer from terminating or refusing to renew the franchise of a dealer who is not providing the manufacturer with adequate representation. Nor does the bill curtail the manufacturer's right to cancel or not to renew an efficient or undesirable dealer's franchise.
>
> The bill does not freeze present channels or methods of automobile distribution and would not prohibit a manufacturer from appointing an additional dealer in a community provided that the establishment of the new dealer is not a device by the manufacturer to coerce or intimidate an existing dealer. The committee emphasizes that the bill does not afford the dealer the right to be free from competition from additional franchise dealers. Appointment of added dealers in an area is a normal competitive method, for securing better distribution and curtailment of this right would be inconsistent with the antitrust objectives of this legislation. Under the bill, a manufacturer does not guarantee the dealer profitable operation or freedom from depletion of investment.
>
> The manufacturer's obligation to act in good faith extends to all of his franchised dealers, including: dealers who sell automobiles to other dealers, franchised or not, for resale to the public; dealers who sell outside of a 'zone of influence' or 'territory'; and dealers who sell automobiles at less than the manufacturer's suggested resale prices. Contract provisions restricting an automobile dealer from transacting business with customers of his choice, or from selling outside a specified territory could violate the antitrust laws. Any restriction on a dealer's right to sue based on the fact that he is selling to another dealer, franchised or not, for resale to the public or based on the fact that he sells outside of a territory or sells at cut rates would contravene the Congressional purposes underlying Section 4 of this bill which provides that this measure shall not repeal, modify, or supersede, directly or indirectly, any provision of the antitrust laws.
>
> Similarly, a manufacturer, in a dealer's suit for damages stemming from a manufacturer's refusal to supply adequate cars, could not set up by way of defense, as lack of good faith, the fact that the dealer sold new cars to other new or used car dealers for resale to the public. Also, a dealer located near another franchised dealer who was sold new cars to used car dealers for resale would not be authorized under this measure to sue a manufacturer for supplying dealers who sell cars to other dealers for resale.

Thus, it appears that it was not the intention of Congress to provide the dealer with a local monopoly and to raise barriers to efficient automobile marketing.

Effect of the act on marketing patterns

The Day in Court Act may be challenged for denying a workable means of controlling the dealer-manufacturer relationship. The act's opponents have argued that the franchise has continuously been improved, that the inevitable consequence of the act will be "to encourage the parties to regard themselves as legal antagonists rather than as participants in a [joint] business venture" and that the climate of cooperation prevailing until the advent of the new legislation will be replaced by a "litigious atmosphere." [26] Some critics of the act have questioned whether the franchise system of distribution—heretofore regarded as "the approach best suited to [the] type of product and the mutuality of interests existing between the manufacturer and dealer"—should be retained.[27]

Thus, despite the assurances the House Report gives, the act may freeze present channels and methods of distribution and restrain manufacturers from removing inefficient dealers. When sued, unless the manufacturer can secure a verdict on the pleadings or a directed verdict, he must run a grave juridical risk. Juries are not notorious for their sympathy toward corporations with deep pockets, especially when the corporation is foreign and the plaintiff a local business man. Thus, the act may function *in terroram,* and while it may inhibit borderline coercive behavior, at the same time it might inhibit manufacturers from eliminating inefficient elements in their distribution systems. To the extent that the latter occurs, inflexibility in the automobile industry integration system would be increased, and the beneficial effects of contract integration over status integration would be diminished. Nevertheless, this does not compel the conclusion that the act goes too far. Any remedial legislation is bound to create new juridical risks. The question of whether the act creates more problems than it solves is one of fact which only experience can answer. The workability of the law will depend on the ability of the judiciary to apply the statute in a manner which accords the dealer a greater degree of independence without destroying manufacturer and consumer interests in an efficient dealership system.

[26] *H. R. Hearings, Dealer Franchises* 284 (Ford Motor Co. statement).
[27] 1 *S. Hearings, Marketing Practices* 686 (Curtice statement).

The interpretation the courts give to the term "coercion" in the act will probably determine how much benefit dealers secure from the new law. If courts take a conservative position and give the term a narrow interpretation, dealers will not secure the benefit they desire. Of course, courts *could* take the other extreme and convert the franchise system from one of contract integration to status integration, making franchises permanent relationships. However, neither extreme is likely. It is to be anticipated that courts will follow the interpretation suggested, *supra,* that the term "coercion" includes not only the threat of or the carrying out of the threat to do acts wrongful in themselves, but it includes as well acts not wrongful as such but which are part of an illegal scheme, acts adopted to further an unlawful plan—specifically, the plan of violation of the antitrust laws.

Given this interpretation of the act, not all dealers who desire legal redress for cancellation will gain it. Indeed, many if not most of the canceled dealer antitrust suits would come out the same way as before. Hence, under this interpretation, the dealer community may feel that the act does not go far enough. Nevertheless, it is submitted that such a construction of the act would most further the public interest. One can quarrel with the proposition that the dealer should recover damages only if by so doing he vindicates the public interest. But one should not quarrel with the proposition that dealer should not take damages if his suit will result in injury to the public. Extending the scope of the term "coercion" beyond unlawful acts which will further an unlawful purpose will so hamper the distribution of automobiles that the ultimate consumer will be injured, and will be forced to foot the bill for preserving inefficient means of distribution. It is submitted that this is not a social cost which should be borne by the car buyer. Hence, it is the position of the authors that the act does go far enough.[28]

Conclusions

Manufacturer-dealer relations have been marked by a continuous conflict of interests. In their desire to achieve greater sales volume, manufacturers have sought vigorous competition among dealers who, in turn, have pursued an independence denied them by the economic power of their suppliers. To the extent the Day in Court Act pro-

[28] A bill identical to the Day in Court Act has been proposed for gasoline distribution, (H.R. 425, 85th Cong., 1st Sess., 1957). The Senate Select Committee on Small Business has considered the extension of the Day in Court Act to other industries.

hibits manufacturers from unwarranted intervention in the day-to-day business of dealers, it seems a worthy statute. But in so far as the bill provides a means of lessening competition in the chain of distribution, it deserves all the criticism applied to fair trade laws. Protection for the middle man against the evils of "cut-throat" competition is always achieved at the consumer's expense. Moreover, any legislation constricting the freedom of contracting parties to adjust to new conditions by dictating their conduct deprives them and society of the flexibility inherent in contractual relationships and fosters the rigidity of status arrangements. Thus, while dealers claim to represent the most satisfactory channel for the distribution and service of automobiles, in the event they seek further congressional action, it would seem wiser to let the marketplace determine which elements are most efficient rather than by legislation lend support to the existing distribution pattern.

Appendix

Automobile Dealer's Day in Court Act of 1956

An Act

To supplement the antitrust laws of the United States, in order to balance the power now heavily weighted in favor of automobile manufacturers, by enabling franchise automobile dealers to bring suit in the district courts of the United States to recover damages sustained by reason of the failure of automobile manufacturers to act in good faith in complying with the terms of franchises or in terminating or not renewing franchises with their dealers.

Be it enacted by the Senate and House of Representatives of the United States of America in Congress assembled, That as used in this Act—

(a) The term "automobile manufacturer" shall mean any person, partnership, corporation, association, or other form of business enterprise engaged in the manufacturing or assembling of passenger cars, trucks, or station wagons, including any person, partnership, or corporation which acts for and is under the control of such manufacturer or assembler in connection with the distribution of said automotive vehicles.

(b) The term "franchise" shall mean the written agreement or contract between any automobile manufacturer engaged in commerce and any automobile dealer which purports to fix the legal rights and liabilities of the parties to such agreement or contract.

(c) The term "automobile dealer" shall mean any person, partnership, corporation, association, or other from of business enterprise resident in the United States or in any Territory thereof or in the District of Columbia operating under the terms of a franchise and engaged in the sale or distribution of passenger cars, trucks, or station wagons.

(d) The term "commerce" shall mean commerce among the several States of the United States or with foreign nations, or in any Territory of the United States or in the District of Columbia, or among the Territories or between any Territory and any State or foreign nation, or between the District of Columbia and any State or Territory or foreign nation.

(e) The term "good faith" shall mean the duty of each party to any franchise, and all officers, employees, or agents thereof to act in a fair and equitable manner toward each other so as to guarantee the one party freedom from coercion, intimidation, or threats of coercion or intimidation from the other party: Provided, That recommendation, endorsement, exposition, persuasion, urging or argument shall not be deemed to constitute a lack of good faith.

SEC. 2. An automobile dealer may bring suit against any automobile manufacturer engaged in commerce, in any district court of the United States in the district in which said manufacturer resides, or is found, or has an agent, without respect to the amount in controversy, and shall recover the damages by him sustained and the cost of suit by reason of the failure of said automobile manufacturer from and after the passage of this Act to act in good faith in performing or complying with any of the terms or provisions of the franchise, or in terminating, canceling, or not renewing the franchise with said dealer: Provided, That in any such suit the manufacturer shall not be barred from asserting in defense of any such action the failure of the dealer to act in good faith.

SEC. 3. Any action brought pursuant to this Act shall be forever barred unless commenced within three years after the cause of action shall have accrued.

SEC. 4. No provision of this Act shall repeal, modify, or supersede, directly or indirectly, any provision of the antitrust laws of the United States.

SEC. 5. This Act shall not invalidate any provision of the laws of any State except insofar as there is a direct conflict between an express provision of this Act and an express provision of State law which can not be reconciled.

67. MERCHANDISING PRACTICES OF DISCOUNT HOUSES *

John W. Gwynne

I appear here today, in response to the request of your Chairman, to discuss the merchandising practices of discount houses.

The typical discount house is a retail store which is engaged principally in conducting over-the-counter sales, usually for cash and often unaccompanied by certain traditional services such as free delivery. They have been described by their proponents as a merchandising innovation which brings economies to the consumer; and by their opponents as unfair to established retailers doing business by more traditional methods. My purpose today is not to evaluate discount houses or to compare their virtues with those of nondiscount retailers. My purpose is to discuss discount selling in the light of existing law.

Mere selling at reduced prices does not violate any law administered by the Federal Trade Commission. A retail seller, or any seller, is generally free to fix the price at which he will sell his goods. There are some exceptions. It is clearly understood that if a number of discount houses in commerce agreed among themselves to sell at a specific low price this would violate the Federal Trade Commission Act and the Sherman Act. Further, if any discount house deliberately made sales in commerce at unreasonably low prices in order to destroy competition or a competitor, this would violate the Federal Trade Commission Act and Section 3 of the Robinson-Patman Act.

An important requirement for violation of the Federal Trade Commission Act is that the questioned sales must take place in the course of interstate commerce. Since most discount house sales are made over the counter in intrastate commerce, they are not within the scope of the Commission's jurisdiction.

Insofar as discount house operations are concerned, the most important statutory enactments have been the so-called "fair trade" laws which have been enacted for the purpose of permitting pro-

* Reprinted by permission of John W. Gwynne from a statement before the Subcommittee on Retailing Distribution and Fair Trade Practices, Senate Small Business Committee, June 25, 1958.
John W. Gwynne, Former Chairman, Federal Trade Commission.

ducers and distributors to maintain prices for the resale of goods produced or distributed by them.

Resale Price Maintenance

Prior to 1937, systematic attempts to interfere with the general freedom of a retailer to sell his goods at whatever price he deemed suitable were held to violate the antitrust laws. In that year the Miller-Tydings Act was passed.

Amending the Sherman Act, the Miller-Tydings Act provided that nothing in the antitrust laws shall render illegal contracts or agreements prescribing minimum prices for described commodities when such contracts or agreements are lawful as applied to intrastate transactions under any statute, law or public policy in effect in any State, territory or the District of Columbia. Thereafter, many States enacted fair trade laws.

On May 21, 1951, in the case of *Schwegmann Bros., et al.* v. *Calvert Distilleries Corp.*, 341 U. S. 384, the Supreme Court held that the exemption in the Miller-Tydings Act extended only to the making of fair trade contracts and did not legalize the efforts of persons fair trading commodities to impose their prices on persons not party to the contracts. The Court said, therefore, that the exercise of this right, when interstate commerce was involved, was not protected by the exemption in the Act.

It was primarily this leading decision by the Supreme Court that led to the enactment of the McGuire Act on July 14, 1952. The McGuire Act, which amends the Federal Trade Commission Act, is in many respects similar to the Miller-Tydings Act, but is broader in scope.

The McGuire Act legalizes contracts prescribing both minimum and stipulated prices, whereas the Miller-Tydings Act provided only for minimum prices. Moreover, the McGuire Act provides for non-signer clauses making it lawful to compel, by an action under State fair trade laws, noncontracting as well as contracting parties to abide by fair trade prices established in the State.

What has happened in the courts since the passage of the McGuire Act? The constitutionality of the Act has never been squarely tested in the United States Supreme Court, although certiorari was denied in one case. (Schwegmann Bros., Giant Supermarket and Eli Lilly & Co., 74 S. Ct. 71) However, the highest courts in fourteen states have held that their fair trade acts, insofar as they applied to nonsigners, are unconstitutional. In four more states there are lower court decisions to the same effect, making a total of eighteen states in which the nonsigner aspect has been declared unconstitutional. Since three states have no fair trade laws, and in nine more states the laws have not been tested by the courts, these figures become even more significant. Moreover, courts in four states have declared their fair trade acts in general unconstitutional.

The primary reason given by most State Supreme Courts for holding the fair trade laws, as applied to nonsigners, unconstitutional was that they violated the due process clause of the state constitution. Among other reasons given for its unconstitutionality were that it was an unlawful delegation of legislative power to private persons, and that it granted to a certain class of citizens privileges which were not equally given to all citizens.

With the breakdown of fair trade at the state level, there have been new attempts to enact federal legislation, which would accomplish the purposes of the Miller-Tydings and the McGuire Acts. One such bill is H. R. 10527, which was made the subject of hearings before the House Committee on Interstate and Foreign Commerce earlier this year. A similar bill has been introduced in the Senate.

In a statement presented April 30, 1958, the Federal Trade Commission unanimously opposed this legislation. The Federal Trade Commission has traditionally opposed resale price maintenance. This position was expressed in complaints filed by the Commission prior to 1920.

Many years later, in 1945, the Federal Trade Commission completed an exhaustive study on resale price maintenance and submitted to Congress an 872-page report. The conclusions reached are far too long and detailed to discuss here, but, speaking quite generally, the Commission found that resale price maintenance was unsound economically, tended to destroy competition, and, at least in certain areas, favored the large concerns.

Again in 1952 the Commission reaffirmed its opposition to the principle of resale price maintenance. At that time the Commission described resale price maintenance as "contrary to the public policy expressed by Congress in the antitrust laws since 1890," and "contrary to the public policy expressed by Congress in the Federal Trade Commission Act."

For the reasons which are outlined above and because the concept of resale price maintenance contravenes the traditional ideas of the American system of free competitive enterprise, the Federal Trade

Commission has reaffirmed its position of opposition to the principles involved in pending resale price maintenance legislation.

Loss Leader Selling

Another practice of which discount houses have been accused is loss leader selling, but this complaint has often been lodged against traditional businesses. There is no federal statute prohibiting loss leader selling as such. Section 3 of the Robinson-Patman Act prohibits the sale of goods at "unreasonably low prices" under certain circumstances. The last clause of the first paragraph of Section 3 of the Robinson-Patman Act makes it illegal to sell, or contract to sell, goods at unreasonably low prices for the purpose of destroying competition or eliminating a competitor. Thus this section forbids certain predatory pricing practices. Section 3 provides also that "any person violating any of the provisions of this section shall, upon conviction thereof, be fined not more than $5,000 or imprisoned not more than one year, or both.

Section 3 of the Robinson-Patman Act is enforced by the Department of Justice. However, under certain circumstances violation thereof may also constitute violation of one or more statutes administered by the Federal Trade Commission. The discriminatory type of practice forbidden by Section 3 will usually be found to violate Section 2 of the Robinson-Patman Act, which is enforced by the Federal Trade Commission. Under certain circumstances the last clause of Section 3 prohibiting sales at unreasonably low prices to destroy competition or to eliminate a competitor may also violate Section 5 of the Federal Trade Commission Act.

The practice of selling below cost, in and of itself, does not constitute a violation of the Federal Trade Commission Act. In *Sears, Roebuck & Co.* v. *F. T. C.*, 258 Fed. 307, the Seventh Circuit Court of Appeals stated as follows: "We find no intent on the part of Congress, even if it has the power, to restrain an owner of property from selling it at any price that is acceptable to him or from giving it away."

In order to constitute an unfair method of competition in violation of Section 5 of the Federal Trade Commission Act, the sales in question must have been made with the intent and purpose and must have the actual or probable effect of eliminating competition or creating a monopoly. In proving such intent, purpose and effect, it has been held necessary for the Commission to show that the seller engaged in numerous unfair acts and practices which constitute a course of conduct deliberately and intentionally followed for the purpose of injuring or eliminating competition.

In one of the few cases in which the Commission has successfully challenged the practice of selling below cost (*E. B. Muller & Co., et al.*, v. *F. T. C.*, 142 Fed. (2) 255), the court stated that "the Commission could not prove a course of conduct for the period charged by picking out a few instances of isolated sales." It continued by evidence of many transactions considered as a group and involving a comparison of prices and costs over a substantial period of time.

These stringent legal requirements make it very difficult for the Commission to take corrective action with respect to sporadic, isolated loss leader promotional offers of the "week-end special" variety.

From time to time bills have been introduced in Congress to prohibit loss leader selling and predatory pricing practices. Several have been introduced in the instant Congress and are now pending. Insofar as such bills would prohibit selling below cost or at unreasonably low prices *for the purpose of destroying competition or a competitor,* I would be inclined to favor the legislation.

Deceptive Practices

From time to time, complaints come to the attention of the Commission alleging that discount houses have indulged in various forms of deceptive acts or practices. The Commission's statutory functions clearly extend to any unfair or deceptive practice in commerce employed by discount houses or other merchandisers.

Specifically, in numerous cases involving so-called fictitious price marking the Commission has issued orders requiring the respondents to cease representing that a price is the regular price when it is in reality in excess of that price at which said merchandise is regularly and customarily sold.

The Commission has also taken action in cases involving the practice of "switching" the customer from certain advertised merchandise, which is low in price, to higher priced merchandise. These tactics are usually associated with so-called "bait" advertising which involves the use of advertisements of sales plans which are designed to obtain leads or prospects for the sales of other or higher priced merchandise. In such instances the Commission has required these retailers to discontinue representing certain merchandise is for sale when such offer is not a bona fide offer to sell the merchandise offered. These orders sometimes contain prohibitions that merchandise should not be represented as being floor samples, models of a certain year, or as being new, unless such is a fact.

An example of a Commission action against deceptive acts and practices by a discount house is the Commission's order to cease and desist in the matter of *George's Radio & Television Company, Inc., et al.,* Docket 6411.

To the extent of its authority, the Commission will continue to police the activities of discount houses under existing statutes. Since the practice of doing business at something less than the traditional return does not, in and of itself, violate any statute we administer, our primary effectiveness can be expected to be most noticeable in the field of deceptive acts or practices, predatory pricing practices or price fixing in commerce.

68. FEDERAL POLICY ON ANTITRUST MATTERS *

Victor R. Hansen

I am delighted to meet with you to discuss current antitrust policies. I am particularly pleased to address an economic group, so that I may promote a better understanding among you of our legal objectives as well as the legislative tools at our command to accomplish those objectives.

Economic policies and antitrust policies in one sense have a common goal. Both strive to achieve an economy which gives freedom of opportunity. Both strive to help the consumer.

Economists as such are concerned with numerous factors which contribute to our economic welfare. They seek to evaluate the trends of the economy. They study wage and price levels and design measures to check inflationary trends.

* Reprinted by permission of Victor R. Hansen from an address before the Metropolitan Economic Association, New York City, October 31, 1958.

Victor R. Hansen, Former Assistant Attorney General of the United States in charge of the Antitrust Division, Department of Justice, Washington, D. C.; Regent of the University of California.

Antitrust policies are also concerned with the public welfare. But they arrive at this objective by a different route. Ours is not the function of economic regulation. We are not concerned basically with whether prices are high or low. We are in essence a law-enforcement, as distinguished from a fact-finding, body. Our aim is to preserve competition and to create conditions which permit competition to flourish. To put it succinctly, the antitrust laws cannot compel competition; they only make it possible.

In carrying out our functions, we must act within our legislative frame of reference. That frame of reference includes, however, a great deal more than the mere language of the statutes that we administer. The boundaries of the antitrust laws are marked by judicial interpretation. The numerous decisions of the federal courts and the Supreme Court which interpret the antitrust laws provide the guideposts which we must follow in planning and executing the antitrust program.

The principal antitrust statutes, as most of you know, which the Antitrust Division of the Department of Justice enforces, are the Sherman Act [1] and the Clayton Act.[2] Although there are numerous provisions contained in these two statutes, the major part of our work centers on three sections. They are Sections 1 and 2 of the Sherman Act and Section 7 of the Clayton Act.[3]

We share responsibility with the Federal Trade Commission for enforcing Section 7, which, as you are aware, deals with mergers. Other provisions of the Clayton Act are enforced primarily by the Commission. Charges under these provisions sometimes are combined with charges brought in Sherman Act cases.

In discussing our current antitrust policies, I shall address myself first to the principal problems arising in cases brought under the Sherman Act. Second, I shall sketch some of the problems and novel situations arising in our increasingly important Section 7 merger cases.

[1] The Sherman Act, enacted on July 2, 1890, c. 647, 26 Stat. 209, was amended by the Miller-Tydings Act of August 17, 1937, c. 690, 50 Stat. 693, and by the Act of July 7, 1955, c. 281, 69 Stat. 282, increasing fines from $5,000 to $50,000.

[2] The Clayton Act was enacted on October 15, 1914, c. 323, 38 Stat. 730, and has been amended on a number of occasions.

[3] Section 3 of the Sherman Act is equally important but applies only to the District of Columbia, the Territories, and between them and the states or foreign countries.

I.

Perhaps the best description of the general purposes of the Sherman Act is contained in a statement made by the Supreme Court in a recent opinion:[4]

> The Sherman Act was designed to be a comprehensive charter of economic liberty aimed at preserving free and unfettered competition as the rule of trade. It rests on the premise that the unrestrained interaction of competitive forces will yield the best allocation of our economic resources, the lowest prices, the highest quality, and the greatest material progress, while at the same time providing an environment conducive to the preservation of our democratic political and social institutions. But even were that premise open to question, the policy unequivocally laid down by the Act is competition.

Courts are frequently called upon in Sherman Act cases to measure the actual or probable effect of particular business conduct upon competition. Unreasonable restraints upon competition fall within the ban of Section 1 of the Sherman Act. Extensive economic information and data may be introduced at trial in order to establish that a particular restraint upon competition is unreasonable.

Economic testimony concerning the effect of challenged business practices upon competition is not necessary or even appropriate in many of the familiar types of cases brought under Section 1 of the Sherman Act. Let me illustrate. If a group of companies is charged with fixing prices for the sale of a product the group manufactures, the issue is simple. Either the companies agreed to fix prices or they did not. If the government proves that they did agree, its proof is complete. Such an agreement is presumed as a matter of law to have a deleterious effect upon competition and no further inquiry into the disastrous effects upon competition is made.

Criticism has sometimes been leveled at the Antitrust Division for too much emphasis upon price-fixing cases. By contrast, more recently, some thought has been voiced that we should have brought a price-fixing case for the recent steel industry price rise. Let me hasten to point out that while the issue in a price-fixing case is a comparatively basic one, its proof is not always simple. Proof there may be, as there was in the steel situation, that prices rise in quick succession. Proof there may also be that prices are administered in that they respond not to supply and demand but to the prices adopted by the price leaders of the industry. Yet all of this may fall short as proof of a price-fixing violation. The law still requires evidence that

[4] *Northern Pacific R. Co.* v. *United States*, 356 U.S. 1, 4.

the parties conspired, namely, that they agreed to adopt the price increases.

Where an industry consists of only a few sellers, administered pricing becomes not only possible, but generally results. As the President of the American Economic Association said in his book on *Monopoly and Free Enterprise,* "the fewer the sellers the easier it is for them to reap the fruits of conspiracy without actually entering into what the courts say is conspiracy." [5] And as one noted antitrust lawyer aptly phrased it: "The price announcement of one of the companies in the field, typically the dominant concern, or principal producer, is *loyally* followed by most of its competitors." [6]

But the greater challenge from an economic standpoint may be found in the so-called monopoly cases brought under Section 2 of the Sherman Act. At the heart of these cases are generally found problems dealing with the nature of the industry, the number of firms competing therein, their comparative size, and the ease of entry into the business. All of these factors—to use an economic term—deal with market structure. This, however, is not the whole of the picture.

Market structure, in itself, is not the only subject of inquiry in monopolization cases. Market behavior or market conduct still plays a part—although a less important part—in cases brought under Section 2 of the Sherman Act. This is understandable. The Sherman Act does not prohibit monopoly in a passive sense. It prohibits what it terms "monopolization," or active monopoly.

To meet this requirement of monopolization as distinguished from monopoly, the courts have evolved the principle that there must be a showing of both monopoly power and an intangible something called "intent." This element known as "intent" may not mean the same thing to an antitrust lawyer that it does to an economist. Actually, it does not mean the same thing today that it meant ten or fifteen years ago. It may mean something else tomorrow from what it means today. The Sherman Act has the breadth of a constitutional provision, as indeed it should have if it is to keep pace with the demands of a changing economy.

To make a showing of intent in monopolization cases, antitrust lawyers throughout the years have generally produced whatever evidence could be found illustrating the use of so-called predatory

[5] Stocking and Watkins, *Monopoly and Free Enterprise,* Twentieth Century Fund (1951), pp. 110-111.

[6] Milton Handler, *A Study of the Construction and Enforcement of the Federal Antitrust Laws,* TNEC Monograph No. 38 (1941), pp. 40-41.

practices. This has been done more out of an abundance of caution than out of reluctance to push ahead for new frontiers in the law. In more recent cases,[7] the courts have held that the business conduct from which intent will be inferred need not be so drastic as to be considered predatory. Nor, in fact, need it even amount to a restraint of trade. It is sufficient that the conduct employed by a monopolist, either singly or in combination with others, be exclusionary.

Thus, to quote Judge Wyzanski's holding in the United Shoe case, given a showing of monopoly power, it is sufficient to establish a violation of Section 2 "for one having effective control of the market to use, or plan to use, any exclusionary practice, even though it is not a technical restraint of trade." [8]

What then is this quality of intent and what is the evidence from which its existence shall be inferred? In the United Shoe case, the court described the exclusionary practices as "contracts, arrangements, and policies which, instead of encouraging competition based on pure merit, further the dominance of a particular firm." "In this sense," the court said, "they are unnatural barriers; they unnecessarily exclude actual and potential competition; they restrict a free market." [9]

This type of evidence is certainly a great deal less than evidence of predatory business behavior as that term was generally understood in antitrust parlance. Yet it may still be something other than mere evidence of market control. One antitrust lawyer writes today: [10]

> Our faith in the antitrust laws will probably continue to be somewhat blind since it is unlikely that economics will ever develop tools to measure accurately the truth or falsity of the basic premises on which our allegiance to the laws of competition rest. But this is no reason why we should permit new verbalism such as "oligopolistic competition" to disguise the fact that the ultimate thrust of the Sherman and Clayton Acts is at the mere possession of power to exclude or lessen competition.

In discussing the necessity of showing the possession of power over price or competition in the case now popularly known as the Cellophane case,[11] the Supreme Court said:

[7] *United States* v. *United Shoe Machinery Corporation* 110 F. Supp. 295, affirmed 347 U.S. 521; *United States* v. *Aluminum Co. of America*, 148 F.2d 416 (C.A. 2).

[8] 110 F. Supp. 295, 342.

[9] *Id.*, pp. 344-345.

[10] William L. McGovern, "The Power and the Glory: The duPont-GM Decision," *The Georgetown Law Journal*, Vol. 46, No. 4 (1958), pp. 655, 670.

[11] *United States* v. *E. I. du Pont de Nemours and Company*, 351 U. S. 377, 392.

> It is inconceivable that power could be controlled without power over competition or vice versa. This approach to the determination of monopoly power is strengthened by this Court's conclusion in prior cases that when an alleged monopolist has power over price and competition, an intention to monopolize in a proper case may be assumed.

Whatever the ultimate outgrowth of the trend may be, judicial interpretation of the law has certainly come a long way from the now thoroughly discredited doctrine that monopoly power or market control is only bad when accompanied by predatory business conduct.

Aside from the questions of market structure and market behavior, we sometimes meet with the suggestion—grounded in economics—that if the market performance of an industry is good, we should do nothing to upset the good performance applecart. When I speak of good market performance I speak of an industry which is regarded as efficient, which has progressed in a technological sense, and which provides the consumer with a choice of good products at reasonable prices. Some economists express the view that if the industry is relatively stable and ease of entry is not too difficult, this in itself is the ultimate good to be desired. Here again the underlying reason for analysis may color the approach to the problem.

An economist, for example, making a study of a particular industry to recommend investments may find that the market performance of an industry is excellent. If there are only a few firms in the business, if these firms have a history of collaborating on prices, dividing territories, or allocating customers, the industry may be an excellent candidate for an investment program.

But an examination of market performance is not the ultimate end from a legal antitrust standpoint. The industry may be efficient. It may engage in research which gives birth to many new products. Antitrust policies do not conflict with such good market performance. But antitrust policies strive to promote competition as such and not only desirable economic performance. Additionally, the antitrust laws assume that products or the service might be better and the prices lower if no illegal restraints and none of the attributes of monopoly were present. And it is not a foregone conclusion that comparable research and comparable economies of production and distribution would not result if there were a large number of sellers. For these very reasons, good market performance is in itself no defense to a charge of violation of the Sherman Act.

The basic question in all monopolization cases from the legal as well as from the economic standpoint is a determination whether monopoly power exists. What, you may ask, are the elements of monopoly power as defined in a legal sense. On this point the law is certain. Monopoly power may be found either in power to exclude competition or power to fix or control prices.

In order to determine whether power to exclude does exist, market structure may come in for considerable economic analysis. A large percentage command of an industry may in itself be an earmark of power to exclude. Other factors, such as comparative size measured against a number of smaller competitors may be equally compelling. Strategic advantages may be such as to give command over the entry of potential competitors. Thus, in the Aluminum case,[12] Judge Learned Hand adverted to the great organization which Alcoa possessed, having the advantage of experience, trade connections and the elite of personnel. It was the misuse of these strategic advantages by the constant and progressive increasing of capacity each time that a newcomer threatened to enter the aluminum industry which caused the court to find Alcoa's course of conduct to be exclusionary.

Power to control prices is, the Supreme Court has said, equally important as an indicia of monopoly power. In a now famous case against all of the leading manufacturers of cigarettes,[13] this power to control prices was found in a combination of factors. Prominent among these was the ability to raise prices arbitrarily in times of depression and to lower prices to below cost and hold them there until the competition of cheaper cigarettes had been eliminated.

Extensive economic data, charts, and graphs are prepared and presented in monopolization cases to depict price trends, price changes and their effect upon sales, as well as profit margins of defendants and their competitors. This veritable sea of economic data must usually be analyzed and related in the first instance to a particular market. Definition of the market as such may be said to be the initial step that must be undertaken in a monopolization case. At the outset we must determine the product or products which are to be included as being within the relevant market. This subject has many facets and could be discussed ad infinitum. However, let me mention but briefly the principal case out of which this problem arises.

Many of you may have heard and undoubtedly participated in the debate concerning the meaning of the Cellophane case.[14] There the Supreme Court held that the production of cellophane had not been

[12] *United States* v. *Aluminum Co. of America*, 148 F.2d 416, 429 (C.A. 2).
[13] *American Tobacco Co.* v. *United States*, 328 U.S. 781, 804-09.
[14] *United States* v. *E. I. du Pont de Nemours and Company*, 351 U.S. 377.

monopolized because cellophane competed with other flexible wrapping materials. Thus, the subject of substitute materials, so dear to an economist's heart, was brought forcefully to the fore. No more definite rule can be declared, the Supreme Court said, than that commodities reasonably interchangeable by consumers for the same purposes must be considered when determining whether control of price and competition exists.

Suffice it to say that the question of what substitute materials should be considered as being competitive with any given commodity in a monopolization case is not an easy matter. In due time subsequent decisions may pave the way for a clearer understanding of the tests which we must meet and the type of evidence which we must produce.

Before I leave this topic, however, I must point out that this type of analysis may not be essential in all monopolization cases. The words of the Supreme Court in the Cellophane case that: "Illegal monopolies under § 2 may well exist over limited products in narrow fields where competition is eliminated," [15] give promise of surmounting the market problem at least in situations where exclusionary market behavior has taken place.

On this note I turn to some of the timely problems presently confronting us in merger cases under Section 7 of the Clayton Act.

II.

The question of mergers has become an ever more important subject in the antitrust field. Opinions may differ among economists on the advisability of this constant march toward concentration. But from the legal standpoint, our philosophy is guided by our responsibilities to enforce Section 7 of the Clayton Act.

As I mentioned earlier, we share responsibility for Section 7 enforcement with the Federal Trade Commission. Both agencies cooperate to prevent duplication of merger investigations. Both actively pursue those investigations which they initiate. A word concerning the respective powers of the two agencies may be accordingly in order here.

The Antitrust Division has no subpoena power by which to compel the production of material from which to ascertain the facts underlying a merger. The Commission, on the other hand, has subpoena power by which it may compel not only production of docu-

[15] *Ibid.*, at 395.

mentary material but also the testimony of witnesses. Additionally, the Commission has statutory power to require corporations, other than banks and certain common carriers, to furnish reports or answers to specific questions. You may well ask why the Department then does not utilize the functions of a grand jury to obtain evidence concerning proposed mergers. The answer is that Section 7 is not a criminal statute. That avenue is closed to us.

I mention this because it has long been my thought that the Antitrust Division could do a better job not only on merger matters but also in Sherman Act cases if it had subpoena power similar to that of the Commission. We have urged Congress to enact legislation giving us what for convenience we have labeled a "civil investigative demand." Possession of such a civil investigative demand would eliminate the prime difficulty arising in merger cases of being dependent upon the voluntary cooperation of those companies who are actively seeking to merge.

All this assumes, of course, that we are fortunate in learning of the merger before it occurs. Frequently, the merger is not disclosed until it is accomplished and the eggs are thoroughly scrambled. The frequency of this situation has caused the Department to seek the passage of a prenotification merger bill. A number of such bills were introduced in both houses of Congress at the last session and various hearings were held thereon. We feel that the bill to which we have lent our support should be fairly acceptable to all parties. The economic report of the President recommended its passage. Former Attorney General Brownell testified in its favor, as did other officials of the Department. But the bill did not pass.

Some time ago we instituted a merger clearance program. Under this program we encourage businessmen to come to the Antitrust Division to discuss their merger plans in advance. Should we find after voluntary and full disclosure by the parties of all the facts that the merger will not lessen competition substantially or tend to create a monopoly in any line of commerce in any section of the country, we may grant assurance that the parties can proceed. We invite complete and full cooperation under this program in the hope that it will serve the mutual advantage of the government and those desiring to merge.

Section 7 of the Clayton Act, you will recall, was passed by Congress originally in 1914. More recently, in 1950, Congress became so concerned with the increasing number of mergers that it amended Section 7 to make the legal tests less stringent and to clarify the types of situations which it embraced. Prior to 1950, Section 7 prohibited acquisition of the stock of one corporation by another where the effect of such acquisition may be to substantially lessen competition between the acquiring and the acquired company.[16]

Section 7, as amended in 1950, deleted the reference to competition between the acquiring and the acquired firms. It now prohibits acquisitions of stock or assets by any of the stock or assets of another corporation engaged in interstate commerce, namely a corporation not necessarily a competitor, where the acquisition has the proscribed effects. Section 7, as it now stands, thus prohibits mergers between one corporation and another where the effect may be substantially to lessen competition or to tend to create a monopoly in (1) any line of commerce, or (2) any section of the country.

The Senate, in its Report on the 1950 bill, stated it is not essential that the line of commerce which may be lessened substantially be a large part of the business of any of the corporations involved in the acquisition.[17] The House Judiciary Committee, in its Report, hastened to comment that acquisitions of stock or assets have a cumulative effect. The bill was intended, the Committee said, to permit intervention in such a cumulative process.[18]

Since the 1950 amendment to Section 7, it is clear that the merger prohibition applies not only to those mergers which substantially lessen competition between the acquiring and the acquired company, but also to those whose impact is felt by competitors of either the acquiring or the acquired company. To put it in the words of the House Judiciary Committee, the change was made "to make it clear that the bill applies to all types of mergers and acquisitions, vertical and conglomerate as well as horizontal, which have the specificed effects of substantially lessening competition . . . or tending to create a monopoly." [19]

Horizontal mergers between competitors on the same level of industry are, of course, familiar to everyone. Vertical mergers which freeze competitors out of a source of supply or foreclose a customers' market are becoming increasingly common. Conglomerate mergers have not as yet been precisely defined. One source describes them as the "all other" category of mergers and acquisitions not included within horizontal or vertical.[20] An example, perhaps, of a conglom-

16 38 Stat. 731.

17 S. Rep. No. 1775, 81st Cong., 2d Sess., 1950, p. 5.

18 H. Rep. No. 1191, 81st Cong., 1st Sess., 1949, p. 8.

19 H. Rep. No. 1191, 81st Cong., 1st Sess., 1949, p. 11.

20 John M. Blair, "The Conglomerate Merger in Economics and Law," *The Georgetown Law Journal*, Vol. 46, No. 4, p. 672.

erate merger may be found in the Gillette Company, until recently primarily a manufacturer of razors and razor blades. This company, I am told, has acquired such varied interests as the Toni home permanent business, the Papermate pen business and some proprietary drugs. Perhaps a more dubious example of a conglomerate merger is one that recently caught my antitrust eye. I understand that a manufacturer of specialty foods has obtained an option to purchase a company which manufacturers what the press described as "seamless women's girdles." [21] The nature of this conglomeration, I admit, is not entirely clear to me.

In two of the major merger cases presently in the process of litigation, the nature of the line of commerce has become a major issue. The Bethlehem Steel merger case, presently awaiting decision, involves a merger between Bethlehem Steel Corporation and the Youngstown Sheet and Tube Company, the second and the sixth largest steel producers.[22] In that case we have taken the position that the line of commerce may constitute any product line that is distinguishable from, or has a separate use from, any other product line. In the Brown Shoe case, which is presently at trial,[23] the defendants have argued that the line of shoes produced by Brown is not competitive with the line of shoes produced by the Kinney Company; that the two lines sell in a different price range and are therefore complementary rather than competitive.

I cannot dwell upon the merits of the contentions raised in these cases at this time. But I should like to make clear that in our opinion the line of commerce test of Section 7 is a far less rigid test than the one required by Section 2 of the Sherman Act under the doctrine of the Cellophane case.

All of you are undoubtedly thoroughly familiar with the duPont-General Motors decision, where the Supreme Court held that du Pont and General Motors had violated Section 7 through the stock acquisition of du Pont of 23 per cent of the stock of General Motors.[24] It is interesting to observe that while the case had been brought under both the Sherman Act and Section 7, as it read prior to the 1950 amendment, the Supreme Court made no mention of the Cellophane case in rendering its decision.

[21] I. Rokeach & Sons, Inc., a manufacturer of kosher foods, acquired an option to purchase Silf Skin, Inc.

[22] *United States* v. *Bethlehem Steel Corporation and the Youngstown Sheet and Tube Company,* (S.D.N.Y., Civil No. 115-328).

[23] *United States* v. *Brown Shoe Company, Inc., and G. R. Kinney Co., Inc.,* (E.D. No., Civil No. 10527).

[24] *United States* v. *E. I. du Pont de Nemours & Company,* 353 U. S. 586.

While in Cellophane, under the Sherman Act, the Court found that the relevant market was the market for flexible wrapping materials rather than cellophane, in duPont-General Motors it rejected the argument that the relevant market was the market of all sales of finishes and fabrics to industrial users. On the contrary, it held [25] that:

> The record shows that automobile finishes and fabrics have sufficient peculiar characteristics and uses to constitute them products sufficiently distinct from all other finishes and fabrics to make them a line of commerce within the meaning of the Clayton Act.

I do not mean to imply that in view of the du Pont-General Motors case all of our problems under Section 7 have been solved. Quite the contrary. New decisions seeking to interpret or follow this decision are bound to emerge. During this month a decision was rendered under Section 7 by the Court of Appeals for the Second Circuit in a case to which the government was not a party.[26] Because of the bearing which it may have on the merger program, let me mention briefly what occurred. A refiner of cane sugar acquired stock in Crystal, a refiner of beet sugar, and demanded representation on Crystal's board of directors. The combination of the two companies would rank fourth in the sugar industry. Crystal sued for an injunction and divestiture. Upon appeal from the court's action in granting the requested injunction, the Court of Appeals said that the relevant market was the market for both cane and beet sugar.

The decision holds that the substantial lessening of competition in any line of commerce requires for determination (1) a definition of a relevant market, and (2) analysis of the nature and extent of the competition within that market. This has a familiar ring. It may speak more in tones of Cellophane than of du Pont-General Motors. The decision speaks also of "quantitative substantiality" and "qualitative substantiality," but without giving any clear enunciation of the context in which the terms were being used.

Whether this decision will prove to be a boon or a hindrance to the merger program, it is too early to say. That may depend partly upon the scrutiny, analysis, and dissection which will surely be made of this opinion by economists, by scholars and by those of us in the antitrust field who must seek to apply it. But, finally, it will depend

[25] *United States* v. *E. I. du Pont de Nemours & Company,* 353 U. S. 586, 593-94.

[26] *American Crystal Sugar Company* v. *The Cuban-American Sugar Company,* (C.A. 2, 1958).

upon the judicial gloss which may ultimately be placed thereon by the courts.

These then are some of the problems that we face. It is my sincere hope that this hour with you may provide, through your leadership in the economic field, a clearer insight into the problems, the policies, and the aims of the Antitrust Division in enforcing the antitrust laws.

In my invitation to speak here today, it was indicated that you would be interested in hearing something concerning the current policy of the Division pertaining to the selection and filing of cases, and the conduct of the Division in the prosecution of cases. It is the policy of the Division to file on the criminal side in cases of price-fixing or so-called *per se* cases. Grand juries are impaneled to receive evidence in possible criminal cases when there are reasonable grounds to believe that an offense has been committed. Indictments are sought against individuals when they are the moving force or leader of the conspiracy. When indictments are sought against individuals, indictments are also sought against the corporation of which they are officers. Indictments are sought against a corporation where it appears that the individual officer of the corporation merely carried out instructions in performing his duties as an employee of the corporation.

Criminal indictments are not sought with an effort to obtain a civil consent decree. After an indictment has been returned and a civil suit has also been filed, discussions concerning a consent decree of the civil action will not be carried on while the criminal action is pending. In other words, the pending criminal action will not be used to force a civil consent decree.

As for criminal cases, it is the policy of the Division not to accept nolo pleas. And when they are offered, opposition will be made by the Division before the Court.

The Division's policy concerning consent decrees is that consent decrees will be entered into only where in the opinion of those of responsibility in the Division are satisfied that the relief secured is adequate. It is also the policy of the Division that no case will be filed unless there is probable cause to believe there has been a violation of one or more of the antitrust laws. In other words, cases are not filed on suspicion alone with the hope that a case may be developed during discovery. I do not mean to infer from this that cases are not filed until sufficient evidence has been secured to assure a government victory.

Now concerning the policy of the Division on Section 7 cases. By virtue of the fact that appropriations and manpower are not adequate to justify a filing of all cases where it may appear there is a probable cause that there has been a violation, particularly in Section 7 cases, selection must be the rule. Selection is based upon several considerations. One, does there appear to be a violation of Section 7 measured by the language of the Section and the legislative intent back of the passage of the 1950 amendment. Secondly, does the case involve new points of law that have not been determined or are not also included in pending Section 7 cases. Third, is the case of real economic importance. And, fourth, will a determination of the case tend to clarify the law. Or, in other words, will it contribute to making ground rules or affording yardsticks from which industry might be guided in its actions.

Formerly, all Section 7 cases were assigned to one section of the Division. In view of the fact that there are often commingling of alleged violations of the Sherman Act, Section 1 or 2, with alleged Section 7 violations, it was felt that it was better that all sections of the Division become familiar with Section 7 cases. When the change was made, personnel was disbursed among all the litigating sections and personnel from litigating sections were transferred to the former section concerned only with Section 7 cases, and now all sections of the Division handle Section 7 cases.

It is my firm belief that the same courtesies that are expected of a general practitioner should also be expected from the government lawyer. It is my firm belief that a government attorney is bound by the same rules of practice and ethics that bind the general practitioner, and that the government attorney dealing with the Court should deal with the Court as all lawyers are expected to with courtesy, respect, and without assuming privileges other than those afforded to all practitioners. Therefore, it is the definite policy of the Division that government attorneys in the Antitrust Division will not discuss matters involving pending litigation with the Court without first giving notice and affording an opportunity for opposing counsel to be present.

Finally, we feel that it is our sworn duty to enforce the antitrust laws as they now stand and as we understand the cases to interpret them. It is up to the Congress to make any amendments it desires.

SECTION 7. INTERNATIONAL MARKETING

The several articles in this section strengthen the hypothesis that the role of marketing in economic development is of much greater importance than that presently assigned by current economic literature.

Peter F. Drucker in his Parlin Memorial Lecture, "Marketing and Economic Development," develops the thesis that marketing is the most important multiplier of development, particularly in regard to the underdeveloped countries. While marketing is not a cure-all, it does contribute to the outstanding need of the underdeveloped areas. That need as identified by Professor Drucker is "for the rapid development of entrepreneurs and managers." He also suggests that the establishment of modern marketing institutions, such as Sears Roebuck in Brazil, can trigger and channel investment so as to result in the multiplication of new industrial business.

Economic reform of internal marketing systems must be evaluated in the light of historical and cultural distinctions prevailing in each underdeveloped area. Anthropologist Sidney W. Mintz in his article, "The Role of the Middleman in the Internal Distribution System of a Caribbean Peasant Economy," supplies evidence which indicates that the Jamaican higglers or middlemen may not be technically efficient when judged by modern marketing standards, but when given the economic background of the British West Indies, higglers are economically efficient. The elimination of inefficient marketers in countries already characterized by a labor surplus also raises the question of whether there are available alternative economic opportunities. Unless this displaced labor can be absorbed by other sectors, the economy may not have benefited at all.

In "Developments in Self-Service Food Distribution Abroad" William Applebaum surveys the growth and characteristics of self-service food stores abroad and projects likely developments for the next five years. After examining some of the obstacles confronting the expansion of self-service food stores, Professor Applebaum concludes that, "this international development will snowball, just as it did in the United States." The people of an underdeveloped area are very much like an individual family. They want to increase their standard of living, but the family income is not large enough to buy all of the things that are needed or desired. If some priority must be assigned in terms of programming economic reform of a marketing system, then revitalization of food retailing should be at the top of any list of proposed marketing projects.

Richard H. Holton in "Food Retailing and Economic Growth" discusses the reasons for expecting that it may be easier to invest in mass distribution before investment is made in mass production. The giant supermarket will probably play a secondary role to the "pine board" grocery chains in any major food retailing innovation in the low income countries. Professor Holton contends that such low investment projects could effect significant economies and permit the majority of a population to enjoy lower food costs and hence higher real incomes. The noninflationary impact of this approach as compared to wage increases would also seem to strengthen the case for rationalization of food distribution in underdeveloped areas.

Professor Karl H. Stein's paper, "Some Observations on the Evolving Retail Pattern in Europe," is based on discussions which took place at the International Congress of Ruschlikon near Zurich, Switzerland. Some 220 retail, wholesale, and manufacturing representatives from the food and consumer goods areas operating primarily in European countries attended. This article examines the development and present status in Europe of self-service operations and the shopping center movement. Professor Stein concludes that though receptive to United States retail innovations, Western Europe has been cautious in adopting and adapting retail innovations to their environment. In the author's opinion, self-service, "Will make further progress, but it is unlikely that it will invade as many of the non-food fields as it has in the United States. Shopping centers will likely spread, but they probably will be built on a scale and in a manner benefiting an area lacking the conditions necessary for the explosive expansion of the regional type common in the United States."

69. MARKETING AND ECONOMIC DEVELOPMENT *

Peter F. Drucker

In the "underdeveloped" countries of the world, the more "glamorous" fields such as manufacturing or construction are generally high-lighted while marketing is treated with neglect, if not with contempt. Yet marketing holds a key position in these countries. It is generally the most backward of all areas of economic life.

Marketing is also the most effective engine of economic development, particularly in its ability rapidly to develop entrepreneurs and managers. And it contributes what is the greatest need of an "underdeveloped" country: a systematic discipline in a vital area of economic activity . . . a discipline which is based on generalized, theoretical concepts and which can, therefore, be both taught and learned.

Marketing as a Business Discipline

The distinguished pioneer of marketing, whose memory we honor today, was largely instrumental in developing marketing as a systematic business discipline:

—In teaching us how to go about, in an orderly, purposeful and planned way to find and create customers;

—To identify and define markets; to create new ones and promote them;

—To integrate customers' needs, wants, and preferences, and the intellectual and creative capacity and skills of an industrial society, toward the design of new and better products and of new distributive concepts and processes.

On this contribution and similar ones of other Founding Fathers of marketing during the last half century rests the rapid emergence of marketing as perhaps the most advanced, certainly the most "scientific" of all functional business disciplines.

But Charles Coolidge Parlin also contributed as a Founding Father toward the development of marketing as a *social discipline*. He helped give us the awareness, the concepts, and the tools that

* From *The Journal of Marketing*, Vol. XXII, No. 3 (January, 1958), pp. 252-259. Reprinted with permission from *The Journal of Marketing*, published quarterly by the American Marketing Association.

Peter F. Drucker, Professor of Management, Graduate School of Business Administration, New York University.

make us understand marketing as a dynamic process of society through which business enterprise is integrated productively with society's purposes and human values. It is in marketing, as we now understand it, that we satisfy individual and social values, needs, and wants—be it through producing goods, supplying services, fostering innovation, or creating satisfaction. Marketing, as we have come to understand it, has its focus on the customer, that is, on the individual making decisions within a social structure and within a personal and social value system. Marketing is thus the process through which economy is integrated into society to serve human needs.

I am not competent to speak about marketing in the first sense, marketing as a functional discipline of business. I am indeed greatly concerned with marketing in this meaning. One could not be concerned, as I am, with the basic institutions of industrial society in general and with the management of business enterprise in particular, without a deep and direct concern with marketing. But in this field I am a consumer of marketing alone—albeit a heavy one. I am not capable of making a contribution. I would indeed be able to talk about the wants and needs I have which I, as a consumer of marketing, hope that you, the men of marketing, will soon supply:—a theory of pricing, for instance, that can serve, as true theories should, as the foundation for actual pricing decisions and for an understanding of price behavior; or a consumer-focused concept and theory of competition. But I could not produce any of these "new products" of marketing which we want. I cannot contribute myself. To use marketing language, I am not even "effective demand," in these fields as yet.

The Role of Marketing

I shall today in my remarks confine myself to the second meaning in which marketing has become a discipline: The role of marketing in economy and society. And I shall single out as my focus the role of marketing in the economic development, especially of underdeveloped "growth" countries.

My thesis is very briefly as follows. Marketing occupies a critical role in respect to the development of such "growth" areas. Indeed marketing is the most important "multiplier" of such development. It is in itself in every one of these areas the least developed, the most backward part of the economic system. Its development, above all others, makes possible economic integration and the fullest utilization of whatever assets and productive capacity an economy already possesses. It mobilizes latent economic energy. It contributes to the greatest needs: that for the rapid development of entrepreneurs and managers, and at the same time it may be the easiest area of managerial work to get going. The reason is that, thanks to men like Charles Coolidge Parlin, it is the most systematized and, therefore, the most learnable and the most teachable of all areas of business management and entrepreneurship.

International and Interracial Inequality

Looking at this world of ours, we see some essentially new facts.

For the first time in man's history the whole world is united and unified. This may seem a strange statement in view of the conflicts and threats of suicidal wars that scream at us from every headline. But conflict has always been with us. What is new is that today all of mankind shares the same vision, the same objective, the same goal, the same hope, and believes in the same tools. This vision might, in gross over-simplification, be called "industrialization."

It is the belief that it is possible for man to improve his economic lot through sytematic, purposeful, and directed effort—individually as well as for an entire society. It is the belief that we have the tools at our disposal—the technological, the conceptual, and the social tools—to enable man to raise himself, through his own efforts, at least to a level that we in this country would consider poverty, but which for most of our world would be almost unbelievable luxury.

And this is an irreversible new fact. It has been made so by these true agents of revolution in our times: the new tools of communication—the dirt road, the truck, and the radio, which have penetrated even the furthest, most isolated and most primitive community.

This is new, and cannot be emphasized too much and too often. It is both a tremendous vision and a tremendous danger in that catastrophe must result if it cannot be satisfied, at least to a modest degree.

But at the same time we have a new, unprecedented danger, that of international and interracial inequality. We on the North American continent are a mere tenth of the world population, including our Canadian friends and neighbors. But we have at least 75 per cent of the world income. And the 75 per cent of the world population whose income is below $100 per capita a year receive together perhaps no more than 10 per cent of the world's income. This is inequality of income, as great as anything the world has ever seen. It is accompanied by very high equality of income in the developed countries, especially in ours where we are in the process of proving that an industrial society does not have to live in extreme tension between the few very rich and the many very poor as lived all earlier societies of man. But what used to be national inequality and economic tension is now rapidly becoming international (and unfortunately also interracial) inequality and tension.

This is also brand new. In the past there were tremendous differences between societies and cultures: in their beliefs, their concepts, their ways of life, and their knowledge. The Frankish knight who went on Crusade was an ignorant and illiterate boor, according to the standards of the polished courtiers of Constantinople or of his Moslem enemies. But economically his society and theirs were exactly alike. They had the same sources of income, the same productivity of labor, the same forms and channels of investment, the same economic institutions, and the same distribution of income and wealth. Economically the Frankish knight, however much a barbarian he appeared, was at home in the societies of the East; and so was his serf. Both fitted in immediately and without any difficulty.

And this has been the case of all societies that went above the level of purely primitive tribe.

The inequality in our world today, however, between nations and races, is therefore a new—and a tremendously dangerous —phenomenon.

What we are engaged in today is essentially a race between the promise of economic development and the threat of international world-wide class war. The economic development is the opportunity of this age. The class war is the danger. Both are new. Both are indeed so new that most of us do not even see them as yet. But they are the essential economic realities of this industrial age of ours. And whether we shall realize the opportunity or succumb to danger will largely decide not only the economic future of this world—it may largely decide its spiritual, its intellectual, its political, and its social future.

Significance of Marketing

Marketing is central in this new situation. For marketing is one of our most potent levers to convert the danger into the opportunity.

To understand this we must ask: What do we mean by "underdeveloped"?

The first answer is, of course, that we mean areas of very low income. But income is, after all, a result. It is a result first of extreme agricultural over-population in which the great bulk of the people have to find a living on the land which, as a result, cannot even produce enough food to feed them, let alone produce a surplus. It is certainly a result of low productivity. And both, in a vicious circle, mean that there is not enough capital for investment, and very low productivity of what is being invested—owing largely to misdirection of investment into unessential and unproductive channels.

All this we know today and understand. Indeed we have learned during the last few years a very great deal both about the structure of an under-developed economy and about the theory and dynamics of economic development.

What we tend to forget, however, is that the essential aspect of an "under-developed" economy and the factor the absence of which keeps it "under-developed," is the inability to organize economic efforts and energies, to bring together resources, wants, and capacities, and so to convert a self-limiting static system into creative, self-generating organic growth.

And this is where marketing comes in.

Lack of development in "under-developed" countries

(1) First, in every "under-developed" country I know of, marketing is the most under-developed—or the least developed—part of th economy, if only because of the strong, pervasive prejudice against the "middleman."

As a result, these countries are stunted by inability to make effective use of the little they have. Marketing might by itself go far toward changing the entire economic tone of the existing system—without any change in methods of production, distribution of population, or of income.

It would make the producers capable of producing marketable products by providing them with standards, with quality demands, and with specifications for their product. It would make the product capable of being brought to markets instead of perishing on the way. And it would make the consumer capable of discrimination, that is, of obtaining the greatest value for his very limited purchasing power.

In every one of these countries, marketing profits are characteristically low. Indeed the people engaged in marketing barely eke out a subsistence living. And "mark-ups" are minute by our standards. But marketing costs are outrageously high. The waste in distribution and marketing, if only from spoilage or from the accumulation of unsalable inventories that clog the shelves for years, has to be seen to be believed. And marketing service is by and large all but nonexistent.

What is needed in any "growth" country to make economic development realistic, and at the same time produce a vivid demonstration of what economic development can produce, is a marketing system:

—A system of physical distribution;
—A financial system to make possible the distribution of goods; and
—Finally actual marketing, that is, an actual system of integrating wants, needs, and purchasing power of the consumer with capacity and resources of production.

This need is largely masked today because marketing is so often confused with the traditional "trader and merchant" of which every one of these countries has more than enough. It would be one of our most important contributions to the development of "under-developed" countries to get across the fact that marketing is something quite different.

It would be basic to get across the triple function of marketing:

—The function of crystallizing and directing demand for maximum productive effectiveness and efficiency;
—The function of guiding production purposefully toward maximum consumer satisfaction and consumer value;
—The function of creating discrimination that then gives rewards to those who really contribute excellence, and that then also penalize the monopolist, the slothful, or those who only want to take but do not want to contribute or to risk.

Utilization by the entrepreneur

(2) Marketing is also the most easily accessible "multiplier" of managers and entrepreneurs in an "under-developed" growth area. And managers and entrepreneurs are the foremost need of these countries. In the first place, "economic development" is not a force of nature. It is the result of the action, the purposeful, responsible, risk-taking action, of men as entrepreneurs and managers.

Certainly it is the entrepreneur and manager who alone can convey to the people of these countries an understanding of what economic development means and how it can be achieved.

Marketing can convert latent demand into effective demand. It cannot, by itself, create purchasing power. But it can uncover and channel all purchasing power that exists. It can, therefore, create rapidly the conditions for a much higher level of economic activity than existed before, can create the opportunities for the entrepreneur.

It then can create the stimulus for the development of modern, responsible, professional management by creating opportunity for the producer who knows how to plan, how to organize, how to lead people, how to innovate.

In most of these countries markets are of necessity very small. They are too small to make it possible to organize distribution for a single-product line in any effective manner. As a result, without a marketing organization, many products for which there is an adequate demand at a reasonable price cannot be distributed; or worse, they can be produced and distributed only under monopoly conditions. A marketing system is needed which serves as the joint and common channel for many producers if any of them is to be able to come into existence and to stay in existence.

This means in effect that a marketing system in the "under-developed" countries is the *creator of small business,* is the only way in which a man of vision and daring can become a businessman and an entrepreneur himself. This is thereby also the only way in which a true middle class can develop in the countries in which the habit of investment in productive enterprise has still to be created.

Developer of standards

(3) Marketing in an "under-developed" country is the developer of standards—of standards for product and service as well as of standards of conduct, of integrity, of reliability, of foresight, and of concern for the basic long-range impact of decisions on the customer, the supplier, the economy, and the society.

Rather than go on making theoretical statements let me point to one illustration: The impact Sears Roebuck has had on several countries of Latin America. To be sure, the countries of Latin America in which Sears operates—Mexico, Brazil, Cuba, Venezuela, Colombia, and Peru—are not "under-developed" in the same sense in which Indonesia or the Congo are "under-developed." Their average income, although very low by our standards, is at least two times, perhaps as much as four or five times, that of the truly "under-developed" countries in which the bulk of mankind still live. Still in every respect except income level these Latin American countries are at best "developing." And they have all the problems of economic development—perhaps even in more acute form than the countries of Asia and Africa, precisely because their development has been so fast during the last ten years.

It is also true that Sears in these countries is not a "low-price" merchandiser. It caters to the middle class in the richer of these countries, and to the upper middle class in the poorest of these countries. Incidentally, the income level of these groups is still lower than that of the worker in the industrial sector of our economy.

Still Sears is a mass-marketer even in Colombia or Peru. What is perhaps even more important, it is applying in these "underdeveloped" countries exactly the same policies and principles it applies in this country, carries substantially the same merchandise (although most of it produced in the countries themselves), and applies the same concepts of marketing it uses in Indianapolis or Philadelphia. Its impact and experience are, therefore, a fair test of what marketing principles, marketing knowledge, and marketing techniques can achieve.

The impact of this one American business which does not have more than a mere handful of stores in these countries and handles no more than a small fraction of the total retail business of these countries is truly amazing. In the first place, Sears' latent purchasing power has fast become actual purchasing power. Or, to put it less theoretically, people have begun to organize their buying and to go out for value in what they do buy.

Secondly, by the very fact that it builds one store in one city, Sears forces a revolution in retailing throughout the whole surrounding area. If forces store modernization. It forces consumer credit. It forces a different attitude toward the customer, toward the store clerk, toward the supplier, and toward the merchandise itself. It forces other retailers to adopt modern methods of pricing, of inventory control, of training, of window display, and what have you.

The greatest impact Sears has had, however, is in the multiplication of new industrial business for which Sears creates a marketing channel. Because it has had to sell goods manufactured in these countries rather than import them (if only because of foreign exchange restrictions), Sears has been instrumental in getting established literally hundreds of new manufacturers making goods which, a few years ago, could not be made in the country, let alone be sold in adequate quantity. Simply to satisfy its own marketing needs, Sears has had to insist on standards of workmanship, quality, and delivery—that is, on standards of production management, of technical management, and above all of the management of people—which, in a few short years, have advanced the art and science of management in these countries by at least a generation.

I hardly need to add that Sears is not in Latin American for reasons of philanthropy, but because it is good and profitable business with extraordinary growth potential. In other words, Sears is in Latin America because marketing is the major opportunity in a "growth economy"—precisely because its absence is a major economic gap and the greatest need.

The discipline of marketing

(4) Finally, marketing is critical in economic development because marketing has become so largely systematized, so largely both learnable and teachable. It is the discipline among all our business disciplines that has advanced the furthest.

I do not forget for a moment how much we still have to learn in marketing. But we should also not forget that most of what we have learned so far we have learned in a form in which we can express it in general concepts, in valid principles and, to a substantial degree, in quantifiable measurements. This, above all others, was the achievement of that generation to whom Charles Coolidge Parlin was leader and inspiration.

A critical factor in this world of ours is the learnability and teachability of what it means to be an entrepreneur and manager. For it is the entrepreneur and the manager who alone can cause economic development to happen. The world needs them, therefore, in very large numbers; and it needs them fast.

Obviously this need cannot be supplied by our supplying entrepreneurs and managers, quite apart from the fact that we hardly have the surplus. Money we can supply. Technical assistance we can supply, and should supply more. But the supply of men we can offer to the people in the "under-developed" countries is of necessity a very small one.

The demand is also much too urgent for it to be supplied by slow evolution through experience, or through dependence on the emergence of "naturals." The danger that lies in the inequality today between the few countries that have and the great many countries that have not is much too great to permit a wait of centuries. Yet it takes centuries if we depend on experience and slow evolution for the supply of entrepreneurs and managers adequate to the needs of a modern society.

There is only one way in which man has ever been able to short-cut experience, to telescope development, in other words, to *learn something*. That way is to have available the distillate of experience and skill in the form of knowledge, of concepts, of generalization, of measurement—in the form of *discipline*, in other words.

The Discipline of Entrepreneurship

Many of us today are working on the fashioning of such a discipline of entrepreneurship and management. Maybe we are further along than most of use realize.

Certainly in what has come to be called "Operation Research and Synthesis" we have the first beginnings of a systematic approach to the entrepreneurial task of purposeful risk-taking and innovation —so far only an approach, but a most promising one, unless indeed we become so enamored with the gadgets and techniques as to forget purpose and aim.

We are at the beginning perhaps also of an understanding of the basic problems of organizing people of diversified and highly advanced skill and judgment together in one effective organization, although again no one so far would, I am convinced, claim more for us than that we have begun at last to ask intelligent questions.

But marketing, although it only covers one functional area in the field, has something that can be called a discipline. It has developed general concepts, that is, theories that explain a multitude of phenomena in simple statements. It even has measurements that record "facts" rather than opinions. In marketing, therefore, we already possess a learnable and teachable approach to this basic and central problem not only of the "under-developed" countries but of all countries. All of us have today the same survival stake in economic development. The risk and danger of international and interracial inequality are simply too great.

Marketing is obviously not a cure-all, not a paradox. It is only one thing we need. But it answers a critical need. At the same time marketing is most highly developed.

Indeed without marketing as the hinge on which to turn, economic development will almost have to take the totalitarian form. A totalitarian system can be defined economically as one in which economic development is being attempted without marketing, indeed as one in which marketing is suppressed. Precisely because it first looks at the values and wants of the individual, and because it then develops people to act purposefully and responsibly—that is, because of its effectiveness in developing a free economy—marketing is suppressed in a totalitarian system. If we want economic development in freedom and responsibility, we have to build it on the development of marketing.

In the new and unprecedented world we live in, a world which knows both a new unity of vision and growth and a new and most dangerous cleavage, marketing has a special and central role to play. This role goes:

—Beyond "getting the stuff out the back door";
—Beyond "getting the most sales with the least cost";
—Beyond "the optimal integration of our values and wants as customers, citizens, and persons, with our productive resources and intellectual achievements"—the role marketing plays in a developed society.

In a developing economy, marketing is, of course, all of this. But in addition, in an economy that is striving to break the age-old bondage of man to misery, want, and destitution, marketing is also the catalyst for the transmutation of latent resources into actual resources, of desires into accomplishments, and the development of responsible economic leaders and informed economic citizens.

70. THE ROLE OF THE MIDDLEMAN IN THE INTERNAL DISTRIBUTION SYSTEM OF A CARIBBEAN PEASANT ECONOMY *

Sidney W. Mintz

I.

This paper seeks to provide evidence for the economic efficiency, under present conditions, of small-scale middlemen in Caribbean economies. By "small-scale middlemen" is meant here those persons who buy and resell mainly agricultural produce which they convey from rural areas to open town and city markets. While some work has been done on the internal marketing systems of Mexico,[1] Guatemala,[2] and Perú,[3] Caribbean specialists have largely neglected the vigorous internal distribution systems which operate in such islands as Haiti, Jamaica, Trinidad and Barbados.[4] This paper adds little in the way of comprehensive information, but may serve to underline the importance of internal marketing systems in the study of "underdeveloped" areas.

The economy of the Caribbean area today is dominated by a system of plantation agriculture devoted to the production of such crops as sugar cane and bananas for the world market. In marked contrast to the plantation sectors of the islands' economies, however, is the existence of large numbers of peasant farmers who produce a

* Reprinted by permission from *Human Organization*, Vol. 15, No. 2 (Summer, 1956), pp. 18-23. Copyright 1957 by The Society for Applied Anthropology.
Sidney W. Mintz, Associate Professor of Anthropology, Department of Anthropology, Yale University.

[1] Cf., for instance, Foster, G., "The Folk Economy of Rural Mexico with Special Reference to Marketing," *The Journal of Marketing*, Vol. 13, No. 4, October 1948, pp. 153-162. A study of the Oaxaca market by Bronislaw Malinowski and Julio de la Fuente has never been published, but some of the data collected are reported in Whetten, N., *Rural Mexico*, University of Chicago Press, Chicago, 1948, pp. 357-360.

[2] Cf., for instance, McBryde, F. W., *Sololá*, Tulane University, Middle American Research Series, Publication No. 5, New Orleans, 1933. The same author's *Cultural and Historical Geography of Southwest Guatemala*, Smithsonian Institution, Institute of Social Anthropology, Publication No. 4, Washington, 1945, is also relevant. Cf. also Mosk, S. A., "Indigenous Economy in Latin America," *Inter-American Economic Affairs*, Vol. 8, No. 3, Winter 1954, pp. 3-26.

[3] Cf., for instance, Valcarcel, L. E., "Indian Markets and Fairs in Perú," *Handbook of South American Indians*, Vol. 2 ("The Andean Civilizations"), Bull. 143, Bureau of American Ethnology, Washington, 1946, pp. 477-482.

[4] Specific materials dealing with Carribean internal marketing and middlemen are cited at subsequent points in this paper.

variety of crops on small farms. Some of the produce of these small farms is used by their peasant producers for subsistence, some is sold within the internal economy, and some on the world market. Frequently, a single small farm will produce crops for all three of these purposes. In Puerto Rico, for instance, the peasant producer may grow tobacco for export, coffee for the internal market, and food crops for his own consumption.[5] In Jamaica, bananas and pimentos are among the main cash crops produced on small farms, while root crops (e.g., yams, sweet potatoes, cassava), tree crops (e.g., ackees, avocados, coconuts), and garden vegetables and fruits are produced on these same farms for sale within the internal economy and for subsistence.[6] A similar picture holds for Haiti. These arrangements, of course, occur only in those regions where large-scale production of cash crops for the world market has not wholly supplanted peasant production. On the south coast of Puerto Rico,[7] in some parishes of Jamaica,[8] and in much of Cuba,[9] the development of plantation agriculture, particularly of sugar cane, has supplanted or prevented the growth of diversified peasant farming patterns.

The peasant cultivator gains very real advantages by producing goods destined for three different purposes. By producing for two very different kinds of market—a world market and an internal market—he reduces the risks involved in producing for sale only to one; and by producing for subsistence, he holds his cash expenditures for foodstuffs to a culturally standardized minimum.[10] The marketing of those items produced for export is handled by various arrangements not relevant here. But means must also be found to distribute the cash crops which are produced for sale within the domestic economy. In most cases, distribution within the internal economies

[5] Cf. *The People of Puerto Rico* (ed. by J. H. Steward), University of Illinois Press, Urbana, 1956. See also Picó, R., *The Geographic Regions of Puerto Rico*, University of Puerto Rico Press, Río Piedras, Puerto Rico, 1950, pp. 132-140.

[6] Cf. "West Indian Agriculture," Carribean Affairs Pamphlet, University College of the West Indies, Mona, Jamaica (n.d.), pp. 6-11. See also Beckwith, M., *Black Roadways*, University of North Carolina Press, Chapel Hill, 1929, pp. 13-28.

[7] Cf. Mintz, S., "The Culture History of a Puerto Rican Sugar-Cane Plantation," *Hispanic American Historical Review*, Vol. 33, No. 2, May 1953, pp. 224-251. See also Picó, *op. cit.*, pp. 100-103.

[8] Cf. Cumper, G., "A Modern Jamaican Sugar Estate," *Social and Economic Studies*, Vol. III, No. 2, Sept. 1954, pp. 119-160.

[9] Cf. Guerra y Sánchez R., *Azúcar y Población en las Antillas*, Havana, 1944.

[10] Cf. Firth, R., *Elements of Social Organization, London*, 1951, pp. 97-98. The present writer has discussed such diversifications at some length in an earlier paper. See Mintz, S., "The Jamaican Internal Marketing Pattern," *Social and Economic Studies*, Vol. IV, No. 1, March 1955, pp. 95-103.

of the Caribbean is accomplished via an established system of open markets. Markets of this kind are particularly important in the internal economies of Haiti [11] and Jamaica.[12]

In some cases within these market settings, the seller of goods is also their producer. More commonly, however, producer and distributor are different persons, for various kinds of specialist middlemen have emerged to carry on the distributive role. In the case of Jamaica, these specialists—called higglers—are usually but not invariably women. They operate in a market situation in which both supply and demand are uncertain, and they deal for the most part with foodstuffs which cannot be stored indefinitely. This combination of conditions—unsure supply and demand, and trade in perishables—makes higgling a risky business, one which calls for considerable shrewdness in day-to-day operations. Operational cost (e.g., transportation fees, market fees, and interest on small loans) are high relative to the profit margin, and a glut in the market can easily wipe out the investment of a higgler who has planned badly or who has had a stroke of bad luck in her choice of goods. By skillful operations, the higgler can earn some profits on her original investment in a series of fortunate trips; but she cannot put a high premium on her time or insist on a high or steady rate of profit, for competition is usually severe.

If his expenditure of time is not too great, and if the costs of transport are minimal, the producer may find it worth his while to do his own selling in the nearest market places. The producer may also choose to serve as his own distributor when he processes some of his produce. An example of this—a farmer who grows and processes his own sugar cane—is described below. The producer-distributor will not necessarily sell directly to the final consumer, however. Middlemen will still enter importantly into the distribution of the items involved.

II.

The conditions under which the distributive process functions in Jamaica have led to the rise of many different types of distributors:

[11] Cf. Leyburn, J., *The Haitian People*, New Haven, 1941, pp. 202-206. See also Metraux, A., *Making a Living in Marbial Valley (Haiti)*, UNESCO Occasional Papers in Education, Paris, 1951, pp. 117-124; and Herskovits, M., *Life in a Haitian Valley*, New York, 1937, pp. 81-84.

[12] For Jamaica, cf. Beckwith, *op. cit.* Also see Olivier, S., *Jamaica: The Blessed Island*, London, 1936, pp. 158-163. The best report on internal marketing in the context of the Jamaican village is in Davenport, W., "A Comparative Study of Two Jamaican Fishing Communities," unpublished doctoral dissertation, Dept. of Anthropology, Yale University, 1956.

some specialist middlemen, some producer-distributors. The characteristics of the items handled in terms of bulk, unit price, perishability, fragility, seasonality, etc.; the character and amplitude of the demand; the seasonal and regional variation in supply; and the means and costs of transport all influence the form which the distribution of a given product will take. Two types of producer-distributors and three types of middlemen are described in the following section of the present paper. These five types appear frequently in the Jamaican internal marketing system, but they are only a sample of the great variety functioning within the system.

The first type of distributor to be described is the cultivator who is close enough to market to make it profitable for him to do his own selling regularly. On three successive market days, a group of seven people came to the Brown's Town (St. Ann Parish) market from a village about four miles distant. The four men and three women who composed the group were all members of one extended family: five siblings consisting of three men and two women, and one man and woman who were siblings, and first cousins to the other five. On one occasion, they carried a load of yams, "Breeze Blow" sweet potatoes, scallions, rosemary, and a few odds and ends of other produce. The main load is the "food," or yams and sweet potatoes. This group regularly brought four donkeyloads, or eight hampers, of produce and paid market fees of ninepence per donkeyload. The selling prices for the produce the group carried were set by the oldest brother of the larger group of siblings. Direct or variable costs of transport were negligible since the produce was carried to market by donkey rather than by truck. (Part of the cost and maintenance of the donkeys, of course, has to be debited to the cost of transport, and would enter into the long period supply price of this service.) Under such an arrangement as this, however, both the risks of production and of primary distribution are carried by the same parties. Some of the risks are diminished by the variety of produce carried and by the fact that the costs of the marketing operation for this group are kept to a minimum. In addition to producing what they sell, these people make most of their own marketing equipment: ropes of trumpet vine, plaiting and donkey pads of banana fiber, and even the box saddles of mahoe wood. The hampers are the only carrying equipment they obtain by purchase. The donkeys are tethered free of charge in the market and are fed with the guinea grass which is stuffed in and over the hampers, thus serving as protection as well as for fodder. A group of this kind illustrates in some ways what must have been one of the older Jamaican marketing patterns.[13]

One buyer who approached this group was not an ultimate consumer but a woman who intended to buy for resale. This woman is an example of a genuine higgler—a nonproducing specialist middleman. She bargained for a hamper of "Breeze Blow" sweet potatoes priced by the seller at 14 shillings. She failed to buy at first, checking with other sellers before she returned to consummate the purchase. The hamper weighed 60-70 pounds. If she were able to resell the total lot at the Brown's Town price per pound that morning, she would have earned about 16 shillings on the transaction; if she trucked the sweet potatoes to Kingston, she might have been able to triple her investment. Sometimes such a higgler will try to resell in small quantities in the local market, perhaps selling the entire purchase if the price remains high and reinvesting in another lot; but she is much more likely to retail only until she can catch a truck to Kingston where she will seek to resell the remainder of her stock to still another higgler there. The Brown's Town woman who buys a whole hamper at a time usually is accumulating produce sufficient to make her trip to Kingston what she considers a worthwhile risk. Depending on her capital and her estimate of the Kingston market situation, the more she buys for resale in Kingston the more profitable her trip can be. In one instance observed by the writer, a woman in the Brown's Town market accumulated four hampers of "food" at her feet—an investment of about two pounds, sixteen shillings—without making any effort to resell. Such a higgler is either confident of her ability to resell in bulk and at a profit, or has an assured buyer awaiting her elsewhere. For their operations to be potentially profitable, the amount of stock these higglers carry must be considerable. But they must pay transport costs not only for themselves but also for their stock, and the price of the trip rises with the quantity of stock they carry. They are faced with the need, therefore, to make fine judgments in estimating potential demand at a distant market and the amount of capital they ought to invest in a single operation.[14]

[13] Cf., for instance, Bacon, E. M. and Aaron, E. M., *The New Jamaica*, New York, 1890, pp. 94-96; Beckford, W., *A Descriptive Account of the Island of Jamaica*, London, 1790, Vol. II, p. 153; Bickell, R., *The West Indies as They Are*, London, 1835, p. 66.

[14] The writer failed to get much information on how current prices in town and Kingston markets are communicated to higglers in the rural areas. This question among others is being studied at present in Jamaica by Mrs. Margaret Katzin, a graduate student from Northwestern University's Dept. of Anthropology.

Another case of a combined produced-distributor role is exemplified by a farmer-sugarmaker who travels regularly from Ulster Spring (Trelawney Parish) to the Brown's Town market, making the trip in his own mule-drawn dray. This man is primarily a produce farmer who carries sugar in addition to other produce; his load usually consists of root crops, bananas, breadfruit, and brown sugar of both the "wet" and the dry "head" variety.[15]

The retailers of this sugar in the Brown's Town market are local women who represent another type of higgler. These women buy "wet" sugar by the tin and sell it by the pound, making a profit of from ten to sixteen shillings on the tin. The wholesale and retail prices of this sugar vary, not only in terms of supply, but also in inverse relation to the supply of fresh mangoes available in a market on a given day; when mangoes are plentiful, the demand for sugar seems to decline. Usually the retailers buy their "wet" sugar on credit, "dig" sugar all day, and at the end of the day pay the sugar-maker in proportion to the part of the total tin they have sold. The remainder of the sugar is stored in the market storeroom at twopence per tin. The selling continues the following market day, when the sugar-maker receives the rest of his money. This arrangement affords some protection to the retailer's investment, although it ties up part of the investment of the sugar-maker. It seems likely that this practice occurs in sugar rather than in foodstuffs such as yams, cocos and breadfruit because sugar is less perishable and the unevenness of demand is therefore not so threatening to the investment of any of the parties concerned.[16]

A final illustration perhaps comes closest to what is usually thought of in Jamaica when one speaks of a higgler. Mrs. N. is the wife of a peasant, who cultivates about four acres of land, and the mother of five children, of whom four are still at home, the oldest a girl twelve years old, the youngest a baby not yet weaned. Until recently, Mrs. N. traveled only to the Brown's Town market, carrying supplies she and her daughter would buy in the surrounding countryside, in addition to produce from her husband's farm. But Brown's Town, she says, is a "cheap" market—that is, the rate of return for

[15] Unrefined sugar of these types is slightly cheaper than refined sugar, and is preferred by many Jamaican country people.

[16] An interesting aspect of this arrangement is the fact that the price paid the sugar-maker for his tin of sugar is fixed at the time of sale. This price remains the same, regardless of the supply of sugar which may be available in the market on the following market day. In other words, the sugar-maker's investment is guaranteed even though full payment is delayed for a week, whereas retailer cannot tell in advance what her margin of profit will be on the following market day.

selling locally produced foodstuffs is low. Several months before she was interviewed, Mrs. N. decided to undertake trips to the Kingston market in an attempt to realize a greater return on her efforts. These trips require a great deal of planning, for not only must capital be borrowed or accumulated for investment, demand estimated, produce acquired, and the actual trip worked out, but arrangements must be made for the care of the family during the mother's absence. On one typical trip, Mrs. N. took eggs (purchased at two shillings threepence, sold at three shillings), soursop (purchased for a penny, sold for sixpence), pumpkins (purchased at one shilling or one shilling sixpence, resold at two shillings), and pineapples (grown on her husband's farm, and sold at one shilling sixpence). On other occasions, Mrs. N. has carried fowls (purchased at about one shilling ninepence per pound, and sold at two shillings threepence per pound), avocados (purchased at from one penny to sixpence, and sold at from sixpence to ninepence), and a few other products. She does not carry "food" (yams, sweet potatoes, cocos, etc.) to Kingston because the price of truck trip to the city rises with the size of the load, and "food" is bulky at the same that the unit price is relatively low. In this regard, Mrs. N.'s approach differs from that of some other higglers. Mrs. N. picks her items on the basis of their yielding a high return relative to their bulk, and this is likely to mean that they are items which are fragile, highly perishable, or both. Many items, such as eggs, avocados, and breadfruit, must be packed in a basket rather than in a burlap sack, and handled with care during a long, rough trip. Mrs. N. buys her stock in and near the village in which she lives. When she is ready to leave, the stock is packed on a donkey. Mrs. N.'s daughter accompanies her mother from the village to a place off the road where a Kingston-bound truck passes regularly on Sunday afternoon. The daughter then returns home with the donkey and with instructions regarding the care of the house and the baby. The cost of Mrs. N.'s trip to Kingston is about twelve shillings, depending on the exact nature of her load, and the cost of return is six shillings. The Kingston market to which she goes opens at midnight Sunday night. If she can, Mrs. N. seeks to sell her goods before that time just outside the market place, for once the market opens she must go inside, paying a gate fee (approximately one shilling sixpence—again, depending on the nature of her load) and a handcart fee (one shilling sixpence). Thus, transport costs about 18 shillings, fees for service and market about three shillings—over one pound sterling is spent or committed for services usually before the first sale is made; in addition, Mrs. N. has other minor expenses, such as her food during her trip. Mrs. N. spends about three pounds in accumulating produce for resale and estimates that she must gross about five pounds to make her trip worth while; that is, a pound or less profit, a pound or more for expenses, and three pounds for reinvestment in the next trip. She may make a slightly larger profit by carrying back a few small articles, such as earrings, bangles, or tinware, for resale in the village, but she rarely does this unless she has an order for the goods. She has several regular buyers at the Kingston market to which she goes who buy from her to resell to ultimate consumers in Kingston. She herself does not dare to sell retail in the residential neighborhoods of Kingston, for she says that she would get lost and also that she doesn't know how to deal with the people who live there.

The early morning trading for a higgler like Mrs. N. is usually brisk and competitive. Prices, particularly of the more perishable items, rise and fall according to the abundance or scarcity of the goods, and one must have chosen well to be sure of a profit. The cheap foodstuffs which are a boon to the consumer may be a catastrophe for the market woman who has miscalculated. Her capital is limited, often borrowed from market butchers at a rate of one shilling per pound for three days' use. A loss of profits on several successive trips can put her out of business. Kingston market women, buying either for wholesale or retail, frequently hold back on their purchases, awaiting the decline in prices which may occur as the hour approaches when many sellers must board trucks to return home. There is little point in carrying the same produce home again (particularly since it would increase the cost of the return trip—a partial explanation of the frequently high amount of wastage in perishable foodstuffs), and Mrs. N. must be ready to go when her truck leaves. The out-of-town higgler, accordingly, can only hope that the Kingston retailer or wholesaler will want to start vending locally earlier than when she, the out-of-towner, must leave, as well as that there is not too big a supply in the market of the items she carries. Price in this situation, as in almost all higgling transactions, is usually determined by bargaining. Out-of-town marketers peg their selling prices somewhat higher than they expect to get, while Kingston higglers offer less than they may expect to pay. The prices which emerge are usually a compromise; but the quoted too-high and two-low figures with which the haggling begins are not haphazard figures; they stand for the bargainer's skilled estimate of the range of variation of the price of a given item in a given market on a given day.[17] Because of their common knowledge of these matters, market women are not likely to outrage each other in the way that a less-knowing housewife may outrage a higgler by offering an unrealistic buying price.

III.

As stated earlier, the cases described above by no means exhaust the variety of produce-distributor and higgler types in the total Jamaican internal marketing system. The distributive role is shaped by such factors as whether marketing is combined with production, the kind of transportation available, and the quantity and type of goods—perishability emerges as an especially important determinant, particularly in a situation where transport is still relatively poor, demand uncertain, and storage or refrigeration facilities practically nonexistent. Roughly speaking, the more perishable the food, the more prices will fluctuate, and also the greater is the chance of wastage. Breadfruit, mangoes, avocados, lettuce, and tomatoes are illustrations of foods which must be sold quickly if they are to be sold at all. Yams and cocos, sweet potatoes and cassava are more stable; still more stable are such items as sugar "heads" and "wet" sugar.[18]

It can be seen from these facts that the term "middleman" in a market situation like Jamaica's does not stand for an economically homogenous class carrying out a uniform economic function. Frequently the middleman is the producer's wife, sister, or other relative; in these cases, the risks of both production and distribution fall upon the same individual or family. It would be incorrect, therefore, to assume that the primary distributor, in such instances, is

[17] The writer does not claim to be able to analyze the actual pricing process in these situations. In spite of a number of 24-hour sessions in the market place, he was never able to isolate precisely the way in which offering prices are established, maintained, or changed, apparently without deliberate price-fixing agreements, by scores or hundreds of independent higglers selling dozens of different items. The market place resembles a stock exchange or an organized commodity market in this regard.

[18] Tinware, clay ware ("yabba"), jippi-jappa products, basketry, and cloth, unlike the items of the food and vegetable market, do not vary significantly in price over short periods. They are not normally subject to scarcity, and they are little affected by glut, seasonality, or regional variation. Yet they are frequently sold in the market place, rather than in regular stores. The sellers of such goods are much more like small shopkeepers than they are like higglers. They carry on their business in the open market rather than in stores probably because they lack the capital for opening a small shop, but also because of the nature of the demand for their particular wares: a demand originating with the poor, rural Jamaicans who come to town primarily to go to market.

exploiting producer and consumer in return for a minor service. Even when the middleman is a specialist completely divorced from production, he or she not only is rendering a very necessary distributive service, but is paying highly for the right to fill this role in the form of transport fees, marketing fees, interest, etc.[19]

The absence of more efficient marketing arrangements seems to be characteristic of many world areas where transportation is poor, storage facilities undeveloped, demand dispersed, capital reserves limited, and production on small farms predominant.[20] Given the low level of the total economy, the internal marketing arrangements in such areas cannot be called inefficient insofar as they do not absorb larger quantities of scarce resources than are needed for the performance of the services required by the customers. The multiplicity of traders is an aspect of the generally low level of such economies. It seems doubtful that the forcible elimination of these trades would be economically advisable. Given the scarcity of capital for economic development, use of available capital to eliminate higglers might adversely affect other existing economic arrangements. Shephard, who has studied Caribbean internal economies, warns against any *a priori* judgments that, regardless of local conditions, the middleman is economically deleterious:

> "It is dangerous to assume as some cooperative enthusiasts do, that middlemen are parasites who interpose themselves between producer and consumer and levy a toll on both without rendering any service. . . . We must not lose sight of the fact that middlemen come into existence in response to a demand by producers and consumers for the essential services they perform. They are induced to undertake these services in the expectation of profit and if the prospect of profit permanently ceases, they cease to operate. The fact that many middlemen earn profits cannot be accepted as conclusive evidence of inefficiency or of excessive charges for the services they perform. . . . It is possible, of course to eliminate particular types of middlemen, but . . . [their] services are indispensable and the question is whether these services can be performed more efficiently by specialist middlemen or by organizations of producers." [21]

[19] Rottenberg, in describing the services performed by the middleman of agricultural products in the Carribean, puts the case dramatically when he writes: "At negative earnings, the self-employed worker pays the buyer of his services for permitting him to render them." Cf. Rottenberg, S., "A Note on Economic Progress and Occupational Distribution," *Review of Economics and Statistics*, Vol. 35, No. 2, May 1953, p. 169.

[20] Cf. Bauer, P. T., *West African Trade*, Cambridge, England, 1954, p. 388.

[21] Shephard, C., "The Small Scale Farmer: Marketing and Processing Problems," *Caribbean Commission Monthly Information Bulletin*, Vol. VIII, No. 3, October 1954, p. 61. See also Bauer, P. T. and Yamey, B. S., "The Economics of Marketing Reform," *Journal of Political Economy*, Vol. LXII, No. 3, June 1954, pp. 211-212. The works of Bauer have proved of particular value to the writer, providing as they have great illumination and significant corroboration of his own findings from a different geographical area.

IV.

No clearly formulated plan for the reform of the internal marketing system or for the elimination of higglers has been prepared in Jamaica, so far as is known to the writer. But many criticisms of the existing system are made, primarily by middle-class observers, in conversation and in the daily press. Thus, for instance, "H.P.J.," writing in the (Kingston, Jamaica) *Daily Gleaner* for June 8, 1955, states:

> ". . . some of us are increasingly vocal on what we regard as 'bad' and 'uneconomic' methods of marketing . . . proposals to change the marketing system are not the result of any wish to impose a new way of life—they are the ideas, for example, of harassed Marketing Department officials confronted with the lamentations of the small farmer himself as his system collapses and the high prices paid by the consumer fail to improve the producer's lot."

The implications of this criticism are clear: producers get too little for their goods, while consumers pay too much for the same goods; what makes the system inefficient lies somewhere between primary production and ultimate purchase. "H.P.J." avoids saying that the higgler gets too much for her services; but no other conclusion seems possible under the circumstances. At the same time that the higgler is not efficient enough, however, she also manages to be too efficient. "H.P.J." again, writing in the *Daily Gleaner* for June 23, 1955, tells us:

> "Few [higglers] in any category make much money. That all perform a function in the absence of green-grocers with telephones and delivery vans and costermongers with vehicles, I do not deny. But here we have an example of the poverty of one class communicating itself to another, since the natural evolution of the greengrocer and the costermonger has been checked by the operation of higglers in search of tiny margins, with a consequent restriction of opportunity for *petit bourgeois* enterprise in an important sector of the home market and (inevitably) high living costs for precisely the class on whom high costs press most hardly. . . ."

Here the higgler is at fault, not because she pays too little and charges too much, but rather because, through her willingness to sell her services so cheaply, she prevents truckers, wholesalers and greengrocers from competing with her successfully, and thereby hampers the growth of the economy.

This curious dilemma—that the higgler manages simultaneously to be too efficient and not efficient enough—is in fact no dilemma at all. The higgler is more efficient, given the present level of the

Jamaican economy, than any would-be competitors. That is why she has survived and has not been supplanted. At the same time, it is true that her services are inefficiently rendered, *if we use as our standard comparable services in more developed economies.* The logical difficulty comes in assuming that the Jamaican economy is not much different from, say, the British or United States economies.

Proponents of economic reform of internal marketing systems in less developed countries must answer three fundamental questions, put from the point of view of the total economy, to justify their proposals: 1) where will the capital come from to effect the reforms, and are these the best ways to employ that capital; 2) what shall be done to employ economically the labor freed by the reforms if they are successful; and 3) will the reforms broaden economic opportunities for the primary producers, or disadvantage some producers by favoring others? Most reforms suggested to increase the efficiency of an internal marketing system such as Jamaica's stem from the assumption that bulk production, transport in bulk, and retailing outlets which can purchase in bulk for resale are more efficient economically than existing practices. This might be true as a general rule in the more "developed" countries. In economies like Jamaica's, however, the greatest savings such reforms would permit—even assuming that capital were available to make them and that they were successful—would be of labor. Yet in these same economies the most abundant resource is labor, and the people likely to lose the most by having their labor "saved for them" are the higglers and the small-scale peasants. Their elimination, or the reduction of their economic opportunities, must therefore raise the question whether the increased efficiency which would allegedly be achieved thereby would then enable other sectors of the economy to make efficient use of the labor saved. Put another way, the question becomes whether the services now performed by middlemen should be eliminated without attention to the economic alternatives open for the people who would thereby be deprived of a means of self-employment.[22] In the case of Jamaica,

[22] Bauer (*op. cit.*, 1954, pp. 26-27) has stated the case very precisely for British West Africa, which has certain qualified similarities to the Jamaican situation:

"The large number of intermediaries and links in the chain of distribution accords with expectations; and it is the result of basic underlying circumstances.

"There is an extensive demand for the services of intermediaries . . . in the marketing of agricultural produce, whether for export or for local consumption. . . . There are many people available to perform these services at a low supply price in terms of daily earnings. Few other profitable channels of employment exist, because of the relative scarcity of suitable land, technical skill and, above all, capital . . . women and children are available to act as intermediaries even for very low earnings.

literally thousands of women without other sources of income except possibly domestic labor depend on higgling entirely or in part for their livings.[23]

Even assuming that alternative gainful employment could be found for the higglers, elimination of this group will make good economic sense only if access to market for the small-scale peasant producer is still maintained. The small-scale producer depends heavily for cash upon the sale of some part of his produce. While he may at times market his own stock, higglers carry on most such distributive activity, as the present paper has sought to indicate. It is sometimes said that greater growth for the Jamaican economy as a whole is possible only if both higgling and small-scale farming are eliminated from the economic picture. But proponents of this position should be reminded that it will take considerable capital to transform the distributive system of the Jamaican economy and still more to transform its agricultural system—capital which might better be employed in developing the industrial sector of the economy. These general points appear to apply to some degree to the internal marketing situation in West Africa as decribed by Bauer.[24] In Jamaica as in West Africa, the higgler is not economically redundant but actually essential to the distributive process as it is presently constituted. The large number of individual higglers—each operating with limited capital, on a narrow profit margin, and apparently without organized price-fixing schemes—intensifies competition and

"The intermediaries are productive as they conserve real resources, especially capital, substituting for it semi-skilled and unskilled labour, which is abundant, stimulate production, and provide employment. Their trading methods are economic in that they use resources which are redundant. . . .

"These considerations dispose of the belief that the value of agricultural or manufacturing output could be increased by compulsory reduction in the number of traders. Such measures would only serve to add to the numbers of redundant and unemployed or under-employed unskilled Africans (especially women and children), and to aggravate the low level of capital and the lack of employment opportunities. The volume of production would not be increased, since the resources set free would be of the type already redundant, while the enforced adoption of uneconomic trading methods would absorb resources (notably capital) in distribution which would otherwise be available for use in agriculture and industry.

"Thus it is clear that the large number of traders, and more especially the large number of stages in the distributive process, are not simply redundant. If the traders were superfluous, and their services unnecessary, the customers would by-pass them to save the price of their services, that is, the profit margin of the intermediaries."

[23] Many Jamaican lower-class women prefer the uncertainty of higgling to the drudgery of domestic work. Cf. Mintz, 1955, p. 102. In a society only a century removed from slavery this is not difficult to understand. In contrast, a number of middle-class Jamaicans, in expressing to the writer their dissatifaction with the existing market system, criticized not only the high cost of food but also the "rudeness" of the higglers. Social attitudes such as these are economically relevant.

[24] Bauer, *op. cit., loc. cit.*

reduces the chances for monopolistic control over the supply by any individuals or groups. In practice, the market place in Jamaica is an example of true competition when compared to much of the economies of marketing in more "developed" countries.

The implications of these data for applied anthropologists should be apparent. Bauer, in commenting on the West African internal marketing situation, writes:

> "The criticisms which neglect these considerations [the economic background of a market situation in which higglers are very numerous] possibly derive from a confusion between technical and economic efficiency. It is true that marketing arrangements in West Africa are primitive technically when compared with those in industrialized societies. But, given the vastly different economic features of West Africa, any attempt to force marketing arrangements more closely into line with those in other societies is certain to waste resources. A set of arrangements which are economically efficient in one society will not be economically efficient in another in which the availability of resources is different. The criticisms may also partly stem from a widespread and influential desire for tidy and controllable economic arrangements; those who share this desire regard the existing unorganized and *seemingly* chaotic arrangements as irrational." [25]

This statement holds as fully for Jamaica and for much of the rest of the Caribbean as it does for British West Africa. It properly emphasizes the importance of viewing reform measures in the context of the particular resources of particular whole economies, before undertaking to change historically and culturally distinctive societies of the Jamaican and West African kind.

[25] Bauer, *op. cit.*, p. 27.

71. DEVELOPMENTS IN SELF-SERVICE FOOD DISTRIBUTION ABROAD *

William Applebaum

This paper deals with the following three questions:

1. How far has self-service and supermarket development in food distribution progressed to date abroad?
2. What are the major differences in conditions abroad compared with the United States (and Canada) affecting self-service and supermarket developments?
3. How far is self-service and supermarket development likely to go abroad in the next five years?

I.

Self-service and supermarkets are manifestations of the American way of life that have captured the imagination of many people throughout the world, and those who have tried it, or have been exposed to it, like it. To be sure, perhaps 90 per cent of the world's people haven't been near a self-service food store. Most of them may have never heard of a supermarket. But the situation is and will be changing. There are stirrings even behind the Iron Curtain, with at least a superette in operation in Tiflis and a supermarket under construction (perhaps already in operation) in Leningrad.

The National Cash Register Company, an advocate of self-service, has been compiling data on the number of self-service food stores outside the United States and Canada. As of two months ago there were nearly 10,000 such stores in more than 40 countries. This represents an increase of 28 per cent in ten months. There were practically no self-service food stores outside the United States and Canada before 1947.

About three fourths of these self-service food stores are in Western and Northern Europe. No self-service food stores are known

* Reprinted by permission from the *Journal of Farm Economics*, Vol. XXXVIII, No. 2 (May, 1956), pp. 348-355.

William Applebaum, Lecturer on Food Distribution and Comparative Marketing, Harvard University Graduate School of Business Administration.

at present in Southern Europe and probably none exist in Central Europe.

In relation to population, Sweden, Norway, and Switzerland lead at present in Europe. These three small countries with a combined population of fifteen million people account for 45 per cent of the self-service food stores in Europe. New Zealand and Australia are also leaders in the self-service movement. They account for about one sixth of the total abroad.

Suggestions have been made that the self-service food stores, and especially the supermarket, thrives best in areas of high standards of living. In the main, the record to date appears to support this.

About half of the self-service food stores abroad are operated by consumer cooperatives; the balance, both chains and independents. The chains that were more cautions to get started are stepping up the tempo of their activities.

Although there are no statistics, it is probably a valid conclusion that most of the present self-service food stores abroad are conversions from service stores. Thus they are stores *in situ,* with some remodeling and perhaps a bit of enlarging. They are small stores averaging about 1,000 square feet, located in congested, densely populated urban areas, without parking and with the inadequate, cramped storage and service areas and facilities. Such superettes cannot carry a large selection of merchandise.

My guess would be that less than 300 of the 10,000 self-service food stores abroad are complete food stores, with a wide selection of groceries, fresh fruits and vegetables, dairy products, baked, smoked and fresh meat and fish. These stores will range in size from 3,000 square feet to more than 10,000 square feet and their sales volume is large enough to be considered supermarkets.

II.

The development of self-service in food distribution abroad has been hampered more or less by several handicaps. To begin with, there is tradition to overcome. Tradition means a myriad of small or tiny food-specialty stores and stands, and it means customer service. Tradition has deep fears of customer pilferage under conditions of self-service merchandising. Tradition induces the businessman to spin out a long list of reasons why housewives in his country are so different from those in the United States and consequently wouldn't respond favorably to the self-service way of life. Finally, tradition

SELF-SERVICE FOOD STORES IN OPERATION OUTSIDE USA AND CANADA

Continent and Country	Population in Millions	Self-Service Food Stores October 31, 1955 †	Self-Service Food Stores Per Million Population	Increase Over December 31, 1954 †
Europe				
England	50	2,413	48	24%
Sweden	7	2,100	300	19
Norway	3	701	250	61
Germany (West)	48	529	11	89
Switzerland	5	500*	100	10
France	43	386	9	21
Netherland	10	302	30	31
Denmark	4	195*	49	4
Belgium	9	97	11	36
Finland	4	44	11	7
Austria	7	35	5	118
Subtotal	190	7,302	38	28
Australia	9	1,156	128	20
New Zealand	2	554	277	35
Subtotal	11	1,710	156	24
Central and South America	150	662	4	28
All others	...	78	...	170
Total		9,752		28

† Data supplied by The National Cash Register Company.
* Revised on basis of data from other sources.

sees no urgent need for changing anything when one can still make a profit, or a living of sorts, by doing things the tried and known way.

Then, there are all the problems of the aftermath of war: destruction, shortages, rationing, restrictions, and a bit of general confusion. These were all real difficulties that tried the courage and patience and ingenuity of even the most enterprising and progressive businessman. Raising capital to finance new enterprises is not easy abroad, and finding suitable locations even for superettes is troublesome. As for getting supermarket sites and buildings, the difficulties multiply in geometric progression with the increase in size of the store desired. It is a sad fact that in reconstruction the war-bombed cities of Europe, the local governments, the city planners, and the property owners all combined to rebuild the shopping facilities essentially on the prewar scale and needs. They looked at the dead past and planned accordingly for the future. And the businessmen failed to organize a movement to prevent this blunder.

Prepackaging is essential for self-service. In the United States the suppliers are now performing the prepackaging of nearly all products except fresh fruits, vegetables, meats, and fish. This is not the case abroad. There prepackaging is still far behind, and in many parts of the world it is primitive by U. S. standards. The cost of packaging material is higher abroad than in the United States and people can less afford to pay for it. Consequently, self-service food distribution abroad is beset with far more problems of getting pre-packaged merchandise before the customer than is the case in the United States. Fortunately, packaging by retailers and suppliers is improving rapidly and suppliers are taking over more of the pre-packaging function.

Self-service is a convenient way to shop, with part of the work in the store done by the customer. This cuts operating expense and the savings can be passed on to the customer as an added inducement. The supermarket is essentially a marriage of self-service and low prices. Unfortunately, abroad it is customary for suppliers of leading grocery brands to insist on resale price maintenance. This of course eliminates competitive pricing from a substantial proportion of lines sold in food stores and thus retards flexibility of pricing as a means of attracting trade. The aggressive merchant tries to meet this situation either by giving cash rebates to his customers on all items purchased, or, in some instances, he features his own private label brands. The supermarket is a strong challenge to the supplier's right to fix retail resale prices.

The supermarket aims at one-stop shopping. It does away with the traditional going to the butcher, the fish monger, the baker, the vegetable shop, the dairy store, and the grocery to buy all the products needed to feed the family. This is the antithesis of the guild laws in food retailing, which protect fragmentized specialization in varying degrees in many places abroad. Until these guild laws are repealed the consumer must pay heavily for every attempt at progress.

The problem of selling fresh meats in supermarkets is especially troublesome in a number of countries, and the only solution permissible at present is to enclose the meat department behind a glass wall with a glass door entrance from the other food departments. An ingenious merchant in Argentina noted that the law in his country said nothing about a butcher selling groceries, so he opened a meat market with a temporary partition to screen off the rear three-fourths of the store. A couple of months later he removed the partition, moved the meat department to the rear, and installed a complete self-service grocery section in the front. The frustrated authorities are still considering whether the merchant is a butcher or a lawbreaker.

Mrs. Consumer abroad who shops in self-service food stores does so more frequently than her American cousin. She is still hampered by lack of refrigeration or very limited refrigeration facilities in the home, and she does not generally have the convenience of an automobile to go shopping. Consequently, her average purchase is relatively small. She assembles her total purchase in a small store basket and carries it home in her personal shopping bag, because even super markets abroad do not as yet provide the convenience of large, strong paper bags in which to take the groceries home.

Complete self-service in all food departments is so rare abroad that it is still practically nonexistent. One or another of all of the perishable departments are on a service or semiservice basis. Self-service fresh meat merchandising is being introduced very cautiously, chiefly because mechanical refrigeration equipment and the necessary transparent wrapping materials are considered very expensive.

Supermarkets abroad do not carry the large variety of food items available in the United States. The differences are to be found in much less products with built-in services, very little frozen foods, less variety in fresh fruits and vegetables throughout the year. Also supermarkets abroad do not offer a wide duplication of brands and sizes of the same product, with the exception of chocolates and wines.

Self-service food merchants abroad point to much higher sales experience per square foot of store selling area than in the United States. This is so because they carry fewer items and less duplication of brands, and sizes, make more frequent grocery deliveries, and customer purchases are better distributed throughout the week, especially since these stores abroad are not open evenings or Sunday.

Food retailers abroad are almost inactive in the use of mass advertising media. Most of the advertising is done by window displays and some newspaper ads. The window displays are very attractive and effective in arresting the attention of pedestrian traffic. There is much window shopping.

Self-service food store personnel abroad are hardworking, but not always well trained in the concepts and methods of self-service merchandising. This is particularly noticeable in the care and handling of perishable products. Because labor is still relatively cheap, mechanization and labor saving devices are not nearly as widely employed abroad as in the United States.

In spite of the high rents and store space limitations, the utilization of the available selling area is not always highly efficient. On the other hand, supermarket operators abroad are imaginative and very resourceful in utilizing a second store to provide additional selling area. Some of the staircases leading to the upper floors are remarkably attractive and impressive.

One must not fail to mention that nonfood lines have found their way in self-service food stores and supermarkets abroad as they have in the United States. In some instances, more space is devoted to a larger number of nonfood items than to food products. These, of course, are exceptional stores, generally in a very important shopping-center location. However, their experience is still too brief to foretell what the shakedown in nonfood lines in supermarkets will be.

In my recent travels abroad, I have seen many peculiarities in self-service food operations. These, pieced together, would make an interesting story. But the situations are probably unusual and perhaps ephemeral. Hence I pass them up, aware that some exception might be found to every generalization I have made.

III.

Having taken a quick and sketchy look at self-service and supermarkets abroad, let us now turn briefly to likely developments in the next five years. Here I would like to present some views from several friends abroad who are up to their necks in the supermarket movement. The following quotes are almost verbatim but somewhat abbreviated. In the case of two, the text represents my free translation of the original in German. Although the names of these contributors are omitted, their countries are carefully identified to give more meaning to their views. In so far as there is repetition, it reveals that these keen European merchants think alike.

IN DENMARK. The independents prefer status quo and are pecularily resistant to dynamic growth. They place their trusts more in protection than in free competition. Therefore, the consumer cooperatives and a few chains are the only competition elements in the retail trade. But Denmark is "underdeveloped" with respect to chain store organizations. The Danish trade law provides that a retailer may operate only one store in a municipality. A manufacturer may open as many stores as he wants but then only sell his own merchandise and similar products from other manufacturers. A consumer cooperative may operate many stores but is permitted to deal only with members.

It is obvious that this very strange legislation sets strong limitations on competition. The big organizations are the only elements today in Denmark open-minded enough to understand that the interests of Mrs. Housewife, low prices, good quality, right type of stores, etc. are the only healthy road for all business. We have tried for years to change this legislation and perhaps we will succeed within the next five years.

I believe that the self-service system will have a better future in Denmark in the coming five years. The supermarkets will also come. I am optimistic because every time I hear in Europe that the American housewives have "another mentality" than their European sisters, I know it is a great lie. All human beings want a better life, a better standard of living. Everything we do here to make it easier for Mrs. Housewife is received with enthusiasm. She is happier in a supermarket than in an old store. She gets more time for her family. She wants progress. She will press her will through.

In England. The larger food retail organizations are known to be engaged in close study and preparing plans for further extensions into the self-service field. Stimulus to more rapid development is being provided by a number of firms with only minor previous interests in the retail food trade and these firms are actually leading the trade at the moment in the development of supermarkets.

There is little doubt that the next five years will see an acceleration of the switch from service to self-service types of shops. Rising overheads, particularly wages, and difficulty of finding suitable staff will provide a strong stimulus. The trend will be for more new shops to be opened up as self-service shops, particularly in new shopping parades. Supermarkets will increase rapidly in number and in size and one company is already planning to open over the next two years a number of units in excess of 10,000 sq. ft. but the majority are likely to be in the 3,000 to 5,000 sq. ft. range.

Lack of mobility and the shopping habits of the British public are handicaps in any attempt to repeat in this country the pattern of American supermarket development.

The most likely field for supermarket development over the next five years will be in main shopping centers; and if in addition to the natural advantage of supermarket shopping such as wide stock assortment, bright surroundings, ease and speed of shopping, the supermarkets succeed in underselling their service trade competitors, even by a small margin, and they establish a reputation for good value, they will be able to establish themselves in off-peak positions. If this is so, the problem of finding right sites will be made a little easier, otherwise lack of suitable sites in good positions in main shopping centers will limit the expansion plans of those companies likely to specialize in supermarkets.

By 1960, most probably 12 per cent to 18 per cent of the food trade in England will be done by self-service lines and supermarkets will play an important part in increasing the self-service section of the total trade.

IN GERMANY. Within the next five years, we may expect at least 5,000 self-service food stores, of which about a thousand will be of supermarket rank. During this period will be made the first attempts to establish suburban markets with parking areas for automobile shoppers. Complete self-service meat and produce will be introduced gradually. The industry is heading toward complete prepacking and the progressive companies will capitalize on the opportunities.

IN SWITZERLAND. During the next five years, cooperatives, chains and large concerns in the food distribution industry will go 80 to 100 per cent self-service. The small independents will stick essentially to service, but will also introduce semi-self-service so that the customer can help herself or be served, as she may wish. As for real supermarkets, I doubt if there will be more than fifty in five years. Opportunities are too limited and store locations are too expensive. Nonetheless, I can foresee supermarkets emerging on the periphery of large cities and even in the country. It is quite possible that even several shopping centers will be built before 1960.

Our friend from Denmark is enthusiastic and hopeful, the Englishman is conservatively optimistic, the German is determined and confident, and the Swiss has no intentions to let a good thing pass by. In short, they expect more and better self-service and supermarkets in the next five years, and so do I.

This international development will snowball, just as it did in the United States. The skepticism, the hesitation, and some of the obstacles abroad parallel, in the main, our own experience. It took us ten to fifteen years to get fully warmed up and in high gear. The same, at varying velocities, will be happening abroad, especially as more people acquire home refrigeration and motorized transportation. Sweden has 300 self-service food stores for every million population. New Zealand has 277. These are the two top performers to date abroad. The United States has about 600 self-service food stores per million population—of these about 150 are supermarkets. Even

Sweden still has a long way to go, and things are far from standing still in the United States.

Elsewhere, I have pointed out that in the postwar years the United States has shared generously with other people the fruits of her way of life and that someday the world may yet proclaim the supermarket as one of the great American contributions to the betterment of standards of living everywhere. Food merchants abroad who are deeply interested in self-service and supermarkets—and their number is rapidly multiplying—are most grateful for all the help they have been receiving from our supermarket industry, from our excellent food trade press, and from many manufacturers of goods and equipment.

Fortunately for all of us, this is not going to remain a one-way street. Those who are now benefiting from our experience and know-how are also acquiring know-how from their own experience. They have minds just as good as ours, and they will come up with ideas and innovations that will supplement and enrich ours, and this will be our reward. The excellent mutual relationships will lead to an international exchange of information that will benefit all people and will result in better nutrition, better health and more for all.

72. FOOD RETAILING AND ECONOMIC GROWTH *

Richard H. Holton

I would like to discuss the "dynamics of food retailing" as it applies to the low-income countries of the world. As a means of accelerating the economic growth of the underdeveloped areas, we have seen the federal government give increased encouragement to investment abroad by private firms and individuals in the United States. Private United States capital has been flowing abroad in recent years, especially into petroleum production. I would like to discuss the possibility that we may see within the next ten years a marked increase in the amount of United States investment in food retailing in these low-income areas.

The pattern of United States direct investment abroad appears to be shifting significantly. As of 1950, 44 per cent of this country's direct investment holdings in foreign countries other than Canada and the western European states were invested in petroleum and mining and smelting; 15 per cent of our direct investment in these countries was in transportation, communications and public utilities; 13 per cent in manufacturing; 8 per cent in agriculture and but 4 per cent in trade.[1] Let me repeat: but 4 per cent in trade. The striking fact is that in 1950, however, 15 per cent of United States net capital movements were accounted for by investment in trade. In other words, the trade sector's share of the increment in our direct investment in these areas was much greater than that sector's share of the total United States direct investment holdings as of 1950. This would seem to support the hypothesis that private United States capital is being attracted increasingly into the trade sector of the low-income countries.

A few preliminary remarks about these data are in order. First, I do not mean to imply that most, or even much, of this investment

* Reprinted by permission from the *Journal of Farm Economics*, Vol. XXXVII, No. 2 (May, 1956), pp. 356-360.

Richard H. Holton, Professor of Business Administration, University of California, Berkeley.

[1] *Foreign Investment in the United States*, a supplement to the *Survey of Current Business*, U. S. Department of Commerce, 1953, Appendix Table 4, p. 44.

in the trade sector is represented by food retailing. About 70 per cent of the trade sector investment is accounted for by wholesaling and another 25 per cent by retailing. Secondly, some of the 1950 net investment in trade was surely a result of the Korean War inventory build-up, but presumably a similar inventory investment occurred in other industries and so did not distort unduly the relative importance of the trade sector investment. It should also be pointed out that the trade sector's greater share of investment in 1950 was due in part to net disinvestment in two of the sectors, namely, agriculture and transportation, communications and public utilities. Finally, it might be mentioned parenthetically, that since the capital coefficient is lower, i.e., the capital turnover is higher in trade than in the extractive industries and in manufacturing generally, the relative significance of our investment in the trade sectors of low-income countries would be even greater if the amount of sales, rather than the amount of investment, were compared.

This statistical impression of increasing United States investment in the trade sector of the low-income countries is supported by knowledge of the experience of various United States firms, Sears-Roebuck providing perhaps the best known example.

I would like to discuss the possible reasons for this apparent shift of our foreign investment toward retailing and wholesaling and to ask especially whether we can expect more United Stated capital to be attracted into food retailing in these low-income areas.

The historical attraction of private United States capital into petroleum, mining and smelting abroad is readily understandable. Much of this investment resulted from the search of United States companies for cheap and reliable sources of raw material supplies. Under such circumstances, of course, there was no problem of finding a market for the output. Furthermore, the almost certain long-run increase in the United States demand for minerals was an impelling force, and in many cases the low-income countries were happy to have their natural resources developed by foreign capital. The virtual absence of import duties on raw materials also facilitated the sale of minerals on the world market.

The historical importance of transportation, communications and public utilities sector as an overseas outlet for United States investment funds can be explained in several ways. Frequently some investment in railways, harbors, and other shipping facilities was a prerequisite to mineral exploitation. Furthermore, since the transportation facilities were selling a service largely to domestic buyers there were no trade barrier problems. Perhaps of greater significance is the fact that railroads historically in most low-income countries have been in a position to cash in on economic growth. In recent years, however, private United States funds have been extruded, as it were, from this sector by nationalization or by government control approaching nationalization.

Why is a smaller proportion of United States direct investment abroad routed into the manufacturing and agricultural sectors? First of all, in some individual countries, such as Cuba, there has been considerable United States direct investment in agricultural production for export, perhaps because large-scale production methods are appropriate and the product can be readily marketed in the United States. More frequently the agricultural sector produces primarily for the local market and United States capital is reluctant to invest. United States investment funds move abroad only when the marketing channel for the commodity to be produced is reasonably clear and unobstructed.

Unfortunately for the economic development of the low-income countries, private United States capital is far less interested in manufacturing operations than in mineral exploitation even though the former is held up, somewhat erroneously, as the *sine qua non* of development. Unlike agriculture, the manufacturing sector as an investment opportunity frequently is as unpopular with the local people as it is with foreigners. In large measure the development of manufacturing is retarded in underdeveloped areas because of market and marketing problems. International trade barriers restrict the movement of manufactured goods far more than the movement of raw materials; the limited size of the local market frequently makes mass production, as the industrialized countries of the western world know it, impossible without an assured export market. Commonly the problem of obtaining an adequate and satisfactorily skilled labor force is a strong deterrent. In an underdeveloped economy also a manufacturer may miss the service industries that facilitate and lower the cost of factory production in mature industrial communities. In contrast with the manufacturing sector, we may see the trade sector account for an increased share of private United States investment funds flowing abroad. These funds may be attracted especially into food retailing and the retailing of other basic consumer goods. Several reasons can be cited for this expectation. First, in many low-income areas the income per capita is rising, expanding the purchasing power of the average family. Furthermore, the population increases are serving to increase the size of the market. In Latin America, for example, the population has been growing since 1920 at about twice the world rate. So the market is broadening both in terms of number of people and purchasing power per person. Insofar as economic growth is associated with industrialization and consequent urbanization, the concentration of population established a context attractive to modern retailing. The tariff barriers that shackle development of manufacturing in low-income areas are not as serious for retailing and wholesaling, since the "product" here is a service for sale on the domestic market. Furthermore, the distributor in any of the underdeveloped areas is a good bit more flexible than the manufacturer who attempts to establish there. It is more difficult for the manufacturer than for the distributor to shift from one good to another. Also the problem of recruiting the sort of labor required is probably not as great in trade as in manufacturing operation.

But more important, retailing in general but food retailing in particular in low-income areas is notably inefficient, as a rule. I have just published an attempt to measure the extent of this excess capacity in the case of Puerto Rico by estimating the cost functions of food retailers and wholesalers.[2] There it was found that really striking economies can be effected by the reduction of excess capacity in food retailing. It seems that the current average return over cost of 23 per cent could feasibly be reduced to about 12 per cent. That there is room for such improvements in food retailing is testified to by the experience of the Rockfeller International Basic Economy Corporation in Venezuela and of certain firms in Puerto Rico. The Rockefeller IBEC investment history, as a matter of fact, would seem to support the notion that opportunity for successful investment in food retailing in the low-income areas is considerably greater, relative to the other sectors, than has generally been appreciated. It is now reported that IBEC will concentrate its efforts on food processing and distribution rather than industrial production.

Finally, the food retailing sector of certain low-income areas would seem to provide attractive investment opportunities for United States firms because successful investment in this area requires not capital as much as knowledge of and experience with the managerial techniques necessary for mass distribution. By these techniques I mean, of course, the single price policy, the large-scale buying, vertical and horizontal integration, intense price competition and the high

[2] John Kenneth Galbraith and Richard H. Holton in collaboration with C. S. Bell, R. E. Bronson and J. A. Robinson, *Marketing Efficiency in Puerto Rico*, (Cambridge, Massachusetts: Harvard University Press, 1955).

volume, low price policy which characterize present-day food retailing in the United States.

We know that local consumers would be responsive to such retailing methods. Again the IBEC experience can be cited as well as that of certain low-margin food retailers in Puerto Rico. Low-income people are apparently as price conscious as one would expect. A significant proportion of them welcome the opportunity to buy for less by foregoing some services. A few years ago I studied a sample of consumers in a Massachusetts town and there the price consciousness of the low-income people stood out very clearly. It would seem that we can generalize to say that poor people are price conscious, wherever they are. If this is true, our mass distribution techniques would seem to be quite salable in the low-income areas of the world.

In sum, then, I am suggesting that in low-income areas we might find it easier to invest in mass distribution before we invest in mass production because fewer obstacles lie in the way of investment in distribution.

Having set forth this hypothesis with such confidence, I must conclude with a few of the many qualifications that should be stressed. First, the food retailing innovation in the low-income countries will probably not be characterized by the giant supermarket as we know it. Some of the major cities may warrant a few scaled-down supermarkets, but the great need is for chains of the old "pine board" grocery stores, selling the basic necessities at a minimum mark-up. Incomes are simply not high enough to support a modern United States supermarket with the usual wide selection of items. The low automobile population requires that the chain outlet be relatively small.

Secondly, efficient distribution of food may appear after integrated distribution has been established for other basic consumer goods. Clothing, shoes, and simple home furnishings in some respects offer fewer distribution problems than does food and may attract integrated distribution before food distribution does.

Thirdly, the big difficulty lies in the training of managerial personnel. But experience gained here in the United States can be applied to this problem, and the general desire on the part of young men abroad to learn United States managerial methods would seem to prevent this obstacle from becoming too great.

Fourthly, United States distributors may well refuse to look to these low-income areas as possible investment outlets until the current boom in shopping centers and supermarkets slows down. It is always simpler to expand in relatively well known territory than to establish stores of a different sort in an unknown market area.

Also, it might be mentioned that rationalization of food distribution may not be an unmixed blessing for the country in question. Presumably many high-margin retailers would be driven out of business and would add to what is typically a chronic unemployment problem. Also the demand stimulation resulting from the development of an aggressive distribution system may increase the demand for imports and create or intensify a balance-of-trade problem. But the risk might be worth taking. Certainly the great bulk of the population would enjoy the lower food costs and therefore higher real income. Also the development of a stronger distributive system can facilitate the production of local goods by removing some of the difficulties of marketing. The impact of more economical food distribution would seem quite clearly to rebound to the great benefit of the typical underdeveloped area in the long run.

73. SOME OBSERVATIONS ON THE EVOLVING RETAIL PATTERN IN EUROPE *

Karl H. Stein [1]

During the past twenty-five years a number of crucial changes in our retail structure and practices—including integrated retailing, private branding, self-service operations, and the shopping center movement—have developed.[2] The underlying causes of these developments seem to relate essentially to a desire to reap the benefits arising from large-scale operations, which has brought the retailer into traditional wholesale functions and manufacturing or, at the least, labeling operations.

The large-scale retail operator relies on volume combined with slim margins for the return on his investment. His assurance of heavy traffic and patronage loyalty would be greater if he could add to low-price appeal a high quality private brand appeal. If, through self-service or self-selection, he can transfer part of the selling function to the customer and part to the manufacturer who presells through prepackaging, he might increase profits by reducing labor costs, while at the same time increasing the potential dollar purchase per customer through the self-service layout which stimulates impulse buying.

The shopping center movement has been stimulated by the accelerating migration to the suburbs.[3] Distributive agencies generally are market-oriented in choice of location.[4] In addition, there appears to have been a transfer of costs to the consumer in this type of operation in that by locating on relatively undeveloped sites, shopping center retailers have escaped higher city taxation, higher public utility service charges, and the more irksome zoning restrictions of the downtown areas. By providing ample parking space, they have

* Reprinted with permission from the *Economics and Business Bulletin*, Vol. 10, No. 3 (March, 1958), pp. 6-17, Bureau of Economic and Business Research, Temple University, Philadelphia.

Karl H. Stein, Associate Professor of Marketing, College of Business Administration, Roosevelt University.

[1] The writer of this article attended the 1957 Congress.

[2] E. Paterson, "Retailing in Ferment," *Printers' Ink* (December 12, 1952).

[3] Clair James Reilly, "The Changing Retail Structure of Metropolitan Areas," *The Economics and Business Bulletin* (September, 1957), pp. 3-15.

[4] G. T. Renner, "Geography of Industrial Localization," *Economic Geography* (July, 1947); Vol. 23, No. 167, p. 169 ff.

invited customers to ignore transportation costs in favor of the unhurried atmosphere and one-stop shopping convenience of the shopping center.

This paper attempts to describe the development and present status in Europe of the last two mentioned elements of the American retail revolution; that is, self-service operations and the shopping center movement.

Food Retailing—An Index of Self-Service Operations

Two types of self-service operations, store self-service and automatic vending will be discussed. Store self-service methods have been applied in a variety of merchandise fields, but in no other field have they enjoyed such acceptance and popularity as in food distribution. In the United States supermarkets and superettes have captured 90 per cent of the dollar volume of food retail sales. Most food products are convenience goods and are therefore purchased quite frequently by brand and by proximity of the retail outlet. The average customer therefore requires less sales assistance than he would in the purchase of shopping or specialty goods.

There are several conditions necessary to the adoption of self-service food distribution. For purposes of analysis these may be distinguished as attitudinal, financial, operational, and institutional at the several stages in the chain of distribution from the ultimate consumer back to the manufacturer.

European consumer attitudes toward self-service

European consumers are not yet as conditioned to self-service food retailing as Americans are. Self-service substitutes for an interpersonal relation in the selling process, a relation between a buyer and his inanimate merchandise environment. It lacks the paternalistic-directive element characteristic of clerk-service operations and substitutes for these personal ingredients the impersonal preselling appeals of package, shelf position, and display. In short, "visual selling" techniques rely in much greater measure on the customer's planned and particularly his impulsive buying initiative cultivated by the permissive atmosphere of the supermarket. Europeans still resist giving up their friendly chat with the corner grocer.[5]

[5] R. Morenil (General Discussion), *Proceedings of the Sixth International Congress of the Green Meadow Foundation,* July 17, 1957, p. 3. This and all subsequent references to the Fifth and Sixth Congress *Proceedings* are to be mimeographed English editions of these *Proceedings.*

From a purely operational viewpoint, self-service transfers to the consumer part of the functions of breaking bulk (especially in the case of eggs and produce) and order filling. The latter confronts him with problems of brand choice and price and package-size comparisons. Europeans are not as yet prepared to assume these tasks to the same extent that Americans have. Financially speaking, although per capita food expenditures in some European countries approximate those of the United States, food expenditures there represent a larger proportion of the family budget, and therefore standards of living are lower than here. (See Tables 1 and 2.) Europeans have far less discretionary spending power for household appliances and automobiles. The present state of ownership of home refrigerators in Europe may be compared with conditions in this country in the early 1930s,[6] private automobile ownership with that of the early 1920s.[7] Although self-service food retailing does not depend on home refrigeration and car ownership, the European lag in these respects is bound to hamper its growth; less frequent and larger food purchases are predicated on a flexible means of transportation and householders' ownership of facilities for food preservation.

It would be wrong, however, to exaggerate the dependence of the further growth of self-service on European home refrigeration and automobile ownership. Most European institutional adaptations of the American self-service supermarket anticipate the relatively smaller average purchase by providing shoppers with wire baskets rather than pushcarts to collect their purchases and handy shopping bags for taking them home, with the alternative in some cases of prompt home delivery at a nominal charge. By way of contrast, the popularity of the "store-on-wheels," especially in Switzerland, points the way to alternative methods for overcoming the present lack of private automotive transportation by taking the merchandise to the customer instead of coaxing him to make a trip to the store. As for food preservation at home, since mean temperatures in most of Europe are considerably lower than in many parts of the United States, there is less need for home refrigeration, and perhaps in the foreseeable future progress in food irradiation will displace this method of food preservation.

[6] R. F. Werner, "General Report on European Area," *Proceedings of the Fifth International Congress of the Green Meadow Foundation* (1956), p. 5.
[7] *Newsweek* (November 4, 1957), p. 58.

European retailer attitudes toward self-service

The attitude of the European grocer toward self-service selling has gradually changed from one of suspicious rejection of this Yankee

TABLE 1

MINUTES OF WORK REQUIRED TO BUY SELECTED FOOD AND SHELTER ITEMS IN SELECTED COUNTRIES, OCTOBER, 1955

	Unit	Belgium 3 Cities	Denmark Copenhagen	France 4 Cities	Germany Fed. Rep.	Italy Large Cities	United Kingdom 7 Cities	United States 46 Large Cities
MEATS AND FISH:								
Beef, sirloin	Kg.	253	96	309	156	329	145	34
Pork, loin chops	Kg.	191	108	211	172	350	139	56
Fresh fish, misc. types	Kg.	130	26	83	57	278	62	29
DAIRY PRODUCTS AND EGGS:								
Butter	Kg.	216	105	332	225	403	127	49
Milk, pasteurized	liter	16	8	18	13	29	15	7
Eggs, fresh	1	8	5	11	8	13	7	2
FRESH FRUITS AND VEGETABLES:								
Apples, eating	Kg.	24	23	42	34	41	36	9
Cabbage, green or red	Kg.	9	6	16	9	..	13	5
Onions	Kg.	12	19	24	18	17	15	6
Potatoes	Kg.	5	7	7	6	13	9	3
MISCELLANEOUS:								
Cigarettes	20	21	45	33	54	51	54	7
Coal, household, misc. types	50 Kg.	234	127	348	115	738	96	44
Electricity, lighting	Kwh	8	1	11	7	14	2	2
Gas, cooking	50 cu.m.	375	239	632	423	571	220	63

Source: Sixth International Congress of the Green Meadow Foundation, 1957, H. J. Onnes, "Prospects For the Deep-Freezing Industry and the Deep-Freezing Chain In Europe," annex, pp. 5 and 6.

TABLE 2

RELATIVE "MEAL PURCHASING POWER" OF EARNINGS IN SELECTED COUNTRIES, OCTOBER, 1955

	Percent of Meal Obtained by 44 Minutes Work	Index of Hourly Earnings[1] (U. S.=100)	Cost of Meal in U. S. Cents	Worktime Required to Obtain Meal (minutes)
United States	100	100	138.4	44
Canada	63	79	174.0	69
Denmark	45	34	105.5	97
United Kingdom	30	29	136.0	146
Germany (federal Republic)	28	23	112.4	154
Belgium	21	27	177.0	204
Austria	18	16	125.0	244
France	17	22	182.7	264
Italy	15[2]	15	137.0[2]	284[2]

Source: *Ibid.*

[1] After conversion of average hourly earnings into U.S. currency by official New York bank rates.

[2] Excluding apples.

TABLE 3

NUMBER OF SELF-SERVICE SHOPS IN EUROPEAN RERAIL FOOD DISTRIBUTION

Country	1948	1953	1955	1957 [1]	Per 100,000 Inhabitants
Belgium	2	60	100	138	1.6
Denmark	..	130	225	...	5.0
Finland	..	30	45	...	1.0
France	1	?	400	...	0.9
Great Britain	1	1700	2500	3300	6.4
Italy	..	1	1	...	...
The Netherlands	1	134	334	...	3.0
Norway	2	373	700	850-900	25.0
Austria	..	13	35 [2]	...	0.5
Sweden	22	1732	2425	over 3000	40.5
Switzerland	5	350	600	900	18.0
West Germany	..	225	500	1500 [3]	2.8
Total	34	4600	7900	...	3.2

Source: H. J. Onnes, *loc. cit.*, page 2 f.

[1] Approximate figures.
[2] Probably too high; it might only be 25.
[3] Including West Berlin.

TABLE 4

ESTIMATED VALUE OF ALL FROZEN FOODS SOLD AT RETAIL IN EUROPE, 1941-1956

1941	$142,000,000	1949	$ 375,000,000
1942	162,000,000	1950	500,000,000
1943	178,000,000	1951	700,000,000
1944	197,000,000	1952	875,000,000
1945	257,000,000	1953	1,200,000,000
1946	324,000,000	1954	1,450,000,000
1947	245,000,000	1955	1,700,000,000
1948	292,000,000	1956	2,106,000,000

Includes all sales of frozen vegetables, fruits, concentrates, poultry, seafoods, meats and prepared foods projected at retail prices. Actual retail sales are 70% of total figures; 74% in 1956. Of total retail dollar volume of frozen food sales, chains (two or more stores) account for an estimated 72%.

Source: H. J. Onnes, *loc. cit.*, page 1.

novelty to its constructive adaptation to European conditions. He has recognized that future hope of profit accretion lies in cutting costs rather than padding margins.[8] In the mild climate of relative prosperity evident since 1950, European retailers have tended to cling less strenuously to antiquated methods and have opened their eyes to opportunities of rationalization. They have given up their dog-in-the-manager view for the attitude of a bird dog.[9] Even so, because of the slower European progress in prepackaging, retailers show

[8] R. F. Werner, "Progress in Distribution," *Proceedings of the Sixth Annual Congress of the Green Meadow Foundation* (1957), p. 13.

[9] R. Nieschlag, "Progress in Distribution," *Proceedings of the Sixth Annual Congress of the Green Meadow Foundation*, 1957, p. 98.

considerable hesitancy in investing in "visual sales" fixtures. Rising labor costs have forced them to search for efficiency improvements, but they usually have looked for them in areas other than total elimination of clerk service.

At the retail level, financial obstacles loom larger than attitudinal ones. Retailers labor under grave difficulties of securing adequate financing. Costs of business real estate are high, stores suitable for remodeling few, and permits for the construction of commercial buildings hard to obtain. Unfortunately, much of the immediate postwar rebuilding failed to take proper account of this facet of the retail revolution.[10]

From an operational viewpoint, in the United States self-service tends to maintain price competition and to compel retailers to stock nationally advertised manufacturers' brands because of their preselling ability. At the same time, self-service encourages retailers to complement the brand loyalty appeal of manufacturers' brands with a patronage loyalty appeal derived from their own private brands. In Europe retail price cutting is probably less common than in the United States, and processor-advertised prices are more strictly adhered to. Moreover, many products remain unbranded and therefore rely on the customer's loyalty to the retailer's personal business reputation.

In some countries the spread of supermarketing has been inhibited primarily by the institutional obstacle of government regulations. In Belgium, for example, the so-called "padlock law" of 1937 prevents retailers in towns of less than 50,000 inhabitants from enlarging existing branch stores, enlarging their operations beyond three branches, and operating other stores as subsidiaries. Since large scale and branch operations are vital to exploiting the operational advantages of self-service methods, clearly such a law inhibits experimentation and growth. As a result, Belgium has the largest number of retailers per capita in Europe.[11] In Denmark and some other Scandinavian countries, meat, bread and/or milk cannot be sold in regular grocery stores and meat products must not be factory-packaged. On the other hand, in the Netherlands, government aids cooperative organizations of medium-sized retailers in obtaining sites and buildings for their members.

[10] R. F. Werner, "General Report on the European Area," *Proceedings of the Fifth International Congress of the Green Meadow Foundation* (1959), p. 3.

[11] In Belgium there is one dealer per 29 inhabitants by comparison with 54 in France, 70 in Switzerland and 83 in Germany. Belgium also has fewer self-service retail food stores per capita than all other European countries except Austria, France, and Finland. (See Table 3.)

Attitudes of processors towards self-service

One of the obstacles to the more rapid spread of self-service methods in Europe most commonly cited is the slow progress made by European food manufacturers and processors in prepackaging their products. "Visual packaging" as Europeans like to call it is a *sine qua non* for self-service or even "half-self-service" or "visual selling." [12] Because no one country represents a sufficiently large selling area, packaging costs, in the absence of application of the latest packaging machinery and materials, have stayed high.

Europe has lagged behind the United States even more when it comes to the preparation and distribution of frozen foods. Due to agricultural customs barriers and reliance of various countries on home-grown foods for everyday consumption, lack of refrigeration at home as well as in stores,[13] manufacturers' difficulties in financing processing and storage plants as well as refrigerated transportation equipment and retail freezer cabinets,[14] lack of consumer education and consumer resistance to high frozen food prices for mediocre quality,[15] the distribution and consumption of frozen foods in Europe has shown only moderate growth. (See Table 4.)

Progress in European self-service food retailing

In this account of the progress of self-service food retail distribution in Europe the term supermarket has been avoided. There are in current use in the United States two definitions of supermarkets stated in terms of annual dollar volume. One requires a minimum of $1 million and is used by the Supermarket Institute and *Supermarket Merchandising*. The other, used by the *Progressive Grocer*, sets the minimum at $375,000. It has been estimated that, even by

[12] R. F. Werner, *op. cit.*, *Proceedings of the Fifth International Congress of the Green Meadow Foundation* (1956), pp. 3 and 19.

[13] Development of refrigeration in Sweden, for example, is shown by the approximate numbers of shops with refrigerated display cases, as follows:

1947	200
1951	2,500
1952	3,000
1953	5,000
1954	7,000
1955/1956	10,000

(of which 3,300 were cooperatives) See H. J. Onnes, "Prospects for the Deep Freezing Industry in France," *Proceedings of the Sixth International Congress of the Green Meadow Foundation* (1957), Annex 2, p. 1.

[14] H. J. Onnes (General Discussion), *Proceedings of the Sixth International Congress of the Green Meadow Foundation* (July 16, 1957), p. 8.

[15] E. F. Gasser (General Discussion), *Proceedings of the Sixth International Congress of the Green Meadow Foundation* (1957), p. 8.

the more modest definition, there are in operation in Europe today probably not more than about 150 supermarkets.[16]

Most European self-service food stores, therefore, would here be classed as superettes. Moreover, insufficient volume alone does not make this description appropriate. Many, if not most, European self-service establishments are converted clerk-service stores.[17]

The most growth has occurred in Switzerland, Sweden, the United Kingdom, Norway, and West Germany. In Switzerland, 80 per cent of the stores of one of the largest food retail chains (260 stores), the Migros Federation of Cooperatives, are operated on a self-service basis. In Sweden cooperatives own 1,800 of more than 3,000 self-service stores. In contrast with conditions in the United States, consumer cooperatives in Europe are among the most-up-to-date retailing institutions. Sweden represents a special case in that this relatively thinly populated country has the largest number of self-service grocery stores per capita in Europe—over 3,000 in total compared with 25 in Austria with almost the same population. In Sweden, manpower shortages combined with the success of small-scale self-service operations were responsible for this remarkable showing.[18] In the United Kingdom, 60 per cent of 3,300 self-service food stores belong to cooperatives, 25 per cent to regional chains, the remainder are independent.

If one were to hazard a guess, it might be said that Europe would gradually overcome present obstacles to the spread of self-service and that it would develop a lush market for refrigeration equipment and frozen foods, both domestic and American in the foreseeable future. Rising consumer incomes and a resulting taste for higher quality foods and "built-in maid service" give additional emphasis to this trend.[19]

On the other hand, Europeans view self-service with some reservations. They see the American supermarket as it entered the

[16] R. F. Werner, *op. cit., Proceedings of the Fifth International Congress of the Green Meadow Foundation* (1956), p. 2.

[17] *Ibid.*, p. 3. One of the major exceptions to this description is the Migros chain in Switzerland which has a number of units doing a typical supermarket business. The first supermarket in Zurich with 1,600 square feet does almost $1 million a year. (Zimmerman, "Surveying Europe's Food Picture," *Super Market Merchandising*, reprint from May—June issues, p. 8.)

Migros has pioneered the addition of many nonfood lines not yet found in our supermarkets, such as a sizeable book selection, a wide assortment of textiles and woolens, men's haberdashery and selected men's and women's under and outer-wear items, lamps and tools, leather goods and many other goods traditional to junior department stores. (See "Migros Gives Switzerland the Most Spectacular Market," *Super Market Merchandising*, February, 1953, p. 6 ff.)

[18] R. Nieschlag, *op. cit., Proceedings of the Sixth International Congress of the Green Meadow Foundation* (1956), p. 6.

[19] E. Nieschlag, *op. cit.*, p. 2.

European scene as a mature institution which has higher margins and more frills than the original prototype. They question whether this is an ultimate or merely a transitory phase in the growth of food distribution.[20] Even so, Europeans generally acknowledge that at the present stage of distribution techniques the extent of supermarketing is one significant indicator of a country's economic development.[21]

Automatic merchandising in Europe

Just as shelf self-service has been adapted to European conditions, so *automatic merchandising* must be viewed against the backdrop of European retail and consumer mores. Except for periodically resurrected keedoozles and present automat cafeterias, American vending machines have been supplementary to store sales although competing to some degree with them. Sweden's and Germany's "vitrinomats" sell a wider assortment of merchandise including groceries, drugs, photographic accessories, tobacco, hosiery, stationery, and books. Vitrinomats are located outside stores and in the usual high traffic spots such as shopping arcades, transportation terminals, and office buildings. Their sales are more truly supplementary to store sales than are those of automatic vending machines of the United States because store hours are more limited and more strictly regulated by local ordinances in Europe.

This peculiar role of automatic vending in contrast with that of the United States and the "store-on-wheels" movement referred to previously gives a clear indication that Europe will find institutional adaptations of the ingredients of the American retail revolution suited to its own psychological attitudes and economic conditions.

This lesson can be driven home by another illustration, a discussion of the shopping center movement in Europe, which forms the second part of this paper.

The Shopping Center Movement and Location Theory

Among the major factors triggering the shopping center movement in the United States have been metropolitan land use, the trek to the suburbs, and automotive transportation. As regards metropolitan land use, industries tend to locate near points of optimum access to that element which would be most expensive or most difficult

[20] Cf. R. F. Werner (General Discussion), *Proceedings of the Sixth International Congress of the Green Meadow Foundation*, July 16 (1957), p. 15.

[21] R. F. Werner, "General Progress in Distribution," *Proceedings of the Sixth International Congress of the Green Meadow Foundation* (1957), p. 5.

to transport and which, therefore, becomes the causative location factor for the industry in question.[22] Thus facilitative and service industries tend to be located by the distribution of markets for their services. If buyers making up those markets are individually very mobile by virtue either of private automotive transportation or frequent and convenient public transportation, the degree of proximity to the markets loses value as the major causative factor for retailing institution location.

The importance of proximity to markets as a causative factor in location is also predicated upon the categories of goods involved. By this reasoning convenience goods, especially food stores, should be located as close to residential complexes as possible, whereas shopping and specialty good stores should tend to be located in an area central to, and/or accessible to a number of residential areas.

The conventional metropolitan retail site pattern conforms to a large extent with this reasoning. The shopping center, especially the regional center, seems to deviate from this position because instead of locating at the hub of transportation facilities and in the heart of a city's social and economic life, it locates on vacant land with good road accessibility, thus creating a new artificial focus of activity which springs mainly from the attractions of leisurely one-stop family shopping.

Europe, at present, does not have any form comparable to the American regional shopping center. There is some evidence of the development of smaller types. These, however, have many traits which differentiate them from those in the United States.

The role of the central business district in Europe

In accounting for this difference in conditions between Europe and the United States, one may note that the downtown plays a different role in Europe than in many American cities. In the second place, suburbanization has proceeded along different lines in Europe, and finally, private automobile ownership in Europe has lagged far behind that in the United States.

The central business district in Europe, frequently to a greater extent than in the United States, represents the cultural focus of a city. Furthermore, not only is the merchandise selection in downtown department and specialty stores wider than in suburban branches, but the merchandise carried downtown is of better quality

[22] G. T. Renner, *op. cit.*, p. 169.

and is more up-to-date fashionwise than that sold on the periphery. It is not surprising, therefore, that the drawing power of big cities continues unabated and that people housed in temporary dwellings after the close of World War II have tended to remigrate into the cities in considerable numbers.[23] For these reasons it is understandable that where this was necessary, Europeans regarded the rapid rebuilding of their city centers after World War II as a welcome symbol of economic and social revival. In this process the need for modern distribution methods and opportunities were in many cases ignored.[24]

In America the idea of one-stop suburban shopping arose out of the growing inaccessibility of the traditional central business district due to traffic congestion and deteriorating public transportation despite the greater distances, greater public transportation difficulties, and higher private costs involved in reaching the suburban or regional shopping centers. Another factor was the "double life" which many married women have come to lead as homemakers and breadwinners, so that their shopping time has been severely curtailed.

In Europe, none of these factors is applicable to anything like the same degree as in the United States. Because of the much lower extent of private car ownership, downtown congestion is not as severe; and public transportation facilities have been maintained more adequately than in the United States. Lagging motorization makes the prospect of shopping far from home, even only once a week, unacceptable to the average European homemaker who, if not gainfully employed, spends much of her time on her daily shopping trips to nearby shopping centers.

European students of the subject tend to view the relationship between downtown and their smaller sized shopping centers as complementary[25] rather than competitive.[26] Downtown must continue to provide the best and most complete selections of shopping and specialty goods, particularly fashion merchandise and appliances, while stores located nearer residential quarters cater primarily to the population's daily routine needs.

23 S. L. Gabriel, "Demographic Developments," *Proceeding of the Sixth International Congress of the Green Meadow Foundation* (1957), p. 2.

24 W. J. Meijer (General Discussion), *Proceedings of the Sixth International Congress of the Green Meadow Foundation* (July 17, 1957), p. 2.

25 C. Billard (General Discussion), *Proceedings of the Sixth International Congress of the Green Meadow Foundation* (July 18, 1957), p. 11. See also R. Nieschlag, *op. cit.*, p. 8.

26 C. T. Jonassen, *The Shopping Center v. Downtown*, Bureau of Business Research, Ohio State University, Columbus, Ohio, *passim*.

Suburbanization and the shopping center movement

Another factor which accounts for this difference in viewpoint is the radically different development of the process of suburbanization in Europe as compared with the United States. In the United States the suburban family, sometimes referred to as the "fringe family," has developed socio-economic traits peculiar to itself. This family is generally more prosperous than those living in most parts of the city; it has more children; and, it is in an age group in which the latest labor-saving home appliances are sought. In short, the suburban family is an ideal potential customer for the one-stop shopping center.[27]

In Europe the suburban family is not necessarily of the middle or upper income groups,[28] especially in some unplanned developments and/or in most of the community housing projects in countries such as West Germany. This is in contrast with the English "garden cities," some of which are as prosperous as many American suburbs. In the war-scarred countries of Europe, such as Germany and Holland, large-scale destruction of urban residential quarters has been a major impetus for suburbanization [29] and the erection of apartments instead of one-family dwellings. In such low income developments it became more important to plan for limited facilities for convenience goods shopping nearby rather than ambitious one-stop shopping centers at too great a distance to be readily reached by existing public transportation facilities.

The integration of a great variety of retail institutions within the newly developed "Satellite towns" represents perhaps one of the most significant departures of the European pattern from the American model. These towns have been planned to include not only modern living quarters with adequate shopping malls and store clusters but new industries to provide employment for the satellite dwellers.[30]

Another basic spark in our shopping center movement lacking in Europe has been the explosive reversal of population trends since the beginning of World War II. Never reaching comparative levels

[27] Sylvia Fleis Fava, "Suburbanism as a Way of Life," *American Sociological Review*, (1956), p. 34 ff. E. Gartly Jaco and Ivan Belknap, "Is a New Family Form Emerging in the Urban Fringe?", *Ibid.* (1953), 551 ff. Bureau of the Census, *Statistical Abstract of the United States* (Washington, D. C., 1951), Table 24, page 20. See also p. 25.

[28] Twenty-Third International Congress on Housing and Town-Planning, Vienna. 1956 Recommendation No. 32.

[29] S. L. Gabriel, op. cit., *Proceedings of the Sixth International Congress of the Green Meadow Foundation,* (1957), p. 2.

[30] Ibid., p. 6. See also H. Carol (General Discussion), *Proceedings of the Sixth International Congress of the Green Meadow Foundation* (July 18, 1957), p. 2.

with those in the United States, European populations have tended toward stability since 1951 with relatively lower birth rates and low mortality resulting in small but stable increases. In many countries the trend toward smaller families continues unbroken, despite the drop in average marriage age.[31]

Europeans can rarely find sufficient economic justification to convert 50- to 200-acre tracts that might still be available into regional shopping centers. It appears that they would rather relieve the apartment shortage and promote industrial decentralization by building a new town according to a rational plan. Convenient and adequate retail facilities, accessible from all parts of such a community and providing adequate off-street parking on the one hand and safe pedestrian malls and children's play areas on the other form an organic part of this kind of integration of living, working and shopping facilities and opportunities.

Automobile ownership as a factor

Widespread automobile ownership has been a powerful factor in the growth of the American shopping center movement. Europe is lagging far behind America in this respect. Although traffic congestion in European downtown areas is increasing, it will likely be a long time before it will drive shoppers away from them into the suburban centers.[32]

Whereas in the United States one private passenger car serves an average of three people, there is only one car for twenty Europeans. Yet Western European countries are presently spending 3 per cent of their gross national product on automobiles; and registrations in many countries have doubled between 1950 and 1954, a percentage increase greater than that which occurred during the previous twenty years.[33] The psychological, practical, social, and technological factors promising further to accelerate this trend are similar to those prevailing in the United States. The automobile represents an important social prestige symbol; it is the most flexible means of transportation from suburban dormitory communities to work.

Obstacles to European motorization

With fifteen sizeable automobile manufacturing organizations in Western Europe, it appears that no one of them can hope to reap the

[31] S. L. Gabriel, *op. cit.*, p. 1.

[32] C. Billard, "Experiences in France," *Proceedings of the Sixth International Congress of the Green Meadow Foundation,* (1957), p. 1.

[33] W. Rootes, "The Prospects of Motorization in Europe," *Proceedings of the Sixth International Congress of the Green Meadow Foundation,* (1957), p. 2.

full benefits of mass production to the extent that American automobile producers have, especially the big three. However, fragmentation of the Western European market area is not the most significant impeding factor; the influence of taxes and import restrictions loom larger. Automobile sales taxes range from 6 per cent of the sales price in Germany and Switzerland to the 75 per cent which is imposed on Denmark's more expensive cars; in Britain the tax amounts to 60 per cent of the factory sales price.[34] Eleven West European countries,[35] mainly as a result of their balance of payments positions, have imposed quantitative import restrictions on automobiles. This forces West European manufacturers into special barter deals within Europe and aggressive competition outside it.

Highway construction has lagged behind in Europe as well. Traffic accident rates in some countries far exceed ours; as a result, insurance premiums are higher. With a population density in Britain, West Germany and the Benelux countries, ten to fifteen times greater than in the United States, increasing motorization over the long run will demand traffic solutions adapted to those conditions such as "fly-overs," freeways, and clover leaves as well as ample vertical-urban parking, both above and below ground.

Although broadening the ownership of private passenger cars will be a crucial factor in the growth of European economies generally, and the development of European outlying shopping centers in particular, one should not forget that the European automobile industry has other important contributions to make. The small petroleum-powered vehicle—the scooter, "moped," and motorcycle—is making Europe more mobile at least over short distances. Improvement of flexible public transportation facilities represents another worth-while effort in this direction. Finally, there is still much to be done in improving trucking equipment used in food distribution as well as enlarging the scope of "service-on-wheels" to include not only merchandise groups other than food products but consumer services such as snack bars, clinics, libraries and the like.[36]

Factors modifying the European shopping center movement

By way of preliminary summary, one might say that the European retail revolution has had to adapt itself to and work with peculiarly European conditions. Lack of private automobile transportation,

[34] *Ibid.*, p. 5.

[35] Belgium, Britain, Denmark, Eire, Finland, France, Iceland, Italy, Luxemburg, Norway, and Spain.

[36] W. Rootes, *loc. cit.*, p. 2.

lower suburban incomes, and lower birth rates all have combined to reduce the impetus to this kind of development in Europe. A greater desire for shopping in a commercial center with a full range of social, professional, governmental and cultural services and facilities and more frequent shopping trips to centers easily accessible by public transportation, as well as the lack of large undeveloped sites suitable for regional centers, have tended to maintain the importance of downtown shopping areas.

Illustrations from European shopping center adaptations

One of the most forward looking examples of a successful adaptation of the shopping center concept to European conditions is represented by the Vällingby Shopping Center in Sweden. Vällingby, a suburb of Stockholm, was planned and built as an independent unit or center. Built for 55,000 people, it boasts one of the most complete suburban-size shopping centers in Europe. Every kind of human want can be satisfied there. In addition to two full-line department stores, there are 72 other stores selling anything from food and clothing to automobiles and furniture. The center also contains medical and dental offices, a legitimate theater, a movie theater, libraries, assembly halls, and a youth center. (See Figure 1). All housing consists of apartments, and shoppers can reach the center on safe pedestrian sidewalks or canopied malls as well as by special access roads with adequate parking. As a result of such a balanced and integrated operation, Vällingby has become a genuine substitute for downtown, not only for its inhabitants but for many people living close to the heart of the city.[37]

Vällingby is also of interest for the research that went into the planning of it. In order to ascertain service needs, for example, the "average customer base" was obtained by dividing the number of a specific type of store into the total population. Turnover was increased by planning for slightly fewer stores in each category than would have been required to meet the planned customer base. Shopping habits were investigated to ascertain Vällingby's drawing power in various categories of goods and contour lines were established to determine potential buying power for each of them. Store structures were oriented toward multi-purpose use in case of miscalculations of subsequent changes in consumer tastes and buying habits. Parking

[37] G. Lindblad, "Experiences in Sweden," *Proceedings of the Sixth International Congress of the Green Meadow Foundation*, (1957), p. 3.

FIGURE 1

Plan of Vällingsby Center

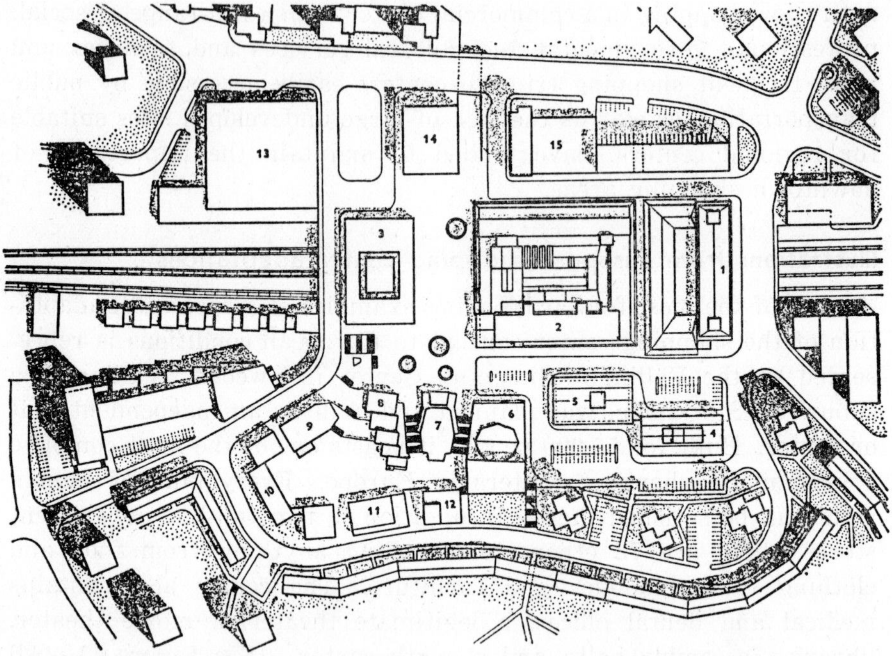

Block No. 1: Wireless, Wines and Spirits, Gentlemen's Outfitting, Coffee, Meat, Hardware, Footware, Fruit and Confectionery; Laundry, Barber, Post Office, Travel Agency, Exhibition Halls and Restaurant.
Block No. 2: 2 Departmental Stores and 2 Banks, Gift Shop, Drug Store, China-ware, Toys, Dairy Produce, Books, Millinery, Footware, Furs, Chocolates, Ladies' Underwear, Gentlemen's Outfitting, Music, and Fish. Further Motor-Car Show Rooms, a Florist, a Watchmaker, and a Restaurant.
Block No. 3: Shops for Groceries and Fruit, Cosmetics, Ladies' and Children's Outfitting, Ladies' Dresses and Zoological Specimens, two Banks, a Dry Cleaner, a Barber, a Florist and a Newspaper Office.
Block No. 4: contains a Butcher, an Electrician, a Rescue Station, a Dry Cleaner, a Sports Goods Shop, Tobacconist, an Optician, a Camera and Film shop, a Photographer's Studio, a Newspaper Office, a Sports Hall, a Dentist, Child and Mother Welfare Centre and Health Centre.
Block No. 5: Ladies' and Children's Clothing, a Café, a Chemist, a Newspaper Office, Motor-Car Show Room, Social Bureau, Pensioners' Office and Labour Exchange.
Block No. 6: Theatre (planned).
Block No. 7: Cinema.
Block No. 8: Assembly Halls.
Block No. 9: Church.
Block No. 10: Parochial Halls.
Block No. 11: Library.
Block No. 12: Youth Centre.
Block No. 13: Reserve.
Block No. 14: Parking.
Block No. 15: Offices, shops and workshops.

requirements were counterchecked by interviewing a sample of drivers using the Center during an early phase of its construction.[38]

Lulea represents another type of shopping center in Europe. In this case downtown was recreated along rational lines in an existing community. Its thirty minute isochronous perimeter based on bus or railway transportation included more or less the former trading area of the town. The sixty minute isochronous perimeter included two small towns and their trading areas, and the hundred and twenty

[38] *Ibid.*, p. 2.

minute perimeter included the entire coastal area. These time-distance figures could be reduced if they were based on private automotive transportation.

Swedish analysts reckoned that people do not shop beyond a radius of three hundred meters for food products for everyday use. Some food products, however, may be acquired within a radius of fifteen hundred meters or even to the limit of the "proximity" zone delineated by the thirty minute isochronous perimeter. Their studies showed that shopping goods are brought by customers living in the "middle zone" lying between the thirty and sixty minute perimeters; thus, local shops carrying these goods do not offer the same breadth of selection. Experience shows that people within the "outer zone," between the sixty and hundred and twenty minute perimeters, have to be coaxed to shop in Lulea by reduced shoppers' fares and by mail order service.

As a result of its drawing power the Lulea center, located in a community of 28,000 inhabitants, serves over 630,000 customers per year. A study of shopping habits showed the need for parking for 20 per cent of the customers or an average of 420 per day. With an even stream of customers, 85 parking places would have sufficed, but to cover peak shopping periods parking for 170 cars was planned. Lulea is also interesting from the point of view of the services it provides for tenants, including carefully coordinated outdoor, catalogue, and pamphlet advertising for the entire center, collective organization of maintenance work, mail order business, credit extension, and shopping tours around the surrounding area.

The Lulea shopping center includes 72 stores covering an area of 9,000 square meters. The nucleus of the center consists of larger stores, the largest being a supermarket of 1,400 square meters. The smallest shop is only 8 square meters. A comfortable temperature is maintained throughout the year in the roofed streets and open squares by means of a hot air curtain. Among other facilities, the center boasts an attractive baby parking lot, a hotel for 150 guests, a movie theater, rest rooms, and a ballroom.

Great Britain provided another example of integrated residential, industrial and commercial planning. The new satellite towns near London visualize a total population of 60,000 inhabitants divided into nine units with a total of a hundred "selling points," mostly individual stores, and, in addition, a full-fledged suburban shopping center of the size of a typical American regional center at the heart of the city.

Finland has evolved a suburban center in which 20 to 50 shops are placed under one roof with approximately 50 square meters alloted to each. It includes a travel agency, bank, beauty parlor, bar, and the usual assortment of stores.

France boasts a "Grand Passage" at Tours consisting of 30 independent stores situated in a shopping arcade. A collective discount of 5 per cent is given on all merchandise bought within the center. While the "Grand Passage" is privately financed, the "Verte Bois" at Sant-Dizier is a government project consisting of 200 stores and serving 20,000 inhabitants. This is another European post-war adaption of shopping center merchandising.

"Lijmbaan" near Rotterdam, Holland, consists of 65 stores built on a street closed to vehicular traffic. The "Nieuwe Market" consists of 190 stores and includes 65 square meters of selling space. Rotterdam's "Twelve Provinces Center" is a single building in which some 200 independent stores are housed on six floors most of which cover only four square meters. Denmark's "Centromes Gwardem" consists of 25 stores with cooperative display facilities.[39]

European shopping centers thus are mainly of a type smaller than American regional centers and, due to European preference for pedestrian access, are located in or near existing newly-planned communities.

Conclusion

It appears that while Western Europe is clearly receptive to the innovations of the American retail revolution, it tends to transplant them with considerable caution and to adapt them to the psychological attitudes of the inhabitants of the various countries as well as to their economic potentials and social organization.

It also appears that self-service will make further progress, but it is unlikely that it will invade as many of the non-food fields as it has in the United States. Shopping centers will likely spread, but they will probably be built on a scale and in a manner befitting an area lacking the conditions necessary for the explosive expansion of the regional type common in the United States. Thus, it seems likely that they will be well-planned, medium-sized centers integrated into the rehabilitation of existing and the planning of new residential and industrial urban and suburban complexes.

[39] R. F. Werner, *Proceedings of the Fifth International Congress of the Green Meadow Foundation* (1956), p. 28.